The Convention on International Trade of Endangered Species

Local Authority and International Policy

The Convention on International Trade of Endangered Species

Local Authority and International Policy

Jonathan Liljeblad

qp

QUID PRO BOOKS

New Orleans, Louisiana

THE CONVENTION ON INTERNATIONAL TRADE OF ENDANGERED SPECIES

Published in 2014 by Quid Pro Books, as part of the *Dissertation Series*. Originally cited in its previous versions as "The Elephant and the Mouse that Roared: The Prospects of International Policy and Local Authority in the Case of the Convention on International Species."

ISBN 978-1-61027-216-2 (pbk.)
ISBN 978-1-61027-217-9 (eBook)

QUID PRO BOOKS

5860 Citrus Blvd., Suite D-101
New Orleans, Louisiana 70123
www.quidprobooks.com

qp

Publisher's Cataloging-in-Publication

Liljeblad, Jonathan.

The Convention on International Trade of Endangered Species : Local Authority and International Policy / Jonathan Liljeblad.

    p. cm. — (Dissertation series)

Includes bibliographical references.

    ISBN 978-1-61027-216-2 (softcover edition)

1. Endangered species—Law and legislation. 2. Wild animal trade—Law and legislation.
3. Convention on International Trade in Endangered Species of Wild Fauna and Flora
(1973). 4. Endangered species—Law enforcement. I. Title. II. Series.

K 3522 .L26 2014

342.123'7—dc22

2014014237

CONTENTS

Foreword

In the fall of 1989 I found myself in the uncomfortable position of being a federal government employee detailed to the state of Maryland to help implement a policy at the county level. At the time I was a young analyst at the Office of Management and Budget, and I was working on a project to test the practicality and cost-effectiveness involved in the delivery of government benefits to recipients using plastic cards, automated teller machines and point of sale devices, a process that is now known as Electronic Benefit Transfer (EBT).

I learned a great deal working on that project, but what has stuck with me most after all these years is the great difficulty of implementing national government policy in a system of federalism, where 50 states plus other sovereign units have competing interests, differing levels of capabilities and varying political and policy cultures. The challenges of coordinating and communicating between the levels of government and across the different federal, state and local agencies were enormous. It is still remarkable to me that EBT was able to overcome all of these hurdles to become a universally accepted way to deliver both federal and state benefits. But it is the hurdles that confronted implementation that I remember most.

Implementation of federal laws, regulations and policies in an environment of federalism is frequently difficult. Implementing federal laws that flow out of international law adds a whole new layer of complexity to implementation, one that is almost always ignored by scholars. However, in this book Jonathan Liljeblad offers an enlightening and long-overdue look at the issue of local implementation of international policy. Using a case study of the implementation of the Convention on the International Trade in Endangered Species (CITES) and its domestic analogue in the U.S., the Endangered Species Act (ESA) by the Port of Los Angeles Police, Liljeblad is able to arrive at insightful conclusions as well as concrete recommendations for policymakers wishing to improve coordination and execution of international policies that rely on local governments for their implementation. Using both qualitative and quantitative approaches, Liljeblad explores how the complexity of federalism is exacerbated by the presence of an international component. Liljeblad finds that law enforcement personnel tend to view international law more negatively than domestic law even when they are dealing with the same issue. He also demonstrates that the views of street level bureaucrats vary greatly depending on the policy in question, and that implementation of CITES confronts many more challenges than other international policies enforced by the Port of Los Angeles Police.

Perhaps this book's greatest contributions are the real world policy recommendations that flow from its analysis. In an environment of increasing devolution, implementing international policies is more and more the responsibility of local authorities acting as agents of state governments in the United States.

Liljeblad calls for greater linkages between federal officials in the Fish and Wildlife Service who are nominally responsible for ensuring that the provisions of the Endangered Species Act are carried out, and the local authorities who do the actual work of enforcing the law. This recommendation applies not only to CITES, but every policy that has its origins in an international agreement. He likewise argues that granting greater authority to local officials to carry out the law would strengthen the linkages between the levels of government. Local law enforcement needs to understand the connections between international law and domestic policies which share a common goal, yet may be construed differently by agents of government. Cross level communication and education are essential. Liljeblad's recommendations would foster a climate of greater understanding of the connections between international and domestic policy and should be heeded by all levels of government to remove unnecessary roadblocks that can derail implementation.

Scott A. Frisch
Professor and Chair of Political Science
California State University
Channel Islands

November 2013

Preface

Prevailing U.S. government philosophy espouses the devolution of authority from federal to local levels. This trend opens the possibility of greater local involvement in policy implementation, and provides international policymakers the opportunity to improve global policies by adding the efforts of local actors to their implementation framework. Much of international policy involves enforcement through international-to-national linkages, but devolution offers the potential to extend the implementation chain by providing national-to-local linkages.

This book explores the nature of such linkages, using the case study on the Convention on the International Trade in Endangered Species (CITES) via its domestic analogue, the Endangered Species Act (ESA). The analysis employs both quantitative and qualitative methods, including interviews, survey research, statistical analysis, and legal document review. The research finds that while the framework of CITES enforcement in the U.S. allows for a national-to-local extension in the CITES implementation chain, it also presents challenges that should be addressed by international policymakers who consider devolution as a way of improving global policy.

JONATHAN LILJEBLAD
Postdoctoral Fellow,
Law School,
University of New England
New South Wales

Australia
January 2014

Acknowledgments

Scholarly work is a product of time, energy, and resources applied with diligence, discipline, and dedication to the process of analysis. It is important to note, however, that scholarship is not a solo endeavor but rather a social one: scholarship is not the product of the scholar alone, but also the many people associated with the scholar whose support constitutes a major, if not the majority, of the time, energy, and resources consumed in advancing the research process. As a result, some recompense should be given to the sacrifices made by the many and not the one.

For this scholarly work, no amount of recompense can make up for the sacrifices made by the many who assisted me. What I can do and wish to do is to offer recognition of those who have helped me, and share the product of the research with them.

To begin, I express my deepest gratitude to the professionals who provided me with guidance and patience during what proved to be a very long path towards growth and maturity. Thanks go to the members of my dissertation committee: Alison Renteln, Richard Dekmejian, and Robert Keim. Without them, I never would have finished this research. Additional gratitude also goes to Sheldon Kaminiecki. Without him, I never would have started this research. It is from these scholars that I learned the craft of my profession.

I also dedicate this work to my parents, Eileen Aye Liljeblad and Kjell Liljeblad, whose love and encouragement sustained me throughout the course of this research. I also dedicate this to my brother, Moe Win, who preceded me into academia and provided me with many lessons on the way. We are a family, and we did what families do: share, commiserate, support, differ, bicker, separate, but always come back together and advance forward as one.

Last, I wish to honor my grandparents, Roma and Lester Blaschke. They may not have been related to me according to a scientific definition based on genetics. But their undying faith and continued devotion to the project that is my life—even when such faith and devotion was not warranted—inspired and motivated me through the darkest moments, and that makes them all the family I could have ever wished to have. That makes us related, and it makes them part of me. My biggest regret is that the people who were so instrumental in my life are not here to share in the fruits of what is really their labor. I wish they were here now. I want to live as a testament to them. This work is in their memory. Thank you.

JL

The Convention on International Trade of Endangered Species

Local Authority and International Policy

1

Statement of Problem

I. Argument

In the prevailing political climate the U.S. has witnessed a shift in federal power, with a trend of decentralization in authority to state and local governments. This is often labeled as devolution, and grouped within discussions on federalism and state and local jurisdictions. Some areas affected by this mindset include those dealing with national security, traffic across U.S. borders, and environmental issues. Steps have already been taken towards allocating what was formerly deemed exclusive federal jurisdiction onto individual communities, with discussions in popular and government circles over enforcement of national laws using not only federal agencies but also local ones.[1] Implicit behind these moves is the belief that implementation of national laws can be served through greater utilization of local government agencies.

The trend to devolution to local law enforcement seems to open a bridge of greater community-level inclusion in larger-scale policy implementation—not only in terms of the local now interacting with the national, but the local now connecting with the global. This is because national laws are sometimes expressions of U.S. obligations to international instruments. Hence, enforcement of a national law effectively means enforcement of an international one.

For global policymakers, such a scenario suggests another level of linkages in policy creation. To ensure effectiveness, they must now follow an "implementation chain" starting from an instrument's creation, continuing to support of

---

[1] Robert Block. "Politics & Economics: Fighting Terrorism By Sharing Data; Homeland Security Plans To Improve Cooperation With Police Departments", Wall Street Journal (Eastern Edition). New York, N.Y.: Oct. 16, 2006, p. A6; R. Steven Brown. "States Put Their Money Where Their Environment Is." Environmental Council of the States. April 1999. URL: http://www.ecos.org/section/publications. Accessed November 12, 2007; *Fact Sheet: Improving Border Security and Immigration Within Existing Law*. Department of Homeland Security. August 10, 2007. URL: http://www.dhs.gov/xnews/releases/pr_1186757867585.shtm. Accessed Sept. 26, 2007; Tom Fitton. "Local Law Enforcement Effective in Fighting Illegal Immigration", *The Conservative Voice*, July 24, 2006. URL: http://www.theconservativevoice.com/articles/article.html?id=16389. Accessed Sept. 25, 2007; Timothy Lawrence. *Devolution and Collaboration in the Development of Environmental Regulations*. Dissertation. Ohio State University (2005); Patrick Poole. "Local Law Enforcement and Homeland Security." *American Thinker*. August 9, 2007. URL: http://www.americanthinker.com/2007/08/local_law_enforcement_and_ home.html. Accessed Sept. 26, 2007; Gretchen Randall. "Devolution to the States is Working for Welfare; It Can Work for Public Lands", National Policy Analysis. National Center for Public Policy Research. June 2001. URL: http://www. nationalcenter.org/NPA340.html. Accessed Sept. 25, 2007; Barry Rabe. "Permitting, Prevention and Integration: Lessons from the States," in *Environmental Governance: A Report on the Next Generation of Environmental Policy*, Donald Kettl (ed.). Brookings Institution Press (2002); Denise Scheberle. *Federalism and Environmental Policy*. Georgetown University Press (2004); Zoe Tillman. "Crackdown: Immigration supporters react to a resolution passed July 10 in Prince William County, Va., that empowers local police to determine the status of residents and to arrest illegal immigrants", *Christian Science Monitor*. July 17, 2007. URL: http://www.csmonitor.com/2007/0717/p01s05-ussc.html. Accessed Sept. 25, 2007; "U.S. Wants Local Help in Human Trafficking", *Juvenile Justice Digest*. Washington: July 6, 2004. Vol. 32, No. 12, p. 6.

signatory members, and then extending to the subordinate authorities within each signatory. This chain can be seen as involving two links between three levels. The first link is global-to-national, in terms of going from international instruments to participating national signatories. The second link is national-to-local, extending from national government to local government.

Much of international policy implementation involves discussions of the first link. The trend to devolution, however, means a greater role for local government in global policy, since devolution calls for greater local participation in enforcement of national laws—national laws which sometimes enunciate U.S. obligations as a signatory to international law. This suggests an increasing significance for the second, national-to-local link in discussions over international policy, and also points out the need to pay more attention to issues at the local level, particularly for policymakers who hope to incorporate local agencies in international policy implementation efforts.

This analysis addresses the potential for involving local government in global policy implementation, and so encompasses both links between these three levels, with particular focus on the local level. For this research, this means beginning with a review of CITES as an international treaty, briefly detailing its framework, continuing on to an introduction of the ESA and related government agencies, and finally discussing the nature of connections to Port of Los Angeles Police.

Such speculation, however, assumes that there are, in fact, linkages between local and national government with respect to international policy. This is not clear. In order to accept the existence of such linkages, and hence their implications for policymakers, there needs to be assurance through analysis. Analysis entails investigation through theory supported by factual or experimental study to confirm the nature of local-to-global connections.

This research is a step towards such requirements, and endeavors to provide a method testing the relationship between international instruments and local enforcement. The approach will be to utilize a selection of international treaties to which the United States is a signatory, and for each of which the federal government has enacted national laws. The selection will provide a case study, with a specific treaty being utilized for in-depth review, and the others serving as controls. The analysis will then conduct the case study by investigating relevant theory and conducting field research, with the intent of reviewing both de jure and de facto connections between local implementation and global policy within the case. The goal is to obtain results to assess the state of the linkages, and then discuss implications to theory and policy.

In rough terms, the argument is that the speculations regarding linkages between local and global levels are not only plausible, but very much true. The hope is that improving such relationships will assist with the implementation of international policies. The details of the argument, as well as the research method, are presented below.

II. Case Study

This analysis adopts the Convention on the International Trade of Endangered Species (CITES) as a case study. The U.S. is a signatory to CITES, and has implemented the federal Endangered Species Act (ESA) in obligation to its signatory duties to CITES. In terms of the local-to-global linkage for the U.S., this turns the research into a study of the relationship between international efforts to manage the trade of endangered species and the actions of local enforcement agencies to support them. In so doing, the research becomes an assessment of the potential the local level has for aiding in the implementation of an international policy instrument such as CITES.

CITES is a particularly useful treaty for a case study, since its enforcement ultimately devolves to a local level. The design of CITES makes the treaty dependent on the actions of its signatory members. As a result, it is inherently tailored toward the inclusion of actors operating below the global level, and allows the freedom for signatories to incorporate local communities in enforcement of the treaty. Because CITES revolves around a fundamental principle that each signatory should be responsible for protecting endangered species within their borders, CITES creates a decentralized management structure wherein the bulk of enforcement responsibility and power is retained by the treaty's member nation-states and a limited administrative role is reserved in a central CITES Secretariat restricted to coordinating information and scheduling treaty conferences. This raises the issue of CITES being dependent on local enforcement for its implementation, with the danger of failures at the local level degrading the effectiveness of the treaty at the international level.

III. Methodology

The research method consists of a hypothesis, theory to provide context, a research sample for study, specification of variables to draw from the sample, and the research tools to perform the analysis. From this, results are expected that will evaluate the strength of the hypothesis. The goal is to find insights relevant to theory with implications for practical policymaking, as well as offer directions for further useful research.

Hypothesis

Following from the argument, the general expectation of this investigation is that with respect to international policies there are linkages between local implementation and global instruments, and hence that there are opportunities to strengthen enforcement of those instruments through greater use of local agents. In terms of the specified case study, which consists of CITES expressed in the U.S. through the ESA, this rough statement can be clarified into the hypothesis that there is a connection between CITES and local law enforcement agencies, and that CITES success can be improved by greater inclusion of such agencies.

In terms of individual questions, this can be viewed as a set:

3

- What is the nature of the current relationship between CITES and relevant law enforcement?
- If the relationship is to be improved, what issues are there to be rectified?
- If the relationship is to be improved, what are the most effective ways to integrate local agencies in international policy implementation?

Theory

For theory, the analysis will provide context for the hypothesis and research method. The analysis will first provide an overview of the arguments regarding trends of both globalization of topics to international levels and devolution of them to local ones. After this, the discussion will then present theoretical perspectives of international politics, and highlight those aspects that address linkages between the global and local—particularly those aspects with insights useful for considering the dependence of international environmental instruments like CITES upon local law enforcement agencies subordinate to the U.S. federal government.

Research Sample

The research method utilizes a research sample in two different senses: a sample in terms of the treaty used for study and a sample from which data was gathered. In terms of treaty samples, the analysis selects treaties all comparable to each other, in the sense that they each 1) deal with international traffic in a particular field, 2) have the U.S. as a signatory member, and 2) have an analogue in U.S. federal law. With CITES being chosen as the instrument for in-depth analysis because of the amenability of its structure to test local-to-global linkages, this meant that other treaties became controls. Based on the criteria, the other treaties adopted are as follows:

- Convention on the International Trade in Endangered Species (CITES)
- Convention Against Illicit Traffic in Narcotics Drugs and Psychotropic Substances (CNDPS)
- Nuclear Nonproliferation Treaty, Biological Weapons, Chemical Weapons Convention (CNBC)
- Convention for the Suppression of Traffic in Persons (CSTP)
- Trade-Related Intellectual Property Agreements (TRIPS)

Each treaty has a domestic analogue, which are, respectively:

- Endangered Species Act (ESA)
- Controlled Substances Import and Export Act (CSIE)
- Defense Against Weapons of Mass Destruction Act (DWMD)
- Trafficking Victims Protection Act (TVP)
- U.S. Customs and Border Patrol Regulations (CBP)

For a data sample, the research involves field data delineated by geography and sample subjects. The case study here, too, specifies a singular geographic location and particular set of subjects with characteristics amenable to study testing the questions of the hypothesis.

Geographically, the analysis focuses on the Port of Los Angeles. Los Angeles is a major point of entry for international traffic to the United States, being one of only two major international seaports on the West Coast (the other being Seattle, Washington). Indeed, it is the busiest port in the western U.S. coast in terms of incoming tonnage of cargo, receiving more than 50,000,000 tons per year, with over 45,000,000 coming from foreign sources.[2] This domination extends beyond shipping traffic to alternative air traffic: in comparison, Miami International Airport, the busiest U.S. airport in terms of international freight, receives only approximately 1.68 million tons of cargo per year, and Los Angeles International Airport, the third busiest U.S. airport in terms of international freight, only processes a little over 2,000,000 tons per year.[3] The comparative volume of trade at the Port of Los Angeles, relative to air traffic or other sea ports, makes it a major nexus point for law enforcement agencies facing international smuggling.

In addition, because of its location on the West Coast, Los Angeles has a greater proximity relative to most other U.S. cities to international trade from the Pacific Rim, which is considered one of the greatest sources of endangered species trafficking.[4] This is compounded by the significant ethnic diversity, containing populations originating from cultures known for being consumers of endangered species parts.[5] With respect to local law enforcement, Los Angeles features agencies that may encounter violations of international trade laws, in particular those at the Port of Los Angeles.

For data, the study entailed use of publicly available documents on CITES and ESA enforcement within the U.S., and the Port of Los Angeles in particular. In addition, it also required the use of interviews and surveys from federal and local agencies: the Fish and Wildlife Service (FWS) and the Port of Los Angeles Police. The FWS is named by the federal government as the CITES administrative office for the U.S., and is also responsible for managing the ESA. The Port of Los Angeles Police was selected because it is the local law enforcement agency monitoring the Port of Los Angeles. Under the concept of "local" the agents of interest for this study are those non-federal field personnel operating at the community level. For the U.S., the field personnel for community law enforcement under are

---

[2] Port of Los Angeles website, URL: http://www.portoflosangeles.org. Accessed: August 1, 2007; U.S. Army Corps of Engineers, Waterborne Commerce Statistics Center, URL: http://www.iwr.usace.army.mil/ndc/wcsc/portname02.htm. Accessed: October 19, 2007; Vanderbilt Center for Transportation Research, URL: http://transp20.vuse.vanderbilt.du/vector/worldkit/index.html. Accessed October 19, 2007.

[3] Miami International Airport Cargo Rankings website, URL: http://miami-airport.com/html/cargo_rankings_.html. Accessed: January 1, 2008; Los Angeles World Airports Cargo website, URL: http://www.lawa.org/lax/cargo.cfm. Accessed January 1, 2008.

[4] Stefan Lovgren. "Wildlife Smuggling Bloom Plaguing L.A., Authorities Say", *National Geographic News*. July 26, 2007. URL: http://news.nationalgeographic.com/news/2007/07/070725-animal-smuggle.html. Accessed Oct. 1, 2007.

[5] Ibid.

municipal police, sheriffs, airports, and port authorities. These bodies operate on a municipal and county level, counties being the larger-encompassing body with boundaries containing municipal police departments, the county sheriff, and county ports and airports—and hence, the Port of Los Angeles Police.

Variables

With respect to the hypothesis and related theories linking local and international levels, the variables for study are those indicating the nature of relationship between local law enforcement and CITES via the ESA, the weaknesses in that relationship, as well as the perceptions of local actors regarding challenges to their support of CITES.

Because evaluation of the CITES-local law enforcement relationship and its weaknesses is a qualitative one, there is no explicit declaration of dependent or independent variables. However, for study of the perceptions of local actors as to the issues in the relationship, a survey is applied allowing descriptive and statistical analysis using dependent and independent variables. The dependent variables are: the perceptions of local law enforcement of CITES in terms of its effectiveness and deterrence value, as well as their satisfaction level over their efforts to enforce it domestically via the ESA. The independent variables are: the perceptions of local law enforcement in terms of challenges to their enforcement efforts, cooperation with other domestic and international law enforcement agencies, and also their knowledge and recognition of CITES.

Both the qualitative and quantitative variables are used to test the hypothesis. The hope is that the analysis will utilize them to generate an assessment from the collected data regarding the potential role for local actors in international policy implementation.

Research Tools

This study primarily uses qualitative and quantitative data. Determination of the de jure existence of linkages between local law enforcement and international policy utilized qualitative information. Evaluation of the de facto nature of such linkages adopted both quantitative surveys and qualitative interviews.

Qualitative data on de jure relationships is drawn from existing documents regarding CITES, the ESA, and government actions on devolution. In terms of de facto connections, interviews come from discussions with representatives of the FWS and the Port of Los Angeles Police.

Quantitative data is obtained from anonymous surveys administered to the patrol officers at the Port of Los Angeles Police. Compiling the survey results allows identification of what patrol officers consider to be major issues in enforcement of national and international laws. Testing the survey results for correlation and causal relationships help to indicate areas for mitigation to better integrate port police in the international policy. As a whole, the quantitative analysis helps evaluate the capacity of patrol officers to accept the potentially greater duty of enforcing national laws like CITES—laws whose responsibility was originally outside their jurisdiction but which are increasingly likely to be allocated to them. Because a national law like the ESA is tied to CITES, this means that the data may also show the capacity of local law enforcement to play a greater role in implementing international policy.

In terms of structure, the surveys gather data indicating the nature of respondent perceptions towards the varying levels of analysis: international policy, the domestic law equivalent, and the issue addressed by those instruments in general. This allows better assessment as to whether respondent views are reflective of their relative personal knowledge of domestic laws, international laws, or related subject matter.

In addition, the survey also asks respondents with their views to a number of treaties in addition to CITES. This is meant to provide a "control" to check respondent answers indicate their own personal feelings regarding the issue of endangered species traffic, or if they indicate their perceptions towards international law in general.

IV. Expected Findings and Significance

The research is expected to provide data useful in support of the hypothesis, by producing findings indicating local-to-global linkages. Particularly for CITES, this would be demonstrated by insights about the connections between local agencies and CITES implementation.

In terms of answering the research questions of the hypothesis, the expectation is for the following:

- There are current linkages between local law enforcement and CITES implementation, and that such linkages are likely to increase

- Local law enforcement perceive manageable challenges to their involvement in CITES implementation

- It is possible to identify the ways the linkages can be strengthened

The implication of these findings is that international policymakers should integrate local actors in designing international policy to improve their effectiveness and potential for success. In addition, it also implies that policymakers accept that international legal instruments are inextricably intertwined with local levels, and that success at a global level requires success at a local one.

By doing so, the research hopes to contribute to the body of policy studies that endeavor to improve the effectiveness of legal instruments by increasing their relevancy to practical implementation issues. This relates to arguments that policy's ultimate goal is to affect change in the real world, and hence should have some orientation towards useful application. For those policies based on theory, this means theory must be translated so as to engage reality, or otherwise it risks being instruments de jure but never de facto—and thereby principles in words but not in life.[6]

---

[6] For examples, see generally: William Evan. *Social Structure and Law*. Sage Publications (1990); Eugene Kamenka, et al. *Law and Society: The Crisis in Legal Ideals*. St. Martin's Press (1978); Stewart Macaulay, et al. *Law and Society: Readings on the Social Study of the Law*. W.W. Norton & Company (1995); Austin Sarat and Jonathan Simon (eds.). *Cultural Analysis,*

V. Structure

In summary, this analysis follows a method composed of a hypothesis, context-relevant theory, a research sample, variables of data types to be taken from the sample, the research tools to study the data, and then a discussion of the results from the research. In keeping with the method, the investigation is divided into the following chapters:

- Chapter 1: statement of the problem
- Chapter 2: presentation of theory
- Chapter 3: review of existing literature on CITES
- Chapter 4: qualitative study of linkages between CITES and local law enforcement
- Chapter 5: descriptive presentation of challenges to linkages with CITES perceived by local law enforcement
- Chapter 6: quantitative statistical analysis indicating possible influences on local perceptions
- Chapter 7: findings and discussions

Cultural Studies, and the Law. Duke University Press (2003); Peter Schuck. *The Limits of the Law.* Westview Press (2000).

2

Literature Review

Within environmental studies, the Convention on the International Trade in Endangered Species (CITES) falls under the domain of biodiversity. Because it deals with one of the largest drivers of species loss, CITES is commonly viewed as an instrument of global policy against ongoing extinction rates. The significance of the treaty is better seen in the context of biodiversity issues.

I. Biodiversity

Biodiversity covers the topics of endangered species, extinction, wildlife conservation, and ecological preservation. Biodiversity addresses the wide array of biological life within the Earth's biosphere which exists in an ecology that relates one species to another. Generally, biodiversity is considered significant to the sustained health of the planet's ecology, first because research increasingly suggests that each biological species serves critical roles in ecosystems, and second because diversity in species ensures the biosphere's ability to adapt to changing stresses upon it.[7] Scientists largely accept that the ecological system of the biosphere relies on the constant maintenance through the interactions of species within it. While the role of each species is not entirely understood, it is clear that the disappearance of species may unravel the complex ecological relationships harboring them, leading to a breakdown of the Earth's ecology, and hence the collapse of the Earth's ability to support life.[8] In conjunction with this, scientists also understand that the environment's ability to adjust to stress is dependent on widespread genetic diversity. This is because genetic diversity ensures that the biosphere will have a source of characteristics or traits from which to draw upon in evolving responses to changes within it. Bereft of biodiversity, the environment would be less able and less likely to survive changing conditions or shocks to it.[9]

Unfortunately, scientific data indicate that the planetary wealth of biodiversity is being eradicated at an alarming rate. While there continues to be ongoing debate regarding the magnitude of species loss relative to past extinction events,

---

[7]   See generally: Ronald Bailey (ed.). *Earth Report 2000*, McGraw-Hill (2000); World Resources Institute. Earthtrends. URL: http://www.earthtrends.wri.org; UNEP. *Global Environmental Outlook 3*. Earthscan (2002); Brian Groombridge and M.D. Jenkins. *Global Biodiversity*. UNEP (2000); Charles Harper. *Environment and Society*. Prentice Hall (2001); Bjorn Lomborg, *The Skeptical Environmentalist*, Cambridge University Press (2001).

[8]   Ibid.

[9]   Ibid.

there is general consensus that current rates are profound—enough so as to warrant questions as to dangers to the global eco-system and genetic diversity.[10]

Biodiversity losses are largely attributable to habitat destruction. Habitat destruction is a direct result of human population growth and its hunger to exploit new land and new resources.[11] Industrial activities, agricultural practices, and the raw need for living space incurs increased consumption of natural resources, generation of pollutants, and eradication of natural environments. Human population growth also drives a need for additional food sources, encouraging the profligate consumption of plant and animal life in a way which decreases species populations for use by burgeoning human populations. The end result is the elimination of habitat harboring indigenous flora and fauna. The combination of these factors has been the dramatic escalation in species extinction rates, and the destabilization of plant and animal populations to levels tenuous for their long-term survival.[12]

Habitat conservation at the level of international policy has been frustrated by the norms of sovereignty, which assert that each nation-state has the responsibility and power to manage its own internal affairs. As a corollary, no nation-state has the right to interfere directly with any other nation-state's internal affairs. Formal international attempts for global habitat conservation conflict with this, as they would invariably require that international limits exist on a country's domestic land-use, and hence act as an external curb on a country's internal governance and land-use policies. This indicates why so few treaties address habitat conservation, and those that do frequently provide only general guidelines and principles with little formal enforcement mechanisms or supporting institutional organization.

Another major source of biodiversity loss has been "takings," through hunting and trade of species. While trading in flora and fauna between nations is a legal component of global economics, there are significant portions of the global economy fostering takings of endangered species in ways that are illegal. This illegal market has grown in conjunction with the liberalization of the global economy, from an estimated annual $50-100 million in the 1970s to approximately $1.5 billion in the 1980s to potentially $5 billion in the 1990s. As of 2007, the value has risen to approximately $15-25 billion per year, second in value behind only narcotics smuggling in terms of illegal black markets.[13] For the U.S. alone, the estimated value is around $1.4 billion per year.[14]

---

10 Groombridge; Ellen Thomas. Lecture, Environmental Studies Course EES 199. Wesleyan University. URL: http: ethomas.web.wesleyan.edu/ees123/mass_extinctions.htm. Accessed December 9, 2003; UNEP *Global Environmental Outlook 3*.

11 Bailey; Jessica Forrest. "Protecting Ecosystems on a Changing Planet." Earthtrends. URL: http://www.earthtrends.wri.org. Accessed December 12, 2003; Groombridge; Harper; Lomborg; UNEP *Global Environmental Outlook 3*.

12 Bailey; Forrest; Groombridge; Harper; Lomborg; UNEP *Global Environmental Outlook 3*; World Resources Institute. *World Resources 2000-2001*. URL: http://www.wri.org. Accessed December 12, 2003.

13 Levy, Adrian and Cathy Scott-Clark, "Poaching for Bin Laden", *The Guardian*. May 5, 2007. URL: http://www.guardian.co.uk/alqaida/story/0,,2073168,00.html. Accessed May 20, 2007; Lovgren, Stefan, "Wildlife Smuggling Bloom Plaguing L.A., Authorities Say", *National Geograph-*

Restrictions on "takings" has been a more opportune ground for international policy compared to habitat conservation. This is because takings of species often result in the transportation of captured or destroyed specimens across nation-state boundaries and international waters, providing international policymakers with a means of gaining jurisdiction over the problem without having to negotiate restrictive issues of sovereignty. The result has been an array of international treaties dealing with endangered species poaching, hunting, and trade relative to the number in existence addressing habitat conservation, with CITES being just one of many.

The spectrum of international efforts to address biodiversity loss is vast, with action from state and non-state actors being directed at both habitat conservation and takings. Private groups have bought out natural wilderness to create conservation preserves, with the intent of acquiring species-rich habitats before commercial interests destroyed them. Other entities have pursued "sustainable use" initiatives, educating governments and communities on the benefits of consuming plant and animal life in ways which would allow species populations to renew themselves. There are also "gene banks" to store genetic material of threatened species, as well as "debt-for-nature" swaps, in which the debt of developing countries are forgiven in exchange for combating habitats and takings.[15] In addition, there has been a proliferation in "clearinghouses" to coordinate policies and aid in communication of scientific and administrative information.[16]

Significant treaty instruments include the 1916 Canadian-American Treaty for Protection of Migratory Birds, the 1933 African Convention Relative to the Preservation of Flora and Fauna in their Natural State, and the 1946 International Whaling Commission. These were joined by such notable international environmental regimes as the 1971 Convention on Wetlands of International Importance Especially as Waterfowl Habitat (CWIIWH, more commonly referred to as the "Ramsar Convention"), the 1973 Convention on the International Trade of Endangered Species (CITES), the 1982 United Nations Convention on Law of the Sea (UNCLOS), the 1987 International Tropical Timber Organization, and the 1992 Caracas Declaration on National Parks. Along with these have been the 1968 Biosphere Conference, the 1972 United Nations Conference on the Human Environment (more commonly referred to as the "Stockholm Conference"), the 1987 Report on the World Commission on Environment and Development (more commonly referred to as the "Brundtland Commission"), and the 1992 International Conference on the Environment (the Earth Summit), held in Rio de Janeiro.[17]

---

ic News. July 26, 2007. URL: http://news.nationalgeographic.com/news/2007/07/070725-animal-smuggle.html. Accessed Oct. 1, 2007.

[14] "Congressional Funding For Enforcement of Wildlife Trade Grossly Inadequate". World Wildlife Fund Press Release. World Wildlife Fund. July 17, 2003. URL: http://worldwildlife.org/news/displayPR.cfm?prID=73. Accessed: Oct. 24, 2007.

[15] See generally: Caldwell.

[16] Ibid.

[17] The full list of international biodiversity treaties is extensive and not all are listed here. For a more complete compilation, please see generally Caldwell.

As an exemplar of international policy on biodiversity, CITES has displayed some successes. Since its inception in 1975, it has grown from 21 signatory member nations to over 172 parties as of 2007.[18] In doing so, it has marked a rise in international attention to the welfare of endangered species, as well as worldwide consciousness regarding environmental issues.

CITES is designed to regulate the international trade in endangered species—as either living or dead flora and fauna specimens and parts.[19] Intended to control the international trade in endangered species, the convention curries international efforts from members while still recognizing the individual parties' sovereignty over their own endemic biological resources. CITES, in asserting regulatory norms, makes an implicit recognition of the global market in endangered species trade, noting its existence and the scale of its reach. As a result, it is a significant international treaty in that it not only encourages global participation in endangered species protection, but also as it focuses on the trade of endangered species itself as a means of protecting them from extinction—that is, rather than concerning itself with the number and type of "takings" allowed, the convention instead ostensibly deals with the number and types of species traded between nations.[20] This makes CITES unique in that it is one of the few international environmental treaties related to endangered species to do so.[21]

Despite such optimism, however, the convention has found itself at the center of controversy. Scholars have argued that its effectiveness is questionable. In particular, they have noted weaknesses in its operation which frustrate its ability to achieve its stated purpose: to regulate and control endangered species trade.

II. CITES

Study on CITES has come from a variety of disciplines: the social sciences, including political science and public administration; law; and economics. Invariably, the research revolves around the treaty's enforcement issues, with varying degrees of depth and scope in analysis. Existing studies of CITES and its implementation have appeared in a wide number of scholarly journal articles,[22] gov-

---

[18]   CITES. CITES.org. URL: http://www.cites.org/eng/disc/parties/index.shtml. Accessed November 12, 2007. CITES is reprinted here in a section following the Conclusions chapter.

[19]   Ginette Hemley (ed.). *International Wildlife Trade: A CITES Sourcebook*. World Wildlife Fund (1994).

[20]   Ibid.

[21]   Other international environmental treaties that deal with trade in endangered species include the International Convention for the Regulation of Whaling (IWRC) and the African Convention of 1968 (see generally Cyrille de Klemm, *Biological Diversity Conservation and the Law*. IUCN (1993)).

[22]   Specifically, there are: Yale Environmental Protection Clinic. *Improving Enforcement and Compliance with the Convention on International Trade in Endangered Species*. URL:// http://www.yale.edu/envirocenter/clinic/cities.html. Accessed September 23, 2007; Kevin Eldridge, "Whale for Sale?", 24 *Georgia Journal of International & Comparative Law* 549-565 (1995); Kathryn Fuller, Ginette Hemley, and Sarah Fitzgerald, "Wildlife Trade Law Implementation in Developing Countries: the Experience in Latin America", 5 *Boston University International Law Journal* 289-310 (1987); Michael J. Glennon, "Has International Law Failed the Elephant?", 84 *American Journal of American Law* 1-43 (1990); Andrew J. Heimert, "How the Elephant Lost His Tusks", 104 *Yale Law Journal* 1473-1506 (1995); Valerie Karno, "Protection

ernment-sponsored agency reports,[23] doctoral dissertations,[24] as well as books,[25] produced by a wide range of sources which include students, professors, non-governmental organizations (NGOs), government agencies, and interested individuals. In general, these materials are directed at several critical elements related to treaty implementation which can be summarized in three major categories of criticism: 1) textually-related formulation problems, 2) operational issues in practical enforcement, and 3) participation barriers. For formulation, the existing scholarship indicates that CITES suffers from: 1) obscure or ill-defined wording,

of Endangered Gorillas and Chimpanzees in International Trade: Can CITES Help?", 14 *Hastings International & Comparative Law Review* (1991); Laura Kosloff and Mark Trexler, "The Convention on International Trade in Endangered Species: Enforcement Theory and Practice in the U.S.", 5 *Boston University International Law Journal* 327-361 (1987); Catharine L. Krieps, "Sustainable Use of Endangered Species under CITES: Is It a Sustainable Alternative?", 17 *University of Pennsylvania Journal of International Economic Law* 461-504 (1996); Susan Lieberman, "Improving International Controls on Wildlife Trade", 20 *Endangered Species Bulletin* (1995); Karl Jonathan Liwo, "The Continuing Significance of the Convention on International Trade in Endangered Species of Wild Fauna and Flora in the 1990's", 15 *Suffolk Transnational Law Journal* 989-1015 (1991); Paul Matthews, "Problems Related to the Convention on the International Trade in Endangered Species", 45 *International & Comparative Law Quarterly* 421-431 (1996); Eric McFadden, "Asian Compliance with CITES: Problems and Prospects", 5 *Boston University International Law Journal* 311-325 (1987); Jeffrey Melick, "Regulation of International Trade in Endangered Wildlife", 1 *Boston University International Law Journal* 249-275 (1982); Bill Padgett, "The African Elephant, Africa, and CITES: The Next Step", 2 *Global Legal Studies Journal* 529-552 (1995); Shennie Patel, "The Convention on International Trade in Endangered Species: Enforcement and the Last Unicorn," 18 *Houston Journal of International Law* 157-173 (1995); Michelle Ann Peters, "The Convention on International Trade of Endangered Species: An Answer to the Call of the Wild?", 10 *Connecticut Journal of International Law* 169-191 (1994); Philippe J. Sands and Albert P. Bedecarre, "Convention on International Trade in Endangered Species: the Role of Public Interest in Non-governmental Organizations in Ensuring the Effective Enforcement of the Ivory Trade Ban", 17 *Boston College Environmental Affairs Law Review* 799-822 (1990); Alan Schonfeld, "International Trade in Wildlife: How Effective is the Endangered Species Treaty?", 15 *California Western International Law Journal* 111-160 (1985); Gwyneth Stewart, "Enforcement Problems in the Endangered Species Convention: Reservations Regarding the Reservation Clauses", 14 *Cornell International Law Journal* 429-455 (1981).

23 Convention on International Trade in Endangered Species of Wild Fauna & Flora European Community Annual Report 1995, European Communities (1998); United States Fish & Wildlife Service. URL:http://www.fws.gov. Accessed: October 1, 2007.

24 Joni Baker. *A Substantive Theory of the Relative Efficiency of Environmental Treaty Compliance Strategies: The Case of CITES.* Texas A&M University (1998); Ian Andrew MacDonald. *Towards a General Theory of Environmental Treaties.* Simon Fraser University (1999); Steve McMullin, *Approaches to Management Effectiveness in State Fish and Wildlife Agencies.* Virginia Polytechnic Institute and State University (1993); Phyllis Ann Mofson, *The Behavior of States in an International Wildlife Conservation Regime: Japan, Zimbabwe, and CITES.* University of Maryland (1996); Mark Charles Trexler, *The Convention on the International Trade of Endangered Species of Wild Flora and Fauna: Political or Conservation Success?* University of California, Berkeley (1990).

25 Jon Hutton and Barnabas Dickson (eds.). *Endangered Species, Threatened Convention: The Past, Present and Future of CITES.* Earthscan Publications (2000); Sarah Fitzgerald. *International Wildlife Trade: Whose Business Is It?* World Wildlife Fund (1989); Andrea L. Gaski and Kurt A. Johnson. *Prescription for Extinction: Endangered Species and Patented Oriental Medicines in Trade.* TRAFFIC USA (1994); Ginette Hemley (ed.). *International Wildlife Trade: A CITES Sourcebook.* World Wildlife Fund (1994); Simon Lyster. *International Wildlife Trade.* Grotius Publications, Ltd. (1985); Rosalind Reeve. *Policing International Trade in Endangered Species: The CITES Treaty and Compliance.* Earthscan Publications (2002); Willem Wijnstekers. *The Evolution of CITES.* CITES Secretariat (2003).

and 2) omissions or loopholes. For operation, research asserts that CITES is hampered in its actual application by: 1) politics between signatory members, and 2) a lack of understanding regarding the realities of implementation. With respect to participation, the literature indicates that there are barriers which affect the ability of potential signatories to enforce CITES.

Formulation Problems

CITES contains several problems produced as a result of unclear or incomplete language. Encompassing confusion over terminology and definitions, these also include actual loopholes inherent in treaty provisions as well as "tension points" regarding content interpretation between parties. More specifically, these difficulties may be listed formally as: 1) linguistic problems over individual phrases, 2) allowance of trade with and among non-parties, 3) abuses of reservations, and 4) the existence of a "denunciation" option for parties.[26]

Phrasing

First, the linguistic questions which have arisen throughout the existence of CITES generally tend to center around the meanings of the terms "species", "endangered" or "threatened", and "commercial trade".[27] First, the word "species" may taxonomically refer to an animal group native to several different countries. But this contrasts with the CITES definition in Article I of "species" as "any species, subspecies, or geographically separate population thereof"—a definition which requires the distinction of different animal groups in differing geographic areas that may be taxonomically identical. If the CITES definition is applied and the species in question is subdivided into further "species" despite being taxonomically identical, then how is the distinction made in taxonomic terms, and how is this distinction made clear for inspection and trade purposes?[28]

Second is the problem that CITES does not define what constitutes an "endangered" or "threatened" species. It leaves unspecified thresholds of any sort to indicate at which point a species is to be considered Appendix I or Appendix II. This leaves two important questions unanswered by the CITES Secretariat. In relation to the preceding definition of "species," a species may be endangered in one country but not necessarily so in another. Does this situation mean that the species in question is considered endangered intentionally, or not endangered? Turning to pure delimitation, the absence of definition leaves no consistent means of determining "endangered" or "threatened" situations. Does this leave individual states with the discretion to set their own criteria? While the CITES Secretariat has issued guidelines attempting to clarify the confusion produced by these two terms that called for a consideration of "biological data" and "probabil-

---

[26] Hemley.

[27] Eldridge; Fitzgerald; Karno; Krieps; Liwo; Matthews; Melick; Peters.

[28] CITES, Article I; Hemley; Liwo.

ity of trade", it still has left the obscure nature of the language intact and subject to continual discussion.[29]

Another question is what constitutes "commercial" trade. This term is never defined explicitly in the CITES text, however, this word critical. Under Article III of the convention the granting of trade in any Appendix I (endangered) species is partially reliant on its determination. Any trade deemed "commercial" would automatically NOT qualify to receive a trade permit. As a result, this implicitly means that the breadth of whatever definition is adopted to delimit "commercial" will also delimit the quantity of trade allowed for Appendix I species. While the CITES Secretariat did release guidelines to define the term "...as broadly as possible", it still did not specify what the exact definition is, making it open to individual state determination,[30] thereby allowing the possibility for abuses in application of what trade is to be deemed "commercial".[31]

These linguistic issues are problematic. The terminology leaves the treaty bereft of uniform specific guidelines to be followed by each signatory member. Instead, it provides ground for dissension between participants over definition and standards to be used in controlling endangered species trade.[32] Differing values and text interpretations allows endangered species traffickers operating under CITES to follow the lowest common denominator (i.e., the most lenient definitions) in exploiting flora and fauna. More than this, it gives signatory parties uncertain legal grounds to pursue traffickers, as the handling of the international trade of endangered species implicitly assumes the involvement of multiple nations—and so, too, multiple legal systems—and hence requires some measure of legal commonality to pursue and capture illegal traffickers trading from one country to another.

Non-Parties

Following this is the question of trade between parties and non-parties to CITES. Article X requires "comparable documentation" from "competent authorities" in non-parties to be shown to CITES parties when trading flora and fauna listed under the convention. Unfortunately, the treaty does not define these terms, nor does it even indicate what minimum standard would be required to fulfill such terms, but instead leaves them open for determination by trading CITES parties. The net result is that non-parties, depending upon the rigor which treaty signatories interpret and enforce its language regarding trade with countries not members to CITES, may effectively operate free of CITES requirements. This allows several problems to limit the treaty: 1) it enables endangered species traffickers to flaunt treaty regulations simply by declaring their products' coun-

---

[29] CITES, Article II; Hemley; Liwo.

[30] CITES, Article III; Hemley; Karno.

[31] An example of this importation of endangered primates to Polish zoos for non-commercial purposes, but which were then re-exported by those zoos in what for all intents and purposes were commercial operations (Karno).

[32] This is a definite fact and not mere speculation. CITES, in order to observe the sovereignty of member nations, allows signatories the right to self-determine any phrases or terms that are not defined in the treaty text (see Hemley).

tries of origin as being non-signatory states, 2) ensures havens from which endangered species traffickers may base with impunity trade operations which violate CITES, and 3) preserves avenues through which the global endangered species trade may conduct business without regard to CITES requirements.[33]

Reservations

There is also the problem arising from abuses of the "reservation" clause in Article XXIII. Under this article, parties are able to claim reservations to CITES for which ever species they wish to exercise trade in, free of the provisions in the convention. Nowhere in the treaty is there a limit as to the number of reservations which a country can claim. Originally, when the drafts of the convention were first being introduced, it was expected that the reservation clause would only be used sparingly. Intended largely to aid in attracting international signatories, the clause was based on assumptions of sincere and earnest compliance with CITES and did not presuppose the possibility of abuse, leaving such a possibility open for exploitation via excessive and unconstrained numbers of reservations.[34] But more than this, the mere existence of such a clause allows for serious markets in endangered species trade to continue unmitigated free of CITES attempts at control and regulation. In effect, the reservation clause enables continued assurance of such trade, serving for all intents and purposes as a self-imposed, self-maintained impediment to CITES success.[35]

Denunciation

The "denunciation" clause in Article XXIV is also an issue. Under this section, any party may choose to withdraw from membership—and hence participation—from CITES simply by issuing a written notice to the Secretariat. Such a clause allows any party no longer interested in compliance to the provisions of the treaty to withdraw un-impeded and without justification, allowing the potential for abandonment of the convention by any number and type of the members concerned.[36]

The net effect of all the preceding CITES text issues is the politicization of the convention. The vagueness leaves open significant areas of discussion in which states may formulate and assert their own definitions and criteria, thus

---

[33]   CITES, Article X; Eldridge; Fitzgerald; Hemley; Karno; Krieps; Liwo; Matthews; Melick; Peters; Gary Meyers, "Surveying the Lay of the Land, Air, and Water: Features of Current International Environmental and Natural Resources Law, and Future Prospects for the Protection of Species Habitat to Preserve Global Biological Diversity," 3 *Colorado Journal of International Environmental Law and Policy* 479-634 (Summer 1992).

[34]   As an example of how states may claim unconstrained numbers of reservations, Switzerland has claimed as many as 32 species, Canada 13, Japan 14, and France 7 (see Karno and Stewart).

[35]   CITES, Article XXIII; Fitzgerald; Favre; Glennon; Heimert; Hemley; Krieps; Liwo; Matthews; Padgett; Peters; Sands and Bedecarre; Stewart.

[36]   Patricia Birnie and Alan Boyle. *International Law and the Environment*. Clarendon Press (1992); CITES, Article XXIV; Favre; Fitzgerald; Glennon; Heimert; Hemley; Krieps; Liwo; Matthews; Padgett; Peters; Sands and Bedecarre; Stewart; Oran Young. *International Cooperation*. Cornell University Press (1989).

preserving opportunities for significant inter-member debate and disagreement. The allowance of trade predominately absent of CITES requirements with and among non-parties to the treaty ensures the preservation of major avenues for illegal endangered species trade. The reservation options allow states to exercise trade free of CITES compliance at their own discretion, offering them participation without obligation. The denunciation clause gives states a final option of departure and its attendant threat of CITES breakdown. Combined together, these three factors produce a situation in which bargaining, negotiation, and interaction will have to occur for any resolution of ambiguities or differences in treaty interpretation, with the chances of reservations or even denunciation being the leverage in these processes. Taking into consideration the lack of an overarching authority with any level of binding or sanctioning power, CITES becomes less a "hard law" instrument of binding international convention and more a "soft law" example of international regimes.

Operational Problems

Not only does CITES have textual vagaries, it also suffers from challenges endemic to the nature of its subject matter. Arising from the mundane realities of public policy at both the international and national level, these problems pose a significant threat to CITES enforcement. Specifically, they are: 1) inspection complexities for participating national authorities, 2) scientific problems in data assessment for those authorities, 3) the inherent obstacles which exist whenever natural phenomenon coincide with policy structures, and 4) the challenges of operation under signatory conditions.

Inspection

First, the enforcement of CITES provisions relies largely on the ability of individual states to accurately and comprehensively inspect all flora and fauna trade that passes through their borders. The years of CITES existence have revealed serious shortcomings in this critical requirement. TRAFFIC investigations reveal that inspectors cannot accurately recognize the endangered species products passed to them, or even ascertain which species are listed in the CITES appendices. In addition, inspectors often experience great difficulty in properly differentiating between authentic export/import permits and false ones. Compounding the situation, inspectors have been found to be generally unaware of other nations' or even their own nation's domestic conservation laws—knowledge of which is critical in determining the issuance and validity of trade permits. While these problems are not solely the fault of inspectors (indeed, the mere task of being able to recognize and distinguish the more than 700 species listed in CITES appendices as well as the individual domestic endangered species laws of every nation on the earth is a task of overwhelming proportions), the fact remains that the aforementioned problems are a significant threat to effective CITES implementation. Such deficiencies are serious, as they allow trade in endangered species listed in CITES appendices to be allocated export/import permits regardless of the existence of relevant wildlife laws.[37]

Data Assessment

Second, there is the simple problem of basic scientific data collection, particularly with regards to obtaining correct population counts for CITES purposes. Accurate numbering of species populations is a notoriously frustrating challenge, as it often requires the estimation of population numbers in their native habitats in situations where they cannot be isolated or sampled in a rigorous, empirically absolute manner. Even with a wealth of financial, administrative, field operative, technical, or technological resources, the surmising of total population counts has often proved to be capable of defying complete estimation.[38] Such absence or weakness of biological population data severely hampers CITES enforcement, as the Scientific Authority of each state relies on them to determine listing in appendices, and therefore protection under CITES provisions. This leaves the question of species status open to non-scientific debate between member nations, and susceptible to political manipulation and determination rather than empirical biological assessment. Hence, species for which no accurate population figures may be gained may find themselves being improperly listed or even excluded from listing in CITES appendices even while their true numbers would require it.[39]

Nature

Third, there are the obstacles which are inherent any time policy—particularly international policy—structures are utilized in an attempt to interact with natural phenomenon. These difficulties occur because of the simple fact that flora and fauna behave as biological organisms irrespective of national boundaries. A specific endangered species may be endangered within the borders of one country but exist in healthy numbers elsewhere. The African elephant, for example, is considered on the verge of extinction in Kenya but is yet prospering in South Africa. Such differences in species welfare has led to confusion and debate between signatory members as to which species should be given protection under CITES and which should not. Because CITES is an international treaty assumed to offer guidelines to be followed by all participants, this lack of consensus erodes CITES protection of dwindling flora and fauna species. Overall, the treaty is incapable of exercising full control over the endangered species trade.[40]

---

[37] Karno; Liwo; Melick; Schonfeld; Trexler.

[38] Raymond Bonner. *At the Hand of Man: Peril and Hope for Africa's Wildlife*. Alfred A. Knopf (1993); Brian Groombridge (ed.). *Global Biodiversity*. UNEP (2000); William Robinson and Eric Bolen. *Wildlife Ecology and Management*. MacMillan Publishing Company (1989).

[39] Karno.

[40] Karno; Padgett.

Signatory

Finally, there is the issue of signatory conditions. The literature observes that because of its efforts to garner international support from potential signatory members, CITES was forced to address participant concerns regarding state sovereignty and hence had to construct a regulatory structure which preserved each signatory's sovereign power over its own internal affairs. As a result, CITES gave each member nation the right and responsibility to enforce the treaty to the extent to which it was capable. Because of this, despite being an ostensibly international treaty, CITES is only effective if its participants are committed to its enforcement. Unfortunately, not all participants are equally willing or able, as some countries either do not consider endangered species protection as a national priority, or do not have the financial, organizational, human, or information resources needed to fully regulate all endangered species trading activity crossing their borders. In "under-developed" regions, these realities have a greater proclivity to appear relative to developed nations due to the extensive pressures which exist in the developing world form the burdens of income inequality, political and socio-economic instability, poor health and social services, and widespread poverty. Such conditions cause the persistence of CITES deficiencies via corruption, inadequate or inconsistent funding, insufficient or unqualified administration, or outright inattention. Thus, because of these realities, CITES is considered to be a convention subject to inconsistent enforcement.[41]

Participation Problems

In addition to textual and operational problems, CITES is confronted with challenges impeding the membership of signatories. CITES, as an international treaty, is an expression of international cooperation between members. For each member, however, the decision to join CITES may involve a cost-benefit calculation, involving the weighing of costs and benefits incurred by joining the treaty. In situations where costs are greater than benefits, potential signatories are discouraged from supporting the treaty.[42]

The costs brought by membership in CITES include the financial, time, and labor resources committed to maintaining the management authority, scientific authority, permit office, prohibition and punishment mechanisms, and annual report filing required under the treaty. Other costs are the transaction costs generated by interactions between countries in support of CITES, such as negotiations, information-sharing, or enforcement assistance. Additional costs include the opportunity costs incurred by a country which surrenders the benefits brought by endangered species trade in lieu of complying with treaty restrictions.[43]

---

[41]   Bonner; Fitzgerald; Fuller et al.; Karno; Krieps; Liwo; Lyster; McFadden; Melick; Padgett; Peters; Reeve; Schonfeld; Trexler; Yale Environmental Protection Clinic.

[42]   Baker; MacDonald.

[43]   Ibid.

The benefits brought by membership are the general benefits of improved endangered species survival, which provides biological gains from biodiversity, emotional and spiritual gains from ecological preservation, scientific gains from potential biological discoveries, and economic gains from sustainable trade in conserved natural resources. Further benefits include improved international cooperation and communication brought by participation in CITES with other signatories.[44]

The result of the above-referenced series of implementation problems is that they hamper the success of CITES as an international legal instrument, essentially blunting the primary tools CITES is reliant upon to regulate and control the international trade in endangered species: accurate and timely CITES appendices listings, accurate and comprehensive trade inspection, and accurate and competent export/import permitting. The challenges, however, also illustrate the telling and continuing problem of CITES as a legal instrument attempting to deal with the practical world—that is, they show the difficulties in linking intention to reality, and the hurdles which inevitably rise in applying international treaties to large-scale issues such as global endangered species conservation and trade. In so doing, they highlight the issues which must be addressed in attempting to establish CITES as an effective international treaty, and whose presence perhaps also indicate the areas of international law in need of further development.[45]

IV. Literature Critique

This review of existing scholarship suggests that a better understanding of CITES problems might be achieved through research beyond the current predilection on nation-state or international levels and further into its implementation at a more fundamental, basic level: enforcement at the local level, not by the government which signed and ratified the treaty, but by the entities that may be expected by the government to actually apply it on a daily basis. Tailoring this analysis to focus on local actors requires guidance from the research literature, since it can point out areas that benefit from this study's contribution. Based on the available body of current work to date, the issues that could utilize this dissertation's attention can be organized into the following themes: limitations caused by level-of-analysis problems in terms of "local" enforcement, excessive breadth which sacrifices close inspection of a single geographic area in favor of an overarching generalized review, an emphasis on non-enforcement issues, a restrictive focus on particular species, and a lack of timeliness in data and analysis.

Level-of-Analysis

Some of the research literature, while ostensibly targeted at successful CITES enforcement, focuses on a level-of-analysis that precludes effective understanding of CITES enforcement in the field. This is due to their attention away

---

44 Ibid.

45 Birnie and Boyle, pp. 1-31; Alexander Kiss (ed.). *Living with Wildlife: Wildlife Resource Management with Local Participation in Africa.* World Bank (1990).

from "local" implementation in lieu of higher level analysis with nation-states or federal bureaucracies as actors under review. A number of studies concentrate exclusively on nation-states as actors, and do not devote attention to alternative levels-of-analysis.[46]

This poses some issues, in that by staying at the nation-state level, such studies lose awareness as to the particularities of enforcement, especially for the issues confronted by administrative personnel tasked with enforcing CITES on a day-to-day basis below the operations of national governments. A study addressing CITES implementation below the nation-state level might better illuminate the specific problems that impact the effective enforcement of CITES-related national regulations. This information is important, as it is ultimately the activities of dedicated personnel in the "field," defined as the lowest levels below national government at which CITES enforcement is at its most personal, that determine the effectiveness and ability of national government to meets its CITES obligations. Information regarding field-level implementation might allow nation-states to engage in self-mitigation and self-improvement without the external oversight of CITES Secretariat or Conference of the Parties (COP). A more useful analysis addressing this aspect of CITES implementation would deal primarily on the issues of day-to-day CITES enforcement confronting field personnel.

Some scholars do extend their work to actors below the nation-state level, with analysis on government agencies tasked with implementing CITES in local communities.[47] But these studies utilize definitions that are constrained, in that "local enforcement" is interpreted as being the activities of the U.S. Fish and Wildlife Service—a federal agency—operating with federal jurisdiction in counties and municipalities. However, under the possible implications of devolution, such a definition ignores the potential roles county and municipal entities may play in federal policy. CITES, as enacted via the ESA, is dependent on reports and referrals from law enforcement agencies to supplement the reach of Fish and Wildlife Service inspectors. Hence, U.S. implementation of CITES extends further than the federal jurisdiction of the FWS, and penultimately reaches the domain of non-federal law enforcement.[48] A more accurate definition of "field" enforcement would encompass these local, non-federal entities.

Beyond the constraints in definition, current research on community-level CITES implementation do not entirely relate local enforcement to national or international levels. In particular, they do not clearly explain how local "field" enforcement problems create a schism between the realities of implementation and CITES' objectives.[49] A study of greater value to CITES would investigate the impact and relationship of "field" problems to the treaty's success.

In addition, in dealing with the "field," existing scholarship retains a focus on leadership, and shies away from patrol personnel. This level-of-analysis cre-

---

[46] Baker; Liwo; MacDonald; Melick; Mofson; Schonfeld.

[47] McMullin; Melick; Schonfeld; Trexler.

[48] McMullin; Melick; Schonfeld; Trexler.

[49] Trexler.

ates a possible gap in knowledge, in that the responses and perceptions of senior management may not be the same as their field staff, and the problems confronting senior management may not be the same as the challenges facing personnel engaged in patrolling CITES-related traffic.[50] Even for the times when the literature does provide attention to field issues encountered by lower-level patrol officers, the analysis is somewhat limited in sampling, with infrequent interviews or surveys. Instead, the investigations rely on anecdotes or observations from single subordinates, missing the opportunity to gather more comprehensive feedback from a larger cohort of patrol personnel.[51] A more appropriate study would employ a larger research sample restricted exclusively to field-level CITES-related enforcement, particularly the issues they face in the day-to-day implementation of CITES.

Breadth of Review

Some literature, while addressing CITES enforcement at the field level below that of national governments, unfortunately do not directly review enforcement within the United States. As a result, the work is rendered less germane insofar as it compounds the level-of-analysis problem by bypassing potential insights of immediate relevancy to U.S. enforcement. Several scholars target regions other than the U.S.[52] In doing so, they engage comparative studies of multiple countries. While useful in summarizing the difficulties confronted by field personnel around the world, this decreases the depth of their study towards uncovering nuances of domestic policy environments. A more useful study for understanding enforcement nuances would devote attention to one nation-state, and dedicate its energies exclusively to the field-level enforcement problems within that country, with the goal of performing an investigation comprehensive in its review of field-level CITES implementation issues but singular in constraining its level-of-analysis to the CITES-related activities of field personnel.

Even when the literature does focus on the U.S., it employs methodology that is still comparative, with the focus on state-by-state analysis. Such an approach misses the deeper insight that could come from a study targeted solely on a single geographic location.[53] A single location-specific, issues-identifying case might unveil more subtle problems of comparable, if not equal, significance to CITES implementation, as it would afford greater attention and closer inspection into the challenges of CITES-related field enforcement.

Emphasis on Non-Enforcement Issues

Some of the research fails to deal with CITES enforcement altogether. Instead, the literature presents a factual description of CITES operation as presented by the treaty, or turns to philosophical or textual nuances in the treaty. While

---

[50] McMullin; Melick; Schonfeld.

[51] Liwo; Schonfeld.

[52] Fuller; Hemley; Fitzgerald; McFadden.

[53] McMullin.

relevant, and in some ways insightful for CITES enforcement, this work does not aid in understanding the day-to-day "field" issues.[54]

Admittedly, a few scholars attempt to provide a more comprehensive method, combining factual presentation with abstract discourse supplemented with implementation review. But these works tend to present enforcement incidentally to their main concern, which tend to relate more to questions of treaty semantics, goals, and administration between signatories, as opposed to field operations supporting CITES.[55] A study more suited towards policy implementation would put more emphasis on the problems encountered by patrol personnel.

Focus on Particular Species or Particular Types of Trade

Several of the studies restrict their attention to specific endangered species or limited types of endangered species trade (such as exotic medicines).[56] These studies help provide understanding about CITES in practice, but their restrictions decrease the cross-application of their observations to other types of flora and fauna, or other categories of trade. In particular, they do not fully illuminate the nature of CITES-related enforcement activities pursued by each nation-state signatory, and do not yield insights into the issues of actual enforcement in the field that must be addressed to ensure control over endangered species trade as a whole. A more appropriate study would be more comprehensive, covering the full range of endangered species protected by CITES, while still being constrained in other ways to field-level CITES-related enforcement activities.

Need for Current Data and Updated Analysis

Finally, while some of the research is related to CITES enforcement, it suffers from a lack of timeliness in data. Because of their publication dates, the literature contains data from the 1980s.[57] Even when the analysis is more recent, it tends to collect data that is limited in sampling size, making it difficult to extrapolate identifiable trends to compare against current policy trends.[58] The current state of knowledge would benefit from data regarding wildlife trade and enforcement resources that was more current and more readily tied to current implementation efforts.

The preceding discussion calls for a study of the highlighted gaps in research. Specifically, it points out potential areas of research for further understanding into treaty implementation: 1) analysis focused on the issues of day-to-day field-level CITES enforcement, 2) a constrained breadth in review targeting a small geographic area so as to produce more nuances and detail as opposed to

---

54 Hemley; Krieps; Sands and Bedecarre.

55 Baker; Lieberman; Liwo; Matthew; Peters; Schonfeld; Stewart.

56 Eldridge; Gaski; Glennon; Heimert; Johnson; Karno; Padgett.

57 Fitzgerald.

58 Trexler.

broad generalization, 3) an emphasis on CITES-related enforcement issues, 4) a scope that encompasses a relatively comprehensive variety of endangered species being transported in violation of CITES in a particular geographic area, and 5) updated literature with more timely data reflecting current trends in CITES enforcement issues. Analysis tailored to addressing these areas may yield further insights into the nature of CITES enforcement, serving either to expand on prior research or uncovering further dimensions in problems. Delving into a field-based analysis of enforcement issues would provide the basis for an in-depth study, with a potentially rich supply of detail offered by the intricacies of field enforcement, while still affording a basis for contextual breadth, in that such detail could exist for the myriad range of enforcement issues. As a dissertation topic, such a target would require some constraints in scope, beginning with a declaration of theory to define a rubric and an objective of analysis, a selection of tools to apply the analysis, a statement of variables upon which the tools are to be applied, and the framework which is to tie the preceding into a coherent body of investigative research fulfilling the objective of analysis.

VI. Conclusion

The existing research literature on CITES ignores the dependence of CITES enforcement upon local law enforcement. This analysis hypothesizes that local actors have an awareness of treaties and see an interest in participating in their enforcement. The hypothesis is tested using a case study centered around CITES, with additional smuggling treaties used for comparison, with data gathered from a local law enforcement agency in Los Angeles dealing with international trafficking covered by the treaties in the study. The case study first utilizes qualitative techniques to determine the nature of the linkage between local law enforcement and CITES along the implementation chain. Subsequently, the analysis then turns to quantitative techniques to identify issues and possible mitigation in the linkage by drawing data from the Port of Los Angeles Police regarding their perceptions of international law, the domestic laws which express international laws within the United States, and the subject issues they were intended to address.

3
Theory

The goal of this study is to highlight the relevance of an additional level of analysis in international policy: the local level. The nature of international policy has tended to ignore this area, with the bulk of study utilizing frameworks involving other conceptualizations of the global arena such as nation-states or transnational non-governmental organizations (i.e., a "higher" level view). In contrast, this research explores the community level by following developing threads in national-to-community allocation of law enforcement responsibilities (i.e., a "lower" level perspective). The intent is to demonstrate the linkage between local and global realms, and the manner in which potential devolution of authority to local enforcement may pose issues to international policy implementation.

To better understand this connection, it is somewhat helpful to survey current theoretical conceptions of international politics. This helps place the study within the context of international policy. Furthermore, it sets the stage to understand the implications of the analysis to current theory.

I. Ideas of the Local

Notions of local involvement in larger-scale government actions are not new with respect to national policy. Both within popular media and research literature, there has been a discourse of utilization by national policy of local actors. Calls for greater local authority in administering national policy have echoed in other countries, even with respect to environmental issues.[59] Within the U.S., this has revolved around a readjustment of authority, with greater allocation of re-

---

59   For examples, see generally: Raymond Bonner. *At the Hand of Man: Peril and Hope for Africa's Wildlife*. Alfred A. Knopf (1993); R. Steven Brown. "States Put Their Money Where Their Environment Is." Environmental Council of the States. April 1999. URL: http://www.ecos.org/section/publications. Accessed November 12, 2007; Alexander Kiss and Dinah Shelton. *International Environmental Law*. Transnational Publishers, Inc. (1991); Clark Gibson and Stuart Marks, "Transforming Rural Hunters into Conservationists: An Assessment of Community-Based Wildlife Management Programs in Africa," *World Development*, Vol. 23 No. 6 (June 1995), pp. 941-957; Jeffrey Hackel, "Community Conservation and the Future of Africa's Wildlife," *Conservation Biology*, Vol. 13 No. 4 (Aug. 1999), pp. 726-734; Mark Infield, "Cultural Values: A Forgotten Strategy for Building Community Support for Protected Areas in Africa," *Conservation Biology*, Vol. 15 No. 3 (June 2001), pp. 800-802; Timothy Lawrence, *Devolution and Collaboration in the Development of Environmental Regulations*. Dissertation. Ohio State University (2005); Barry Rabe, "Permitting, Prevention and Integration: Lessons from the States," in *Environmental Governance: A Report on the Next Generation of Environmental Policy*, Donald Kettl (ed.). Brookings Institution Press (2002); Denise Scheberle. *Federalism and Environmental Policy*. Georgetown University Press (2004); Kirsten M. Silvius, et al. (eds.). *People in Nature: Wildlife Conservation in South and Central America*. Columbia University Press (2004); Oswald Braken Tisen, et al. "Wildlife Conservation and Local Communities in Sarawak, Malaysia". Paper presented to Second Regional Forum for Southeast Asia of the IUCN World Commission For Protected Areas. Dec. 1999. URL: http://www.mered.org.uk/ mike/ papers/Communities_Pakse_99.htm. Accessed Oct. 24, 2007; David Western, et al. (eds.). *Natural Connections: Perspectives in Community-Based Conservation*. Island Press. 1994.

sponsibilities and powers to local communities. Areas where this is more frequently discussed include border security, human trafficking, and national security.[60]

This process of devolution reflects a modification of traditional rules of jurisdiction, which tend to hold that enforcement of national laws fall under exclusive jurisdiction of federal agencies while local laws are the exclusive jurisdiction of local agencies. As suggested by popular and scholarly literature, current trends presume that enforcement of national laws will benefit from the addition of resources at the local level, and look to the opportunities for local actors to gain greater jurisdiction over federal laws.[61]

II. Encompassing the Local within the Global

Given the prospects for greater enforcement of national law by local actors implied by the increasing calls for devolution, it would appear a potential equally beneficial concept for supporting international instruments. Unfortunately, the notion that local authority can assist policy implementation, while prevalent within the discourse on national policy, is not so apparent with global ones. The concept of devolution is largely discussed within the framework of national laws, but less so for international law.

The absence of devolution with international policy may be a reflection of prevailing scholarship. Modern investigations of international policy, as reflected in the discourse over globalization, utilize a "higher" level-of-analysis paradigm focusing more on the relations between transnational forces and less on the role of local actors.

---

[60] For examples, see generally: Robert Block, "Politics & Economics: Fighting Terrorism By Sharing Data; Homeland Security Plans To Improve Cooperation With Police Departments", *Wall Street Journal* (Eastern Edition), New York, New York, Oct 16, 2006, p. A6; *Fact Sheet: Improving Border Security and Immigration Within Existing Law*. Department of Homeland Security. August 10, 2007. URL: http://www.dhs.gov/xnews/releases/pr_1186757867585.shtm. Accessed Sept. 26, 2007; Tom Fitton, "Local Law Enforcement Effective in Fighting Illegal Immigration", *The Conservative Voice*, July 24, 2006. URL: http://www.theconservativevoice .com/articles/ article.html?id=16389. Accessed Sept. 25, 2007; Patrick Poole, "Local Law Enforcement and Homeland Security", *American Thinker*, August 9, 2007. URL: http:// www.americanthinker.com/2007/08/ local_law_enforcement_and_home.html. Accessed Sept. 26, 2007; Gretchen Randall, "Devolution to the States is Working for Welfare; It Can Work for Public Lands", National Policy Analysis. National Center for Public Policy Research. June 2001. URL: http://www.nationalcenter.org/ NPA340.html. Accessed Sept. 25, 2007; Zoe Tillman, "Crackdown: Immigration supporters react to a resolution passed July 10 in Prince William County, Va., that empowers local police to determine the status of residents and to arrest illegal immigrants", *Christian Science Monitor*. July 17, 2007. URL: http://www.csmonitor.com/2007/ 0717/p01s05-ussc.html. Accessed Sept. 25, 2007; "U.S. Wants Local Help in Human Trafficking", *Juvenile Justice Digest*, Vol. 32 No. 12 (July 6, 2004), p. 6.

[61] For examples, see generally: Kathleen Anders and Curtis Shook, "New Federalism: Impact on State and Local Governments", *Journal of Public Budgeting, Accounting, & Financial Management*, Vol. 15 No. 3 (Fall 2003). pp. 466-486; Fred Collie. *21st Century Policing: The Institutionalization of Homeland Security in Local Law Enforcement Organizations*. Master's Thesis, Naval Postgraduate School. Monterey: Department of National Security Affairs (2006); David Thacher, "The Local Role in Homeland Security", *Law & Society Review*. Vol. 39 No. 3 (Sept. 2005), pp. 635-676; Charles Wise and Rania Nader, "Organizing the Federal System for Homeland Fecurity: Problems, issues, and Dilemmas", *Public Administration Review*, Vol. 62 Special Issue (Sept. 2002), pp. 44-58.

This is apparent in the literature, which addresses globalization from varying perspectives, including world history, economics, politics, culture, security and environment, and concerns itself with the impact globalization in these areas has on human society.[62] Historical research explores the thread of international relations throughout the past, and compares it to the current era.[63] Economic globalization studies the proliferation of trans-national trade regimes and multi-national integrated markets.[64] Political globalization observes how states are increasingly interacting with both supra-state organizations, which tie them together in a horizontal arrangement of power, as well as sub-state actors, who interact with states and supra-states in vertical arrangements of power.[65] Cultural

---

[62] For examples, see generally: Bonaventura de Sousa Santos and Cesar Rodriguez-Garavito (eds.). *Law and Globalization from Below*. Cambridge University Press (2005); Robert Gilpin. *The Challenge of Global Capitalism: The World Economy in the 21st Century*. Princeton University Press (2000); Paul Kennedy, et al. *Global Trends and Global Governance*. Pluto Press (2002); Richard Langhorne. *The Coming of Globalization*. Palgrave (2001); Jan Aart Scholte. *Globalization: A Critical Introduction*. St. Martin's Press (2000); P.J. Simmons and Chantal De Jonge Oudraat (eds.). *Managing Global Issues*. Carnegie Endowment for International Peace (2001).

[63] For examples, see generally: Ian Clark. *Globalization and Fragmentation*. Oxford University Press (1997); Michael Hanagan, "States and Capital", in *Ends of Globalization*, Don Kalb, Marco Van Der Land, et al. (eds.). Rowman and Littlefield (2000), pp. 67-86; Giovanni Arrighi, "Globalization, State Sovereignty, and the Endless Accumulation of Capital", in *Ends of Globalization*, Don Kalb, Marco Van Der Land, et al. (eds.). Rowman and Littlefield (2000), pp. 125-150; Paul Hirst and Grahame Thompson, "Globalization and the History of the International Economy", in *Global Transformation Reader*, David Held and Anthony McGrew (eds.). Polity (2000), pp. 68-75; Robert K. Schaeffer. *Understanding Globalization*. Rowman and Littlefield (2d ed. 2003); Manfred B. Steger. *Globalization*. Oxford University Press (2003).

[64] For examples, see generally: C.F. Bergsten, "Globalizing Free Trade", *Foreign Affairs*, Vol. 75 No. 3 (May/June 1996), pp. 105-120; Albert Berry, "Who Wins and Who Loses? An Economic Perspective", in *Civilizing Globalization*, Richard Sandbrook (ed.). SUNY Press (2003), pp. 15-26; Robin Broad (ed.). *Global Backlash*. Rowman and Littlefield Publishers (2002); Michel Chossudovsky. *The Globalization of Poverty*. Zed (1997); Tony Clarke, "Mechanisms of Corporate Rule", in *The Case Against the Global Economy*, Jerry Mander and Edward Goldsmith (eds.). Sierra Club Books (1996), pp.78-91; Giovanni Cornia, "Poverty and Inequality in the Era of Liberalization and Globalization", in Hans Van Ginkel et al., *Human Development and Environment*. United Nations University Press (2002), pp. 55-87; CQ Researcher. *Global Issues*. Congressional Quarterly Press (2001); de Sousa Santos; Edward Goldsmith, "Global Trade and the Environment", in *The Case Against the Global Economy*, Jerry Mander and Edward Goldsmith (eds.). Sierra Club Books (1996), pp. 78-91; William Greider. *One World, Ready or Not*. Allen Lane (1997); Andrew Hurrell and Nagaire Woods (eds.). *Inequality, Globalization, and World Politics*. Oxford University Press (1999); Martin Kohr. *Rethinking Globalization*. Zed (2001); Martin Khor. "Global Economy and the Third World", in *The Case Against the Global Economy*, Jerry Mander and Edward Goldsmith (eds.). Sierra Club Books (1996), pp. 47-59; Langhorne; Kennedy, et al.; Scholte; Simmons and Oudraat; Charles Tilly, "Globalization Threatens Labor's Rights", *International Labor and Working Class History*, Vol. 47 No. 1 (Spring 1995), pp. 1-23; Hans van Ginkel, et al. *Human Development and Environment*. United Nations University Press (2002), pp. 55-87; Jeremy Rifkin, "New Technology and the End of Jobs", in *The Case Against the Global Economy*, Jerry Mander and Edward Goldsmith (eds.). Sierra Club Books (1996), pp. 108-121; Caroline Thomas and Peter Wilkin (eds.). *Globalization and the South*. MacMillan (1997); Adrian Wood. *North-South Trade, Employment and Inequality*. Clarendon Press (1994).

[65] For examples, see generally: Tony Clarke; Ronald Cox, "An Alternative Approach to Multilateralism for the 21st Century", *Global Governance*, Vol. 3 No.1 (Jan.-April 1997), pp. 103-116; David Held. *Democracy and the Global Order*. Polity Press (1995); Kennedy, et al.; Langhorne; Eric Lee. *The Labour Movement and the Internet: the New Internationalism*. Pluto (1997); Anthony McGrew. *The Transformation of Democracy? Globalization and Territorial Democra-*

globalization deals with the increasing integration of values and aesthetics irrespective of national boundaries or geographic range.[66] Security concerns address the questions of a growing prevalence of violence conducted by non-state entities with objectives unrelated to self-determination or state sovereignty.[67] Environmental globalization research studies issues of ongoing natural degradation and resulting international responses.[68]

All of these areas of the globalization discourse bypasses focus on local actors, as much as they are defined as those entities which are not nation-states nor

---

cy. Polity Press (1997); Ralph Nader and Lori Wallach, "GATT, NAFTA, and The Subversion of the Democratic Process", in *The Case Against the Global Economy*, Jerry Mander and Edward Goldsmith (eds.). Sierra Club Books (1996), pp. 92-107; James Rosenau. *Along the Domestic-Foreign Frontier*. Cambridge University Press (1997); Simmons and Hopkins; Scholte; Beth Simmons and Daniel Hopkins, "The Constraining Power of International Treaties: Theory and Methods", *American Political Science Review*, Vol. 99 No. 4 (November 2005), pp. 623-632; Simmons and Oudraat; Jana von Stein, "Do Treaties Constrain or Screen? Selection Bias and Treaty Compliance", *American Political Science Review*, Vol. 99 No. 4 (November 2005), pp. 611-622; Susan Strange. *The Retreat of the State*. Cambridge University Press (1996); Andrew Vandenberg (ed.). *Citizenship and Democracy in a Global Era*. MacMillan (2000).

[66] For examples, see generally: Broad; Ronald Brown, "Globalization and the End of the National Project", in *Boundaries in Question*, John MacMillan and Andrew Linklater (ed.). Pinter (1995), pp. 28-60; Mark Duffield. *Global Governance and the New Wars*. Zed (2001); Kennedy, et al.; Scholte; Michael Shapiro, "Moral Geographies and the Ethics of Post-Sovereignty", *Public Culture*, Vol. 6 No. 3 (Spring 1994), pp. 479-502; John Tomlinson, "Homogenisation and Globalisation", *History of European Ideas*, Vol. 20 No. 4-6 (Feb. 1995), pp. 891-897; Alan Warde, "Eating Globally: Cultural Flows and the Spread of Ethnic Restaurants", in *The Ends of Globalization*, Marco Van Der Land, et al. (eds.). Rowman and Littlefield (2000), pp. 219-316.

[67] For examples, see generally: Congressional Quarterly; Duffield; Robert Harvey. *Global Disorder*. Carroll and Graff Publishers (2003); Hans Holm and Georg Sorenson, "International Relations Theory in a World of Variation", in *Whose World Order?*, Georg Sorensen and Hans Holm (eds.). Westview (1995), pp. 187-206; Samuel Huntington. *Clash of Civilizations*. Touchstone (1997); Robert Kaplan, "The Coming Anarchy", *Atlantic Monthly*, Vol. 273 No. 2 (Feb. 1994), pp. 44-76; Kennedy, et al.; Langhorne; Paul Richards. *Fighting for the Rainforest*. Heinemann (1996); Simmons and Oudraat; Susan Willett, "Globalization and the Means of Destruction", in *Globalization and Insecurity*, Barbara Harriss-White (ed.). Palgrave (2002), pp. 184-202.

[68] For examples, see generally: Broad; Lynton Keith Caldwell. *International Environmental Policy*. Duke University Press (1996); Akiko Domoto, "International Environment Governance—Its Impact on Social and Human Development", in *Human Development and the Environment*, Hans Van Ginkel et al. (eds.). United Nations University Press (2002), pp. 284-301; Hilary French, "Challenging the WTO", *Worldwatch*, Vol. 12 No. 6 (Nov./Dec. 1999), pp. 22-27; Edward Goldsmith, "Global Trade and the Environment", in *The Case Against the Global Economy*, Jerry Mander and Edward Goldsmith (eds.). Sierra Club Books (1996), pp. 78-91; Inter-Parliamentary Union. Final Declaration of the Parliamentary Meeting on the Occasion of UNCTAD X, Bangkok. UNCTAD (February 2000); Joseph G. Jabbra and Onkar P. Dwivedi (eds.). *Governmental Response to Environmental Challenges in Global Perspective*. IOS Press (1998); Martin Khor, "Global Economy and the Third World", in *The Case Against the Global Economy*, Jerry Mander and Edward Goldsmith (eds.). Sierra Club Books (1996), pp. 47-59; Bjorn Lomborg. *The Skeptical Environmentalist*. Cambridge University Press (2001); Scholte; Simmons and Oudraat; Matthew Stilwell, *Governance, Globalization and the Need for WTO Reform*. Centre for International Environmental Law (1999); UNDP. *Human Development Report 1999*. Oxford University Press (1999); Hans van Ginkel, et al. (eds.). *Human Development and the Environment: Challenges for the United Nations in the New Millenium*. United Nations University Press (2002); Gerd Winter (ed.). *Multilevel Governance of Global Environmental Change*. Cambridge University Press (2006); World Commission on Environment and Development. *Our Common Future*. Oxford University Press (1987).

trans-national non-governmental organizations but are still within the sovereign borders of nation-states. To the extent the research does review the local, it does so within analysis of how global and local arenas interact, and does not delve into notions of the function local actors may play in international policy.

This opens an area for analysis, particularly for policymakers seeing to improve the effectiveness of international instruments. In light of federal efforts at devolution of authority once deemed exclusive to national government jurisdiction, there appears to be an opening to utilize local actors in international policy implementation. As the federal government moves to allocate enforcement of national laws to local government, linkages are created between "lower-level" communities and larger-scale policies. Because some of the national laws are domestic expressions of international treaties, these linkages extend from lower-level law enforcement to "higher-level" global policies. The result is that local actors may be seen as potential participants in the enforcement of international instruments.

III. Linkages from Global Perspectives to Local Communities

Similar to the research addressing global phenomenon, the focus on higher-level actors at the expense of lower-level actors is a prevailing feature in international political theory. Within the context of existing theory, lower-level (including community-level) actions are overshadowed by perspectives dealing with trans-national or supra-national activities. Despite this, there are facets of the scholarship that offer direction regarding sub-nation-state actors and their relationships with global politics. Understanding them assists in placing community-level operations within the context of international policy implementation, and allows connection between local levels to global ones.

Theories of the Global

International political theory is built upon several generally recognized major schools, with each school exercising differing perspectives in studying the world. As interpreted by the field, such perspectives may be divided into the following distinct bodies: the realist/neo-realists, liberals/neo-liberals, international legalists, and structuralists. Realists/Neo-Realists generally view the world as a largely anarchical system consisting of nation-states as the primary international actors.[69] Liberalists/Neo-Liberalists view the world as composed of nation-states and non-governmental actors interacting in interdependent relationships.[70] Structuralists, sometimes labeled "post-behavioral", "post-modern", or

---

[69] See generally: David Baldwin (ed.). *Neorealism and Neoliberalism*. Columbia University Press (1993); Ken Booth and Steve Smith (eds.). *International Relations Theory Today*. Pennsylvania State University Press (1995); James Der Derian (ed.). *International Theory: Critical Investigations*. New York University Press (1995); James Dougherty and Robert Pfaltzgraff, Jr. (eds.). *Contending Theories of International Relations*. HarperCollins Publishers (1990); Joshua Goldstein. *International Relations*. Addison Wesley Longman (4th ed. 2001); Phil Williams, et al. (eds.). *Classic Readings of International Relations*. Wadsworth Publishing Co. (1994).

[70] Ibid.; Gerhard von Glahn. *Law Among Nations*. MacMillan Publishing Co. (1992); Ann-Marie Slaughter-Burley, "International Law and International Relations Theory: A Dual Agenda",

"critical studies," argue that the global arena is essentially an historical construction created and maintained by actors who have power over actors who do not, with the international community being a structure organized to preserve and encourage the unequal relationships between the elites and non-elites.[71]

All of the aforementioned theoretical schools, while distinct from each other, nevertheless tend to emphasize a higher-level worldview, both in terms of their scale of analytical boundaries and their classification of actors operating within those boundaries. All the schools, without exception, generally deal with the world as a single international arena with nation-states and assorted non-governmental organizations (NGOs) as the primary actors. This suggests that international policy structures based on such theories are constructions drawn exclusively from these actors.

Alternatives, however, do exist within the scholarship. The history of international political theory has sustained a "level-of-analysis" controversy, over whether the world should be interpreted as a single massive system, a community of nation-states and NGOs, or as an array of sub-national groups and peoples.[72] Proponents of the latter state that the adoption of a "macro"-level view incorrectly ignores "micro"-level phenomenon in which the roles of human society and domestic populations are assumed to be fully capable of influencing global activity. If not this, then the world should at least be construed as consisting of multiple, interacting levels in which domestic groups have as vital a role in international relations as the political institutions which stand above them.[73]

Local Connections to the Global

Lower-level perspectives—particularly in relation to environmental issues—have accompanied the development of international politics research on globalization, with studies addressing the shifts in authority between global and nation-state levels, as well as between nation-state and local levels. A dominant concern is how complex, interconnected, trans-boundary environmental problems have affected changes in the international landscape, with a proliferation of actors

---

American Journal of International Law, Vol. 87 No. 2 (April 1993), pp. 205-255; Steven Schneebaum, "The Enforceability of Customary Norms of Public International Law", *Brooklyn Journal of International Law*, Vol. 8 No. 1 (1982), pp. 289-315.

71 See generally: Der Derian; Goldstein.

72 For introduction, see generally: J. David Singer, "The Level-of-Analysis Problem in International Relations", *World Politics*, Vol. 14 No. 1 (October 1961), pp. 77-92.

73 The literature on this is extensive. For examples, see generally: Yale Ferguson and Richard Mansbach, "Between Celebration and Despair: Constructive Suggestions for Future International Theory", *International Studies Quarterly*, Vol. 35 No. 4 (December 1991), pp. 363-386; Peter Haas, "Introduction: Epistemic Communities and International Policy Coordination", *International Organization*, Vol. 46 No. 1 (Winter 1992), pp. 1-35; Samuel Huntington. *Clash of Civilizations*. Touchstone (1997); David Putnam, "Diplomacy and Domestic Politics: The Logic of Two-Level Games", *International Organization*, Vol. 42 No. 3 (Summer 1988), pp. 427-460; James Rosenau, "The Relocation of Authority in a Shrinking World", *Comparative Politics*, Vol. 24 No. 3 (April 1992), pp. 253-272; Ian Rowlands, "The International Politics of Environment and Development: The Post-UNCED Agenda", *Millenium*, Vol. 21 No. 2 (Summer 1992), pp. 209-224; Peter Skalnik, "On the Inadequacy of the Concept of the 'Traditional State'", *Journal of Legal Pluralism and Unofficial Law*, Vol. 25 & 26 (1987), pp. 301-325.

accompanied by changes in power across traditional notions of international, national, and local areas of authority.[74]

Research emphasizing the local level within international environmental policy features the works of Elinor Ostrom and Ronnie Lipschutz, who conceptualize environmental issues as multi-level phenomenon, and dedicated portions of their research to investigating "micro"-level phenomenon as it operates with respect to trans-national environmental problems. Both assert the importance of local activities in influencing the success or failure of "macro"-level policy instruments. Ostrom primarily addresses the subject of common pool resources (CPRs), and studies the role of local solutions relative to national policy. Her work has been extended to deal with the relationship between local activities and international policies. Lipschutz similarly focuses on the challenges of environmental problems, and writes on the importance of local authority in implementing international policy. His research has also been applied in studying the interaction of actors in the hierarchy of local and national authority.

Elinor Ostrom argues that much of the environment composes "common pool resources" which are accessible for use by communities of people, who interact with the environment as a shared resource. Such CPRs, she notes, are susceptible to over-exploitation and depletion. Solutions to this problem have tended to center around debates between those who believe that CPRs are best managed by privatization and the resulting efficiencies of free market forces versus those who believe that CPRs are best managed by centralized authorities capable of creating and enforcing laws on natural resource use. She asserts that there is a third option: local management.[75] Ostrom believes that effective solutions to CPR problems can be created by actors at the local level through the development of cooperative natural resource use rules independent of free market economic principles and being enforceable without non-local government authority.[76] She believes that actors at the local level are better suited to managing CPRs, since they are 1) more familiar with the environment in their commu-

[74]   For examples, see generally: Lamont Hempel. *Environmental Governance: The Global Challenge*. Island Press (1996); Sheila Jasanoff and Marybeth Martello (eds.). *Earthly Politics: Local and Global in Environmental Governance*. MIT Press (2004); Ronnie Lipschutz, "From Place to Planet: Local Knowledge and Global Environmental Governance", *Global Governance*, Vol. 3 No. 1 (Jan.-Apr. 1997), pp. 83-102; Ronnie Lipschutz and Judith Mayer. *Global Civil Society and Global Environmental Politics: The Politics of Nature from Place to Planet*. SUNY Press (1996); Matthew Paterson, "Interpreting Trends in Global Environmental Governance", *International Affairs*. Vol. 75 No. 4 (October 1999). pp. 793-802; James Rosenau. "Governance, Order, and Change in World Politics", in James Rosenau and Ernst-Otto Czempiel (eds.), *Governance Without Government: Order and Change in World Politics*. Cambridge University Press (1992); Daniel Press, et al., "The Role of Local Government in the Conservation of Rare Species", *Conservation Biology*, Vol. 10 No. 6 (December 1996), pp. 1538-1548; James Rosenau. "Environmental Challenges in a Turbulent World", in Ronnie Lipschutz and Ken Conca (eds.), *The State and Social Power in Global Environmental Politics*. Columbia University Press (1993); Ion Bogdan Vasi, "Thinking Globally, Planning Nationally and Acting Locally: Nested Organizational Fields and the Adoption of Environmental Practices", *Social Forces*, Vol. 86 No. 1 (September 2007), pp. 113-137; Oran Young (ed.). *Global Governance: Drawing Insights from the Environmental Experience*. MIT Press (1997).

[75]   Elinor Ostrom. *Governing the Commons*. Cambridge University Press (1990).

[76]   Ibid.

nities, 2) more familiar with the nature of their interaction with local environments, and 3) capable of developing and adapting management rules that are built of community consensus, and hence more likely to be self-sustaining.[77]

Ronnie Lipschutz, compared to Ostrum, extends the arguments for more "micro"-level conceptions to the notion of international environmental policy structures. In his work on global environmentalism, Lipschutz notes that existing international policy dealing with environmental issues is largely implemented with nation-states and major NGOs as their primary participants. Such action implies that the creators of such policies, either consciously or unconsciously, are following a "macro"-level worldview in which nation-states and NGOs are the most effective actors in the international arena. This ignores the existence of local communities and social groups, where "local" consists of areas of operation beneath national governments or nation-states.[78] Lipschutz argues that increasing levels of globalization is leading to fragmentation and diffusion in political authority. This, he asserts, increases the role of "local" authority, since "local" authority possesses greater familiarity and greater knowledge of community-level conditions and concerns, and "local" authority is also more responsive to community-level issues.[79]

Lipschutz continues by asserting that international policy structures, being the product of "macro"-level thinking, are inherently incapable of being fully applicable to local, sub-nation-state situations. This is because international policy requires a level of abstraction and generalization in which action must be appropriate to all the situations in which it is to be implemented. Given the inevitable variety of situations which exist throughout the reaches of the world, and given their propensity to change in unpredictable manners, the requirement of generalization reduces international policy to relatively simplistic mechanisms which are insufficiently flexible or responsive to local contexts. The end result is a gap between policy goals and actual policy performance.[80]

Both Ostrum and Lipschutz share the contention that there is potential for contributions from the local level to the successful operation of international institutions. Ostrum asserts this by arguing for greater inclusion of local communities in resolving global CPR issues because of the greater sensitivity local communities have to local issues. In contrast, Lipschutz does the same by calling for greater allocation of authority to local communities in implementing global policy because of the better responsiveness local communities have to local contexts. For both Ostrum and Lipschutz, the underlying belief is that local commu-

---

[77] Nives Dolsak and Elinor Ostrom (eds.). *Commons in the New Millenium*. MIT Press (2003); Robert Keohane and Elinor Ostrom (eds.). *Local Commons and Global Interdependence: Heterogeneity and Cooperation in Two Domains*. Sage Publications (1995).

[78] See generally: Ronnie Lipschutz, "Reconstructing World Politics: The Emergence of Global Civil Society", *Millenium*, Vol. 21 No. 3 (Winter 1992), pp. 389-420; Ronnie Lipschutz and Ken Conca (eds.). *The State and Social Power in Global Environmental Politics*. Columbia University Press (1992); Ronnie Lipschutz, "From Place to Planet: Local Knowledge and Global Environmental Governance", *Global Governance*, Vol. 3 No. 1 (Jan.-Apr. 1997), pp. 83-102.

[79] Ibid.

[80] Ibid.

nities have the capacity and awareness to direct their actions in a way which supports larger-scale international policy instruments. The implication of their research is essentially this: there are connections between lower-level community actions and higher-level international policy, and so implementation at the local level can influence the efforts of international treaties.

IV. Conclusion

Devolution concepts highlight the use of local actors to help implement policy—including international ones. While existing research regarding international policy tends to bypass the function of local actors in supporting international instruments, it does not refute the possibility, and leaves the question open. International politics theory provides some threads for investigating the opportunities posed by having local actors participate in international policy implementation.

Following the directions from international politics theory, particularly from Ostrum and Lipschutz, this analysis hypothesizes that there are linkages between local actors and global policy, such that local actors can contribute to their enforcement. The next chapters conduct the investigation evaluating this hypothesis.

4
Linkage

Understanding the linkage between local law enforcement and international policy within the context of CITES involves following a chain of evidence from the design of the instrument itself to its expression within the U.S., and then onto local communities. The first link is global-to-national, in terms of going from international instruments to participating national signatories. The second link is national-to-local, extending from national government to local government. This analysis addresses the potential for involving local government in global policy implementation, and so encompasses both links between these three levels, with particular focus on the local level. For this research, this means beginning with a review of CITES as an international treaty, briefly detailing its framework, continuing on to an introduction of the ESA and related government agencies, and finally discussing the nature of connections to Port of Los Angeles Police.

The nature of the local-to-global linkage manifests itself in ways different to the intentions of textual legality, with the de jure guidelines differing from the de facto expression. The de jure linkage is apparent from the language of the treaty, as well as the ESA. The de facto linkage is one deduced from discussions with government officials at both federal and local levels.

I. De Jure Linkages

Information regarding de jure connections between local and global levels is taken from publicly available documents for CITES and the ESA. The full text of both are accessible on the internet, as is the official websites for the administrative offices responsible for both. These resources, along with available scholarly commentaries, indicate linkages going beyond the dual international-national connection to an additional national-local one.

Global to National: CITES Design and Operation

The main objective of CITES is to ensure the continuing existence of endangered species of fauna and flora. To accomplish this, it attempts to regulate the international trade of specimens, managing the traffic of species and taking action when necessary to ensure their survival.

Generally, the treaty design involves the statement of requirements which each signatory nation-state is assumed to abide by as its obligatory terms of membership, with the recognition that "international cooperation is essential for the protection of certain species of wild fauna and flora against over-exploitation through international trade."[81] In addition, the treaty design compels each member with the authority and responsibility to implement the laws it deems necessary to ensure fulfillment of CITES requirements and objectives. The reasoning

---

[81] CITES, Preamble.

behind this is two-fold: 1) that the "peoples and states are and should be the best protectors of their own wild fauna and flora"[82] for reasons of familiarity over endemic ecological conditions and socio-cultural particularities; and 2) to guarantee some measure of respect for each state's sovereignty and thereby assuage any possible fears held by existing or potentially new members of the dangers of acceding powers of political self-determination to external international entities.

In delegating its signatory members with the authority and responsibility for enforcement of the treaty, CITES make little effort to create an international institutional structure. With its deference to each member nation-state's sovereignty, the treaty avoids the implementation of any independent entity to enforce its language, but rather prefers to focus on only creating CITES-specific administrative organizations to support signatories with information and communication.

The CITES text approaches the endangered species trade as consisting of two areas: 1) the international business of specimens and parts involving transportation and transactions crossing national boundaries, and 2) the domestic business composed of takings, transportation, and possession of specimens and parts. The treaty itself is ostensibly aimed primarily at the international trade in endangered species, and dedicates the bulk of its content to this issue. Treaty language regarding domestic trade, while clear, is succinct and contained in several unique sections. To explicate the operation of CITES in these two areas, it is necessary to summarize the body of the text and to highlight critical areas in its language.

International Trade

CITES deals with the international trade of endangered species specimens and parts through several major mechanisms: 1) the use of permits and certificates, 2) the call for "Scientific Authorities" and "Management Authorities" within each member party, 3) the listing of species into one of three appendices, and 4) creation of CITES organizations intended to assist in maintenance and support of the treaty. The following discussion reviews each of these elements.

1) PERMITS AND CERTIFICATES

Permits and certificates are meant to facilitate determination of trade goods as being legal or illegal. Under CITES, they are needed for any action involving the trans-national transaction or possession of species listed as being under the protection of the treaty—both in terms of export and import. Permits and certificates are issued by the Management Authority of each signatory member, and apply only to the consignment of specimens and parts for which they were issued. The requirements for obtaining a permit or certificate vary according as to which CITES appendix the species in a consignment are listed under, as well as according to whether or not the issuance of permits and certificates contravene the laws of a signatory state regarding the species in that consignment. Officially, each

---

[82] Ibid.

permit or certificate must contain identification listing: 1) title of the convention, 2) the name of the Management Authority granting it, and 3) a control number.[83]

2) SCIENTIFIC AND MANAGEMENT AUTHORITIES

The call for separate Scientific and Management Authorities is intended to facilitate state control over both 1) the issuing of permits and certificates, as well as 2) the gathering and organization of scientific information relevant to endangered species. Each signatory is required to create at least one Management Authority representative of the signatory with the power to grant permits and certificates. Similarly, each signatory is also required to create at least one Scientific Authority whose function is to offer information and advice needed to determine if and to what extent the trade in a particular species is detrimental to its survival.[84]

3) CITES APPENDICES

The appendices provide a standardized hierarchy of endangered species, organized by the extent to which the survival of species has been determined and agreed upon by CITES parties at regularly scheduled CITES conventions. Appendix I contains the names of those species considered in danger of imminent extinction, and which "are or may be affected by trade." Species listed under Appendix I "must be subject to particularly strict regulation in order not to endanger further their survival and must only be authorized in exceptional circumstances." Any trade in an Appendix I species requires the grant and presentation of import and export permits and certificates which have been issued by Management Authorities under the consultation and approval of Scientific Authorities regarding 1) the particular welfare of the specimens and parts being traded and 2) the general welfare of the species to which those specimens and parts belong.[85]

Appendix II holds the names of species which are either 1) not necessarily in danger of extinction but may become so unless trade in them is placed under control or 2) needed to be placed under regulation in order to assist the control of species belonging to 1). In contrast to Appendix I, trade in an Appendix II species only requires the grant and presentation of permits and certificates for purposes of export. In addition, trade in Appendix II species only requires Scientific Authorities to determine that the general welfare of a species is not threatened by the trade of specimens and parts belonging to it before authorizing Management Authorities to issue permits and certificates.[86]

Appendix III lists those species which "any Party identified as being subject to regulation for the purposes of restricting exploitation, and as needing the

---

[83] CITES, Article VI.

[84] CITES, Article IX. See also Articles III-VII.

[85] CITES, Article III.

[86] CITES, Article IV.

cooperation of other parties in the control of trade." Similar to Appendix II, trade in Appendix III species only requires the grant and presentation of export permits and certificates. Unlike Appendix II, however, it eliminates the need for Management Authorities to seek the approval of Scientific Authorities in issuing permits and certificates.[87]

4) CITES ORGANIZATIONS

CITES also calls for the existence of the organizations dedicated to supporting its maintenance and operation. Under the treaty text, "a Secretariat shall be provided by the Executive Director of the United Nations Environment Programme." The Secretariat may be "assisted by suitable intergovernmental or nongovernmental, international or national agencies and body technically qualified in protection, conservation and management of wild fauna and flora."[88]

The duties of the Secretariat involve the holding of CITES meetings, coordination of CITES-relevant data and discussions, the undertaking of research needed for successful CITES implementation, and any other activities necessary to organize the signatory states in support of the treaty. In line with the treaty language quoted above, the Secretariat is supported by the World Conservation Monitoring Centre (WCMC), which collects and analyzes wildlife trade information, and the network of Trades Record Analysis of Flora and Fauna in Commerce (TRAFFIC) offices, who monitor worldwide flora and fauna trade and conduct investigations in regards to CITES.[89]

Domestic Trade

CITES deals with the domestic trade in endangered species through implicit means stated briefly within its text. Consistent with its structure, which was designed to preserve the sovereignty of member states, the treaty offers little in terms of explicit language regarding how or in what manner signatories are expected to implement endangered species laws. It does, however, note the following:

> The provisions of the present Convention shall in no way affect the right of Parties to adopt:
>
> > a) stricter domestic measures regarding the conditions for trade, taking, possession or transport of specimens and species included in Appendices I, II, and III, or the complete prohibition thereof; or

---

[87] CITES, Article V.

[88] CITES, Article XII.

[89] World Conservation Monitoring Center. URL: http://wcmc.org.uk. Accessed December 1, 2003; Geoffrey Lean and Don Hinrichsen. *Atlas of the Environment*. HarperCollins Publishers (1994).

b) domestic measures restricting or prohibiting trade, taking, possession or transport of species not included in Appendices I, II, or III.[90]

In addition, CITES also states:

> The provisions of the present Convention shall in no way affect the provisions of any domestic measures or the obligations of Parties deriving from any treaty, convention, or international agreement relating to other aspects of trade, taking, possession or transport of specimens which is in force or subsequently may enter into force for any Part...[91]

The text goes on to observe that CITES requirements must be met by a signatory regardless of the pre-existing presence or subsequent enactment by that signatory of other endangered species-related treaties or agreements. Moreover, the text asserts that CITES may not be interpreted as contravening or contradicting any other endangered species-related treaties or agreements, and that it should not be construed as affecting the obligations by CITES parties to the requirements of any such treaties or agreements of which they are members.[92]

On cursory review, it would appear that the treaty is affirming what is already self-evident, and is repeating what should already be clear from its initial declaration that "peoples and States are and should be the best protectors of their own wild fauna and flora" and from its general intentions to respect each member's sovereignty. Closer inspection, however, suggests that the formal statement of the above rights and provisions may be taken as a subtle indication that CITES recognizes and accepts the fact that the international business in endangered species specimens and parts is predicated on—or at the very least connected to—the takings and transactions of specimens and parts occurring within the domestic boundaries of each signatory nation-state.

In particular, the nature of the language in the first quote given above implies an awareness that regulation and control of the international endangered species trade inherently involves regulation and control of domestic trade—in other words, that CITES is dependent on domestic laws dealing with species listed within the treaty's appendices. More than this, the quote suggests by its mere presence that the treaty is reminding its members that there is a need to enact laws which extend beyond CITES requirements to fully achieve CITES' ulterior objective: the continued survival of endangered species. This reveals that the treaty is asking signatories to abide by the "spirit" of its text as much as it is asking them to abide by the language of it. Indeed, it may be considered as offering an implicit suggestion for member nation-states to implement and enforce laws addressing all aspects of domestic endangered species conservation issues as part of their obligations as signatory parties to CITES.

---

[90] CITES, Artice XIV, Paragraph 1.

[91] CITES, Article XIV, Paragraph 2.

[92] CITES, Article XIV, Paragraphs 3-6.

National to Local: CITES Enforcement in the U.S.

Enforcement of CITES in the U.S. is based on a combination of legal and administrative instruments. Legal implementation is conducted via the Endangered Species Act (ESA), which serves to fulfill U.S. obligations as a signatory to CITES, and thereby establishes a link between the treaty's international level and U.S. national level. The ESA was created in 1973 as a federal response to CITES, and dealt directly with the U.S. implementation of CITES. It is not identical to CITES in terms of species protected, since species listings within the ESA are determined by the federal government (for CITES, this is done by the signatories) and often deal with species native to the U.S. The ESA, however, does have considerable overlap with CITES-listed flora and fauna in fulfillment of U.S. obligations to the international treaty.

The ESA executes the U.S. duties under CITES by specifying what federal bodies are to serve as the country's Management Authority, Scientific Authority, Permit Office, and prohibitions and penalties. The Department of Interior has responsibility to implement the treaty.[93] Within the department, with respect to fauna, the Fish and Wildlife Service (FWS) and National Marine Fisheries Service (NMFS) are charged as administrators of CITES, with the FWS having the duty of enforcement.[94] Holding the role of both Management Authority and Scientific Authority, the FWS contains the Wildlife Permit Office (WPO) and the Office of Scientific Authority (OSA).[95] With respect to flora, the Department of Agriculture functions as administrator of CITES, with the Animal and Plant Health Inspection Service (APHIS) carrying out the duties of Management Authority and Scientific Authority.[96]

Like CITES, the ESA is based on a listing of endangered and threatened species.[97] However, the ESA applies different listing criteria and also expands the scope of species protection beyond just trafficking to more encompassing habitat conservation.[98] Nonetheless, the ESA does specifically prohibit any trade which is in violation of CITES.[99] With respect to permits, the ESA applies the CITES system of permits, requiring licenses for any import or export of species listed under the ESA.[100]

Beyond CITES, the ESA specifies penalties for contravention of the act. Violations of the ESA are subject to a range of penalties, ranging from those classified as criminal violations to those falling under civil penalties or administrative

---

[93] 16 U.S.C. Section 1537a(a).

[94] Ibid.

[95] Ibid.

[96] Laura Kosloff and Mark Trexler, "The Convention on International Trade in Endangered Species: Enforcement Theory and Practice in the U.S.", *Boston University International Law Journal*, Vol. 5 No. 3 (1987), pp. 327-361.

[97] Ibid., p. 345.

[98] Ibid.

[99] 16 U.S.C. Section 1538(c).

[100] 16 U.S.C. Section 1538(d).

remedies.[101] Violations of the ESA are treated as misdemeanor, with sanctions being levied under strict liability, so that violators can still be prosecuted even if they were not aware of the ESA.[102]

The ESA comprises the main regulatory instrument through which the U.S. implements CITES regulations.[103] The ESA is enforced by the U.S. Department of Interior, which assigns administration of the acts to the Fish and Wildlife Service (FWS). To fulfill its mission, the FWS employs two classes of officers: special agents and wildlife inspectors. Special agents are responsible for conducting investigations, undercover operations, and court prosecutions, while wildlife inspectors process commercial cargo shipments and personal travel goods. Both types of personnel receive ten weeks of training covering the wildlife trade, including CITES and the ESA, as well as identification of illegally traded species. In addition, special agents undergo the standard ten week training required of all federal law enforcement personnel.

With respect to local law enforcement agencies, the linkage is not so explicit. While the ESA functions to connect federal authority to CITES as a treaty, and so bridge the national and global levels, there is nothing so specific to tie local communities to national ones in the U.S. Based on interviews with both FWS and the Port of Los Angeles Police, no formal instruments exist connecting the two entities together in ESA implementation.

This, however, is not to say that there is no linkage between local and national levels. While being a federal agency, the FWS maintains multiple field offices in each state, with special agents and wildlife inspectors at each one to maintain FWS duties, including monitoring of endangered species trade under the ESA and CITES. Because such field offices deliver FWS representatives to points-of-entry, from a certain perspective the agency provides its own presence at the local level, in effect enacting a connection between the federal government and local communities—albeit not local law enforcement—through which federal authority is projected at a community level.[104]

In addition, while there is no formal instrument between local agencies and federal ones, there is an informal one, in that there are referrals whereby port police—and any local law enforcement agency—can contact FWS with information on suspected illegal species trade that violates the ESA. In conjunction with this, local officers are also able to detain suspected violating material until arrival by FWS representatives.[105]

If the current movements by the federal government towards devolution were to become more substantial, it is conceivable that the aforementioned link-

---

[101] Kosloff and Trexler, pp. 347-348.

[102] Shennie Patel, "The Convention on International Trade in Endangered Species: Enforcement and the Last Unicorn", *Houston Journal of International Law*, Vol. 18 No. 1 (1995), pp. 157-173.

[103] Congressional Research Service. "The Endangered Species Act in the 109 Congress: Conflicting Values and Difficult Choices". The Library of Congress. URL: usinfo.state.gov/infousa/ government/branches/docs/IB10144_2006Jan25.pdf. Accessed January 25, 2008.

[104] Fish and Wildlife Service. URL:http://www.fws.gov. Accessed October 1, 2007.

[105] Anonymous Interview, Fish & Wildlife Service, October 9, 2007; Anonymous Interviews, Port of Los Angeles Police, December 16, 2005.

age could become stronger. Federal adaptation of local police to enforce U.S. immigration laws sets a precedent for use of local law enforcement in implementing federal law. It would be a logical extension to consider using local police such as those at the Port of Los Angeles in upholding the ESA. In principle, the avenues for linkage between local-to-national levels exist on an informal basis, and so offer extensions with respect to CITES between international instruments to local communities.

II. De Facto Linkages

Reviewing CITES and ESA documentation may provide the framework for implementation in principle, but it does not confirm the nature of the linkage between local law enforcement and international policy. For this, discussions were arranged with government officials to determine the extent of local-federal interactions, with the topics for conversation including enforcement operations and coordination between the federal and local levels. It was through these interviews that a number of issues were revealed regarding the local-federal linkages with respect to endangered species trafficking under CITES and the ESA—issues which indicate that while such linkages may exist in principle from local to national to global, they may do so to a lesser degree in reality.

Referral

Conceptually, FWS stations accept communications regarding potential violations of the ESA, which indicates that patrol officers at the Port of Los Angeles can readily contact FWS representatives whenever suspected illegal endangered species products are observed entering or leaving the port. To some degree, this is supported by the FWS, which admitted their use of referrals (or "tips" and "leads") to seize illegally trafficked goods and their responsible parties. The Port of Los Angeles Police confirms the act of referrals for any potential smuggling of species its officers happen to come across.

However, records of referrals in terms of their frequency or percentage out of total seizures are not kept either by the FWS or the Port of Los Angeles Police. This makes it difficult to gauge to what extent this connection between Port of Los Angeles Police and FWS exists. For its part, FWS sources note that the reliance on referrals from other law enforcement agencies (federal, state, and local) by the agency was significant.[106] Similarly, the Port of Los Angeles Police indicated that no formal records are kept for referrals, holding instead only records of coordinated interdiction operations with the FWS—something which is a much lower occurrence than "tips" or "leads" of smuggled species.[107]

The result is that there is no definitive way in terms of numbers to estimate the strength of the linkage between federal and local levels with respect to the FWS and Port of Los Angeles Police. At present, there are only the subjective perceptions of both entities. A record of referrals would be helpful in demonstrat-

---

[106] Anonymous Interview, Fish & Wildlife Service.

[107] Anonymous Interviews, Port of Los Angeles Police.

ing a linkage in objective terms of the extent of communication between the agencies, as well as reflective of the level of coordination between the two.

Education

Even if there was an accurate record of referrals between the FWS and the Port of Los Angeles Police, it might still not be entirely enough to create an effective linkage. For referrals to the FWS to be useful, they have to be accurate, in the sense that they lead to discovery of genuine violations of the ESA. Otherwise, the connection becomes inefficient, indicating a weak linkage between the agencies.

There is reason for concern regarding this issue. FWS personnel receive training in identifying illegal traded species, but local police do not. FWS special agents and wildlife inspectors each receive ten weeks of training in identifying violations of federal wildlife laws, including the ESA and CITES. In addition, when requested, they provide such training to other federal agencies. However, there is no training given for local law enforcement at the state or local level, including the Port of Los Angeles Police.[108]

CITES appendices list over 700 species for which trade is illegal. These are in addition to species listed in the ESA. Identifying suspected illegal trafficking from this list out of the myriad numbers of general flora and fauna being transported through the Port of Los Angeles would appear to be a significant challenge for a trained person. For an untrained one—particularly a patrol officer monitoring other forms of criminal activity, it would be overwhelming. Expecting untrained personnel to make accurate referrals to the FWS under such circumstance seems be a tenuous proposition.

But here, too, there is a paucity of available information. Accuracy in giving leads about species smuggling requires accuracy in identifying suspects. Unfortunately, neither the FWS nor the Port of Los Angeles Police compile records identifying the number or percentage of referrals that prove to be positive (i.e., leading to apprehension of goods and parties involved in ESA violations) or false. The best estimate is subjective, with FWS sources assuring that the majority of tips it receives are accurate.[109]

Without these numbers, there is an open question as to how effective the connection is between the FWS and Port of Los Angeles Police. While not necessary in establishing existence of a linkage, it is relevant in assessing the capacity of local law enforcement to support the efforts of a federal agency to fulfill ESA responsibilities.

Jurisdiction

Another issue is the division in jurisdiction between the federal and local agencies. The FWS holds jurisdiction for violations of federal law, and reserves to state and local agencies activities covered under their respective laws. The Port of

---

[108]   Anonymous Interview, Fish & Wildlife Service.

[109]   Anonymous Interview, Fish & Wildlife Service; Anonymous Interviews, Port of Los Angeles Police.

Los Angeles Police, as local law enforcement, exercises jurisdiction for state and local crimes, but defers violations of federal law to the federal agencies.

This division in jurisdiction manifests itself in endangered species operations. Because the ESA is a federal law, the port police do not make seizures citing it, but instead make referrals to the FWS, whose representatives then respond to inspect the suspected violation. In addition, the police do not initiate investigations with the express purpose of catching illegal endangered species being transported through the port, but instead maintain their focus on crimes under state and local law. Federal crimes, including those involving species smuggling, are treated as incidental, and so ones requiring action only if discovered in the course of pursuing a state or local crime. Even then, the expectation is that the local agency will refer the potential federal violation to the appropriate federal agency.[110]

Jurisdictional issues means that apprehension of ESA violations requires coordination between FWS and the Port of Los Angeles Police, with a linkage of sufficient strength to ensure 1) local law enforcement has the requisite expertise to identify a potential ESA crime, 2) local law enforcement can readily contact FWS, and 3) FWS responds to make the apprehension. While both FWS and the Port of Los Angeles Police offer subjective evaluations to the affirmative that such a linkage indeed exists, the lack of objective measures makes it difficult to accurately confirm it.

Field Operations

Apart from the aforementioned issues, there is an added one of field operations to locate species smuggling. Expectations for a strong local-national linkage would entail coordination of efforts to identify illegal shipments of flora and fauna, including inspections of general trade going through the Port of Los Angeles.

However, the depth of such activities is somewhat limited. FWS special agents, because their jobs focus primarily on investigations, undercover work, and legal prosecution, do not engage in physical patrol of goods going through the Port of Los Angeles. FWS wildlife inspectors, who carry a greater responsibility to identify ESA violations, also do not engage in physical patrol. Instead, they fulfill their duties by comparing shipping manifests with trade declarations of the shipping parties. FWS sources assert that both special agents and wildlife inspectors do conduct on-site search and seizure operations, but that this does not consume the majority of their time, with physical inspections taking place on a random basis and aimed for specific issues.[111]

---

[110] Anonymous Interview, Fish & Wildlife Service; Anonymous Interviews, Port of Los Angeles Police.

[111] Anonymous Interview, Fish & Wildlife Service; FWS. *Inspector Brochure*. Fish & Wildlife Service. URL: http://library.fws.gov/Pubs/Inspector02.pdf. Accessed October 28, 2007. FWS Wildlife Inspectors. URL: http://www.fws.gov/le/AboutLE/wildlife_inspectors.htm. Accessed October 1, 2007; FWS Special Agents. URL: FWS Special Agents, URL: http://www.fws.gov/le/AboutLE/special_agents.htm. Accessed October 1, 2007.

The lack of such inspections is reasonable given the magnitude of traffic relative to the number of inspectors. According to the FWS 2006 Annual Report, there are only 202 special agents and 112 wildlife inspectors spread throughout the United States among 36 field offices, whose time must be shared between 38 ports, airports, and border crossing stations receiving international traffic.[112] With respect to case load, for 2006, the special agents and wildlife inspectors investigate roughly 15,000 cases, processing nearly 183,000 wildlife shipments requiring approximately 145,000 inspections.[113] During this time, the special agents and inspectors located in the Southern California Torrance and Ventura offices were involved more than 23,000 inspections, which marked only a fraction of the approximately 50,000,000 tons of material which passed through the Port of Los Angeles for the year.[114] Given such numbers, it would be difficult, if not inefficient, to require FWS personnel to physically inspect every item entering the United States, let alone the port.

In contrast, the Port of Los Angeles Police do conduct regular physical patrols of harbor facilities, including shipping containers. But their patrols are directed at a wide array of potential crimes, rather than just ESA violations alone, meaning that their attention must cover a much broader range of priorities than carried by FWS. Moreover, they do not physically enter shipping containers or goods to uncover potential species smuggling; as law enforcement agents, their capacity to make entrance is limited by legal restrictions requiring probable cause and warrants to investigate private property, meaning that discovery of ESA violations are made incidental to pursuit of other crimes. Even then, because of jurisdiction issues, Port of Los Angeles Police cannot initiate seizures for ESA-related species, but must make a referral to FWS.

This situation is one with a disjuncture in coverage, in that the entity with the power to make searches and seizures under the ESA does not regularly conduct physical patrols, and the entity that does do so does not have the jurisdiction to perform searches and seizures. This makes enforcement of the ESA reliant on the coordination between FWS and the Port of Los Angeles Police. But as indicated by the previous discussion, the strength of such linkage is rife with questions and not entirely affirmative.

---

[112] FWS. URL:http://www.fws.gov. Accessed October 1, 2007; FWS Annual Report 2006. URL: http://www.fws.gov/le/AboutLE/annual.htm. Accessed October 1, 2007; FWS Inspector Brochure; FWS Special Agents.

[113] FWS Annual Report 2006.

[114] FWS Annual Report 2006; FWS Torrance Office Directory. URL: http://www.fws.gov/ offices/directory/ListOffices.cfm?statecode=6. Accessed October 28, 2007; FWS Ventura Staff List. URL://http://www.fws.gov/ventura/textonly/stafflisting.html. Accessed October 28, 2007; Port of Los Angeles website. URL: http://www.portoflosangeles.org. Accessed August 1, 2007; U.S. Army Corps of Engineers, Waterborne Commerce Statistics Center. URL: http://www. iwr.usace .army.mil/ndc/wcsc/portname02.htm. Accessed October 19, 2007; Vanderbilt Center for Transportation Research. URL: http://transp20.vuse.vanderbilt.edu/vector/worldkit/index .html. Accessed October 19, 2007.

III. Discussion

As evidenced by the above observations, the nature of local-to-global connections with respect to CITES and the ESA is somewhat mixed between de jure and de facto perspectives. De jure, there is a measure of understood linkage between the Port of Los Angeles Police as local agencies and the FWS as the federal entity, with the actions of the two organizations supporting CITES as an international instrument via their support for the ESA. This arrangement is not explicit, with an operative law dictating cooperation under CITES or the ESA, but there is an informal one, in that there are referrals whereby port police can contact FWS with information on suspected illegal species trade that violates the ESA, or detain suspected violating material until arrival by FWS representatives.

De facto conditions, however, clearly show that the state of this linkage is still questionable, with a number of unresolved issues regarding potential challenges that may be responsible for frustrating implementation of CITES and the ESA, particularly in terms of available information about enforcement and also disjunctures between federal and local enforcement. Without some resolution, the situation makes it uncertain as to whether local actors can be incorporated into the implementation chain that starts from the international level and then descends downward to the local level.

Regarding the lack of information, the paucity of information regarding referrals and training prevents determination of the frequency and accuracy of those referrals, making it difficult to fully ascertain the connections between the Port of Los Angeles Police and the ESA. Subjective assertions by both organizations suggest that referrals to indeed occur, but data on frequency and accuracy would indicate the extent of referrals, and hence help assess the strength of the linkage between the two organizations. It would also clarify what actions could be used to improve the local-to-national connections. If evidence showed that the frequency of referrals by port police to the FWS was low relative to the scale of endangered species trade, it would suggest that the connection between them would benefit from greater coordination in terms of more communication or better sharing of information resources. On the other hand, if the evidence showed that the frequency of referrals was acceptable, but that their accuracy in uncovering actual ESA violations was not, it would point to a need for better education of the port police officers sending the referrals to FWS.

With respect to disjunctures, the greater availability of information on jurisdiction and field operations clearly shows a division in terms of enforcement. Because the Port of Los Angeles Police and FWS both observe the demarcation in federal versus local jurisdiction, actions against illegal wildlife shipments requires coordination between the two, with the port police referring suspected cases to FWS—a condition whose suspect nature casts doubt as to the effectiveness of the linkage between the agencies. This problem is compounded by the nature of field operations, since the entity (the port police) with routine patrols defers ESA violations to the jurisdiction of an entity that does not (FWS). Because it maintains a more active field presence, the port police pose a greater level of local expertise in terms of familiarity with port operations, nuances about law enforcement in the port, and timeliness in responding to newly discovered crimes.

The net result of the current de jure and de facto situation can be summarized as follows in five major points. First, at the present time, because ESA is a federal law with an affiliated federal agency and no authority to local actors, formal de jure CITES implementation extends only to a national level, and not to a local one. Second, local involvement in ESA enforcement appears de facto informal through a referral system to FWS. Third, under the de facto conditions, the informal linkage of local actors (Port of Los Angeles Police) to the national one (FWS) in support of a national law (ESA) is suspect. Fourth, as a result, ESA and CITES enforcement misses an opportunity for improvement by avoiding the contributions of a local law enforcement agency with the potential to assist it. Fifth, integrating local law enforcement into CITES implementation requires enabling the domestic linkage, which means that local actors (port police) have greater authority to support a federal law (ESA) and related federal agency (FWS)—something that is not currently the case

A possible solution to this is greater coordination between Port of Los Angeles Police and FWS. But here, too, this means better information about referrals and training, returning to the issues of incomplete data held by the two agencies.

Another potential solution would be an adjustment in jurisdiction and operational capabilities. This could be achieved under different philosophical approaches: increasing federal power, or increasing local power. If the approach is to rely upon federal authority, the consistent prescription would be to allow FWS to maintain its jurisdiction, but then empower it with greater resources (perhaps in personnel, as well as communication and information retrieval) so that it could gain the capability to maintain a greater, more consistent field presence to identify potential ESA and CITES violations.

In contrast, if the approach is to turn to local authority, the natural procedure would to grant local law enforcement, including the Port of Los Angeles Police, more jurisdiction to follow-up (via investigations, entrance to goods, etc. —actions they are jurisdictionally currently forbidden to conduct) on suspected ESA and CITES cases its regular patrols uncover. This way, while they would still ultimately relay these cases to the federal jurisdiction of FWS, port police officers would be better able to exploit their local expertise.

The latter solution is more in keeping with the purpose of this research. It is sometimes known as devolution, and one that seems to be gaining greater attention within the federal government. But whether this is a viable option for ESA and CITES is unclear. It makes a number of assumptions regarding local law enforcement in terms of capabilities, particularly with respect to their willingness to accept additional duties and their capacity to do so. It is not clear that steps have been taken discover if local agencies, particularly the Port of Los Angeles Police in the present case, can meet these assumptions. Given the question introduced here as to the level of coordination between the Port of Los Angeles Police and FWS, the prospect of federal inquiry to the port police is not optimistic.

Verifying these assumptions is important. Gaining the feedback from the local entity upon which more duties may be given would be a logical step in enhancing policymaking; the success of a policy is dependent on effectively responding to the problem it is meant to solve, and that means recognizing pre-existing conditions related to the problem. For ESA and CITES, this means recognizing the observations of the port police who can offer first-person information about a major conduit for ESA and CITES violations. Simply ignoring local authorities is a debatable proposition—that is the current situation, and the success of it is readily apparent in the ongoing CITES controversy. Ameliorating the problem calls for a more sensitive approach involving more incorporation of local law enforcement.

The subsequent steps in this research endeavor to follow through on this call. The analysis will investigate the Port of Los Angeles Police to determine if its officers are willing and able to accept greater responsibilities to the ESA and CITES. In essence, the study will do what it is unclear (and perhaps unlikely) the federal government has not: ask local actors for feedback regarding issues in their enforcement of domestic and international policy, to help policymakers determine whether—and how—local actors can be given greater responsibility to enforcing federal law supporting an international implementation framework.

5
Descriptive Review of Data

Policymakers intent on utilizing local law enforcement to aid in implementation of the Convention on International Trade in Endangered Species (CITES) are extending the implementation chain an additional link, from the treaty's international-to-national framework to a national-to-local extension. Based on the current framework within the United States, which fulfills U.S obligations to CITES through the domestic Endangered Species Act (ESA) and the federal government's Fish and Wildlife Service (FWS), creating the national-to-local extension may be accomplished through three methods: increasing coordination between local officers and the FWS, adjusting jurisdictional and operational capabilities to increase federal power, or to adjust jurisdictional and operational capabilities to increase local power.

This study showed that the first method is obstructed by the presence of incomplete data necessary to improve referrals and training between the FWS and the Port of Los Angeles Police. The second method to increase federal power by empowering the FWS with greater resources to enforce of the ESA is viable, but not one consistent with current philosophical orientation in federal government policy. Current policy philosophy seems to pursue the third method, which turns to local authority and looks to add the resources of local actors such as the Port of Los Angeles Police to existing enforcement framework for CITES.

The latter option is a reflection of the ongoing trend towards devolution, wherein authority is shifted to the local level. While the concept normally applies to redistribution in power from federal to local agencies, it serves a similar purpose for international policymakers looking to grant more responsibilities to local actors.

Whether this can be a viable strategy for CITES, however, is unclear. Unfortunately, the scholarly literature on CITES largely eschews discussions of local law enforcement agencies. For those times the body of research addresses local enforcement of CITES, it does so using FWS branch offices as the "local" level, even as such offices are still representatives of federal government. In contrast, the concept of devolution uses the word "local" in jurisdictional terms, with local actors being those entities with authority over geographically immediate territory outside of federal jurisdiction. As a result, because the research literature on CITES does not fully delve into the potential of actors with local jurisdiction, it offers little guidance about the opportunities for devolution as an international policy strategy.

This stage of the analysis is a step towards mitigating the situation. To generate assistance for efforts at devolution, this section of the study endeavors to continue the analysis by further investigating jurisdictionally "local" actors as utilized by the concept of devolution. For this case study, this means gathering information about the conditions for the Port of Los Angeles Police. This analysis accomplishes this by direct research, using a survey instrument administered to port police, and then reviewing survey data to evaluate devolution and generate recommendations for policymakers.

The investigation at this stage presents a description of the results to identify general trends found from the survey responses gathered from local law enforcement. Such a descriptive analysis involves use of histograms showing the distribution of answers to the survey questions to infer trends. The histograms are contained within the appendices. Comments about the highlights from the histograms are given in within this review, to help outline the larger trends. The discussion at the end notes the major points of relevance taken from the histogram highlights.

Generally speaking, the survey was administered via hard-copy to the patrol officers at the Port of Los Angeles Police during their morning roll call, and included anyone licensed to carry a firearm and make arrests under the organization's jurisdiction. The results were entered into SPSS to create a codebook of responses. SPSS then created histograms of the survey results, with each question being assigned a variable for statistical analysis and a histogram for descriptive analysis. The histograms were exported as graphic files into the appendices of this manuscript for purposes of publication.

I. Survey Design and Administration

The survey endeavored to gather data regarding attitudes and perceptions of law enforcement personnel regarding smuggling issues, domestic laws dealing with each issue, and international treaties connected with each domestic law. To accomplish this, the survey organized questions into sections covering each of the three areas, and added a fourth dealing with demographics, resulting in the following structure:

- Section I: Smuggling
- Section II: Domestic Law
- Section III: International Law
- Section IV: Demographics

For purposes of comparison across fields, the survey took responses for endangered species traffic while also taking responses for other smuggling issues. The intent was to gauge the existence of potential differences or consistency in attitudes and perceptions across various fields, which would indicate if survey participant responses were the result of bias over endangered species traffic relative to other topics, or the result of their interactions with domestic or international legal instruments. In essence, endangered species served as the subject of analysis, and the other topics served as control groups. Towards this end, a range of smuggling issues was selected based on 1) the existence of international treaties addressing them and 2) domestic laws implementing those international treaties. In this survey, this resulted in selection of the following topics:

Table 3-1: Topics

Smuggling Issue	International Instrument	Domestic Instrument
Endangered species traffic	Convention on the International Trade in Endangered Species (CITES)	Endangered Species Act (ESA)
Narcotics traffic	Convention Against Illicit Traffic in Narcotic Drugs and Psychotropic Substances (CNDPS)	Controlled Substances Import and Export Act (CSIE)
Weapons traffic	Nuclear Nonproliferation Treaty, Biological Weapons Convention, Chemical Weapons Convention (CNBC)	Defense Against Weapons of Mass Destruction Act (DWMD)
Human traffic	Convention for the Suppression of the Traffic in Persons (CSTP)	Trafficking Victims Protection Act (TVP)
Contraband/gray market traffic	Trade-Related Intellectual Property Agreements (TRIPs)	U.S. Customs and Border Patrol Regulations (CBP)

For questions, the survey endeavored to gather quantitative measures of participant levels of attitudes and perceptions for each of the above items. Questions gauged a range of factors dealing with awareness, knowledge, and confidence for each domestic and international law, as well as identifying perceived challenges to their enforcement. The survey held a total of 57 questions with each asking for responses for either the five specified sets of issues and laws or a selected list of factors. Overall, the survey questions gathered data on 275 variables. Each variable marked a respondent's answer that was either ordinal (e.g., from "not at all knowledgeable" set as a value of 1 to "extremely knowledgeable" set as a value of 7) or scalar (e.g, "increased," "decreased," or "constant"). These variables were distributed among the questions, with the questions organized into major groups identified as follows:

Table 3-2: Question Groups

Section	Question Groups
Section I: Smuggling	Level of importance of smuggling
	Level of knowledge regarding smuggling
	Legitimacy of duty to deal with smuggling
	Resource challenges to performance
Section II: Domestic Law	Level of knowledge of domestic U.S. laws dealing with smuggling
	Level of effectiveness of domestic efforts regarding smuggling
	Level of deterrence of domestic laws
	Level of cooperation of domestic agencies to enforce domestic laws
	Level of satisfaction over results of personal efforts to control smuggling
	Level of satisfaction over results of organization's efforts to control smuggling
Section III: International Law	Level of knowledge of international laws dealing with smuggling
	Level of effectiveness of international efforts regarding smug-

	gling
	Level of deterrence of international laws
	Level of cooperation between domestic and international agencies to enforce international laws
Section IV: General	*Demographics*

The survey instrument itself is available in Appendix 1. The survey was anonymous, with identification of respondent. The survey was given blind, with respondents filling out the hard-copy form without interaction with researchers during roll call meetings at the beginning of their daily work shifts; law enforcement personnel who completed the survey returned them anonymously to management, who delivered them to researchers in batches by U.S. mail. Respondents were Port of Los Angeles police officers licensed to carry firearms and make arrests under port police jurisdiction. The questions given to these officers were time-independent, in that the instrument posed questions asking for responses based on each participant's accumulated lifetime of experience.

It should be noted that the survey was a comprehensive questionnaire intended to get data across a range of international treaties and attendant domestic instruments for different types of smuggling issues. The goal was to gather information that could be available for later subsequent research beyond the confines of the research design constructed for this analysis. As a result, this study draws upon a selected number of variables in the survey instrument rather than all.

II. Histograms

Review of the raw data offers some direction in finding trends of relevance to the hypothesis. The raw data is the mass of survey responses from participants, summaries for which are produced graphically as histograms that make it easier to observe survey results. Trends, as so far in the nature of responses to survey questions, are reflected in the histograms, particularly in the distributions of answers given for each survey question.

For this study, recognition of trends can begin by observing the behavior of the means from the histogram of responses for each survey question. Observing the trends in the data for each of these categories makes it easier to perceive and interpret the sentiments of respondents regarding local enforcement of international law. To help find trends from the means relevant to the hypothesis, the study organized the means into differing subject matter: questions related to issue area, performance challenges, those related to domestic law, and those related to international law.

Comments for each are presented below.

Issues

For respondent data regarding smuggling issues, the survey asked personnel to provide answers on a ratings scale from 1 to 7, with 1 being the lowest (e.g., "not at all important" for Level of Importance) and 7 being the highest (e.g., "extremely" important for Level of Importance). The questions posed the following:

1) The level of importance for smuggling (for each of 5 smuggling issues)

2) The level of respondent's knowledge (for each of the 5 smuggling issues)

Histograms were generated from the respondent's answers to each of these questions. Each histogram was used to produce a mean and an assessment of respondent's perspectives with respect to the questions.

For the question asking each survey participant to provide their perspective on the level of importance for each smuggling topic, the histograms (see Appendix 2) showed a distribution of responses largely skewed towards the higher values of 6 or 7, with the one exception being endangered species smuggling, which had a much more ambivalent distribution closer to the middle value of 4. The distinction in levels of importance accorded to each smuggling area is illustrated by the following table:

Histograms - Level of Importance of Smuggling	Mean
Endangered Species Traffic	4.33
Narcotics Traffic	6.44
Weapons Traffic	6.53
Traffic in Human Beings	6.19
Contraband/Gray Market Traffic	5.75

This suggests that respondents tended to view the smuggling of endangered species as being less important than other forms of smuggling, and that endangered species do not warrant a high level of priority while other types of smuggling do.

Similarly, with the question asking participants for their level of knowledge of each area of smuggling, the histograms (see Appendix 2) shows a distribution of responses placed among the higher values above the middle point of 4, with endangered species smuggling again being the exception. Endangered species smuggling received a distribution heavily marked towards the low values of 1 and 2. The difference in distribution is illustrated by the following table showing the relative means of the histograms for each smuggling issue:

Histograms - Level of Respondent's Knowledge of Smuggling	Mean
Endangered Species Traffic	2.17
Narcotics Traffic	4.83
Weapons Traffic	4.28
Traffic in Human Beings	4.28
Contraband/Gray Market Traffic	4.14

This indicates that with respect to the level of knowledge, respondents generally considered themselves as having fair knowledge of each smuggling topic apart from endangered species traffic, which most of them admitted little familiarity.

The dichotomy in responses between endangered species smuggling and the others presented in the survey were somewhat consistent with the question of legitimacy. On the question of whether participants believed each smuggling issue to be a legitimate issue for enforcement by them or their organization, the majority marked all 5 (endangered species, narcotics, weapons, humans, contraband) to be legitimate duties, but did so in varying degrees. A significant majority recognized narcotics, weapons, humans, and contraband as legitimate, with only 1 claim being registered for "no" for narcotics, weapons, and human traffic and only 6 claims of "no" for contraband.

For endangered species, however, the margin was much closer. While 20 respondents recognized it as a legitimate duty, fully 12 said it was not, producing a much narrower margin relative to other issues in the extent to which participants accepted it as a worthy cause for law enforcement.

Performance Challenges

The questionnaire also asked respondents to indicate on the 1-to-7 ratings scale their perception of:

1) Resource challenges to personal performance

2) Resource challenges to organizational performance

For each question, survey participants were provided a list of 17 potential challenges and asked to rate each with respect to their level of harm to personal or organizational performance, with 1 being "not at all harmful" and 7 being "extremely harmful." The 17 potential challenges were:

- Lack of money
- Lack of time
- Lack of knowledge
- Lack of training
- Lack of personal interest
- Excessive administrative paperwork
- Ineffective technology
- Ineffective strategic focus on organizational mission and purpose by employer
- Ineffective tactical policy to achieve organizational mission and purpose by employer
- Lack of clarity in employee duties and responsibility by employer
- Conflict or lack of communication between leadership and employees
- Conflict or lack of communication with co-workers
- Conflict or lack of communication with international and foreign entities
- Conflict or lack of communication with domestic government agencies

Histograms for each of the 17 potential challenges, with a set of 17 histograms for the question of challenges to personal performance and another set of 17 for the question of challenges to organizational performance (see Appendix 2). The histograms display the distribution of results for personnel perceptions of their weakest and greatest challenges.

For what factors participants identified as being weakest and greatest challenges to their personal or organizational performance, the trends of the histograms are indicated by the following table showing the means for each set of histograms, with one set of means for the question of personal performance and another set of means for organizational performance:

Histograms - Resource Challenges	Mean - Personal	Mean - Organization
Lack of Money	2.94	2.88
Lack of Time	4.47	4.46
Lack of Knowledge	4.81	4.11
Lack of Training	4.56	4.29

Lack of Personal Interest	2.83	3.35
Excessive Administrative Paperwork	4.03	4.17
Ineffective Technology	4.22	4.29
Ineffective Strategic Focus by Employer	4.28	4.34
Ineffective Tactical Policy by Employer	4.14	4.11
Lack of Clarity in Employee Duties by Employer	3.97	4.17
Conflict or Lack of Communication between Leadership & Employees	4.31	4.11
Conflict or Lack of Communication with Co-Workers	3.56	3.49
Conflict or Lack of Communication with International Entities	4.61	4.66
Conflict or Lack of Communication with Domestic Agencies	4.78	4.54

With respect to personal performance, the factors that were considered least harmful by respondents to their personal performance were "lack of money," "lack of personal interest," and "conflict or lack of communication with co-workers." Factors that were considered of mediocre or moderate harm were "excessive administrative paperwork," "ineffective technology," "ineffective strategic focus," "ineffective tactical policy," "lack of clarity in duties," "conflict or lack of communication between leaders and employees." Factors that were found to be very harmful were "lack of time," "lack of knowledge," "lack of training," "conflict or lack of communication with international and foreign entities," and "conflict or lack of communication with domestic government agencies."

In comparison to perceived challenges to personal performance, respondents found slight degrees of harm to their organization's performance. Similar to personal performance challenges, respondents indicated that the least harmful challenges to their organization's performance was "lack of money," "lack of personal interest," and "conflict or lack of communication with co-workers."

In contrast to challenges to personal performance, however, respondents showed a greater number of factors were considered moderately harmful. These were "lack of knowledge," "lack of training," "excessive administrative paper-work," "ineffective technology," "ineffective strategic focus," "ineffective tactical policy," "lack of clarity in duties," "conflict or lack of communication between leaders and employees."

In addition, while participants identified 5 factors as very harmful to personal performance, they identified 3 factors as being harmful to organizational performance: "lack of time," "conflict of lack of communication with international and foreign entities," and "conflict or lack of communication with domestic government agencies."

These differences between what respondents perceived as challenges to personal and organizational performance indicate that with respect to the most harmful factors, participants tended to distinguish themselves separately from their organization, with the view that their organization's available time and training is more adequate than what they could offer individually. But apart from this distinction, respondents indicated that they viewed the challenges to roughly the same for them individually as they were for the organization.

Domestic Laws

With respect to personnel attitudes and perceptions towards domestic laws, the survey utilized the 1-to-7 ratings scale for the following questions:

1) The level of knowledge regarding U.S. laws (for each of 5 smuggling issues)

2) The level of effectiveness of domestic efforts to enforce U.S. laws (for each of 5 smuggling issues)

3) The level of deterrence of U.S. laws (for each of 5 smuggling issues)

4) The level of cooperation between domestic agencies to enforce U.S. laws (for each of 5 smuggling issues)

5) The level of satisfaction over personal efforts to control smuggling (for each of 5 smuggling issues)

6) The level of satisfaction over organization's efforts to control smuggling (for each of 5 smuggling issues)

Results for each question are given by histograms giving the distribution of responses to each question.

For the level of knowledge given by respondents for each U.S. smuggling law, the histograms (see Appendix 3) show that respondents perceived themselves as having a relatively low level of knowledge regarding the domestic laws affiliated with each of the 5 smuggling issues, with the ESA being the lowest. This is exemplified by the following table showing the means of the histogram distributions for each question:

Histograms - Level of Knowledge of Domestic Laws	Mean
ESA	1.97
CSIE	3.94
DWMD	3.71
TVP	3.23
CBP	2.97

This shows that while survey participants in general admitted to a low level of knowledge about U.S. smuggling laws, they hold a dramatically lower level of knowledge with respect to the Endangered Species Act relative to the other laws.

This pattern is somewhat paralleled by the respondent histograms (see Appendix 3) for the question of how survey participants viewed the effectiveness of each U.S. smuggling law, wherein again the participants gave U.S. smuggling laws low ratings, with the ESA being the lowest. This is reflected in the table of the means of each histogram:

Histograms - Level of Effectiveness of Domestic Laws	Mean
ESA	2.83
CSIE	3.89
DWMD	3.83
TVP	3.14
CBP	3.11

This demonstrates that participants tended to view the laws as having a low level of effectiveness, but with the ESA have a clearly lower perceived level of effectiveness.

For deterrence value, the histograms (see Appendix 3) indicate the distinction between the domestic laws is not so clearly pronounced. While the respondents continued to mark the domestic laws covered in the study with low ratings for deterrence, the ESA's ratings were much closer to the others laws. This is illustrated by the following table of means:

Histograms - Level of Deterrence of Domestic Laws	Mean
ESA	2.66
CSIE	3.31
DWMD	3.22
TVP	2.86
CBP	2.83

This suggests that participants hold all domestic smuggling laws with the same level of deterrence: very low. It also suggests that they consider the ESA to be similar in deterrence value to other smuggling laws—albeit the least deterrent.

For cooperation, the histograms (see Appendix 3) generate a trend comparable to that for deterrence value. Respondents perceive U.S. smuggling laws as receiving little cooperation between domestic agencies in enforcement, with the ESA being ranked the lowest. This is shown in the following table of means:

Histograms - Level of Cooperation in Enforcing Domestic Laws	Mean
ESA	3.25
CSIE	4.11
DWMD	4.11
TVP	3.94
CBP	3.44

Consistent with the trend for deterrence value, but differing in absolute ratings, it is evident by the closeness of the means to the middle value of 4 that participants held ambivalent feelings about the level of cooperation between domestic agencies for the CSIE, DWMD, and TVP. In contrast, the perceived the CBP and the ESA as having distinctly lower levels of cooperation.

Next, the survey asked respondents to mark their level of satisfaction over the monthly amounts of searches and seizures they were personally involved in. For both searches and seizures, the histograms (see Appendix 3) display roughly the same levels of satisfaction for all the laws in this study. This is confirmed by the table of means for both searches and seizures given below:

Histograms - Level of Personal Satisfaction over Searches & Seizures	Mean - Searches	Mean - Seizures
ESA	2.97	2.53
CSIE	3.38	2.91
DWMD	2.94	2.67
TVP	3	2.67
CBP	3	2.75

It is apparent here that participants held a low level of satisfaction over the monthly number of searches or seizures they conducted individually, and that the levels of satisfaction were roughly the same for all the smuggling laws in this study.

The search and seizure question was posed again, but asking each respondent for their level of satisfaction in their organization's involvement in searches and seizures per month. The histograms (see Appendix 3) yield comparable low satisfaction ratings, but with the ESA having the lowest. This is seen in the following table of means for both searches and seizures given below:

Histograms - Level of Organizational Satisfaction over Searches & Seizures	Mean - Searches	Mean - Seizures
ESA	2.55	2.65
CSIE	3.36	3.29
DWMD	3.03	3.15
TVP	2.66	2.82
CBP	2.71	2.94

Again, it is apparent that participants held low satisfaction ratings for the monthly number of searches and seizures performed by their organization. But compared to personal satisfaction above, it is also apparent that participants held a slightly lower level of satisfaction in their organization's searches and seizures in enforcing the ESA.

International

For respondent's attitudes and perceptions towards international laws, the survey continued applying a 1-to-7 ratings scale, using the following questions:

1) The level of knowledge regarding international laws (for each of 5 smuggling issues)

2) The level of effectiveness of international efforts to enforce international laws (for each of 5 smuggling issues)

3) The level of deterrence of international laws (for each of 5 smuggling issues)

4) The level of cooperation between domestic & international agencies to enforce international laws (for each of 5 smuggling issues)

Results for each question are given by the histograms for each. The histograms are contained in Appendix 4.

For the question asking each respondent for their knowledge of international laws, the histograms generated distributions skewed towards the low end of the 1-to-7 ratings scale, with values well below the middle point of 4. This reflects a perception held by respondents that they held little knowledge of international smuggling treaties. Of the 5 international treaties covered in the survey, CITES received the lowest marks. This is demonstrated in the following table of the means from the histogram of each treaty:

Histograms - Level of Knowledge of International Laws	Mean
CITES	1.89
CNDPS	3.08
CNBC	2.69
CSTP	2.56
TRIPS	2.31

This clearly demonstrates that survey participants admitted to having a low level of knowledge of international smuggling laws, with a distinctly lower level of knowledge of CITES than they did other international treaties. Such low levels of knowledge were marked even though each of these treaties held a corresponding match in the domestic laws mentioned in the survey.

Somewhat similar results were found for the question asking respondents for the perceived effectiveness of domestic and international attempts to enforce the treaties posed in the survey. The question was divided into 2 components, with one directing participants to rate the effectiveness of domestic agencies in enforcing each international smuggling treaty, and the other directing them to rate the effectiveness of international agencies to enforce each treaty. The histogram results for both were generally low, with the majority of responses going towards the low end of the scale below the middle point of 4 on the 1-to-7 ratings scale. This is scene in the table below:

Histograms - Level of Effectiveness of International Laws	Mean - Domestic Support	Mean - International Support
CITES	3.09	2.86
CNDPS	3.67	3.23
CNBC	3.6	3.26
CSTP	3.29	3
TRIPS	3.29	3.17

Comparable to the numbers for knowledge of international treaties, the values for the histograms display a low level of perceived effectiveness for both domestic and international support, with slightly lower levels for CITES relative to the other treaties. However, there is a trend apparent in comparison of the above means, in that survey takers seemed to believe that domestic government support for international treaties is greater than international support for those treaties.

The low ratings continued with the question asking respondents to mark the level of deterrence for each international treaty. Here again, the histograms produced numbers leaning towards the low end of the ratings scale, with means well below the middle value of 4. The means of the histograms are given in the table below:

Histograms - Level of Deterrence of International Laws	Mean
CITES	2.35
CNDPS	2.86
CNBC	2.85
CSTP	2.56
TRIPS	2.5

This shows just how low the ratings were, with all of the international smuggling treaties in the survey being given ratings well below the mediocre value of 4, with CITES having only slightly lower values than the others. This suggests that respondents tended to view international treaties as generally having low deterrence value.

There was little change in the nature of the numbers with the question asking respondents to rate the level of cooperation in enforcing the treaties at both the domestic and international levels. The question was divided into 2 parts, with one part asking participants to mark how much cooperation they perceived from domestic agencies and another part asking them how much cooperation they perceived from international agencies. For both parts, the histograms again displayed low numbers below the middle value of 4, with CITES having slightly lower numbers. This is indicated by the table of means from the histograms:

Histograms - Level of Cooperation of International Laws	Mean - Domestic Cooperation	Mean - International Cooperation
CITES	2.73	2.6
CNDPS	3.46	3.22
CNBC	3.23	3.17
CSTP	3.31	2.89
TRIPS	2.97	2.86

This displays how low the ratings were. It also shows that CITES, consistent with the other questions on international treaties, received lower marks relative to the other treaties in the survey. This suggests that respondents generally perceived little cooperation—from either domestic agencies or international entities—in enforcing international treaties, with CITES being seen as gaining less cooperation than others.

Demographics

For demographic data, the survey used a number of different scales of differing units, arranged as follows:

1) Years Employed – LA Port Police used a scale based on years

2) Years Employed – Law Enforcement also used a scale based on years

3) Age used the respondent's age in years

4) Ethnic Group used a scale with Caucasian-American being 1, Hispanic-American being 2, African-American as 3, Asian-American as 4, and Other being 5

5) Gender was assigned values of 1 for Male, 2 for Female, and 3 for Other

6) Years Education followed a scale given in years

7) Annual Income followed a scale of 1-to-10, with 1 representing a bracket of $0-10,000 per year and 10 representing a bracket of $100,000 or more per year

8) Years Lived in U.S. is given in years

9) Years Lived in California is given in years

10) Years Lived in LA is given in years

11) Religious Attendance used a scale of 1-to-4, with 1 being once each week, 2 being once each month, 3 being a few times each year, and 4 being never

12) Political Ideology used a scale of 1-to-7 representing a continuum from liberal to conservative, with 1 being extremely liberal and 7 being extremely conservative

The mean and standard deviation for the results for each demographic variable are given in the table below:

Demographic	Mean	Standard Deviation
Years Employed - LA Port Police	11.54	9.63
Years Employed - Law Enforcement	14.76	10.65
Age	40.68	9.82
Ethnic Group	2.3	1.43
Gender	1.11	0.4
Years Education	4.92	4.27
Annual Income	8.2	1.89
Years Lived in U.S.	39.25	9.73
Years Lived in California	36.25	10.34
Years Lived in LA	31.23	15.26
Religious Attendance	2.15	1.06
Political Ideology	4.58	1.2

Generally, this shows a number of trends:

- Respondents had a wide range of experience both as Port of Los Angeles Police and as law enforcement professionals, with the standard deviations showing a significant variation in the range of experience (9.63 years and 10.65 years, respectively). However, the histograms for both did not yield a normal distribution curve, but instead show a slightly heavier weight towards fewer years, with fully half (18) respondents saying they had less than 10 years in the Port of Los Angeles Police and almost as many (13) saying they had less than 10 years of law enforcement experience. This makes sense, considering that managers with more extensive experience would be fewer in number relative to subordinates with less experience.

- Age, while also having a large range (as indicated by the standard deviation of 9.82) yielded a normal distribution curve, with fewer respondents being under 30 or over 50, and the bulk being within the 30-50 age range.

- For Ethnic group, the overwhelming majority were either Caucasian-American (12 responses) or Hispanic-American (11 responses out of), with less than half indicating they were anything else.

- For Gender, the vast majority were male (32 out of 36 respondents).

- With Years of Education, there was a marked bifurcation in the responses. As a result, while there is a mean of 4.92 years of education, the histogram shows a divide skewed towards less education, with 30 respondents having less than 8 years of education and 6 having more than 12. This is commensurate with the idea that managers with more education would be fewer in number relative to the number of less educated subordinates.

- Annual Income showed a heavy weight towards the higher income brackets, with the mean of 8.2 on the 1-to-10 scale showing an overall annual salary of roughly $80,000 per year. The low standard deviation (1.89) indicates that a majority of respondents earned around this figure.

- For Years Lived in U.S., Years Lived in California, and Years Lived in LA, the histograms yielded rough normal distribution curves, with the majority of respondents grouped around the means for each question (39.25, 36.25, and 31.23, respectively). However, the range was extensive, as indicated by the standard deviations (9.73, 10.34, 15.26, respectively).

- For Religious Attendance, even though the mean of 2.15 suggests monthly attendance, the histogram distribution clearly shows a bifurcation, with larger numbers attending either weekly (13 respondents) or a few times each year (12).

- For Political Ideology, there is a distinct normal distribution curve, with the majority of respondents grouped around the mean of 4.58. The standard deviation of 1.58 shows that most respondents placed themselves around the mean, and very few marked either extreme.

III. Data Trends

With respect to the hypothesis, the next step in the analysis is to generate an overview from the raw data and determine if there are any patterns demonstrating similarities or disparities between 1) domestic and international levels, and 2) endangered species traffic and other areas. Observing the nature of such patterns will help guide further investigation into the extent of relationships between international law and local enforcement.

This section begins the discussion with a comparison of data trends between the domestic and international levels, drawing upon the means calculated for the histograms in the previous section. In particular, it compares histogram means of respondent answers to questions regarding:

1) Knowledge of topic issue, domestic law on issue, and international law on issue

2) Perceived effectiveness of domestic and international law for each issue

3) Perceived deterrence value of domestic and international law for each issue

4) Perceived cooperation to support domestic and international law for each issue

The section continues the discussion with a comparison of data trends between endangered species traffic and other topic issues covered by the survey instrument. This is accomplished by utilizing the means for the histograms of the above questions, but organizing them so as to better display the differences and similarities between responses to endangered species traffic and the other types of smuggling in this study.

Level of Analysis (variables across differing levels)

Reviewing the histogram means for respondent impressions about attitudes on knowledge, effectiveness, deterrence, and cooperation yield some observable differences between domestic and international laws. These differences are clear when the means are organized for each of these question areas according to differing levels of analysis. This is seen in the following:

Knowledge (issue, domestic, international)

There was a noticeable disparity between each of the 5 sets of issues, domestic laws, and international laws regarding how respondents perceived their level of knowledge. This is plainly evident in comparison of the means from each set of histograms covering the question of each respondent's level of knowledge with respect to a specific smuggling issue, the domestic law addressing that issue, and the international law connected to the issue.

Smuggling Issue	International Instrument	Domestic Instrument
Endangered species Mean:2.17	CITES Mean: 1.89	ESA Mean: 1.97
Narcotics Mean: 4.83	CNDPS Mean: 3.08	CSIE Mean: 3.94

Weapons:	CNBC	DWMD
Mean: 4.28	Mean: 2.69	Mean: 3.71
Human:	CSTP	TVP
Mean: 4.28	Mean: 2.56	Mean: 3.23
Contraband/gray market:	TRIPS:	CBP
Mean: 4.14	Mean: 2.31	Mean: 2.97

Setting aside the issue of knowledge held by law enforcement personnel of laws they would conceivably be expected to enforce, there is a consistent difference between international treaties versus domestic ones, with the survey participants consistently perceiving their level of knowledge about international laws to be lower than domestic ones. In addition, despite the low claims of knowledge about domestic and international laws, for both levels participants still perceived themselves as having somewhat more knowledge about the general smuggling issues addressed by each law than they did the laws themselves.

It is interesting to contrast these self-assessments in light of the level of importance participants assigned to each issue:

Smuggling Issue	*Mean*
Endangered species	4.33
Narcotics	6.44
Weapons	6.53
Human traffic	6.19
Contraband/gray market	5.75

Despite the higher values indicating respondent belief in the importance of the issues, they still claimed a lower level of knowledge about the laws connected to each one.

Effectiveness (domestic, international)

For effectiveness, there was not a consistent difference between the perceived effectiveness of domestic laws versus international laws. This is evident by comparison of the means for each category given below:

International Instrument - International Support	International Instrument - Domestic Support	Domestic Instrument
CITES Mean: 2.86	3.09	ESA Mean: 2.83
CNDPS Mean: 3.23	3.67	CSIE Mean: 3.89
CNBC Mean: 3.26	3.6	DWMD Mean: 3.83
CSTP Mean: 3	3.29	TVP Mean: 3.14
TRIPS: Mean: 3.17	3.29	CBP Mean: 3.11

However, there was a consistent difference between the perceived effectiveness of international support from non-domestic entities for international treaties versus the perceived effectiveness from domestic entities for international treaties. The means domestic support for international laws was consistently higher, indicating that respondents perceived domestic agencies as being more effective in their support for international treaties than international agencies.

Deterrence (domestic, international)

There was a marked difference between the perceived level of deterrence of domestic laws relative to international laws on corresponding issues. The means for each set of domestic-international laws are given below:

International Instrument	Domestic Instrument
CITES Mean: 2.35	ESA Mean: 2.66

CNDPS Mean: 2.86	CSIE Mean: 3.31
CNBC Mean: 2.85	DWMD Mean: 3.22
CSTP Mean: 2.56	TVP Mean: 2.86
TRIPS: Mean: 2.5	CBP Mean: 2.83

The means for the perceived effectiveness of domestic laws, while low, are consistently higher than those for international laws. This suggests that while respondents viewed laws on smuggling issues as having low deterrence effect, they viewed international laws as having much less deterrence value than domestic ones—even though the domestic laws are the mechanisms for the international ones.

Cooperation (domestic, international)

The bifurcation between the international and domestic levels continued for the perceived level of cooperation in the enforcement of each respective law. This is evident from the means given below:

International *Instrument -* *International* *Cooperation*	*International* *Instrument -* *Domestic* *Cooperation*	*Domestic* *Instrument*
CITES Mean: 2.6	CITES Mean: 2.73	ESA Mean: 3.25
CNDPS Mean: 3.22	CNDPS Mean: 3.46	CSIE Mean: 4.11

CNBC	CNBC	DWMD
Mean: 3.17	Mean: 3.23	Mean: 4.11
CSTP	CSTP	TVP
Mean: 2.89	Mean: 3.31	Mean: 3.94
TRIPS:	TRIPS:	CBP
Mean: 2.86	Mean: 2.97	Mean: 3.44

Overall, the means for cooperation between domestic entities in the enforcement of domestic laws was perceived by respondents as being consistently higher than for equivalent international laws. Moreover, the cooperation between domestic entities in the enforcement of international laws was perceived as being greater than the cooperation with international ones. This suggests that, while still viewed as low, cooperation between domestic agencies in the enforcement of laws is still considered by respondents as being better than the cooperation with foreign entities.

Issue: Issue v. issue (variables across differing issues)

The previous section presented histogram means in a way highlighting the distinctions between domestic and international levels for a variety of question topics: knowledge, effectiveness, deterrence, and cooperation. The discussion, however, also benefits by organizing the means in a way which shows the differences between endangered species traffic and the other forms of smuggling. Doing so clarifies the nature of the relationship between international law and local enforcement, especially whether it is issue-specific or if endangered species (and thereby CITES and the ESA) are different from the other issues. The differences are displayed in the following:

Environment v. others

With respect to the larger topics related to illegal trade covered in this survey, endangered species traffic had lower ratings relative to the other topics. This is seen by comparing the mean values of the histograms from the questions in the survey that dealt with each topic. The means are given in the table below:

Trade Issue	Endan-gered Species	Narcot-ics	Weap-ons	Hu-man Beings	Contra-band	Mean of Means	Stand-ard Devia-tion
Histogram Mean - Importance of Issue	4.33	6.44	6.53	6.19	5.75	6.19	0.9009
Histogram Mean - Level of Respond-ent's Knowledge of Issue	2.17	4.83	4.28	4.28	4.14	4.28	1.0242

For both questions in the survey that dealt with the topics of illegal trade, endangered species traffic had a lower mean compared to the other topics, indicating that survey participants viewed it less favorably relative to other forms of illegal trade.

The extent of these lower ratings can be inferred by using statistical calculations for the overall mean value of the means for each topic on each survey question (given in the table above as "mean of means"), as well as statistical calculations for standard deviation on each question.

For the question asking each participant to rate the importance of each topic (given in the table above as "Importance of Issue"), the mean of means was 6.19 and the standard deviation was 0.9009. The mean on the question for endangered species trade was 4.33, which was well below the low end of the standard deviation at 5.2891 (since 1 standard deviation around 6.19 is 6.19+/-0.9009).

With respect to the level of respondent's knowledge (given in the table as "Level of Respondent's Knowledge of Issue"), the mean of means was 4.28 and the standard deviation was 1.0242. The mean for endangered species trade was well outside the low end of the standard deviation at 3.2558 (4.28+/-1.0242).

The implication for endangered species falling outside the standard deviation is that survey participants viewed the topic of endangered species with significantly greater negativity than they did the other issues, and that the subject of endangered species was a unique one outside the purview of the respondents.

ESA v. others

Among the domestic laws covered in this study, the ESA consistently ranked as the lowest in the ratings it received from respondents. This is plainly evident in comparison of the means gathered from the histograms for each question and each domestic law. The means are given in the table below:

Domestic Law	ESA	CSIE	DWMD	TVP	CBP	Mean of Means	Standard Deviation
Histogram Mean - Level of Knowledge of Domestic Laws	1.97	3.94	3.71	3.23	2.97	3.23	0.7694
Histogram Mean - Level of Effectiveness of Domestic Laws	2.83	3.89	3.83	3.14	3.11	3.14	0.4727
Histogram Mean - Level of Deterrence of Domestic Laws	2.66	3.31	3.22	2.86	2.83	2.86	0.2765
Histogram Mean - Level of Cooperation in Enforcing Domestic Laws	3.25	4.11	4.11	3.94	3.44	3.94	0.3998

Histogram Mean - Level of Personal Satisfaction over Searches	2.97	3.38	2.94	3	3	3	0.1817
Histogram Mean - Level of Personal Satisfaction over Seizures	2.53	2.91	2.67	2.67	2.75	2.67	0.1389
Histogram Mean - Level of Organizational Satisfaction over Searches	2.55	3.36	3.03	2.66	2.71	2.71	0.3307
Histogram Mean - Level of Organizational Satisfaction over Seizures	2.65	3.29	3.15	2.82	2.94	2.94	0.2552

Based on the mean values from the histograms, the ESA was clearly perceived as deserving of lower rankings by survey respondents. The extent to which participants marked the ESA lower relative to other domestic laws can be inferred by using the statistical calculations for the mean of the mean values for each domestic law from the histograms for each survey question (given in the table above as "mean of means"), as well as the statistical calculation for standard deviation for the mean of means.

For example, taking the survey question asking for participants' levels of knowledge for each domestic law, the mean of the responses for the ESA was 1.97. The mean on this question for all the domestic laws in the survey was 3.23, with a standard deviation of 0.7694. This indicates that the ESA was well outside the standard deviation, since 1.97 is below the low standard deviation mark of 2.4606 (1 standard deviation around 3.23 is 3.23+/- 0.7694).

Repeating this for the other questions results in finding that the ESA was inside the standard deviation for perceived effectiveness (2.83, which is within the low end of 1 standard deviation of 3.14, or 2.6673), perceived deterrence (2.66, which is within the low end of the standard deviation of 2.5835), "level of personal satisfaction over searches" (2.97, which is within 1 standard deviation of 3.0, or .1817), and "level of organizational satisfaction over searches" (2.55, which is within the low end of the standard deviation of 2.3793).

The ESA falls outside the standard deviation for the remaining questions, with means outside the low end of the standard deviation for perceived "cooperation in enforcing domestic laws" (3.25, which is outside the low end of 1 standard deviation from 3.94, or 3.5402), just outside the standard deviation for "personal satisfaction over seizures" (2.53, with the low end of the standard deviation being 2.5311), and also just outside the standard deviation for "organizational satisfaction over seizures" (2.65, versus the low end of the standard deviation being 2.6848).

The implications of the means for the ESA falling outside or within the standard deviation of the "mean of means" for each survey question is that respondents evidently had more negative views of the ESA with respect to some questions than they did others. Taking the questions where the means for the ESA fell outside the standard deviations, respondents felt dramatically more poorly about the ESA relative to other domestic laws in the survey with respect to the level of cooperation with other domestic agencies in its enforcement, and felt likewise regarding seizures made under the ESA by respondents as individually and by their organization as a whole. In contrast, taking the questions where the means for the ESA fell within the standard deviations, respondents felt negatively about ESA—but not substantially so relative to other domestic laws—in perceived effectiveness, deterrence value, or levels of satisfaction regarding searches under the law by the respondents individually or their organization as a whole.

CITES v. others

CITES had a consistently lower rating than the other international treaties involved in this survey, as is demonstrated by a comparison of the means gathered from the histograms for each international treaty for each of the survey questions involved in this analysis. The value of the mean for the histogram for each survey question for each international treaty is given below:

International Law	CITES	CNDPS	CNBC	CSTP	TRIPS	Mean of Means	Standard Deviation
Histogram Mean - Level of Knowledge of Int'l Laws	1.89	3.08	2.69	2.56	2.31	2.56	0.4428

Histogram Mean - Effectiveness of Domestic Support for Int'l Law	3.09	3.67	3.6	3.29	3.29	3.29	0.2411
Histogram Mean - Effectiveness of Int'l Support for Int'l Law	2.86	3.23	3.26	3	3.17	3.17	0.1695
Histogram Mean - Level of Deterrence of Int'l Laws	2.35	2.86	2.85	2.56	2.5	2.56	0.2243
Histogram Mean - Level of Domestic Cooperation for Int'l Laws	2.73	3.46	3.23	3.31	2.97	3.23	0.2900
Histogram Mean - Level of Domestic & Int'l Cooperation for Int'l Laws	2.6	3.22	3.17	2.89	2.86	2.89	0.2527

For each survey question posed for 5 international treaties in this study, CITES had the lowest mean, indicating that out of the 5 international treaties it was perceived by respondents as generally being ranked the lowest.

The extent to which CITES received the lowest ratings in each survey question is indicated in the above table by the statistical calculations for the mean of the 5 treaties for each respective survey question (given in the table above as "mean of means"), along with the attendant standard deviation (given in the table above as "standard deviation").

Beginning with the survey question asking respondents for their level of knowledge of a particular treaty, responses for CITES resulted in a mean of 1.89. For the 5 treaties overall, the mean for that particular question was 2.56, and the standard deviation was 0.4428. This shows to be within 1 standard deviation of the overall mean (i.e., "mean of means") of 2.56, each treaty would have had to have a mean value within a range of 2.1172 or 3.0028 (essentially, 2.56 +/- 0.4428). CITES, with 1.89, was very clearly outside of this standard deviation.

Going through similar calculations for each of the other questions in the survey, comparison of CITES mean values to those of the overall mean values finds that CITES is within the standard deviation for the mean of means for "effectiveness of domestic support for international law" (3.09, which is within the low end of the standard deviation of 3.0489), and is also within the standard deviation for "level of deterrence of international laws" (2.35, which is within of the low end of the standard deviation of 2.3357).

CITES, however, falls outside the standard deviation of the mean of means for the remaining questions: "effectiveness of international support for international law" (2.86, which is outside the low end of the standard deviation of 3.0005), "level of domestic cooperation for international laws" (2.73, which is well outside of the low end of the standard deviation of 2.94), and "level of domestic and international cooperation for international laws" (2.6, which is well below the low end of the standard deviation of 2.6373).

The implication of CITES falling outside or within the standard deviations for the above questions is that respondents see CITES as being significantly lower ratings—that, relative to the other international treaties in this survey, CITES is perceived as being much less known by survey participants and as suffering from significantly less effective international efforts at enforcement, markedly less cooperation between domestic agencies for enforcement, and dramatically less cooperation between domestic and international agencies in enforcement. By comparison, for the questions where CITES falls within the standard deviation, the implication is that respondents see CITES as having less domestic support and offering much lower deterrence relative to the other treaties in this study.

II. Discussion

To summarize the findings of this discussion, the comparison of histograms means highlights a number of intriguing points regarding the relationship between international treaties and local enforcement that warrant further investigation to determine the nature of the relationship. In particular, they show distinctions between domestic and international laws (i.e., level-of-analysis)as well as distinctions between endangered species traffic and other illegal traffic (i.e., issue-by-issue). These differences point to issues for policymakers hoping to use linkages from the international levels to local ones as a tool to improve implementation of international instruments. The issues and policy implications are dealt with separately below.

Level-of-Analysis

With respect to the level-of-analysis between domestic and international law, it is clear that international laws tended to receive lower marks from respondents relative to domestic law for the following variables:

- level of knowledge held by the respondent of international treaty versus its domestic law equivalent

- perceived effectiveness of support for international treaty by international organizations versus support by domestic agencies
- perceived cooperation in enforcement of international treaty versus co-operation in enforcement of domestic law equivalent
- perceived deterrence value of international treaty versus domestic law equivalent
- perceived cooperation in enforcement of international treaty between international organizations versus domestic agencies
- perceived cooperation in enforcement of international treaty versus domestic law equivalent

Based on the respondent answers, it is apparent that there is a gap in how local personnel perceive domestic instruments versus international ones, even though both are dealing with the same issue. More than this, the gap is one that has local law enforcement largely viewing international law more negatively than domestic law. The net effect is that local actors, such as the Port of Los Angeles Police, may be less motivated to support what they consider to be ineffectual international policy so long as they do not see connections between such policy and the domestic laws to which they are focused.

Issue-by-Issue

With respect to endangered species traffic compared to other smuggling areas, it is apparent that respondents tended to give endangered species smuggling, and its related domestic law (ESA) and international treaty (CITES), lower ratings for the following variables:

- perceived importance
- respondent's level of knowledge
- perceived effectiveness
- respondent's level of satisfaction of enforcement, both personally and by employing organization
- perceived support for enforcement
- perceived cooperation for enforcement

From the survey responses, it is evident that endangered species, along with its related instruments the ESA and CITES, hold less support from local law enforcement compared to other issues. This suggests that as subject matter, endangered species smuggling may be an aberration for law enforcement, particularly for the Port of Los Angeles Police, and hence that observations drawn from CITES as a case for international policymaking may not necessarily apply to other international instruments.

Policy Implications

The underlying purpose of this analysis is to help policymakers intent on utilizing local actors in international policy implementation recognize potential issues in linking global enforcement to the local level. The descriptive review of the data is intended to highlight what local actors professed to be issues in their law enforcement activities with respect to domestic and international laws. The above discussion points draws upon these highlights to pose several warnings for policymakers aspiring for linkages to local actors to strengthen enforcement of international policy.

The concept of devolution promises a means of aiding international instruments by incorporating local actors into implementation. By shifting additional authority to local entities, devolution extends the implementation chain beyond the global-to-national link further to national-to-local one. While body of research literature on CITES focuses primarily on global and national jurisdictions, and thereby leaves the application of devolution to CITES enforcement an open question, the results of the histograms here provide some insights as to the potential for greater local jurisdiction over international treaties.

To begin, it is evident from this research that local entities sometimes disconnect domestic and international laws, in that their views towards one are not consistent with their views towards the other—even when both a domestic and international law are connected to each other. This, however, is not necessarily a problem for policy implementation. So long as a domestic law is an analogue of an international one, local support can be transposed between the two, with local views of more familiar domestic laws influencing views of less well-known international ones. In this case study, the data shows that Port of Los Angeles Police consider the domestic law ESA more favorably than the international treaty CITES. Because the ESA is the domestic analogue of CITES, this means that policymakers can still expect positive police support for CITES, with local favorable sentiments of the ESA acting as a mechanism to indirectly transfer such perspectives to CITES.

The risk in this situation for policymakers is that the relationship may act negatively. This case study presented survey data wherein local law was considered more favorable than analogous international law. It is, however, conceivable that there are domestic policies held in lower esteem than equivalent international ones, resulting in a situation where dissatisfaction with domestic laws would transpose to prejudice against equivalent international laws. This would contradict the hope of policymakers relying on the greater familiarity with local law over international law held by local actors.

Another option is to ameliorate the disconnect so that local actors see that their support for one is connected to the other. Following the devolution concept, this calls for strengthening the national-to-local linkage. The histograms of the survey data shows this involves several issues. Based on the observations of level-of-analysis data, these largely revolve around a lack of awareness or understanding by local actors of international instruments, and also a dearth of coordination with policy actors at the national and international levels. The former could be addressed through a greater commitment to education of local actors regarding their connection to global policy. The latter could be treated by improving coordination through greater communication, sharing of resources, and adjustment in jurisdiction. All these measures, in effect, are ones previously prescribed in this research as mechanisms for improving the linkages in the policy chain from international to domestic, and from domestic to local levels.

Prescribing which measures to apply, as well as the manner in which to apply them, requires a better understanding of the factors influencing the disconnect between views on domestic and international levels. This suggests a need to better understand the nuances driving the perspectives of local actors. The next stage of the analysis aims to fulfill this objective, applying statistical methods to the survey data to determine if there are potential explanatory or causal factors influencing local officers. The study will then use the results to make policy recommendations.

Regardless of the action taken—to either ignore the disconnect in views between domestic and international policy and rely on local sentiments towards more familiar domestic instruments, or to try and ameliorate the disconnect—actions in extending the policy chain to the local level should be cognizant of issue-specific idiosyncrasies. From the issue-by-issue data, it is clear that some topics like endangered species smuggling, along with their attendant domestic and international instruments, are viewed in markedly different ways by local actors relative to other topics. As a result, the policy action taken should vary by topic issue on a case-by-case basis.

The next step in the analysis will investigate if there are any inter-related influences within the data, with some variables having a determinative relationship with any of the others. This will determine if the observations made in this discussion are subject to behavioral connections between the data. The presence of such connections may affect the policy implications, in the sense that they may point to different explanations for the descriptive trends drawn from the data histograms. The research will take the descriptive analysis presented here and continue with statistical analysis. This will involve specification of independent and dependent variables using the survey questions, calculation of correlations to find potential causal relationships, and performance of regression analysis to determine the strength of such possible causal relationships.

6
Statistical Analysis of Data

International policymakers hoping to utilize local actors in support of policy are seeking to extend the implementation chain from an international-to-national level to a national-to-local one. Devolution promises to enable the creation of the national-to-local linkage by distributing greater authority from federal government to local agencies with respect to enforcement of national laws that are analogues of international ones.

A challenge to such aspirations is the potential unwillingness of local actors to participate in the implementation of international policy. While local actors may be supportive of domestic policies, and thereby ripe for receiving greater authority to enforce national laws under devolution, it is not clear that this automatically means the same for international laws. The analysis showed that there are sometimes disconnections between local interest in domestic laws versus international instruments.

For those situations, however, where local views are biased towards domestic laws, policymakers can still expect to integrate local actors into the implementation chain, so long as the domestic law and international laws are equivalent. Under this condition, local preferences towards the domestic instrument can be transposed to international policy. Unfortunately, this prescription is qualified, since there is a risk that local views are negative towards domestic policies, and that such attitudes would be transposed towards equivalent international policies.

Policymakers hoping to avoid such complications have the option of ameliorating the disconnect in views between domestic and international instruments. But doing so requires better understanding of the factors driving local perspectives towards policy. This is necessary to tailor appropriate actions to mitigate the factors producing the disconnect.

Following the observations of the histograms, the next stage in the study is to determine potential relationships between the variables, specifically those that might demonstrate the connections between the level of success of the legal instruments in the survey versus potential explanatory factors. In doing so, the analysis may indicate if respondent views on the efficacy of their enforcement of international or domestic laws has some basis in their apparent backgrounds or working environment. If true, it would supply policymakers with a greater understanding of what issues they would need to address in strengthening the linkage to local actors so as to incorporate them into implementation efforts for global instruments.

To accomplish this, the study targets those variables in the survey that dealt with the level-of-analysis and issue-by-issue disconnections highlighted by the descriptive analysis, particularly those indicative of respondent views regarding local law enforcement operations, domestic laws, international laws, and personal characteristics. By survey section this meant the following variables:

83

- Section I: Smuggling
  - QIA1—Importance of Smuggling
  - QIB1—Knowledge of Smuggling
  - QIE1—Challenges to Personal Performance
  - QIE3—Challenges to Organizational Performance
- Section II: Domestic Law
  - QIIA1—Knowledge of Domestic Law
  - QIIB1—Effectiveness of Domestic Efforts to Enforce Domestic Law
  - QIIC1—Deterrence of Domestic Law
  - QIID1—Cooperation of Domestic Agencies
  - QIIF1—Satisfaction Over Personal Efforts in Searches
  - QIIF3—Satisfaction Over Personal Efforts in Seizures
  - QIIH1—Satisfaction Over Organizational Efforts in Searches
  - QIIH3—Satisfaction Over Organizational Efforts in Seizures
- Section III: International Law
  - QIIIA1—Knowledge of International Law
  - QIIIB1—Effectiveness of International Efforts to Enforce International Law
  - QIIIB2—Effectiveness of Domestic Efforts to Enforce International Law
  - QIIIC1—Deterrence of International Laws
  - QIIID1—Cooperation of Domestic Agencies
  - QIIID2—Cooperation of International Agencies
- Section IV: Demographics
  - QIV—Demographics

Generally, the study applied statistical analysis to the above. The statistical investigation began with transformation of the data set to allow application of standard statistical methods, determination of correlation values between the variables, and then regression analysis to find determinative relationships for those variable pairs for which there was significant correlation.

The statistical calculations were conducted using a dedicated commercial software suite: SPSS. All data was entered into SPSS, and all calculations, as well as graphic output, were produced using SPSS.

I. Transformed Dataset

Because the dataset produced histograms which were frequently skewed, the analysis performed data transformation. This is because statistical calculations involve parametric tests and functions which assume a normal distribution (i.e., the traditional bell curve), and as a result tend to produce misleading results when applied to distributions that do not follow the normal curve. The histograms in this study did not match a normal distribution curve, and so called for methods that would allow statistical techniques while reducing the danger of misleading results.

Ordinarily, the choice when confronted by skewed data is to either transform the data so that it more closely matches a bell curve and hence becomes ripe for parametric statistical analysis, or to avoid the use of parametric statistical techniques altogether and instead apply non-parametric ones. Given the tendency for non-parametric techniques to be less sensitive in detecting potential relationships in the data, the analysis chose to persist with parametric tests. In an effort to preserve the applicability of the parametric techniques, the data had to be transformed to more closely follow a normal distribution curve.

The histograms did present a few data points following bell curves. However, they frequently displayed distribution curves that were either skewed to the left (i.e., lower end of the 1-to-7 ratings scale) or to the right (i.e., the higher end of the 1-to-7 ratings scale). These skewed curves were subjected to transformations, with curves skewed to the left being transformed via a square root formula (where xtransformed = sqrt(x)) and curves skewed to the right being transformed via a reflection and square root formula (where the xtransformed = sqrt (1-x)).

The goal was to produce a dataset for statistical analysis composed entirely of histograms that followed—as much as possible—normal distribution curves, so as to maximize the efficacy of the parametric techniques. It was this transformed dataset that was used for the subsequent parametric tests and functions to find correlations and explore the possibility of causal relationships between differing variables.

II. Correlations

The initial step in the statistical analysis was an initial determination of the level of correlation for all the variables, with the goal of using the correlations to identify promising relationships for further statistical calculations and eliminating less promising ones from review.

SPSS, in order to calculate correlations, requires specification of scalar independent and dependent variables. In the data selected for this analysis, dependent variables are taken as those that were indicative of participant attitudes on efficacy of the laws included in the survey, and the independent variables are taken as perhaps those that were indicative of participant demographics and working environment. This produces the following arrangement of dependent and independent variables:

Independent Variables	Dependent Variables
QIA1--Importance of Smuggling	QIIB1--Effectiveness of Domestic Efforts to Enforce Domestic Law
	QIIC1--Deterrence of Domestic Laws
QIB1--Knowledge of Smuggling	
QIE1--Challenges to Personal Per-formance	QIIF1--Satisfaction Over Personal Efforts in Searches
QIE3--Challenges to Organizational Performance	QIIF3--Satisfaction Over Personal Efforts in Seizures
QIIA1--Knowledge of Domestic Law	QIIH1--Satisfaction Over Organiza-tional Efforts in Searches
QIID1--Cooperation Domestic Agencies	QIIH3--Satisfaction Over Organiza-tional Efforts in Seizures
	QIIIB1--Effectiveness of Interna-tional Efforts to Enforce Internation-al Law
QIIIA1--Knowledge of International Law	
QIIID1--Cooperation of Domestic Agencies	QIIIB2--Effectiveness of Domestic Efforts to Enforce International Law
QIIID2--Cooperation of International Agencies	QIIIC1--Deterrence of International Laws
QIV--Demographics	

The above tables list 10 independent variables and 9 dependent variables, for a total of 19. However, the actual total of variables is significantly higher.

Among the listings above, 2 deal with challenges to personal and organizational performance, for which the survey listed 14 for both personal and organizational performance, making 28 variables. One, demographics, had 7 variables used in this analysis. In addition, the remaining 16 of the 19 given in the table actually represent the questions posed to each respondent by the survey, and each question encompassed the 5 topic issues (endangered species, narcotics, weapons human traffic, or gray market) or laws (ESA/CITES for endangered species, CSIE/CNDPS for narcotics, DWMD/CNBC for weapons, TVP/CSTP for human traffic, and CBP/TRIPs for gray market) covered by this study, making 80 variables. As a result, the actual total of variables that are involved in the analysis is 115, with 70 falling under the category of independent variables and 45 under dependent variables.

SPSS allows only 100 variables to be involved in correlation calculations. This means that SPSS, in generating a correlation matrix, will only allow inclusion of 100 variables. Since the analysis exceeds this with 115, it was necessary to divide the variables into groups. In an effort to generate correlation matrices useful to comparison between dependent variables, the independent variables were retained as a whole to provide a common point of reference, leaving the dependent variables to be divided into two groups. This meant that the correlation analysis was done twice, so that there were two correlation matrices. Each matrix contains all the independent variables specified in the table. However, one matrix was generated for the dependent variables addressing domestic law, and another matrix was generated for dependent variables addressing international law. The reasoning is that this still allowed all dependent variables (both domestic and independent) to be compared on the basis of the same independent variables. The correlation matrices are presented in Appendix 6 and 7.

The level of correlation was determined using Pearson's product-moment correlation coefficient of r, which indicates the apparent predictive capability of one variable upon another in the sense that it gives the level of correlation between the behavior of different variables. An r>0.5 suggests a non-trivial level of predictive capability, and hence the potential of a causal relationship, thereby warranting additional statistical analysis to verify or disprove such a potential relationship.

Attendant with correlation is the approximation of variance, which was found using the coefficient of determination, given by r^2. This indicates how much of the variance in one variable can be attributed to the variance of another variable. It is a measure in percent, and so approximates just how closely connected the behaviors of 2 separate variables are.

All data for all variables were subjected to correlation calculations using SPSS, resulting in a correlation matrix presenting the Pearson's correlation value (r) and a coefficient of determination for each variable pair. The Pearson product-moment correlation coefficient measured the relationship between the variables. Those variable pairs with Pearson's correlation values greater than 0.5 (r>0.5) were taken as indicative of potential relationships, and the coefficient of determination observed for the level of variance.

Of the 115 variables in the study, only a few produced r>0.5. The Pearson's values for all the data are given in Appendix 6, which presents the correlation matrix for variables involved in this research. Out of these correlation values, the variable pairs that had Pearson's r>0.5 are presented in the following table, along with their coefficients of determination:

Variables Pairs (Transformed)	Correlation: Pearson's r	Coefficient of Determination: r^2
Level of Deterrence International Law-CITES Years in California	0.508	0.258
Level of Deterrence International Law-CNDPS Level Cooperation Domestic Orgs to Enforce Int'l Law-CNDPS	0.513	0.263
Deterrence International Law-TRIPS Level Cooperation Domestic Orgs to Enforce Int'l Law-TRIPs	0.518	0.268
Level Effectiveness Domestic Law-CBP Level Cooperation Domestic Orgs to Enforce Domestic Law-CBP	0.66	0.436
Level Effectiveness Domestic Law-CBP Level Cooperation Int' Orgs to Enforce Int'l Law-TRIPs	0.529	0.280
Level Effectiveness Domestic Law-CBP Level Cooperation Domestic Orgs to	0.579	0.335

Enforce Int'l Law-TRIPs		
Level Effectiveness Domestic Law-ESA Level of Knowledge-Smuggling	0.527	0.278
Level Effectiveness Domestic Law-ESA Level of Cooperation Domestic Orgs to Enforce Domestic Law-ESA	0.569	0.324
Level Effectiveness Domestic Law-ESA Level of Cooperation Domestic Orgs to Enforce Int'l Law-CITES	0.532	0.283
Level Effectiveness Domestic Law-ESA Level of Cooperation Int'l Orgs to Enforce Int'l Law-CITES	0.502	0.252

This is a total of 10 variable pairs, out of a dataset of 115 variables. This suggests that only a small fraction of the dataset had any relationship, since based on the Pearson's r values only a few of the variables shows produced any substantial level of correlation.

Without exception, the few variable pairs that had r>0.5 also yielded substantial coefficients of determination. For example, the pair of "Level of Effectiveness Domestic Law-ESA" and "Level of Cooperation Int'l Orgs to Enforce Int'l Law-CITES" had the lowest coefficient of determination of 0.252, which meant that 25% of the variation in one variable is attributable to the variation in the other. This is a non-trivial sum. The highest coefficient of determination was 0.436, or 43.6% of variance, between "Level Effectiveness Domestic Law-CBP" and "Level Cooperation Domestic Orgs to Enforce Domestic Law-CBP."

Given that there exists a significant level of correlation and related variance in these 10 variable pairs, the next step is to determine if a readily identifiable formula exists delineating the relationships. This can be found by performing regression analysis.

III. Regression Analysis

Regression analysis began with an analysis of variance (ANOVA), and proceeded with a determination of possible coefficients (beta and sig.).

The ANOVA test determines if the variance between different groups of variables is statistically significant, with a value of significance (sig.) close to 0 indicating greater potential for a relationship between variables in a variable cluster which warrants investigation for an appropriate equation with coefficients (beta) representing the relationship. In other words, ANOVA helps identify variable relationship clusters between individual dependent variables and multiple potential independent variables whose behavior can be modeled by linear equations with coefficients of beta (e.g., $x = (beta_1)(y_1) + (beta_2)(y_2) + (beta_n)(y_n)$), where x represents a particular dependent variable, and y_n represents potential independent variables and $beta_n$ the coefficients for each independent variable. Note that variable relationships involve clusters of variables, so that there may be one dependent variable (x) with multiple independent variables (y_1, y_2, etc.), each of which needs its own beta ($beta_1$, $beta_2$, etc.).

The results of the ANOVA tests for the dependent variables with significant correlation values are given in the table below, with each F and sig. value assigned for each dependent variable and its set of independent variables:

Dependent Variable	Independent Variables	F	sig.
Level Effectiveness Domestic Law-CBP	Level Cooperation Domestic Orgs to Enforce Domestic Law-CBP	10.75	0.000
	Level Cooperation Domestic Orgs to Enforce Int'l Law-TRIPS		
	Level Cooperation Int'l Orgs to Enforce Int'l Law-TRIPS		
Level Effectiveness Domestic Law-ESA	Level Knowledge Smuggling	5.272	0.003
	Level Cooperation Domestic Orgs to Enforce Domestic Law-ESA		
	Level Cooperation Domestic Orgs to Enforce Int'l Law-CITES		

	Level Cooperation Int'l Orgs to Enforce Int'l Law-CITES		
Level of Deterrence International Law-CITES	Years in California	8.713	0.007
Level of Deterrence International Law-CNDPS	Level Cooperation Domestic Orgs to Enforce Int'l Law-CNDPS	11.807	0.002
Deterrence International Law-TRIPS	Level Cooperation Domestic Orgs to Enforce Int'l Law-TRIPs	11.755	0.002

To determine the hierarchy of influence each set of independent variables had upon each appropriate dependent variable, the regression analysis found coefficients and sig. values for each individual independent variable. Beta values for each set of independent variables are useful for showing the relative power of each variable in determining the behavior of a dependent variable, with the variable having the highest beta exerting the greatest determinative influence and the variable with the lowest beta exerting the least. Beta values with sig.>.05 tend to indicate that the respective variable is not making a significant unique contribution in terms of helping predict the behavior of the dependent variable.

With these factors, the beta and sig. values for the above variables are given in the table below:

Dependent Variable	Independent Variables	beta	sig.
Level Effectiveness Domestic Law-CBP	Level Cooperation Domestic Orgs to Enforce Domestic Law-CBP	0.66	0.000
	Level Cooperation Domestic Orgs to Enforce Int'l Law-TRIPS	0.511	0.001
	Level Cooperation Int'l Orgs to Enforce Int'l Law-TRIPS	0.341	0.018
Level Effectiveness Domestic Law-ESA	Level Knowledge Smuggling	0.282	0.143
	Level Cooperation Domestic Orgs to Enforce Domestic Law-ESA	0.569	0.001

	Level Cooperation Domestic Orgs to Enforce Int'l Law-CITES	0.33	0.055
	Level Cooperation Int'l Orgs to Enforce Int'l Law-CITES	0.253	0.179
Level of Deterrence International Law-CITES	Years in California	0.508	0.007
Level of Deterrence International Law-CNDPS	Level Cooperation Domestic Orgs to Enforce Int'l Law-CNDPS	0.513	0.002
Deterrence International Law-TRIPS	Level Cooperation Domestic Orgs to Enforce Int'l Law-TRIPs	0.518	0.002

Based on these numbers, the statistically significant relationships can be further narrowed down, to just 6 statistically predictive relationships:

- Level effectiveness of domestic law-CBP v. Level cooperation domestic orgs. to enforce domestic law-CBP
- Level effectiveness of domestic law-CBP v. Level cooperation domestic orgs. to enforce international law-TRIPS
- Level effectiveness of domestic law-ESA v. Level cooperation domestic orgs. to enforce domestic law-ESA
- Level deterrence of international law-CITES v. Years in California
- Level deterrence of international law-CNDPS v. Level cooperation domestic orgs. to enforce international law-CNDPS
- Level deterrence of international law-TRIPS v. Level cooperation domestic orgs. to enforce international law-TRIPS

The existence of just these 6 relationships out of the entire quantity of variables measured by the survey poses some material for discussion.

IV. Discussion

The results of the regression indicate some patterns in the predictive relationships of interest to the hypothesis. The hypothesis offered the argument that there is a relationship between domestic law enforcement and international treaties, as expressed in terms of implementation via domestic laws that fulfill treaty obligations. The study tested this hypothesis using a domestic law (the ESA) that met US obligations to an international treaty (CITES) with respect to a specific issue (endangered species). For comparison, the study also reviewed 5 other sets of domestic laws-international treaties-issue areas.

Based on the regression analysis of the data for all these sets, there are some points of discussion in terms of both domestic and international-level relationships. The data yielded predictive relationships between variables at the domestic level, with 2 out of the 6 dealing with domestic enforcement of domestic laws. There was no comparable relationship found for international enforcement of international laws. With respect to predictive relationships between domestic enforcement and international laws, there were 4 variable pairs.

These results pose a number of issues for policymakers attempting to extend policy linkages to local communities with the goal of involving local actors in implementation of international instruments. Comments for the confirmed predictive relationships are given below, and followed by a review of policy implications.

Predictive relationships — domestic enforcement and domestic law

For domestic enforcement of domestic law, the data established predictive relationships for a specific connection for 2 different issue areas. This was a positive relationship between perceived cooperation between domestic law enforcement agencies and perceived effectiveness of domestic law. The relationship was found for 2 different domestic laws: CBP and ESA.

The replication of the same connection between 2 different issue areas supports assertion of reasoning that a law becomes more effective the more resources are organized to enforce it. This assertion is qualified, since the 3 remaining issue areas (narcotics, weapons, and humans trafficking) found no such predictive relationship. It is, however, supportive of this research's case study of CITES, since it does show a relationship between law enforcement and domestic law with respect to the ESA, which is the domestic law implementing US obligations to CITES.

Predictive relationships — domestic enforcement and international laws

The data did yield relationships between international and domestic levels, with predictive relationships evident between international treaties and domestic laws for 4 out of the 6 variable pairs. Of these 4, 1 demonstrated a connection between the effectiveness of international law (CITES) and a respondents' term of residency in California. This is largely irrelevant to the hypothesis, and can be discarded from discussion. Of the other 3 variable pairs, predictive relationships were found for 1) perceived cooperation between domestic agencies to enforce international law and perceived effectiveness of international law, and 2) perceived cooperation between domestic agencies to enforce domestic law and perceived effectiveness of domestic law. For the first set of predictive relationships, the connections were for narcotics traffic (CNDPS) and gray market traffic (TRIPS). For the second set, the predictive relationship was found for gray market traffic (CBP).

These relationships all involve the level of cooperation between domestic agencies to enforce international law, and they show that this variable has a predictive connection to the effectiveness of both the international law (shown for both TRIPS and CNDPS) and the domestic law fulfilling US obligations to it (shown for the CBP). This suggests that the domestic law enforcement personnel in this survey perceive a relationship between the activities of domestic law enforcement and international law, and believe that there are predictive consequences between actions of domestic law enforcement and an international treaty.

This indicates that respondents see a connection between themselves and international policy, and that they believe local actions can influence global ones. Such support, however, is tempered by the dearth of similar relationships in the other issue areas, especially for the treaty within this case study: CITES. The topic of endangered species generated nothing in terms of predictive relationships confirming comparable connections to those for CBP-TRIPS or the CNDPS. The lack of such a relationship for CITES is at odds with the findings for the ESA, since the ESA is ostensibly the US effort to meet its obligations to CITES. The implication of this disparity is grounds for discussion in the conclusion.

Policy Implications

The above results can perhaps be better reviewed if organized in terms of 2 different categories: 1) the disparity in results between local and international levels, and 2) the disparity between CITES and other international treaties. For the first, it is apparent that the statistical analysis produced mixed results in terms of finding a significant determinative relationship between local perspectives of domestic laws and the equivalent international law. For the second, it is evident that the issue of endangered species trafficking, along with its respective domestic and international instruments of the ESA and CITES, was perceived differently by local actors relative to the other topic areas encompassed in the survey.

For policymakers aspiring to incorporate local actors into implementation of international instruments via extension of policy linkages from global to national to local, the issues revealed in this discussion point to a number of suggestions. First, based on the feedback in the survey, there is a determinative relationship between how local law enforcement perceives cooperation between domestic law enforcement agencies and how they perceive effectiveness of domestic law. This means that their dedication to domestic laws can be improved by expanding the interaction between them and other relevant domestic organizations. This can be translated as involving greater coordination—a point which confirms the policy findings from the descriptive analysis of the histograms: the linkage between local actors and national government can be strengthened by improving the coordination between them, since it acts to increase the authority of local actors in relation to national laws.

Second, the data yields a determinative relationship between how respondents perceive domestic cooperation and the deterrence level of international law. This shows that local actors see a connection between their activities and international policy, particularly when their activities are coordinated with other national agencies. This again confirms the policy findings of the descriptive analysis, and reiterates that the linkage from international instruments to local actors may be directly enhanced by improving their coordination with other domestic law enforcement organizations.

Finally, the statistical findings, much like the descriptive review, still shows a disparity by issue topic, with CITES having markedly different results than others. This leads to the same policy suggestion of the descriptive analysis: extending the policy chain to the local level should be cognizant of issue-specific idiosyncrasies, meaning that the level of effort involved in improving coordination between local actors and national agencies will vary by topic issue.

Having found agreement between this statistical analysis and the previous descriptive analysis, the next stage is to summarize the results of the research and the policy recommendations. This will be done in the conclusion, which will extend the study's findings to present further implications for theory, and then note additional areas of potentially beneficial research.

7
Conclusions

I. Summary of Analysis and Discussion

This research investigated the potential of incorporating local actors in the implementation of international policy via devolution of authority to local levels that served to extend the implementation chain from an international-to-national to an additional national-to-local one. Taking a specific treaty as a case study, it framed the hypothesis as being that there is a connection between the treaty and local law enforcement, and that such a connection allows the addition of local law enforcement to the current national and international implementation efforts sustaining the treaty. For a subject, the analysis focused on the Convention on the International Trade in Endangered Species (CITES), which by its language places implementation duties upon its signatory nation-states, with each one holding sovereign authority to define the means of implementation. The goal of the study was to make findings that could be enunciated as policy recommendations regarding international law.

Following these guidelines, the case study distilled to several specific questions for investigation. First, what is the nature of the current relationship between CITES and local law enforcement? Second, if the relationship is to be improved, what issues are there needing rectification? Third, if the relationship is to be improved, what are the most effective ways to integrate local agencies in international policy implementation?

The methodology adopted to answer these questions began with a review of theory and research literature to develop a context as to existing understanding about CITES as an international instrument. Based on the literature, both for international politics and for CITES enforcement, it was apparent that much of the focus on global policy dealt with the first link in the implementation chain, which involved international-national interactions. This left relatively open the purview of this study, which turned on the second link in the implementation chain, which extends global policy to national-local interactions.

Subsequently, the analysis utilized direct research involving qualitative materials from public documents and interviews with national and local agencies related to CITES enforcement within the U.S., from which discussion turned to the nature of the linkage between the national-local levels with respect to the treaty. The discussion determined that, based on the current federal-local jurisdictional structure within the United States, policymakers intent on utilizing local law enforcement to aid in CITES implementation may do so through three methods: increasing coordination between local officers and the FWS, adjusting jurisdictional and operational capabilities to increase federal power, or to adjust jurisdictional and operational capabilities to increase local power. The first was problematic, because of incomplete data that impeded improvement of referrals and training between the FWS and the Port of Los Angeles Police. The second was contrary to current government philosophy, which favors decentralization of federal power. The third was most consistent with ongoing policy perspectives, which call for devolution of power to local authorities.

Taking the concept of devolution as a direction for creation of the national-to-local link in the implementation chain, the research proceeded to the next stage of the research to determine what issues would be involved at the local level if local law enforcement were to be expected to help support CITES. Much of the CITES research literature offered little guidance in this area, as it focused primarily on the international-to-national link, and less so on the national-to-local link. This study addressed this gap in the literature by using a descriptive discussion of survey results from local law enforcement personnel regarding their observations of international and domestic laws, and found that there was a bifurcation in local perspectives between domestic and international laws, as well as variation in perspectives depending on the subject matter of the laws. The analysis noted that it is possible that local views towards international laws could be irrelevant, so long as they maintained support for domestic laws that were the analogues of international ones. This condition, however, presupposed local support for domestic law, and hence was vulnerable to situations where local officers held negative views of domestic analogues. The study observed than an alternative option to avoid such risk was to bridge differences in views between domestic and international policies.

To help those policymakers who chose to connect the divide between domestic and international levels, the study turned to regression analysis to investigate if there were any determinative factors producing the trends in the survey data. The goal at this juncture was to find what aspects, if any, could be exploited to improve local law enforcement support for a greater role in international policy, with the determinative factors impacting local views on global instruments highlighting the aspects to be exploited for mitigation. The discussion of the regression results determined that according to local actors the major determinative factors were the level of interaction between local and national agencies, with greater levels of communication and coordination producing greater levels of interest in implementing laws, both domestic and international.

The findings of the preceding steps are given here, and are taken from the discussions given in each of the preceding chapters outlined above in the study. This conclusion also relates the findings to the theory involved in the methodology. In addition, it offers recommendations based on the findings that can help policymakers currently formulating international instruments. To finish, the discussion notes a number of caveats about the analysis, and poses additional areas for potential further study.

II. Findings

The findings are best understood by organizing them in relation to the questions associated with the hypothesis. This makes for three sections: the nature of the relationship between CITES and local port police, the issues faced by the police in terms of their inclusion in CITES enforcement, and the potential targets for solution to mitigate such problems.

Nature of linkage

The first stage in analysis endeavored to clarify the nature of the linkage to local law enforcement. For CITES, this meant investigating the relationship of the local Port of Los Angeles Police to the federal Fish & Wildlife Service (FWS) in de jure and de facto perspectives.

De jure, the research found that there is a measure of understood linkage between the Port of Los Angeles Police as local agencies and the FWS as the federal entity. It is not formally enunciated in law, but rather informally maintained, with port police making referrals, with either information on suspected illegal species trade contravening the ESA, or detainment of suspected violations until timely arrival by FWS representatives.

De facto conditions, however, clearly show that the state of this linkage is still uncertain, with a number of unresolved issues regarding potential challenges that may be responsible for frustrating implementation of CITES and the ESA, particularly in terms of available information about enforcement and also disjunctures between federal and local enforcement. The first issue is that the paucity of information regarding referrals and training prevents determination of the frequency and accuracy of those referrals, making it difficult to fully ascertain the connections between the Port of Los Angeles Police and the ESA. The second issue is that the available information on jurisdiction and field operations shows a division in terms of enforcement between federal and local levels.

Because the Port of Los Angeles Police and FWS both observe the demarcation in federal versus local jurisdiction, actions against illegal wildlife shipments requires coordination between the two, with the port police referring suspected cases to FWS. The nature of such a condition is made suspect under this analysis, casting doubt as to the effectiveness of the linkage between the agencies. The problem is compounded by the nature of field operations, since the entity (the port police) that conducts routine patrols defers ESA violations to the jurisdiction of an entity that does not (FWS). Because it maintains a more active field presence, the port police pose a greater level of local expertise in terms of familiarity with port operations, nuances about law enforcement in the port, and timeliness in responding to newly discovered crimes—factors which policymakers pursuing devolution to foster a national-to-local link in the implementation chain would likely seek to utilize.

The findings regarding de jure and de facto aspects of the local-to-national linkage generated a number of consequent points relevant to the policy goals of incorporating local actors into international policy. First, because the ESA is a federal law with an affiliated federal agency and no authority to local actors, formal de jure CITES implementation extends only to a national level, and not to a local one. Second, local involvement by the Port of Los Angeles Police in ESA enforcement appears to be de facto informal through a referral system to FWS. Third, de facto conditions suggest that the informal linkage between local actors to the national level in support of a national law (ESA) is weak. Fourth, this situation means that ESA and CITES enforcement misses an opportunity to include the contributions of a local law enforcement.

The above leads to the fifth point, which is that solutions to the de jure and de facto issues may be: increasing coordination between local officers and the FWS, adjusting jurisdictional and operational capabilities to increase federal power, or to adjust jurisdictional and operational capabilities to increase local power. Increasing coordination is frustrated by incomplete agency record preventing diagnosis and improvement of referrals and training between the FWS and the Port of Los Angeles Police. Increasing federal power is contrary to current government philosophy, which favors decentralization of federal authority. Allocating greater capability to local levels is most consistent with prevailing policy preferences for devolution of power to local authorities.

Sixth, and finally, the concept of devolution acts to enable the national-to-local linkage in the implementation chain. Policymakers seeking to integrate local law enforcement into CITES enforcement are extending the implementation chain from international-to-national down to national-to-local. To accomplish this, they can enable the domestic linkage through devolution, which means that local actors (port police) should gain greater authority to support a federal law (ESA) and related federal agency (FWS)—something that is not currently the case.

Issues in incorporating local police

To use devolution for creation of the national-to-local link in the implementation chain, it was useful to determine what issues would be involved at the local level if local actors were integrated into CITES enforcement. Because existing CITES research literature focused primarily on the international-to-national link, the second phase in this study delved into local perspectives to better understand a potential national-to-local connection. This involved a descriptive study of data regarding local law enforcement perspectives regarding efforts in relation to domestic and international law. The data came from a survey administered to Port of Los Angeles Police, the local agency ripe for devolution of federal ESA authority. For control purposes, the survey gathered responses regarding endangered species smuggling in general, ESA as a domestic law, and CITES as an international one. Also for control purposes, these types of questions were applied for other smuggling issues and international-domestic laws.

The results highlight a number of points regarding the relationship between international treaties and local enforcement. They show distinctions between domestic and international laws (i.e., level-of-analysis disconnection) as well as distinctions between endangered species traffic and other illegal traffic (i.e., issue-by-issue disconnection).

With respect to the level-of-analysis results, the histograms of the survey data show a gap in terms of how local personnel perceive domestic instruments versus international ones, even though both deal with the same issue. Generally, local law enforcement viewed international law more negatively than domestic law. This suggests that local actors may be less motivated to support what they consider to be ineffectual international policy because they do not see connections between such policy and domestic laws.

In some ways, this is not a problem for policy implementation, because if a domestic law is an analogue of an international one, local support can be transposed between the two, with local views of more familiar domestic laws influencing views of less well-known international ones. The study finds that Port of Los Angeles Police consider the domestic law ESA more positive than the international treaty CITES. Since the ESA is the analogue of CITES, this means that policymakers can still expect police support for CITES, with local views of the ESA acting as a mechanism to indirectly transfer enforcement interest in the ESA to CITES.

Such findings should be considered with caution. They are relevant when local law is perceived more favorably than analogous international law. For situations where the domestic law is regarded less favorably than its international counterpart, it is risky for policymakers to rely on local perspectives of the domestic instrument to engender support for international policy. Policymakers would be advised to adopt a case-by-case approach in applying these findings.

The perceptions of local actors towards CITES is important. This is because for CITES, domestic law means federal, not local, and thus limits ESA jurisdiction and operations to a federal agency: the Fish and Wildlife Service. The result is that the U.S. policy framework limits the implementation chain to the international-to-national linkage, and also prevents CITES implementation from taking advantage of port police sympathies towards the ESA.

Greater linkage between local actors and the federal ESA would render moot the disparities in local views towards domestic versus international laws. By granting greater authority to local actors to support federal law, a stronger national-to-local linkage would be added to the implementation chain incorporating local actors into ESA enforcement. Because the ESA is the domestic equivalent of CITES, it would enable CITES policymakers to exploit local sympathies towards the ESA in support of CITES, and thereby render port police views towards CITES irrelevant from an implementation perspective.

Apart from the level-of-analysis results from the histograms, there are also the disparities in data going issue-by-issue. The histograms show that endangered species, along with the related ESA and CITES, are deemed by local law enforcement to be lower in priority compared to other subjects like weapons, gray-market, narcotics, or human trafficking. This suggests that local perspectives towards international policy are subject to a case-by-case variation by issue topic, and that policymakers looking to devolution to build the national-to-local link in the implementation chain need to monitor the characteristics of the legal framework involved in a particular issue area.

Targets for solution

For policymakers seeking to address the disconnect in viewpoints between domestic and international policy, the final step in the research was to try and identify specific areas through which policymakers could attempt to improve the linkages to the local level. This involved regression analysis to find determinative factors producing the trends in the survey data, with the expectation that such factors would highlight what aspects could be exploited to improve local support for participation in international policy implementation.

The analysis found that there is a determinative relationship in terms of how local law enforcement perceives cooperation between domestic law enforcement agencies and how they perceive effectiveness of domestic law. This means that their dedication to domestic laws can be achieved by increasing the coordination between them and other relevant domestic organizations, which would serve to increase their authority in support of federal laws—which may be U.S. domestic expressions of international law.

In addition, the data yields a determinative relationship between how respondents perceive domestic cooperation and the deterrence level of international law. This suggests local actors see a connection between their activities and international policy, especially when their activities are coordinated with other national agencies.

Finally, there is a disparity by issue topic in terms of local views on laws, with endangered species having markedly different results than other topics. This indicates that hopes to strengthen linkages between local actors and national agencies for the sake of improving policy implementation should be adjusted depending on the topic issue.

III. Caveats

The findings of the research were hampered by a number of factors which prevented more conclusive or compelling analysis. Specifically, these were the limited nature of the data set, the restriction from specific types of data, and the inability to get security clearance for access to other agencies.

Limited data

The data set in this study was composed of surveys returned from 36 respondents representing all the armed patrol officers at the Port of Los Angeles. The survey gathered data for 115 variables, from which correlation calculations produced a regression analysis containing 70 independent variables and 45 dependent variables. This meant that the ratio between the number of independent variables and the number of respondents was roughly 2:1.

Statistical methods typically employ a rule of 10 entries for each independent variable, or in this case, a ratio of independent variables to respondents of 1:10. Statistical methods require a requisite number of data points to yield reliable results, with the trend being a larger data set yielding more verifiable and robust statistics and a smaller data set yielding greater chances for error or misleading statistics. The ratio of 1:10 is taken as a rough threshold value indicating a point of reasonable reliability or risk of error.

In this study, the data set clearly fell below the requisite threshold ratio. However, this was somewhat unavoidable for a number of reasons: 1) the quantity of data points could not be increased, because the survey was taken from an agency that employed only 36 law enforcement officers, and so comprised the entire potential data set of the available field sample, and 2) the reduction of independent variables to reach the desired ratio would have reduced the scope of the analysis to an extent that it undermined its relevancy to the hypothesis.

Types of data

The research method in this study was largely comprised of interviews and survey data. However, both federal and local agencies involved in the case study did not retain data regarding the nature of referrals made between them. Specifically, there were not quantitative data kept regarding the frequency and accuracy of those referrals made by the Port of Los Angeles Police to FWS for CITES-related violations. This made it difficult to fully ascertain the connections between the Port of Los Angeles Police and the ESA, particularly in terms of the level of communication between the two and the level of training required by local law enforcement in the event there were allocated more authority in CITES implementation.

Security clearance

The focus of this analysis was on local law enforcement. This was because the research revolved around the question of integrating local actors into the international policy implementation, and hence attention to the implementation chain. In the implementation chain, the first link is global-to-national, in terms of going from international instruments to participating national signatories, and the second link is national-to-local, extending from national government to local government. This analysis, while encompassing both links between these three levels, focused on the local level. This meant that the research concentrated on local law enforcement at the Port of Los Angeles, rather than the federal government offices with comparable jurisdiction over the port.

There are many law enforcement organizations responsible for protection of the Port of Los Angeles. Each organization has jurisdiction not just geographically, but also by subject matter. This means that while all may share jurisdiction over a common area, each one will have exclusive jurisdiction over a specific issue area. For example, the Coast Guard maintains jurisdiction over the waterways within the port, and Customs also retains jurisdiction in terms of interdicting commercial shipping.

While not crucial to the case study of CITES involved in this analysis, the research would have benefited from a more expansive inclusion of these other agencies and their jurisdictional issues, since it would have offered a more comprehensive assessment of the nature of law enforcement activities over international trade. For this study, this would have meant pursuing survey data with respondents from the other law enforcement agencies covering the Port of Los Angeles: the Coast Guard, FBI, etc.

Some effort was made to contact these federal agencies. Unfortunately, responses were not forthcoming. Despite the sponsorship of the law enforcement agency involved in this study (the Port of Los Angeles Police), there was no approval granted for study from the other organizations protecting the Port of Los Angeles. In large part, this is attributable to the nature of the data, which quite possibly infringed on information considered a matter of security by the agencies in question. Security clearance, while requested, was either denied or simply not answered, yielding to a suppression of attempts to gain further data.

IV. Directions for future research

The results of the data were somewhat encouraging, if in some ways mixed. While the regression analysis showed little connection between local levels and international treaties, it nevertheless showed a connection between local levels and domestic laws which were enacted to enforce those international treaties. This pattern was displayed for not only the case in this study (CITES as the international treaty and the ESA as the domestic law implementing it within the US), but also for others. This would warrant additional analysis to further investigate the nature of connections between international instruments and domestic enforcement.

There are some qualifications to make. In particular, there were constraining factors in regards to the limited data sample, restrictions in data gathering, and lack of security clearance. All these factors leave much of the analysis and its findings susceptible to questions.

However, while such questions are cause for reservations about the regression analysis, the correlation calculations for the data clearly showed compelling connections between variables suggesting some relationship between international instruments and domestic enforcement. As a result, even though the regression analysis was not conclusive, the correlation values still suggest some value for additional investigations in the future.

With respect to the hypothesis and the methodology in this study, the statistical calculations support the possibility of more conclusive results through the extension of the scope of the data. The data was limited in that the lack of response from other domestic law enforcement agencies with jurisdiction over international trafficking at the Port of Los Angeles constrained the analysis to just a single agency. This leaves unanswered questions as to the nature of responses that might have been found from the other domestic agencies, even if federal. Such responses may have indicated whether different federal agencies treat U.S. obligations to international law differently, and whether such differences are displayed in agency behavior. This would demonstrate that domestic implementation of international treaties is partially a function of which agencies are involved in treaty enforcement, and could possibly reveal more about the nature of the national-to-local linkage within the implementation chain of international instruments.

In addition, the data was also limited in that the analysis largely utilized interviews and survey data. While appropriate for the methodology in this research, it could benefit from study of other types of data. In particular, it would be illuminating to find line-item annual budgets, as well as annual search and seizure rates categorized by the smuggling issues encompassed in this analysis (i.e., weapons, narcotics, humans, endangered species, gray market goods) for each agency. This would provide empirical data to compare to the attitudinal measures of the survey, allowing better determination of the accuracy of attitudes held by survey respondents, as well as an opportunity to perform time-series studies of relationships between empirical variables. This would help to determine if international treaties are dependent on not only the attitudes of local law enforcement, but also the resources available to local law enforcement.

Further, the scope of the study generated implications regarding the nature of international treaties relative to local law enforcement using only smuggling-related instruments. Verification of such implications could be accomplished by repetition of the study using non-smuggling international treaties, to determine if the relationship between international treaties and local enforcement is partially a function of the nature of the treaty itself.

Moreover, the analysis was constrained by a hypothesis that approached local level implementation through the views of local law enforcement personnel towards international policy instruments. The opposite approach, however, might prove useful, in terms of how international policymaking institutions view implementation at the local level. This would supplement this study in terms of providing insight as to the relationship between global and local policy from the global perspective. In particular, it would indicate that, to the extent that local law enforcement holds a role in implementing international policy, international policymakers also see the role that local enforcement may have on the existence of international treaties.

Finally, the data in this study was a single-time sample of respondents. It would be useful, however, to gather time-series data to see if the perspectives of local law enforcement changes over time, and if such changes produce a corresponding result in implementation or perspectives towards international instruments. This would provide compelling support for the argument that local law enforcement has an influence on the successful implementation of international policy.

V. Implications for theory

The implications of the findings are this: there is a connection between international treaties and local enforcement affecting the enforcement of those treaties, international policy should reach out to local law enforcement, and international policy is perhaps more principle while the local is more practical.

The hypothesis was posed as an articulation of an underlying element of theories of Elinor Ostrum and Ronnie Lipschutz. Ostrum's and Lipschutz's theories share the contention that local actors have the potential to contribute to the successful implementation of international policy. Their common belief is that actors at the local level have the capacity to direct their actions to support policy at the global level.

The research produced findings whose significance to Ostrum and Lipschutz are mixed. To some degree, the research validated the hypothesis and in so doing provides support for their theories. But this is qualified by the nature of the survey question answers and the nuances between the different treaties involved in the survey.

With respect to the survey question answers, it was readily apparent from the histograms that respondents felt a low level of knowledge regarding the international treaties in this study, and also perceived them as being largely ineffective and of low deterrence value. These are discouraging to the underlying theory that local actors would hold any interest in the enforcement of international policy. In addition, the histograms showed respondents claiming a low level of cooperation between domestic agencies in supporting treaties, which further damages the theory that local actors see a connection between the local level and the global level.

However, these implications are mitigated by other histograms that present survey participants as holding the treaty topics of international smuggling to be highly important, and which also present the participants as having low levels of satisfaction over their personal and organizational efforts in support of the treaties in the survey. In contrast to the histograms above, these results support the theory that local actors are aware of global issues, and that they do see a connection between local actions and international policy.

The differences between the varying histogram results may be that the survey participants involved in this analysis do see themselves and local level efforts in ways conducive to Ostrum's and Lipschutz's concepts of local contributions to international enforcement, but that they just do not hold the treaties involved in the survey in high regard. That is, the respondents see a role for themselves—and local law enforcement—in international policy conceptually, but are not optimistic for such roles in relation to the treaties encompassed here specifically.

For the various treaties in the survey, the nuances in findings between them generate implications as mixed as the ones generated from the histograms. The study consistently found differences between CITES and the other smuggling treaties in the survey. This disparity was evident in the histograms, the correlation calculations, and the regression analysis. In all 3 areas of this study, CITES and the subject of endangered species smuggling yielded a much lower level of respondent awareness, support, and confidence, as well as a much weaker level of connection between local actors and international law. This did little to buttress the theories of Ostrum and Lipschutz.

In contrast to CITES, the other treaties in the survey did more to support the theory. For the other treaties, the histograms showed there was a higher level of awareness, support, and confidence. In addition, the correlation calculations and regression analysis showed 2 of them produced a strong connection between local actors and international law. As a result, unlike CITES, the other treaties are more supportive of the theory that local law enforcement are cognizant of global issues, and hold a connection between the local level and international law.

The nuances between the treaties suggest that the strength of Ostrum's and Lipschutz's ideas may be issue-specific and even instrument-specific, with local recognition and perception of a particular issue area and particular law determining their responses to questions over local-to-global relationships. That is, respondents may see a connection between local and international levels as a concept, but their ability to see or support it is subject dependent.

VI. Ramifications to policy

Continuing from the implications to theory, the findings from this case study also point to larger ramifications for general international policy. They present a number of considerations in terms of implementation, particularly for those policymakers with aspirations of incorporating the efforts of local actors to those at national and international levels. Based on the findings from this research, these considerations can be grouped into several categories: whether local actors can truly be linked to the implementation chain from the global-to-local level, the challenges in creating such linkages, and what ways they can be realized.

Building the implementation chain

The incorporation of local actors into international policy implementation essentially means extension of the implementation chain beyond the international-to-national level to the national-to-local one. The findings indicate that creation of this linkage is possible through devolution of authority from federal government to local law enforcement agencies. For those situations where there is existing disjunctures in jurisdiction or operation, and for those situations where policy preferences eschew centralized federal power, devolution offers a viable option for integrating local efforts into international policy.

Possibilities of the local

The findings support the contention that local actors have the capacity to recognize international policy and to connect local-level activities to it. To some degree, there is acceptance of a determinative relationship, with local actions—especially those coordinated between local entities and national ones—influencing the participation in the implementation of global instruments. This suggests there is a pre-existing awareness of larger-scale international policy at the local level, and a recognition of how the two are connected to each other.

For situations where domestic analogues are seen negatively compared to international ones, the alternative is for more direct engagement of local sentiments towards international policy. But even in situations where international policy is viewed negatively compared to domestic policy, there is still a possibility of reaching local actors. In conditions where domestic laws are seen more positively than international ones, it is still possible to harness local support by exploiting their sympathies to domestic laws. The findings indicate that while a domestic law may be an expression of larger international policy, local actors tend to maintain a bias favoring a domestic instrument over the equivalent international treaty. Consequently, global policy can still gain local support so long as a consistent national law exists.

The alternative is to avoid the challenges of adjusting policy framework to match disparate views between domestic and local levels, by instead focusing on amelioration of the disconnect itself. This can be achieved by increasing levels of communication and coordination between local and federal as well as local and international agencies.

Challenges in linking to the local

The study demonstrated aspirations of encompassing local efforts to global policy face a number of challenges. Attempts to add a national-to-local link in implementation requires recognition of the nature of interactions between the two levels and the manner by which authority is allocated between them. The findings showed that these issues include the de jure design of national law with respect to local involvement, as well as the de facto problems of demarcations in jurisdiction between national and local governments along with the nature of coordination between national and local actors.

Another aspect that poses difficulty is the variation in local attitudes by issue. The findings clearly showed differences in sentiment towards international and domestic laws depending on the issue involved. Some topics clearly garnered different responses than others.

Policymakers at the international level, if they are intent on involving local support, would need to familiarize themselves with these kinds of issues. This would mean investigating the national-to-local dynamics unique to each country, and adjusting policy design to accommodate for the full spectrum of nation-state signatories involved in most treaties. It would also mean doing this on a case-by-case basis for each treaty involving a specific subject matter.

Ways of linking to the local

This research suggests that there are potentially productive ways of extending international instruments to local levels. Following the findings, the areas determinative of improving local acceptance of increased involvement in global policy appear to be authority in terms of enforcement and coordination in terms of information. De jure, these can be achieved formally in the language of law, either international or—in cases where local biases favor domestic ones—national, where the law states the mechanisms by which local actors are involved in implementation and defines their jurisdiction. De facto, these can be achieved informally via greater coordination of resources and communications with other organizations—local, national, or international—to unify energies against specific issues.

The Convention on the International Trade in Endangered Species (CITES)

The Convention on International Trade
in Endangered Species
of Wild Fauna and Flora

Signed at Washington, D.C., on 3 March 1973
Amended at Bonn, on 22 June 1979

The Contracting States,

Recognizing that wild fauna and flora in their many beautiful and varied forms are an irreplaceable part of the natural systems of the earth which must be protected for this and the generations to come;

Conscious of the ever-growing value of wild fauna and flora from aesthetic, scientific, cultural, recreational and economic points of view;

Recognizing that peoples and States are and should be the best protectors of their own wild fauna and flora;

Recognizing, in addition, that international co-operation is essential for the protection of certain species of wild fauna and flora against over-exploitation through international trade;

Convinced of the urgency of taking appropriate measures to this end; Have agreed as follows:

Article I
Definitions

For the purpose of the present Convention, unless the context otherwise requires:

(a) "Species" means any species, subspecies, or geographically separate population thereof;

(b) "Specimen" means:

(i) any animal or plant, whether alive or dead;

(ii) in the case of an animal: for species included in Appendices I and II, any readily recognizable part or derivative thereof; and for species included in Appendix III, any readily recognizable part or derivative thereof specified in Appendix III in relation to the species; and

(iii) in the case of a plant: for species included in Appendix I, any readily recognizable part or derivative thereof; and for species included in Appendices II and III, any readily recognizable part or derivative thereof specified in Appendices II and III in relation to the species;

(c) "Trade" means export, re-export, import and introduction from the sea;

(d) "Re-export" means export of any specimen that has previously been imported;

(e) "Introduction from the sea" means transportation into a State of specimens of any species which were taken in the marine environment not under the jurisdiction of any State;

(f) "Scientific Authority" means a national scientific authority designated in accordance with Article IX;

(g) "Management Authority" means a national management authority designated in accordance with Article IX;

(h) "Party" means a State for which the present Convention has entered into force.

Article II
Fundamental Principles

1. Appendix I shall include all species threatened with extinction which are or may be affected by trade. Trade in specimens of these species must be subject to particularly strict regulation in order not to endanger further their survival and must only be authorized in exceptional circumstances.

2. Appendix II shall include:

(a) all species which although not necessarily now threatened with extinction may become so unless trade in specimens of such species is subject to strict regulation in order to avoid utilization incompatible with their survival; and

(b) other species which must be subject to regulation in order that trade in specimens of certain species referred to in sub-paragraph (a) of this paragraph may be brought under effective control.

3. Appendix III shall include all species which any Party identifies as being subject to regulation within its jurisdiction for the purpose of preventing or restricting exploitation, and as needing the co-operation of other Parties in the control of trade.

4. The Parties shall not allow trade in specimens of species included in Appendices I, II and III except in accordance with the provisions of the present Convention.

Article III
Regulation of Trade in Specimens of Species Included in Appendix I

1. All trade in specimens of species included in Appendix I shall be in accordance with the provisions of this Article.

2. The export of any specimen of a species included in Appendix I shall require the prior grant and presentation of an export permit. An export permit shall only be granted when the following conditions have been met:

(a) a Scientific Authority of the State of export has advised that such export will not be detrimental to the survival of that species;

(b) a Management Authority of the State of export is satisfied that the specimen was not obtained in contravention of the laws of that State for the protection of fauna and flora;

(c) a Management Authority of the State of export is satisfied that any living specimen will be so prepared and shipped as to minimize the risk of injury, damage to health or cruel treatment; and

(d) a Management Authority of the State of export is satisfied that an import permit has been granted for the specimen.

3. The import of any specimen of a species included in Appendix I shall require the prior grant and presentation of an import permit and either an export permit or a re-export certificate. An import permit shall only be granted when the following conditions have been met:

(a) a Scientific Authority of the State of import has advised that the import will be for purposes which are not detrimental to the survival of the species involved;

(b) a Scientific Authority of the State of import is satisfied that the proposed recipient of a living specimen is suitably equipped to house and care for it; and

(c) a Management Authority of the State of import is satisfied that the specimen is not to be used for primarily commercial purposes.

4. The re-export of any specimen of a species included in Appendix I shall require the prior grant and presentation of a re-export certificate. A re-export certificate shall only be granted when the following conditions have been met:

(a) a Management Authority of the State of re-export is satisfied that the specimen was imported into that State in accordance with the provisions of the present Convention;

(b) a Management Authority of the State of re-export is satisfied that any living specimen will be so prepared and shipped as to minimize the risk of injury, damage to health or cruel treatment; and

(c) a Management Authority of the State of re-export is satisfied that an import permit has been granted for any living specimen.

5. The introduction from the sea of any specimen of a species included in Appendix I shall require the prior grant of a certificate from a Management Authority of the State of introduction. A certificate shall only be granted when the following conditions have been met:

(a) a Scientific Authority of the State of introduction advises that the introduction will not be detrimental to the survival of the species involved;

(b) a Management Authority of the State of introduction is satisfied that the proposed recipient of a living specimen is suitably equipped to house and care for it; and

(c) a Management Authority of the State of introduction is satisfied that the specimen is not to be used for primarily commercial purposes.

Article IV
Regulation of Trade in Specimens of Species Included in Appendix II

1. All trade in specimens of species included in Appendix II shall be in accordance with the provisions of this Article.

2. The export of any specimen of a species included in Appendix II shall require the prior grant and presentation of an export permit. An export permit shall only be granted when the following conditions have been met:

(a) a Scientific Authority of the State of export has advised that such export will not be detrimental to the survival of that species;

(b) a Management Authority of the State of export is satisfied that the specimen was not obtained in contravention of the laws of that State for the protection of fauna and flora; and

(c) a Management Authority of the State of export is satisfied that any living specimen will be so prepared and shipped as to minimize the risk of injury, damage to health or cruel treatment.

3. A Scientific Authority in each Party shall monitor both the export permits granted by that State for specimens of species included in Appendix II and the actual exports of such specimens. Whenever a Scientific Authority determines that the export of specimens of any such species should be limited in order to maintain that species throughout its range at a level consistent with its role in the ecosystems in which it occurs and well above the level at which that species might become eligible for inclusion in Appendix I, the Scientific Authority shall advise the appropriate Management Authority of suitable measures to be taken to limit the grant of export permits for specimens of that species.

4. The import of any specimen of a species included in Appendix II shall require the prior presentation of either an export permit or a re-export certificate.

5. The re-export of any specimen of a species included in Appendix II shall require the prior grant and presentation of a re-export certificate. A re-export certificate shall only be granted when the following conditions have been met:

(a) a Management Authority of the State of re-export is satisfied that the specimen was imported into that State in accordance with the provisions of the present Convention; and

(b) a Management Authority of the State of re-export is satisfied that any living specimen will be so prepared and shipped as to minimize the risk of injury, damage to health or cruel treatment.

6. The introduction from the sea of any specimen of a species included in Appendix II shall require the prior grant of a certificate from a Management Authority of the State of introduction. A certificate shall only be granted when the following conditions have been met:

(a) a Scientific Authority of the State of introduction advises that the introduction will not be detrimental to the survival of the species involved; and

(b) a Management Authority of the State of introduction is satisfied that any living specimen will be so handled as to minimize the risk of injury, damage to health or cruel treatment.

7. Certificates referred to in paragraph 6 of this Article may be granted on the advice of a Scientific Authority, in consultation with other national scientific authorities or, when appropriate, international scientific authorities, in respect of periods not exceeding one year for total numbers of specimens to be introduced in such periods.

Article V
Regulation of Trade in Specimens of Species Included in Appendix III

1. All trade in specimens of species included in Appendix III shall be in accordance with the provisions of this Article.

2. The export of any specimen of a species included in Appendix III from any State which has included that species in Appendix III shall require the prior grant and presentation of an export permit. An export permit shall only be granted when the following conditions have been met:

(a) a Management Authority of the State of export is satisfied that the specimen was not obtained in contravention of the laws of that State for the protection of fauna and flora; and

(b) a Management Authority of the State of export is satisfied that any living specimen will be so prepared and shipped as to minimize the risk of injury, damage to health or cruel treatment.

3. The import of any specimen of a species included in Appendix III shall require, except in circumstances to which paragraph 4 of this Article applies, the prior presentation of a certificate of origin and, where the import is from a State which has included that species in Appendix III, an export permit.

4. In the case of re-export, a certificate granted by the Management Authority of the State of re-export that the specimen was processed in that State or is being re-exported shall be accepted by the State of import as evidence that the provisions of the present Convention have been complied with in respect of the specimen concerned.

Article VI
Permits and Certificates

1. Permits and certificates granted under the provisions of Articles III, IV, and V shall be in accordance with the provisions of this Article.

2. An export permit shall contain the information specified in the model set forth in Appendix IV, and may only be used for export within a period of six months from the date on which it was granted.

3. Each permit or certificate shall contain the title of the present Convention, the name and any identifying stamp of the Management Authority granting it and a control number assigned by the Management Authority.

4. Any copies of a permit or certificate issued by a Management Authority shall be clearly marked as copies only and no such copy may be used in place of the original, except to the extent endorsed thereon.

5. A separate permit or certificate shall be required for each consignment of specimens.

6. A Management Authority of the State of import of any specimen shall cancel and retain the export permit or re-export certificate and any corresponding import permit presented in respect of the import of that specimen.

7. Where appropriate and feasible a Management Authority may affix a mark upon any specimen to assist in identifying the specimen. For these purposes "mark" means any indelible imprint, lead seal or other suitable means of identifying a specimen, designed in such a way as to render its imitation by unauthorized persons as difficult as possible.

Article VII
Exemptions and Other Special Provisions Relating to Trade

1. The provisions of Articles III, IV and V shall not apply to the transit or transhipment of specimens through or in the territory of a Party while the specimens remain in Customs control.

2. Where a Management Authority of the State of export or re-export is satisfied that a specimen was acquired before the provisions of the present Convention applied to that specimen, the provisions of Articles III, IV and V shall not apply to that specimen where the Management Authority issues a certificate to that effect.

3. The provisions of Articles III, IV and V shall not apply to specimens that are personal or household effects. This exemption shall not apply where:

(a) in the case of specimens of a species included in Appendix I, they were acquired by the owner outside his State of usual residence, and are being imported into that State; or

(b) in the case of specimens of species included in Appendix II:

(i) they were acquired by the owner outside his State of usual residence and in a State where removal from the wild occurred;

(ii) they are being imported into the owner's State of usual residence; and

(iii) the State where removal from the wild occurred requires the prior grant of export permits before any export of such specimens; unless a Management Authority is satisfied that the specimens were acquired before the provisions of the present Convention applied to such specimens.

4. Specimens of an animal species included in Appendix I bred in captivity for commercial purposes, or of a plant species included in Appendix I artificially propagated for commercial purposes, shall be deemed to be specimens of species included in Appendix II.

5. Where a Management Authority of the State of export is satisfied that any specimen of an animal species was bred in captivity or any specimen of a plant species was artificially propagated, or is a part of such an animal or plant or was derived therefrom, a certificate by that Management Authority to that effect shall be accepted in lieu of any of the permits or certificates required under the provisions of Article III, IV or V.

6. The provisions of Articles III, IV and V shall not apply to the non-commercial loan, donation or exchange between scientists or scientific institutions registered by a Management Authority of their State, of herbarium specimens, other preserved, dried or embedded museum specimens, and live plant material which carry a label issued or approved by a Management Authority.

7. A Management Authority of any State may waive the requirements of Articles III, IV and V and allow the movement without permits or certificates of specimens which form part of a travelling zoo, circus, menagerie, plant exhibition or other travelling exhibition provided that:

(a) the exporter or importer registers full details of such specimens with that

Management Authority;

(b) the specimens are in either of the categories specified in paragraph 2 or 5 of this Article; and

(c) the Management Authority is satisfied that any living specimen will be so transported and cared for as to minimize the risk of injury, damage to health or cruel treatment.

Article VIII
Measures to Be Taken by the Parties

1. The Parties shall take appropriate measures to enforce the provisions of the present Convention and to prohibit trade in specimens in violation thereof. These shall include measures:

(a) to penalize trade in, or possession of, such specimens, or both; and

(b) to provide for the confiscation or return to the State of export of such specimens.

2. In addition to the measures taken under paragraph 1 of this Article, a Party may, when it deems it necessary, provide for any method of internal reimbursement for expenses incurred as a result of the confiscation of a specimen traded in violation of the measures taken in the application of the provisions of the present Convention.

3. As far as possible, the Parties shall ensure that specimens shall pass through any formalities required for trade with a minimum of delay. To facilitate such passage, a Party may designate ports of exit and ports of entry at which speci-

mens must be presented for clearance. The Parties shall ensure further that all living specimens, during any period of transit, holding or shipment, are properly cared for so as to minimize the risk of injury, damage to health or cruel treatment.

4. Where a living specimen is confiscated as a result of measures referred to in paragraph 1 of this Article:

(a) the specimen shall be entrusted to a Management Authority of the State of confiscation;

(b) the Management Authority shall, after consultation with the State of export, return the specimen to that State at the expense of that State, or to a rescue centre or such other place as the Management Authority deems appropriate and consistent with the purposes of the present Convention; and

(c) the Management Authority may obtain the advice of a Scientific Authority, or may, whenever it considers it desirable, consult the Secretariat in order to facilitate the decision under sub-paragraph (b) of this paragraph, including the choice of a rescue centre or other place.

5. A rescue centre as referred to in paragraph 4 of this Article means an institution designated by a Management Authority to look after the welfare of living specimens, particularly those that have been confiscated.

6. Each Party shall maintain records of trade in specimens of species included in Appendices I, II and III which shall cover:

(a) the names and addresses of exporters and importers; and

(b) the number and type of permits and certificates granted; the States with which such trade occurred; the numbers or quantities and types of specimens, names of species as included in Appendices I, II and III and, where applicable, the size and sex of the specimens in question.

7. Each Party shall prepare periodic reports on its implementation of the present Convention and shall transmit to the Secretariat:

(a) an annual report containing a summary of the information specified in sub-paragraph (b) of paragraph 6 of this Article; and

(b) a biennial report on legislative, regulatory and administrative measures taken to enforce the provisions of the present Convention.

8. The information referred to in paragraph 7 of this Article shall be available to the public where this is not inconsistent with the law of the Party concerned.

Article IX
Management and Scientific Authorities

1. Each Party shall designate for the purposes of the present Convention:

(a) one or more Management Authorities competent to grant permits or certificates

on behalf of that Party; and

(b) one or more Scientific Authorities.

2. A State depositing an instrument of ratification, acceptance, approval or accession shall at that time inform the Depositary Government of the name and address of the Management Authority authorized to communicate with other Parties and with the Secretariat.

3. Any changes in the designations or authorizations under the provisions of this Article shall be communicated by the Party concerned to the Secretariat for transmission to all other Parties.

4. Any Management Authority referred to in paragraph 2 of this Article shall, if so requested by the Secretariat or the Management Authority of another Party, communicate to it impression of stamps, seals or other devices used to authenticate permits or certificates.

Article X
Trade with States not Party to the Convention

Where export or re-export is to, or import is from, a State not a Party to the present Convention, comparable documentation issued by the competent authorities in that State which substantially conforms with the requirements of the present Convention for permits and certificates may be accepted in lieu thereof by any Party.

Article XI
Conference of the Parties

1. The Secretariat shall call a meeting of the Conference of the Parties not later than two years after the entry into force of the present Convention.

2. Thereafter the Secretariat shall convene regular meetings at least once every two years, unless the Conference decides otherwise, and extraordinary meetings at any time on the written request of at least one-third of the Parties.

3. At meetings, whether regular or extraordinary, the Parties shall review the implementation of the present Convention and may:

(a) make such provision as may be necessary to enable the Secretariat to carry out its duties, and adopt financial provisions;

(b) consider and adopt amendments to Appendices I and II in accordance with Article XV;

(c) review the progress made towards the restoration and conservation of the species included in Appendices I, II and III;

(d) receive and consider any reports presented by the Secretariat or by any Party; and

(e) where appropriate, make recommendations for improving the effectiveness of the present Convention.

4. At each regular meeting, the Parties may determine the time and venue of the next regular meeting to be held in accordance with the provisions of paragraph 2 of this Article.

5. At any meeting, the Parties may determine and adopt rules of procedure for the meeting.

6. The United Nations, its Specialized Agencies and the International Atomic Energy Agency, as well as any State not a Party to the present Convention, may be represented at meetings of the Conference by observers, who shall have the right to participate but not to vote.

7. Any body or agency technically qualified in protection, conservation or management of wild fauna and flora, in the following categories, which has informed the Secretariat of its desire to be represented at meetings of the Conference by observers, shall be admitted unless at least one-third of the Parties present object:

(a) international agencies or bodies, either governmental or non-governmental, and

national governmental agencies and bodies; and

(b) national non-governmental agencies or bodies which have been approved for this purpose by the State in which they are located. Once admitted, these observers shall have the right to participate but not to vote.

Article XII
The Secretariat

1. Upon entry into force of the present Convention, a Secretariat shall be provided by the Executive Director of the United Nations Environment Programme. To the extent and in the manner he considers appropriate, he may be assisted by suitable inter-governmental or non-governmental international or national agencies and bodies technically qualified in protection, conservation and management of wild fauna and flora.

2. The functions of the Secretariat shall be:

(a) to arrange for and service meetings of the Parties;

(b) to perform the functions entrusted to it under the provisions of Articles XV and XVI of the present Convention;

(c) to undertake scientific and technical studies in accordance with programmes authorized by the Conference of the Parties as will contribute to the implementation of the present Convention, including studies concerning standards for appropriate preparation and shipment of living specimens and the means of identifying specimens;

(d) to study the reports of Parties and to request from Parties such further information with respect thereto as it deems necessary to ensure implementation of the present Convention;

(e) to invite the attention of the Parties to any matter pertaining to the aims of the present Convention;

(f) to publish periodically and distribute to the Parties current editions of Appendices I, II and III together with any information which will facilitate identification of specimens of species included in those Appendices;

(g) to prepare annual reports to the Parties on its work and on the implementation of the present Convention and such other reports as meetings of the Parties may request;

(h) to make recommendations for the implementation of the aims and provisions of the present Convention, including the exchange of information of a scientific or technical nature;

(i) to perform any other function as may be entrusted to it by the Parties.

Article XIII
International Measures

1. When the Secretariat in the light of information received is satisfied that any species included in Appendix I or II is being affected adversely by trade in specimens of that species or that the provisions of the present Convention are not being effectively implemented, it shall communicate such information to the authorized Management Authority of the Party or Parties concerned.

2. When any Party receives a communication as indicated in paragraph 1 of this Article, it shall, as soon as possible, inform the Secretariat of any relevant facts insofar as its laws permit and, where appropriate, propose remedial action. Where the Party considers that an inquiry is desirable, such inquiry may be carried out by one or more persons expressly authorized by the Party.

3. The information provided by the Party or resulting from any inquiry as specified in paragraph 2 of this Article shall be reviewed by the next Conference of the Parties which may make whatever recommendations it deems appropriate.

Article XIV
Effect on Domestic Legislation and International Conventions

1. The provisions of the present Convention shall in no way affect the right of Parties to adopt:

(a) stricter domestic measures regarding the conditions for trade, taking, possession or transport of specimens of species included in Appendices I, II and III, or the complete prohibition thereof; or

(b) domestic measures restricting or prohibiting trade, taking, possession or transport of species not included in Appendix I, II or III.

2. The provisions of the present Convention shall in no way affect the provisions of any domestic measures or the obligations of Parties deriving from any treaty, convention, or international agreement relating to other aspects of trade, taking, possession or transport of specimens which is in force or subsequently may enter

into force for any Party including any measure pertaining to the Customs, public health, veterinary or plant quarantine fields.

3. The provisions of the present Convention shall in no way affect the provisions of, or the obligations deriving from, any treaty, convention or international agreement concluded or which may be concluded between States creating a union or regional trade agreement establishing or maintaining a common external Customs control and removing Customs control between the parties thereto insofar as they relate to trade among the States members of that union or agreement.

4. A State party to the present Convention, which is also a party to any other treaty, convention or international agreement which is in force at the time of the coming into force of the present Convention and under the provisions of which protection is

afforded to marine species included in Appendix II, shall be relieved of the obligations imposed on it under the provisions of the present Convention with respect to trade in specimens of species included in Appendix II that are taken by ships registered in that State and in accordance with the provisions of such other treaty, convention or international agreement.

5. Notwithstanding the provisions of Articles III, IV and V, any export of a specimen taken in accordance with paragraph 4 of this Article shall only require a certificate from a Management Authority of the State of introduction to the effect that the specimen was taken in accordance with the provisions of the other treaty, convention or international agreement in question.

6. Nothing in the present Convention shall prejudice the codification and development of the law of the sea by the United Nations Conference on the Law of the Sea convened pursuant to Resolution 2750 C (XXV) of the General Assembly of the United Nations nor the present or future claims and legal views of any State concerning the law of the sea and the nature and extent of coastal and flag State jurisdiction.

Article XV
Amendments to Appendices I and II

1. The following provisions shall apply in relation to amendments to Appendices I and II at meetings of the Conference of the Parties:

(a) Any Party may propose an amendment to Appendix I or II for consideration at the next meeting. The text of the proposed amendment shall be communicated to the Secretariat at least 150 days before the meeting. The Secretariat shall consult the other Parties and interested bodies on the amendment in accordance with the provisions of sub-paragraphs (b) and (c) of paragraph 2 of this Article and shall communicate the response to all Parties not later than 30 days before the meeting.

(b) Amendments shall be adopted by a two-thirds majority of Parties present and voting. For these purposes "Parties present and voting" means Parties present and casting an affirmative or negative vote. Parties abstaining from voting shall not be counted among the two-thirds required for adopting an amendment.

(c) Amendments adopted at a meeting shall enter into force 90 days after that meeting for all Parties except those which make a reservation in accordance with paragraph 3 of this Article.

2. The following provisions shall apply in relation to amendments to Appendices I and II between meetings of the Conference of the Parties:

(a) Any Party may propose an amendment to Appendix I or II for consideration between meetings by the postal procedures set forth in this paragraph.

(b) For marine species, the Secretariat shall, upon receiving the text of the proposed amendment, immediately communicate it to the Parties. It shall also consult inter-governmental bodies having a function in relation to those species especially with a view to obtaining scientific data these bodies may be able to provide and to ensuring co-ordination with any conservation measures enforced by such bodies. The Secretariat shall communicate the views expressed and data provided by these bodies and its own findings and recommendations to the Parties as soon as possible.

(c) For species other than marine species, the Secretariat shall, upon receiving the text of the proposed amendment, immediately communicate it to the Parties, and, as soon as possible thereafter, its own recommendations.

(d) Any Party may, within 60 days of the date on which the Secretariat communicated its recommendations to the Parties under sub-paragraph (b) or (c) of this paragraph, transmit to the Secretariat any comments on the proposed amendment together with any relevant scientific data and information.

(e) The Secretariat shall communicate the replies received together with its own recommendations to the Parties as soon as possible. (f) If no objection to the proposed amendment is received by the Secretariat within 30 days of the date the replies and recommendations were communicated under the provisions of sub-paragraph (e) of this paragraph, the amendment shall enter into force 90 days later for all Parties except those which make a reservation in accordance with paragraph 3 of this Article.

(g) If an objection by any Party is received by the Secretariat, the proposed amendment shall be submitted to a postal vote in accordance with the provisions of sub-paragraphs (h) , (i) and (j) of this paragraph.

(h) The Secretariat shall notify the Parties that notification of objection has been received.

(i) Unless the Secretariat receives the votes for, against or in abstention from at least one-half of the Parties within 60 days of the date of notification under sub-paragraph (h) of this paragraph, the proposed amendment shall be referred to the next meeting of the Conference for further consideration.

(j) Provided that votes are received from one-half of the Parties, the amendment shall be adopted by a two-thirds majority of Parties casting an affirmative or negative vote.

(k) The Secretariat shall notify all Parties of the result of the vote.

(l) If the proposed amendment is adopted it shall enter into force 90 days after the date of the notification by the Secretariat of its acceptance for all Parties except those which make a reservation in accordance with paragraph 3 of this Article.

3. During the period of 90 days provided for by sub-paragraph (c) of paragraph 1 or sub-paragraph (l) of paragraph 2 of this Article any Party may by notification in writing to the Depositary Government make a reservation with respect to the amendment. Until such reservation is withdrawn the Party shall be treated as a State not a Party to the present Convention with respect to trade in the species concerned.

Article XVI
Appendix III and Amendments thereto

1. Any Party may at any time submit to the Secretariat a list of species which it identifies as being subject to regulation within its jurisdiction for the purpose mentioned in paragraph 3 of Article II. Appendix III shall include the names of the Parties submitting the species for inclusion therein, the scientific names of the species so submitted, and any parts or derivatives of the animals or plants concerned that are specified in relation to the species for the purposes of sub-paragraph (b) of Article I.

2. Each list submitted under the provisions of paragraph 1 of this Article shall be communicated to the Parties by the Secretariat as soon as possible after receiving it. The list shall take effect as part of Appendix III 90 days after the date of such communication. At any time after the communication of such list, any Party may by notification in writing to the Depositary Government enter a reservation with respect to any species or any parts or derivatives, and until such reservation is withdrawn, the State shall be treated as a State not a Party to the present Convention with respect to trade in the species or part or derivative concerned.

3. A Party which has submitted a species for inclusion in Appendix III may withdraw it at any time by notification to the Secretariat which shall communicate the withdrawal to all Parties. The withdrawal shall take effect 30 days after the date of such communication.

4. Any Party submitting a list under the provisions of paragraph 1 of this Article shall submit to the Secretariat a copy of all domestic laws and regulations applicable to the protection of such species, together with any interpretations which the Party may deem appropriate or the Secretariat may request. The Party shall, for as long as the species in question is included in Appendix III, submit any amendments of such laws and regulations or any interpretations as they are adopted.

Article XVII
Amendment of the Convention

1. An extraordinary meeting of the Conference of the Parties shall be convened by the Secretariat on the written request of at least one-third of the Parties to con-

sider and adopt amendments to the present Convention. Such amendments shall be adopted by a two-thirds majority of Parties present and voting. For these purposes "Parties present and voting" means Parties present and casting an affirmative or negative vote. Parties abstaining from voting shall not be counted among the two-thirds required for adopting an amendment.

2. The text of any proposed amendment shall be communicated by the Secretariat to all Parties at least 90 days before the meeting.

3. An amendment shall enter into force for the Parties which have accepted it 60 days after two-thirds of the Parties have deposited an instrument of acceptance of the amendment with the Depositary Government. Thereafter, the amendment shall enter into force for any other Party 60 days after that Party deposits its instrument of acceptance of the amendment.

Article XVIII
Resolution of Disputes

1. Any dispute which may arise between two or more Parties with respect to the interpretation or application of the provisions of the present Convention shall be subject to negotiation between the Parties involved in the dispute.

2. If the dispute can not be resolved in accordance with paragraph 1 of this Article, the Parties may, by mutual consent, submit the dispute to arbitration, in particular that of the Permanent Court of Arbitration at The Hague, and the Parties submitting the dispute shall be bound by the arbitral decision.

Article XIX
Signature

The present Convention shall be open for signature at Washington until 30th April 1973 and thereafter at Berne until 31st December 1974.

Article XX
Ratification, Acceptance, Approval

The present Convention shall be subject to ratification, acceptance or approval. Instruments of ratification, acceptance or approval shall be deposited with the Government of the Swiss Confederation which shall be the Depositary Government.

Article XXI
Accession

The present Convention shall be open indefinitely for accession. Instruments of accession shall be deposited with the Depositary Government.

Article XXII
Entry into Force

1. The present Convention shall enter into force 90 days after the date of deposit of the tenth instrument of ratification, acceptance, approval or accession, with the Depositary Government.

2. For each State which ratifies, accepts or approves the present Convention or accedes thereto after the deposit of the tenth instrument of ratification, acceptance, approval or accession, the present Convention shall enter into force 90 days after the deposit by such State of its instrument of ratification, acceptance, approval or accession.

Article XXIII
Reservations

1. The provisions of the present Convention shall not be subject to general reservations. Specific reservations may be entered in accordance with the provisions of this Article and Articles XV and XVI.

2. Any State may, on depositing its instrument of ratification, acceptance, approval or accession, enter a specific reservation with regard to:

(a) any species included in Appendix I, II or III; or

(b) any parts or derivatives specified in relation to a species included in Appendix III.

3. Until a Party withdraws its reservation entered under the provisions of this Article, it shall be treated as a State not a Party to the present Convention with respect to trade in the particular species or parts or derivatives specified in such reservation.

Article XXIV
Denunciation

Any Party may denounce the present Convention by written notification to the Depositary Government at any time. The denunciation shall take effect twelve months after the Depositary Government has received the notification.

Article XXV
Depositary

1. The original of the present Convention, in the Chinese, English, French, Russian and Spanish languages, each version being equally authentic, shall be deposited with the Depositary Government, which shall transmit certified copies thereof to all States that have signed it or deposited instruments of accession to it.

2. The Depositary Government shall inform all signatory and acceding States and the Secretariat of signatures, deposit of instruments of ratification, acceptance,

approval or accession, entry into force of the present Convention, amendments thereto, entry and withdrawal of reservations and notifications of denunciation.

3. As soon as the present Convention enters into force, a certified copy thereof shall be transmitted by the Depositary Government to the Secretariat of the United Nations for registration and publication in accordance with Article 102 of the Charter of the United Nations.

In witness whereof the undersigned Plenipotentiaries, being duly authorized to that effect, have signed the present Convention.

Done at Washington this third day of March, One Thousand Nine Hundred and Seventy-three.

Bibliography

Alagappan, Meena. "The United States' Enforcement of the Convention on International Trade in Endangered Species." Northwestern Journal of International Law & Business. Vol. 10 No. 3 (1990). pp. 541-568.

Anders, Kathleen and Curtis Shook. "New Federalism: Impact on State and Local Governments." Journal of Public Budgeting, Accounting, & Financial Management. Vol. 15 No. 3 (Fall 2003). pp. 466-486.

Arrighi, Giovanni. "Globalization, State Sovereignty, and the Endless Accumulation of Capital", in *Ends of Globalization*, Don Kalb, Marco Van Der Land, et al (eds.). Rowman and Littlefield (2000). pp. 125-150.

Bacon, Brad. "Enforcement Mechanisms in International Wildlife Agreements and the United States: Wading Through the Murk." Georgetown International Environmental Law Review. Vol. 12 No. 3 (Fall 1999). p. 331-390.

Bailey, Ronald (ed.). *Earth Report 2000*. McGraw-Hill (2000).

Baker, Joni. *A Substantive Theory of the Relative Efficiency of Environmental Treaty Compliance Strategies: The Case of CITES*. Texas A&M University (1998).

Baldwin, David (ed.). *Neorealism and Neoliberalism*. Columbia University Press (1993).

Bergsten, C.F. "Globalizing Free Trade." Foreign Affairs. Vol. 75 No. 3 (May/June 1996). pp. 105-120.

Berry, Albert. "Who Wins and Who Loses? An Economic Perspective", in *Civilizing Globalization*, Richard Sandbrook (eds.). SUNY Press (2003). pp. 15-26.

Birnie, Patricia and Alan Boyle. *International Law and the Environment*. Clarendon Press (1992).

Block, Robert. "Politics & Economics: Fighting Terrorism By Sharing Data; Homeland Security Plans To Improve Cooperation With Police Departments." Wall Street Journal. (Eastern Edition). New York, New York. Oct 16, 2006. p. A6.

Bonner, Raymond. *At the Hand of Man: Peril and Hope for Africa's Wildlife*. Alfred A. Knopf (1993).

Booth, Ken and Steve Smith (eds.). *International Relations Theory Today*. Pennsylvania State University Press (1995).

Boyd, Ronald, Chief, Port of Los Angeles Police. Personal Interview. December 16, 2005.

Broad, Robin (ed.), *Global Backlash*. Rowman and Littlefield Publishers (2002).

Brown, Ronald. "Globalization and the End of the National Project", in *Boundaries in Question*, John MacMillan and Andrew Linklater (ed.). Pinter (1995). pp. 28-60.

R. Steven Brown. "States Put Their Money Where Their Environment Is." Environ-mental Council of the States. April 1999. URL: http://www.ecos.org/section/publications. Accessed November 12, 2007

Caldwell, Lynton Keith. *International Environmental Policy*. Duke University Press (1996).

Carey, Jay E. "Improving the Efficacy of CITES by Providing the Proper Incentives to Protect Endangered Species." Washington University Law Quarterly. Vol. 77 No. 4 (1999). pp. 1291-1322.

Chossudovsky, Michel. *The Globalization of Poverty*. Zed (1997).

Clark, Ian. *Globalization and Fragmentation*. Oxford University Press (1997).

Clarke, Tony. "Mechanisms of Corporate Rule", in *The Case Against the Global Econ-omy*, Jerry Mander and Edward Goldsmith (eds.). Sierra Club Books (1996). pp.78-91.

CITES.org. URL: http://www.cites.org. Accessed November 12, 2007.

Collie, Fred. *21st Century Policing: The Institutionalization of Homeland Security in Local Law Enforcement Organizations*. Master's Thesis, Naval Postgraduate School. Monterey: Department of National Security Affairs (2006).

Congressional Research Service. "The Endangered Species Act in the 109 Congress: Conflicting Values and Difficult Choices". The Library of Congress. URL: usin-fo.state.gov/infousa/government/branches/docs/IB10144_2006Jan25.pdf. Accessed: January 25, 2008.

Convention on the International Trade of Endangered Species. URL: http://www.cites.org/eng/disc/text.shtml. Accessed November 10, 2007.

Convention on International Trade in Endangered Species of Wild Fauna & Flora European Community Annual Report 1995. European Communities (1998).

"Congressional Funding For Enforcement of Wildlife Trade Grossly Inadequate". World Wildlife Fund Press Release. World Wildlife Fund. July 17, 2003. URL: http://worldwildlife.org/news/displayPR.cfm?prID=73. Accessed: Oct. 24, 2007.

Cornia, Giovanni. "Poverty and Inequality in the Era of Liberalization and Globaliza-tion", in Hans Van Ginkel and et al, *Human Development and Environment*. United Nations University Press (2002). pp. 55-87.

Cox, Kevin (ed.). *Spaces of Globalization*. Guilford (1997).

Cox, Ronald. "An Alternative Approach to Multilateralism for the 21st Century." Global Governance. Vol. 3 No.1 (Jan.-April 1997). pp. 103-116.

CQ Researcher. *Global Issues*. Congressional Quarterly Press (2001).

de Klemm, Cyrille. *Biological Diversity Conservation and the Law*. IUCN (1993).

de Sousa Santos, Bonaventura and Cesar Rodriguez-Garavito (eds.). *Law and Global-ization from Below*. Cambridge University Press (2005).

Der Derian, James (ed.). *International Theory: Critical Investigations*. New York University Press (1995).

Dolsak, Nives and Elinor Ostrom (eds.). *Commons in the New Millenium*. MIT Press (2003).

Domoto, Akiko. "International Environment Governance—Its Impact on Social and Human Development", in *Human Development and the Environment*, Hans Van Ginkel et al (eds.). United Nations University Press (2002). pp. 284-301.

Dougherty, James and Robert Pfaltzgraff, Jr. (eds.). *Contending Theories of International Relations*. HarperCollins Publishers (1990).

Duffield, Mark. *Global Governance and the New Wars*. Zed (2001).

Eldridge, Kevin. "Whale for Sale?" Georgia Journal of International Comparative Law Vol. 24 (1995). pp. 549-565.

Evan, William. *Social Structure and Law*. Sage Publications (1990).

Fact Sheet: Improving Border Security and Immigration Within Existing Law. Department of Homeland Security. August 10, 2007. URL: http://www.dhs.gov/xnews/releases/pr_1186757867585.shtm. Accessed Sept. 26, 2007.

Favre, David. "Tension Points within the Language of the CITES Treaty." Boston University International Law Journal. Vol. 5 No. 3 (1987). pp. 247-258.

Ferguson, Yale and Richard Mansbach. "Between Celebration and Despair: Constructive Suggestions for Future International Theory." International Studies Quarterly. Vol. 35 No. 4 (December 1991). pp. 363-386.

Fish & Wildlife Service. *Annual Report 2006*. Fish & Wildlife Service. URL: http://www.fws.gov/le/AboutLE/annual.htm. Accessed October 1, 2007.

Fish & Wildlife Service. *Inspector Brochure*. Fish & Wildlife Service. URL: http://library.fws.gov/Pubs/Inspector02.pdf. Accessed October 28, 2007.

Fish & Wildlife Service Website.

> Main Page: URL:http://www.fws.gov. Accessed: October 1, 2007;
> Special Agents: URL: http://www.fws.gov/le/AboutLE/special_agents.htm. Accessed October 1, 2007;
> Torrance Office Directory:
> URL: http://www.fws.gov/offices/directory/ListOffices.cfm?statecode=6. Accessed October 28, 2007
> Ventura Office Staff List:
> URL: http://www.fws.gov/ventura/textonly/stafflisting.html. Accessed October 28, 2007
> Wildlife Inspectors:
> URL: http://www.fws.gov/le/AboutLE/wildlife_inspectors.htm. Accessed October 1, 2007

Fitton, Tom. "Local Law Enforcement Effective in Fighting Illegal Immigration." The Conservative Voice, July 24, 2006. URL: http://www.theconservativevoice.com/articles/article.html?id=16389. Accessed Sept. 25, 2007

Fitzgerald, Sarah. *International Wildlife Trade: Whose Business Is It?* World Wildlife Fund (1989).

Forrest, Jessica. "Protecting Ecosystems on a Changing Planet." Earthtrends. URL: http://www.earthtrends.wri.org. Accessed December 12, 2003.

French, Hilary. "Challenging the WTO." Worldwatch. Vol. 12 No. 6 (Nov./Dec. 1999). pp. 22-27.

Fuller, Kathryn, Ginette Hemley, and Sarah Fitzgerald. "Wildlife Trade Law Implementation in Developing Countries: the Experience in Latin America." Boston University International Law Journal. Vol. 5 No. 3 (1987). pp. 289-310.

Gaski, Andrea L. and Kurt A. Johnson. *Prescription for Extinction: Endangered Species and Patented Oriental Medicines in Trade*. TRAFFIC USA (1994).

Gibson, Clark and Stuart Marks, "Transforming Rural Hunters into Conservationists: An Assessment of Community-Based Wildlife Management Programs in Africa." World Development. Vol. 23 No. 6 (June 1995). pp. 941-957.

Gilpin, Robert. *The Challenge of Global Capitalism: The World Economy in the 21st Century*. Princeton University Press (2000).

Glennon, Michael J. "Has International Law Failed the Elephant?" The American Journal of American Law. Vol. 84 No. 1 (January 1990). pp. 1-43.

Goldsmith, Edward. "Global Trade and the Environment", in *The Case Against the Global Economy*, Jerry Mander and Edward Goldsmith (eds.). Sierra Club Books (1996). pp. 78-91.

Goldstein, Joshua. *International Relations (4th ed.)*. Addison Wesley Longman (2001).

Goodland, Robert. "The Case That the World Has Reached Its Limits", in *Population, Technology, and Lifestyle: The Transition to Sustainability*, Robert Goodland et al (eds.). Island Press (1992).

Grace, Edward, Special Agent, Fish & Wildlife Service. Personal Interview. October 9, 2007.

Greider, William. *One World, Ready or Not*. Allen Lane (1997).

Groombridge, Brian (ed.). *Global Biodiversity: Status of the Earth's Living Resources*. Chapman and Hall (1992);

Groombridge, Brian and M.D. Jenkins. *Global Biodiversity*. UNEP (2000).

Hackel, Jeffrey. "Community Conservation and the Future of Africa's Wildlife." Conservation Biology. Vol. 13 No. 4 (Aug. 1999). pp. 726-734.

Haas, Peter. "Introduction: Epistemic Communities and International Policy Coordination." International Organization. Vol. 46 No. 1 (Winter 1992). pp. 1-35.

Hanagan, Michael. "States and Capital", in *Ends of Globalization*, Don Kalb, Marco Van Der Land, and et al (eds.). Rowman and Littlefield (2000). pp. 67-86.

Harper, Charles. *Environment and Society*. Prentice Hall (2001).

Harvey, Robert. *Global Disorder*. Carroll and Graff Publishers (2003).

Heimert, Andrew J. "How the Elephant Lost His Tusks." Yale Law Journal. Vol. 104 No. 3 (April 1995). pp.1473-1506.

Held, David. *Democracy and the Global Order*. Polity Press (1995).

Hemley, Ginette (ed.). *International Wildlife Trade: A CITES Sourcebook*. World Wildlife Fund (1994).

Hempel, Lamont. *Environmental Governance: The Global Challenge*. Island Press (1996).

Hirst, Paul and Grahame Thompson. "Globalization and the History of the International Economy", in *Global Transformation Reader*, David Held and Anthony McGrew (eds.). Polity (2000). pp. 68-75.

Holm, Hans and Georg Sorenson, "International Relations Theory in a World of Variation", in *Whose World Order?*, Georg Sorensen and Hans Holm (eds.), Westview (1995). pp. 187-206.

Huntington, Samuel. "The Clash of Civilizations." Foreign Affairs. Vol. 72 No. 3 (Summer 1993). pp. 22-50.

Huntington, Samuel. *Clash of Civilizations*. Touchstone (1997).

Hurrell, Andrew and Nagaire Woods (eds.). *Inequality, Globalization, and World Politics*. Oxford University Press (1999).

Hutton, Jon and Barnabas Dickson (eds.). *Endangered Species, Threatened Convention: The Past, Present and Future of CITES*. Earthscan Publications (2000).

Infield, Mark. "Cultural Values: a Forgotten Strategy for Building Community Support for Protected Areas in Africa." Conservation Biology. Vol. 15 No. 3 (June 2001). pp. 800-802.

Inter-Parliamentary Union. *Final Declaration of the Parliamentary Meeting on the Occasion of UNCTAD X, Bangkok*. UNCTAD (February 2000).

Jabbra, Joseph G. and Onkar P. Dwivedi (eds.), *Governmental Response to Environmental Challenges in Global Perspective*. IOS Press (1998).

Jasanoff, Sheila and Marybeth Martello (eds.). *Earthly Politics: Local and Global in Environmental Governance*. MIT Press (2004).

Kamenka, Eugene, et al. *Law and Society: The Crisis in Legal Ideals*. St. Martin's Press (1978)

Kaplan, Robert. "The Coming Anarchy." Atlantic Monthly. Vol. 273 No. 2 (Feb. 1994). pp. 44-76.

Karno, Valerie. "Protection of Endangered Gorillas and Chimpanzees in International Trade: Can CITES Help?" Hastings International and Comparative Law Review. Vol. 14 No. 4 (1991). pp. 989-1015.

Kazmar, Jonathan P. "The International Illegal Plant and Wildlife Trade: Biological Genocide?" U.C. Davis Journal of International Law & Policy. Vol. 6 No. 1 (2000). pp. 105-150.

Kennedy, Paul, et al. *Global Trends and Global Governance*. Pluto Press (2002).

Keohane, Robert and Elinor Ostrom (eds.). *Local Commons and Global Interdependence: Heterogeneity and Cooperation in Two Domains*. Sage Publications (1995).

Kiss, Alexander (ed.). *Living with Wildlife: Wildlife Resource Management with Local Participation in Africa*. World Bank (1990).

Kiss, Alexander and Dinah Shelton. *International Environmental Law*. Transnational Publishers, Inc. (1991).

Kohr, Martin. *Rethinking Globalization*. Zed (2001).

Kohr, Martin. "Global Economy and the Third World", in *The Case Against the Global Economy*, Jerry Mander and Edward Goldsmith (eds.). Sierra Club Books (1996). pp. 47-59.

Kosloff, Laura H. and Marc Trexler. "The Convention on International Trade in Endangered Species: Enforcement Theory and Practice in the U.S." Boston University International Law Journal. Vol. 5 No. 3 (1987). pp. 327-361.

Krieps, Catharine L. "Sustainable Use of Endangered Species under CITES: Is It a Sustainable Alternative?" University of Pennsylvania Journal of International Economic Law. Vol. 17 No. 2 (Spring 1996). pp. 461-504.

Langhorne, Richard. *The Coming of Globalization*. Palgrave (2001).

Lawrence, Timothy. *Devolution and Collaboration in the Development of Environmental Regulations*. Dissertation. Ohio State University (2005);

Lean, Geoffrey and Don Hinrichsen. *Atlas of the Environment*. HarperCollins Publishers (1994).

Lee, Eric. *The Labour Movement and the Internet: the New Internationalism*. Pluto (1997).

Lee, Joonmoo. "Poachers, Tigers and Bears...Oh My!", Northwestern Journal of International Law & Business. Vol. 16 No. 2 (Spring 1996). pp. 497-516.

Levy, Adrian and Cathy Scott-Clark, "Poaching for Bin Laden". The Guardian. May 5, 2007. URL: http://www.guardian.co.uk/alqaida/story/0,,2073168,00.html. Accessed May 20, 2007

Lieberman, Susan. "Improving International Controls on Wildlife Trade." Endangered Species Bulletin. Vol. 20 No. 2 (1995). pp. 8-13.

Lin-Heng, L. "The Implementation of the Convention on International Trade in Endangered Species in Singapore." Journal of International Wildlife Law and Policy. Vol. 2 No. 1 (1999). pp. 46-63.

Lipschutz, Ronnie. "Reconstructing World Politics: The Emergence of Global Civil Society." Millenium. Vol. 21 No. 3 (Winter 1992). pp. 389-420.

Lipschutz, Ronnie and Ken Conca (eds.). *The State and Social Power in Global Environmental Politics.* Columbia University Press (1992).

Lipschutz, Ronnie. "From Place to Planet: Local Knowledge and Global Environmental Governance." Global Governance. Vol. 3 No. 1 (Jan.-April 1997). pp. 83-102.

Ronnie Lipschutz and Judith Mayer. *Global Civil Society and Global Environmental Politics: The Politics of Nature from Place to Planet.* SUNY Press (1996).

Liwo, Karl Jonathan. "The Continuing Significance of the Convention on International Trade in Endangered Species of Wild Fauna and Flora in the 1990's." Suffolk Transnational Law Journal. Vol. 15 No. 1 (1991). pp. 122-152.

Lomborg, Bjorn. *The Skeptical Environmentalist.* Cambridge University Press (2001).

Los Angeles World Airports Cargo website. URL: http://www.lawa.org/lax/cargo.cfm. Accessed January 1, 2008.

Lovgren, Stefan. "Wildlife Smuggling Bloom Plaguing L.A., Authorities Say". National Geographic News. July 26, 2007. URL: http://news.nationalgeographic.com/news/2007/07/070725-animal-smuggle.html. Accessed Oct. 1, 2007.

Lyster, Simon. *International Wildlife Trade.* Grotius Publications, Ltd. (1985).

Macaulay, Stewart, et al. *Law and Society: Readings on the Social Study of the Law.* W.W. Norton & Company (1995).

MacDonald, Ian Andrew. *Towards a General Theory of Environmental Treaties.* Simon Fraser University (1999).

Matthews, Paul. "Problems Related to the Convention on the International Trade in Endangered Species." International and Comparative Law Quarterly. Vol. 45 No. 2 (April 1996). pp. 421-431.

McCloskey, Kevin, Sergeant, Port of Los Angeles Police. Personal Interview. . December 16, 2005.

McFadden, Eric. "Asian Compliance with CITES: Problems and Prospects." Boston University International Law Journal. Vol. 5 No. 3. (1987). pp. 311-325.

McGrew, Anthony. *The Transformation of Democracy? Globalization and Territorial Democracy.* Polity Press (1997).

McMullin, Steve. *Approaches to Management Effectiveness in State Fish and Wild-life Agencies.* Virginia Polytechnic Institute and State University (1993).

Melick, Jeffrey. "Regulation of International Trade in Endangered Wildlife." Boston University International Law Journal. Vol. 1 No. 2 (1982). pp. 249-275.

Gary Meyers. "Surveying the Lay of the Land, Air, and Water: Features of Current International Environmental and Natural Resources Law, and Future Prospects for the Protection of Species Habitat to Preserve Global Biological Diversity." Colorado Journal of International Environmental Law and Policy. Vol. 3 No. 2 (Summer 1992). pp. 479-634.

Miami International Airport Cargo Rankings website. URL: http://miami-airport.com/html/cargo_rankings_.html. Accessed: January 1, 2008.

Mofson, Phyllis Ann. *The Behavior of States in an International Wildlife Conserva-tion Regime: Japan, Zimbabwe, and CITES.* University of Maryland (1996).

Nader, Ralph and Lori Wallach, "GATT, NAFTA, and The Subversion of the Demo-cratic Process", in *The Case Against the Global Economy,* Jerry Mander and Edward Goldsmith (eds.). Sierra Club Books (1996). pp. 92-107.

Ostrom, Elinor. *Governing the Commons.* Cambridge University Press (1990).

Padgett, Bill. "The African Elephant, Africa, and CITES: The Next Step." Global Legal Studies Journal. Vol. 2 No. 2 (1995). pp. 529-552.

Patel, Shennie "The Convention on International Trade in Endangered Species: Enforcement and the Last Unicorn." Houston Journal of International Law. Vol. 18 No. 1 (1995). pp. 157-173.

Paterson, Matthew. "Interpreting Trends in Global Environmental Governance." International Affairs. Vol. 75 No. 4 (October 1999). pp. 793-802.

Peters, Michelle Ann. "The Convention on International Trade of Endangered Spe-cies: An Answer to the Call of the Wild?" Connecticut Journal of International Law. Vol. 10 No. 3 (Fall 1994). pp.169-191.

Poole, Patrick. "Local Law Enforcement and Homeland Security." American Thinker. August 9, 2007. URL: http://www.americanthinker.com/2007/08/local_law_enforcement_and_home.ht ml. Accessed September 26, 2007.

Port of Los Angeles website, URL: http://www.portoflosangeles.org. Accessed August 1, 2007.

Press, Daniel, et al. "The Role of Local Government in the Conservation of Rare Spe-cies." Conservation Biology. Vol. 10 No. 6 (December 1996). pp. 1538-1548.

Putnam, David. "Diplomacy and Domestic Politics: The Logic of Two-Level Games." International Organization. Vol. 42 No. 3 (Summer 1988). pp. 427-460.

Rabe, Barry. "Permitting, Prevention and Integration: Lessons from the States," in *Environmental Governance: A Report on the Next Generation of Environmental Policy*, Donald Kettl (ed.). Brookings Institution Press (2002

Randall, Gretchen. "Devolution to the States is Working for Welfare; It Can Work for Public Lands", National Policy Analysis. National Center for Public Policy Research. June 2001. URL: http://www.nationalcenter.org/NPA340.html. Accessed Sept. 26, 2007.

Reeve, Rosalind. *Policing International Trade in Endangered Species: the CITES Treaty and Compliance*. Earthscan (2002).

Richards, Paul. *Fighting for the Rainforest*. Heinemann (1996).

Rifkin, Jeremy. "New Technology and the End of Jobs", in *The Case Against the Global Economy,* Jerry Mander and Edward Goldsmith (eds.), Sierra Club Books (1996). pp. 108-121.

Robinson, William and Eric Bolen. *Wildlife Ecology and Management*. MacMillan Publishing Company (1989).

Rosenau, James. *Along the Domestic-Foreign Frontier*. Cambridge University Press (1997).

Rosenau, James. "The Relocation of Authority in a Shrinking World." Comparative Politics. Vol. 24 No. 3 (April 1992). pp. 253-272.

James Rosenau. "Governance, Order, and Change in World Politics," in James Rosenau and Ernst-Otto Czempiel (eds.), *Governance Without Government: Order and Change in World Politics*. Cambridge University Press (1992).

Rowlands, Ian. "The International Politics of Environment and Development: The Post-UNCED Agenda." Millenium. Vol. 21 No. 2 (Summer 1992). pp. 209-224.

Sands, Philippe J. and Albert P. Bedecarre. "Convention on International Trade in Endangered Species: the Role of Public Interest in Non-governmental Organizations in Ensuring the Effective Enforcement of the Ivory Trade Ban." Boston College Environmental Affairs Law Review. Vol. 17 No. 3 (1990). pp. 799-822.

Sarat, Austin and Jonathan Simon (eds.). *Cultural Analysis, Cultural Studies, and the Law*. Duke University Press (2003)

Schaeffer, Robert K. *Understanding Globalization (2nd Ed.)*. Rowman and Littlefield (2003).

Scheberle, Denise. *Federalism and Environmental Policy*. Georgetown University Press (2004).

Schneebaum, Steven. "The Enforceability of Customary Norms of Public International Law." Brooklyn Journal of International Law. Vol. 8 No. 1 (1982). pp. 289-315.

Scholte, Jan Aart. *Globalization: A Critical Introduction*. St. Martin's Press (2000).

Schonfeld, Alan. "International Trade in Wildlife: How Effective is the Endangered Species Treaty?" California Western International Law Journal. Vol. 15 No. 1 (April 1985). pp. 111-160.

Schuck, Peter. *The Limits of the Law*. Westview Press (2000).

Shapiro, Michael. "Moral Geographies and the Ethics of Post-Sovereignty." Public Culture. Vol. 6 No. 3 (Spring 1994). pp. 479-502.

Kirsten Silvius, et al (eds.). *People in Nature: Wildlife Conservation in South and Central America*. Columbia University Press (2004).

Simmons, Beth and Daniel Hopkins. "The Constraining Power of International Treaties: Theory and Methods." American Political Science Review. Vol. 99 No. 4 (November 2005). pp. 623-632.

Simmons, P.J. and Chantal De Jonge Oudraat (eds.). *Managing Global Issues*. Carnegie Endowment for International Peace (2001)

Singer, J. David. "The Level-of-Analysis Problem in International Relations." World Politics. Vol. 14 No. 1 (October 1961). pp. 77-92.

Skalnik, Peter. "On the Inadequacy of the Concept of the 'Traditional State'." Journal of Legal Pluralism & Unofficial Law. Vol. 25 & 26 (1987). pp. 301-325.

Slaughter-Burley, Ann-Marie. "International Law and International Relations Theory: A Dual Agenda." American Journal of International Law. Vol. 87 No. 2 (April 1993). pp. 205-255.

Steger, Manfred B. *Globalization*. Oxford University Press (2003).

Stewart, Gwyneth. "Enforcement Problems in the Endangered Species Convention; Reservations Regarding the Reservation Clauses." Cornell International Law Journal. Vol. 14 No. 2 (1981). pp. 429-455.

Stilwell, Matthew. *Governance, Globalization and the Need for WTO Reform*. Centre for International Environmental Law (1999).

Strange, Susan. *The Retreat of the State*. Cambridge University Press (1996).

Thacher, David. "The Local Role in Homeland Security". Law & Society Review. Vol. 39 No. 3 (September 2005). pp. 635-676.

Thomas, Caroline and Peter Wilkin (eds.). *Globalization and the South*. MacMillan (1997).

Thomas, Ellen. Lecture, Environmental Studies Course EES 199, Wesleyan University URL: http: ethomas.web.wesleyan.edu/ees123/mass_extinctions.htm. Accessed December 9, 2003.

Tillman, Zoe. "Crackdown: Immigration supporters react to a resolution passed July 10 in Prince William County, Va., that empowers local police to determine the status of residents and to arrest illegal immigrants." Christian Science Monitor. July 17, 2007. URL: http://www.csmonitor.com/2007/0717/p01s05-ussc.html. Accessed Sept. 25, 2007.

Tilly, Charles. "Globalization Threatens Labor's Rights", International Labor and Working Class History. Vol. 47 No. 1(Spring 1995). pp. 1-23.

Tisen, Oswald Braken , et al. "Wildlife Conservation and Local Communities in Sarawak, Malaysia". Paper presented to Second Regional Forum for Southeast Asia of the

IUCN World Commission For Protected Areas. Dec. 1999. URL: http://www.mered.org.uk/mike/papers/Communities_Pakse_99.htm. Accessed Oct. 24, 2007.

Tomlinson, John. "Homogenisation and Globalisation." History of European Ideas. Vol. 20 No. 4-6 (Feb. 1995). pp. 891-897.

Tracy, Ralph, Boyd, Captain, Port of Los Angeles Police. Personal Interview. . December 16, 2005.

Trexler, Mark Charles. *The Convention on the International Trade of Endangered Species of Wild Flora and Fauna: Political or Conservation Success?* University of California, Berkeley (1990).

UNDP. *Human Development Report 1999*. Oxford University Press (1999).

UNEP. *Global Environmental Outlook 3*. Earthscan (2002).

U.S. Army Corps of Engineers. Waterborne Commerce Statistics Center. URL: http://www.iwr.usace.army.mil/ndc/wcsc/portname02.htm. Accessed October 19, 2007.

"U.S. Wants Local Help in Human Trafficking." Juvenile Justice Digest. Vol. 32 No. 12 (Jul 6, 2004). p. 6.

Vandenberg, Andrew (ed.). *Citizenship and Democracy in a Global Era*. MacMillan (2000).

Vanderbilt Center for Transportation Research. URL: http://transp20.vuse.vanderbilt.edu/vector/worldkit/index.html. Accessed October 19, 2007.

van Ginkel, Hans, et al (eds.). *Human Development and the Environment: Challenges for the United Nations in the New Millenium*. United Nations University Press (2002).

van Heijnsbergen, P. *International Legal Protection of Wild Fauna and Flora*. IOS Press (1997).

Vasi, Ion Bogdan. "Thinking Globally, Planning Nationally and Acting Locally: Nested Organizational Fields and the Adoption of Environmental Practices." Social Forces. Vol. 86 No. 1 (September 2007). pp. 113-137.

von Glahn, Gerhard. *Law Among Nations*. MacMillan Publishing Company (1992).

von Stein, Jana. "Do Treaties Constrain or Screen? Selection Bias and Treaty Compliance." American Political Science Review. Vol. 99 No. 4 (November 2005). pp. 611-622.

Wagener, Amy. "Endangered Species: Traded to Death." Earthtrends. World Resources Institute (August 2001). URL: http://earthtrends.wri.org/features/view_feature.php?theme=7&fid=25. Accessed December 12, 2006.

Warde, Alan. "Eating Globally: Cultural Flows and the Spread of Ethnic Restaurants", in *The Ends of Globalization*, Marco Van Der Land, et al (eds.). Rowman and Little-field (2000). pp. 219-316.

Weiss, Edith Brown and Harold K. Jacobson (eds.). *Engaging Countries: Strengthening Compliance with International Environmental Accords*. MIT Press (1998).

Western, David, et al (eds.). *Natural Connections: Perspectives in Community-Based Conservation*. Island Press. 1994.

WijnStekers, Willem. *The Evolution of CITES: A Reference to the Convention on International Trade in Endangered Species of Wild Fauna and Flora*. CITES Secretariat. 2006.

Willett, Susan. "Globalization and the Means of Destruction", in *Globalization and Insecurity*, Barbara Harriss-White (ed.). Palgrave (2002). pp. 184-202.

Williams, Phil, et al (eds.). *Classic Readings of International Relations*. Wadsworth Publishing Company (1994).

Winter, Gerd (ed.). *Multilevel Governance of Global Environmental Change*. Cambridge University Press (2006).

Wise, Charles R and Rania Nader. "Organizing the Federal System for Homeland Security: Problems, Issues, and Dilemmas". Public Administration Review. Vol. 62 Special Issue (September 2002), pp. 44-58.

Wood, Adrian. *North-South Trade, Employment and Inequality*. Clarendon Press (1994).

World Commission on Environment and Development. *Our Common Future*. Oxford University Press (1987).

World Conservation Monitoring Center. *Checklist of CITES Species: A Reference to the Appendices to the Convention on International Trade in Endangered Species of Wild Fauna and Flora*. World Conservation Monitoring Center. 2001.

World Conservation Monitoring Center. URL: http://wcmc.org.uk. Accessed December 1, 2003.

World Resources Institute. *World Resources 2000-2001*. URL: http://www.wri.org. Accessed December 12, 2003.

Yale Environmental Protection Clinic. "Yale Center for Environmental Law & Policy. Improving Enforcement and Compliance with the Convention on International Trade in Endangered Species." URL: http://www.yale.edu/envirocenter/clinic/cities.html. Accessed September 23, 2007.

Young, Oran. *International Cooperation*. Cornell University Press (1989).

Young, Oran (ed.). *Global Governance: Drawing Insights from the Environmental Experience*. MIT Press (1997).

Appendix 1: Survey

Survey Questions

To: _____

From: *Jonathan Liljeblad*

Date: _____

Re: *Instructions & Questionnaire*

I.   INTRODUCTION

I am currently engaged on research for my doctoral dissertation investigating the relationship between smuggling, international treaties, and local law enforcement.

As part of the dissertation research, I am conducting this survey to determine the perceptions and attitudes of field personnel tasked with enforcing international treaties via domestic U.S. laws. The survey focuses on point-of-entry law enforcement personnel and smuggling with respect to the following: a) their awareness of international and domestic laws, b) their understanding of the connection between international and domestic laws, and c) their concern for international and domestic laws in the scheme of their and their organization's priorities and responsibilities. Point-of-entry law enforcement personnel include the Port of Los Angeles Police, LAX Police, and U.S. Customs at both the port and the airport.

II.   INSTRUCTIONS

Please complete this survey, preferably during a time you normally use for reflection and focus (for example, a weekend). You will likely need approximately 30 minutes. Please answer the questions as honestly and personally as possible using your own existing base of experience and knowledge.

This survey will be purely confidential, and respondents should feel free to answer as honestly and personally as possible.

When you are finished, please return this survey and any comments in the attached self-addressed stamped envelope BY _____, 2005 to me at the following location:

1107 Fair Oaks Ave. #264
South Pasadena, CA 91030

Should you have any questions, please feel free to contact me.

Thank You,
Jonathan Liljeblad
JD/PhD Candidate, University of Southern California
liljebla@usc.edu
(818) 209-6915

ACRONYMS AND DEFINITIONS:

Survey questions are oriented to compare question respondent views on a variety of smuggling issues as a means of providing a basis of reference. The survey questions revolve around 5 smuggling issues and test respondents on these issues in terms of their impressions and distinctions between international and domestic instruments, and between themselves and their organizations. The issues and respective international and domestic laws are as follows:

Smuggling Issue	International Instrument	Domestic Instrument
Endangered species traffic	Convention on the International Trade in Endangered Species (CITES)	Endangered Species Act (ESA)
Narcotics traffic	Convention Against Illicit Traffic in Narcotic Drugs and Psychotropic Substances (CNDPS)	Controlled Substances Import and Export Act (CSIE)
Weapons traffic	Nuclear Nonproliferation Treaty, Biological Weapons Convention, Chemical Weapons Convention (CNBC)	Defense Against Weapons of Mass Destruction Act (DWMD)
Human traffic	Convention for the Suppression of the Traffic in Persons (CSTP)	Trafficking Victims Protection Act (TVP)
Contraband/gray market traffic	Trade-Related Intellectual Property Agreements (TRIPs)	U.S. Customs and Border Patrol Regulations (CBP)

In addition, the above smuggling issues are defined as follows:

Endangered species traffic	*illegal importation into the United States of any species (animal or plant) threatened with extinction*
Narcotics traffic	*illegal importation into the United States in narcotic drugs and psychotropic substances (natural or synthetic)*
Weapons traffic	*illegal importation into the United States of weapons of mass destruction (nuclear, biological, or chemical)*
Human traffic	*illegal importation into the United States of human beings who either are intent on criminal activity or are being victimized in terms of sexual acts, involuntary servitude, and slavery*
Contraband/gray market traffic	*illegal importation into the United States of commercial goods*

I. Smuggling Issues

A) Level of Importance for Smuggling

Scale of 1 to 7, 1 being not at all important and 7 being extremely important.

1. In your opinion, how important is each of the following issues? (circle one)

	not at all important					extremely important	
Endangered species smuggling	1	2	3	4	5	6	7
Narcotics smuggling	1	2	3	4	5	6	7
Weapons smuggling	1	2	3	4	5	6	7
Human trafficking	1	2	3	4	5	6	7
Contraband smuggling	1	2	3	4	5	6	7

2. In your opinion, how have these levels of importance changed for each of the issues during your term of employment with your organization? (circle one)

Endangered species smuggling	increased / decreased / constant
Narcotics smuggling	increased / decreased / constant
Weapons smuggling	increased / decreased / constant

Human trafficking	increased / decreased / constant
Contraband smuggling	increased / decreased / constant

B) Level of Knowledge Regarding Smuggling

Scale of 1 to 7, 1 being not at all knowledgeable and 7 being extremely knowledgeable.

1. How knowledgeable are you on each of the following issues? (circle one)

	not at all knowledgeable					extremely knowledgeable	
Endangered species smuggling	1	2	3	4	5	6	7
Narcotics smuggling	1	2	3	4	5	6	7
Weapons smuggling	1	2	3	4	5	6	7
Human trafficking	1	2	3	4	5	6	7
Contraband smuggling	1	2	3	4	5	6	7

2. In your opinion, how has your knowledge changed for each of the issues during your term of employment with your organization? (circle one)

Endangered species smuggling	increased / decreased / constant
Narcotics smuggling	increased / decreased / constant
Weapons smuggling	increased / decreased / constant
Human trafficking	increased / decreased / constant
Contraband smuggling	increased / decreased / constant

C) Perceived Legitimacy of Duty to Deal With Smuggling

1. Do you believe it is appropriate that you/your organization has the responsibility to enforce CITES/ESA, which deal with endangered species smuggling?

| For you | Yes | No | Not Applicable |
| For your organization | Yes | No | Not Applicable |

2. Do you believe it is appropriate that you/your organization has the responsibility to enforce CNDPS/CSIE, which deal with narcotics smuggling?

For you	Yes	No	Not Applicable
For your organization	Yes	No	Not Applicable

3. Do you believe it is appropriate that you/your organization has the responsibility to enforce CNBC/DWMD, which deal with weapons smuggling?

For you	Yes	No	Not Applicable
For your organization	Yes	No	Not Applicable

4. Do you believe it is appropriate that you/your organization has the responsibility to enforce CSTP/TVP, which deal with human smuggling?

For you	Yes	No	Not Applicable
For your organization	Yes	No	Not Applicable

5. Do you believe it is appropriate that you/your organization has the responsibility to enforce TRIPS/CBP, which deal with contraband/gray market smuggling?

For you	Yes	No	Not Applicable
For your organization	Yes	No	Not Applicable

D) Level of Public Awareness

Scale of 1 to 7, with 1 being not at all aware and 7 being extremely aware.

1. In your opinion, how aware is the public of each of the following INTERNATIONAL laws? (circle one)

	not at all aware					extremely aware	
CITES (endangered species)	1	2	3	4	5	6	7
CNDPS (narcotics)	1	2	3	4	5	6	7
CNBC (weapons)	1	2	3	4	5	6	7
CSTP (human traffic)	1	2	3	4	5	6	7
TRIPS (contraband goods)	1	2	3	4	5	6	7

2. In your opinion, how aware is the public of each of the following DOMESTIC laws?
(circle one)

	not at all aware					extremely aware	
ESA (endangered species)	1	2	3	4	5	6	7
CSIE (narcotics)	1	2	3	4	5	6	7
DWMD (weapons)	1	2	3	4	5	6	7
TVP (human traffic)	1	2	3	4	5	6	7
CBP (contraband goods)	1	2	3	4	5	6	7

3. In your opinion, how aware is the public of your organization's role in enforcing laws dealing with each of the following issues? (circle one)

	not at all aware					extremely aware	
Endangered species smuggling	1	2	3	4	5	6	7
Narcotics smuggling	1	2	3	4	5	6	7
Weapons smuggling	1	2	3	4	5	6	7
Human trafficking	1	2	3	4	5	6	7
Contraband smuggling	1	2	3	4	5	6	7

E) Resource Challenges to Personal and Organizational Performance

Scale of 1 to 7, with 1 being not at all harmful and 7 being extremely harmful.

1. How have the following challenges harmed your PERSONAL performance of your professional duties with regards to smuggling? (circle one)

	not at all harmful					extremely harmful	
Lack of Money	1	2	3	4	5	6	7
Lack of Time	1	2	3	4	5	6	7
Lack of Knowledge	1	2	3	4	5	6	7

Lack of Training	1 2 3 4 5 6 7
Lack of Personal Interest	1 2 3 4 5 6 7
Excessive Administrative Paperwork	1 2 3 4 5 6 7
Ineffective Technology	1 2 3 4 5 6 7
Ineffective Strategic Focus on Organizational Mission and Purpose by Employer	1 2 3 4 5 6 7
Ineffective Tactical Policy to Achieve Organizational Mission and Purpose by Employer	1 2 3 4 5 6 7
Lack of Clarity in Employee Duties and Responsibilities by Employer	1 2 3 4 5 6 7
Conflict or Lack of Communication between Leadership and Employees	1 2 3 4 5 6 7
Conflict or Lack of Communication with Co-workers	1 2 3 4 5 6 7
Conflict or Lack of Communication with International & Foreign Entities	1 2 3 4 5 6 7
Conflict or Lack of Communication with Domestic Government Agencies	1 2 3 4 5 6 7

2. How has the harm of the following challenges to your PERSONAL performance changed during your term of employment? (circle one)

Lack of Money	increased / decreased / constant
Lack of Time	increased / decreased / constant
Lack of Knowledge	increased / decreased / constant

Lack of Training	increased / decreased / constant
Lack of Personal Interest	increased / decreased / constant
Excessive Administrative Paperwork	increased / decreased / constant
Ineffective Technology	increased / decreased / constant
Ineffective Strategic Focus on Organizational Mission and Purpose by Employer	increased / decreased / constant
Ineffective Tactical Policy to Achieve Organizational Mission and Purpose by Employer	increased / decreased / constant
Lack of Clarity in Employee Duties and Responsibilities by Employer	increased / decreased / constant
Conflict or Lack of Communication between Leadership and Employees	increased / decreased / constant
Conflict or Lack of Communication with Co-workers	increased / decreased / constant
Conflict or Lack of Communication with International & Foreign Entities	increased / decreased / constant
Conflict or Lack of Communication with Domestic Government Agencies	increased / decreased / constant

Scale of 1 to 7, with 1 being not at all harmful and 7 being extremely harmful.

3. How have the following challenges harmed your ORGANIZATION's performance of its duties with regards to smuggling? (circle one)

	not at all harmful					extremely harmful
Lack of Money	1	2	3	4 5	6	7
Lack of Time	1	2	3	4 5	6	7

Lack of Knowledge	1	2	3	4	5	6	7
Lack of Training	1	2	3	4	5	6	7
Lack of Personal Interest	1	2	3	4	5	6	7
Excessive Administrative Paperwork	1	2	3	4	5	6	7
Ineffective Technology	1	2	3	4	5	6	7
Ineffective Strategic Focus on Organizational Mission and Purpose by Employer	1	2	3	4	5	6	7
Ineffective Tactical Policy to Achieve Organizational Mission and Purpose by Employer	1	2	3	4	5	6	7
Lack of Clarity in Employee Duties and Responsibilities by Employer	1	2	3	4	5	6	7
Conflict or Lack of Communication between Leadership and Employees	1	2	3	4	5	6	7
Conflict or Lack of Communication with Co-workers	1	2	3	4	5	6	7
Conflict or Lack of Communication with International & Foreign Entities	1	2	3	4	5	6	7
Conflict or Lack of Communication with Domestic Government Agencies	1	2	3	4	5	6	7

4. How has the harm of the following challenges to your ORGANIZATION's performance changed during your term of employment? (circle one)

Lack of Money	increased / decreased / constant
Lack of Time	increased / decreased / constant

Lack of Knowledge	increased / decreased / constant
Lack of Training	increased / decreased / constant
Lack of Personal Interest	increased / decreased / constant
Excessive Administrative Paperwork	increased / decreased / constant
Ineffective Technology	increased / decreased / constant
Ineffective Strategic Focus on Organizational Mission and Purpose by Employer	increased / decreased / constant
Ineffective Tactical Policy to Achieve Organizational Mission and Purpose by Employer	increased / decreased / constant
Lack of Clarity in Employee Duties and Responsibilities by Employer	increased / decreased / constant
Conflict or Lack of Communication between Leadership and Employees	increased / decreased / constant
Conflict or Lack of Communication with Co-workers	increased / decreased / constant
Conflict or Lack of Communication with International & Foreign Entities	increased / decreased / constant
Conflict or Lack of Communication with Domestic Government Agencies	increased / decreased / constant

II. Domestic Law Questions

A) Level of Knowledge Regarding DOMESTIC U.S. Laws Dealing with Smuggling

Scale of 1 to 7, 1 being not at all knowledgeable and 7 being extremely knowledgeable.

1. How knowledgeable are you on each of the following domestic laws? (circle one)

	not at all knowledgeable				extremely knowledgeable		
ESA (endangered species)	1	2	3	4	5	6	7
CSIE (narcotics)	1	2	3	4	5	6	7
DWMD (weapons)	1	2	3	4	5	6	7
TVP (human traffic)	1	2	3	4	5	6	7
CBP (contraband goods)	1	2	3	4	5	6	7

2. In your opinion, how has your knowledge changed for each of the domestic laws during your term of employment with your current employer? (circle one)

ESA (endangered species)	increased / decreased / constant
CSIE (narcotics)	increased / decreased / constant
DWMD (weapons)	increased / decreased / constant
TVP (human traffic)	increased / decreased / constant
CBP (gray market goods)	increased / decreased / constant

B) Level of Perceived Overall Effectiveness of DOMESTIC Efforts Regarding Smuggling

Scale of 1 to 7, 1 being not at all effective and 7 being extremely effective.

1. In your opinion, how effective are overall DOMESTIC government efforts in supporting each of the DOMESTIC U.S. laws dealing with smuggling? (circle one)

	not at all effective				extremely effective		
ESA (endangered species)	1	2	3	4	5	6	7
CSIE (narcotics)	1	2	3	4	5	6	7
DWMD (weapons)	1	2	3	4	5	6	7
TVP (human traffic)	1	2	3	4	5	6	7
CBP (contraband goods)	1	2	3	4	5	6	7

C) Level of Deterrence of DOMESTIC Laws

Scale of 1 to 7, with 1 being not at all deterrent and 7 being extremely deterrent.

1. In your opinion, how much of a deterrence is each of the following DOMESTIC laws?
(circle one)

	not at all deterrent					extremely deterrent	
ESA (endangered species)	1	2	3	4	5	6	7
CSIE (narcotics)	1	2	3	4	5	6	7
DWMD (weapons)	1	2	3	4	5	6	7
TVP (human traffic)	1	2	3	4	5	6	7
CBP (contraband goods)	1	2	3	4	5	6	7

D) Level of Cooperation Between Domestic Agencies to enforce DOMESTIC Laws

Scale of 1 to 7, with 1 being not at all cooperative and 7 being extremely cooperative.

1. In your opinion, how cooperative with each other are your organization and other U.S. government agencies in enforcing each of the following DOMESTIC laws?
(circle one)

	not at all cooperative					extremely cooperative	
ESA (endangered species)	1	2	3	4	5	6	7
CSIE (narcotics)	1	2	3	4	5	6	7
DWMD (weapons)	1	2	3	4	5	6	7
TVP (human traffic)	1	2	3	4	5	6	7
CBP (contraband goods)	1	2	3	4	5	6	7

E) Results of PERSONAL Efforts to Control Smuggling

1. Approximately what number of searches & seizures are you PERSONALLY involved in on a monthly basis for each of the following laws:

	# SEARCHES	# SEIZURES
ESA (endangered species)	_____ per month	_____ per month
CSIE (narcotics)	_____ per month	_____ per month
DWMD (weapons)	_____ per month	_____ per month
TVP (human traffic)	_____ per month	_____ per month
CBP (contraband goods)	_____ per month	_____ per month

2. In your opinion, how has the number of SEARCHES you PERSONALLY make under each law changed your term of employment? (circle one)

ESA (endangered species)	increased / decreased / constant
CSIE (narcotics)	increased / decreased / constant
DWMD (weapons)	increased / decreased / constant
TVP (human traffic)	increased / decreased / constant
CBP (gray market goods)	increased / decreased / constant

3. In your opinion, how has the number of SEIZURES you PERSONALLY make under each law changed during your term of employment? (circle one)

ESA (endangered species)	increased / decreased / constant
CSIE (narcotics)	increased / decreased / constant
DWMD (weapons)	increased / decreased / constant
TVP (human traffic)	increased / decreased / constant
CBP (gray market goods)	increased / decreased / constant

F) Level of Satisfaction over Results of PERSONAL Efforts to Control Smuggling

Scale of 1 to 7, with 1 being not at all satisfied and 7 being extremely satisfied.

1. How satisfied are you with the number of SEARCHES you PERSONALLY make under each of the following laws? (circle one)

	not at all satisfied				extremely satisfied		
ESA (endangered species)	1	2	3	4	5	6	7

CSIE (narcotics)	1	2	3	4	5	6	7
DWMD (weapons)	1	2	3	4	5	6	7
TVP (human traffic)	1	2	3	4	5	6	7
CBP (contraband goods)	1	2	3	4	5	6	7

2. How has the number of SEARCHES you PERSONALLY make under each law changed during your term of employment? (circle one)

ESA (endangered species)	increased / decreased / constant
CSIE (narcotics)	increased / decreased / constant
DWMD (weapons)	increased / decreased / constant
TVP (human traffic)	increased / decreased / constant
CBP (gray market goods)	increased / decreased / constant

3. How satisfied are you with the number of SEIZURES you PERSONALLY make under each of the following laws? (circle one)

	not at all satisfied					extremely satisfied	
ESA (endangered species)	1	2	3	4	5	6	7
CSIE (narcotics)	1	2	3	4	5	6	7
DWMD (weapons)	1	2	3	4	5	6	7
TVP (human traffic)	1	2	3	4	5	6	7
CBP (contraband goods)	1	2	3	4	5	6	7

4. How has the number of SEIZURES you PERSONALLY make under each law changed during your term of employment? (circle one)

ESA (endangered species)	increased / decreased / constant
CSIE (narcotics)	increased / decreased / constant
DWMD (weapons)	increased / decreased / constant
TVP (human traffic)	increased / decreased / constant

CBP (gray market goods)	increased / decreased / constant

G) Results of ORGANIZATION's Efforts to Control Smuggling

1. Approximately what number of searches & seizures is your ORGANIZATION involved in on a monthly basis for each of the following laws:

	# SEARCHES	# SEIZURES
ESA (endangered species)	_____ per month	_____ per month
CSIE (narcotics)	_____ per month	_____ per month
DWMD (weapons)	_____ per month	_____ per month
TVP (human traffic)	_____ per month	_____ per month
CBP (contraband goods)	_____ per month	_____ per month

2. In your opinion, how has the number of SEARCHES your ORGANIZATION makes under each law changed during your term of employment? (circle one)

ESA (endangered species)	increased / decreased / constant
CSIE (narcotics)	increased / decreased / constant
DWMD (weapons)	increased / decreased / constant
TVP (human traffic)	increased / decreased / constant
CBP (gray market goods)	increased / decreased / constant

3. In your opinion, how has the number of SEIZURES your ORGANIZATION makes under each law changed during your term of employment? (circle one)

ESA (endangered species)	increased / decreased / constant
CSIE (narcotics)	increased / decreased / constant
DWMD (weapons)	increased / decreased / constant
TVP (human traffic)	increased / decreased / constant
CBP (gray market goods)	increased / decreased / constant

H) Level of Satisfaction over Results of ORGANIZATION's Efforts to Control Smuggling

Scale of 1 to 7, with 1 being not at all satisfied and 7 being extremely satisfied.

1. How satisfied are you with the number of SEARCHES your ORGANIZATION makes under each of the following laws? (circle one)

	not at all satisfied				extremely satisfied		
ESA (endangered species)	1	2	3	4	5	6	7
CSIE (narcotics)	1	2	3	4	5	6	7
DWMD (weapons)	1	2	3	4	5	6	7
TVP (human traffic)	1	2	3	4	5	6	7
CBP (contraband goods)	1	2	3	4	5	6	7

2. How has the number of SEARCHES your ORGANIZATION makes under each law changed during your term of employment? (circle one)

ESA (endangered species)	increased / decreased / constant
CSIE (narcotics)	increased / decreased / constant
DWMD (weapons)	increased / decreased / constant
TVP (human traffic)	increased / decreased / constant
CBP (gray market goods)	increased / decreased / constant

3. How satisfied are you with the number of SEIZURES your ORGANIZATION makes under each of the following laws? (circle one)

	not at all satisfied				extremely satisfied		
ESA (endangered species)	1	2	3	4	5	6	7
CSIE (narcotics)	1	2	3	4	5	6	7
DWMD (weapons)	1	2	3	4	5	6	7
TVP (human traffic)	1	2	3	4	5	6	7
CBP (contraband goods)	1	2	3	4	5	6	7

4. In your opinion, how has the number of SEIZURES your ORGANIZATION makes under each law changed during your term of employment? (circle one)

ESA (endangered species)	increased / decreased / constant
CSIE (narcotics)	increased / decreased / constant
DWMD (weapons)	increased / decreased / constant
TVP (human traffic)	increased / decreased / constant
CBP (gray market goods)	increased / decreased / constant

I) Time to Investigate/Seize/Report/Adjudicate

1. For you personally, out of your total PERSONAL monthly work hours, what is the approximate distribution of hours you devote to each of the following issues:

ESA (endangered species)	_____ % of total monthly hours
CSIE (narcotics)	_____ % of total monthly hours
DWMD (weapons)	_____ % of total monthly hours
TVP (human traffic)	_____ % of total monthly hours
CBP (gray market goods)	_____ % of total monthly hours
Other	_____ % of total monthly hours

2. In your opinion, how has the distribution of your PERSONAL work hours changed for each of the laws during your term of employment? (circle one)

ESA (endangered species)	increased / decreased / constant
CSIE (narcotics)	increased / decreased / constant
DWMD (weapons)	increased / decreased / constant
TVP (human traffic)	increased / decreased / constant
CBP (gray market goods)	increased / decreased / constant

III. International Law Questions

A) Level of Knowledge Regarding INTERNATIONAL Laws Dealing with Smuggling

Scale of 1 to 7, 1 being not at all knowledgeable and 7 being extremely knowledgeable.

1. How knowledgeable are you on each of the following INTERNATIONAL laws? (circle one)

	not at all knowledgeable				extremely knowledgeable		
CITES (endangered species)	1	2	3	4	5	6	7
CNDPS (narcotics)	1	2	3	4	5	6	7
CNBC (weapons)	1	2	3	4	5	6	7
CSTP (human traffic)	1	2	3	4	5	6	7
TRIPS (contraband goods)	1	2	3	4	5	6	7

2. In your opinion, how has your knowledge changed for each of the INTERNATIONAL laws during your term of employment with your organization? (circle one)

CITES (endangered species)	increased / decreased / constant
CNDPS (narcotics)	increased / decreased / constant
CNBC (weapons)	increased / decreased / constant
CSTP (human traffic)	increased / decreased / constant
TRIPS (gray market goods)	increased / decreased / constant

B) Level of Perceived Overall Effectiveness of INTERNATIONAL Efforts Regarding Smuggling

Scale of 1 to 7, with 1 being not at all effective and 7 being extremely effective.

1. In your opinion, how effective are overall INTERNATIONAL government efforts in supporting each of the INTERNATIONAL laws dealing with smuggling? (circle one)

	not at all effective				extremely effective		
CITES (endangered species)	1	2	3	4	5	6	7
CNDPS (narcotics)	1	2	3	4	5	6	7
CNBC (weapons)	1	2	3	4	5	6	7
CSTP (human traffic)	1	2	3	4	5	6	7
TRIPS (contraband goods)	1	2	3	4	5	6	7

2. In your opinion, how effective are overall DOMESTIC government efforts in supporting each of the INTERNATIONAL laws dealing with smuggling? (circle one)

	not at all effective				extremely effective		
CITES (endangered species)	1	2	3	4	5	6	7
CNDPS (narcotics)	1	2	3	4	5	6	7
CNBC (weapons)	1	2	3	4	5	6	7
CSTP (human traffic)	1	2	3	4	5	6	7
TRIPS (contraband goods)	1	2	3	4	5	6	7

C) Level of Deterrence of INTERNATIONAL Laws

Scale of 1 to 7, with 1 being not at all effective and 7 being extremely effective.

1. In your opinion, how much of a deterrence is each of the following INTERNATIONAL laws?
(circle one)

	not at all deterrent				extremely deterrent		
CITES (endangered species)	1	2	3	4	5	6	7
CNDPS (narcotics)	1	2	3	4	5	6	7
CNBC (weapons)	1	2	3	4	5	6	7
CSTP (human traffic)	1	2	3	4	5	6	7
TRIPS (contraband goods)	1	2	3	4	5	6	7

D) Level of Cooperation Between Domestic Agencies to Enforce INTERNATIONAL Laws

Scale of 1 to 7, with 1 being not at all cooperative and 7 being extremely cooperative.

1. In your opinion, how cooperative with each other are your organization and other DOMESTIC government agencies in enforcing each of the following INTERNATIONAL laws?
(circle one)

	not at all cooperative					extremely cooperative	
CITES (endangered species)	1	2	3	4	5	6	7
CNDPS (narcotics)	1	2	3	4	5	6	7
CNBC (weapons)	1	2	3	4	5	6	7
CSTP (human traffic)	1	2	3	4	5	6	7
TRIPS (contraband goods)	1	2	3	4	5	6	7

2. In your opinion, how cooperative with each other are your organization and other INTERNATIONAL agencies (governmental and non-governmental) in enforcing each of the following INTERNATIONAL laws? (circle one)

	not at all cooperative					extremely cooperative	
CITES (endangered species)	1	2	3	4	5	6	7
CNDPS (narcotics)	1	2	3	4	5	6	7
CNBC (weapons)	1	2	3	4	5	6	7
CSTP (human traffic)	1	2	3	4	5	6	7
TRIPS (contraband goods)	1	2	3	4	5	6	7

IV. General Questions

A) Demographic Information, to be used for statistical purposes only.

1. How many years have you been employed by your current employer? _____ years

2. How many years have you been employed in law enforcement? _____ years

3. How many years have you held your current job title? _____ years

4. What is your age in years? _____ years

5. What is your ethnic group? (check one)

      Caucasian-American   _____
      Hispanic-American   _____

African-American	_____
Asian-American	_____
Other	_____

6. What is your gender?   Male   Female   Other

7. How many years of education have you completed? _____

        Less than 12 (did not finish high school)
        12 years (high school or GED)
        14 years (Associate degree)
        16 years (Bachelor's degree)
        18 years (Master's degree)
        19 years (Professional degree such as MBA, JD)
        20 or more years (Doctorate)

8. What is your personal annual income? (check one)

$0-10,000	_____
$10,001-$20,000	_____
$20,001-$30,000	_____
$30,001-$40,000	_____
$40,001-$50,000	_____
$50,001-$60,000	_____
$70,001-$80,000	_____
$80,001-$90,000	_____
$90,001-$100,000	_____
$100,000+	_____

9. How many years have you lived in the following:

U.S.	_____	years
California	_____	years
Los Angeles	_____	years

10. What is your nation of birth? _____

11. Are you a U.S. citizen?   Yes   No

12. What is your first language? _____

13. How often do you attend a religious institution, such as a church, a synagogue, or a temple?

Once each week	_____
Once each month	_____
A few times each year	_____
Never	_____

14. In terms of political ideology, how do you perceive yourself on a scale of 1 to 7, with 1 being extremely liberal and 7 being extremely conservative? (circle one)

extremely liberal						extremely conservative
1	2	3	4	5	6	7

Appendix 2: Histograms – Issues

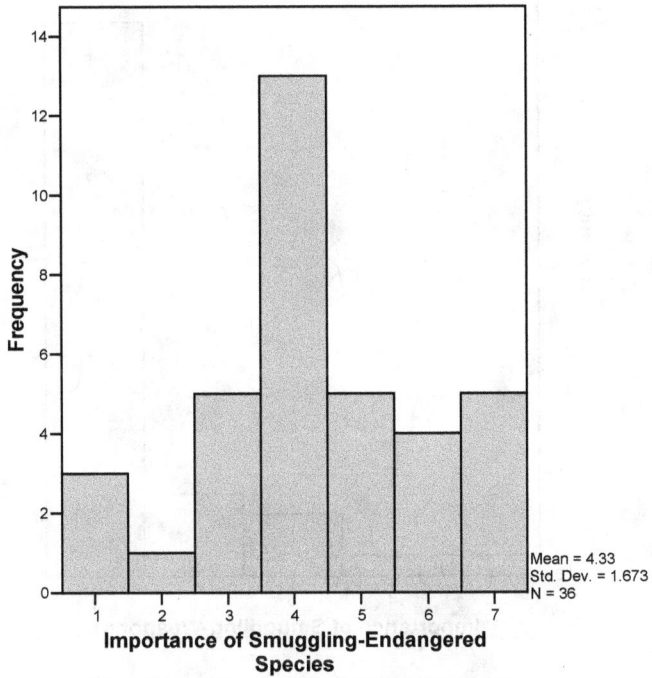

Mean = 4.33
Std. Dev. = 1.673
N = 36

Importance of Smuggling-Endangered Species

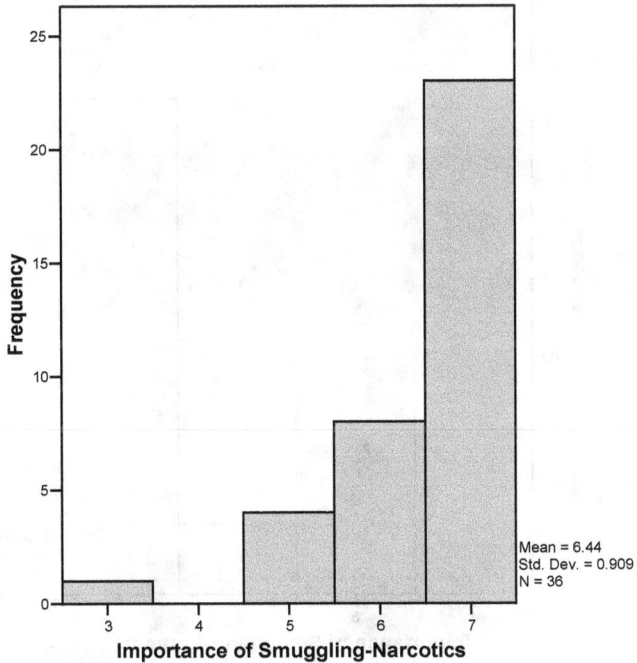

Mean = 6.44
Std. Dev. = 0.909
N = 36

Importance of Smuggling-Narcotics

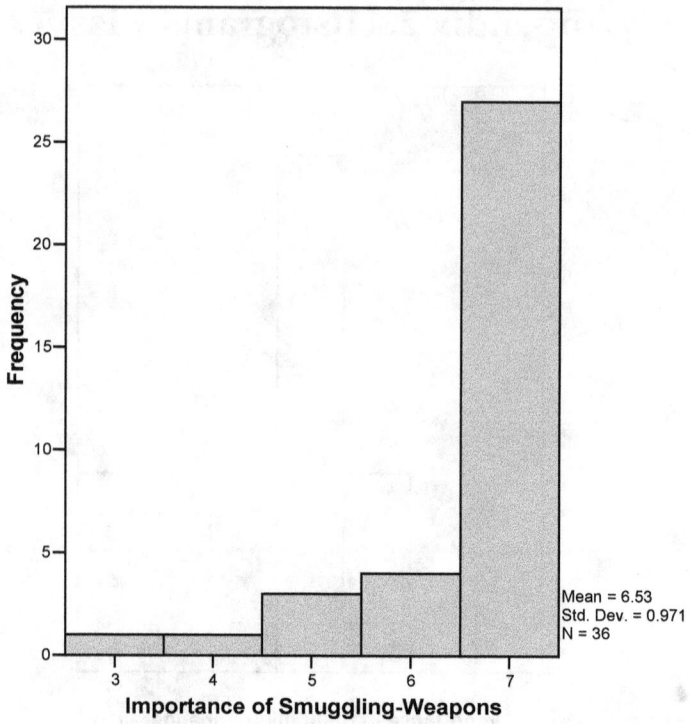

Mean = 6.53
Std. Dev. = 0.971
N = 36

Importance of Smuggling-Weapons

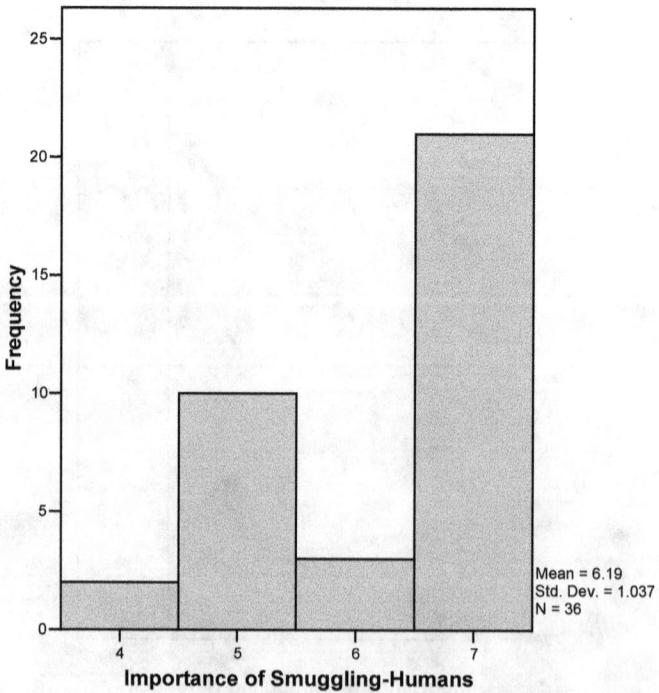

Mean = 6.19
Std. Dev. = 1.037
N = 36

Importance of Smuggling-Humans

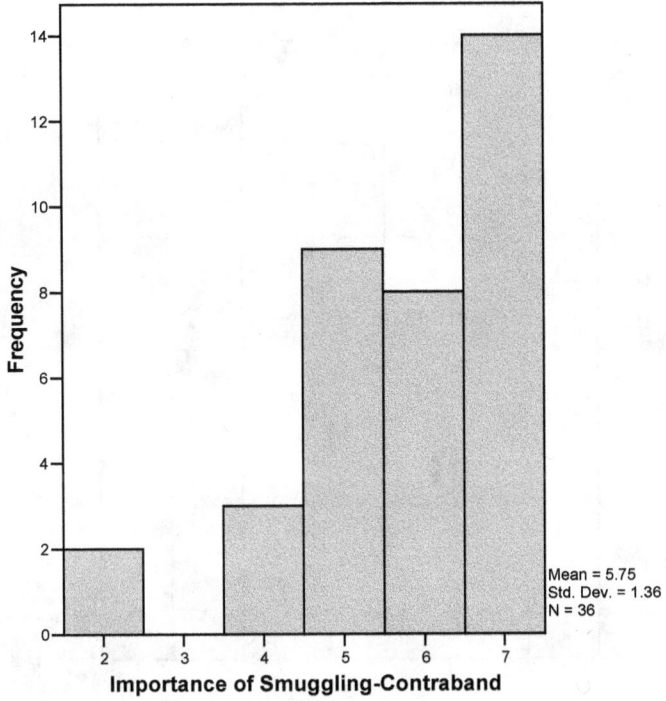

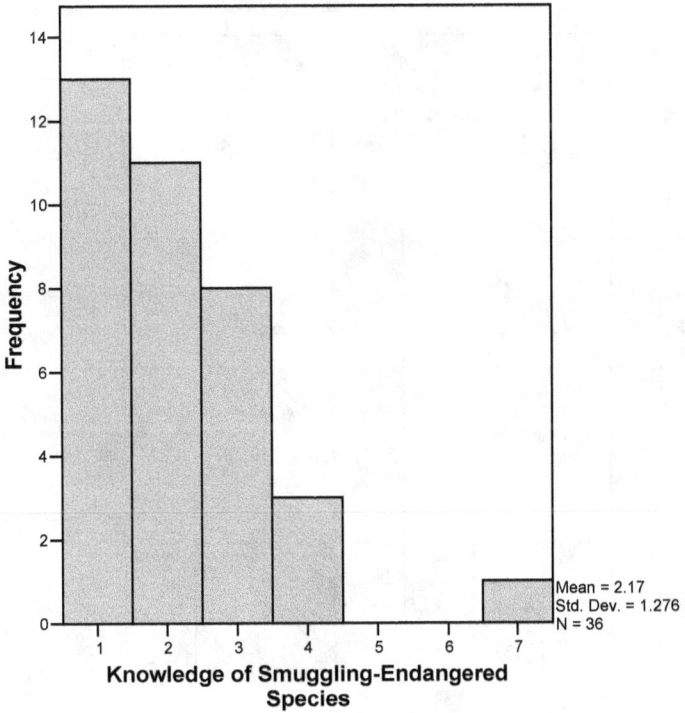

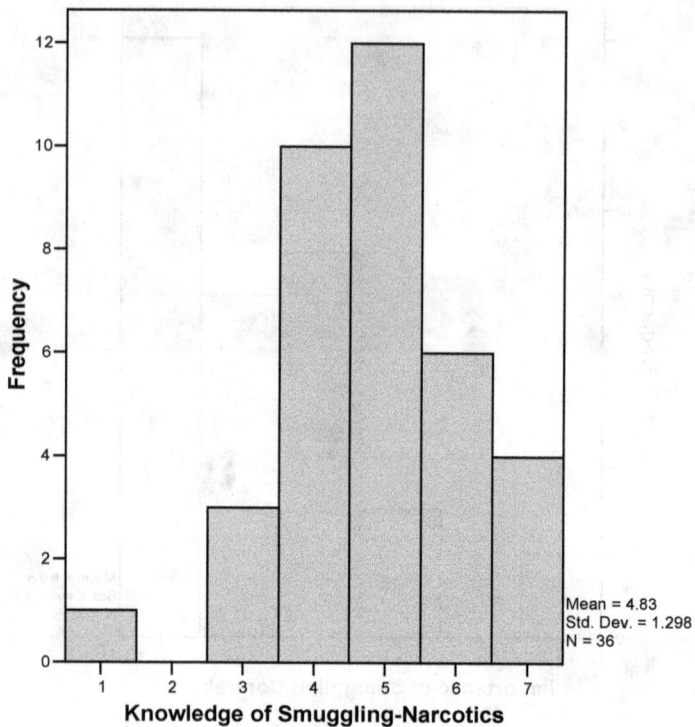

Mean = 4.83
Std. Dev. = 1.298
N = 36

Knowledge of Smuggling-Narcotics

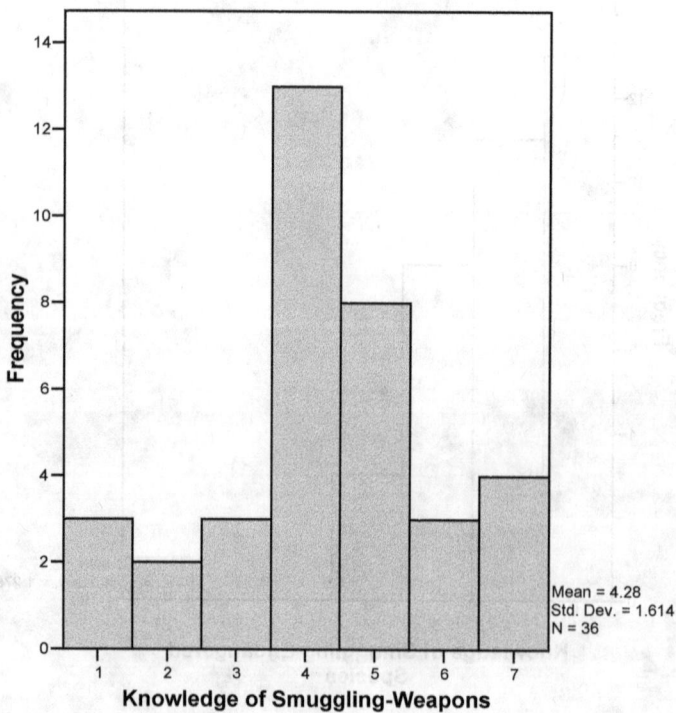

Mean = 4.28
Std. Dev. = 1.614
N = 36

Knowledge of Smuggling-Weapons

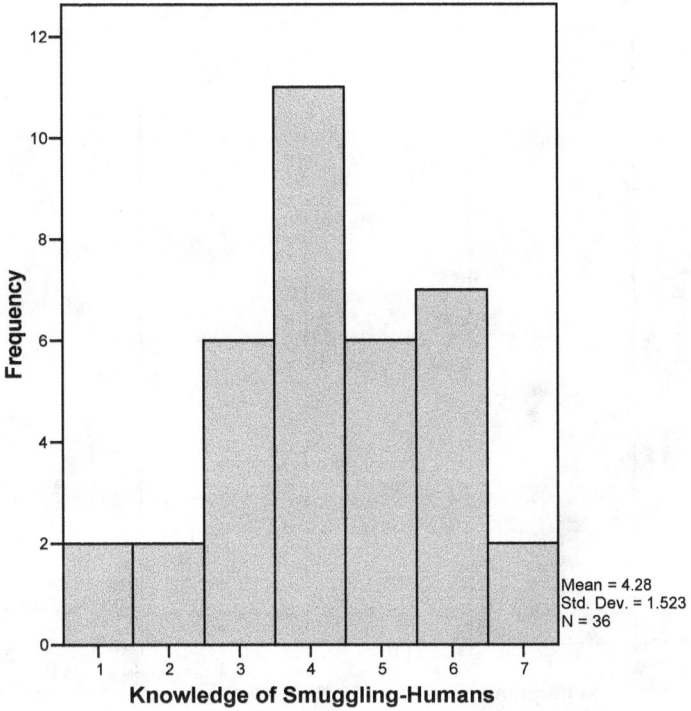

Mean = 4.28
Std. Dev. = 1.523
N = 36

Knowledge of Smuggling-Humans

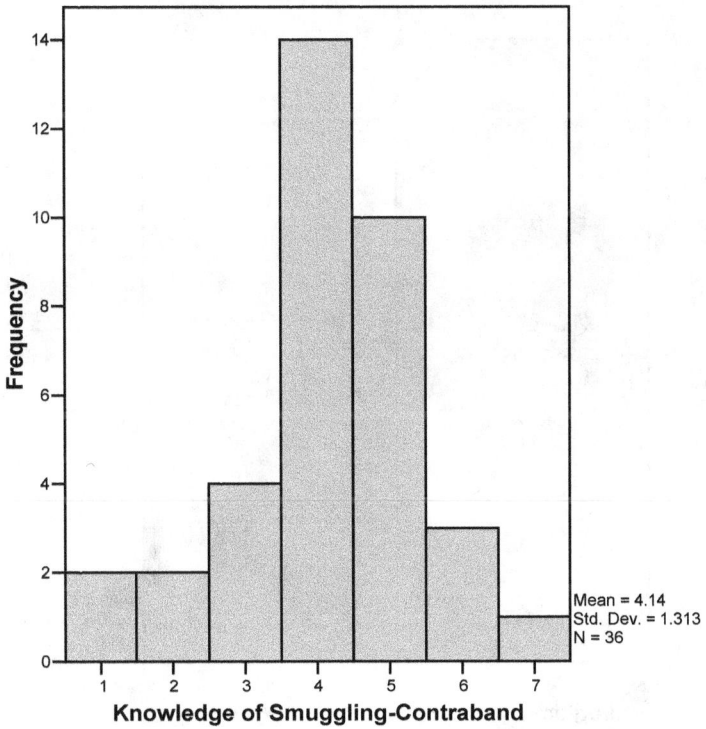

Mean = 4.14
Std. Dev. = 1.313
N = 36

Knowledge of Smuggling-Contraband

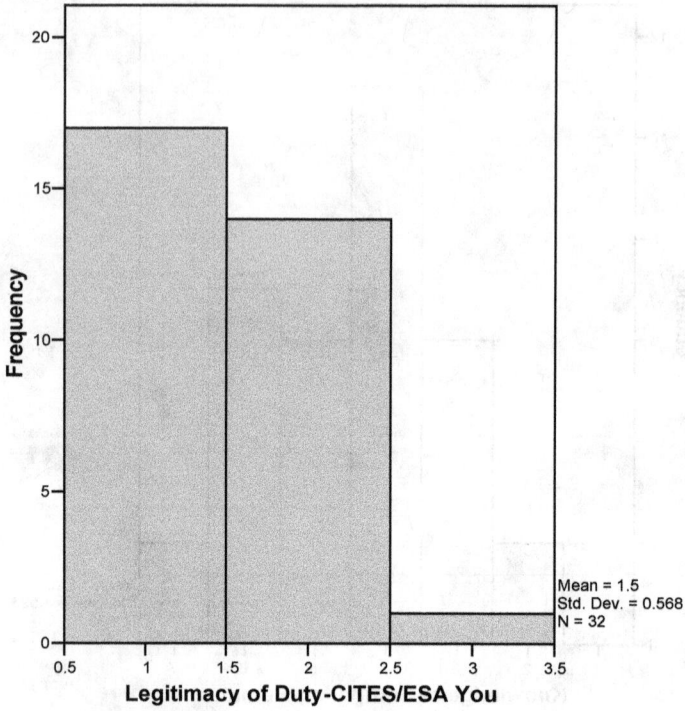

Mean = 1.5
Std. Dev. = 0.568
N = 32

Legitimacy of Duty-CITES/ESA You

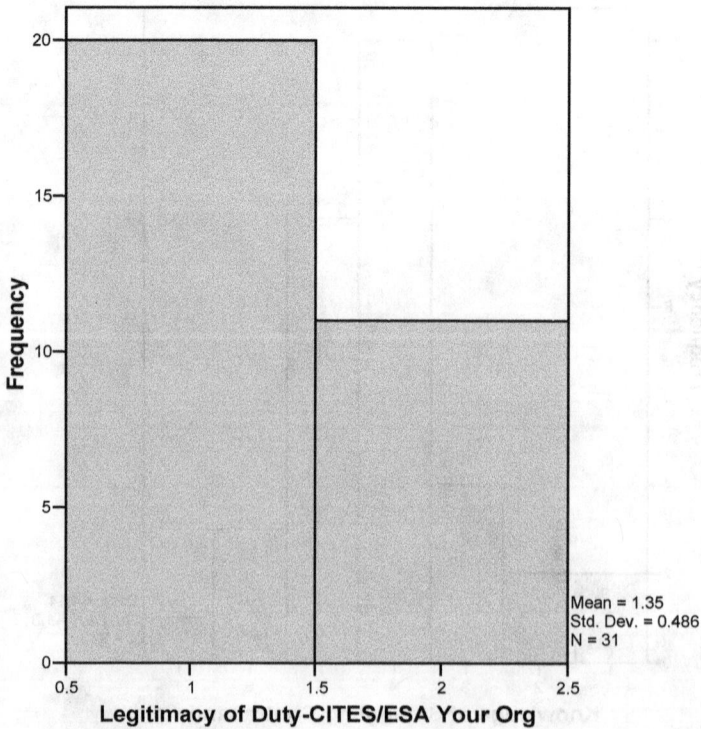

Mean = 1.35
Std. Dev. = 0.486
N = 31

Legitimacy of Duty-CITES/ESA Your Org

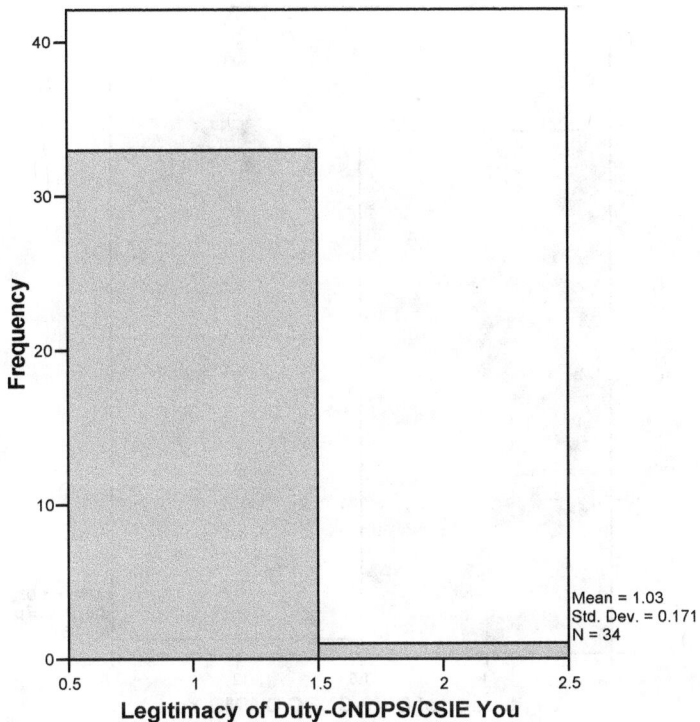

Mean = 1.03
Std. Dev. = 0.171
N = 34

Legitimacy of Duty-CNDPS/CSIE You

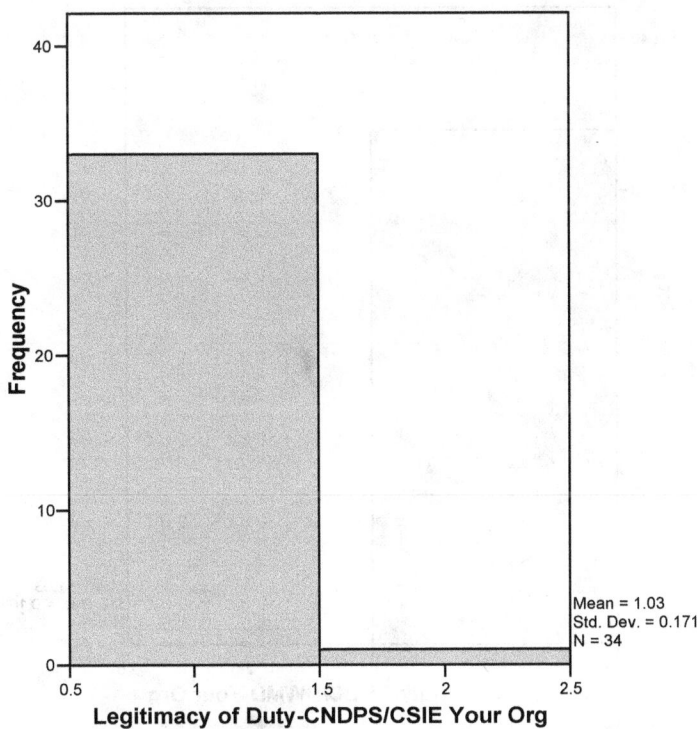

Mean = 1.03
Std. Dev. = 0.171
N = 34

Legitimacy of Duty-CNDPS/CSIE Your Org

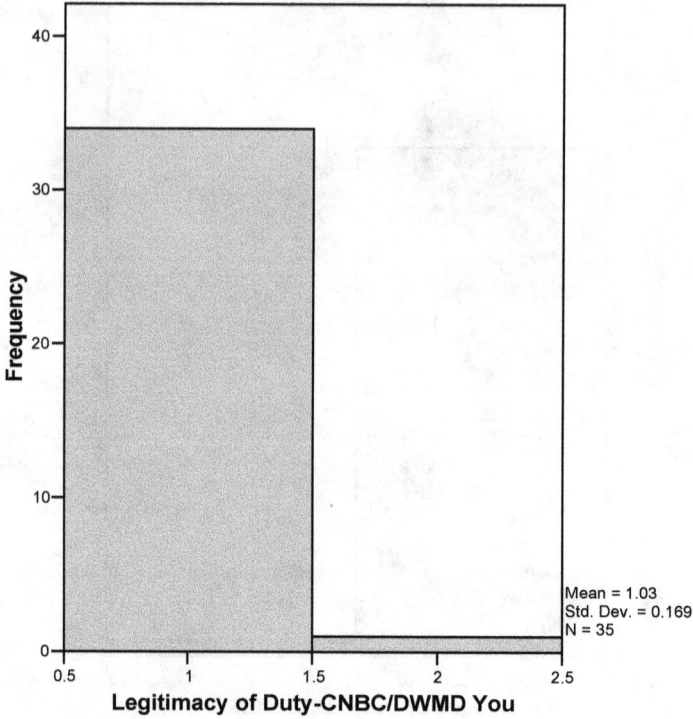

Mean = 1.03
Std. Dev. = 0.169
N = 35

Legitimacy of Duty-CNBC/DWMD You

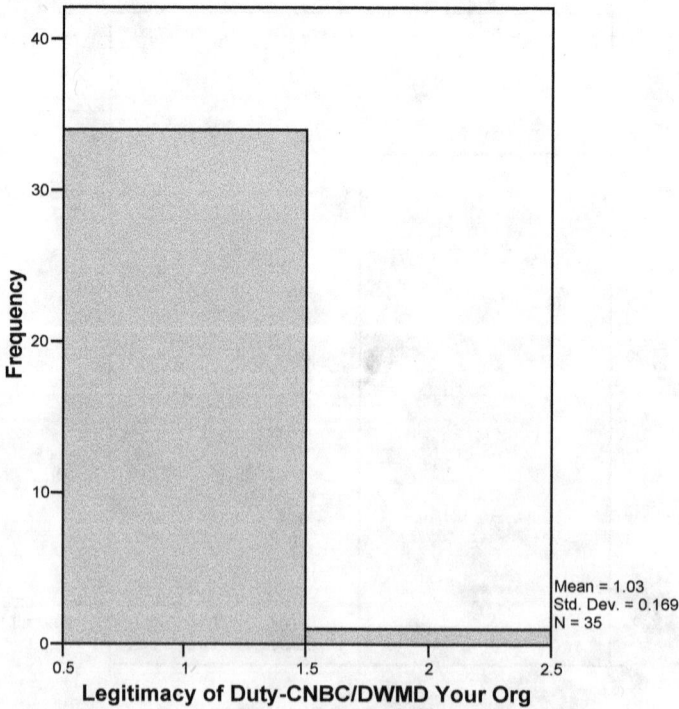

Mean = 1.03
Std. Dev. = 0.169
N = 35

Legitimacy of Duty-CNBC/DWMD Your Org

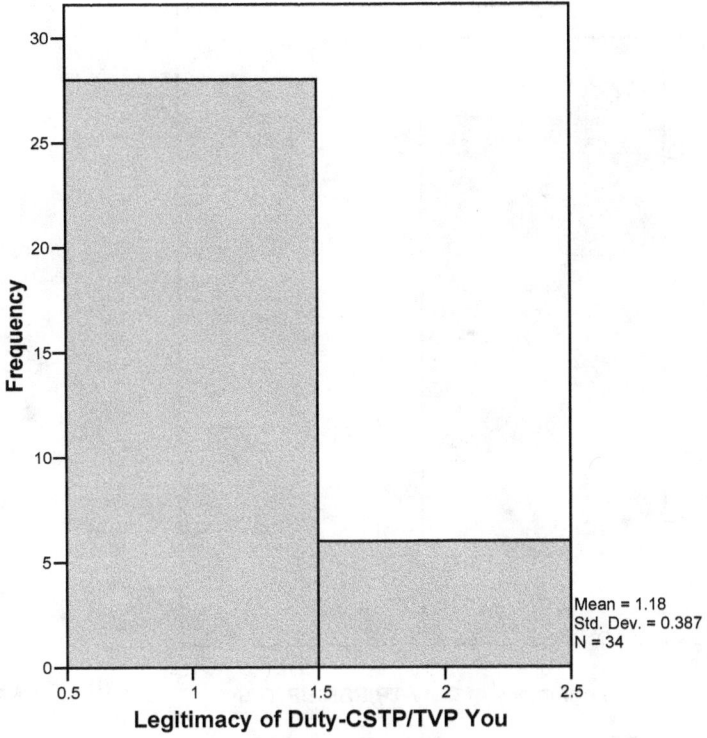

Mean = 1.18
Std. Dev. = 0.387
N = 34

Legitimacy of Duty-CSTP/TVP You

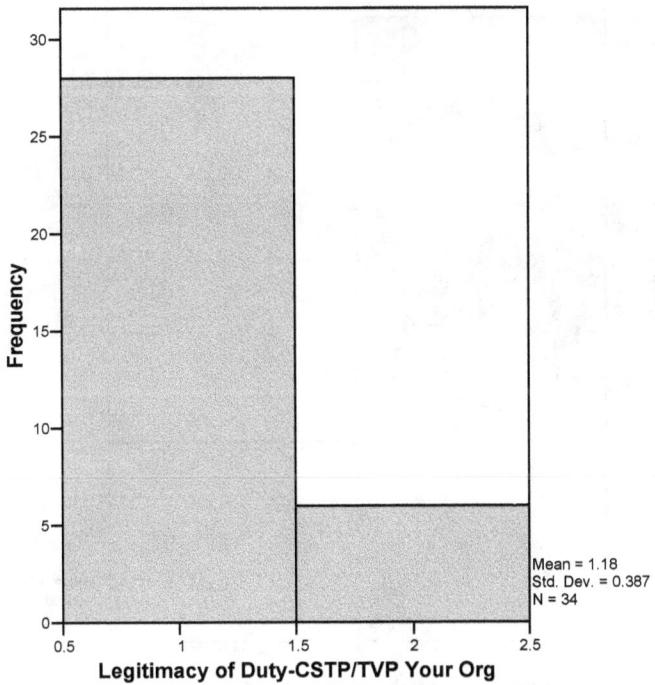

Mean = 1.18
Std. Dev. = 0.387
N = 34

Legitimacy of Duty-CSTP/TVP Your Org

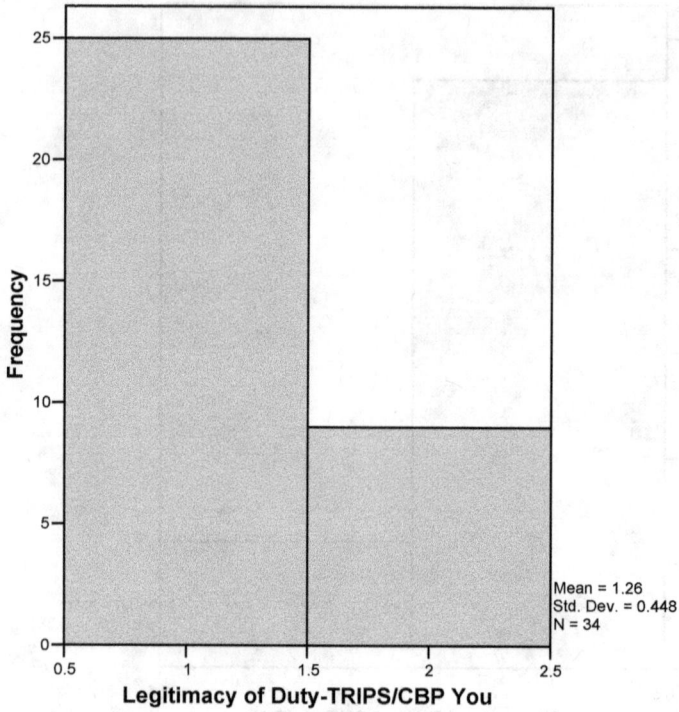

Mean = 1.26
Std. Dev. = 0.448
N = 34

Legitimacy of Duty-TRIPS/CBP You

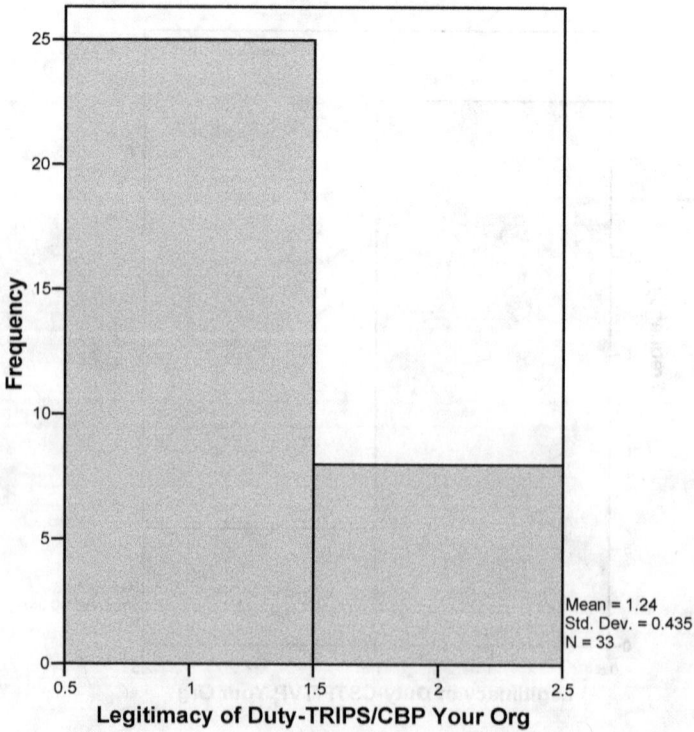

Mean = 1.24
Std. Dev. = 0.435
N = 33

Legitimacy of Duty-TRIPS/CBP Your Org

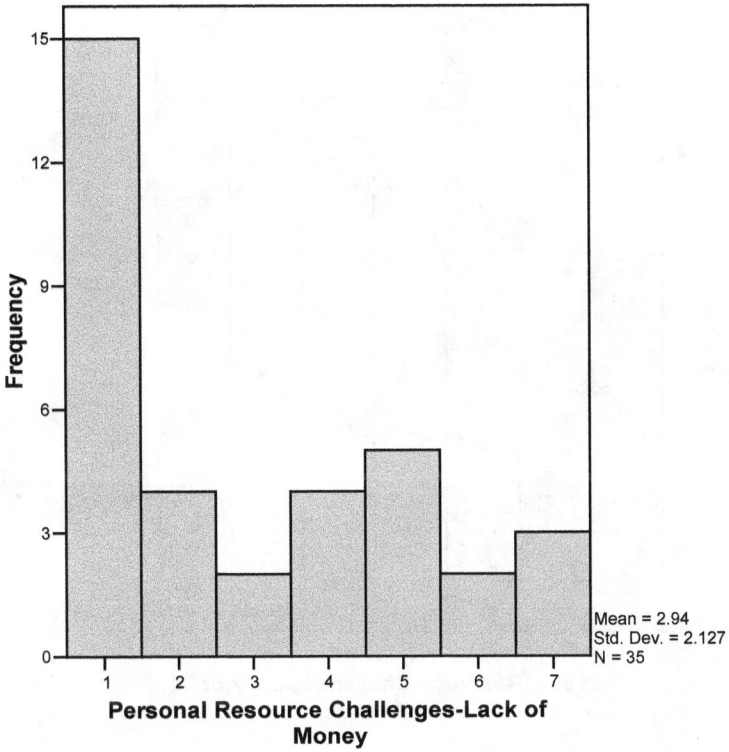

Personal Resource Challenges-Lack of Money

Mean = 2.94
Std. Dev. = 2.127
N = 35

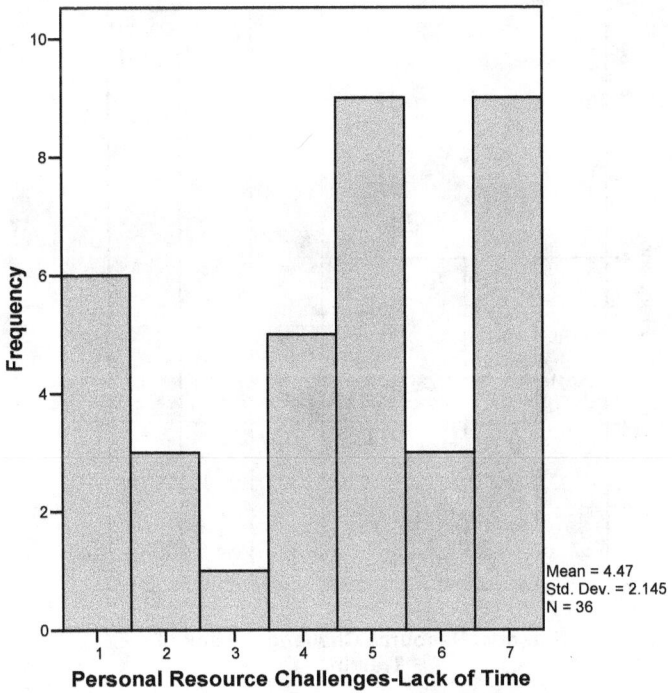

Personal Resource Challenges-Lack of Time

Mean = 4.47
Std. Dev. = 2.145
N = 36

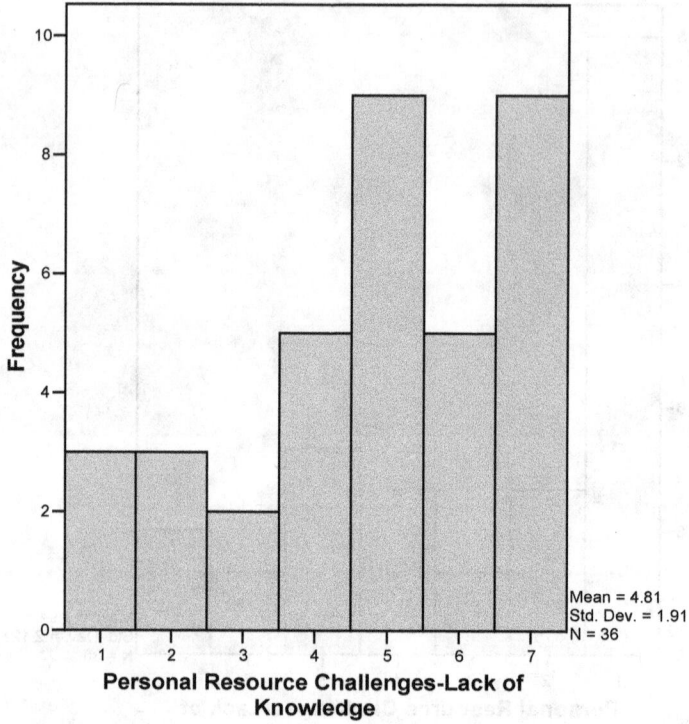

Mean = 4.81
Std. Dev. = 1.91
N = 36

Personal Resource Challenges-Lack of Knowledge

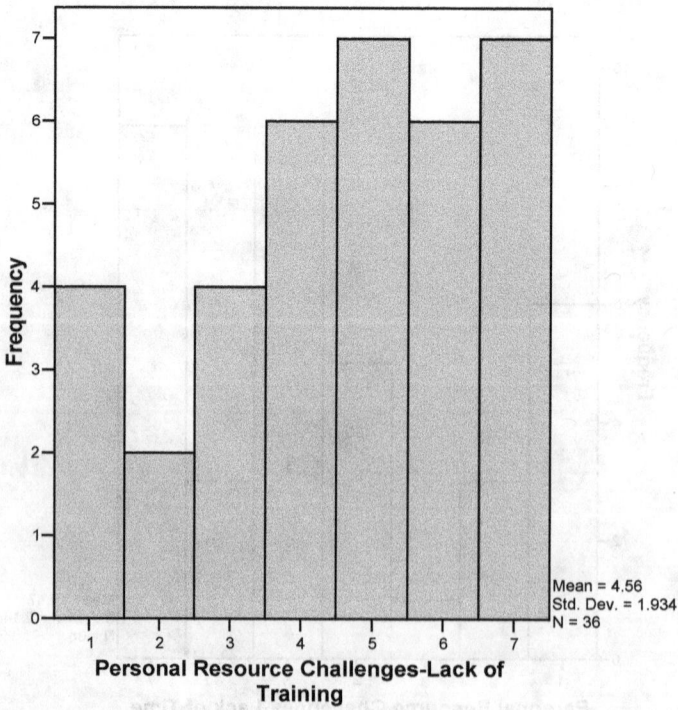

Mean = 4.56
Std. Dev. = 1.934
N = 36

Personal Resource Challenges-Lack of Training

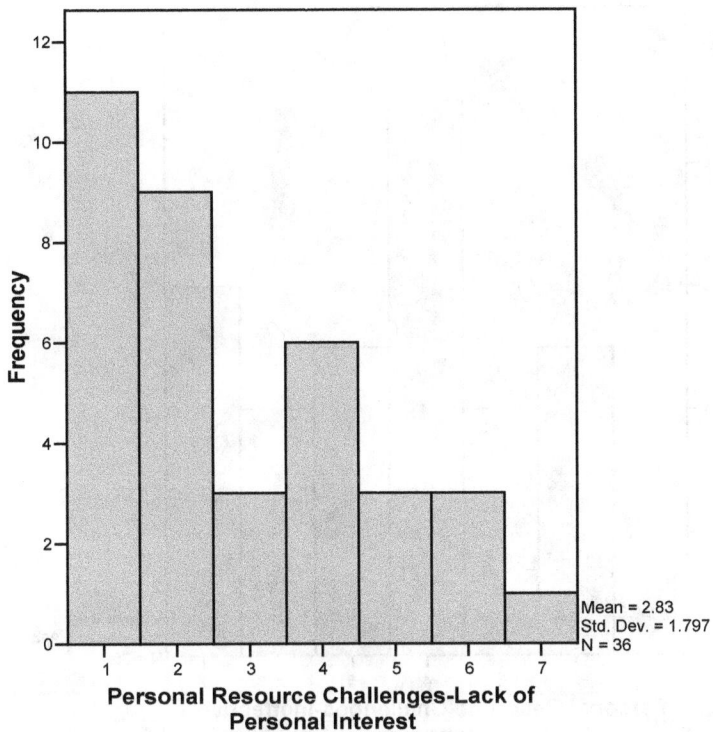

Mean = 2.83
Std. Dev. = 1.797
N = 36

**Personal Resource Challenges-Lack of
Personal Interest**

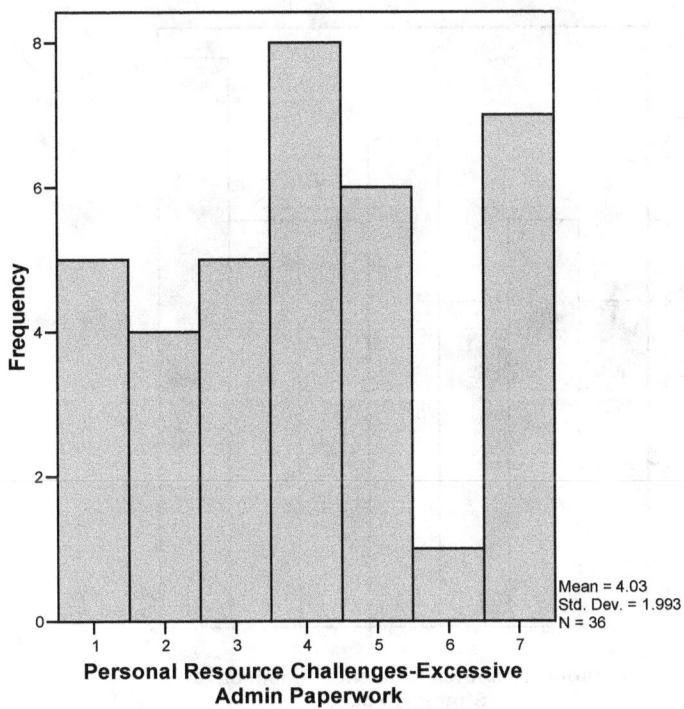

Mean = 4.03
Std. Dev. = 1.993
N = 36

**Personal Resource Challenges-Excessive
Admin Paperwork**

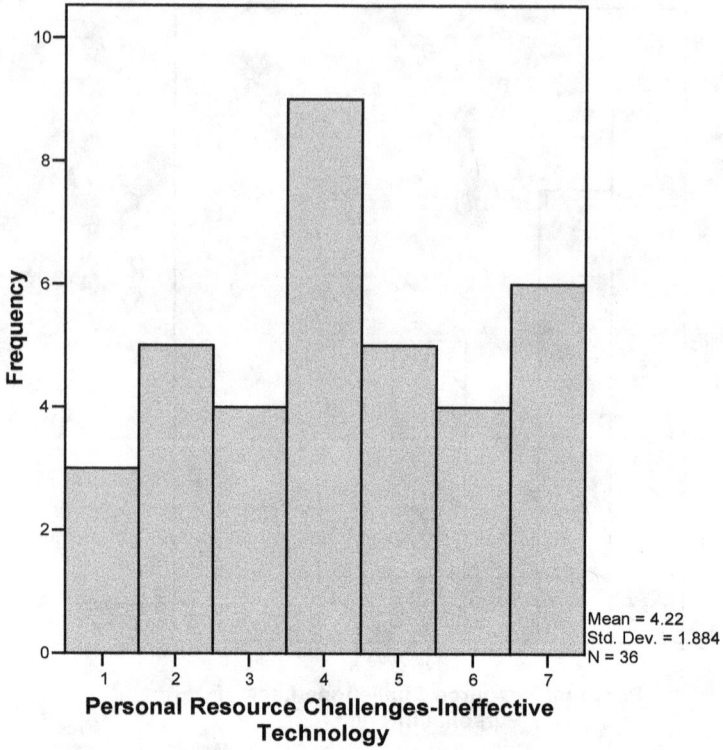

Mean = 4.22
Std. Dev. = 1.884
N = 36

Personal Resource Challenges-Ineffective Technology

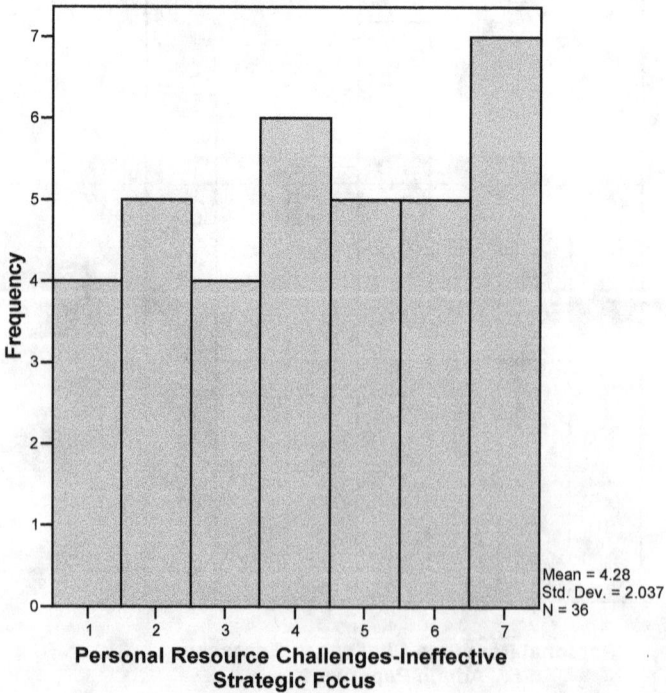

Mean = 4.28
Std. Dev. = 2.037
N = 36

Personal Resource Challenges-Ineffective Strategic Focus

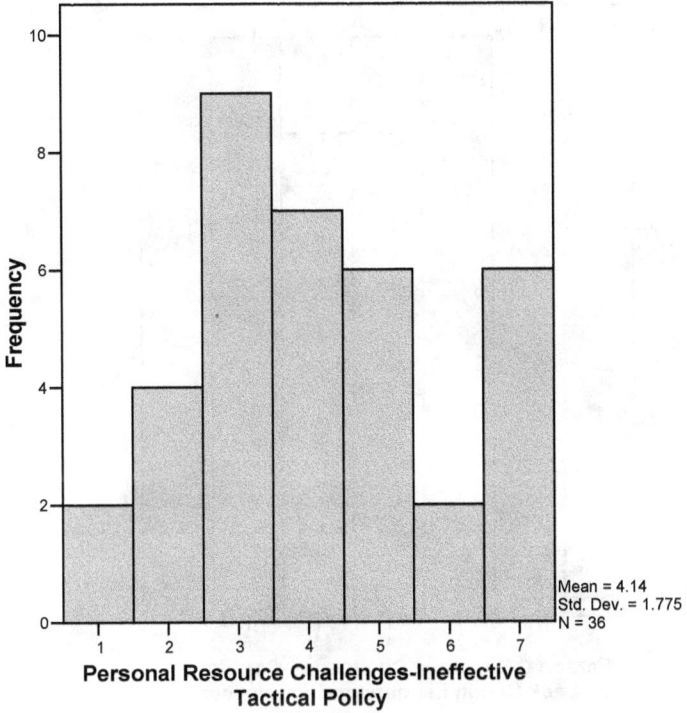

Mean = 4.14
Std. Dev. = 1.775
N = 36

**Personal Resource Challenges-Ineffective
Tactical Policy**

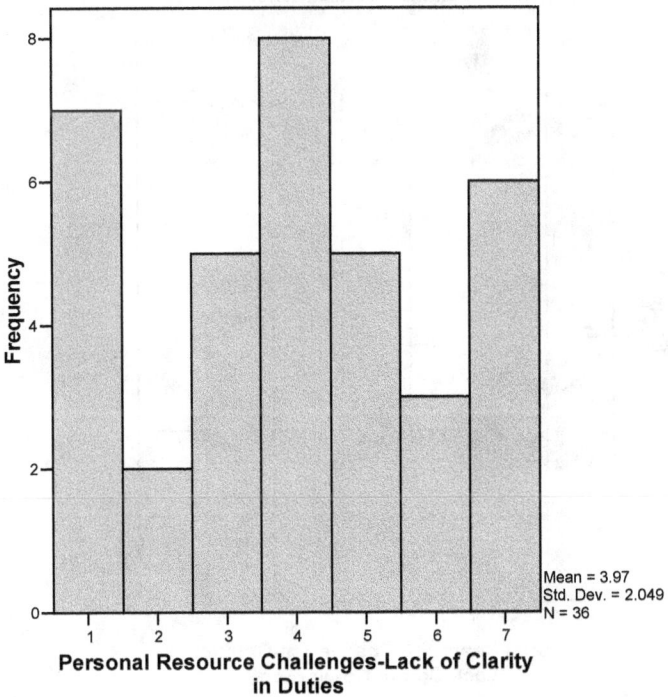

Mean = 3.97
Std. Dev. = 2.049
N = 36

**Personal Resource Challenges-Lack of Clarity
in Duties**

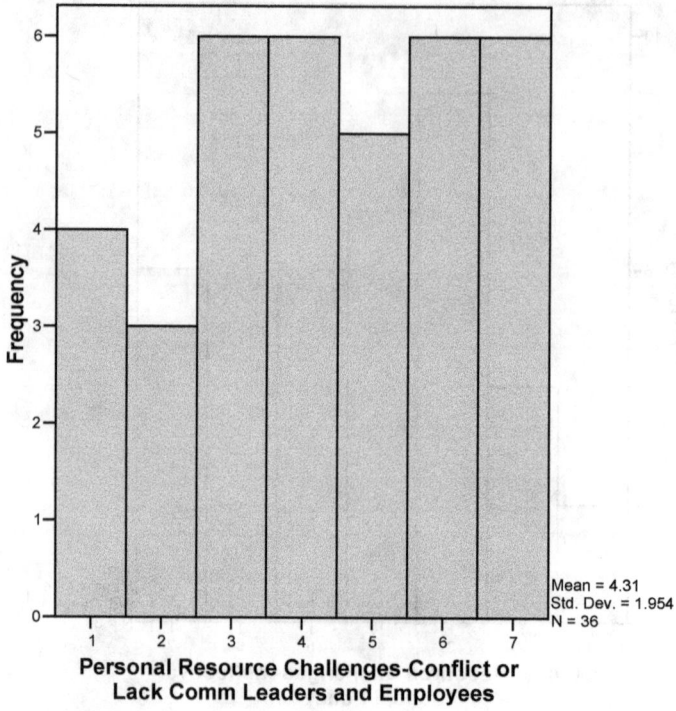

Mean = 4.31
Std. Dev. = 1.954
N = 36

Personal Resource Challenges-Conflict or Lack Comm Leaders and Employees

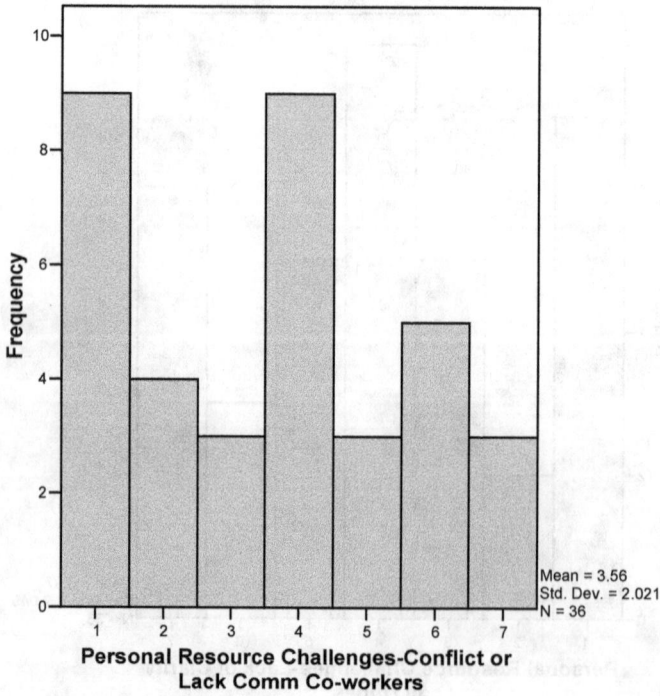

Mean = 3.56
Std. Dev. = 2.021
N = 36

Personal Resource Challenges-Conflict or Lack Comm Co-workers

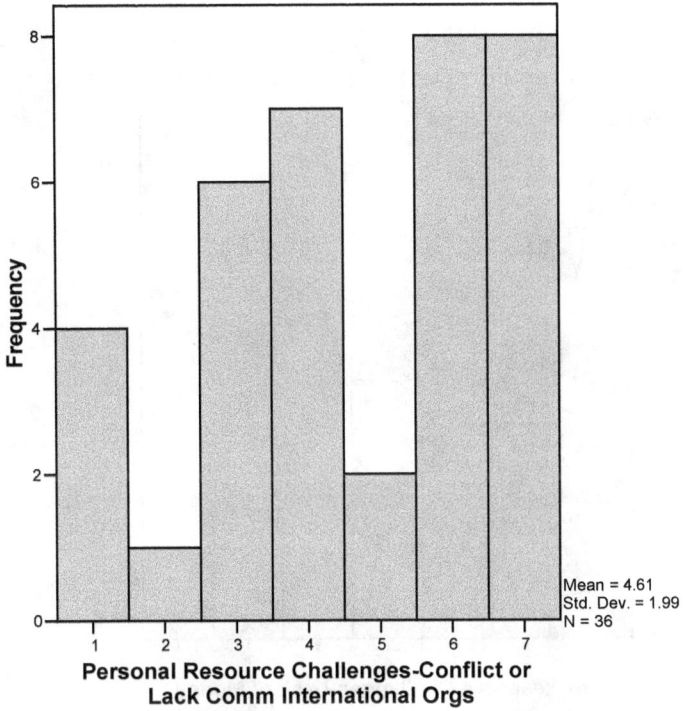

Mean = 4.61
Std. Dev. = 1.99
N = 36

**Personal Resource Challenges-Conflict or
Lack Comm International Orgs**

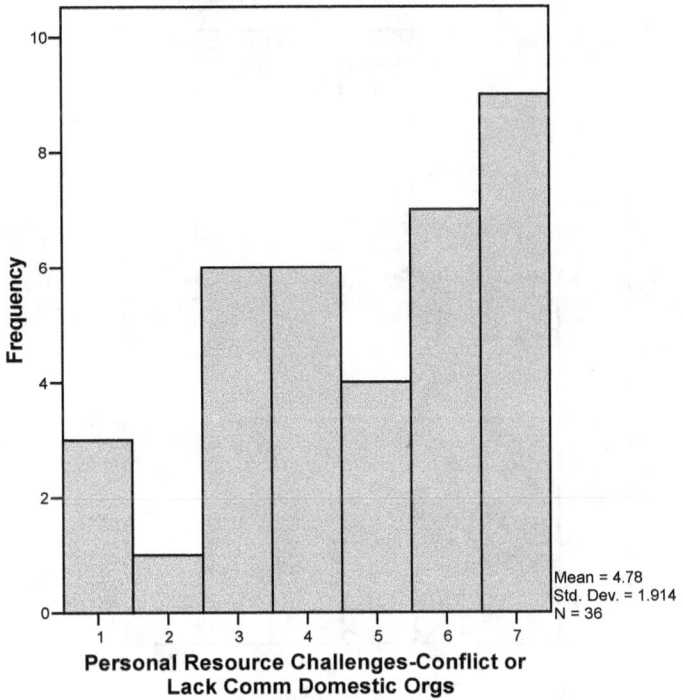

Mean = 4.78
Std. Dev. = 1.914
N = 36

**Personal Resource Challenges-Conflict or
Lack Comm Domestic Orgs**

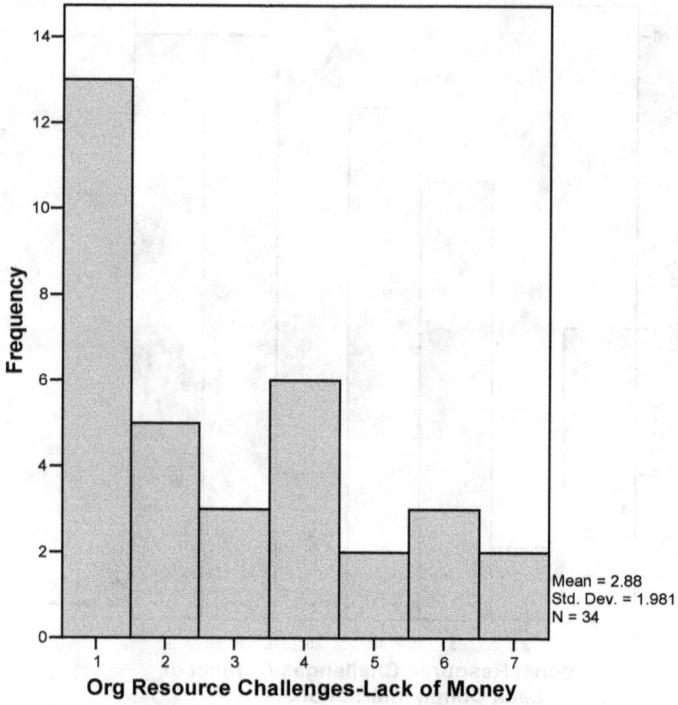

Mean = 2.88
Std. Dev. = 1.981
N = 34

Org Resource Challenges-Lack of Money

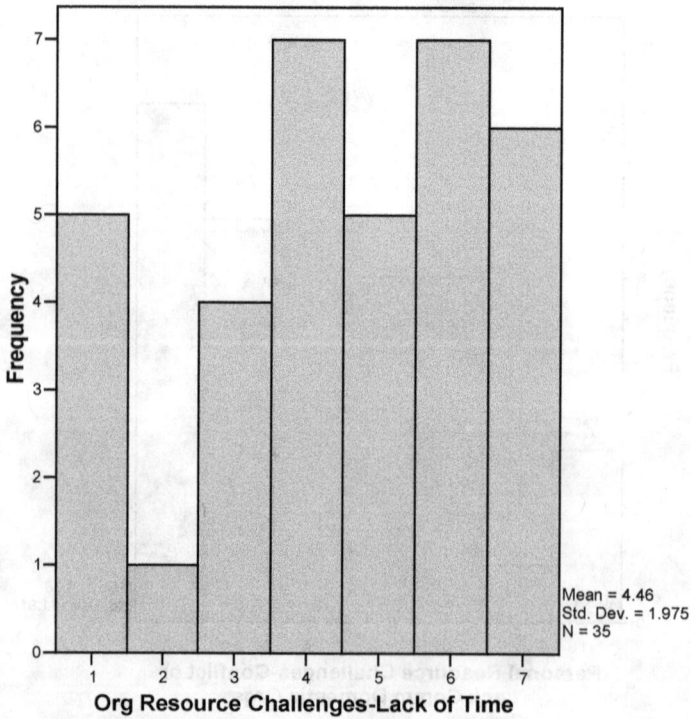

Mean = 4.46
Std. Dev. = 1.975
N = 35

Org Resource Challenges-Lack of Time

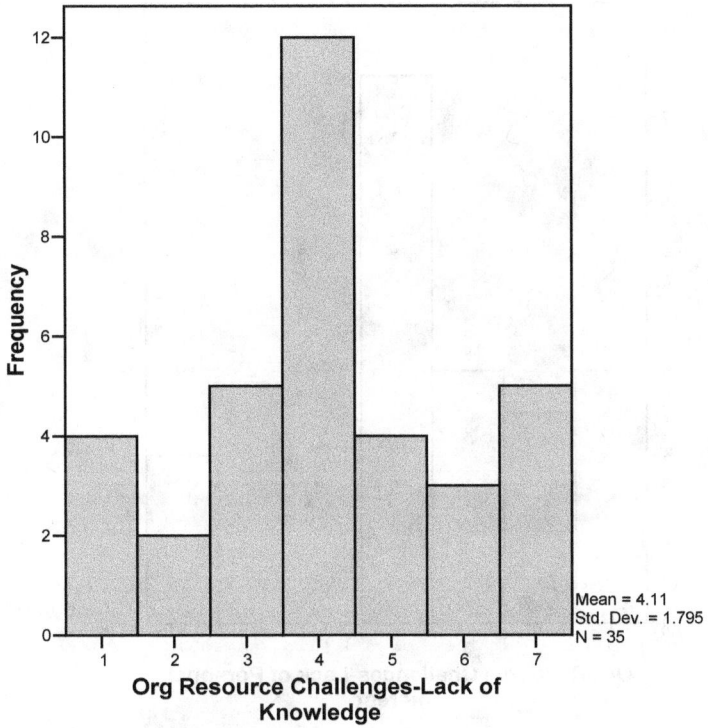

Mean = 4.11
Std. Dev. = 1.795
N = 35

Org Resource Challenges-Lack of Knowledge

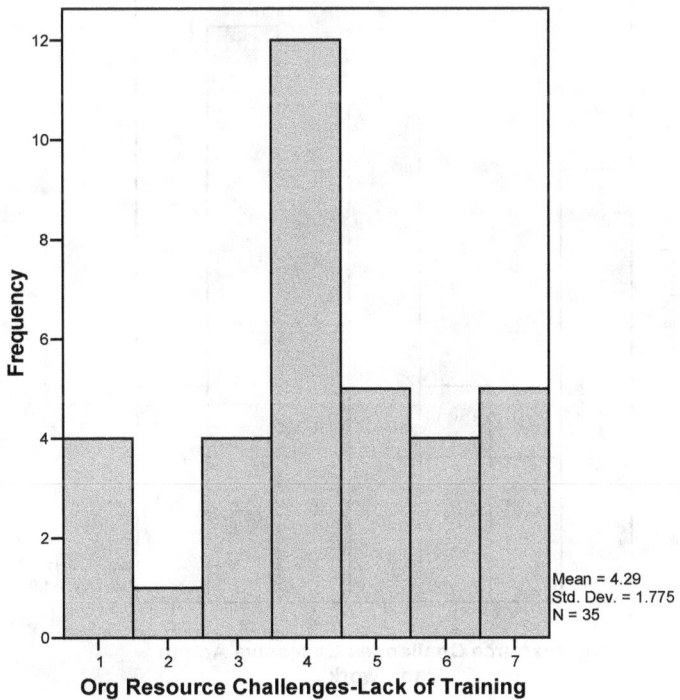

Mean = 4.29
Std. Dev. = 1.775
N = 35

Org Resource Challenges-Lack of Training

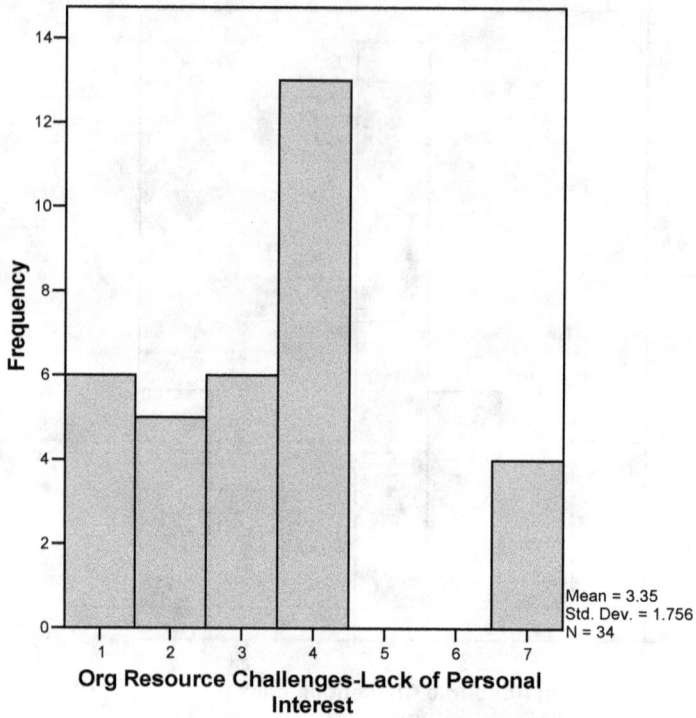

Mean = 3.35
Std. Dev. = 1.756
N = 34

Org Resource Challenges-Lack of Personal Interest

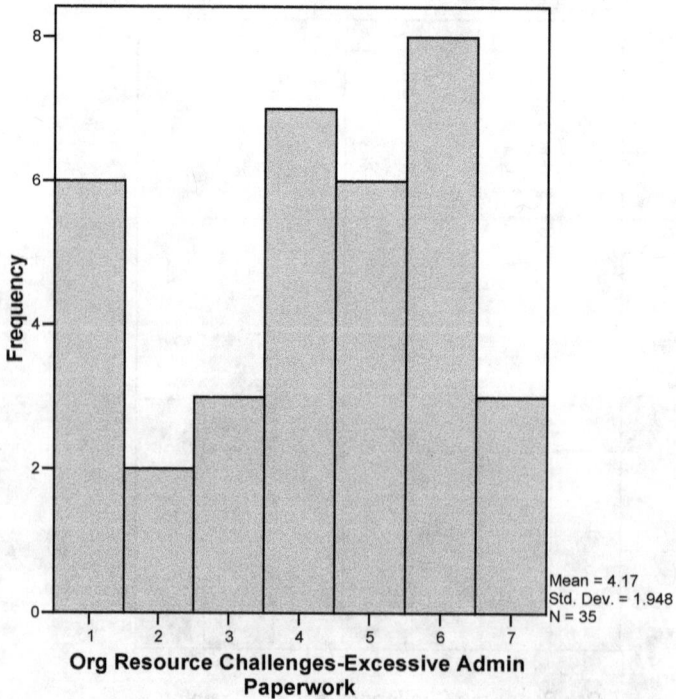

Mean = 4.17
Std. Dev. = 1.948
N = 35

Org Resource Challenges-Excessive Admin Paperwork

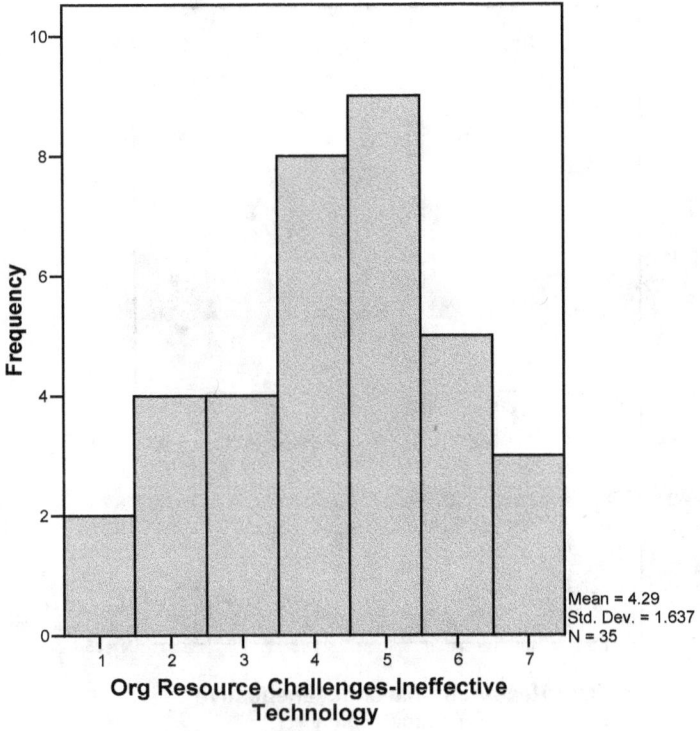

Org Resource Challenges-Ineffective
Technology

Mean = 4.29
Std. Dev. = 1.637
N = 35

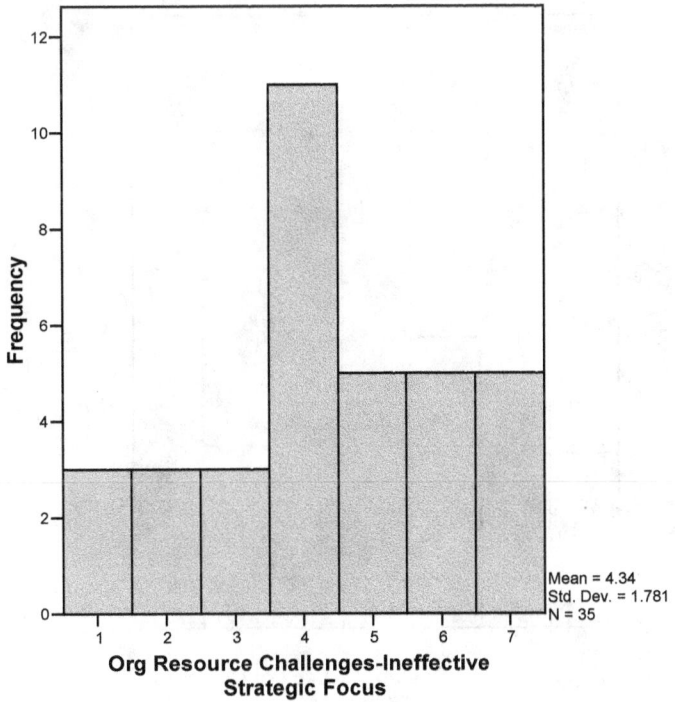

Org Resource Challenges-Ineffective
Strategic Focus

Mean = 4.34
Std. Dev. = 1.781
N = 35

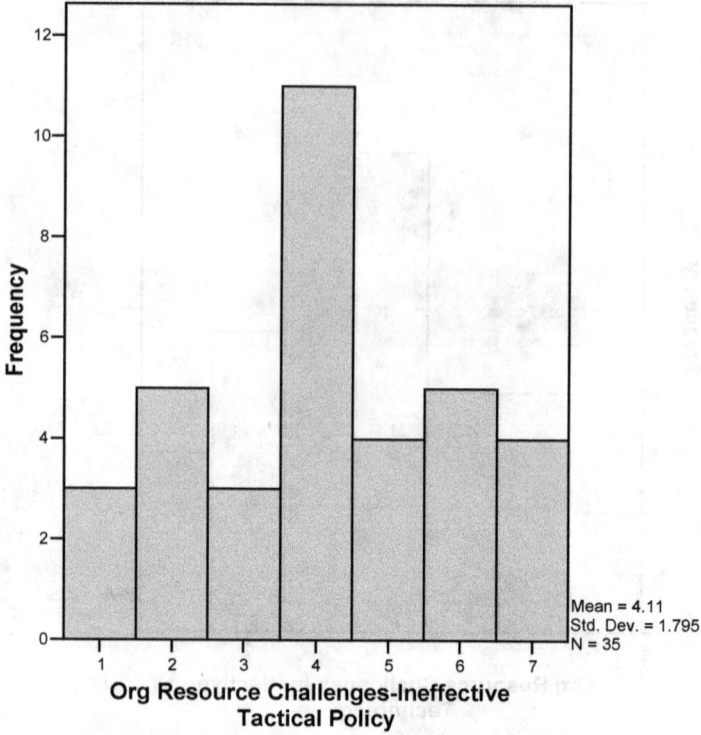

Mean = 4.11
Std. Dev. = 1.795
N = 35

Org Resource Challenges-Ineffective
Tactical Policy

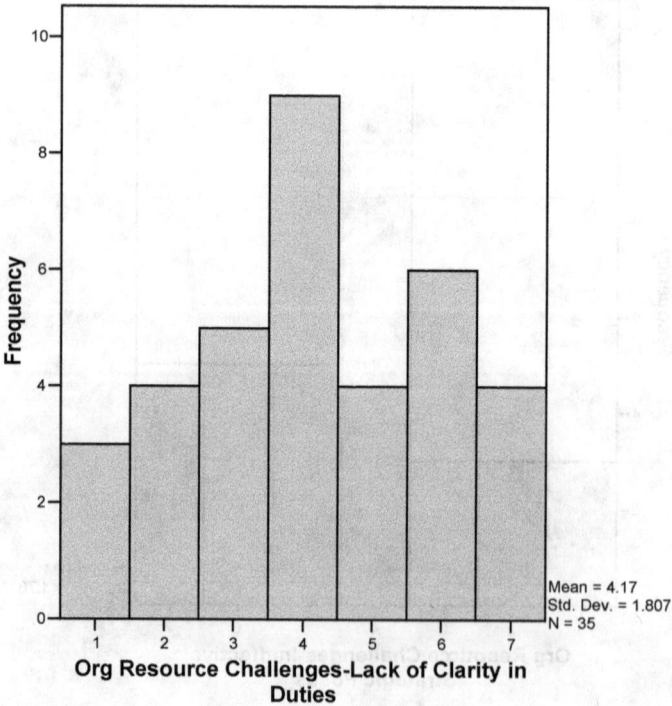

Mean = 4.17
Std. Dev. = 1.807
N = 35

Org Resource Challenges-Lack of Clarity in
Duties

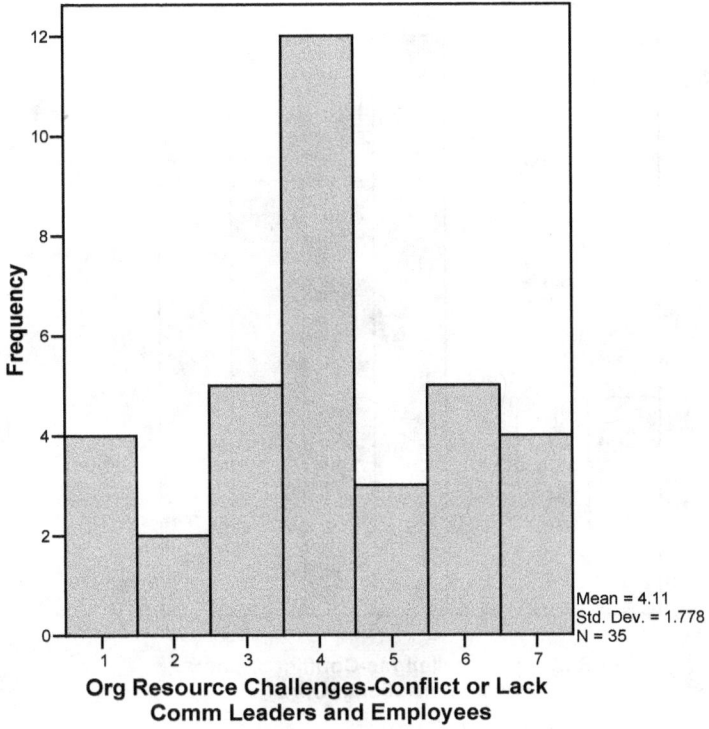

Org Resource Challenges-Conflict or Lack
Comm Leaders and Employees

Mean = 4.11
Std. Dev. = 1.778
N = 35

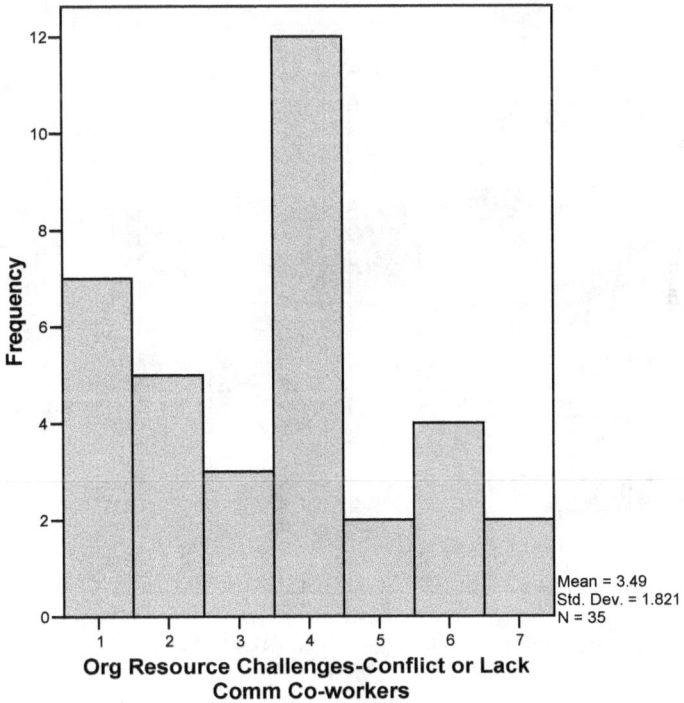

Org Resource Challenges-Conflict or Lack
Comm Co-workers

Mean = 3.49
Std. Dev. = 1.821
N = 35

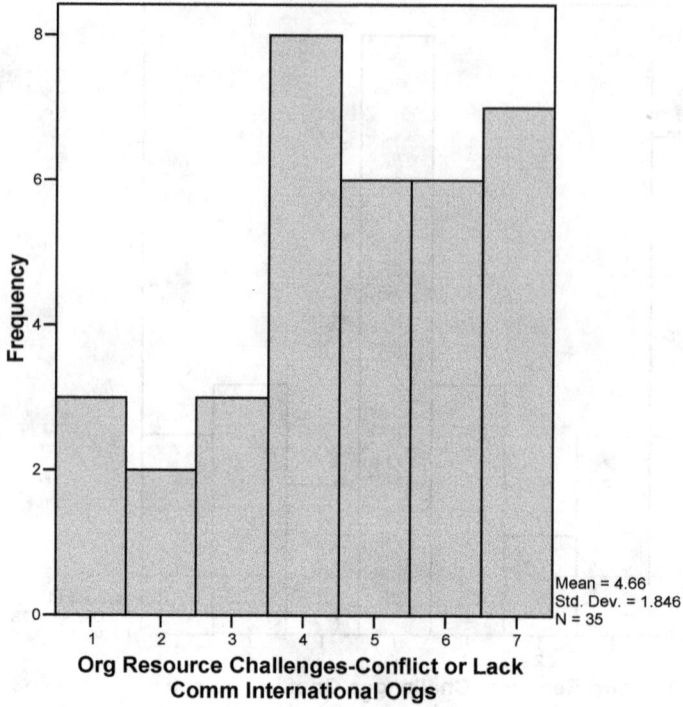

Org Resource Challenges-Conflict or Lack
Comm International Orgs

Mean = 4.66
Std. Dev. = 1.846
N = 35

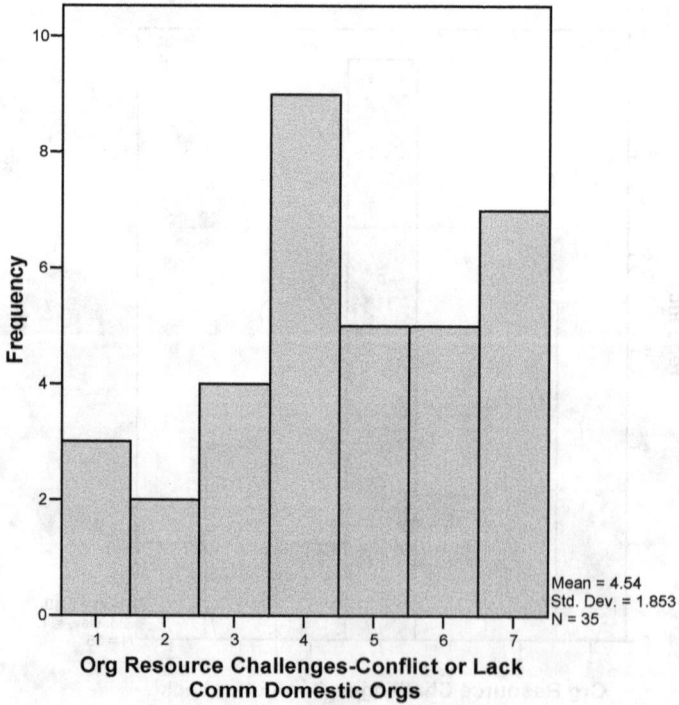

Org Resource Challenges-Conflict or Lack
Comm Domestic Orgs

Mean = 4.54
Std. Dev. = 1.853
N = 35

Appendix 3: Histograms – Domestic Law

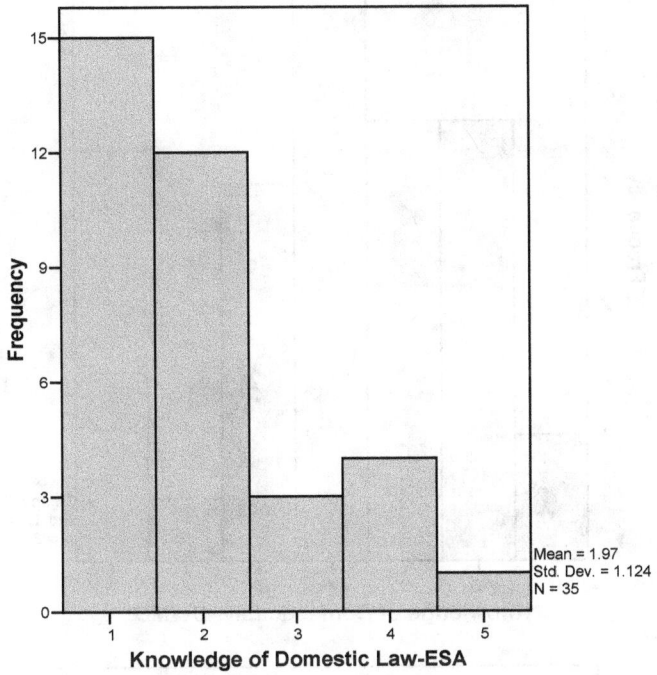

Mean = 1.97
Std. Dev. = 1.124
N = 35

Knowledge of Domestic Law-ESA

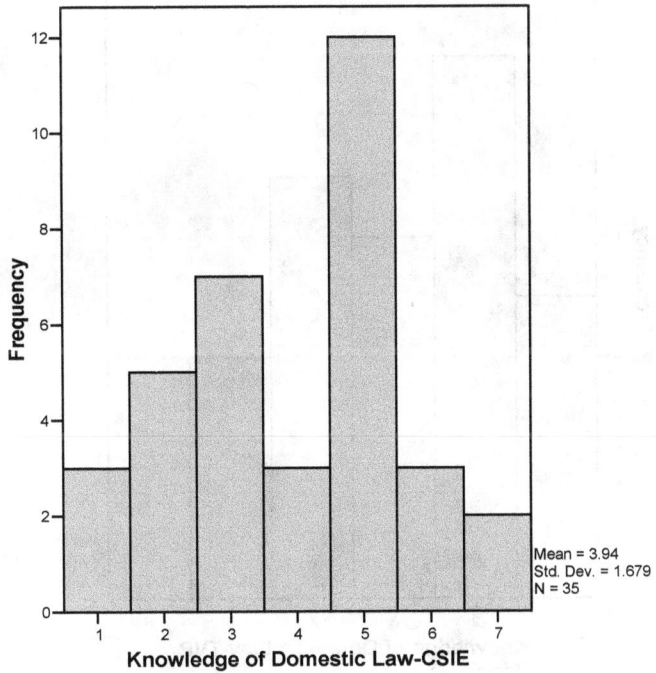

Mean = 3.94
Std. Dev. = 1.679
N = 35

Knowledge of Domestic Law-CSIE

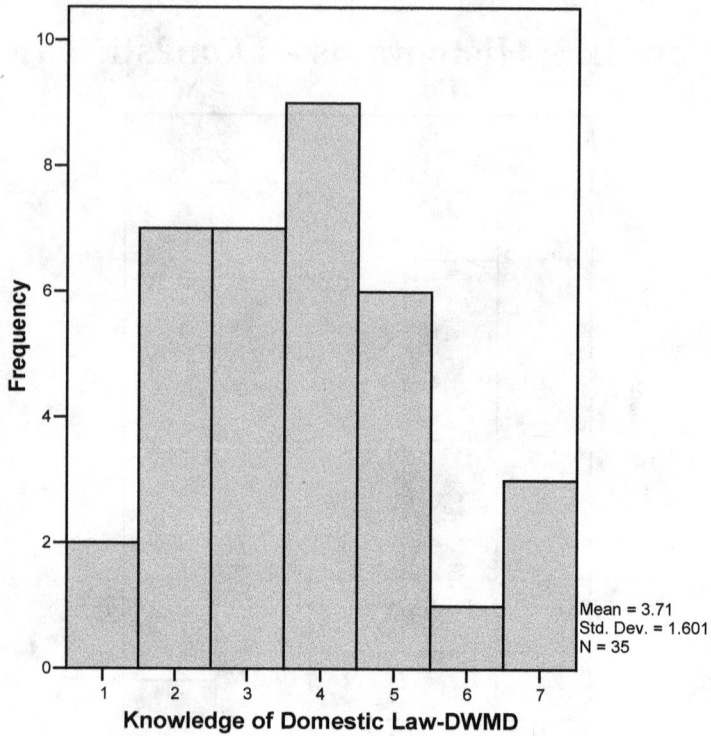

Mean = 3.71
Std. Dev. = 1.601
N = 35

Knowledge of Domestic Law-DWMD

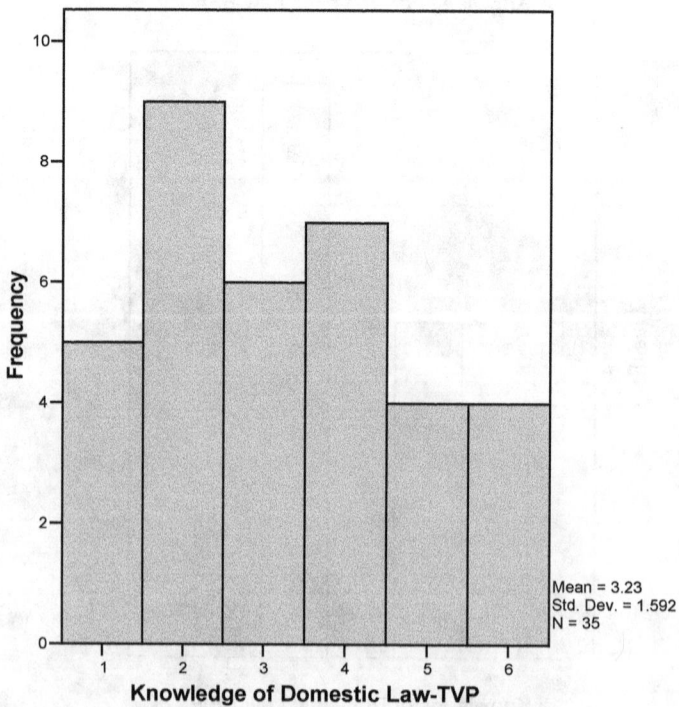

Mean = 3.23
Std. Dev. = 1.592
N = 35

Knowledge of Domestic Law-TVP

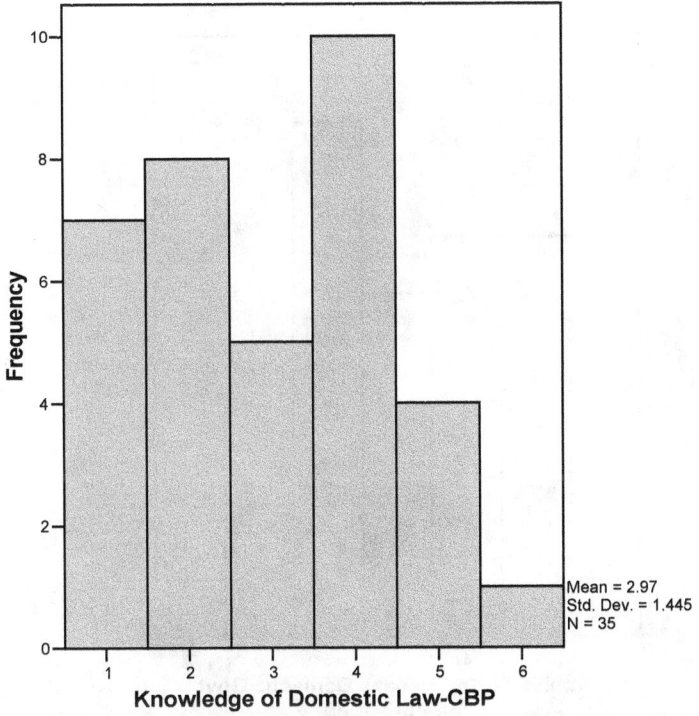

Knowledge of Domestic Law-CBP

Mean = 2.97
Std. Dev. = 1.445
N = 35

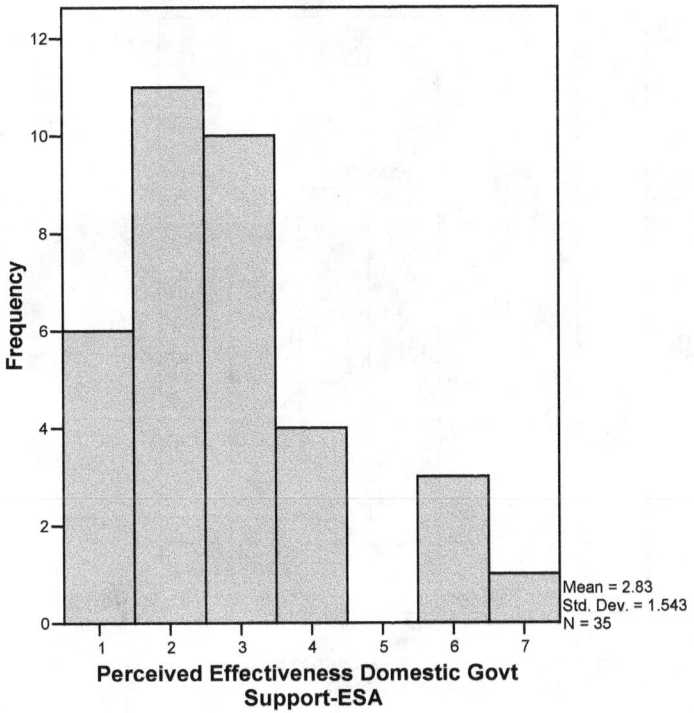

Perceived Effectiveness Domestic Govt
Support-ESA

Mean = 2.83
Std. Dev. = 1.543
N = 35

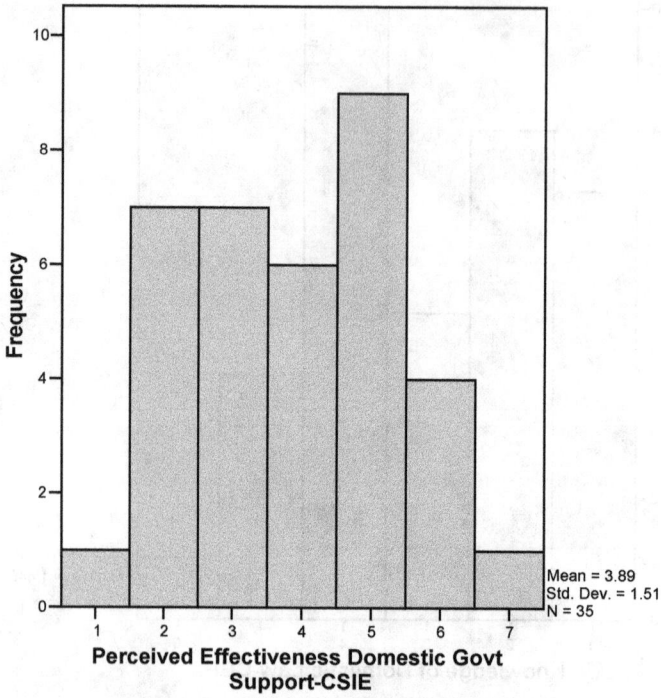

Mean = 3.89
Std. Dev. = 1.51
N = 35

Perceived Effectiveness Domestic Govt Support-CSIE

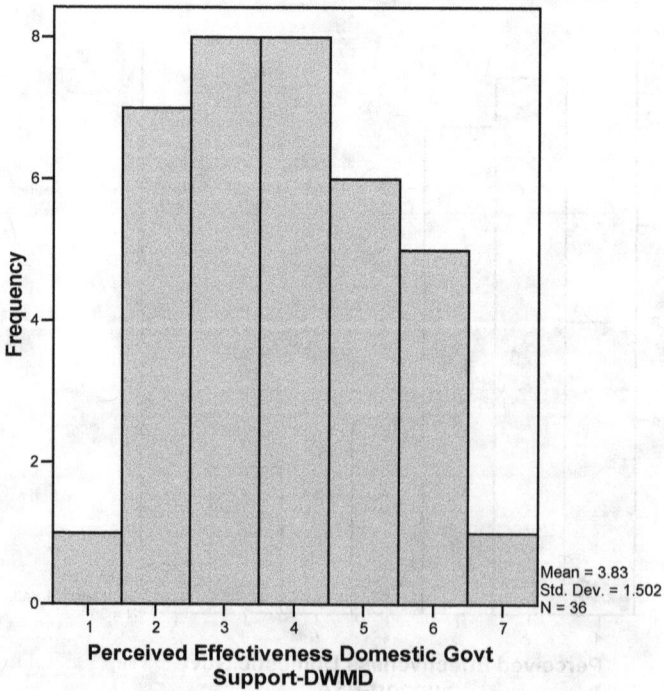

Mean = 3.83
Std. Dev. = 1.502
N = 36

Perceived Effectiveness Domestic Govt Support-DWMD

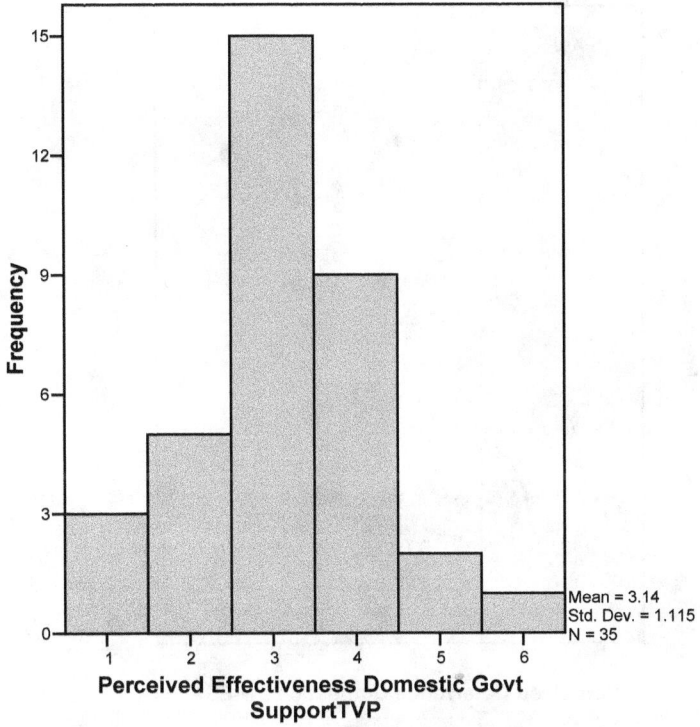

Perceived Effectiveness Domestic Govt
SupportTVP

Mean = 3.14
Std. Dev. = 1.115
N = 35

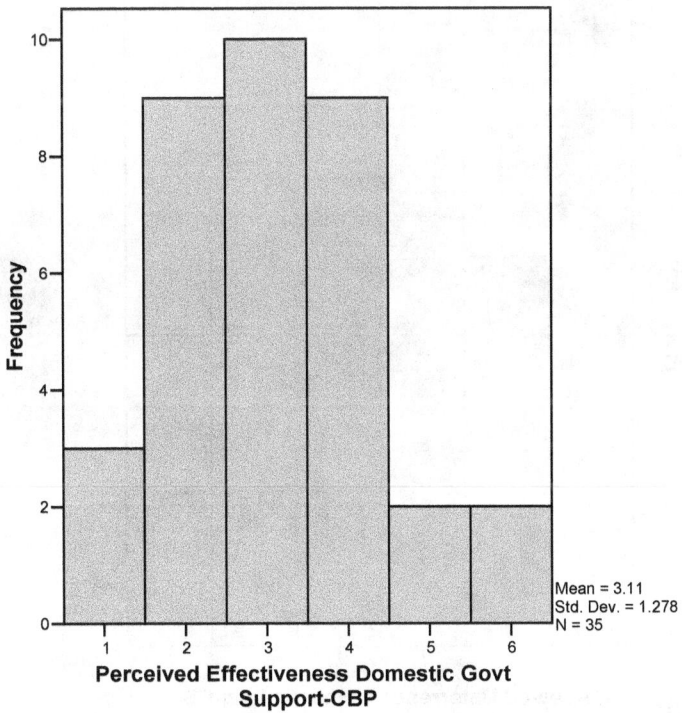

Perceived Effectiveness Domestic Govt
Support-CBP

Mean = 3.11
Std. Dev. = 1.278
N = 35

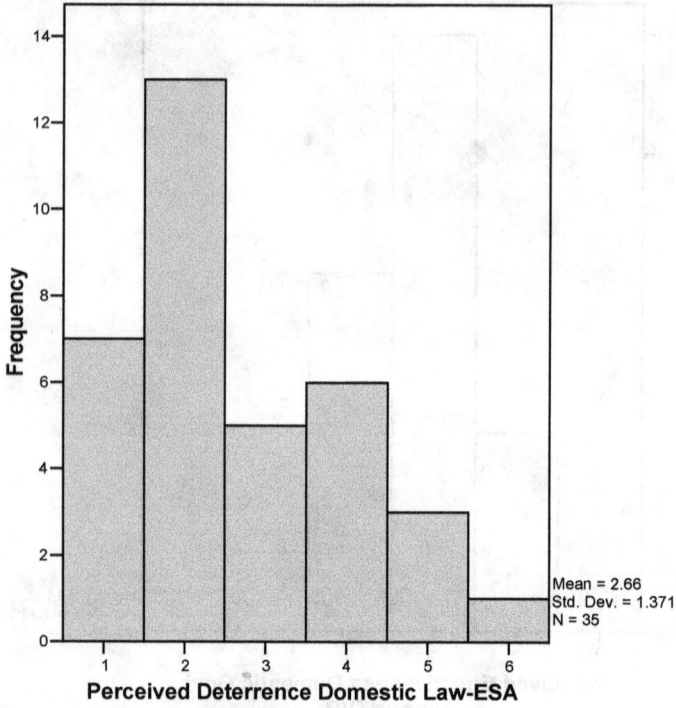

Perceived Deterrence Domestic Law-ESA

Mean = 2.66
Std. Dev. = 1.371
N = 35

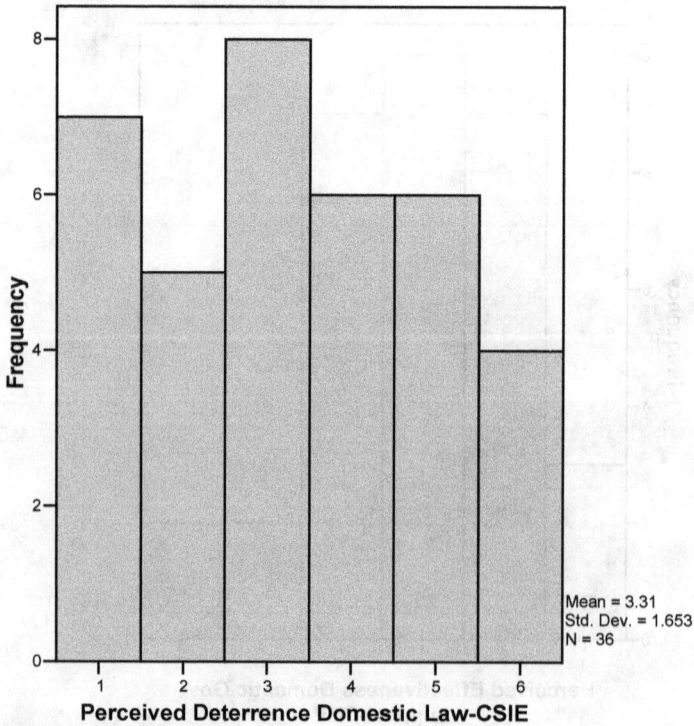

Perceived Deterrence Domestic Law-CSIE

Mean = 3.31
Std. Dev. = 1.653
N = 36

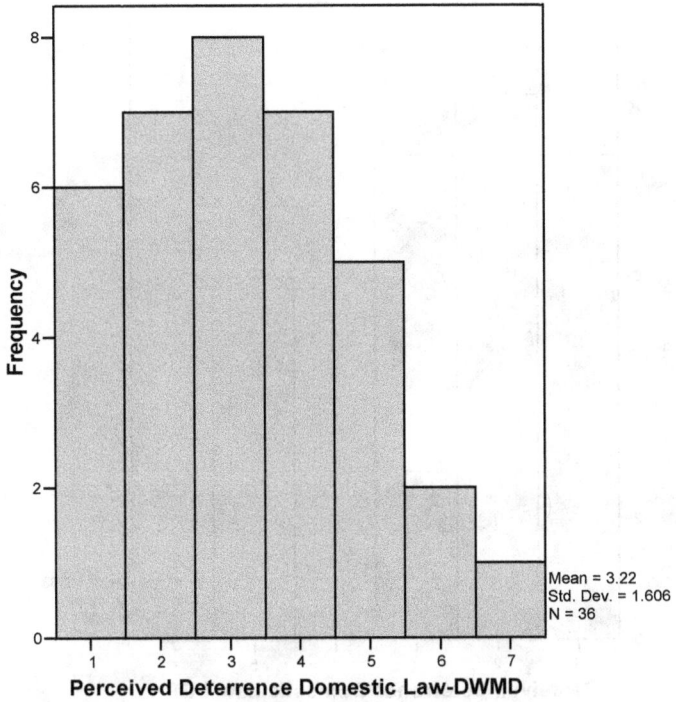

Mean = 3.22
Std. Dev. = 1.606
N = 36

Perceived Deterrence Domestic Law-DWMD

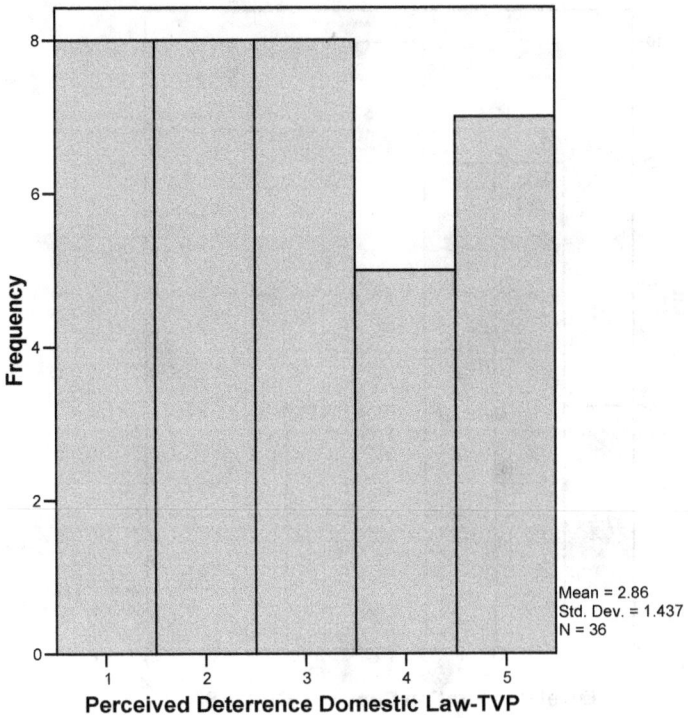

Mean = 2.86
Std. Dev. = 1.437
N = 36

Perceived Deterrence Domestic Law-TVP

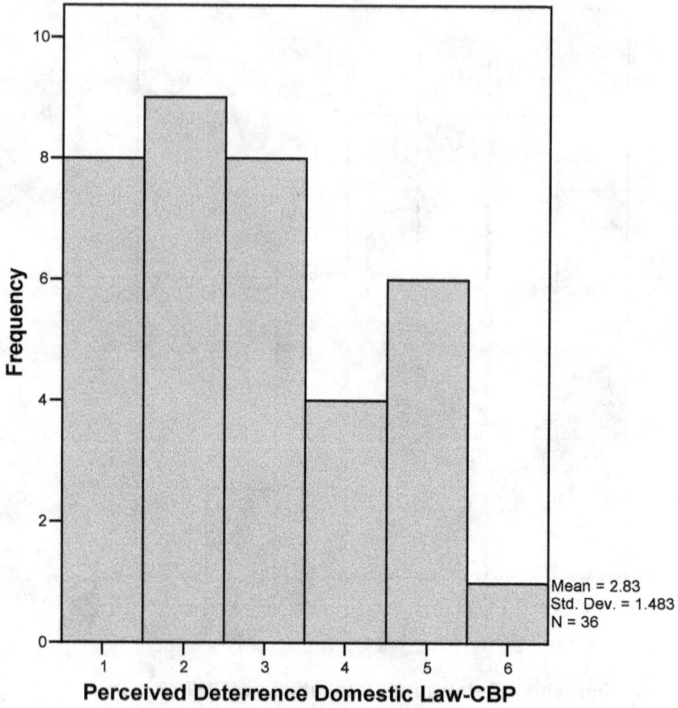

Mean = 2.83
Std. Dev. = 1.483
N = 36

Perceived Deterrence Domestic Law-CBP

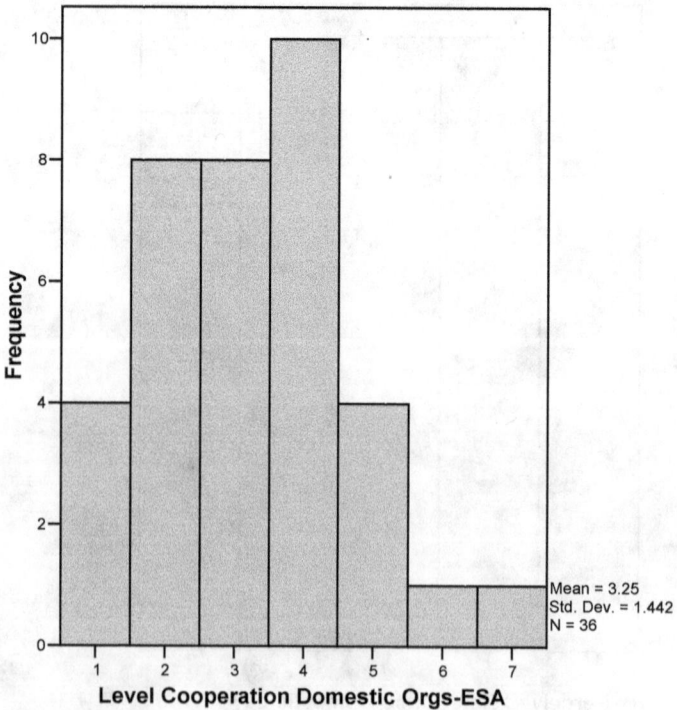

Mean = 3.25
Std. Dev. = 1.442
N = 36

Level Cooperation Domestic Orgs-ESA

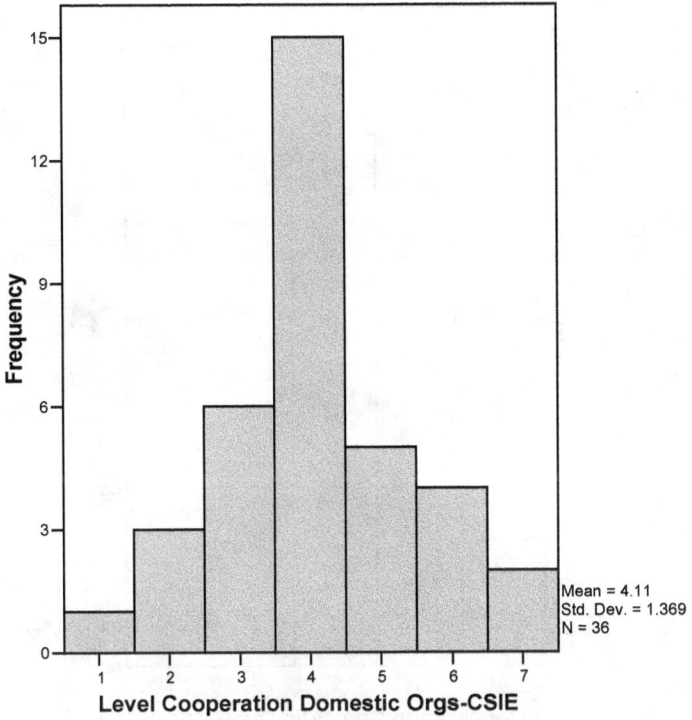

Mean = 4.11
Std. Dev. = 1.369
N = 36

Level Cooperation Domestic Orgs-CSIE

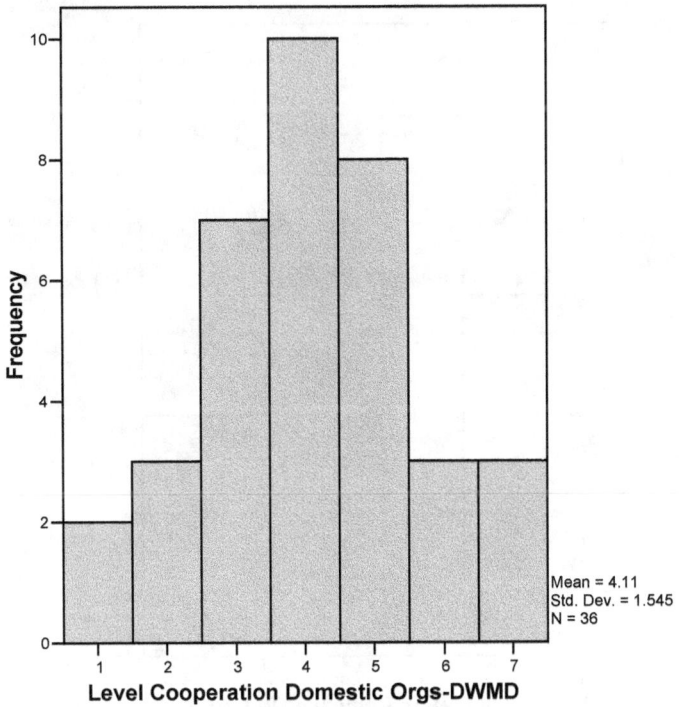

Mean = 4.11
Std. Dev. = 1.545
N = 36

Level Cooperation Domestic Orgs-DWMD

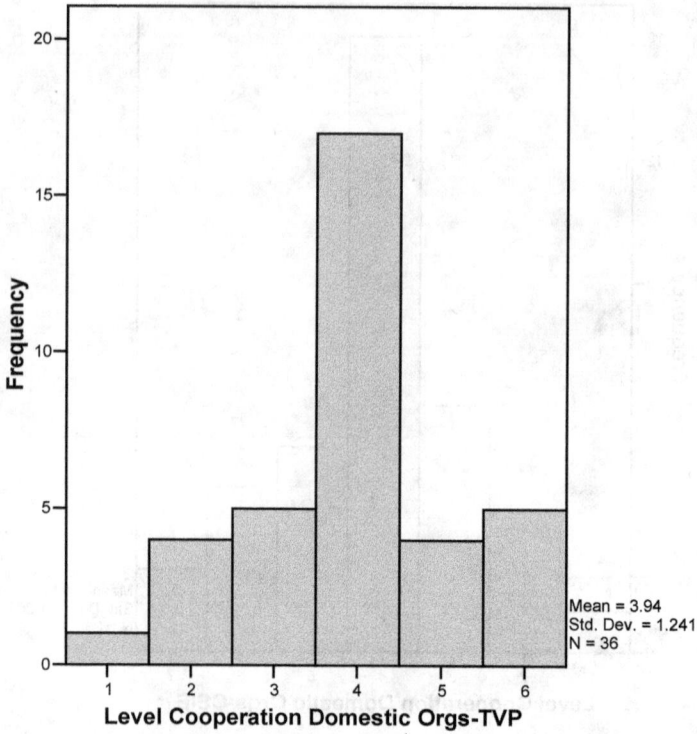

Mean = 3.94
Std. Dev. = 1.241
N = 36

Level Cooperation Domestic Orgs-TVP

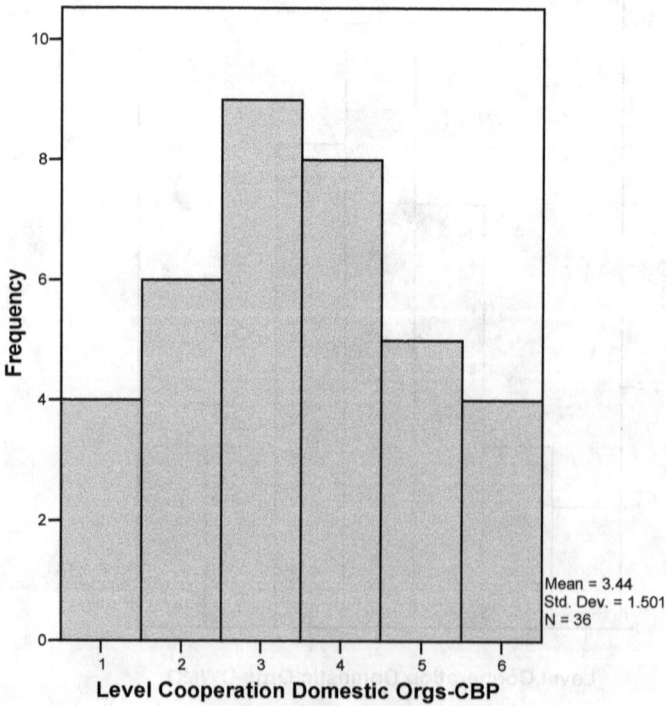

Mean = 3.44
Std. Dev. = 1.501
N = 36

Level Cooperation Domestic Orgs-CBP

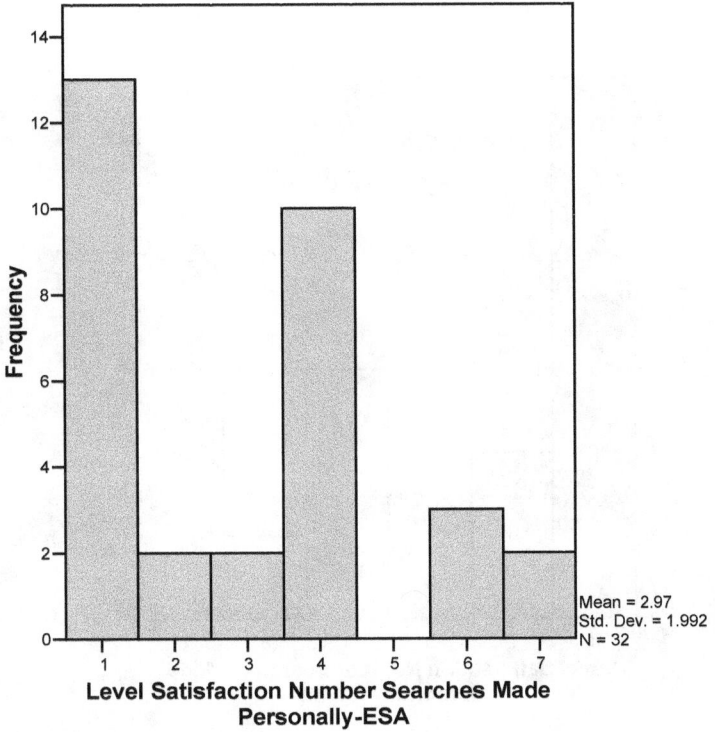

Mean = 2.97
Std. Dev. = 1.992
N = 32

**Level Satisfaction Number Searches Made
Personally-ESA**

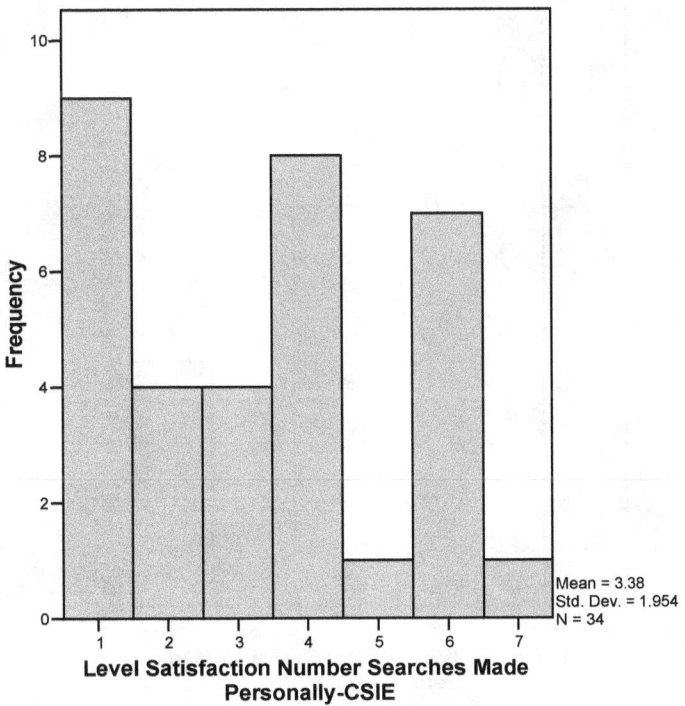

Mean = 3.38
Std. Dev. = 1.954
N = 34

**Level Satisfaction Number Searches Made
Personally-CSIE**

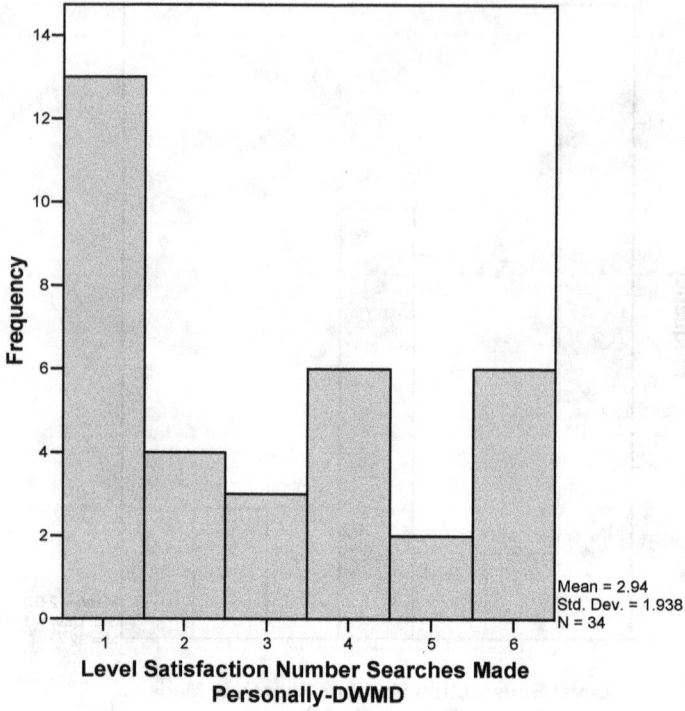

Mean = 2.94
Std. Dev. = 1.938
N = 34

**Level Satisfaction Number Searches Made
Personally-DWMD**

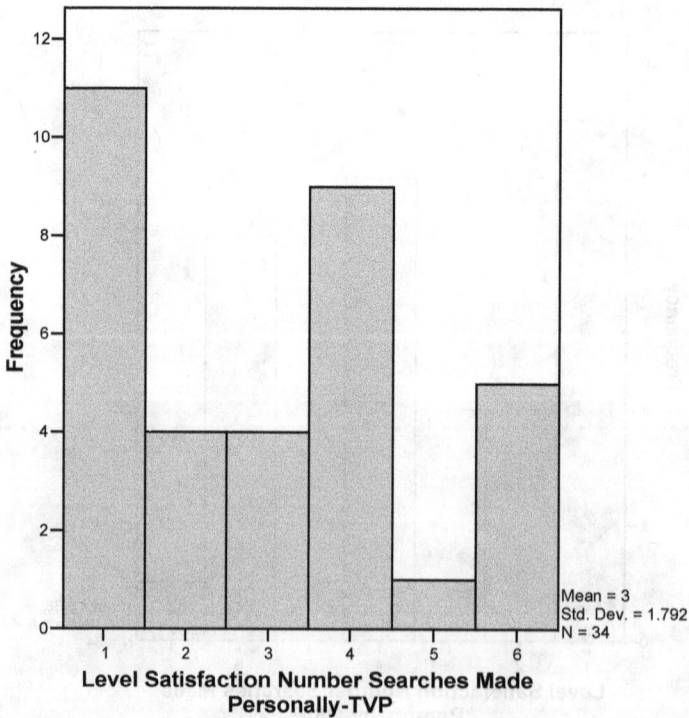

Mean = 3
Std. Dev. = 1.792
N = 34

**Level Satisfaction Number Searches Made
Personally-TVP**

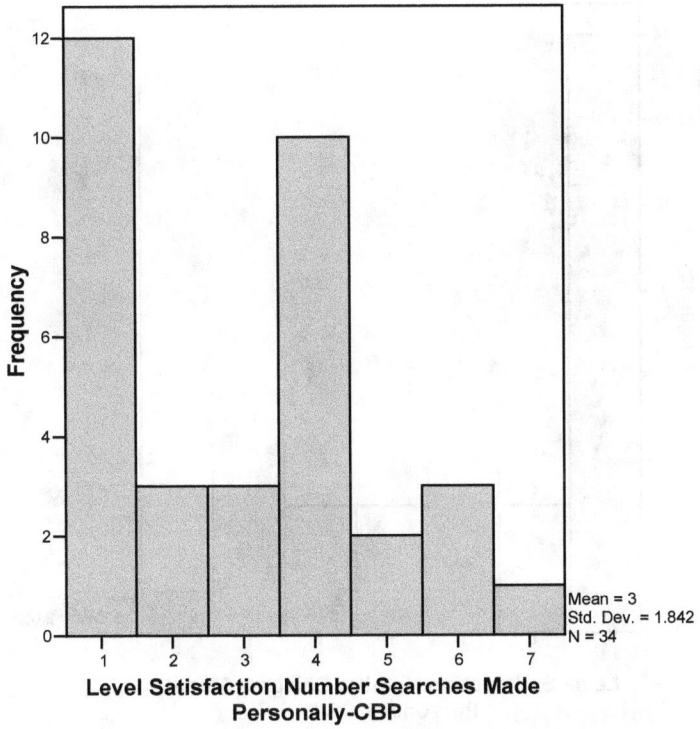

Level Satisfaction Number Searches Made
Personally-CBP

Mean = 3
Std. Dev. = 1.842
N = 34

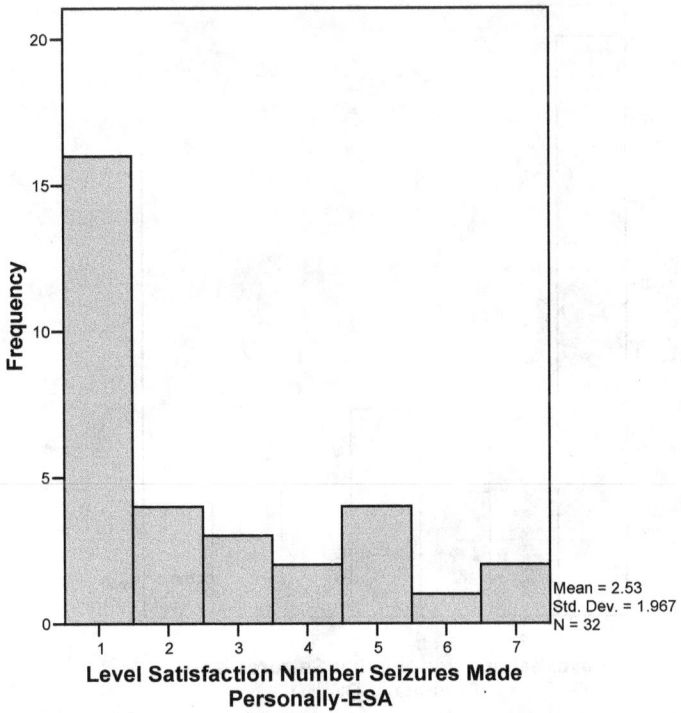

Level Satisfaction Number Seizures Made
Personally-ESA

Mean = 2.53
Std. Dev. = 1.967
N = 32

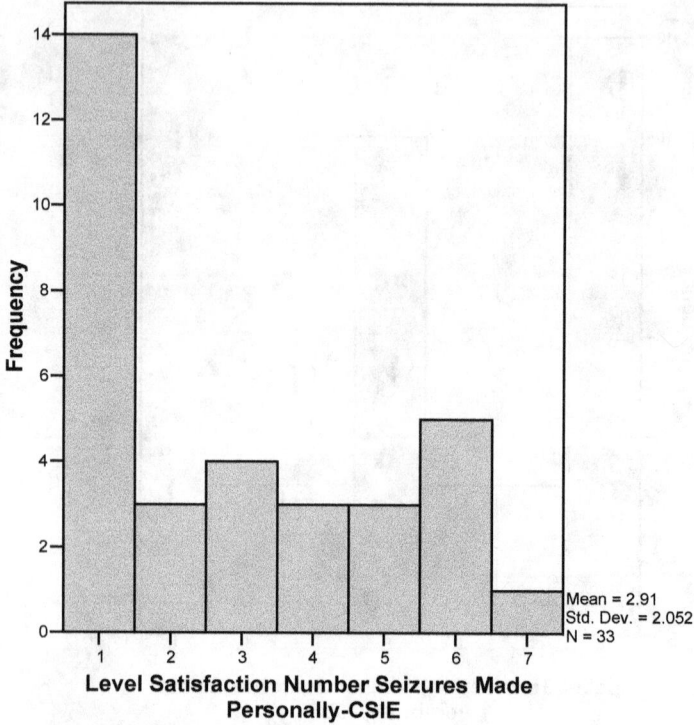

Mean = 2.91
Std. Dev. = 2.052
N = 33

**Level Satisfaction Number Seizures Made
Personally-CSIE**

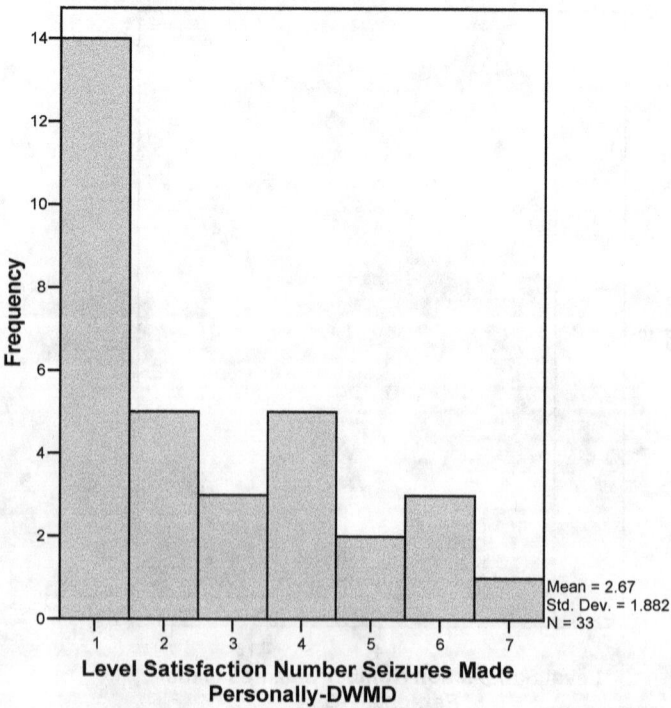

Mean = 2.67
Std. Dev. = 1.882
N = 33

**Level Satisfaction Number Seizures Made
Personally-DWMD**

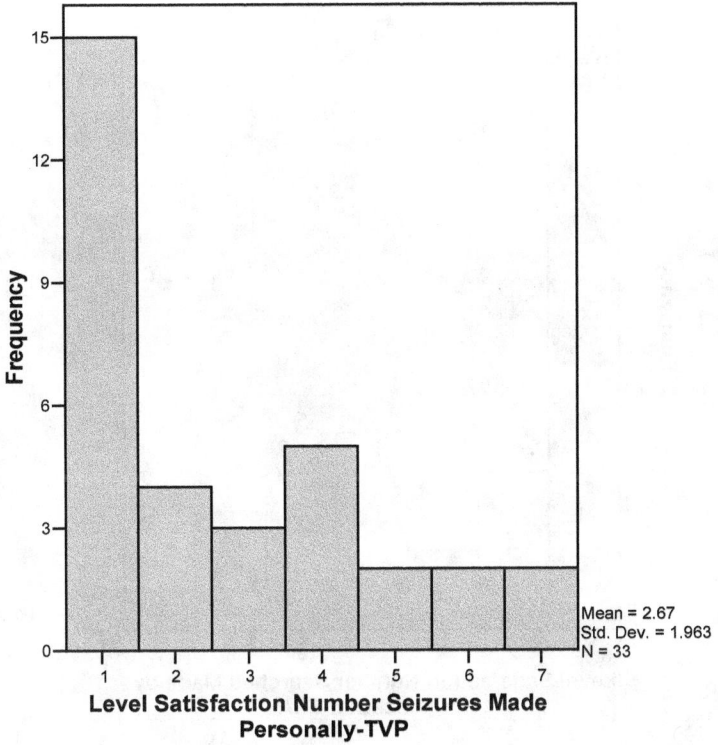

Mean = 2.67
Std. Dev. = 1.963
N = 33

**Level Satisfaction Number Seizures Made
Personally-TVP**

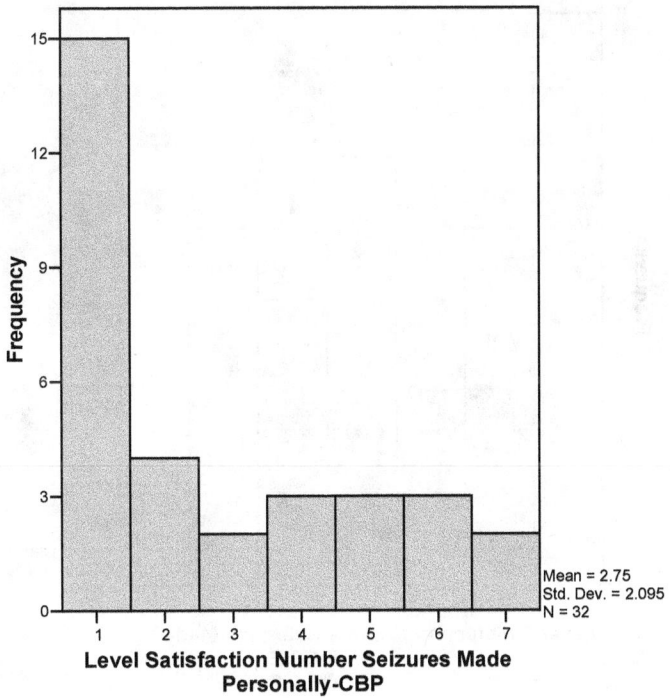

Mean = 2.75
Std. Dev. = 2.095
N = 32

**Level Satisfaction Number Seizures Made
Personally-CBP**

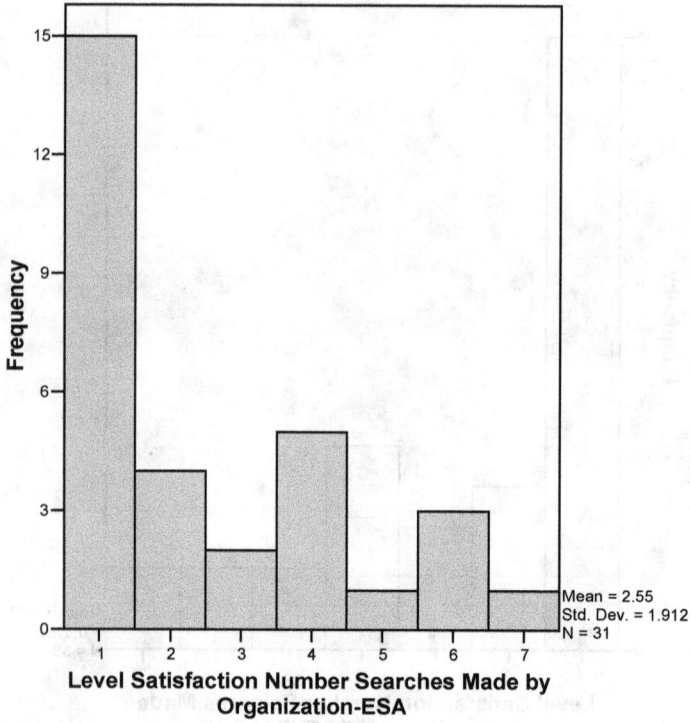

Mean = 2.55
Std. Dev. = 1.912
N = 31

Level Satisfaction Number Searches Made by Organization-ESA

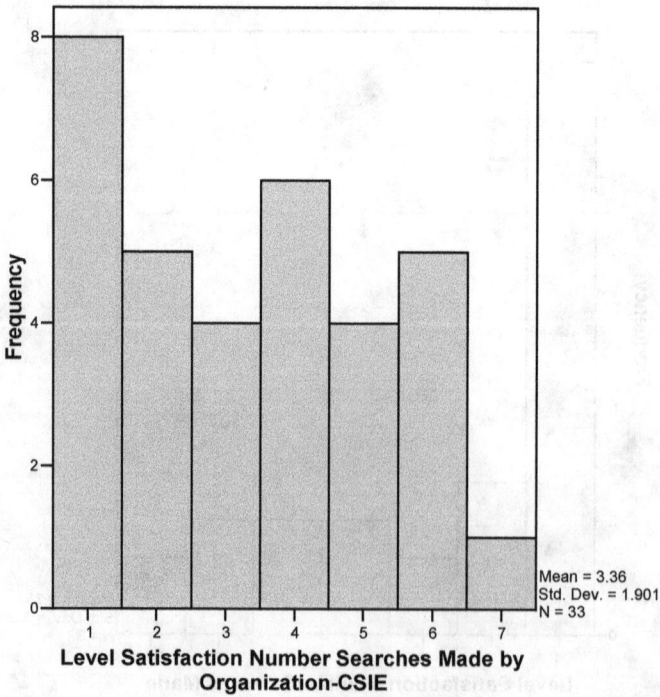

Mean = 3.36
Std. Dev. = 1.901
N = 33

Level Satisfaction Number Searches Made by Organization-CSIE

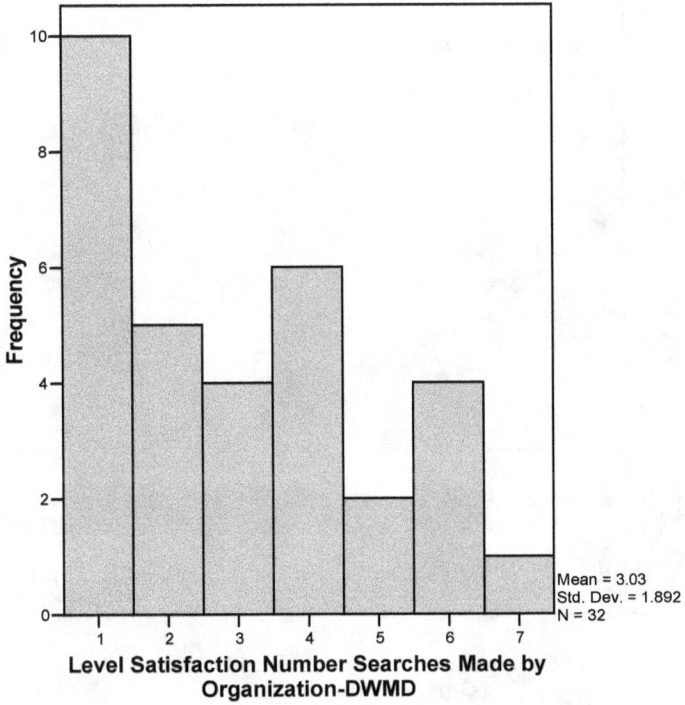

Mean = 3.03
Std. Dev. = 1.892
N = 32

Level Satisfaction Number Searches Made by Organization-DWMD

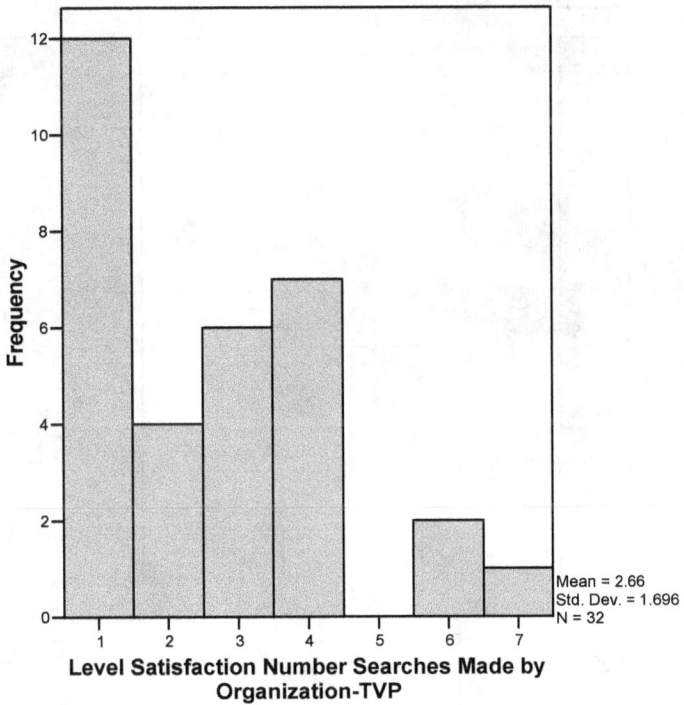

Mean = 2.66
Std. Dev. = 1.696
N = 32

Level Satisfaction Number Searches Made by Organization-TVP

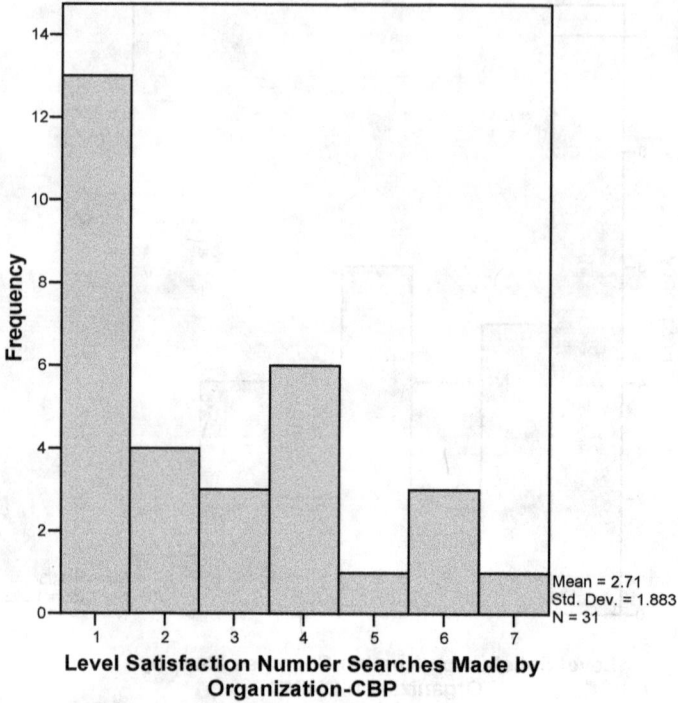

Mean = 2.71
Std. Dev. = 1.883
N = 31

Level Satisfaction Number Searches Made by Organization-CBP

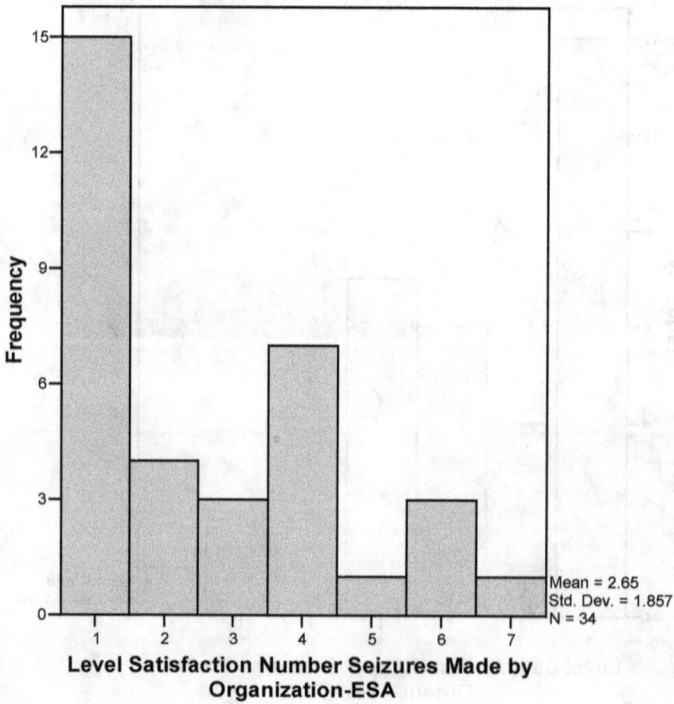

Mean = 2.65
Std. Dev. = 1.857
N = 34

Level Satisfaction Number Seizures Made by Organization-ESA

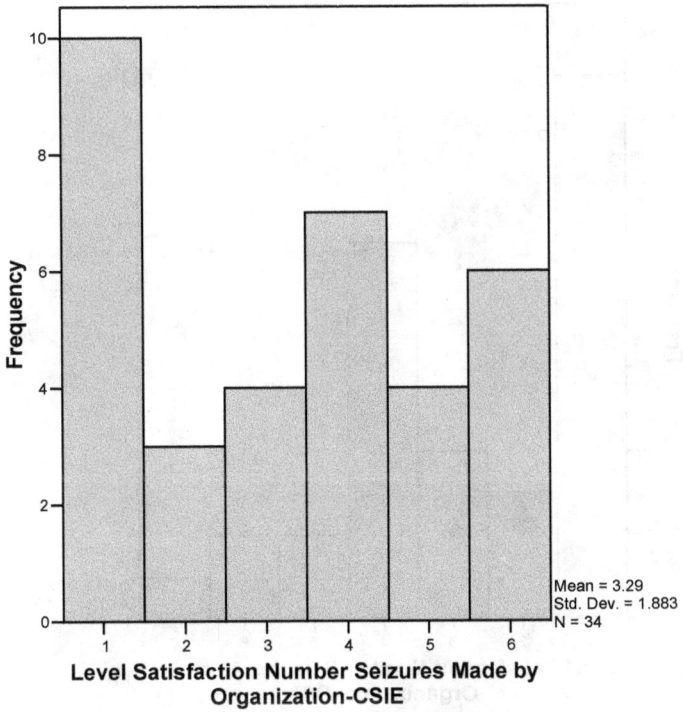

Level Satisfaction Number Seizures Made by
Organization-CSIE

Mean = 3.29
Std. Dev. = 1.883
N = 34

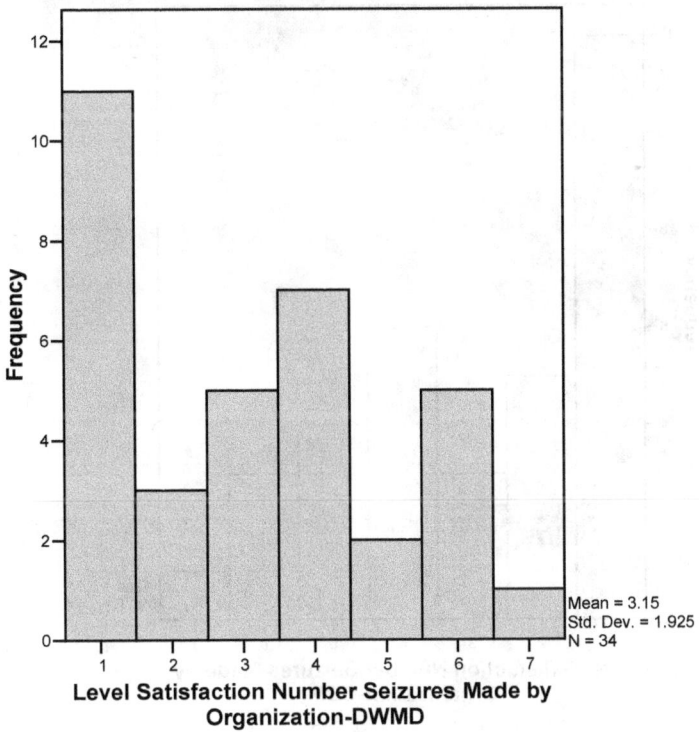

Level Satisfaction Number Seizures Made by
Organization-DWMD

Mean = 3.15
Std. Dev. = 1.925
N = 34

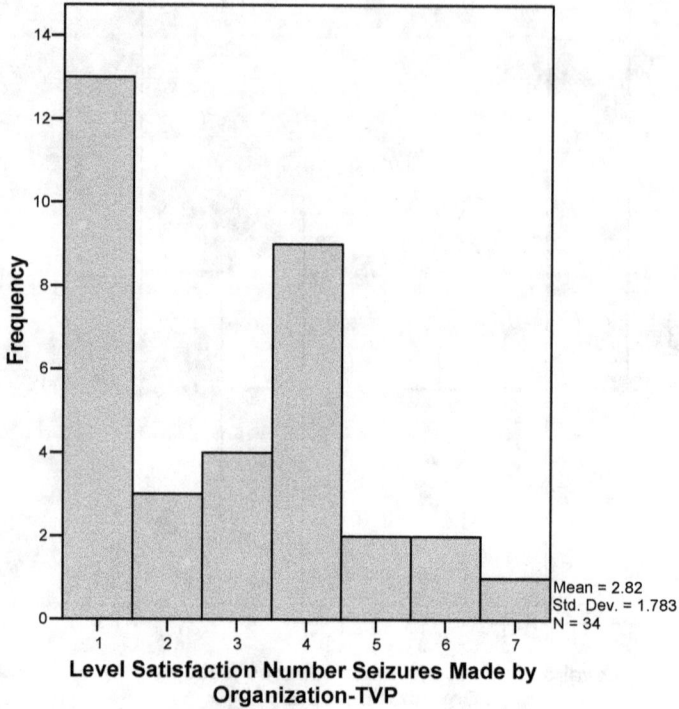

Mean = 2.82
Std. Dev. = 1.783
N = 34

Level Satisfaction Number Seizures Made by Organization-TVP

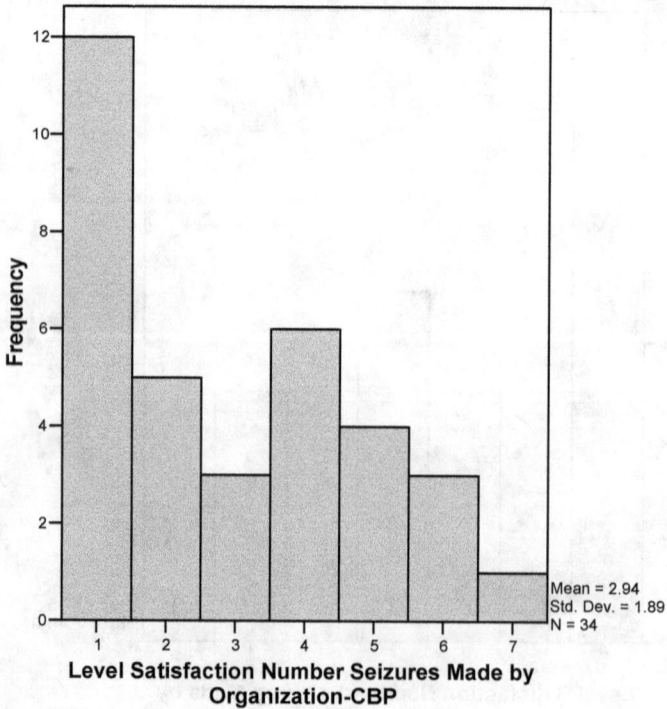

Mean = 2.94
Std. Dev. = 1.89
N = 34

Level Satisfaction Number Seizures Made by Organization-CBP

Appendix 4: Histograms – International Law

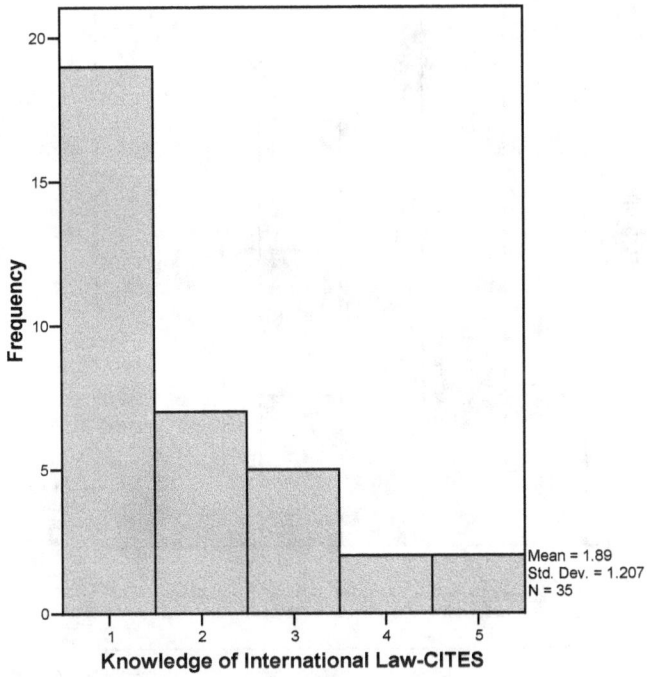

Mean = 1.89
Std. Dev. = 1.207
N = 35

Knowledge of International Law-CITES

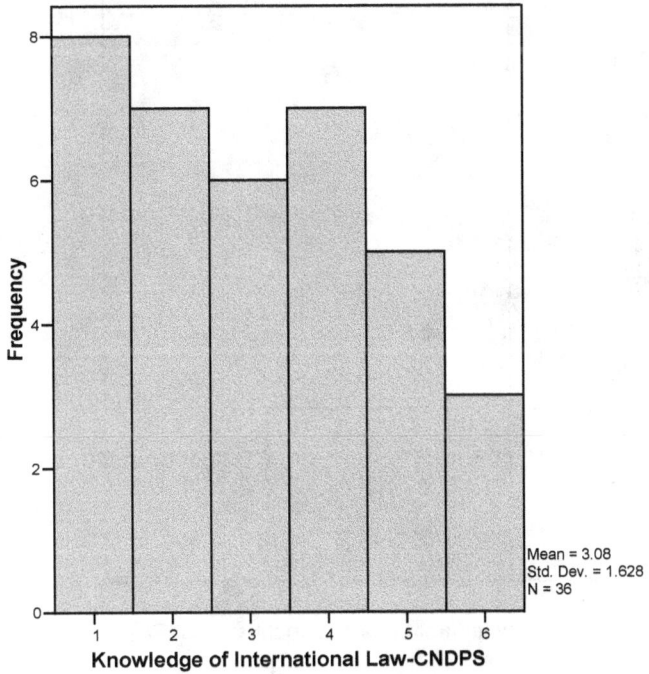

Mean = 3.08
Std. Dev. = 1.628
N = 36

Knowledge of International Law-CNDPS

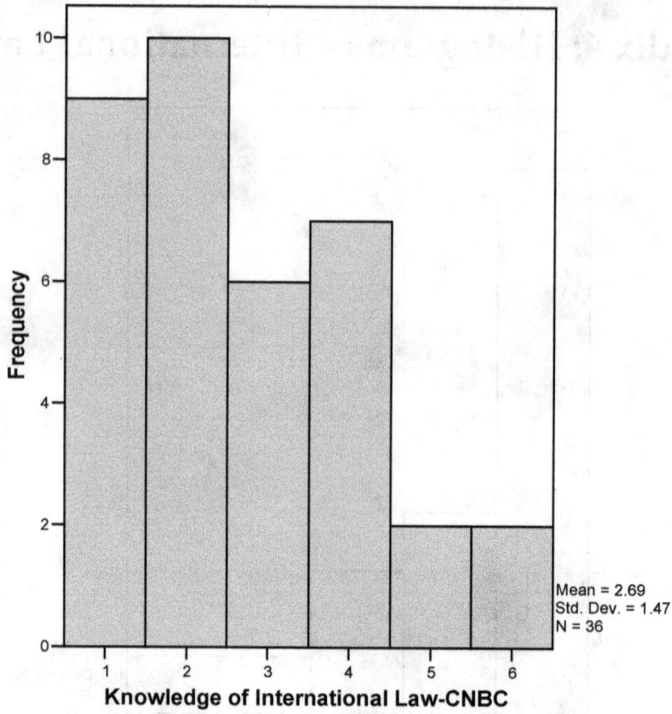

Mean = 2.69
Std. Dev. = 1.47
N = 36

Knowledge of International Law-CNBC

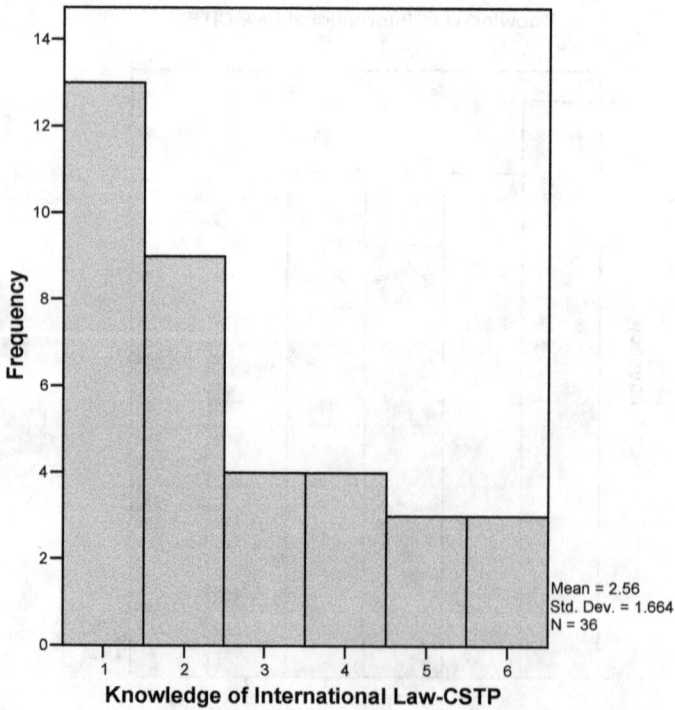

Mean = 2.56
Std. Dev. = 1.664
N = 36

Knowledge of International Law-CSTP

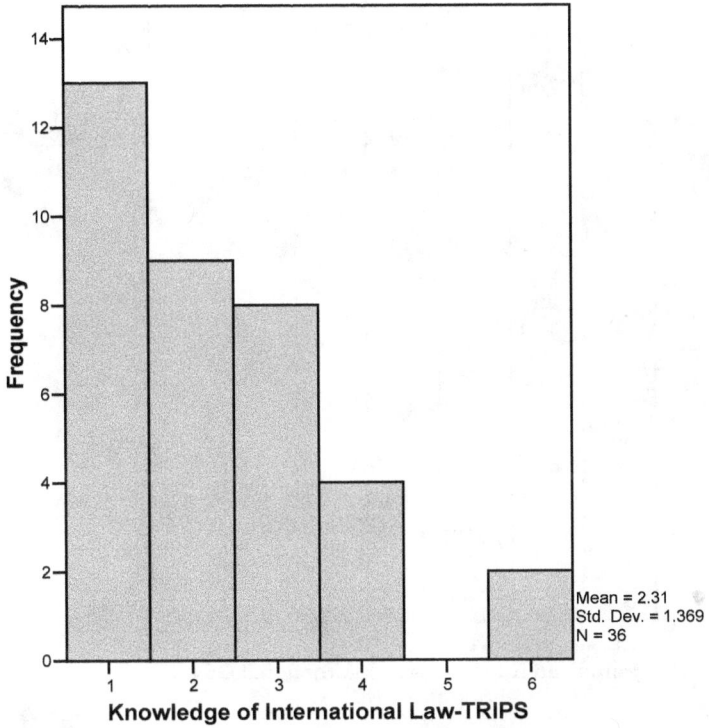

Mean = 2.31
Std. Dev. = 1.369
N = 36

Knowledge of International Law-TRIPS

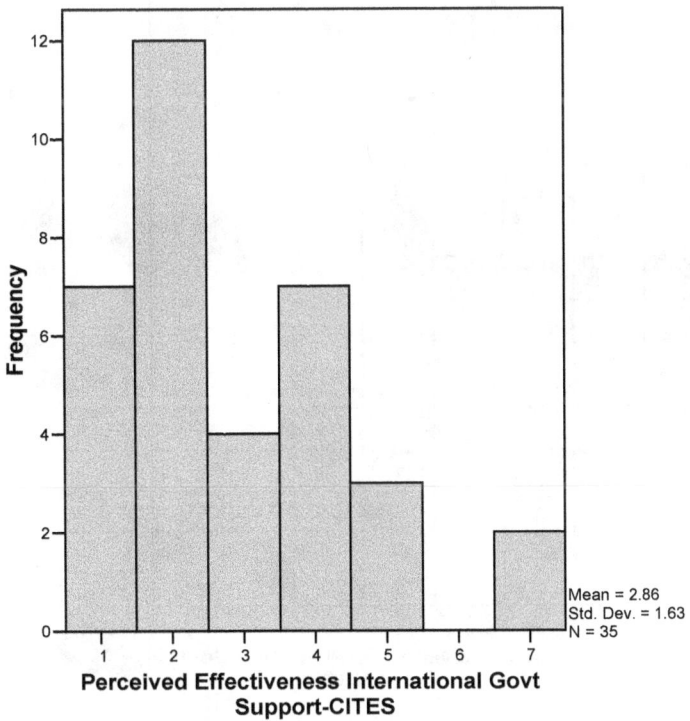

Mean = 2.86
Std. Dev. = 1.63
N = 35

Perceived Effectiveness International Govt Support-CITES

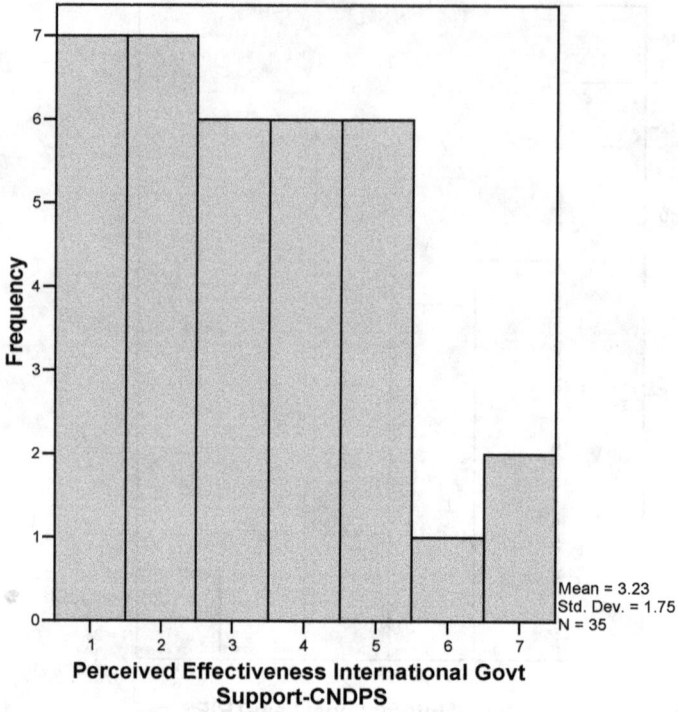

Mean = 3.23
Std. Dev. = 1.75
N = 35

Perceived Effectiveness International Govt Support-CNDPS

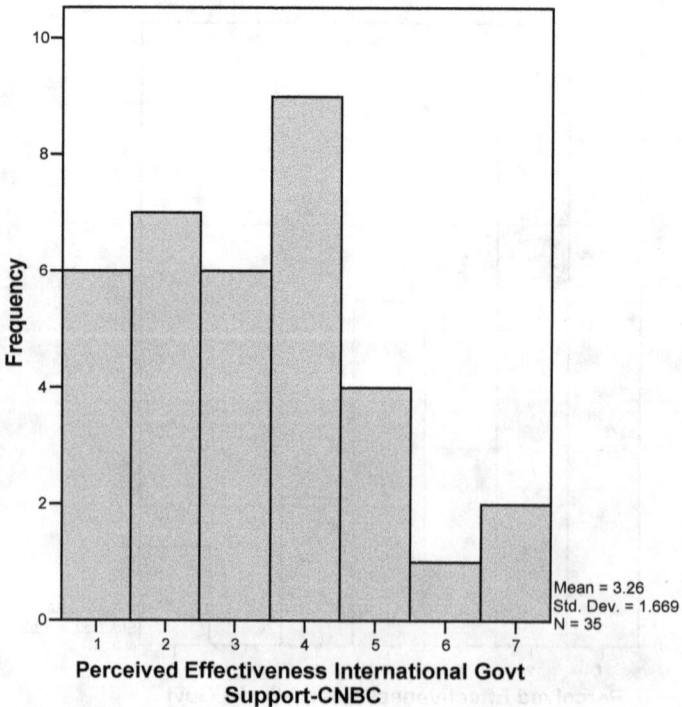

Mean = 3.26
Std. Dev. = 1.669
N = 35

Perceived Effectiveness International Govt Support-CNBC

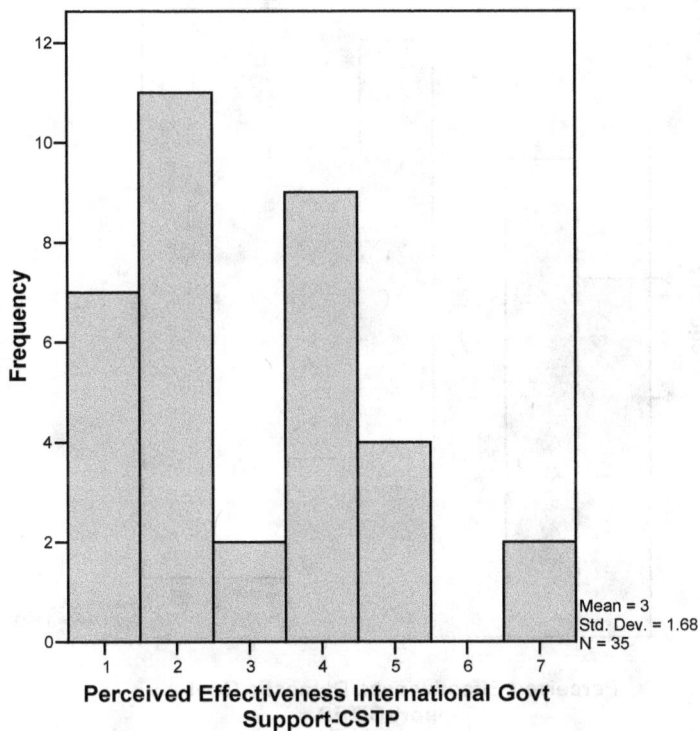

Mean = 3
Std. Dev. = 1.68
N = 35

Perceived Effectiveness International Govt Support-CSTP

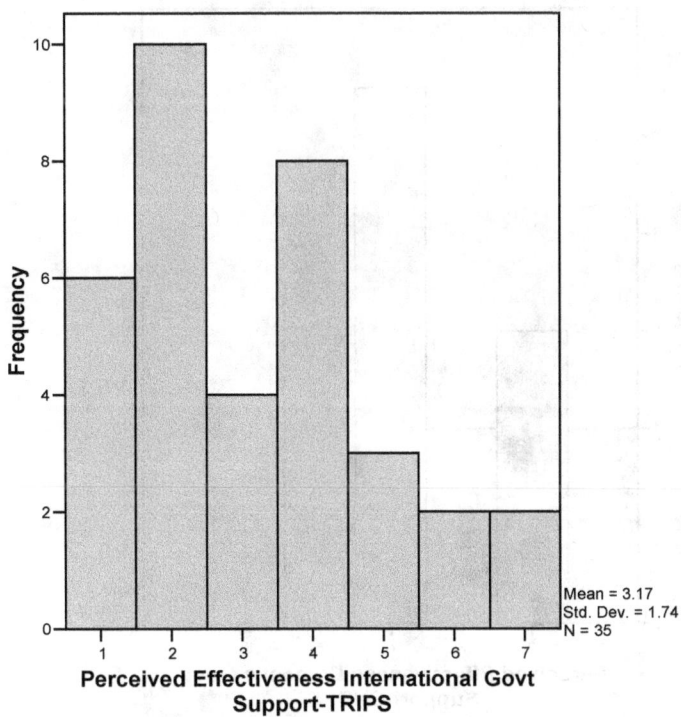

Mean = 3.17
Std. Dev. = 1.74
N = 35

Perceived Effectiveness International Govt Support-TRIPS

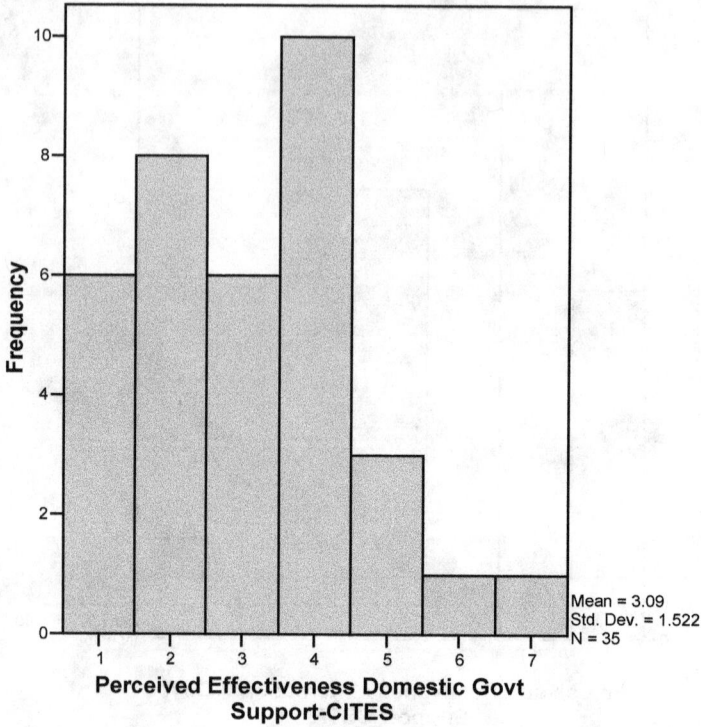

Mean = 3.09
Std. Dev. = 1.522
N = 35

Perceived Effectiveness Domestic Govt Support-CITES

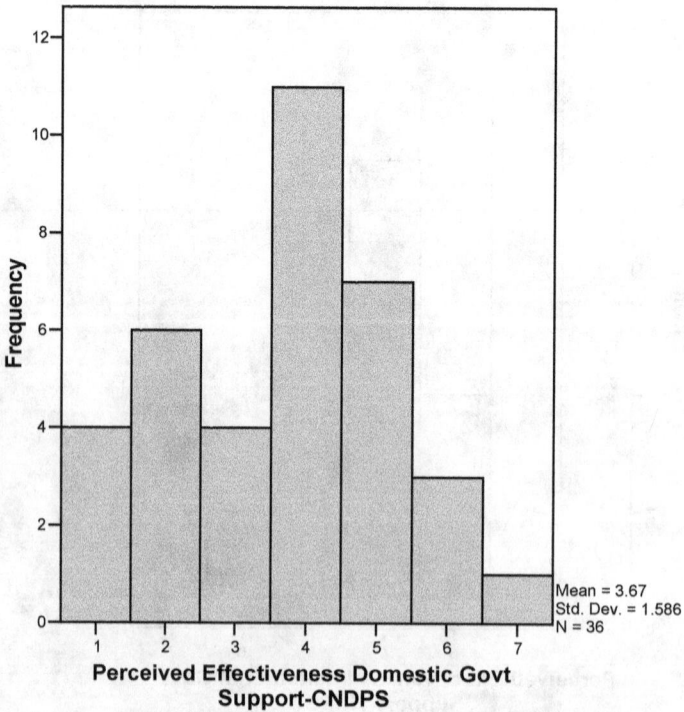

Mean = 3.67
Std. Dev. = 1.586
N = 36

Perceived Effectiveness Domestic Govt Support-CNDPS

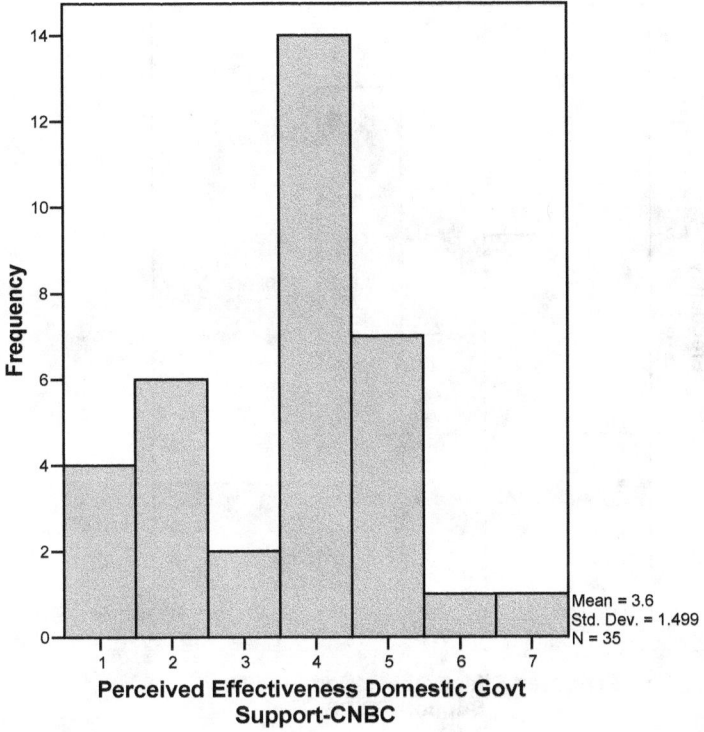

Perceived Effectiveness Domestic Govt Support-CNBC

Mean = 3.6
Std. Dev. = 1.499
N = 35

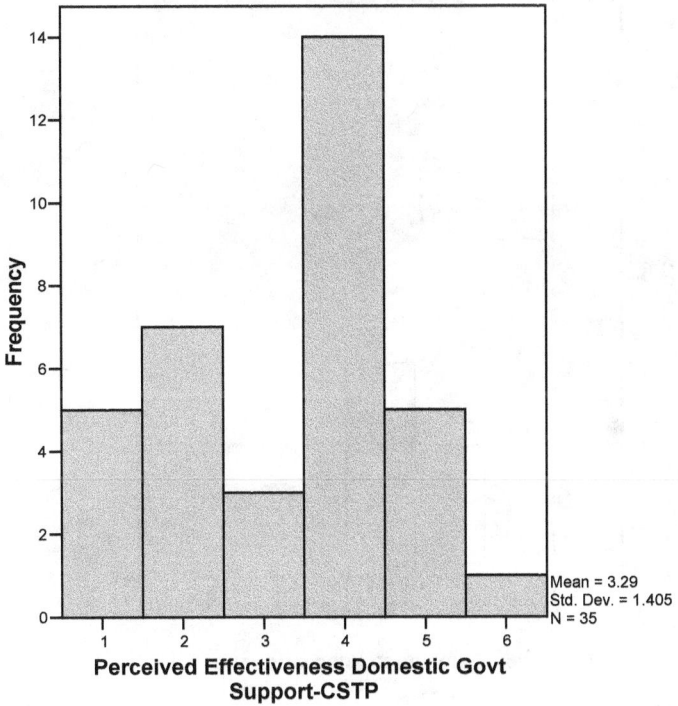

Perceived Effectiveness Domestic Govt Support-CSTP

Mean = 3.29
Std. Dev. = 1.405
N = 35

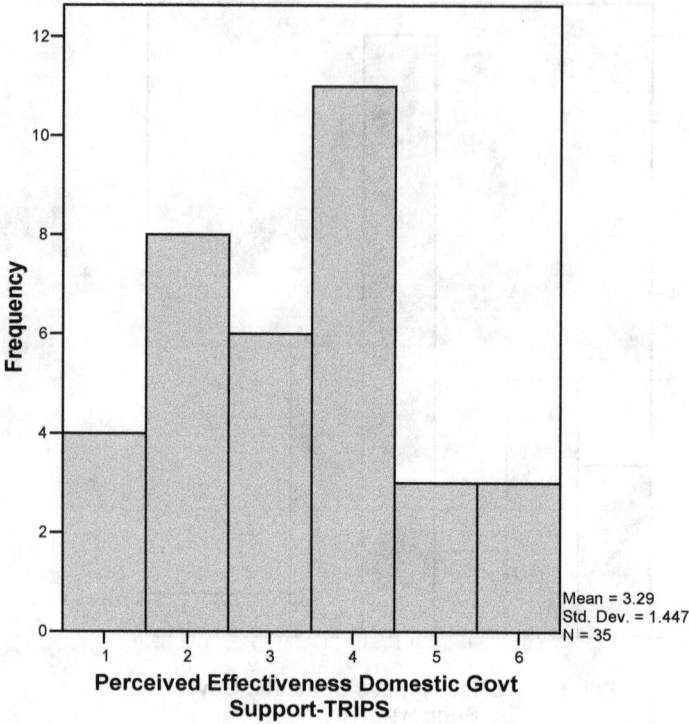

Mean = 3.29
Std. Dev. = 1.447
N = 35

Perceived Effectiveness Domestic Govt Support-TRIPS

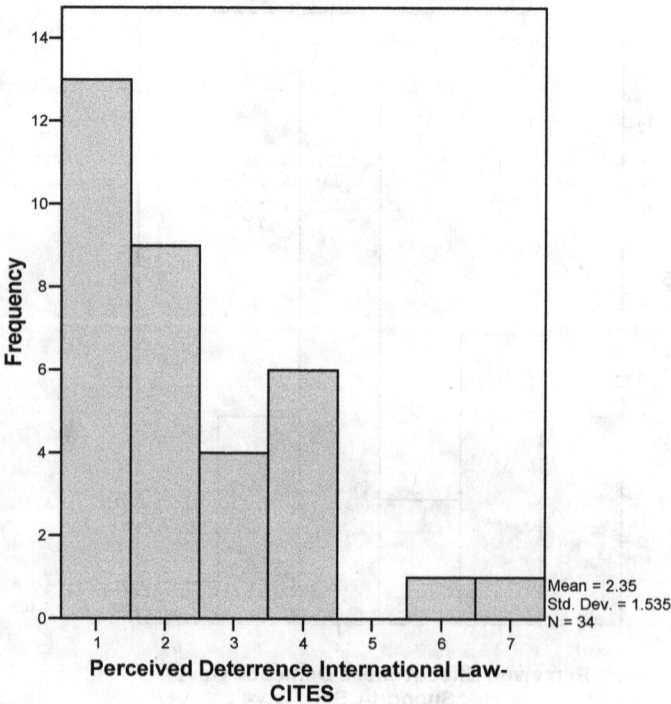

Mean = 2.35
Std. Dev. = 1.535
N = 34

Perceived Deterrence International Law-CITES

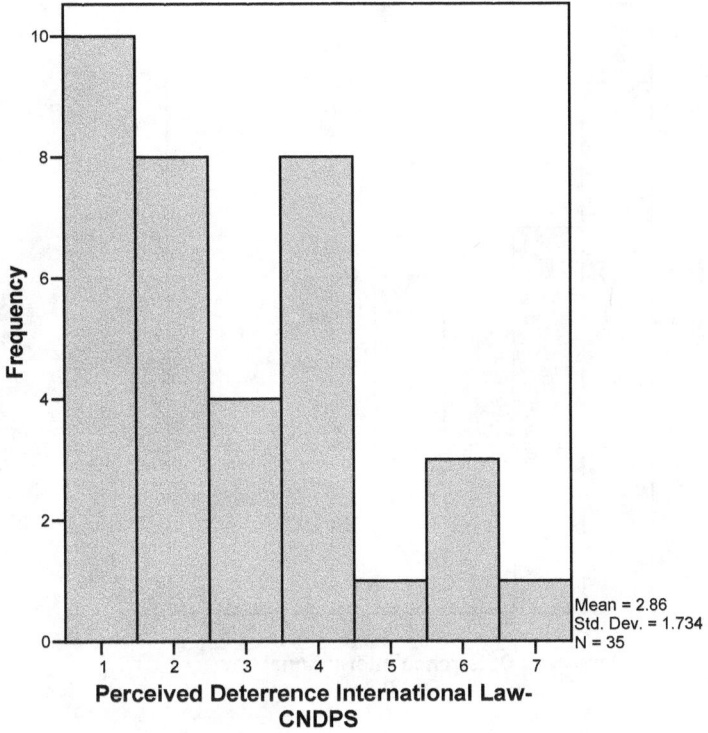

Mean = 2.86
Std. Dev. = 1.734
N = 35

Perceived Deterrence International Law-CNDPS

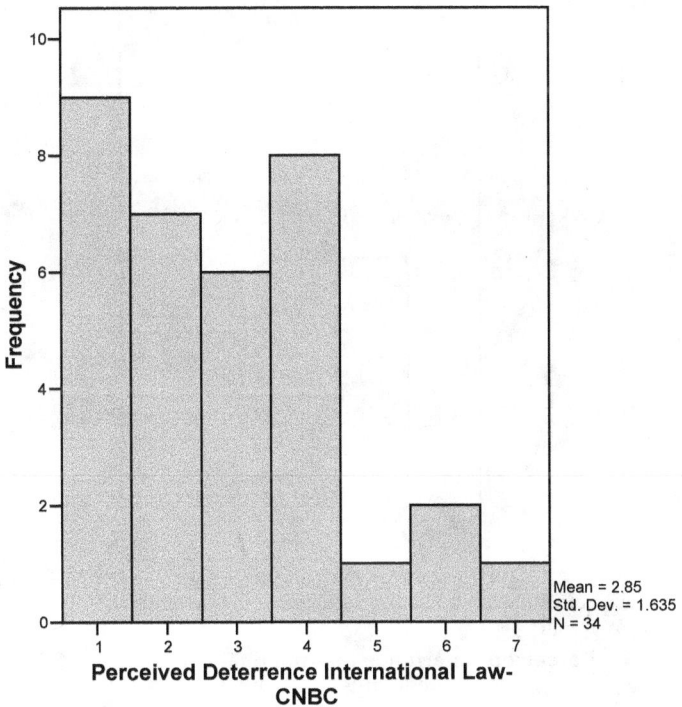

Mean = 2.85
Std. Dev. = 1.635
N = 34

Perceived Deterrence International Law-CNBC

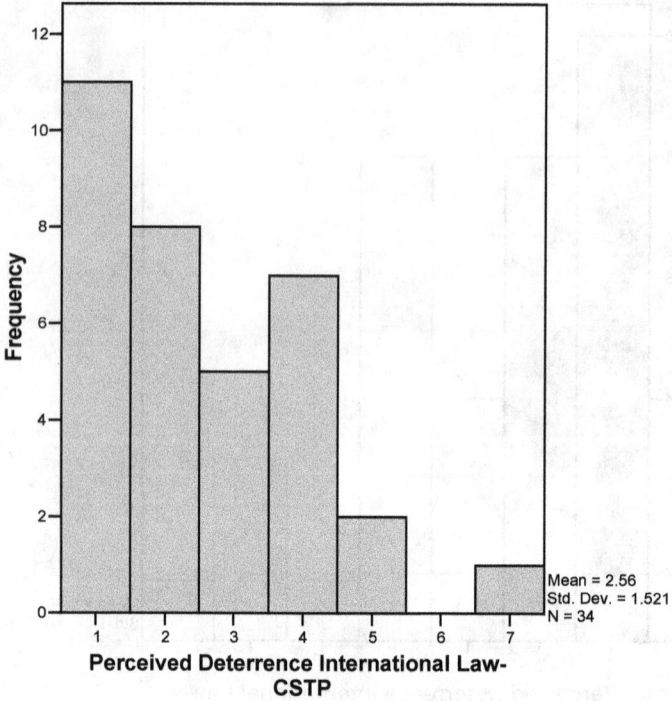

Mean = 2.56
Std. Dev. = 1.521
N = 34

Perceived Deterrence International Law-
CSTP

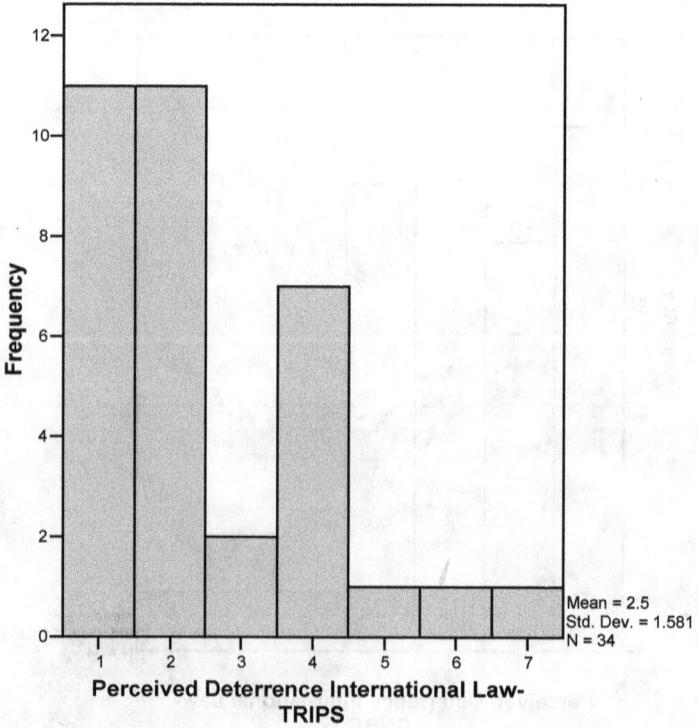

Mean = 2.5
Std. Dev. = 1.581
N = 34

Perceived Deterrence International Law-
TRIPS

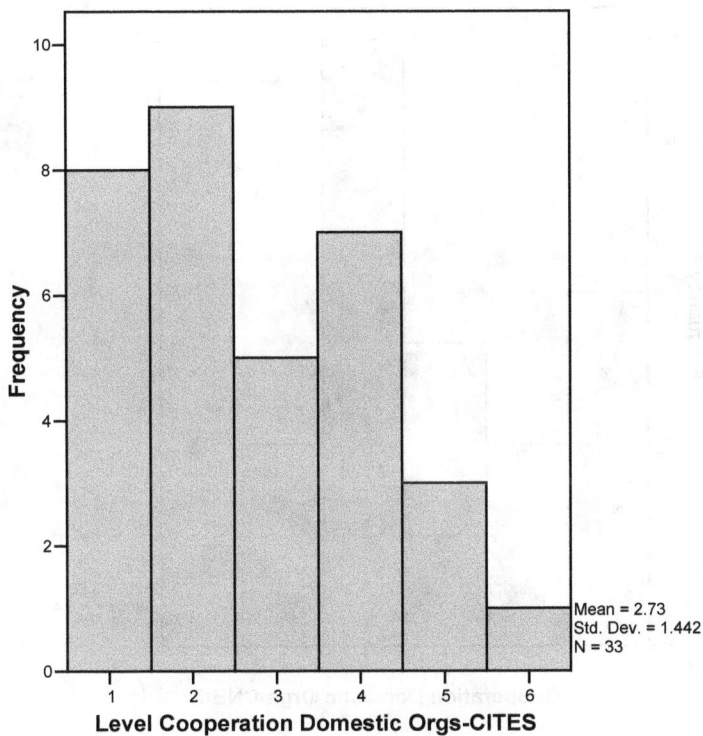

Mean = 2.73
Std. Dev. = 1.442
N = 33

Level Cooperation Domestic Orgs-CITES

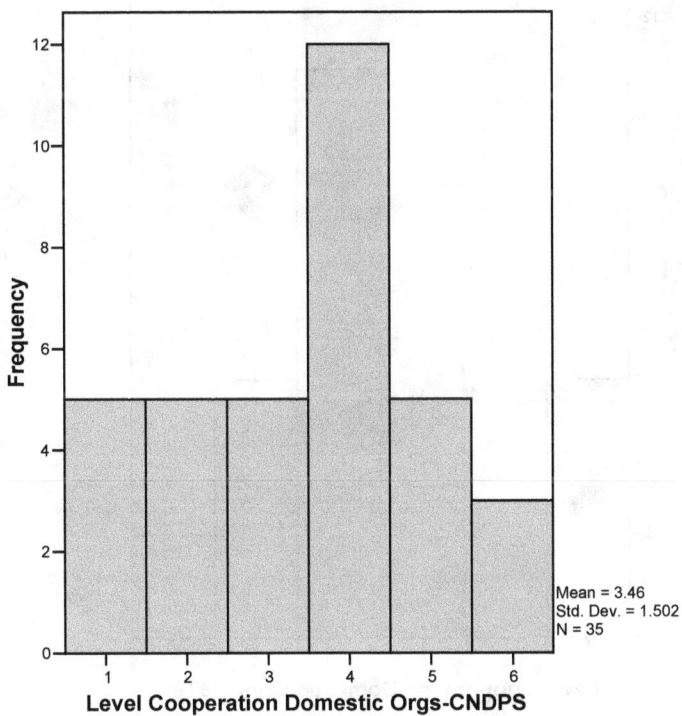

Mean = 3.46
Std. Dev. = 1.502
N = 35

Level Cooperation Domestic Orgs-CNDPS

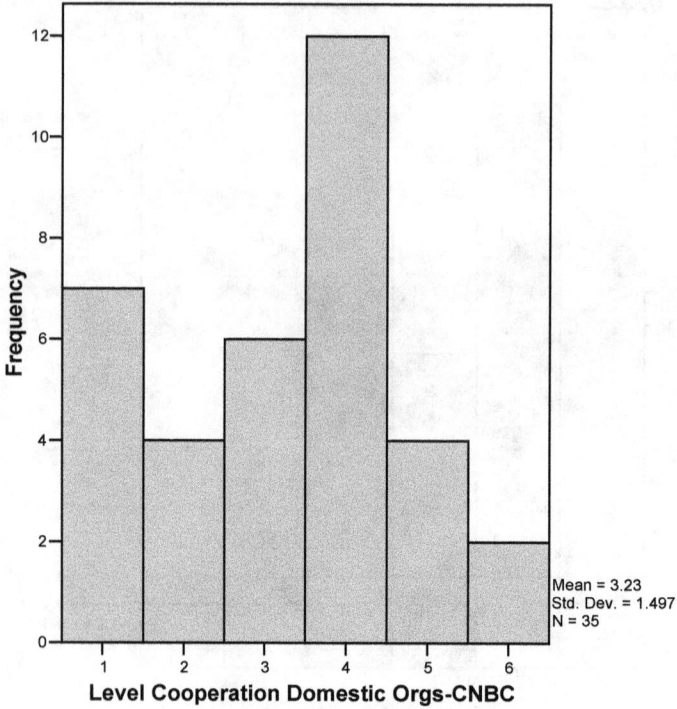

Mean = 3.23
Std. Dev. = 1.497
N = 35

Level Cooperation Domestic Orgs-CNBC

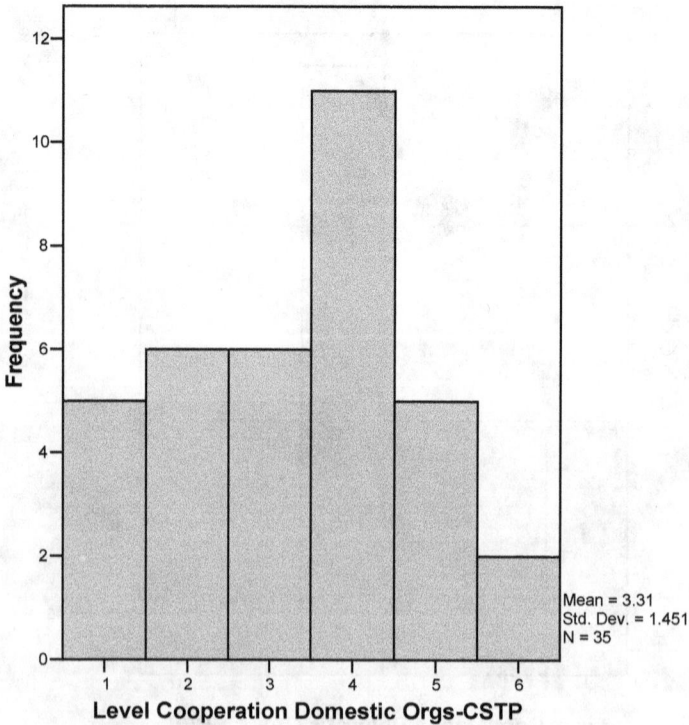

Mean = 3.31
Std. Dev. = 1.451
N = 35

Level Cooperation Domestic Orgs-CSTP

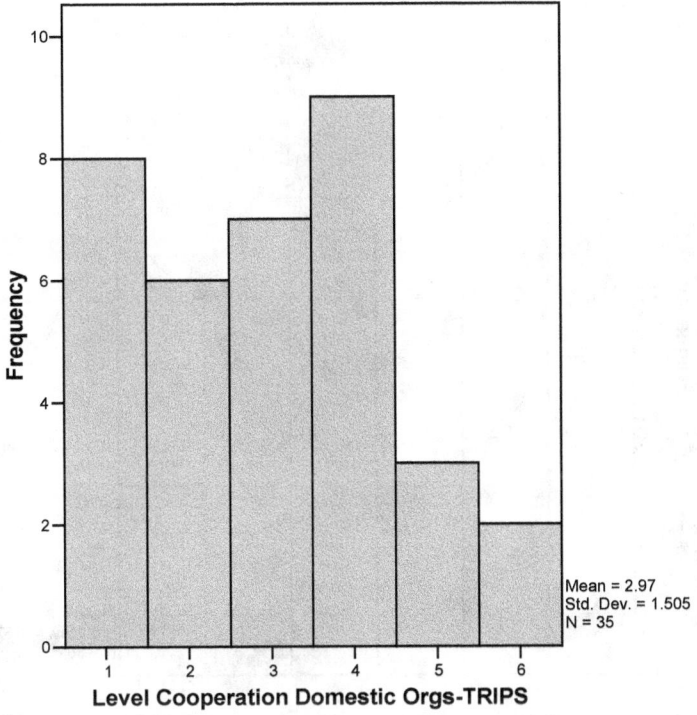

Mean = 2.97
Std. Dev. = 1.505
N = 35

Level Cooperation Domestic Orgs-TRIPS

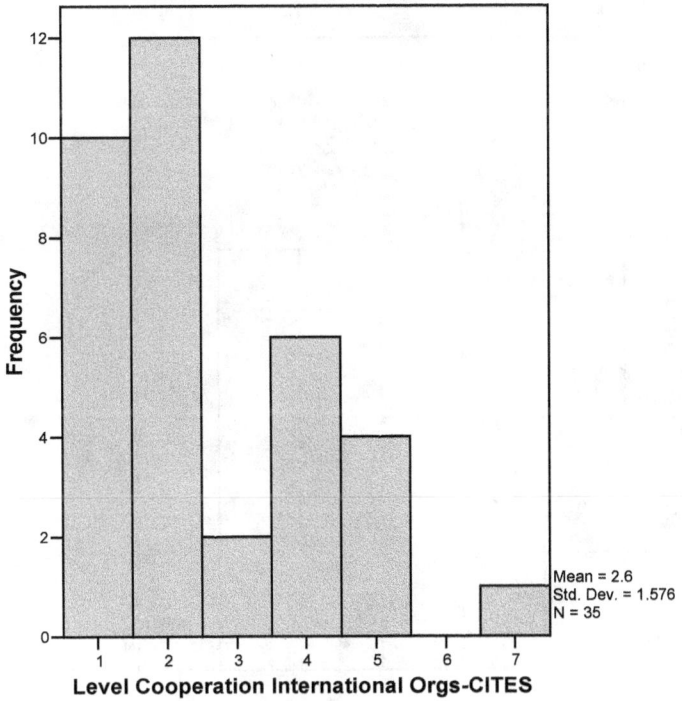

Mean = 2.6
Std. Dev. = 1.576
N = 35

Level Cooperation International Orgs-CITES

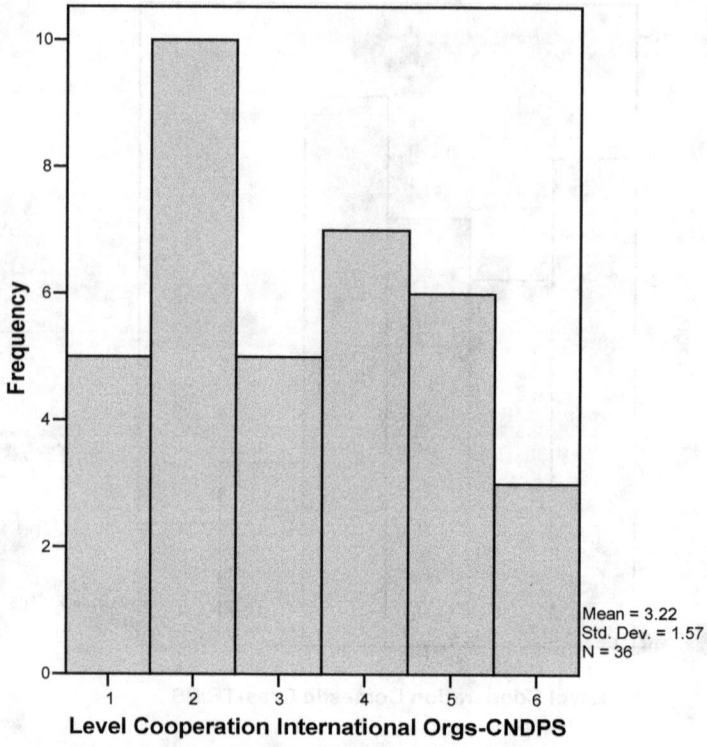

Mean = 3.22
Std. Dev. = 1.57
N = 36

Level Cooperation International Orgs-CNDPS

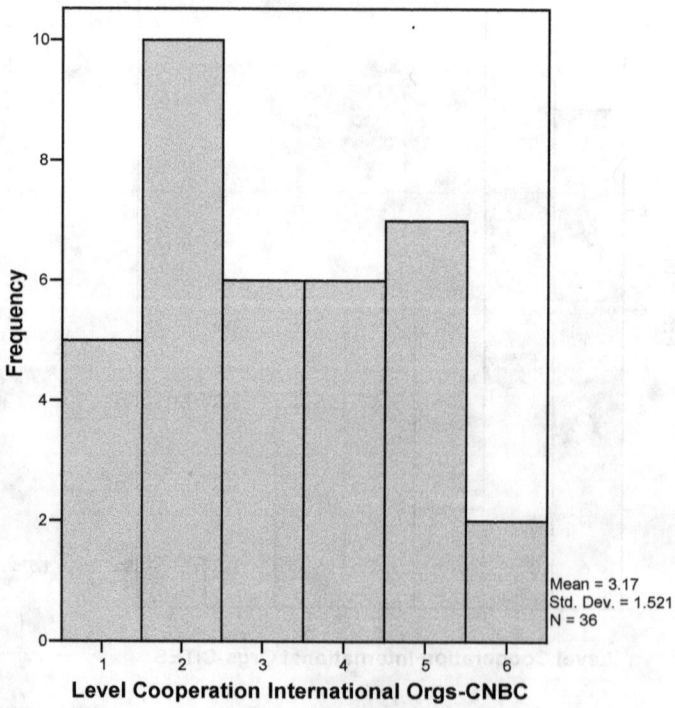

Mean = 3.17
Std. Dev. = 1.521
N = 36

Level Cooperation International Orgs-CNBC

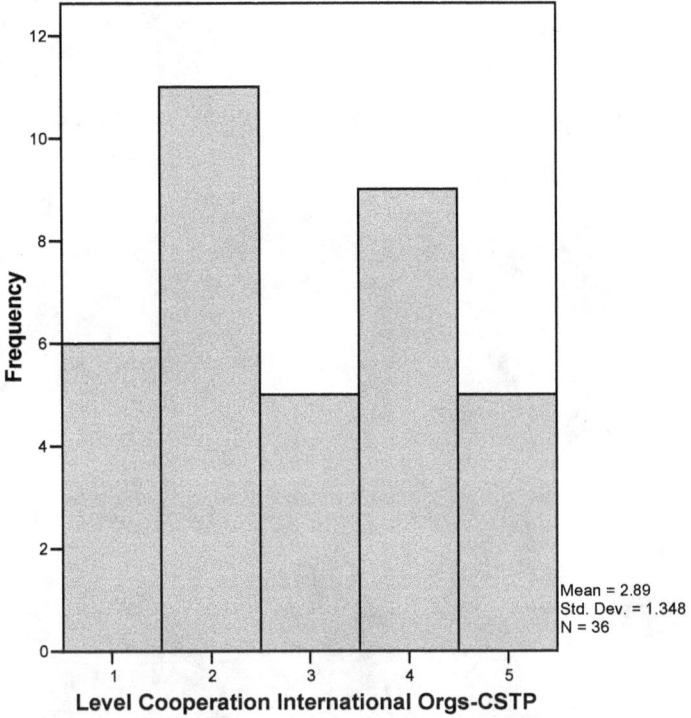

Mean = 2.89
Std. Dev. = 1.348
N = 36

Level Cooperation International Orgs-CSTP

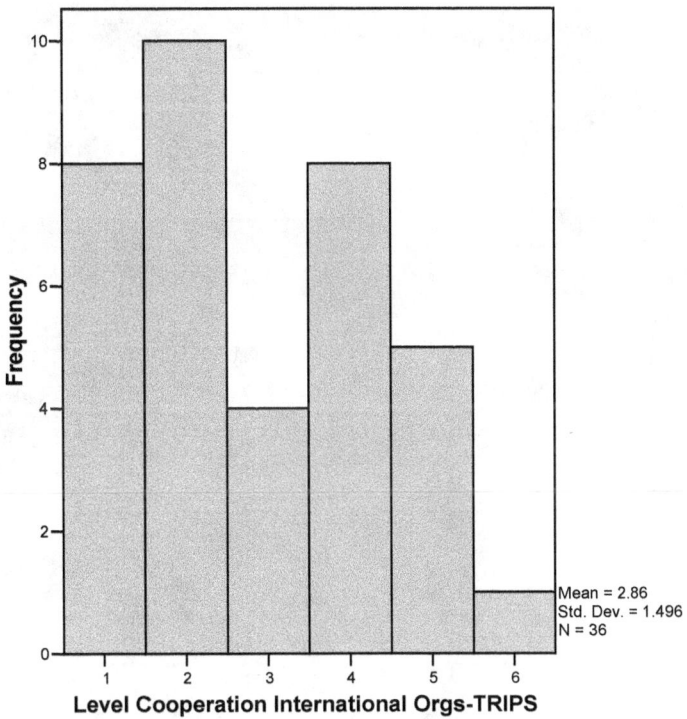

Mean = 2.86
Std. Dev. = 1.496
N = 36

Level Cooperation International Orgs-TRIPS

Appendix 5: Histograms – Demographics

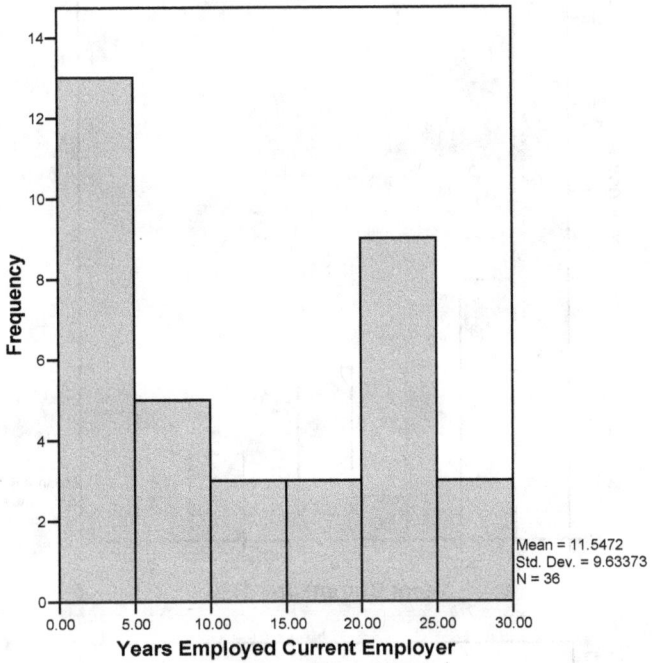

Mean = 11.5472
Std. Dev. = 9.63373
N = 36

Years Employed Current Employer

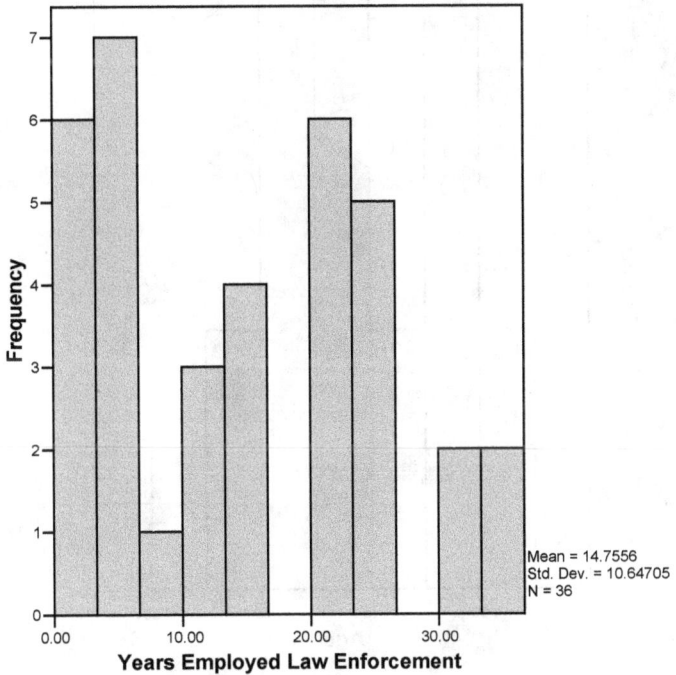

Mean = 14.7556
Std. Dev. = 10.64705
N = 36

Years Employed Law Enforcement

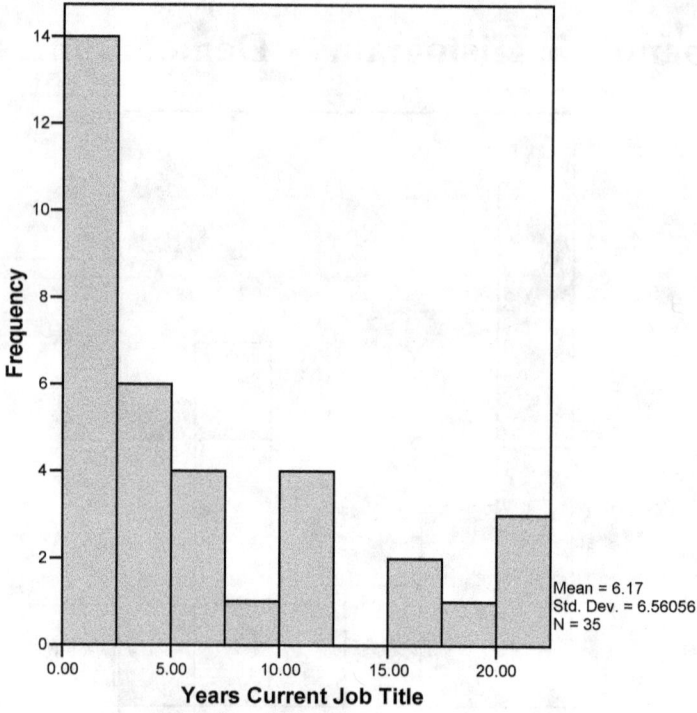

Mean = 6.17
Std. Dev. = 6.56056
N = 35

Years Current Job Title

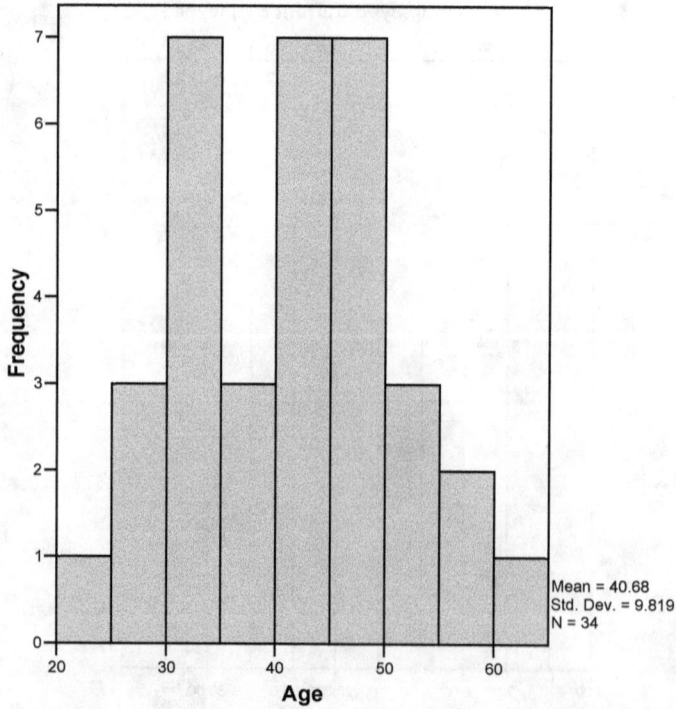

Mean = 40.68
Std. Dev. = 9.819
N = 34

Age

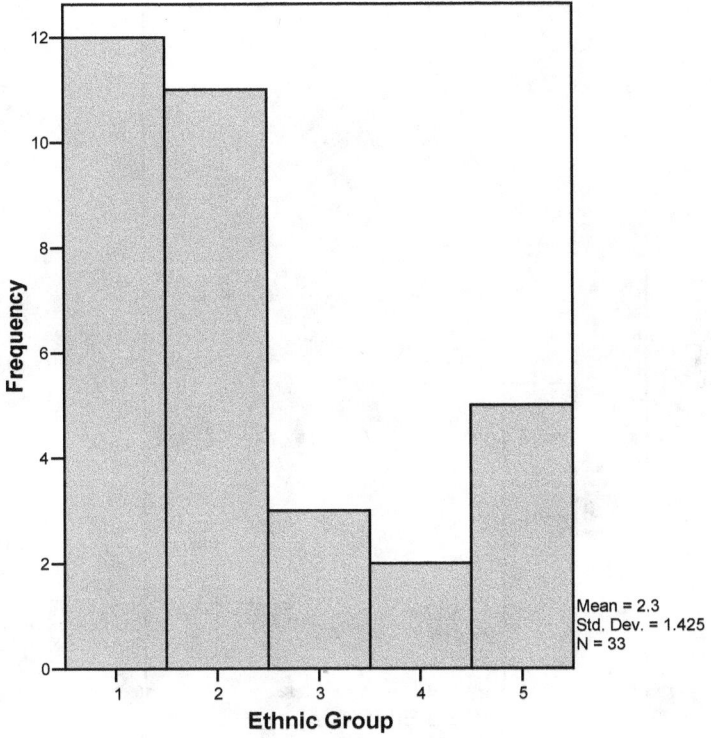

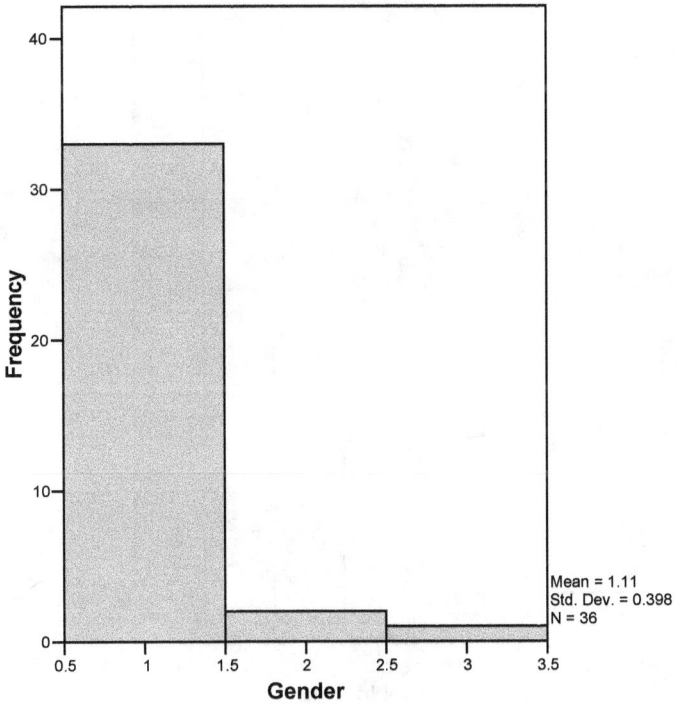

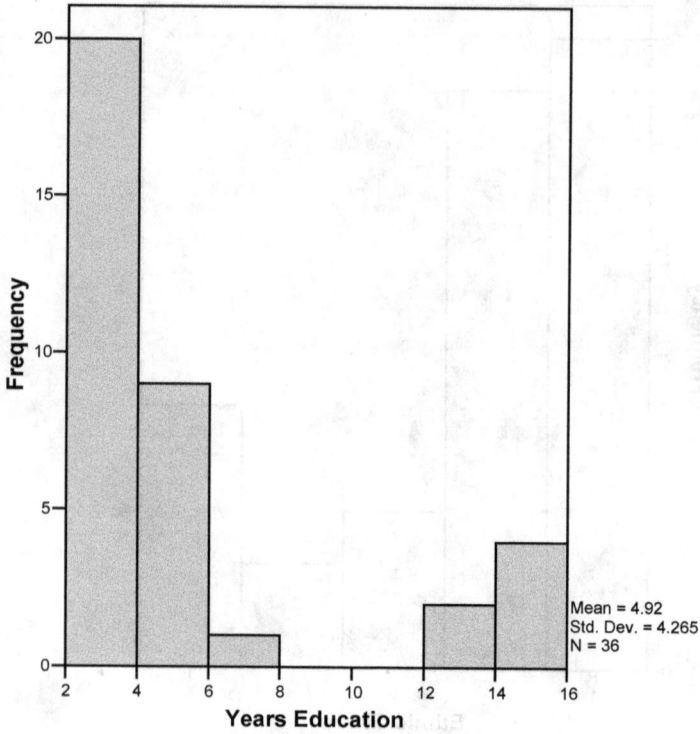

Mean = 4.92
Std. Dev. = 4.265
N = 36

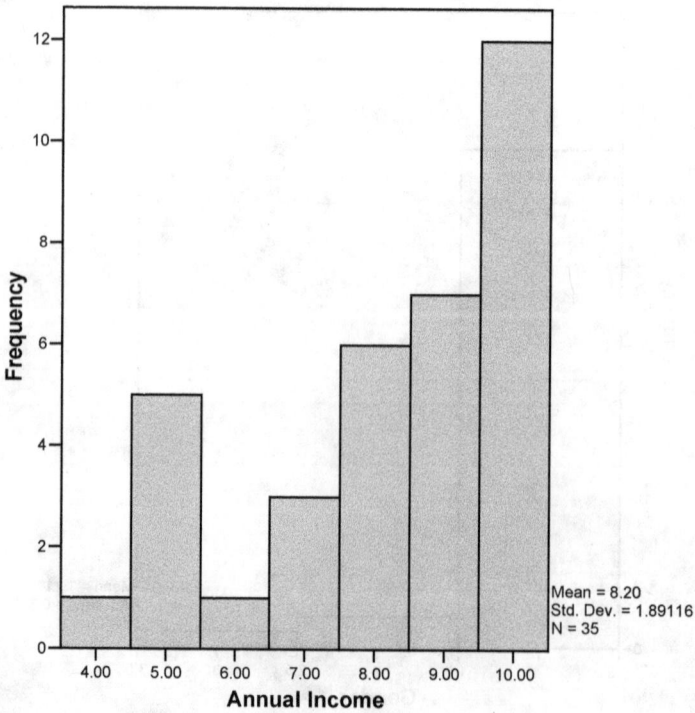

Mean = 8.20
Std. Dev. = 1.89116
N = 35

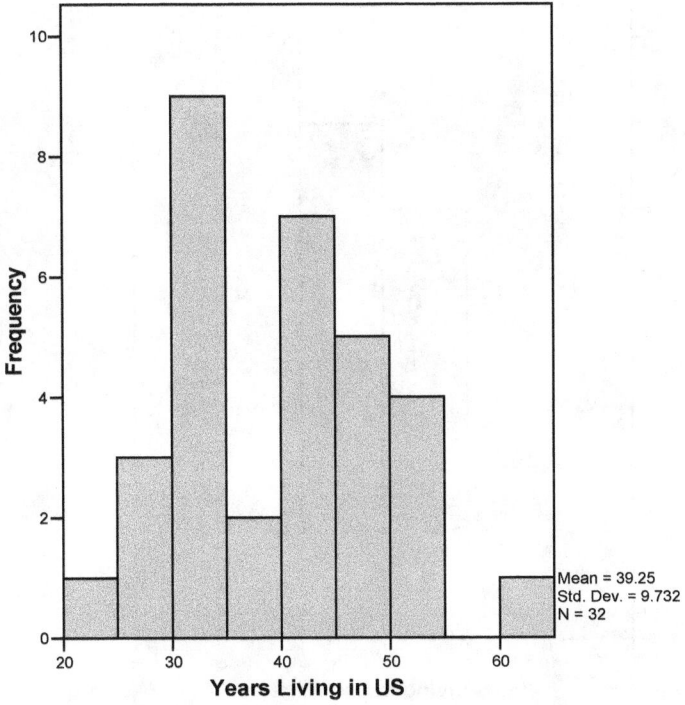

Mean = 39.25
Std. Dev. = 9.732
N = 32

Years Living in US

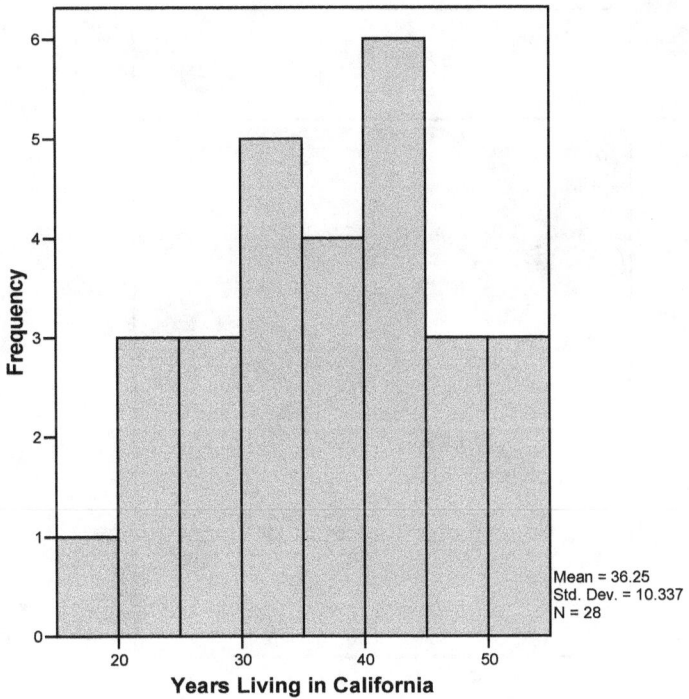

Mean = 36.25
Std. Dev. = 10.337
N = 28

Years Living in California

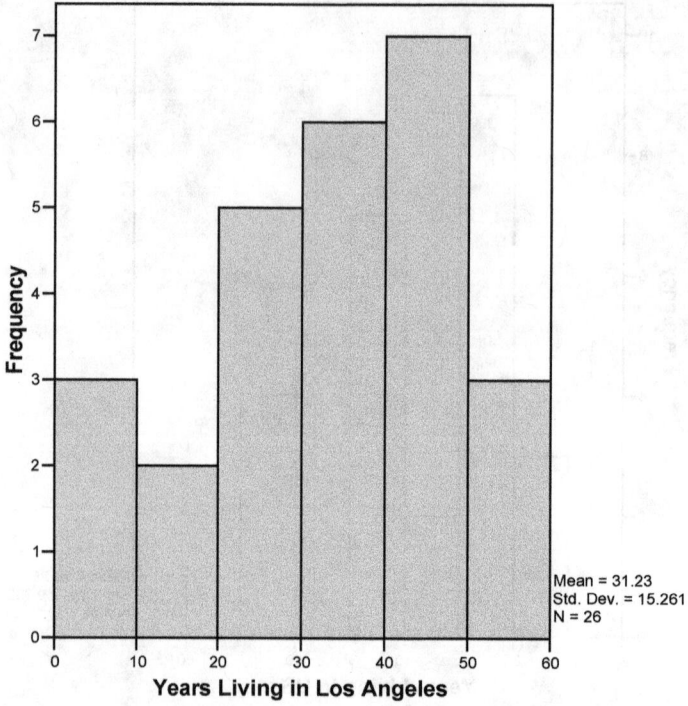

Mean = 31.23
Std. Dev. = 15.261
N = 26

Years Living in Los Angeles

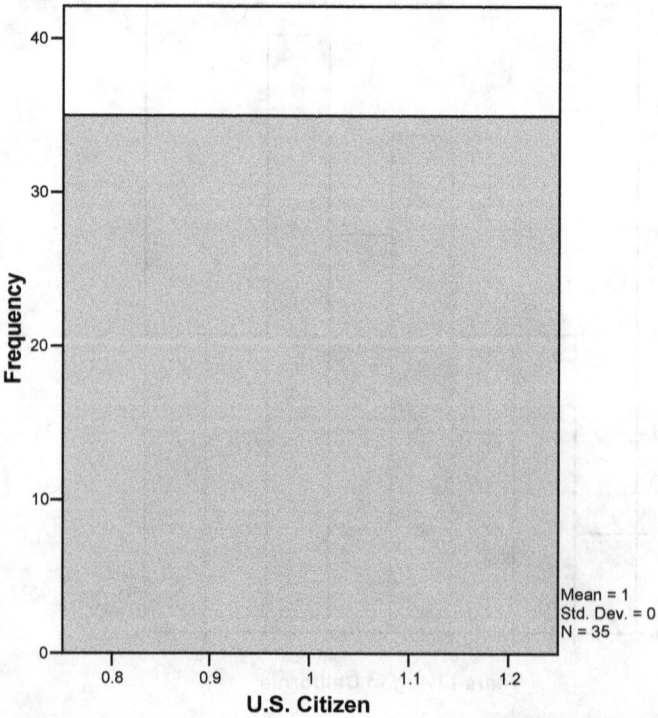

Mean = 1
Std. Dev. = 0
N = 35

U.S. Citizen

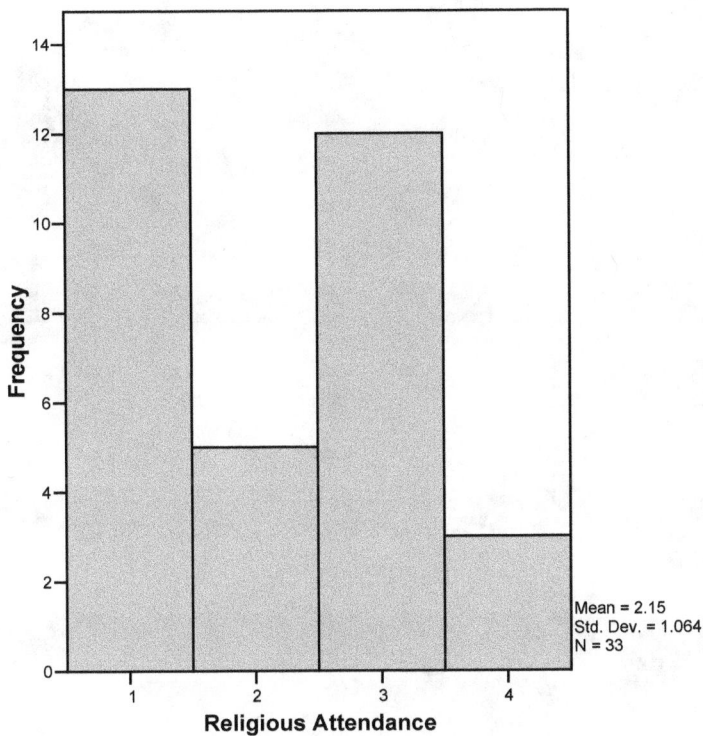

Mean = 2.15
Std. Dev. = 1.064
N = 33

Religious Attendance

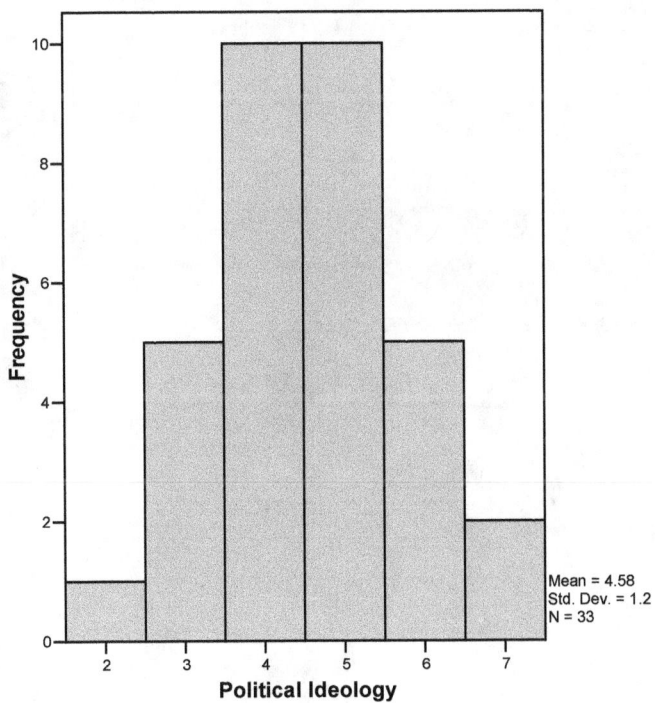

Mean = 4.58
Std. Dev. = 1.2
N = 33

Political Ideology

Appendix 6: Correlation Matrix – Domestic Variables (Parametric)

Table A6 is broken down into the following 90 sub-tables, arranged in a matrix of 9 rows and 10 columns:

Row 1 Col 1	Row 1 Col 2	Row 1 Col 3	Row 1 Col 4	Row 1 Col 5	Row 1 Col 6	Row 1 Col 7	Row 1 Col 8	Row 1 Col 9	Row 1 Col 10
Row 2 Col 1	Row 2 Col 2	Row 2 Col 3	Row 2 Col 4	Row 2 Col 5	Row 2 Col 6	Row 2 Col 7	Row 2 Col 8	Row 2 Col 9	Row 2 Col 10
Row 3 Col 1	Row 3 Col 2	Row 3 Col 3	Row 3 Col 4	Row 3 Col 5	Row 3 Col 6	Row 3 Col 7	Row 3 Col 8	Row 3 Col 9	Row 3 Col 10
Row 4 Col 1	Row 4 Col 2	Row 4 Col 3	Row 4 Col 4	Row 4 Col 5	Row 4 Col 6	Row 4 Col 7	Row 4 Col 8	Row 4 Col 9	Row 4 Col 10
Row 5 Col 1	Row 5 Col 2	Row 5 Col 3	Row 5 Col 4	Row 5 Col 5	Row 5 Col 6	Row 5 Col 7	Row 5 Col 8	Row 5 Col 9	Row 5 Col 10
Row 6 Col 1	Row 6 Col 2	Row 6 Col 3	Row 6 Col 4	Row 6 Col 5	Row 6 Col 6	Row 6 Col 7	Row 6 Col 8	Row 6 Col 9	Row 6 Col 10
Row 7 Col 1	Row 7 Col 2	Row 7 Col 3	Row 7 Col 4	Row 7 Col 5	Row 7 Col 6	Row 7 Col 7	Row 7 Col 8	Row 7 Col 9	Row 7 Col 10
Row 8 Col 1	Row 8 Col 2	Row 8 Col 3	Row 8 Col 4	Row 8 Col 5	Row 8 Col 6	Row 8 Col 7	Row 8 Col 8	Row 8 Col 9	Row 8 Col 10
Row 9 Col 1	Row 9 Col 2	Row 9 Col 3	Row 9 Col 4	Row 9 Col 5	Row 9 Col 6	Row 9 Col 7	Row 9 Col 8	Row 9 Col 9	Row 9 Col 10

To promote accuracy and legibility, all tables are presented in their original printing.

Table A6. Correlation Matrix – Domestic Variables (Parametric) (Row 1, Col 1)

Correlation Matrix, Dependent Variables (Parametric)		Importance of Smuggling-Endangered Species	reflectsqrtQ1A1b	reflectsqrtQ1A1c	reflectsqrtQ1A1d	reflectsqrtQ1A1e	sqrtQ1B1a	Knowledge of Smuggling-Narcotics	Knowledge of Smuggling-Weapons	Knowledge of Smuggling-Humans	Knowledge of Smuggling-Contraband
Importance of Smuggling-Endangered Species	Pearson Correlation	1.0000	-0.0784	-0.0965	-0.0759	-0.1760	0.4053	0.0395	-0.1727	-0.1831	-0.0867
	Sig. (2-tailed)	.	0.6496	0.5757	0.6598	0.3047	0.0142	0.8193	0.3137	0.2852	0.6150
	N	36.0000	36.0000	36.0000	36.0000	36.0000	36.0000	36.0000	36.0000	36.0000	36.0000
reflectsqrtQ1A1b	Pearson Correlation	-0.0784	1.0000	0.6310	0.2015	0.4542	0.2640	-0.2259	-0.1211	0.0181	0.0993
	Sig. (2-tailed)	0.6496	.	0.0000	0.2386	0.0054	0.1198	0.1852	0.4818	0.9165	0.5647
	N	36.0000	36.0000	36.0000	36.0000	36.0000	36.0000	36.0000	36.0000	36.0000	36.0000
reflectsqrtQ1A1c	Pearson Correlation	-0.0965	0.6310	1.0000	0.4053	0.1972	0.2011	-0.2008	-0.1053	-0.0978	0.0536
	Sig. (2-tailed)	0.5757	0.0000	.	0.0142	0.2489	0.2397	0.2403	0.5409	0.5703	0.7560
	N	36.0000	36.0000	36.0000	36.0000	36.0000	36.0000	36.0000	36.0000	36.0000	36.0000
reflectsqrtQ1A1d	Pearson Correlation	-0.0759	0.2015	0.4053	1.0000	0.1431	0.1065	-0.1408	0.0206	-0.1564	0.0659
	Sig. (2-tailed)	0.6598	0.2386	0.0142	.	0.4052	0.5366	0.4126	0.9050	0.3622	0.7024
	N	36.0000	36.0000	36.0000	36.0000	36.0000	36.0000	36.0000	36.0000	36.0000	36.0000
reflectsqrtQ1A1e	Pearson Correlation	-0.1760	0.4542	0.1972	0.1431	1.0000	-0.1598	-0.0782	-0.2644	-0.0633	-0.4163
	Sig. (2-tailed)	0.3047	0.0054	0.2489	0.4052	.	0.3520	0.6505	0.1192	0.7136	0.0115
	N	36.0000	36.0000	36.0000	36.0000	36.0000	36.0000	36.0000	36.0000	36.0000	36.0000
sqrtQ1B1a	Pearson Correlation	0.4053	0.2640	0.2011	0.1065	-0.1598	1.0000	0.2037	0.2523	0.2008	0.3338
	Sig. (2-tailed)	0.0142	0.1198	0.2397	0.5366	0.3520	.	0.2335	0.1376	0.2402	0.0466
	N	36.0000	36.0000	36.0000	36.0000	36.0000	36.0000	36.0000	36.0000	36.0000	36.0000
Knowledge of Smuggling-Narcotics	Pearson Correlation	0.0395	-0.2259	-0.2008	-0.1408	-0.0782	0.2037	1.0000	0.5816	0.4286	0.5001
	Sig. (2-tailed)	0.8193	0.1852	0.2403	0.4126	0.6505	0.2335	.	0.0002	0.0091	0.0019
	N	36.0000	36.0000	36.0000	36.0000	36.0000	36.0000	36.0000	36.0000	36.0000	36.0000
Knowledge of Smuggling-Weapons	Pearson Correlation	-0.1727	-0.1211	-0.1053	0.0206	-0.2644	0.2523	0.5816	1.0000	0.3046	0.6419
	Sig. (2-tailed)	0.3137	0.4818	0.5409	0.9050	0.1192	0.1376	0.0002	.	0.0708	0.0000
	N	36.0000	36.0000	36.0000	36.0000	36.0000	36.0000	36.0000	36.0000	36.0000	36.0000
Knowledge of Smuggling-Humans	Pearson Correlation	-0.1831	0.0181	-0.0978	-0.1564	-0.0633	0.2008	0.4286	0.3046	1.0000	0.5803
	Sig. (2-tailed)	0.2852	0.9165	0.5703	0.3622	0.7136	0.2402	0.0091	0.0708	.	0.0002
	N	36.0000	36.0000	36.0000	36.0000	36.0000	36.0000	36.0000	36.0000	36.0000	36.0000
Knowledge of Smuggling-Contraband	Pearson Correlation	-0.0867	0.0993	0.0536	0.0659	-0.4163	0.3338	0.5001	0.6419	0.5803	1.0000
	Sig. (2-tailed)	0.6150	0.5647	0.7560	0.7024	0.0115	0.0466	0.0019	0.0000	0.0002	.
	N	36.0000	36.0000	36.0000	36.0000	36.0000	36.0000	36.0000	36.0000	36.0000	36.0000
sqrtQ1E1a	Pearson Correlation	-0.0786	0.0433	0.1506	0.0706	0.0150	0.0094	-0.0175	-0.0949	-0.1211	-0.0438
	Sig. (2-tailed)	0.6535	0.8050	0.3879	0.6871	0.9319	0.9572	0.9206	0.5878	0.4883	0.8029
	N	35.0000	35.0000	35.0000	35.0000	35.0000	35.0000	35.0000	35.0000	35.0000	35.0000
Personal Resource Challenges-Lack of Time	Pearson Correlation	-0.2521	0.0491	0.1354	0.1898	0.0699	0.0171	0.1009	-0.0720	0.1074	0.1384
	Sig. (2-tailed)	0.1380	0.7762	0.4311	0.2676	0.6854	0.9213	0.5582	0.6766	0.5331	0.4207
	N	36.0000	36.0000	36.0000	36.0000	36.0000	36.0000	36.0000	36.0000	36.0000	36.0000

Table A6, continued (Row 1, Col 2)

Correlation Matrix, Dependent Variables (Parametric)		sqrtQ1E1a	Personal Resource Challenges-Lack of Time	Personal Resource Challenges-Lack of Knowledge	Personal Resource Challenges-Lack of Training	sqrtQ1E1e	Personal Resource Challenges-Excessive Admin Paperwork	Personal Resource Challenges-Ineffective Technology	Personal Resource Challenges-Ineffective Strategic Focus	Personal Resource Challenges-Ineffective Tactical Policy	Personal Resource Challenges-Lack of Clarity in Duties
Importance of Smuggling-Endangered Species	Pearson Correlation	-0.0786	-0.2521	-0.0060	-0.1118	0.0017	-0.1143	-0.0332	-0.1285	-0.1699	-0.0555
	Sig. (2-tailed)	0.6535	0.1380	0.9725	0.5161	0.9923	0.5070	0.8474	0.4550	0.3218	0.7476
	N	35.0000	36.0000	36.0000	36.0000	36.0000	36.0000	36.0000	36.0000	36.0000	36.0000
reflectsqrtQ1A1b	Pearson Correlation	0.0433	0.0491	-0.1074	-0.0574	0.0673	0.1222	-0.0507	-0.0880	-0.0058	-0.0091
	Sig. (2-tailed)	0.8050	0.7762	0.5329	0.7396	0.6965	0.4777	0.7692	0.6099	0.9732	0.9579
	N	35.0000	36.0000	36.0000	36.0000	36.0000	36.0000	36.0000	36.0000	36.0000	36.0000
reflectsqrtQ1A1c	Pearson Correlation	0.1506	0.1354	-0.1398	-0.1409	-0.0870	0.0631	-0.0964	-0.2280	-0.0994	-0.1168
	Sig. (2-tailed)	0.3879	0.4311	0.4162	0.4125	0.6141	0.7148	0.5758	0.1811	0.5643	0.4976
	N	35.0000	36.0000	36.0000	36.0000	36.0000	36.0000	36.0000	36.0000	36.0000	36.0000
reflectsqrtQ1A1d	Pearson Correlation	0.0706	0.1898	0.0012	-0.0396	-0.1839	-0.0777	-0.2668	-0.2106	-0.1638	-0.1988
	Sig. (2-tailed)	0.6871	0.2676	0.9945	0.8186	0.2829	0.6526	0.1157	0.2177	0.3397	0.2451
	N	35.0000	36.0000	36.0000	36.0000	36.0000	36.0000	36.0000	36.0000	36.0000	36.0000
reflectsqrtQ1A1e	Pearson Correlation	0.0150	0.0699	0.0140	0.0473	0.0016	-0.0052	0.0638	0.0616	0.1821	0.1008
	Sig. (2-tailed)	0.9319	0.6854	0.9356	0.7840	0.9928	0.9760	0.7115	0.7211	0.2879	0.5587
	N	35.0000	36.0000	36.0000	36.0000	36.0000	36.0000	36.0000	36.0000	36.0000	36.0000
sqrtQ1B1a	Pearson Correlation	0.0094	0.0171	0.0056	0.0112	0.2065	0.0536	0.0157	0.1585	0.0430	0.0533
	Sig. (2-tailed)	0.9572	0.9213	0.9743	0.9483	0.2270	0.7560	0.9276	0.3558	0.8033	0.7575
	N	35.0000	36.0000	36.0000	36.0000	36.0000	36.0000	36.0000	36.0000	36.0000	36.0000
Knowledge of Smuggling-Narcotics	Pearson Correlation	-0.0175	0.1009	-0.0019	-0.0190	0.0853	0.2558	0.2258	-0.0792	-0.0393	0.0626
	Sig. (2-tailed)	0.9206	0.5582	0.9911	0.9126	0.6208	0.1320	0.1854	0.6460	0.8202	0.7166
	N	35.0000	36.0000	36.0000	36.0000	36.0000	36.0000	36.0000	36.0000	36.0000	36.0000
Knowledge of Smuggling-Weapons	Pearson Correlation	-0.0949	-0.0720	-0.2415	-0.2339	0.2980	0.2285	-0.0585	-0.1197	-0.1135	-0.1099
	Sig. (2-tailed)	0.5878	0.6766	0.1560	0.1698	0.0775	0.1802	0.7349	0.4868	0.5097	0.5235
	N	35.0000	36.0000	36.0000	36.0000	36.0000	36.0000	36.0000	36.0000	36.0000	36.0000
Knowledge of Smuggling-Humans	Pearson Correlation	-0.1211	0.1074	0.0093	-0.0248	0.0830	-0.0120	0.0177	-0.0164	0.0170	0.0758
	Sig. (2-tailed)	0.4883	0.5331	0.9572	0.8859	0.6301	0.9445	0.9184	0.9245	0.9215	0.6605
	N	35.0000	36.0000	36.0000	36.0000	36.0000	36.0000	36.0000	36.0000	36.0000	36.0000
Knowledge of Smuggling-Contraband	Pearson Correlation	-0.0438	0.1384	-0.0687	-0.1326	0.1690	0.2170	-0.0706	-0.1110	-0.1189	0.0121
	Sig. (2-tailed)	0.8029	0.4207	0.6905	0.4409	0.3243	0.2037	0.6824	0.5192	0.4899	0.9442
	N	35.0000	36.0000	36.0000	36.0000	36.0000	36.0000	36.0000	36.0000	36.0000	36.0000
sqrtQ1E1a	Pearson Correlation	1.0000	0.3118	0.3342	0.2759	0.1914	0.4520	0.3708	0.5510	0.6237	0.5042
	Sig. (2-tailed)	.	0.0683	0.0497	0.1087	0.2708	0.0064	0.0283	0.0006	0.0001	0.0020
	N	35.0000	35.0000	35.0000	35.0000	35.0000	35.0000	35.0000	35.0000	35.0000	35.0000
Personal Resource Challenges-Lack of Time	Pearson Correlation	0.3118	1.0000	0.5812	0.4861	0.3338	0.3445	0.2844	0.4073	0.4851	0.5687
	Sig. (2-tailed)	0.0683	.	0.0002	0.0027	0.0466	0.0396	0.0927	0.0137	0.0027	0.0003
	N	35.0000	36.0000	36.0000	36.0000	36.0000	36.0000	36.0000	36.0000	36.0000	36.0000

231

Table A6, continued (Row 1, Col 3)

Correlation Matrix, Dependent Variables (Parametric)		Personal Resource Challenges-Conflict or Lack Comm Leaders and Employees	sqrtQ1E1I	Personal Resource Challenges-Conflict or Lack Comm International Orgs	Personal Resource Challenges-Conflict or Lack Comm Domestic Orgs	sqrtQ1E3a	Org Resource Challenges-Lack of Time	Org Resource Challenges-Lack of Knowledge	Org Resource Challenges-Lack of Training	sqrtQ1E3e	Org Resource Challenges-Excessive Admin Paperwork
Importance of Smuggling-Endangered Species	Pearson Correlation	-0.0670	0.0461	0.0229	-0.0208	0.0133	-0.2552	-0.1379	-0.1090	-0.2357	-0.2130
	Sig. (2-tailed)	0.6979	0.7894	0.8946	0.9041	0.9404	0.1390	0.4295	0.5331	0.1795	0.2193
	N	36.0000	36.0000	36.0000	36.0000	34.0000	35.0000	35.0000	35.0000	34.0000	35.0000
reflectsqrtQ1A1b	Pearson Correlation	0.0368	-0.0333	0.0465	-0.1078	-0.1596	-0.1996	-0.3436	-0.2567	-0.0838	-0.1647
	Sig. (2-tailed)	0.8314	0.8470	0.7876	0.5314	0.3674	0.2502	0.0433	0.1366	0.6376	0.3445
	N	36.0000	36.0000	36.0000	36.0000	34.0000	35.0000	35.0000	35.0000	34.0000	35.0000
reflectsqrtQ1A1c	Pearson Correlation	-0.0162	-0.0776	-0.0535	-0.0861	-0.2365	-0.1862	-0.3719	-0.2689	-0.0101	-0.0928
	Sig. (2-tailed)	0.9253	0.6528	0.7567	0.6178	0.1782	0.2843	0.0278	0.1184	0.9550	0.5960
	N	36.0000	36.0000	36.0000	36.0000	34.0000	35.0000	35.0000	35.0000	34.0000	35.0000
reflectsqrtQ1A1d	Pearson Correlation	-0.1624	0.0044	-0.1854	-0.2570	-0.3896	-0.0401	-0.1642	-0.1838	0.1432	-0.0628
	Sig. (2-tailed)	0.3439	0.9796	0.2789	0.1303	0.0227	0.8190	0.3458	0.2906	0.4192	0.7202
	N	36.0000	36.0000	36.0000	36.0000	34.0000	35.0000	35.0000	35.0000	34.0000	35.0000
reflectsqrtQ1A1e	Pearson Correlation	0.2367	-0.1415	-0.0606	0.1232	0.0326	0.0005	-0.0840	-0.0341	0.1655	0.0211
	Sig. (2-tailed)	0.1646	0.4104	0.7254	0.4741	0.8548	0.9978	0.6316	0.8458	0.3496	0.9040
	N	36.0000	36.0000	36.0000	36.0000	34.0000	35.0000	35.0000	35.0000	34.0000	35.0000
sqrtQ1B1a	Pearson Correlation	0.0124	0.0984	0.0694	-0.0188	-0.0214	-0.1127	-0.1504	-0.1441	-0.2154	-0.2287
	Sig. (2-tailed)	0.9427	0.5681	0.6876	0.9131	0.9043	0.5192	0.3884	0.4090	0.2211	0.1863
	N	36.0000	36.0000	36.0000	36.0000	34.0000	35.0000	35.0000	35.0000	34.0000	35.0000
Knowledge of Smuggling-Narcotics	Pearson Correlation	-0.0357	-0.0247	0.1843	0.1111	0.2403	0.0762	-0.0412	-0.0791	0.0355	0.1035
	Sig. (2-tailed)	0.8364	0.8862	0.2818	0.5187	0.1711	0.6634	0.8141	0.6516	0.8419	0.5540
	N	36.0000	36.0000	36.0000	36.0000	34.0000	35.0000	35.0000	35.0000	34.0000	35.0000
Knowledge of Smuggling-Weapons	Pearson Correlation	-0.1635	0.0217	-0.0188	-0.1551	0.2145	-0.0246	-0.2739	-0.3116	-0.0703	-0.0973
	Sig. (2-tailed)	0.3406	0.9001	0.9134	0.3663	0.2232	0.8886	0.1114	0.0684	0.6926	0.5783
	N	36.0000	36.0000	36.0000	36.0000	34.0000	35.0000	35.0000	35.0000	34.0000	35.0000
Knowledge of Smuggling-Humans	Pearson Correlation	-0.0869	-0.2842	-0.0105	-0.0370	-0.0719	0.0081	-0.0646	-0.1464	-0.2233	-0.2894
	Sig. (2-tailed)	0.6142	0.0930	0.9517	0.8303	0.6860	0.9632	0.7124	0.4014	0.2043	0.0917
	N	36.0000	36.0000	36.0000	36.0000	34.0000	35.0000	35.0000	35.0000	34.0000	35.0000
Knowledge of Smuggling-Contraband	Pearson Correlation	-0.0616	0.0032	0.1416	-0.0556	-0.1157	-0.0850	-0.1819	-0.2547	-0.1197	-0.1697
	Sig. (2-tailed)	0.7213	0.9854	0.4100	0.7474	0.5145	0.6275	0.2956	0.1398	0.5001	0.3299
	N	36.0000	36.0000	36.0000	36.0000	34.0000	35.0000	35.0000	35.0000	34.0000	35.0000
sqrtQ1E1a	Pearson Correlation	0.5982	0.5175	0.3957	0.4968	0.5355	0.3713	0.2971	0.3371	0.4286	0.6521
	Sig. (2-tailed)	0.0001	0.0015	0.0186	0.0024	0.0013	0.0306	0.0879	0.0512	0.0128	0.0000
	N	35.0000	35.0000	35.0000	35.0000	33.0000	34.0000	34.0000	34.0000	33.0000	34.0000
Personal Resource Challenges-Lack of Time	Pearson Correlation	0.4964	0.1927	0.4594	0.6319	0.2228	0.4499	0.4761	0.4834	0.5283	0.4741
	Sig. (2-tailed)	0.0021	0.2602	0.0048	0.0000	0.2053	0.0067	0.0038	0.0033	0.0013	0.0040
	N	36.0000	36.0000	36.0000	36.0000	34.0000	35.0000	35.0000	35.0000	34.0000	35.0000

Table A6, continued (Row 1, Col 4)

Correlation Matrix, Dependent Variables (Parametric)		Org Resource Challenges-Ineffective Technology	Org Resource Challenges-Ineffective Strategic Focus	Org Resource Challenges-Ineffective Tactical Policy	Org Resource Challenges-Lack of Clarity in Duties	Org Resource Challenges-Conflict or Lack Comm Leaders and Employees	sqrtQ1E3l	Org Resource Challenges-Conflict or Lack Comm International Orgs	Org Resource Challenges-Conflict or Lack Comm Domestic Orgs	sqrtQHA1a	Knowledge of Domestic Law-CSIE
Importance of Smuggling-Endangered Species	Pearson Correlation	-0.1288	-0.0368	-0.0218	0.0492	-0.0220	-0.0396	0.0261	0.0753	0.0714	-0.0032
	Sig. (2-tailed)	0.4609	0.8339	0.9009	0.7792	0.9000	0.8214	0.8818	0.6674	0.6836	0.9852
	N	35.0000	35.0000	35.0000	35.0000	35.0000	35.0000	35.0000	35.0000	35.0000	35.0000
reflectsqrtQ1A1b	Pearson Correlation	-0.2495	-0.2400	-0.2306	-0.3141	-0.1516	-0.0530	-0.3126	-0.3260	0.3292	-0.2346
	Sig. (2-tailed)	0.1483	0.1649	0.1827	0.0661	0.3846	0.7622	0.0675	0.0560	0.0535	0.1750
	N	35.0000	35.0000	35.0000	35.0000	35.0000	35.0000	35.0000	35.0000	35.0000	35.0000
reflectsqrtQ1A1c	Pearson Correlation	-0.1343	-0.2113	-0.2437	-0.3196	-0.1189	-0.0769	-0.3248	-0.2974	0.1555	0.0142
	Sig. (2-tailed)	0.4419	0.2231	0.1584	0.0613	0.4961	0.6604	0.0570	0.0827	0.3724	0.9356
	N	35.0000	35.0000	35.0000	35.0000	35.0000	35.0000	35.0000	35.0000	35.0000	35.0000
reflectsqrtQ1A1d	Pearson Correlation	-0.0683	-0.0591	-0.1340	-0.1009	0.0441	0.0348	-0.0833	-0.1055	0.1382	0.0931
	Sig. (2-tailed)	0.6967	0.7359	0.4429	0.5642	0.8016	0.8425	0.6341	0.5464	0.4284	0.5947
	N	35.0000	35.0000	35.0000	35.0000	35.0000	35.0000	35.0000	35.0000	35.0000	35.0000
reflectsqrtQ1A1e	Pearson Correlation	0.1518	0.0927	0.1423	0.0087	0.1340	-0.1052	0.0119	0.0191	-0.1336	-0.1776
	Sig. (2-tailed)	0.3840	0.5964	0.4147	0.9603	0.4430	0.5474	0.9457	0.9131	0.4440	0.3073
	N	35.0000	35.0000	35.0000	35.0000	35.0000	35.0000	35.0000	35.0000	35.0000	35.0000
sqrtQ1B1a	Pearson Correlation	-0.0945	0.0266	-0.0108	0.0917	-0.0517	0.0804	0.0776	0.0426	0.5077	0.0953
	Sig. (2-tailed)	0.5894	0.8796	0.9507	0.6001	0.7678	0.6460	0.6577	0.8080	0.0018	0.5859
	N	35.0000	35.0000	35.0000	35.0000	35.0000	35.0000	35.0000	35.0000	35.0000	35.0000
Knowledge of Smuggling-Narcotics	Pearson Correlation	0.2007	0.0133	0.0210	0.0127	0.0840	-0.0488	0.1324	0.1116	0.0948	0.6809
	Sig. (2-tailed)	0.2477	0.9398	0.9048	0.9422	0.6316	0.7808	0.4484	0.5233	0.5879	0.0000
	N	35.0000	35.0000	35.0000	35.0000	35.0000	35.0000	35.0000	35.0000	35.0000	35.0000
Knowledge of Smuggling-Weapons	Pearson Correlation	-0.0701	-0.1614	-0.1416	-0.1453	0.0522	0.0348	-0.1213	-0.1315	0.2332	0.5161
	Sig. (2-tailed)	0.6890	0.3543	0.4172	0.4050	0.7657	0.8428	0.4878	0.4513	0.1776	0.0015
	N	35.0000	35.0000	35.0000	35.0000	35.0000	35.0000	35.0000	35.0000	35.0000	35.0000
Knowledge of Smuggling-Humans	Pearson Correlation	-0.0244	-0.0382	-0.1871	-0.0797	-0.2450	-0.4343	0.0368	-0.0734	0.0326	0.1554
	Sig. (2-tailed)	0.8893	0.8277	0.2818	0.6492	0.1560	0.0091	0.8337	0.6753	0.8525	0.3726
	N	35.0000	35.0000	35.0000	35.0000	35.0000	35.0000	35.0000	35.0000	35.0000	35.0000
Knowledge of Smuggling-Contraband	Pearson Correlation	-0.1510	-0.1665	-0.1946	-0.1955	-0.0940	-0.0865	-0.1600	-0.1675	0.4173	0.3006
	Sig. (2-tailed)	0.3867	0.3390	0.2626	0.2604	0.5912	0.6213	0.3587	0.3362	0.0126	0.0793
	N	35.0000	35.0000	35.0000	35.0000	35.0000	35.0000	35.0000	35.0000	35.0000	35.0000
sqrtQ1E1a	Pearson Correlation	0.5895	0.3989	0.4226	0.3674	0.4307	0.4065	0.2378	0.2694	0.1149	-0.0396
	Sig. (2-tailed)	0.0002	0.0194	0.0128	0.0326	0.0110	0.0171	0.1756	0.1234	0.5176	0.8241
	N	34.0000	34.0000	34.0000	34.0000	34.0000	34.0000	34.0000	34.0000	34.0000	34.0000
Personal Resource Challenges-Lack of Time	Pearson Correlation	0.3837	0.4444	0.5063	0.3689	0.4729	0.2147	0.3700	0.3163	0.1779	-0.1054
	Sig. (2-tailed)	0.0229	0.0075	0.0019	0.0292	0.0041	0.2155	0.0287	0.0641	0.3066	0.5467
	N	35.0000	35.0000	35.0000	35.0000	35.0000	35.0000	35.0000	35.0000	35.0000	35.0000

Table A6, continued (Row 1, Col 5)

Correlation Matrix, Dependent Variables (Parametric)		Knowledge of Domestic Law-DWMD	Knowledge of Domestic Law-TVP	Knowledge of Domestic Law-CBP	sqrtQ1B1a	Perceived Effectiveness Domestic Govt Support-CSIE	Perceived Effectiveness Domestic Govt Support-DWMD	Perceived Effectiveness Domestic Govt SupportTVP	Perceived Effectiveness Domestic Govt Support-CBP	sqrtQ1IC1a	Perceived Deterrence Domestic Law-CSIE
Importance of Smuggling-Endangered Species	Pearson Correlation	-0.2227	-0.2041	-0.1039	0.1444	-0.3171	-0.0909	-0.1500	-0.0849	0.0838	-0.2341
	Sig. (2-tailed)	0.1984	0.2396	0.5527	0.4078	0.0634	0.5979	0.3899	0.6276	0.6323	0.1693
	N	35.0000	35.0000	35.0000	35.0000	35.0000	36.0000	35.0000	35.0000	35.0000	36.0000
reflectsqrtQ1A1b	Pearson Correlation	-0.1107	-0.1045	0.1069	0.2197	-0.2167	-0.2119	0.1203	0.1503	0.0825	-0.1871
	Sig. (2-tailed)	0.5268	0.5503	0.5409	0.2047	0.2111	0.2148	0.4912	0.3886	0.6374	0.2746
	N	35.0000	35.0000	35.0000	35.0000	35.0000	36.0000	35.0000	35.0000	35.0000	36.0000
reflectsqrtQ1A1c	Pearson Correlation	0.0084	-0.0642	0.2938	-0.0267	-0.1550	-0.2500	0.0406	0.1898	-0.0479	-0.0832
	Sig. (2-tailed)	0.9620	0.7141	0.0867	0.8791	0.3740	0.1414	0.8168	0.2747	0.7848	0.6295
	N	35.0000	35.0000	35.0000	35.0000	35.0000	36.0000	35.0000	35.0000	35.0000	36.0000
reflectsqrtQ1A1d	Pearson Correlation	0.0954	-0.0603	0.1321	0.1104	-0.0148	0.0844	0.3279	0.3699	-0.0846	-0.3257
	Sig. (2-tailed)	0.5856	0.7308	0.4494	0.5279	0.9327	0.6246	0.0545	0.0287	0.6288	0.0526
	N	35.0000	35.0000	35.0000	35.0000	35.0000	36.0000	35.0000	35.0000	35.0000	36.0000
reflectsqrtQ1A1e	Pearson Correlation	-0.1624	-0.0460	-0.2579	-0.1642	-0.4207	-0.2755	-0.0776	-0.2319	-0.1418	-0.3539
	Sig. (2-tailed)	0.3512	0.7932	0.1347	0.3460	0.0119	0.1039	0.6576	0.1801	0.4164	0.0342
	N	35.0000	35.0000	35.0000	35.0000	35.0000	36.0000	35.0000	35.0000	35.0000	36.0000
sqrtQ1B1a	Pearson Correlation	0.0299	0.1391	0.0992	0.5266	-0.0525	-0.0257	0.0809	0.0167	0.3969	0.1588
	Sig. (2-tailed)	0.8644	0.4256	0.5707	0.0012	0.7644	0.8818	0.6440	0.9242	0.0182	0.3550
	N	35.0000	35.0000	35.0000	35.0000	35.0000	36.0000	35.0000	35.0000	35.0000	36.0000
Knowledge of Smuggling-Narcotics	Pearson Correlation	0.5787	0.5195	0.2628	0.0615	0.3300	0.3662	0.0810	-0.0566	0.1620	0.3838
	Sig. (2-tailed)	0.0003	0.0014	0.1273	0.7258	0.0529	0.0281	0.6435	0.7468	0.3525	0.0208
	N	35.0000	35.0000	35.0000	35.0000	35.0000	36.0000	35.0000	35.0000	35.0000	36.0000
Knowledge of Smuggling-Weapons	Pearson Correlation	0.6878	0.4150	0.5338	0.2414	0.4299	0.3848	0.4147	0.2175	0.1631	0.3848
	Sig. (2-tailed)	0.0000	0.0132	0.0010	0.1623	0.0099	0.0205	0.0133	0.2094	0.3492	0.0205
	N	35.0000	35.0000	35.0000	35.0000	35.0000	36.0000	35.0000	35.0000	35.0000	36.0000
Knowledge of Smuggling-Humans	Pearson Correlation	0.3185	0.5869	0.1776	0.0641	0.1815	0.2580	0.1463	-0.0915	0.1132	0.2830
	Sig. (2-tailed)	0.0622	0.0002	0.3074	0.7145	0.2966	0.1287	0.4016	0.6011	0.5172	0.0944
	N	35.0000	35.0000	35.0000	35.0000	35.0000	36.0000	35.0000	35.0000	35.0000	36.0000
Knowledge of Smuggling-Contraband	Pearson Correlation	0.4673	0.4621	0.6159	0.2397	0.3448	0.3453	0.3833	0.2676	0.2242	0.3749
	Sig. (2-tailed)	0.0047	0.0052	0.0001	0.1655	0.0425	0.0392	0.0230	0.1202	0.1955	0.0243
	N	35.0000	35.0000	35.0000	35.0000	35.0000	36.0000	35.0000	35.0000	35.0000	36.0000
sqrtQ1E1a	Pearson Correlation	-0.2166	-0.1300	-0.1190	-0.0595	-0.2248	-0.2630	-0.2881	-0.1696	-0.1783	-0.0002
	Sig. (2-tailed)	0.2186	0.4636	0.5028	0.7381	0.2013	0.1269	0.0985	0.3377	0.3131	0.9993
	N	34.0000	34.0000	34.0000	34.0000	34.0000	35.0000	34.0000	34.0000	34.0000	35.0000
Personal Resource Challenges-Lack of Time	Pearson Correlation	-0.0797	-0.0226	0.0886	-0.0992	-0.1528	-0.0369	-0.0628	-0.0502	-0.0112	0.0226
	Sig. (2-tailed)	0.6491	0.8976	0.6129	0.5709	0.3809	0.8306	0.7200	0.7744	0.9489	0.8959
	N	35.0000	35.0000	35.0000	35.0000	35.0000	36.0000	35.0000	35.0000	35.0000	36.0000

234

Table A6, continued (Row 1, Col 6)

Correlation Matrix, Dependent Variables (Parametric)		sqrtQIIC1c	Perceived Deterrence Domestic Law-TVP	sqrtQIIC1e	sqrtQIID1a	Level Cooperation Domestic Orgs-CSIE	Level Cooperation Domestic Orgs-DWMD	Level Cooperation Domestic Orgs-TVP	Level Cooperation Domestic Orgs-CBP	sqrtQIIF1a	sqrtQIIF1b
Importance of Smuggling-Endangered Species	Pearson Correlation	-0.1238	-0.1109	-0.2413	0.2661	-0.0291	0.0626	0.1330	0.0417	0.0504	0.0934
	Sig. (2-tailed)	0.4718	0.5197	0.1563	0.1167	0.8662	0.7167	0.4393	0.8092	0.7840	0.5992
	N	36.0000	36.0000	36.0000	36.0000	36.0000	36.0000	36.0000	36.0000	32.0000	34.0000
reflectsqrtQ1A1b	Pearson Correlation	-0.1524	-0.1102	-0.0459	0.2364	-0.1636	-0.1263	-0.1268	0.0764	0.0604	-0.1690
	Sig. (2-tailed)	0.3747	0.5221	0.7905	0.1650	0.3404	0.4630	0.4612	0.6578	0.7427	0.3392
	N	36.0000	36.0000	36.0000	36.0000	36.0000	36.0000	36.0000	36.0000	32.0000	34.0000
reflectsqrtQ1A1c	Pearson Correlation	-0.0944	-0.1419	0.0556	0.1976	0.0149	0.0214	-0.0633	0.1665	-0.1249	-0.1418
	Sig. (2-tailed)	0.5838	0.4089	0.7473	0.2480	0.9312	0.9013	0.7139	0.3317	0.4957	0.4236
	N	36.0000	36.0000	36.0000	36.0000	36.0000	36.0000	36.0000	36.0000	32.0000	34.0000
reflectsqrtQ1A1d	Pearson Correlation	-0.0979	-0.2716	-0.1219	0.2932	0.1377	0.1513	0.0183	0.2144	-0.1993	0.0424
	Sig. (2-tailed)	0.5701	0.1090	0.4788	0.0826	0.4231	0.3783	0.9154	0.2091	0.2741	0.8117
	N	36.0000	36.0000	36.0000	36.0000	36.0000	36.0000	36.0000	36.0000	32.0000	34.0000
reflectsqrtQ1A1e	Pearson Correlation	-0.1055	-0.0945	-0.1092	-0.1569	-0.2225	-0.3094	-0.3146	-0.3942	-0.0240	0.0298
	Sig. (2-tailed)	0.5404	0.5835	0.5259	0.3609	0.1922	0.0663	0.0617	0.0174	0.8965	0.8673
	N	36.0000	36.0000	36.0000	36.0000	36.0000	36.0000	36.0000	36.0000	32.0000	34.0000
sqrtQ1B1a	Pearson Correlation	0.0353	0.0993	-0.0364	0.6200	0.2881	0.1094	0.4848	0.2573	0.1235	-0.0133
	Sig. (2-tailed)	0.8381	0.5645	0.8332	0.0001	0.0884	0.5255	0.0027	0.1297	0.5005	0.9406
	N	36.0000	36.0000	36.0000	36.0000	36.0000	36.0000	36.0000	36.0000	32.0000	34.0000
Knowledge of Smuggling-Narcotics	Pearson Correlation	0.4694	0.3394	0.2517	0.0729	0.5092	0.3940	0.4552	-0.0049	-0.1043	-0.0588
	Sig. (2-tailed)	0.0039	0.0429	0.1386	0.6725	0.0015	0.0174	0.0053	0.9774	0.5701	0.7410
	N	36.0000	36.0000	36.0000	36.0000	36.0000	36.0000	36.0000	36.0000	32.0000	34.0000
Knowledge of Smuggling-Weapons	Pearson Correlation	0.4439	0.4604	0.3294	0.4288	0.5158	0.4225	0.4073	0.3248	-0.0699	-0.0020
	Sig. (2-tailed)	0.0067	0.0047	0.0498	0.0091	0.0013	0.0103	0.0137	0.0532	0.7038	0.9909
	N	36.0000	36.0000	36.0000	36.0000	36.0000	36.0000	36.0000	36.0000	32.0000	34.0000
Knowledge of Smuggling-Humans	Pearson Correlation	0.2701	0.1878	-0.0107	0.0309	0.2726	0.1807	0.4165	-0.0180	0.1561	0.1541
	Sig. (2-tailed)	0.1111	0.2728	0.9505	0.8582	0.1078	0.2915	0.0115	0.9168	0.3935	0.3843
	N	36.0000	36.0000	36.0000	36.0000	36.0000	36.0000	36.0000	36.0000	32.0000	34.0000
Knowledge of Smuggling-Contraband	Pearson Correlation	0.4805	0.2528	0.1780	0.3750	0.3252	0.3303	0.4434	0.3882	-0.0844	-0.1481
	Sig. (2-tailed)	0.0030	0.1368	0.2989	0.0242	0.0530	0.0491	0.0068	0.0193	0.6462	0.4032
	N	36.0000	36.0000	36.0000	36.0000	36.0000	36.0000	36.0000	36.0000	32.0000	34.0000
sqrtQ1E1a	Pearson Correlation	-0.1764	-0.1158	-0.0258	-0.0357	-0.3267	-0.3174	-0.2215	-0.1697	-0.2070	-0.0962
	Sig. (2-tailed)	0.3108	0.5076	0.8832	0.8388	0.0554	0.0632	0.2010	0.3297	0.2638	0.5943
	N	35.0000	35.0000	35.0000	35.0000	35.0000	35.0000	35.0000	35.0000	31.0000	33.0000
Personal Resource Challenges-Lack of Time	Pearson Correlation	0.1106	-0.1264	0.0506	-0.0498	-0.0671	-0.0939	0.0638	-0.0404	-0.1109	-0.2253
	Sig. (2-tailed)	0.5207	0.4625	0.7696	0.7728	0.6976	0.5860	0.7115	0.8149	0.5457	0.2001
	N	36.0000	36.0000	36.0000	36.0000	36.0000	36.0000	36.0000	36.0000	32.0000	34.0000

Table A6, continued (Row 1, Col 7)

Correlation Matrix, Dependent Variables (Parametric)		sqrtQ1F1c	sqrtQ1F1d	sqrtQ1F1e	sqrtQ1F3a	sqrtQ1F3b	sqrtQ1F3c	sqrtQ1F3d	sqrtQ1F3e	sqrtQ1H1a	sqrtQ1H1b
Importance of Smuggling-Endangered Species	Pearson Correlation	0.0165	0.0284	-0.0537	-0.2414	-0.2512	-0.2383	-0.3544	-0.3864	-0.1081	-0.2764
	Sig. (2-tailed)	0.9260	0.8732	0.7628	0.1832	0.1584	0.1817	0.0430	0.0289	0.5628	0.1195
	N	34.0000	34.0000	34.0000	32.0000	33.0000	33.0000	33.0000	32.0000	31.0000	33.0000
reflectsqrtQ1A1b	Pearson Correlation	-0.1062	-0.1074	0.1569	-0.0647	-0.1102	-0.0034	-0.0148	0.0348	-0.0970	0.0090
	Sig. (2-tailed)	0.5502	0.5454	0.3756	0.7248	0.5417	0.9849	0.9348	0.8502	0.6036	0.9606
	N	34.0000	34.0000	34.0000	32.0000	33.0000	33.0000	33.0000	32.0000	31.0000	33.0000
reflectsqrtQ1A1c	Pearson Correlation	-0.1201	-0.1416	0.0686	-0.1281	0.0011	0.0398	0.0272	0.1298	-0.1550	0.1046
	Sig. (2-tailed)	0.4986	0.4245	0.6998	0.4848	0.9953	0.8261	0.8804	0.4790	0.4051	0.5624
	N	34.0000	34.0000	34.0000	32.0000	33.0000	33.0000	33.0000	32.0000	31.0000	33.0000
reflectsqrtQ1A1d	Pearson Correlation	-0.0528	-0.1716	-0.1147	-0.1500	0.1236	0.1548	-0.0797	0.0007	-0.2176	0.0467
	Sig. (2-tailed)	0.7668	0.3318	0.5182	0.4124	0.4930	0.3898	0.6594	0.9971	0.2397	0.7965
	N	34.0000	34.0000	34.0000	32.0000	33.0000	33.0000	33.0000	32.0000	31.0000	33.0000
reflectsqrtQ1A1e	Pearson Correlation	-0.3576	-0.3022	-0.0120	0.0052	0.1371	-0.0259	0.0467	0.0663	0.0715	0.2733
	Sig. (2-tailed)	0.0379	0.0824	0.9462	0.9776	0.4467	0.8863	0.7962	0.7185	0.7024	0.1238
	N	34.0000	34.0000	34.0000	32.0000	33.0000	33.0000	33.0000	32.0000	31.0000	33.0000
sqrtQ1B1a	Pearson Correlation	0.2251	0.1861	0.1549	-0.0668	-0.1502	-0.0322	-0.0703	-0.0543	-0.0600	-0.2608
	Sig. (2-tailed)	0.2006	0.2920	0.3818	0.7166	0.4040	0.8587	0.6975	0.7678	0.7487	0.1427
	N	34.0000	34.0000	34.0000	32.0000	33.0000	33.0000	33.0000	32.0000	31.0000	33.0000
Knowledge of Smuggling-Narcotics	Pearson Correlation	-0.0835	-0.1039	-0.1528	-0.1191	0.0091	0.0473	-0.0908	-0.0659	0.0786	0.0491
	Sig. (2-tailed)	0.6387	0.5587	0.3883	0.5162	0.9600	0.7939	0.6152	0.7202	0.6741	0.7860
	N	34.0000	34.0000	34.0000	32.0000	33.0000	33.0000	33.0000	32.0000	31.0000	33.0000
Knowledge of Smuggling-Weapons	Pearson Correlation	0.1940	0.0901	0.0153	0.0330	0.1041	0.2319	0.0772	0.1019	0.1345	0.0259
	Sig. (2-tailed)	0.2717	0.6124	0.9317	0.8576	0.5642	0.1940	0.6693	0.5788	0.4708	0.8864
	N	34.0000	34.0000	34.0000	32.0000	33.0000	33.0000	33.0000	32.0000	31.0000	33.0000
Knowledge of Smuggling-Humans	Pearson Correlation	0.2198	0.2118	0.1843	0.0503	0.1032	0.1408	0.1034	0.1169	0.0682	0.1668
	Sig. (2-tailed)	0.2116	0.2291	0.2967	0.7844	0.5677	0.4345	0.5669	0.5239	0.7156	0.3535
	N	34.0000	34.0000	34.0000	32.0000	33.0000	33.0000	33.0000	32.0000	31.0000	33.0000
Knowledge of Smuggling-Contraband	Pearson Correlation	0.1269	-0.0415	-0.0458	-0.1160	-0.0951	0.0989	-0.1229	-0.0991	-0.1638	-0.1180
	Sig. (2-tailed)	0.4746	0.8155	0.7971	0.5271	0.5985	0.5840	0.4957	0.5894	0.3787	0.5130
	N	34.0000	34.0000	34.0000	32.0000	33.0000	33.0000	33.0000	32.0000	31.0000	33.0000
sqrtQ1E1a	Pearson Correlation	-0.0437	-0.0732	-0.2009	-0.0570	0.1746	0.1386	0.0894	0.0932	-0.1399	-0.1329
	Sig. (2-tailed)	0.8092	0.6856	0.2622	0.7608	0.3393	0.4493	0.6266	0.6181	0.4611	0.4685
	N	33.0000	33.0000	33.0000	31.0000	32.0000	32.0000	32.0000	31.0000	30.0000	32.0000
Personal Resource Challenges-Lack of Time	Pearson Correlation	-0.2986	-0.1764	-0.1978	0.0787	0.0032	-0.0273	0.0682	0.0585	-0.0793	-0.3969
	Sig. (2-tailed)	0.0863	0.3182	0.2622	0.6686	0.9858	0.8802	0.7060	0.7504	0.6713	0.0222
	N	34.0000	34.0000	34.0000	32.0000	33.0000	33.0000	33.0000	32.0000	31.0000	33.0000

Table A6, continued (Row 1, Col 8)

Correlation Matrix, Dependent Variables (Parametric)		sqrtQIIIH1c	sqrtQIIIH1d	sqrtQIIIH1e	sqrtQIIIH3a	sqrtQIIIH3b	sqrtQIIIH3c	PcHIIQubs	sqrtQIIIH3e	sqrtQIIIA1a	sqrtQIIIA1b
Importance of Smuggling-Endangered Species	Pearson Correlation	-0.2027	-0.3250	-0.2381	-0.0493	-0.2851	-0.2406	-0.2563	-0.3019	0.1539	-0.0319
	Sig. (2-tailed)	0.2659	0.0696	0.1971	0.7820	0.1022	0.1704	0.1434	0.0827	0.3774	0.8535
	N	32.0000	32.0000	31.0000	34.0000	34.0000	34.0000	34.0000	34.0000	35.0000	36.0000
reflectsqrtQ1A1b	Pearson Correlation	-0.1862	-0.0960	0.1926	-0.1360	-0.0175	-0.2103	-0.1407	0.0943	0.1940	0.0782
	Sig. (2-tailed)	0.3075	0.6013	0.2993	0.4430	0.9217	0.2324	0.4275	0.5956	0.2642	0.6503
	N	32.0000	32.0000	31.0000	34.0000	34.0000	34.0000	34.0000	34.0000	35.0000	36.0000
reflectsqrtQ1A1c	Pearson Correlation	-0.0804	-0.0028	0.1787	-0.1850	0.0051	-0.1055	-0.0472	0.0969	0.0303	0.1695
	Sig. (2-tailed)	0.6616	0.9878	0.3360	0.2949	0.9772	0.5525	0.7910	0.5858	0.8627	0.3229
	N	32.0000	32.0000	31.0000	34.0000	34.0000	34.0000	34.0000	34.0000	35.0000	36.0000
reflectsqrtQ1A1d	Pearson Correlation	0.0113	-0.1859	-0.1453	-0.1860	-0.0495	-0.0621	-0.1862	-0.1238	0.1534	0.1824
	Sig. (2-tailed)	0.9510	0.3083	0.4356	0.2922	0.7812	0.7272	0.2917	0.4853	0.3788	0.2870
	N	32.0000	32.0000	31.0000	34.0000	34.0000	34.0000	34.0000	34.0000	35.0000	36.0000
reflectsqrtQ1A1e	Pearson Correlation	0.0988	-0.0266	0.1380	0.1135	0.2423	0.1325	0.1279	0.2300	-0.2490	0.1344
	Sig. (2-tailed)	0.5906	0.8851	0.4592	0.5227	0.1673	0.4551	0.4710	0.1907	0.1492	0.4346
	N	32.0000	32.0000	31.0000	34.0000	34.0000	34.0000	34.0000	34.0000	35.0000	36.0000
sqrtQ1B1a	Pearson Correlation	-0.2745	-0.1833	-0.1340	-0.1723	-0.2976	-0.2605	-0.2476	-0.3064	0.5686	0.0163
	Sig. (2-tailed)	0.1285	0.3152	0.4724	0.3299	0.0874	0.1367	0.1580	0.0780	0.0004	0.9248
	N	32.0000	32.0000	31.0000	34.0000	34.0000	34.0000	34.0000	34.0000	35.0000	36.0000
Knowledge of Smuggling-Narcotics	Pearson Correlation	-0.0001	-0.0615	-0.0256	0.0632	0.0665	0.0367	0.0117	-0.0274	0.0614	0.4628
	Sig. (2-tailed)	0.9996	0.7382	0.8912	0.7225	0.7087	0.8366	0.9478	0.8775	0.7262	0.0045
	N	32.0000	32.0000	31.0000	34.0000	34.0000	34.0000	34.0000	34.0000	35.0000	36.0000
Knowledge of Smuggling-Weapons	Pearson Correlation	-0.0341	0.0282	-0.0302	0.1058	0.0136	0.0256	0.1006	-0.0306	0.1530	0.2114
	Sig. (2-tailed)	0.8531	0.8782	0.8719	0.5514	0.9391	0.8858	0.5713	0.8637	0.3804	0.2159
	N	32.0000	32.0000	31.0000	34.0000	34.0000	34.0000	34.0000	34.0000	35.0000	36.0000
Knowledge of Smuggling-Humans	Pearson Correlation	0.1997	0.2083	0.1067	-0.0003	0.1945	0.2078	0.1212	0.1222	0.2038	0.2662
	Sig. (2-tailed)	0.2733	0.2526	0.5678	0.9989	0.2704	0.2384	0.4949	0.4911	0.2403	0.1166
	N	32.0000	32.0000	31.0000	34.0000	34.0000	34.0000	34.0000	34.0000	35.0000	36.0000
Knowledge of Smuggling-Contraband	Pearson Correlation	-0.1555	-0.1024	-0.0722	-0.1491	-0.1162	-0.1528	-0.1184	-0.0652	0.3504	0.3009
	Sig. (2-tailed)	0.3954	0.5772	0.6997	0.3999	0.5128	0.3884	0.5048	0.7141	0.0390	0.0745
	N	32.0000	32.0000	31.0000	34.0000	34.0000	34.0000	34.0000	34.0000	35.0000	36.0000
sqrtQ1E1a	Pearson Correlation	-0.0513	-0.1180	-0.0339	-0.1628	-0.1273	-0.0821	-0.1608	-0.1548	0.3282	0.2881
	Sig. (2-tailed)	0.7839	0.5274	0.8590	0.3654	0.4803	0.6495	0.3713	0.3898	0.0581	0.0933
	N	31.0000	31.0000	30.0000	33.0000	33.0000	33.0000	33.0000	33.0000	34.0000	35.0000
Personal Resource Challenges-Lack of Time	Pearson Correlation	-0.1848	-0.1055	-0.0919	0.0323	-0.3235	-0.1906	-0.0051	-0.0089	0.3114	0.0694
	Sig. (2-tailed)	0.3112	0.5654	0.6229	0.8563	0.0620	0.2802	0.9770	0.9600	0.0686	0.6877
	N	32.0000	32.0000	31.0000	34.0000	34.0000	34.0000	34.0000	34.0000	35.0000	36.0000

Table A6, continued (Row 1, Col 9)

Correlation Matrix, Dependent Variables (Parametric)		sqrtQIIA1c	sqrtQIIA1d	sqrtQIIA1e	sqrtQIIID1a	Level Cooperation Domestic Orgs-CNDPS	Level Cooperation Domestic Orgs-CNBC	Level Cooperation Domestic Orgs-CSTP	Level Cooperation Domestic Orgs-TRIPS	sqrtQIIID2a	Level Cooperation International Orgs-CNDPS
Importance of Smuggling-Endangered Species	Pearson Correlation	-0.1127	-0.1182	-0.1398	-0.0834	-0.0518	-0.1244	-0.1646	-0.1113	0.0214	0.1124
	Sig. (2-tailed)	0.5128	0.4923	0.4159	0.6445	0.7677	0.4764	0.3448	0.5246	0.9028	0.5139
	N	36.0000	36.0000	36.0000	33.0000	35.0000	35.0000	35.0000	35.0000	35.0000	36.0000
reflectsqrtQ1A1b	Pearson Correlation	-0.0579	-0.0618	0.3553	0.0701	-0.0744	0.0249	0.0051	0.1878	0.2075	0.0021
	Sig. (2-tailed)	0.7373	0.7201	0.0335	0.6984	0.6711	0.8870	0.9767	0.2800	0.2317	0.9902
	N	36.0000	36.0000	36.0000	33.0000	35.0000	35.0000	35.0000	35.0000	35.0000	36.0000
reflectsqrtQ1A1c	Pearson Correlation	0.0782	-0.0557	0.3276	0.1064	0.1564	0.1364	0.1535	0.3916	0.2276	0.1330
	Sig. (2-tailed)	0.6503	0.7470	0.0511	0.5557	0.3696	0.4348	0.3786	0.0200	0.1886	0.4393
	N	36.0000	36.0000	36.0000	33.0000	35.0000	35.0000	35.0000	35.0000	35.0000	36.0000
reflectsqrtQ1A1d	Pearson Correlation	0.2523	-0.0240	0.2496	0.0308	0.1160	0.1835	0.0920	0.2575	0.1701	0.0575
	Sig. (2-tailed)	0.1377	0.8894	0.1421	0.8648	0.5069	0.2913	0.5993	0.1353	0.3285	0.7391
	N	36.0000	36.0000	36.0000	33.0000	35.0000	35.0000	35.0000	35.0000	35.0000	36.0000
reflectsqrtQ1A1e	Pearson Correlation	0.0069	-0.1092	-0.0503	-0.1836	-0.0204	-0.0434	-0.0947	-0.0987	-0.0940	-0.0534
	Sig. (2-tailed)	0.9683	0.5260	0.7708	0.3065	0.9072	0.8045	0.5886	0.5725	0.5913	0.7571
	N	36.0000	36.0000	36.0000	33.0000	35.0000	35.0000	35.0000	35.0000	35.0000	36.0000
sqrtQ1B1a	Pearson Correlation	0.0481	0.1280	0.1387	0.4138	0.2400	0.2866	0.2611	0.2429	0.5361	0.1694
	Sig. (2-tailed)	0.7807	0.4570	0.4197	0.0167	0.1649	0.0951	0.1298	0.1597	0.0009	0.3233
	N	36.0000	36.0000	36.0000	33.0000	35.0000	35.0000	35.0000	35.0000	35.0000	36.0000
Knowledge of Smuggling-Narcotics	Pearson Correlation	0.4045	0.3222	0.1691	0.1939	0.3670	0.2308	0.2171	-0.0035	-0.0078	0.2711
	Sig. (2-tailed)	0.0144	0.0553	0.3241	0.2797	0.0301	0.1821	0.2103	0.9839	0.9646	0.1098
	N	36.0000	36.0000	36.0000	33.0000	35.0000	35.0000	35.0000	35.0000	35.0000	36.0000
Knowledge of Smuggling-Weapons	Pearson Correlation	0.4489	0.2949	0.2459	0.3706	0.2723	0.4812	0.2043	0.2767	0.2198	0.2907
	Sig. (2-tailed)	0.0060	0.0808	0.1483	0.0337	0.1136	0.0034	0.2391	0.1075	0.2044	0.0855
	N	36.0000	36.0000	36.0000	33.0000	35.0000	35.0000	35.0000	35.0000	35.0000	36.0000
Knowledge of Smuggling-Humans	Pearson Correlation	0.2159	0.4759	0.2935	0.1707	0.1638	0.1396	0.2787	0.0033	0.1284	0.1288
	Sig. (2-tailed)	0.2061	0.0033	0.0823	0.3422	0.3471	0.4239	0.1050	0.9852	0.4625	0.4541
	N	36.0000	36.0000	36.0000	33.0000	35.0000	35.0000	35.0000	35.0000	35.0000	36.0000
Knowledge of Smuggling-Contraband	Pearson Correlation	0.3780	0.4396	0.5612	0.3408	0.1460	0.3090	0.2677	0.2737	0.1527	0.0678
	Sig. (2-tailed)	0.0230	0.0073	0.0004	0.0523	0.4028	0.0709	0.1200	0.1117	0.3810	0.6944
	N	36.0000	36.0000	36.0000	33.0000	35.0000	35.0000	35.0000	35.0000	35.0000	36.0000
sqrtQ1E1a	Pearson Correlation	0.3869	0.2685	0.2605	-0.0079	-0.1191	-0.1925	-0.1203	-0.0535	-0.0563	-0.0521
	Sig. (2-tailed)	0.0217	0.1188	0.1307	0.9652	0.4956	0.2680	0.4912	0.7601	0.7519	0.7663
	N	35.0000	35.0000	35.0000	33.0000	35.0000	35.0000	35.0000	35.0000	34.0000	35.0000
Personal Resource Challenges-Lack of Time	Pearson Correlation	0.1221	0.2363	0.1714	0.1206	0.0242	-0.0511	0.1117	0.0041	-0.1385	-0.1679
	Sig. (2-tailed)	0.4779	0.1653	0.3175	0.5039	0.8903	0.7705	0.5231	0.9813	0.4277	0.3277
	N	36.0000	36.0000	36.0000	33.0000	35.0000	35.0000	35.0000	35.0000	35.0000	36.0000

Table A6, continued (Row 1, Col 10)

Correlation Matrix, Dependent Variables (Parametric)		Level Cooperation International Orgs-CNBC	Level Cooperation International Orgs-CSTP	sqrtQIIID2e	sqrtQIVA1	sqrtQIVA2	sqrtQIVA3	sqrtQIVA5	sqrtQIVA7	sqrtQIVA8	Political Ideology
Importance of Smuggling-Endangered Species	Pearson Correlation	0.0449	0.0549	-0.0110	0.1272	0.1038	-0.2036	-0.1126	-0.0287	-0.0400	-0.1693
	Sig. (2-tailed)	0.7949	0.7504	0.9491	0.4597	0.5471	0.2408	0.5259	0.8680	0.8195	0.3464
	N	36.0000	36.0000	36.0000	36.0000	36.0000	35.0000	34.0000	36.0000	35.0000	33.0000
reflectsqrtQ1A1b	Pearson Correlation	0.0023	0.0373	0.0624	-0.1992	0.0760	-0.0784	-0.3136	-0.0640	0.1170	0.3071
	Sig. (2-tailed)	0.9895	0.8292	0.7177	0.2442	0.6595	0.6545	0.0709	0.7108	0.5031	0.0821
	N	36.0000	36.0000	36.0000	36.0000	36.0000	35.0000	34.0000	36.0000	35.0000	33.0000
reflectsqrtQ1A1c	Pearson Correlation	0.0860	0.0793	0.2157	0.0037	-0.0544	-0.0162	-0.1166	0.0205	0.1854	0.2647
	Sig. (2-tailed)	0.6180	0.6459	0.2065	0.9827	0.7528	0.9265	0.5114	0.9057	0.2864	0.1366
	N	36.0000	36.0000	36.0000	36.0000	36.0000	35.0000	34.0000	36.0000	35.0000	33.0000
reflectsqrtQ1A1d	Pearson Correlation	0.1102	0.1459	0.2396	-0.1471	-0.2229	-0.1433	-0.0908	-0.2604	0.1977	0.1013
	Sig. (2-tailed)	0.5222	0.3959	0.1593	0.3919	0.1914	0.4115	0.6095	0.1250	0.2548	0.5750
	N	36.0000	36.0000	36.0000	36.0000	36.0000	35.0000	34.0000	36.0000	35.0000	33.0000
reflectsqrtQ1A1e	Pearson Correlation	-0.0231	-0.0056	-0.1143	-0.2422	-0.0831	-0.0897	-0.1674	-0.1845	-0.0653	0.0011
	Sig. (2-tailed)	0.8936	0.9740	0.5070	0.1546	0.6301	0.6085	0.3440	0.2813	0.7093	0.9951
	N	36.0000	36.0000	36.0000	36.0000	36.0000	35.0000	34.0000	36.0000	35.0000	33.0000
sqrtQ1B1a	Pearson Correlation	0.1797	0.2332	0.1194	0.1477	0.1831	-0.0036	0.1451	-0.1589	0.0121	0.1583
	Sig. (2-tailed)	0.2943	0.1710	0.4880	0.3899	0.2852	0.9835	0.4129	0.3545	0.9450	0.3789
	N	36.0000	36.0000	36.0000	36.0000	36.0000	35.0000	34.0000	36.0000	35.0000	33.0000
Knowledge of Smuggling-Narcotics	Pearson Correlation	0.2604	0.2177	0.0106	0.0975	-0.1039	0.0204	0.1769	-0.1265	0.0783	0.0522
	Sig. (2-tailed)	0.1251	0.2021	0.9511	0.5715	0.5464	0.9073	0.3169	0.4621	0.6548	0.7729
	N	36.0000	36.0000	36.0000	36.0000	36.0000	35.0000	34.0000	36.0000	35.0000	33.0000
Knowledge of Smuggling-Weapons	Pearson Correlation	0.4227	0.2247	0.3393	0.1958	0.0264	0.1837	0.2895	-0.0129	0.0283	0.3089
	Sig. (2-tailed)	0.0102	0.1876	0.0429	0.2525	0.8784	0.2908	0.0968	0.9406	0.8720	0.0802
	N	36.0000	36.0000	36.0000	36.0000	36.0000	35.0000	34.0000	36.0000	35.0000	33.0000
Knowledge of Smuggling-Humans	Pearson Correlation	0.1151	0.2938	0.0382	0.1268	0.0276	0.2654	0.1668	-0.2391	0.1825	0.0541
	Sig. (2-tailed)	0.5040	0.0820	0.8247	0.4610	0.8732	0.1234	0.3458	0.1602	0.2939	0.7649
	N	36.0000	36.0000	36.0000	36.0000	36.0000	35.0000	34.0000	36.0000	35.0000	33.0000
Knowledge of Smuggling-Contraband	Pearson Correlation	0.1025	0.1867	0.1958	0.1346	0.0214	0.1990	0.0464	0.0134	0.2487	0.2656
	Sig. (2-tailed)	0.5518	0.2757	0.2524	0.4339	0.9013	0.2517	0.7946	0.9384	0.1497	0.1352
	N	36.0000	36.0000	36.0000	36.0000	36.0000	35.0000	34.0000	36.0000	35.0000	33.0000
sqrtQ1E1a	Pearson Correlation	-0.1166	-0.0751	-0.1284	0.0884	0.2392	0.3484	-0.0613	-0.0508	-0.1871	-0.1008
	Sig. (2-tailed)	0.5047	0.6679	0.4624	0.6135	0.1663	0.0435	0.7347	0.7719	0.2894	0.5767
	N	35.0000	35.0000	35.0000	35.0000	35.0000	34.0000	33.0000	35.0000	34.0000	33.0000
Personal Resource Challenges-Lack of Time	Pearson Correlation	-0.2175	-0.0209	-0.2123	0.0179	0.0627	0.1729	-0.3000	-0.0716	0.2606	0.1789
	Sig. (2-tailed)	0.2026	0.9038	0.2138	0.9176	0.7164	0.3206	0.0847	0.6782	0.1305	0.3193
	N	36.0000	36.0000	36.0000	36.0000	36.0000	35.0000	34.0000	36.0000	35.0000	33.0000

Table A6, continued (Row 2, Col 1)

Correlation Matrix, Dependent Variables (Parametric)		Importance of Smuggling-Endangered Species	reflectsqrtQ1A1b	reflectsqrtQ1A1c	reflectsqrtQ1A1d	reflectsqrtQ1A1e	sqrtQ1B1a	Knowledge of Smuggling-Narcotics	Knowledge of Smuggling-Weapons	Knowledge of Smuggling-Humans	Knowledge of Smuggling-Contraband
Personal Resource Challenges-Lack of Knowledge	Pearson Correlation	-0.0060	-0.1074	-0.1398	0.0012	0.0140	0.0056	-0.0019	-0.2415	0.0093	-0.0687
	Sig. (2-tailed)	0.9725	0.5329	0.4162	0.9945	0.9356	0.9743	0.9911	0.1560	0.9572	0.6905
	N	36.0000	36.0000	36.0000	36.0000	36.0000	36.0000	36.0000	36.0000	36.0000	36.0000
Personal Resource Challenges-Lack of Training	Pearson Correlation	-0.1118	-0.0574	-0.1409	-0.0396	0.0473	0.0112	-0.0190	-0.2339	-0.0248	-0.1326
	Sig. (2-tailed)	0.5161	0.7396	0.4125	0.8186	0.7840	0.9483	0.9126	0.1698	0.8859	0.4409
	N	36.0000	36.0000	36.0000	36.0000	36.0000	36.0000	36.0000	36.0000	36.0000	36.0000
sqrtQ1E1e	Pearson Correlation	0.0017	0.0673	-0.0870	-0.1839	0.0016	0.2065	0.0853	0.2980	0.0830	0.1690
	Sig. (2-tailed)	0.9923	0.6965	0.6141	0.2829	0.9928	0.2270	0.6208	0.0775	0.6301	0.3243
	N	36.0000	36.0000	36.0000	36.0000	36.0000	36.0000	36.0000	36.0000	36.0000	36.0000
Personal Resource Challenges-Excessive Admin Paperwork	Pearson Correlation	-0.1143	0.1222	0.0631	-0.0777	-0.0052	0.0536	0.2558	0.2285	-0.0120	0.2170
	Sig. (2-tailed)	0.5070	0.4777	0.7148	0.6526	0.9760	0.7560	0.1320	0.1802	0.9445	0.2037
	N	36.0000	36.0000	36.0000	36.0000	36.0000	36.0000	36.0000	36.0000	36.0000	36.0000
Personal Resource Challenges-Ineffective Technology	Pearson Correlation	-0.0332	-0.0507	-0.0964	-0.2668	0.0638	0.0157	0.2258	-0.0585	0.0177	-0.0706
	Sig. (2-tailed)	0.8474	0.7692	0.5758	0.1157	0.7115	0.9276	0.1854	0.7349	0.9184	0.6824
	N	36.0000	36.0000	36.0000	36.0000	36.0000	36.0000	36.0000	36.0000	36.0000	36.0000
Personal Resource Challenges-Ineffective Strategic Focus	Pearson Correlation	-0.1285	-0.0880	-0.2280	-0.2106	0.0616	0.1585	-0.0792	-0.1197	-0.0164	-0.1110
	Sig. (2-tailed)	0.4550	0.6099	0.1811	0.2177	0.7211	0.3558	0.6460	0.4868	0.9245	0.5192
	N	36.0000	36.0000	36.0000	36.0000	36.0000	36.0000	36.0000	36.0000	36.0000	36.0000
Personal Resource Challenges-Ineffective Tactical Policy	Pearson Correlation	-0.1699	-0.0058	-0.0994	-0.1638	0.1821	0.0430	-0.0393	-0.1135	0.0170	-0.1189
	Sig. (2-tailed)	0.3218	0.9732	0.5643	0.3397	0.2879	0.8033	0.8202	0.5097	0.9215	0.4899
	N	36.0000	36.0000	36.0000	36.0000	36.0000	36.0000	36.0000	36.0000	36.0000	36.0000
Personal Resource Challenges-Lack of Clarity in Duties	Pearson Correlation	-0.0555	-0.0091	-0.1168	-0.1988	0.1008	0.0533	0.0626	-0.1099	0.0758	0.0121
	Sig. (2-tailed)	0.7476	0.9579	0.4976	0.2451	0.5587	0.7575	0.7166	0.5235	0.6605	0.9442
	N	36.0000	36.0000	36.0000	36.0000	36.0000	36.0000	36.0000	36.0000	36.0000	36.0000
Personal Resource Challenges-Conflict or Lack Comm Leaders and Employees	Pearson Correlation	-0.0670	0.0368	-0.0162	-0.1624	0.2367	0.0124	-0.0357	-0.1635	-0.0869	-0.0616
	Sig. (2-tailed)	0.6979	0.8314	0.9253	0.3439	0.1646	0.9427	0.8364	0.3406	0.6142	0.7213
	N	36.0000	36.0000	36.0000	36.0000	36.0000	36.0000	36.0000	36.0000	36.0000	36.0000
sqrtQ1E1l	Pearson Correlation	0.0461	-0.0333	-0.0776	0.0044	-0.1415	0.0984	-0.0247	0.0217	-0.2842	0.0032
	Sig. (2-tailed)	0.7894	0.8470	0.6528	0.9796	0.4104	0.5681	0.8862	0.9001	0.0930	0.9854
	N	36.0000	36.0000	36.0000	36.0000	36.0000	36.0000	36.0000	36.0000	36.0000	36.0000
Personal Resource Challenges-Conflict or Lack Comm International Orgs	Pearson Correlation	0.0229	0.0465	-0.0535	-0.1854	-0.0606	0.0694	0.1843	-0.0188	-0.0105	0.1416
	Sig. (2-tailed)	0.8946	0.7876	0.7567	0.2789	0.7254	0.6876	0.2818	0.9134	0.9517	0.4100
	N	36.0000	36.0000	36.0000	36.0000	36.0000	36.0000	36.0000	36.0000	36.0000	36.0000
Personal Resource Challenges-Conflict or Lack Comm Domestic Orgs	Pearson Correlation	-0.0208	-0.1078	-0.0861	-0.2570	0.1232	-0.0188	0.1111	-0.1551	-0.0370	-0.0556
	Sig. (2-tailed)	0.9041	0.5314	0.6178	0.1303	0.4741	0.9131	0.5187	0.3663	0.8303	0.7474
	N	36.0000	36.0000	36.0000	36.0000	36.0000	36.0000	36.0000	36.0000	36.0000	36.0000

Table A6, continued (Row 2, Col 2)

Correlation Matrix, Dependent Variables (Parametric)		sqrtQ1E1a	Personal Resource Challenges-Lack of Time	Personal Resource Challenges-Lack of Knowledge	Personal Resource Challenges-Lack of Training	sqrtQ1E1e	Personal Resource Challenges-Excessive Admin Paperwork	Personal Resource Challenges-Ineffective Technology	Personal Resource Challenges-Ineffective Strategic Focus	Personal Resource Challenges-Ineffective Tactical Policy	Personal Resource Challenges-Lack of Clarity in Duties
Personal Resource Challenges-Lack of Knowledge	Pearson Correlation	0.3342	0.5812	1.0000	0.9275	0.3493	0.3018	0.6239	0.6827	0.5897	0.6849
	Sig. (2-tailed)	0.0497	0.0002	.	0.0000	0.0368	0.0736	0.0000	0.0000	0.0002	0.0000
	N	35.0000	36.0000	36.0000	36.0000	36.0000	36.0000	36.0000	36.0000	36.0000	36.0000
Personal Resource Challenges-Lack of Training	Pearson Correlation	0.2759	0.4861	0.9275	1.0000	0.2734	0.2702	0.5769	0.6850	0.5761	0.6457
	Sig. (2-tailed)	0.1087	0.0027	0.0000	.	0.1066	0.1110	0.0002	0.0000	0.0002	0.0000
	N	35.0000	36.0000	36.0000	36.0000	36.0000	36.0000	36.0000	36.0000	36.0000	36.0000
sqrtQ1E1e	Pearson Correlation	0.1914	0.3338	0.3493	0.2734	1.0000	0.5245	0.3197	0.5547	0.4222	0.4292
	Sig. (2-tailed)	0.2708	0.0466	0.0368	0.1066	.	0.0010	0.0574	0.0004	0.0103	0.0090
	N	35.0000	36.0000	36.0000	36.0000	36.0000	36.0000	36.0000	36.0000	36.0000	36.0000
Personal Resource Challenges-Excessive Admin Paperwork	Pearson Correlation	0.4520	0.3445	0.3018	0.2702	0.5245	1.0000	0.3484	0.4345	0.5723	0.5320
	Sig. (2-tailed)	0.0064	0.0396	0.0736	0.1110	0.0010	.	0.0373	0.0081	0.0003	0.0008
	N	35.0000	36.0000	36.0000	36.0000	36.0000	36.0000	36.0000	36.0000	36.0000	36.0000
Personal Resource Challenges-Ineffective Technology	Pearson Correlation	0.3708	0.2844	0.6239	0.5769	0.3197	0.3484	1.0000	0.5567	0.5629	0.5197
	Sig. (2-tailed)	0.0283	0.0927	0.0000	0.0002	0.0574	0.0373	.	0.0004	0.0004	0.0012
	N	35.0000	36.0000	36.0000	36.0000	36.0000	36.0000	36.0000	36.0000	36.0000	36.0000
Personal Resource Challenges-Ineffective Strategic Focus	Pearson Correlation	0.5510	0.4073	0.6827	0.6850	0.5547	0.4345	0.5567	1.0000	0.8897	0.8164
	Sig. (2-tailed)	0.0006	0.0137	0.0000	0.0000	0.0004	0.0081	0.0004	.	0.0000	0.0000
	N	35.0000	36.0000	36.0000	36.0000	36.0000	36.0000	36.0000	36.0000	36.0000	36.0000
Personal Resource Challenges-Ineffective Tactical Policy	Pearson Correlation	0.6237	0.4851	0.5897	0.5761	0.4222	0.5723	0.5629	0.8897	1.0000	0.8650
	Sig. (2-tailed)	0.0001	0.0027	0.0002	0.0002	0.0103	0.0003	0.0004	0.0000	.	0.0000
	N	35.0000	36.0000	36.0000	36.0000	36.0000	36.0000	36.0000	36.0000	36.0000	36.0000
Personal Resource Challenges-Lack of Clarity in Duties	Pearson Correlation	0.5042	0.5687	0.6849	0.6457	0.4292	0.5320	0.5197	0.8164	0.8650	1.0000
	Sig. (2-tailed)	0.0020	0.0003	0.0000	0.0000	0.0090	0.0008	0.0012	0.0000	0.0000	.
	N	35.0000	36.0000	36.0000	36.0000	36.0000	36.0000	36.0000	36.0000	36.0000	36.0000
Personal Resource Challenges-Conflict or Lack Comm Leaders and Employees	Pearson Correlation	0.5982	0.4964	0.5447	0.4604	0.4211	0.5114	0.4778	0.8107	0.8852	0.8299
	Sig. (2-tailed)	0.0001	0.0021	0.0006	0.0047	0.0105	0.0014	0.0032	0.0000	0.0000	0.0000
	N	35.0000	36.0000	36.0000	36.0000	36.0000	36.0000	36.0000	36.0000	36.0000	36.0000
sqrtQ1E1l	Pearson Correlation	0.5175	0.1927	0.2645	0.1879	0.3410	0.5958	0.2670	0.5559	0.5402	0.4613
	Sig. (2-tailed)	0.0015	0.2602	0.1190	0.2724	0.0418	0.0001	0.1154	0.0004	0.0007	0.0046
	N	35.0000	36.0000	36.0000	36.0000	36.0000	36.0000	36.0000	36.0000	36.0000	36.0000
Personal Resource Challenges-Conflict or Lack Comm International Orgs	Pearson Correlation	0.3957	0.4594	0.5736	0.5330	0.3925	0.6658	0.3591	0.5279	0.5658	0.6280
	Sig. (2-tailed)	0.0186	0.0048	0.0003	0.0008	0.0179	0.0000	0.0315	0.0009	0.0003	0.0000
	N	35.0000	36.0000	36.0000	36.0000	36.0000	36.0000	36.0000	36.0000	36.0000	36.0000
Personal Resource Challenges-Conflict or Lack Comm Domestic Orgs	Pearson Correlation	0.4968	0.6319	0.6835	0.6132	0.4321	0.5785	0.5291	0.7125	0.7745	0.8215
	Sig. (2-tailed)	0.0024	0.0000	0.0000	0.0001	0.0085	0.0002	0.0009	0.0000	0.0000	0.0000
	N	35.0000	36.0000	36.0000	36.0000	36.0000	36.0000	36.0000	36.0000	36.0000	36.0000

Table A6, continued (Row 2, Col 3)

Correlation Matrix, Dependent Variables (Parametric)			sqrtQ1E11	Personal Resource Challenges-Conflict or Lack Comm International Orgs	Personal Resource Challenges-Conflict or Lack Comm Domestic Orgs	sqrtQ1E3a	Org Resource Challenges-Lack of Time	Org Resource Challenges-Lack of Knowledge	Org Resource Challenges-Lack of Training	sqrtQ1E3e	Personal Resource Challenges-Conflict or Lack Comm Leaders and Employees
Personal Resource Challenges-Lack of Knowledge	Pearson Correlation	0.5447	0.2645	0.5736	0.6835	0.2711	0.4688	0.8329	0.8367	0.3772	0.5046
	Sig. (2-tailed)	0.0006	0.1190	0.0003	0.0000	0.1210	0.0045	0.0000	0.0000	0.0279	0.0020
	N	36.0000	36.0000	36.0000	36.0000	34.0000	35.0000	35.0000	35.0000	34.0000	35.0000
Personal Resource Challenges-Lack of Training	Pearson Correlation	0.4604	0.1879	0.5330	0.6132	0.2455	0.3864	0.8421	0.8394	0.3616	0.4976
	Sig. (2-tailed)	0.0047	0.2724	0.0008	0.0001	0.1617	0.0219	0.0000	0.0000	0.0356	0.0024
	N	36.0000	36.0000	36.0000	36.0000	34.0000	35.0000	35.0000	35.0000	34.0000	35.0000
sqrtQ1E1e	Pearson Correlation	0.4211	0.3410	0.3925	0.4321	0.4098	0.0904	0.2760	0.2369	0.4965	0.4340
	Sig. (2-tailed)	0.0105	0.0418	0.0179	0.0085	0.0161	0.6053	0.1085	0.1707	0.0028	0.0092
	N	36.0000	36.0000	36.0000	36.0000	34.0000	35.0000	35.0000	35.0000	34.0000	35.0000
Personal Resource Challenges-Excessive Admin Paperwork	Pearson Correlation	0.5114	0.5958	0.6658	0.5785	0.2648	0.0679	0.1780	0.2168	0.3455	0.5589
	Sig. (2-tailed)	0.0014	0.0001	0.0000	0.0002	0.1302	0.6983	0.3064	0.2110	0.0454	0.0005
	N	36.0000	36.0000	36.0000	36.0000	34.0000	35.0000	35.0000	35.0000	34.0000	35.0000
Personal Resource Challenges-Ineffective Technology	Pearson Correlation	0.4778	0.2670	0.3591	0.5291	0.4635	0.3841	0.5886	0.6681	0.3066	0.4503
	Sig. (2-tailed)	0.0032	0.1154	0.0315	0.0009	0.0058	0.0227	0.0002	0.0000	0.0778	0.0066
	N	36.0000	36.0000	36.0000	36.0000	34.0000	35.0000	35.0000	35.0000	34.0000	35.0000
Personal Resource Challenges-Ineffective Strategic Focus	Pearson Correlation	0.8107	0.5559	0.5279	0.7125	0.3866	0.3242	0.7021	0.6671	0.5175	0.6065
	Sig. (2-tailed)	0.0000	0.0004	0.0009	0.0000	0.0239	0.0575	0.0000	0.0000	0.0017	0.0001
	N	36.0000	36.0000	36.0000	36.0000	34.0000	35.0000	35.0000	35.0000	34.0000	35.0000
Personal Resource Challenges-Ineffective Tactical Policy	Pearson Correlation	0.8852	0.5402	0.5658	0.7745	0.4224	0.3104	0.5752	0.5784	0.5213	0.6251
	Sig. (2-tailed)	0.0000	0.0007	0.0003	0.0000	0.0128	0.0696	0.0003	0.0003	0.0016	0.0001
	N	36.0000	36.0000	36.0000	36.0000	34.0000	35.0000	35.0000	35.0000	34.0000	35.0000
Personal Resource Challenges-Lack of Clarity in Duties	Pearson Correlation	0.8299	0.4613	0.6280	0.8215	0.4139	0.2282	0.6555	0.6437	0.4520	0.5833
	Sig. (2-tailed)	0.0000	0.0046	0.0000	0.0000	0.0150	0.1873	0.0000	0.0000	0.0073	0.0002
	N	36.0000	36.0000	36.0000	36.0000	34.0000	35.0000	35.0000	35.0000	34.0000	35.0000
Personal Resource Challenges-Conflict or Lack Comm Leaders and Employees	Pearson Correlation	1.0000	0.6103	0.5973	0.8361	0.3253	0.2036	0.5026	0.4964	0.4955	0.5537
	Sig. (2-tailed)	.	0.0001	0.0001	0.0000	0.0605	0.2408	0.0021	0.0024	0.0029	0.0006
	N	36.0000	36.0000	36.0000	36.0000	34.0000	35.0000	35.0000	35.0000	34.0000	35.0000
sqrtQ1E11	Pearson Correlation	0.6103	1.0000	0.5245	0.4760	0.1459	0.0786	0.2653	0.3241	0.4006	0.4504
	Sig. (2-tailed)	0.0001	.	0.0010	0.0033	0.4103	0.6537	0.1235	0.0575	0.0189	0.0066
	N	36.0000	36.0000	36.0000	36.0000	34.0000	35.0000	35.0000	35.0000	34.0000	35.0000
Personal Resource Challenges-Conflict or Lack Comm International Orgs	Pearson Correlation	0.5973	0.5245	1.0000	0.7869	0.2008	0.1757	0.5045	0.5332	0.2910	0.4796
	Sig. (2-tailed)	0.0001	0.0010	.	0.0000	0.2548	0.3127	0.0020	0.0010	0.0950	0.0036
	N	36.0000	36.0000	36.0000	36.0000	34.0000	35.0000	35.0000	35.0000	34.0000	35.0000
Personal Resource Challenges-Conflict or Lack Comm Domestic Orgs	Pearson Correlation	0.8361	0.4760	0.7869	1.0000	0.3785	0.2783	0.6298	0.6691	0.4769	0.6087
	Sig. (2-tailed)	0.0000	0.0033	0.0000	.	0.0273	0.1055	0.0001	0.0000	0.0043	0.0001
	N	36.0000	36.0000	36.0000	36.0000	34.0000	35.0000	35.0000	35.0000	34.0000	35.0000

242

Table A6, continued (Row 2, Col 4)

Correlation Matrix, Dependent Variables (Parametric)		Org Resource Challenges-Ineffective Technology	Org Resource Challenges-Ineffective Strategic Focus	Org Resource Challenges-Ineffective Tactical Policy	Org Resource Challenges-Lack of Clarity in Duties	Org Resource Challenges-Conflict or Lack Comm Leaders and Employees	sqrtQ1E3l	Org Resource Challenges-Conflict or Lack Comm International Orgs	Org Resource Challenges-Conflict or Lack Comm Domestic Orgs	sqrtQ1IA1a	Knowledge of Domestic Law-CSIE
Personal Resource Challenges-Lack of Knowledge	Pearson Correlation	0.5715	0.7606	0.6627	0.7468	0.5058	0.2868	0.7712	0.7446	0.1297	-0.1119
	Sig. (2-tailed)	0.0003	0.0000	0.0000	0.0000	0.0019	0.0948	0.0000	0.0000	0.4579	0.5223
	N	35.0000	35.0000	35.0000	35.0000	35.0000	35.0000	35.0000	35.0000	35.0000	35.0000
Personal Resource Challenges-Lack of Training	Pearson Correlation	0.5343	0.7089	0.6414	0.7607	0.4702	0.2943	0.7224	0.6898	0.1362	-0.2222
	Sig. (2-tailed)	0.0009	0.0000	0.0000	0.0000	0.0044	0.0862	0.0000	0.0000	0.4354	0.1996
	N	35.0000	35.0000	35.0000	35.0000	35.0000	35.0000	35.0000	35.0000	35.0000	35.0000
sqrtQ1E1e	Pearson Correlation	0.3100	0.3791	0.4666	0.3853	0.4733	0.3287	0.3387	0.3704	0.1985	0.0135
	Sig. (2-tailed)	0.0699	0.0247	0.0047	0.0223	0.0041	0.0539	0.0465	0.0285	0.2530	0.9384
	N	35.0000	35.0000	35.0000	35.0000	35.0000	35.0000	35.0000	35.0000	35.0000	35.0000
Personal Resource Challenges-Excessive Admin Paperwork	Pearson Correlation	0.3545	0.3099	0.4462	0.2944	0.5096	0.5204	0.3204	0.3419	0.1231	0.1304
	Sig. (2-tailed)	0.0367	0.0700	0.0072	0.0860	0.0018	0.0014	0.0606	0.0444	0.4810	0.4553
	N	35.0000	35.0000	35.0000	35.0000	35.0000	35.0000	35.0000	35.0000	35.0000	35.0000
Personal Resource Challenges-Ineffective Technology	Pearson Correlation	0.7341	0.6454	0.4557	0.5999	0.3705	0.2168	0.5919	0.6206	-0.0890	0.1874
	Sig. (2-tailed)	0.0000	0.0000	0.0059	0.0001	0.0285	0.2108	0.0002	0.0001	0.6113	0.2811
	N	35.0000	35.0000	35.0000	35.0000	35.0000	35.0000	35.0000	35.0000	35.0000	35.0000
Personal Resource Challenges-Ineffective Strategic Focus	Pearson Correlation	0.6251	0.7928	0.7917	0.7915	0.6182	0.5372	0.6129	0.6329	0.1663	-0.2240
	Sig. (2-tailed)	0.0001	0.0000	0.0000	0.0000	0.0001	0.0009	0.0001	0.0000	0.3398	0.1958
	N	35.0000	35.0000	35.0000	35.0000	35.0000	35.0000	35.0000	35.0000	35.0000	35.0000
Personal Resource Challenges-Ineffective Tactical Policy	Pearson Correlation	0.6686	0.7660	0.8024	0.7397	0.6952	0.4737	0.5677	0.5770	0.0529	-0.2112
	Sig. (2-tailed)	0.0000	0.0000	0.0000	0.0000	0.0000	0.0040	0.0004	0.0003	0.7627	0.2234
	N	35.0000	35.0000	35.0000	35.0000	35.0000	35.0000	35.0000	35.0000	35.0000	35.0000
Personal Resource Challenges-Lack of Clarity in Duties	Pearson Correlation	0.5461	0.7172	0.8184	0.6774	0.6451	0.4299	0.5515	0.5381	0.1278	-0.2785
	Sig. (2-tailed)	0.0007	0.0000	0.0000	0.0000	0.0000	0.0100	0.0006	0.0009	0.4645	0.1053
	N	35.0000	35.0000	35.0000	35.0000	35.0000	35.0000	35.0000	35.0000	35.0000	35.0000
Personal Resource Challenges-Conflict or Lack Comm Leaders and Employees	Pearson Correlation	0.6035	0.7479	0.8003	0.6391	0.7390	0.5035	0.4527	0.5411	0.0748	-0.1977
	Sig. (2-tailed)	0.0001	0.0000	0.0000	0.0000	0.0000	0.0020	0.0063	0.0008	0.6692	0.2549
	N	35.0000	35.0000	35.0000	35.0000	35.0000	35.0000	35.0000	35.0000	35.0000	35.0000
sqrtQ1E1l	Pearson Correlation	0.4102	0.4507	0.4718	0.3910	0.5790	0.9287	0.3371	0.4099	0.0207	0.0244
	Sig. (2-tailed)	0.0144	0.0066	0.0042	0.0202	0.0003	0.0000	0.0477	0.0145	0.9059	0.8893
	N	35.0000	35.0000	35.0000	35.0000	35.0000	35.0000	35.0000	35.0000	35.0000	35.0000
Personal Resource Challenges-Conflict or Lack Comm International Orgs	Pearson Correlation	0.3417	0.4554	0.6704	0.5006	0.6766	0.5669	0.5283	0.4958	0.2155	0.0457
	Sig. (2-tailed)	0.0446	0.0060	0.0000	0.0022	0.0000	0.0004	0.0011	0.0025	0.2137	0.7945
	N	35.0000	35.0000	35.0000	35.0000	35.0000	35.0000	35.0000	35.0000	35.0000	35.0000
Personal Resource Challenges-Conflict or Lack Comm Domestic Orgs	Pearson Correlation	0.5933	0.6978	0.8536	0.6819	0.7312	0.4613	0.6075	0.6459	0.1088	-0.1031
	Sig. (2-tailed)	0.0002	0.0000	0.0000	0.0000	0.0000	0.0053	0.0001	0.0000	0.5340	0.5558
	N	35.0000	35.0000	35.0000	35.0000	35.0000	35.0000	35.0000	35.0000	35.0000	35.0000

Correlation Matrix, Dependent Variables (Parametric)		Knowledge of Domestic Law-DWMD	Knowledge of Domestic Law-TVP	Knowledge of Domestic Law-CBP	sqrtQ1IB1a	Perceived Effectiveness Domestic Govt Support-CSIE	Perceived Effectiveness Domestic Govt Support-DWMD	Perceived Effectiveness Domestic Govt SupportTVP	Perceived Effectiveness Domestic Govt Support-CBP	sqrtQ1IC1a	Perceived Deterrence Domestic Law-CSIE
Personal Resource Challenges-Lack of Knowledge	Pearson Correlation	-0.1684	0.0131	-0.1704	-0.0207	-0.1588	-0.0216	-0.2723	-0.1568	-0.0097	-0.0349
	Sig. (2-tailed)	0.3335	0.9404	0.3279	0.9061	0.3621	0.9006	0.1136	0.3684	0.9560	0.8397
	N	35.0000	35.0000	35.0000	35.0000	35.0000	36.0000	35.0000	35.0000	35.0000	36.0000
Personal Resource Challenges-Lack of Training	Pearson Correlation	-0.2745	-0.0242	-0.2953	0.0772	-0.1195	-0.0557	-0.2538	-0.1208	0.1033	-0.0367
	Sig. (2-tailed)	0.1105	0.8901	0.0850	0.6595	0.4940	0.7468	0.1413	0.4895	0.5550	0.8315
	N	35.0000	35.0000	35.0000	35.0000	35.0000	36.0000	35.0000	35.0000	35.0000	36.0000
sqrtQ1E1e	Pearson Correlation	-0.0123	-0.0726	0.1008	0.0554	0.0380	0.0232	-0.0384	-0.0354	-0.0232	0.2299
	Sig. (2-tailed)	0.9439	0.6784	0.5644	0.7519	0.8286	0.8930	0.8265	0.8402	0.8946	0.1773
	N	35.0000	35.0000	35.0000	35.0000	35.0000	36.0000	35.0000	35.0000	35.0000	36.0000
Personal Resource Challenges-Excessive Admin Paperwork	Pearson Correlation	0.0638	0.1009	0.0404	0.2519	0.0177	-0.0175	0.0173	-0.0679	0.1834	0.2142
	Sig. (2-tailed)	0.7156	0.5642	0.8177	0.1444	0.9198	0.9193	0.9212	0.6981	0.2917	0.2097
	N	35.0000	35.0000	35.0000	35.0000	35.0000	36.0000	35.0000	35.0000	35.0000	36.0000
Personal Resource Challenges-Ineffective Technology	Pearson Correlation	0.0578	0.0814	-0.1367	-0.0869	-0.0620	-0.1884	-0.4288	-0.3476	-0.0074	0.0418
	Sig. (2-tailed)	0.7415	0.6421	0.4337	0.6196	0.7234	0.2711	0.0102	0.0408	0.9665	0.8088
	N	35.0000	35.0000	35.0000	35.0000	35.0000	36.0000	35.0000	35.0000	35.0000	36.0000
Personal Resource Challenges-Ineffective Strategic Focus	Pearson Correlation	-0.3036	-0.0651	-0.2731	0.1213	-0.2103	-0.2085	-0.3213	-0.2878	0.0771	0.0674
	Sig. (2-tailed)	0.0762	0.7100	0.1125	0.4875	0.2252	0.2223	0.0598	0.0936	0.6599	0.6961
	N	35.0000	35.0000	35.0000	35.0000	35.0000	36.0000	35.0000	35.0000	35.0000	36.0000
Personal Resource Challenges-Ineffective Tactical Policy	Pearson Correlation	-0.2200	-0.0220	-0.2471	0.0551	-0.2880	-0.2482	-0.2887	-0.3012	0.0662	-0.0343
	Sig. (2-tailed)	0.2040	0.9003	0.1525	0.7534	0.0934	0.1444	0.0926	0.0787	0.7055	0.8424
	N	35.0000	35.0000	35.0000	35.0000	35.0000	36.0000	35.0000	35.0000	35.0000	36.0000
Personal Resource Challenges-Lack of Clarity in Duties	Pearson Correlation	-0.2676	0.0909	-0.1374	0.1344	-0.3218	-0.2057	-0.2773	-0.2312	0.1138	0.0701
	Sig. (2-tailed)	0.1201	0.6036	0.4314	0.4414	0.0594	0.2287	0.1069	0.1815	0.5151	0.6847
	N	35.0000	35.0000	35.0000	35.0000	35.0000	36.0000	35.0000	35.0000	35.0000	36.0000
Personal Resource Challenges-Conflict or Lack Comm Leaders and Employees	Pearson Correlation	-0.2397	-0.1073	-0.1200	0.0178	-0.3135	-0.2352	-0.2338	-0.2236	0.0073	-0.0032
	Sig. (2-tailed)	0.1655	0.5394	0.4922	0.9193	0.0666	0.1673	0.1764	0.1966	0.9669	0.9852
	N	35.0000	35.0000	35.0000	35.0000	35.0000	36.0000	35.0000	35.0000	35.0000	36.0000
sqrtQ1E11	Pearson Correlation	-0.1690	-0.2804	-0.1781	0.2308	-0.0598	-0.1697	-0.0749	-0.1061	0.0877	-0.0424
	Sig. (2-tailed)	0.3317	0.1028	0.3061	0.1822	0.7329	0.3223	0.6688	0.5440	0.6164	0.8060
	N	35.0000	35.0000	35.0000	35.0000	35.0000	36.0000	35.0000	35.0000	35.0000	36.0000
Personal Resource Challenges-Conflict or Lack Comm International Orgs	Pearson Correlation	-0.0794	0.1555	0.0366	0.1476	-0.0264	0.0064	-0.0629	-0.0719	0.1672	0.2196
	Sig. (2-tailed)	0.6502	0.3723	0.8345	0.3973	0.8804	0.9706	0.7195	0.6815	0.3371	0.1982
	N	35.0000	35.0000	35.0000	35.0000	35.0000	36.0000	35.0000	35.0000	35.0000	36.0000
Personal Resource Challenges-Conflict or Lack Comm Domestic Orgs	Pearson Correlation	-0.2276	0.0439	-0.0862	0.0080	-0.2122	-0.1523	-0.1881	-0.2038	-0.0003	0.1395
	Sig. (2-tailed)	0.1885	0.8024	0.6226	0.9636	0.2211	0.3751	0.2793	0.2402	0.9986	0.4172
	N	35.0000	35.0000	35.0000	35.0000	35.0000	36.0000	35.0000	35.0000	35.0000	36.0000

Table A6, continued (Row 2, Col 6)

Correlation Matrix, Dependent Variables (Parametric)		sqrtQIIC1c	Perceived Deterrence Domestic Law-TVP	sqrtQIIC1e	sqrtQIID1a	Level Cooperation Domestic Orgs-CSIE	Level Cooperation Domestic Orgs-DWMD	Level Cooperation Domestic Orgs-TVP	Level Cooperation Domestic Orgs-CBP	sqrtQIIF1a	sqrtQIIF1b
Personal Resource Challenges-Lack of Knowledge	Pearson Correlation	-0.1669	-0.2495	-0.1759	-0.1174	-0.3195	-0.3120	-0.1253	-0.1085	0.1083	-0.0091
	Sig. (2-tailed)	0.3307	0.1422	0.3048	0.4955	0.0575	0.0639	0.4667	0.5287	0.5553	0.9594
	N	36.0000	36.0000	36.0000	36.0000	36.0000	36.0000	36.0000	36.0000	32.0000	34.0000
Personal Resource Challenges-Lack of Training	Pearson Correlation	-0.2088	-0.1770	-0.1284	-0.1545	-0.3802	-0.3942	-0.2011	-0.1170	0.1907	0.0057
	Sig. (2-tailed)	0.2216	0.3017	0.4554	0.3682	0.0222	0.0174	0.2396	0.4968	0.2959	0.9744
	N	36.0000	36.0000	36.0000	36.0000	36.0000	36.0000	36.0000	36.0000	32.0000	34.0000
sqrtQ1E1e	Pearson Correlation	0.0587	0.0541	0.0138	0.2266	-0.0320	-0.0340	0.0283	0.0558	0.0661	0.0388
	Sig. (2-tailed)	0.7339	0.7540	0.9362	0.1839	0.8528	0.8439	0.8701	0.7467	0.7192	0.8277
	N	36.0000	36.0000	36.0000	36.0000	36.0000	36.0000	36.0000	36.0000	32.0000	34.0000
Personal Resource Challenges-Excessive Admin Paperwork	Pearson Correlation	0.1684	0.1810	0.1871	0.1332	0.0093	0.1753	0.0584	-0.0042	-0.1616	-0.2565
	Sig. (2-tailed)	0.3262	0.2909	0.2746	0.4387	0.9570	0.3065	0.7350	0.9804	0.3770	0.1430
	N	36.0000	36.0000	36.0000	36.0000	36.0000	36.0000	36.0000	36.0000	32.0000	34.0000
Personal Resource Challenges-Ineffective Technology	Pearson Correlation	-0.2577	-0.1782	-0.1381	-0.1490	-0.2315	-0.3228	-0.1657	-0.1672	-0.0084	-0.1464
	Sig. (2-tailed)	0.1292	0.2984	0.4219	0.3857	0.1743	0.0548	0.3342	0.3296	0.9637	0.4087
	N	36.0000	36.0000	36.0000	36.0000	36.0000	36.0000	36.0000	36.0000	32.0000	34.0000
Personal Resource Challenges-Ineffective Strategic Focus	Pearson Correlation	-0.1948	-0.1036	-0.1071	-0.0144	-0.3394	-0.4186	-0.1068	-0.0882	0.1466	0.0246
	Sig. (2-tailed)	0.2549	0.5478	0.5340	0.9337	0.0429	0.0111	0.5354	0.6088	0.4234	0.8902
	N	36.0000	36.0000	36.0000	36.0000	36.0000	36.0000	36.0000	36.0000	32.0000	34.0000
Personal Resource Challenges-Ineffective Tactical Policy	Pearson Correlation	-0.1335	-0.0706	-0.0541	-0.0835	-0.3240	-0.3391	-0.1520	-0.1525	0.0448	-0.0462
	Sig. (2-tailed)	0.4377	0.6824	0.7539	0.6284	0.0539	0.0430	0.3760	0.3747	0.8078	0.7952
	N	36.0000	36.0000	36.0000	36.0000	36.0000	36.0000	36.0000	36.0000	32.0000	34.0000
Personal Resource Challenges-Lack of Clarity in Duties	Pearson Correlation	0.0130	-0.0110	0.0157	-0.0795	-0.2536	-0.2787	0.0556	-0.0516	0.0846	-0.0926
	Sig. (2-tailed)	0.9399	0.9490	0.9275	0.6447	0.1357	0.0997	0.7476	0.7651	0.6455	0.6025
	N	36.0000	36.0000	36.0000	36.0000	36.0000	36.0000	36.0000	36.0000	32.0000	34.0000
Personal Resource Challenges-Conflict or Lack Comm Leaders and Employees	Pearson Correlation	-0.0270	-0.0760	-0.0229	-0.1120	-0.3763	-0.3806	-0.1813	-0.1645	-0.0455	-0.1292
	Sig. (2-tailed)	0.8759	0.6595	0.8946	0.5157	0.0237	0.0220	0.2899	0.3377	0.8047	0.4665
	N	36.0000	36.0000	36.0000	36.0000	36.0000	36.0000	36.0000	36.0000	32.0000	34.0000
sqrtQ1E1l	Pearson Correlation	-0.1768	-0.1162	-0.0757	0.0549	-0.2268	-0.0638	-0.0832	-0.0522	0.0422	-0.1154
	Sig. (2-tailed)	0.3023	0.4997	0.6608	0.7504	0.1835	0.7115	0.6294	0.7623	0.8187	0.5157
	N	36.0000	36.0000	36.0000	36.0000	36.0000	36.0000	36.0000	36.0000	32.0000	34.0000
Personal Resource Challenges-Conflict or Lack Comm International Orgs	Pearson Correlation	0.2174	0.1404	0.1757	-0.1358	-0.1725	-0.1342	0.0026	-0.1031	-0.1438	-0.3227
	Sig. (2-tailed)	0.2029	0.4140	0.3054	0.4298	0.3143	0.4350	0.9881	0.5496	0.4323	0.0627
	N	36.0000	36.0000	36.0000	36.0000	36.0000	36.0000	36.0000	36.0000	32.0000	34.0000
Personal Resource Challenges-Conflict or Lack Comm Domestic Orgs	Pearson Correlation	0.1262	0.0092	0.0275	-0.1864	-0.3066	-0.2523	-0.0655	-0.2033	-0.0994	-0.2261
	Sig. (2-tailed)	0.4633	0.9574	0.8735	0.2764	0.0689	0.1377	0.7043	0.2344	0.5883	0.1986
	N	36.0000	36.0000	36.0000	36.0000	36.0000	36.0000	36.0000	36.0000	32.0000	34.0000

Table A6, continued (Row 2, Col 7)

Correlation Matrix, Dependent Variables (Parametric)		sqrtQIIF1c	sqrtQIIF1d	sqrtQIIF1e	sqrtQIIF3a	sqrtQIIF3b	sqrtQIIF3c	sqrtQIIF3d	sqrtQIIF3e	sqrtQIIH1a	sqrtQIIH1b
Personal Resource Challenges- Lack of Knowledge	Pearson Correlation	0.0427	-0.0585	-0.1075	0.1141	-0.0232	-0.0038	-0.0373	-0.0989	-0.0276	-0.1980
	Sig. (2-tailed)	0.8104	0.7422	0.5451	0.5341	0.8979	0.9835	0.8368	0.5903	0.8830	0.2694
	N	34.0000	34.0000	34.0000	32.0000	33.0000	33.0000	33.0000	32.0000	31.0000	33.0000
Personal Resource Challenges- Lack of Training	Pearson Correlation	0.1015	0.0279	-0.0027	0.1976	-0.0366	-0.0206	0.0343	-0.0256	0.0682	-0.1366
	Sig. (2-tailed)	0.5680	0.8756	0.9878	0.2784	0.8397	0.9094	0.8496	0.8893	0.7154	0.4485
	N	34.0000	34.0000	34.0000	32.0000	33.0000	33.0000	33.0000	32.0000	31.0000	33.0000
sqrtQ1E1e	Pearson Correlation	0.0927	0.0833	0.0729	0.0805	0.1213	0.2117	0.0945	0.0923	-0.0718	-0.2252
	Sig. (2-tailed)	0.6020	0.6396	0.6822	0.6612	0.5011	0.2368	0.6008	0.6155	0.7010	0.2077
	N	34.0000	34.0000	34.0000	32.0000	33.0000	33.0000	33.0000	32.0000	31.0000	33.0000
Personal Resource Challenges- Excessive Admin Paperwork	Pearson Correlation	-0.0410	-0.1363	-0.3311	-0.1245	-0.0371	0.0921	-0.1067	-0.1303	-0.1560	-0.2115
	Sig. (2-tailed)	0.8178	0.4423	0.0558	0.4972	0.8378	0.6104	0.5546	0.4772	0.4019	0.2374
	N	34.0000	34.0000	34.0000	32.0000	33.0000	33.0000	33.0000	32.0000	31.0000	33.0000
Personal Resource Challenges- Ineffective Technology	Pearson Correlation	-0.1622	-0.1558	-0.1023	0.0750	-0.1372	-0.1400	-0.0575	-0.0434	-0.1413	-0.1802
	Sig. (2-tailed)	0.3595	0.3788	0.5649	0.6834	0.4466	0.4372	0.7506	0.8136	0.4483	0.3155
	N	34.0000	34.0000	34.0000	32.0000	33.0000	33.0000	33.0000	32.0000	31.0000	33.0000
Personal Resource Challenges- Ineffective Strategic Focus	Pearson Correlation	0.1301	0.0206	0.0108	0.1669	0.0401	0.0107	0.0652	-0.0002	-0.0698	-0.2101
	Sig. (2-tailed)	0.4635	0.9078	0.9515	0.3611	0.8247	0.9528	0.7184	0.9992	0.7093	0.2406
	N	34.0000	34.0000	34.0000	32.0000	33.0000	33.0000	33.0000	32.0000	31.0000	33.0000
Personal Resource Challenges- Ineffective Tactical Policy	Pearson Correlation	-0.0279	-0.0811	-0.0942	0.0477	-0.0116	-0.0994	-0.0059	-0.0514	-0.1009	-0.2229
	Sig. (2-tailed)	0.8753	0.6484	0.5963	0.7956	0.9488	0.5819	0.9739	0.7799	0.5893	0.2125
	N	34.0000	34.0000	34.0000	32.0000	33.0000	33.0000	33.0000	32.0000	31.0000	33.0000
Personal Resource Challenges- Lack of Clarity in Duties	Pearson Correlation	-0.0274	-0.1833	-0.1149	0.0840	-0.1195	-0.1611	-0.1174	-0.1774	-0.0227	-0.2694
	Sig. (2-tailed)	0.8778	0.2995	0.5174	0.6476	0.5077	0.3704	0.5154	0.3315	0.9033	0.1295
	N	34.0000	34.0000	34.0000	32.0000	33.0000	33.0000	33.0000	32.0000	31.0000	33.0000
Personal Resource Challenges- Conflict or Lack Comm Leaders and Employees	Pearson Correlation	-0.1723	-0.2909	-0.1789	-0.0331	-0.0592	-0.1344	-0.1288	-0.1714	-0.1973	-0.2543
	Sig. (2-tailed)	0.3297	0.0951	0.3114	0.8574	0.7436	0.4557	0.4750	0.3483	0.2875	0.1532
	N	34.0000	34.0000	34.0000	32.0000	33.0000	33.0000	33.0000	32.0000	31.0000	33.0000
sqrtQ1E11	Pearson Correlation	0.0713	-0.0724	-0.2049	0.0475	-0.0390	0.0830	-0.0956	-0.1490	-0.1591	-0.1984
	Sig. (2-tailed)	0.6888	0.6839	0.2449	0.7962	0.8295	0.6461	0.5965	0.4156	0.3926	0.2684
	N	34.0000	34.0000	34.0000	32.0000	33.0000	33.0000	33.0000	32.0000	31.0000	33.0000
Personal Resource Challenges- Conflict or Lack Comm International Orgs	Pearson Correlation	-0.0674	-0.2852	-0.3538	-0.2485	-0.2527	-0.0719	-0.3422	-0.3818	-0.2561	-0.4468
	Sig. (2-tailed)	0.7050	0.1021	0.0401	0.1703	0.1559	0.6909	0.0513	0.0311	0.1643	0.0091
	N	34.0000	34.0000	34.0000	32.0000	33.0000	33.0000	33.0000	32.0000	31.0000	33.0000
Personal Resource Challenges- Conflict or Lack Comm Domestic Orgs	Pearson Correlation	-0.2200	-0.3097	-0.3158	-0.0629	-0.1287	-0.1530	-0.1822	-0.2323	-0.1179	-0.3552
	Sig. (2-tailed)	0.2113	0.0747	0.0689	0.7324	0.4752	0.3954	0.3103	0.2008	0.5276	0.0425
	N	34.0000	34.0000	34.0000	32.0000	33.0000	33.0000	33.0000	32.0000	31.0000	33.0000

Table A6, continued (Row 2, Col 8)

Correlation Matrix, Dependent Variables (Parametric)		sqrtQIIIH1c	sqrtQIIIH1d	sqrtQIIIH1e	sqrtQIIIH3a	sqrtQIIIH3b	sqrtQIIIH3c	sqrtQIIIH3d	sqrtQIIIH3e	sqrtQIIIA1a	sqrtQIIIA1b
Personal Resource Challenges- Lack of Knowledge	Pearson Correlation	0.0821	-0.0850	-0.1499	0.0573	-0.1203	0.0261	-0.1690	-0.1839	0.1295	-0.1696
	Sig. (2-tailed)	0.6552	0.6439	0.4210	0.7478	0.4978	0.8837	0.3393	0.2978	0.4584	0.3227
	N	32.0000	32.0000	31.0000	34.0000	34.0000	34.0000	34.0000	34.0000	35.0000	36.0000
Personal Resource Challenges- Lack of Training	Pearson Correlation	0.1364	0.0330	-0.0387	0.1218	-0.0259	0.0917	-0.0896	-0.0900	0.1581	-0.2311
	Sig. (2-tailed)	0.4567	0.8578	0.8362	0.4926	0.8845	0.6059	0.6144	0.6128	0.3642	0.1750
	N	32.0000	32.0000	31.0000	34.0000	34.0000	34.0000	34.0000	34.0000	35.0000	36.0000
sqrtQ1E1e	Pearson Correlation	-0.1211	-0.1269	-0.1392	0.0438	-0.1685	-0.0905	0.0060	-0.0226	0.2187	-0.0790
	Sig. (2-tailed)	0.5091	0.4889	0.4552	0.8058	0.3409	0.6107	0.9732	0.8991	0.2069	0.6468
	N	32.0000	32.0000	31.0000	34.0000	34.0000	34.0000	34.0000	34.0000	35.0000	36.0000
Personal Resource Challenges- Excessive Admin Paperwork	Pearson Correlation	-0.1947	-0.2166	-0.1780	-0.1361	-0.1377	-0.1565	-0.1547	-0.1709	0.3565	0.2407
	Sig. (2-tailed)	0.2856	0.2337	0.3380	0.4427	0.4374	0.3768	0.3822	0.3340	0.0356	0.1573
	N	32.0000	32.0000	31.0000	34.0000	34.0000	34.0000	34.0000	34.0000	35.0000	36.0000
Personal Resource Challenges- Ineffective Technology	Pearson Correlation	-0.0530	-0.1520	-0.2013	-0.0141	-0.0797	-0.0039	-0.1921	-0.1572	-0.0354	0.0213
	Sig. (2-tailed)	0.7734	0.4061	0.2775	0.9371	0.6541	0.9827	0.2765	0.3745	0.8399	0.9020
	N	32.0000	32.0000	31.0000	34.0000	34.0000	34.0000	34.0000	34.0000	35.0000	36.0000
Personal Resource Challenges- Ineffective Strategic Focus	Pearson Correlation	-0.0487	-0.0923	-0.1590	-0.0841	-0.1749	-0.0566	-0.1473	-0.1766	0.3285	-0.1415
	Sig. (2-tailed)	0.7911	0.6155	0.3929	0.6362	0.3226	0.7505	0.4059	0.3177	0.0540	0.4103
	N	32.0000	32.0000	31.0000	34.0000	34.0000	34.0000	34.0000	34.0000	35.0000	36.0000
Personal Resource Challenges- Ineffective Tactical Policy	Pearson Correlation	-0.0750	-0.0966	-0.1189	-0.1267	-0.1559	-0.0755	-0.1363	-0.1435	0.3383	0.0382
	Sig. (2-tailed)	0.6834	0.5988	0.5240	0.4753	0.3785	0.6711	0.4422	0.4181	0.0468	0.8250
	N	32.0000	32.0000	31.0000	34.0000	34.0000	34.0000	34.0000	34.0000	35.0000	36.0000
Personal Resource Challenges- Lack of Clarity in Duties	Pearson Correlation	-0.0687	-0.0852	-0.0667	-0.0320	-0.2148	-0.1023	-0.1130	-0.1166	0.3095	-0.0093
	Sig. (2-tailed)	0.7086	0.6429	0.7214	0.8575	0.2225	0.5646	0.5245	0.5114	0.0704	0.9569
	N	32.0000	32.0000	31.0000	34.0000	34.0000	34.0000	34.0000	34.0000	35.0000	36.0000
Personal Resource Challenges- Conflict or Lack Comm Leaders and Employees	Pearson Correlation	-0.2072	-0.2420	-0.1481	-0.1224	-0.2159	-0.1763	-0.1437	-0.0984	0.2006	0.1294
	Sig. (2-tailed)	0.2552	0.1821	0.4265	0.4906	0.2200	0.3186	0.4175	0.5800	0.2479	0.4521
	N	32.0000	32.0000	31.0000	34.0000	34.0000	34.0000	34.0000	34.0000	35.0000	36.0000
sqrtQ1E1l	Pearson Correlation	-0.2524	-0.2989	-0.2417	-0.1231	-0.1713	-0.1942	-0.1863	-0.1976	0.2261	-0.0278
	Sig. (2-tailed)	0.1635	0.0966	0.1902	0.4881	0.3327	0.2710	0.2915	0.2627	0.1915	0.8719
	N	32.0000	32.0000	31.0000	34.0000	34.0000	34.0000	34.0000	34.0000	35.0000	36.0000
Personal Resource Challenges- Conflict or Lack Comm International Orgs	Pearson Correlation	-0.3581	-0.3934	-0.2447	-0.1401	-0.2608	-0.2933	-0.2497	-0.2169	0.2839	0.1332
	Sig. (2-tailed)	0.0442	0.0259	0.1845	0.4295	0.1363	0.0922	0.1544	0.2179	0.0984	0.4388
	N	32.0000	32.0000	31.0000	34.0000	34.0000	34.0000	34.0000	34.0000	35.0000	36.0000
Personal Resource Challenges- Conflict or Lack Comm Domestic Orgs	Pearson Correlation	-0.1514	-0.1940	-0.1619	0.0276	-0.2020	-0.0826	-0.0254	-0.0713	0.2088	0.0700
	Sig. (2-tailed)	0.4081	0.2874	0.3842	0.8769	0.2518	0.6422	0.8868	0.6887	0.2287	0.6850
	N	32.0000	32.0000	31.0000	34.0000	34.0000	34.0000	34.0000	34.0000	35.0000	36.0000

Table A6, continued (Row 2, Col 9)

Correlation Matrix, Dependent Variables (Parametric)		sqrtQIIIA1c	sqrtQIIIA1d	sqrtQIIIA1e	sqrtQIIID1a	Level Cooperation Domestic Orgs-CNDPS	Level Cooperation Domestic Orgs-CNBC	Level Cooperation Domestic Orgs-CSTP	Level Cooperation Domestic Orgs-TRIPS	sqrtQIIID2a	Level Cooperation International Orgs-CNDPS
Personal Resource Challenges-Lack of Knowledge	Pearson Correlation	-0.1149	-0.0342	-0.1854	0.0284	-0.3494	-0.3097	-0.1833	-0.2496	-0.0454	-0.1854
	Sig. (2-tailed)	0.5044	0.8430	0.2790	0.8754	0.0397	0.0702	0.2919	0.1481	0.7956	0.2791
	N	36.0000	36.0000	36.0000	33.0000	35.0000	35.0000	35.0000	35.0000	35.0000	36.0000
Personal Resource Challenges-Lack of Training	Pearson Correlation	-0.1980	-0.0110	-0.2242	0.1815	-0.3143	-0.2839	-0.1215	-0.1957	0.0772	-0.1642
	Sig. (2-tailed)	0.2471	0.9493	0.1888	0.3122	0.0660	0.0984	0.4870	0.2598	0.6593	0.3386
	N	36.0000	36.0000	36.0000	33.0000	35.0000	35.0000	35.0000	35.0000	35.0000	36.0000
sqrtQ1E1e	Pearson Correlation	0.1071	0.1396	0.0952	0.2646	-0.0257	0.1179	0.0768	0.1020	0.2775	0.2058
	Sig. (2-tailed)	0.5340	0.4166	0.5809	0.1367	0.8833	0.4998	0.6610	0.5600	0.1066	0.2285
	N	36.0000	36.0000	36.0000	33.0000	35.0000	35.0000	35.0000	35.0000	35.0000	36.0000
Personal Resource Challenges-Excessive Admin Paperwork	Pearson Correlation	0.3647	0.2381	0.2494	0.2109	0.0392	0.0146	0.0791	0.0394	0.1931	0.1350
	Sig. (2-tailed)	0.0288	0.1620	0.1424	0.2387	0.8230	0.9334	0.6514	0.8221	0.2663	0.4324
	N	36.0000	36.0000	36.0000	33.0000	35.0000	35.0000	35.0000	35.0000	35.0000	36.0000
Personal Resource Challenges-Ineffective Technology	Pearson Correlation	0.0335	0.0131	-0.1226	-0.1934	-0.3843	-0.4478	-0.3132	-0.3367	-0.1671	-0.1814
	Sig. (2-tailed)	0.8461	0.9398	0.4762	0.2809	0.0227	0.0070	0.0669	0.0479	0.3375	0.2896
	N	36.0000	36.0000	36.0000	33.0000	35.0000	35.0000	35.0000	35.0000	35.0000	36.0000
Personal Resource Challenges-Ineffective Strategic Focus	Pearson Correlation	-0.0162	0.0718	-0.1359	0.0917	-0.2957	-0.2249	-0.1131	-0.1968	0.0834	-0.2790
	Sig. (2-tailed)	0.9254	0.6775	0.4294	0.6117	0.0845	0.1940	0.5179	0.2572	0.6337	0.0994
	N	36.0000	36.0000	36.0000	33.0000	35.0000	35.0000	35.0000	35.0000	35.0000	36.0000
Personal Resource Challenges-Ineffective Tactical Policy	Pearson Correlation	0.1323	0.1710	-0.0048	-0.0591	-0.3184	-0.3398	-0.2203	-0.2806	-0.0788	-0.3088
	Sig. (2-tailed)	0.4418	0.3186	0.9778	0.7439	0.0623	0.0458	0.2034	0.1025	0.6526	0.0669
	N	36.0000	36.0000	36.0000	33.0000	35.0000	35.0000	35.0000	35.0000	35.0000	36.0000
Personal Resource Challenges-Lack of Clarity in Duties	Pearson Correlation	0.0524	0.1479	-0.0612	0.1341	-0.1994	-0.2423	-0.0036	-0.1610	-0.0609	-0.2645
	Sig. (2-tailed)	0.7615	0.3892	0.7228	0.4568	0.2509	0.1608	0.9835	0.3556	0.7280	0.1190
	N	36.0000	36.0000	36.0000	33.0000	35.0000	35.0000	35.0000	35.0000	35.0000	36.0000
Personal Resource Challenges-Conflict or Lack Comm Leaders and Employees	Pearson Correlation	0.1660	0.1161	0.0572	-0.1135	-0.2432	-0.2412	-0.1756	-0.1849	-0.2003	-0.3302
	Sig. (2-tailed)	0.3334	0.5002	0.7403	0.5296	0.1592	0.1628	0.3128	0.2877	0.2487	0.0492
	N	36.0000	36.0000	36.0000	33.0000	35.0000	35.0000	35.0000	35.0000	35.0000	36.0000
sqrtQ1E1l	Pearson Correlation	0.0690	-0.1745	-0.0507	-0.0093	-0.1364	-0.0657	-0.1034	-0.0830	0.0048	-0.2251
	Sig. (2-tailed)	0.6893	0.3088	0.7689	0.9590	0.4346	0.7077	0.5545	0.6355	0.9781	0.1868
	N	36.0000	36.0000	36.0000	33.0000	35.0000	35.0000	35.0000	35.0000	35.0000	36.0000
Personal Resource Challenges-Conflict or Lack Comm International Orgs	Pearson Correlation	0.0944	0.2105	0.0680	0.0776	-0.1258	-0.2421	-0.0921	-0.1925	-0.0771	-0.0630
	Sig. (2-tailed)	0.5840	0.2179	0.6937	0.6677	0.4716	0.1611	0.5988	0.2678	0.6596	0.7150
	N	36.0000	36.0000	36.0000	33.0000	35.0000	35.0000	35.0000	35.0000	35.0000	36.0000
Personal Resource Challenges-Conflict or Lack Comm Domestic Orgs	Pearson Correlation	0.1161	0.2141	-0.0306	0.0771	-0.0970	-0.2036	-0.0198	-0.1262	-0.1538	-0.1353
	Sig. (2-tailed)	0.5001	0.2099	0.8595	0.6697	0.5793	0.2409	0.9102	0.4701	0.3778	0.4315
	N	36.0000	36.0000	36.0000	33.0000	35.0000	35.0000	35.0000	35.0000	35.0000	36.0000

Table A6, continued (Row 2, Col 10)

Correlation Matrix, Dependent Variables (Parametric)		Level Cooperation International Orgs-CNBC	Level Cooperation International Orgs-CSTP	sqrtQIIID2e	sqrtQIVA1	sqrtQIVA2	sqrtQIVA3	sqrtQIVA5	sqrtQIVA7	sqrtQIVA8	Political Ideology
Personal Resource Challenges-Lack of Knowledge	Pearson Correlation	-0.1852	-0.0530	-0.1736	0.2114	0.1892	0.1521	-0.2011	-0.0987	-0.0474	0.1173
	Sig. (2-tailed)	0.2795	0.7586	0.3114	0.2158	0.2690	0.3830	0.2541	0.5670	0.7868	0.5155
	N	36.0000	36.0000	36.0000	36.0000	36.0000	35.0000	34.0000	36.0000	35.0000	33.0000
Personal Resource Challenges-Lack of Training	Pearson Correlation	-0.1489	-0.0524	-0.1508	0.1371	0.0768	0.1250	-0.2275	-0.0693	-0.0792	0.1329
	Sig. (2-tailed)	0.3860	0.7616	0.3800	0.4251	0.6560	0.4742	0.1957	0.6881	0.6510	0.4610
	N	36.0000	36.0000	36.0000	36.0000	36.0000	35.0000	34.0000	36.0000	35.0000	33.0000
sqrtQIE1e	Pearson Correlation	0.2551	0.1915	0.2529	0.2619	0.2009	0.2528	0.0274	-0.0159	-0.1426	0.1533
	Sig. (2-tailed)	0.1333	0.2632	0.1366	0.1228	0.2400	0.1428	0.8780	0.9268	0.4139	0.3945
	N	36.0000	36.0000	36.0000	36.0000	36.0000	35.0000	34.0000	36.0000	35.0000	33.0000
Personal Resource Challenges-Excessive Admin Paperwork	Pearson Correlation	0.0927	0.0969	0.0811	0.3080	0.2318	0.4174	0.0237	-0.0877	0.0388	0.2197
	Sig. (2-tailed)	0.5908	0.5738	0.6380	0.0676	0.1738	0.0126	0.8939	0.6111	0.8251	0.2192
	N	36.0000	36.0000	36.0000	36.0000	36.0000	35.0000	34.0000	36.0000	35.0000	33.0000
Personal Resource Challenges-Ineffective Technology	Pearson Correlation	-0.2226	-0.2263	-0.2817	0.3243	0.2996	0.2555	-0.3674	-0.0528	-0.1169	0.1397
	Sig. (2-tailed)	0.1918	0.1844	0.0960	0.0537	0.0758	0.1385	0.0325	0.7597	0.5037	0.4381
	N	36.0000	36.0000	36.0000	36.0000	36.0000	35.0000	34.0000	36.0000	35.0000	33.0000
Personal Resource Challenges-Ineffective Strategic Focus	Pearson Correlation	-0.2551	-0.1966	-0.2426	0.2088	0.2963	0.3183	-0.0811	0.0901	-0.2959	0.0123
	Sig. (2-tailed)	0.1332	0.2504	0.1540	0.2216	0.0794	0.0624	0.6486	0.6014	0.0843	0.9460
	N	36.0000	36.0000	36.0000	36.0000	36.0000	35.0000	34.0000	36.0000	35.0000	33.0000
Personal Resource Challenges-Ineffective Tactical Policy	Pearson Correlation	-0.3368	-0.2681	-0.3346	0.2928	0.4052	0.4473	-0.1987	-0.0004	-0.2056	0.1382
	Sig. (2-tailed)	0.0446	0.1139	0.0461	0.0831	0.0142	0.0071	0.2599	0.9983	0.2361	0.4431
	N	36.0000	36.0000	36.0000	36.0000	36.0000	35.0000	34.0000	36.0000	35.0000	33.0000
Personal Resource Challenges-Lack of Clarity in Duties	Pearson Correlation	-0.3009	-0.1977	-0.3052	0.2937	0.2994	0.3700	-0.2636	0.1326	-0.1085	0.0998
	Sig. (2-tailed)	0.0745	0.2477	0.0702	0.0821	0.0761	0.0287	0.1320	0.4406	0.5350	0.5805
	N	36.0000	36.0000	36.0000	36.0000	36.0000	35.0000	34.0000	36.0000	35.0000	33.0000
Personal Resource Challenges-Conflict or Lack Comm Leaders and Employees	Pearson Correlation	-0.3636	-0.2689	-0.3400	0.2933	0.3287	0.4069	-0.2154	0.1726	-0.2587	0.0549
	Sig. (2-tailed)	0.0293	0.1128	0.0425	0.0825	0.0503	0.0153	0.2212	0.3140	0.1335	0.7615
	N	36.0000	36.0000	36.0000	36.0000	36.0000	35.0000	34.0000	36.0000	35.0000	33.0000
sqrtQIE11	Pearson Correlation	-0.2286	-0.2462	-0.2096	0.2187	0.2301	0.3031	0.0993	0.1235	-0.2521	-0.0632
	Sig. (2-tailed)	0.1799	0.1477	0.2199	0.2001	0.1770	0.0767	0.5762	0.4729	0.1440	0.7268
	N	36.0000	36.0000	36.0000	36.0000	36.0000	35.0000	34.0000	36.0000	35.0000	33.0000
Personal Resource Challenges-Conflict or Lack Comm International Orgs	Pearson Correlation	-0.1384	-0.0166	-0.1955	0.1870	0.2393	0.2714	-0.0521	-0.0101	0.0640	0.0389
	Sig. (2-tailed)	0.4207	0.9236	0.2531	0.2749	0.1599	0.1148	0.7700	0.9535	0.7150	0.8299
	N	36.0000	36.0000	36.0000	36.0000	36.0000	35.0000	34.0000	36.0000	35.0000	33.0000
Personal Resource Challenges-Conflict or Lack Comm Domestic Orgs	Pearson Correlation	-0.2322	-0.0763	-0.2643	0.2684	0.2483	0.3473	-0.1372	0.0575	-0.1378	0.0614
	Sig. (2-tailed)	0.1729	0.6582	0.1193	0.1134	0.1443	0.0409	0.4391	0.7392	0.4300	0.7343
	N	36.0000	36.0000	36.0000	36.0000	36.0000	35.0000	34.0000	36.0000	35.0000	33.0000

Table A6, continued (Row 3, Col 1)

Correlation Matrix, Dependent Variables (Parametric)		Importance of Smuggling-Endangered Species	reflectsqrtQ1A1b	reflectsqrtQ1A1c	reflectsqrtQ1A1d	reflectsqrtQ1A1e	sqrtQ1B1a	Knowledge of Smuggling-Narcotics	Knowledge of Smuggling-Weapons	Knowledge of Smuggling-Humans	Knowledge of Smuggling-Contraband
sqrtQ1E3a	Pearson Correlation	0.0133	-0.1596	-0.2365	-0.3896	0.0326	-0.0214	0.2403	0.2145	-0.0719	-0.1157
	Sig. (2-tailed)	0.9404	0.3674	0.1782	0.0227	0.8548	0.9043	0.1711	0.2232	0.6860	0.5145
	N	34.0000	34.0000	34.0000	34.0000	34.0000	34.0000	34.0000	34.0000	34.0000	34.0000
Org Resource Challenges-Lack of Time	Pearson Correlation	-0.2552	-0.1996	-0.1862	-0.0401	0.0005	-0.1127	0.0762	-0.0246	0.0081	-0.0850
	Sig. (2-tailed)	0.1390	0.2502	0.2843	0.8190	0.9978	0.5192	0.6634	0.8886	0.9632	0.6275
	N	35.0000	35.0000	35.0000	35.0000	35.0000	35.0000	35.0000	35.0000	35.0000	35.0000
Org Resource Challenges-Lack of Knowledge	Pearson Correlation	-0.1379	-0.3436	-0.3719	-0.1642	-0.0840	-0.1504	-0.0412	-0.2739	-0.0646	-0.1819
	Sig. (2-tailed)	0.4295	0.0433	0.0278	0.3458	0.6316	0.3884	0.8141	0.1114	0.7124	0.2956
	N	35.0000	35.0000	35.0000	35.0000	35.0000	35.0000	35.0000	35.0000	35.0000	35.0000
Org Resource Challenges-Lack of Training	Pearson Correlation	-0.1090	-0.2567	-0.2689	-0.1838	-0.0341	-0.1441	-0.0791	-0.3116	-0.1464	-0.2547
	Sig. (2-tailed)	0.5331	0.1366	0.1184	0.2906	0.8458	0.4090	0.6516	0.0684	0.4014	0.1398
	N	35.0000	35.0000	35.0000	35.0000	35.0000	35.0000	35.0000	35.0000	35.0000	35.0000
sqrtQ1E3e	Pearson Correlation	-0.2357	-0.0838	-0.0101	0.1432	0.1655	-0.2154	0.0355	-0.0703	-0.2233	-0.1197
	Sig. (2-tailed)	0.1795	0.6376	0.9550	0.4192	0.3496	0.2211	0.8419	0.6926	0.2043	0.5001
	N	34.0000	34.0000	34.0000	34.0000	34.0000	34.0000	34.0000	34.0000	34.0000	34.0000
Org Resource Challenges-Excessive Admin Paperwork	Pearson Correlation	-0.2130	-0.1647	-0.0928	-0.0628	0.0211	-0.2287	0.1035	-0.0973	-0.2894	-0.1697
	Sig. (2-tailed)	0.2193	0.3445	0.5960	0.7202	0.9040	0.1863	0.5540	0.5783	0.0917	0.3299
	N	35.0000	35.0000	35.0000	35.0000	35.0000	35.0000	35.0000	35.0000	35.0000	35.0000
Org Resource Challenges-Ineffective Technology	Pearson Correlation	-0.1288	-0.2495	-0.1343	-0.0683	0.1518	-0.0945	0.2007	-0.0701	-0.0244	-0.1510
	Sig. (2-tailed)	0.4609	0.1483	0.4419	0.6967	0.3840	0.5894	0.2477	0.6890	0.8893	0.3867
	N	35.0000	35.0000	35.0000	35.0000	35.0000	35.0000	35.0000	35.0000	35.0000	35.0000
Org Resource Challenges-Ineffective Strategic Focus	Pearson Correlation	-0.0368	-0.2400	-0.2113	-0.0591	0.0927	0.0266	0.0133	-0.1614	-0.0382	-0.1665
	Sig. (2-tailed)	0.8339	0.1649	0.2231	0.7359	0.5964	0.8796	0.9398	0.3543	0.8277	0.3390
	N	35.0000	35.0000	35.0000	35.0000	35.0000	35.0000	35.0000	35.0000	35.0000	35.0000
Org Resource Challenges-Ineffective Tactical Policy	Pearson Correlation	-0.0218	-0.2306	-0.2437	-0.1340	0.1423	-0.0108	0.0210	-0.1416	-0.1871	-0.1946
	Sig. (2-tailed)	0.9009	0.1827	0.1584	0.4429	0.4147	0.9507	0.9048	0.4172	0.2818	0.2626
	N	35.0000	35.0000	35.0000	35.0000	35.0000	35.0000	35.0000	35.0000	35.0000	35.0000
Org Resource Challenges-Lack of Clarity in Duties	Pearson Correlation	0.0492	-0.3141	-0.3196	-0.1009	0.0087	0.0917	0.0127	-0.1453	-0.0797	-0.1955
	Sig. (2-tailed)	0.7792	0.0661	0.0613	0.5642	0.9603	0.6001	0.9422	0.4050	0.6492	0.2604
	N	35.0000	35.0000	35.0000	35.0000	35.0000	35.0000	35.0000	35.0000	35.0000	35.0000
Org Resource Challenges-Conflict or Lack Comm Leaders and Employees	Pearson Correlation	-0.0220	-0.1516	-0.1189	0.0441	0.1340	-0.0517	0.0840	0.0522	-0.2450	-0.0940
	Sig. (2-tailed)	0.9000	0.3846	0.4961	0.8016	0.4430	0.7678	0.6316	0.7657	0.1560	0.5912
	N	35.0000	35.0000	35.0000	35.0000	35.0000	35.0000	35.0000	35.0000	35.0000	35.0000
sqrtQ1E3l	Pearson Correlation	-0.0396	-0.0530	-0.0769	0.0348	-0.1052	0.0804	-0.0488	0.0348	-0.4343	-0.0865
	Sig. (2-tailed)	0.8214	0.7622	0.6604	0.8425	0.5474	0.6460	0.7808	0.8428	0.0091	0.6213
	N	35.0000	35.0000	35.0000	35.0000	35.0000	35.0000	35.0000	35.0000	35.0000	35.0000

Table A6, continued (Row 3, Col 2)

Correlation Matrix, Dependent Variables (Parametric)		sqrtQ1E1a	Personal Resource Challenges- Lack of Time	Personal Resource Challenges- Lack of Knowledge	Personal Resource Challenges- Lack of Training	sqrtQ1E1e	Personal Resource Challenges- Excessive Admin Paperwork	Personal Resource Challenges- Ineffective Technology	Personal Resource Challenges- Ineffective Strategic Focus	Personal Resource Challenges- Ineffective Tactical Policy	Personal Resource Challenges- Lack of Clarity in Duties
sqrtQ1E3a	Pearson Correlation	0.5355	0.2228	0.2711	0.2455	0.4098	0.2648	0.4635	0.3866	0.4224	0.4139
	Sig. (2-tailed)	0.0013	0.2053	0.1210	0.1617	0.0161	0.1302	0.0058	0.0239	0.0128	0.0150
	N	33.0000	34.0000	34.0000	34.0000	34.0000	34.0000	34.0000	34.0000	34.0000	34.0000
Org Resource Challenges- Lack of Time	Pearson Correlation	0.3713	0.4499	0.4688	0.3864	0.0904	0.0679	0.3841	0.3242	0.3104	0.2282
	Sig. (2-tailed)	0.0306	0.0067	0.0045	0.0219	0.6053	0.6983	0.0227	0.0575	0.0696	0.1873
	N	34.0000	35.0000	35.0000	35.0000	35.0000	35.0000	35.0000	35.0000	35.0000	35.0000
Org Resource Challenges- Lack of Knowledge	Pearson Correlation	0.2971	0.4761	0.8329	0.8421	0.2760	0.1780	0.5886	0.7021	0.5752	0.6555
	Sig. (2-tailed)	0.0879	0.0038	0.0000	0.0000	0.1085	0.3064	0.0002	0.0000	0.0003	0.0000
	N	34.0000	35.0000	35.0000	35.0000	35.0000	35.0000	35.0000	35.0000	35.0000	35.0000
Org Resource Challenges- Lack of Training	Pearson Correlation	0.3371	0.4834	0.8367	0.8394	0.2369	0.2168	0.6681	0.6671	0.5784	0.6437
	Sig. (2-tailed)	0.0512	0.0033	0.0000	0.0000	0.1707	0.2110	0.0000	0.0000	0.0003	0.0000
	N	34.0000	35.0000	35.0000	35.0000	35.0000	35.0000	35.0000	35.0000	35.0000	35.0000
sqrtQ1E3e	Pearson Correlation	0.4286	0.5283	0.3772	0.3616	0.4965	0.3455	0.3066	0.5175	0.5213	0.4520
	Sig. (2-tailed)	0.0128	0.0013	0.0279	0.0356	0.0028	0.0454	0.0778	0.0017	0.0016	0.0073
	N	33.0000	34.0000	34.0000	34.0000	34.0000	34.0000	34.0000	34.0000	34.0000	34.0000
Org Resource Challenges- Excessive Admin Paperwork	Pearson Correlation	0.6521	0.4741	0.5046	0.4976	0.4340	0.5589	0.4503	0.6065	0.6251	0.5833
	Sig. (2-tailed)	0.0000	0.0040	0.0020	0.0024	0.0092	0.0005	0.0066	0.0001	0.0001	0.0002
	N	34.0000	35.0000	35.0000	35.0000	35.0000	35.0000	35.0000	35.0000	35.0000	35.0000
Org Resource Challenges- Ineffective Technology	Pearson Correlation	0.5895	0.3837	0.5715	0.5343	0.3100	0.3545	0.7341	0.6251	0.6686	0.5461
	Sig. (2-tailed)	0.0002	0.0229	0.0003	0.0009	0.0699	0.0367	0.0000	0.0001	0.0000	0.0007
	N	34.0000	35.0000	35.0000	35.0000	35.0000	35.0000	35.0000	35.0000	35.0000	35.0000
Org Resource Challenges- Ineffective Strategic Focus	Pearson Correlation	0.3989	0.4444	0.7606	0.7089	0.3791	0.3099	0.6454	0.7928	0.7660	0.7172
	Sig. (2-tailed)	0.0194	0.0075	0.0000	0.0000	0.0247	0.0700	0.0000	0.0000	0.0000	0.0000
	N	34.0000	35.0000	35.0000	35.0000	35.0000	35.0000	35.0000	35.0000	35.0000	35.0000
Org Resource Challenges- Ineffective Tactical Policy	Pearson Correlation	0.4226	0.5063	0.6627	0.6414	0.4666	0.4462	0.4557	0.7917	0.8024	0.8184
	Sig. (2-tailed)	0.0128	0.0019	0.0000	0.0000	0.0047	0.0072	0.0059	0.0000	0.0000	0.0000
	N	34.0000	35.0000	35.0000	35.0000	35.0000	35.0000	35.0000	35.0000	35.0000	35.0000
Org Resource Challenges- Lack of Clarity in Duties	Pearson Correlation	0.3674	0.3689	0.7468	0.7607	0.3853	0.2944	0.5999	0.7915	0.7397	0.6774
	Sig. (2-tailed)	0.0326	0.0292	0.0000	0.0000	0.0223	0.0860	0.0001	0.0000	0.0000	0.0000
	N	34.0000	35.0000	35.0000	35.0000	35.0000	35.0000	35.0000	35.0000	35.0000	35.0000
Org Resource Challenges- Conflict or Lack Comm Leaders and Employees	Pearson Correlation	0.4307	0.4729	0.5058	0.4702	0.4733	0.5096	0.3705	0.6182	0.6952	0.6451
	Sig. (2-tailed)	0.0110	0.0041	0.0019	0.0044	0.0041	0.0018	0.0285	0.0001	0.0000	0.0000
	N	34.0000	35.0000	35.0000	35.0000	35.0000	35.0000	35.0000	35.0000	35.0000	35.0000
sqrtQ1E3l	Pearson Correlation	0.4065	0.2147	0.2868	0.2943	0.3287	0.5204	0.2168	0.5372	0.4737	0.4299
	Sig. (2-tailed)	0.0171	0.2155	0.0948	0.0862	0.0539	0.0014	0.2108	0.0009	0.0040	0.0100
	N	34.0000	35.0000	35.0000	35.0000	35.0000	35.0000	35.0000	35.0000	35.0000	35.0000

Table A6, continued (Row 3, Col 3)

Correlation Matrix, Dependent Variables (Parametric)		Personal Resource Challenges-Conflict or Lack Comm Leaders and Employees	sqrtQ1E11	Personal Resource Challenges-Conflict or Lack Comm International Orgs	Personal Resource Challenges-Conflict or Lack Comm Domestic Orgs	sqrtQ1E3a	Org Resource Challenges-Lack of Time	Org Resource Challenges-Lack of Knowledge	Org Resource Challenges-Lack of Training	sqrtQ1E3e	Org Resource Challenges-Excessive Admin Paperwork
sqrtQ1E3a	Pearson Correlation	0.3253	0.1459	0.2008	0.3785	1.0000	0.5117	0.3452	0.3915	0.3655	0.5827
	Sig. (2-tailed)	0.0605	0.4103	0.2548	0.0273	.	0.0020	0.0455	0.0220	0.0365	0.0003
	N	34.0000	34.0000	34.0000	34.0000	34.0000	34.0000	34.0000	34.0000	33.0000	34.0000
Org Resource Challenges-Lack of Time	Pearson Correlation	0.2036	0.0786	0.1757	0.2783	0.5117	1.0000	0.5157	0.5404	0.3159	0.4224
	Sig. (2-tailed)	0.2408	0.6537	0.3127	0.1055	0.0020	.	0.0015	0.0008	0.0688	0.0115
	N	35.0000	35.0000	35.0000	35.0000	34.0000	35.0000	35.0000	35.0000	34.0000	35.0000
Org Resource Challenges-Lack of Knowledge	Pearson Correlation	0.5026	0.2653	0.5045	0.6298	0.3452	0.5157	1.0000	0.9587	0.4325	0.5495
	Sig. (2-tailed)	0.0021	0.1235	0.0020	0.0001	0.0455	0.0015	.	0.0000	0.0106	0.0006
	N	35.0000	35.0000	35.0000	35.0000	34.0000	35.0000	35.0000	35.0000	34.0000	35.0000
Org Resource Challenges-Lack of Training	Pearson Correlation	0.4964	0.3241	0.5332	0.6691	0.3915	0.5404	0.9587	1.0000	0.4030	0.5554
	Sig. (2-tailed)	0.0024	0.0575	0.0010	0.0000	0.0220	0.0008	0.0000	.	0.0181	0.0005
	N	35.0000	35.0000	35.0000	35.0000	34.0000	35.0000	35.0000	35.0000	34.0000	35.0000
sqrtQ1E3e	Pearson Correlation	0.4955	0.4006	0.2910	0.4769	0.3655	0.3159	0.4325	0.4030	1.0000	0.7700
	Sig. (2-tailed)	0.0029	0.0189	0.0950	0.0043	0.0365	0.0688	0.0106	0.0181	.	0.0000
	N	34.0000	34.0000	34.0000	34.0000	33.0000	34.0000	34.0000	34.0000	34.0000	34.0000
Org Resource Challenges-Excessive Admin Paperwork	Pearson Correlation	0.5537	0.4504	0.4796	0.6087	0.5827	0.4224	0.5495	0.5554	0.7700	1.0000
	Sig. (2-tailed)	0.0006	0.0066	0.0036	0.0001	0.0003	0.0115	0.0006	0.0005	0.0000	.
	N	35.0000	35.0000	35.0000	35.0000	34.0000	35.0000	35.0000	35.0000	34.0000	35.0000
Org Resource Challenges-Ineffective Technology	Pearson Correlation	0.6035	0.4102	0.3417	0.5933	0.5270	0.4404	0.6191	0.6693	0.4891	0.5929
	Sig. (2-tailed)	0.0001	0.0144	0.0446	0.0002	0.0014	0.0081	0.0001	0.0000	0.0033	0.0002
	N	35.0000	35.0000	35.0000	35.0000	34.0000	35.0000	35.0000	35.0000	34.0000	35.0000
Org Resource Challenges-Ineffective Strategic Focus	Pearson Correlation	0.7479	0.4507	0.4554	0.6978	0.3169	0.3804	0.7509	0.7401	0.4064	0.4743
	Sig. (2-tailed)	0.0000	0.0066	0.0060	0.0000	0.0678	0.0242	0.0000	0.0000	0.0171	0.0040
	N	35.0000	35.0000	35.0000	35.0000	34.0000	35.0000	35.0000	35.0000	34.0000	35.0000
Org Resource Challenges-Ineffective Tactical Policy	Pearson Correlation	0.8003	0.4718	0.6704	0.8536	0.3936	0.2420	0.7079	0.6817	0.5428	0.6589
	Sig. (2-tailed)	0.0000	0.0042	0.0000	0.0000	0.0213	0.1614	0.0000	0.0000	0.0009	0.0000
	N	35.0000	35.0000	35.0000	35.0000	34.0000	35.0000	35.0000	35.0000	34.0000	35.0000
Org Resource Challenges-Lack of Clarity in Duties	Pearson Correlation	0.6391	0.3910	0.5006	0.6819	0.3625	0.2906	0.7829	0.7546	0.3878	0.4762
	Sig. (2-tailed)	0.0000	0.0202	0.0022	0.0000	0.0351	0.0904	0.0000	0.0000	0.0234	0.0038
	N	35.0000	35.0000	35.0000	35.0000	34.0000	35.0000	35.0000	35.0000	34.0000	35.0000
Org Resource Challenges-Conflict or Lack Comm Leaders and Employees	Pearson Correlation	0.7390	0.5790	0.6766	0.7312	0.2974	0.1354	0.5025	0.5110	0.5015	0.5461
	Sig. (2-tailed)	0.0000	0.0003	0.0000	0.0000	0.0876	0.4381	0.0021	0.0017	0.0025	0.0007
	N	35.0000	35.0000	35.0000	35.0000	34.0000	35.0000	35.0000	35.0000	34.0000	35.0000
sqrtQ1E3l	Pearson Correlation	0.5035	0.9287	0.5669	0.4613	0.1722	0.1338	0.3496	0.4188	0.4392	0.4573
	Sig. (2-tailed)	0.0020	0.0000	0.0004	0.0053	0.3302	0.4436	0.0395	0.0123	0.0094	0.0057
	N	35.0000	35.0000	35.0000	35.0000	34.0000	35.0000	35.0000	35.0000	34.0000	35.0000

Table A6, continued (Row 3, Col 4)

Correlation Matrix, Dependent Variables (Parametric)		Org Resource Challenges-Ineffective Technology	Org Resource Challenges-Ineffective Strategic Focus	Org Resource Challenges-Ineffective Tactical Policy	Org Resource Challenges-Lack of Clarity in Duties	Org Resource Challenges-Conflict or Lack Comm Leaders and Employees	sqrtQ1E3l	Org Resource Challenges-Conflict or Lack Comm International Orgs	Org Resource Challenges-Conflict or Lack Comm Domestic Orgs	sqrtQIIA1a	Knowledge of Domestic Law-CSIE
sqrtQ1E3a	Pearson Correlation	0.5270	0.3169	0.3936	0.3625	0.2974	0.1722	0.3658	0.3306	0.0390	-0.0192
	Sig. (2-tailed)	0.0014	0.0678	0.0213	0.0351	0.0876	0.3302	0.0334	0.0562	0.8295	0.9157
	N	34.0000	34.0000	34.0000	34.0000	34.0000	34.0000	34.0000	34.0000	33.0000	33.0000
Org Resource Challenges-Lack of Time	Pearson Correlation	0.4404	0.3804	0.2420	0.2906	0.1354	0.1338	0.4475	0.3240	-0.0461	0.0654
	Sig. (2-tailed)	0.0081	0.0242	0.1614	0.0904	0.4381	0.4436	0.0070	0.0576	0.7956	0.7133
	N	35.0000	35.0000	35.0000	35.0000	35.0000	35.0000	35.0000	35.0000	34.0000	34.0000
Org Resource Challenges-Lack of Knowledge	Pearson Correlation	0.6191	0.7509	0.7079	0.7829	0.5025	0.3496	0.7932	0.7503	-0.0605	-0.2321
	Sig. (2-tailed)	0.0001	0.0000	0.0000	0.0000	0.0021	0.0395	0.0000	0.0000	0.7341	0.1865
	N	35.0000	35.0000	35.0000	35.0000	35.0000	35.0000	35.0000	35.0000	34.0000	34.0000
Org Resource Challenges-Lack of Training	Pearson Correlation	0.6693	0.7401	0.6817	0.7546	0.5110	0.4188	0.7846	0.7474	-0.0674	-0.2196
	Sig. (2-tailed)	0.0000	0.0000	0.0000	0.0000	0.0017	0.0123	0.0000	0.0000	0.7050	0.2120
	N	35.0000	35.0000	35.0000	35.0000	35.0000	35.0000	35.0000	35.0000	34.0000	34.0000
sqrtQ1E3e	Pearson Correlation	0.4891	0.4064	0.5428	0.3878	0.5015	0.4392	0.3551	0.3623	-0.0472	-0.0513
	Sig. (2-tailed)	0.0033	0.0171	0.0009	0.0234	0.0025	0.0094	0.0393	0.0352	0.7942	0.7766
	N	34.0000	34.0000	34.0000	34.0000	34.0000	34.0000	34.0000	34.0000	33.0000	33.0000
Org Resource Challenges-Excessive Admin Paperwork	Pearson Correlation	0.5929	0.4743	0.6589	0.4762	0.5461	0.4573	0.4667	0.4788	0.1397	0.0040
	Sig. (2-tailed)	0.0002	0.0040	0.0000	0.0038	0.0007	0.0057	0.0047	0.0036	0.4306	0.9821
	N	35.0000	35.0000	35.0000	35.0000	35.0000	35.0000	35.0000	35.0000	34.0000	34.0000
Org Resource Challenges-Ineffective Technology	Pearson Correlation	1.0000	0.8327	0.6391	0.7585	0.6652	0.4128	0.6756	0.7328	-0.1555	0.1273
	Sig. (2-tailed)	.	0.0000	0.0000	0.0000	0.0000	0.0137	0.0000	0.0000	0.3798	0.4731
	N	35.0000	35.0000	35.0000	35.0000	35.0000	35.0000	35.0000	35.0000	34.0000	34.0000
Org Resource Challenges-Ineffective Strategic Focus	Pearson Correlation	0.8327	1.0000	0.8061	0.9043	0.7485	0.4589	0.7970	0.8421	-0.0550	-0.0390
	Sig. (2-tailed)	0.0000	.	0.0000	0.0000	0.0000	0.0056	0.0000	0.0000	0.7574	0.8266
	N	35.0000	35.0000	35.0000	35.0000	35.0000	35.0000	35.0000	35.0000	34.0000	34.0000
Org Resource Challenges-Ineffective Tactical Policy	Pearson Correlation	0.6391	0.8061	1.0000	0.8464	0.8618	0.5439	0.7400	0.7592	0.0757	-0.1634
	Sig. (2-tailed)	0.0000	0.0000	.	0.0000	0.0000	0.0007	0.0000	0.0000	0.6703	0.3557
	N	35.0000	35.0000	35.0000	35.0000	35.0000	35.0000	35.0000	35.0000	34.0000	34.0000
Org Resource Challenges-Lack of Clarity in Duties	Pearson Correlation	0.7585	0.9043	0.8464	1.0000	0.7352	0.4632	0.8647	0.9029	0.0103	-0.1033
	Sig. (2-tailed)	0.0000	0.0000	0.0000	.	0.0000	0.0051	0.0000	0.0000	0.9539	0.5610
	N	35.0000	35.0000	35.0000	35.0000	35.0000	35.0000	35.0000	35.0000	34.0000	34.0000
Org Resource Challenges-Conflict or Lack Comm Leaders and Employees	Pearson Correlation	0.6652	0.7485	0.8618	0.7352	1.0000	0.6403	0.5766	0.6412	-0.0102	0.0233
	Sig. (2-tailed)	0.0000	0.0000	0.0000	0.0000	.	0.0000	0.0003	0.0000	0.9542	0.8959
	N	35.0000	35.0000	35.0000	35.0000	35.0000	35.0000	35.0000	35.0000	34.0000	34.0000
sqrtQ1E3l	Pearson Correlation	0.4128	0.4589	0.5439	0.4632	0.6403	1.0000	0.4079	0.4448	0.0510	-0.0101
	Sig. (2-tailed)	0.0137	0.0056	0.0007	0.0051	0.0000	.	0.0150	0.0074	0.7743	0.9546
	N	35.0000	35.0000	35.0000	35.0000	35.0000	35.0000	35.0000	35.0000	34.0000	34.0000

Table A6, continued (Row 3, Col 5)

Correlation Matrix, Dependent Variables (Parametric)		Knowledge of Domestic Law-DWMD	Knowledge of Domestic Law-TVP	Knowledge of Domestic Law-CBP	sqrtQIIB1a	Perceived Effectiveness Domestic Govt Support-CSIE	Perceived Effectiveness Domestic Govt Support-DWMD	Perceived Effectiveness Domestic Govt SupportTVP	Perceived Effectiveness Domestic Govt Support-CBP	sqrtQIIC1a	Perceived Deterrence Domestic Law-CSIE
sqrtQ1E3a	Pearson Correlation	-0.0303	-0.0886	-0.1843	-0.2277	-0.0836	-0.1092	-0.3786	-0.3451	-0.0268	0.1820
	Sig. (2-tailed)	0.8672	0.6241	0.3046	0.1953	0.6435	0.5387	0.0272	0.0456	0.8805	0.3028
	N	33.0000	33.0000	33.0000	34.0000	33.0000	34.0000	34.0000	34.0000	34.0000	34.0000
Org Resource Challenges-Lack of Time	Pearson Correlation	0.0926	0.0988	-0.1136	-0.4854	-0.1392	-0.1100	-0.4992	-0.5349	-0.2993	-0.0318
	Sig. (2-tailed)	0.6023	0.5783	0.5224	0.0036	0.4324	0.5294	0.0027	0.0011	0.0855	0.8562
	N	34.0000	34.0000	34.0000	34.0000	34.0000	35.0000	34.0000	34.0000	34.0000	35.0000
Org Resource Challenges-Lack of Knowledge	Pearson Correlation	-0.3174	-0.0808	-0.3351	-0.1021	-0.0383	-0.0571	-0.3467	-0.2541	0.0181	0.0966
	Sig. (2-tailed)	0.0674	0.6494	0.0527	0.5656	0.8297	0.7444	0.0446	0.1470	0.9191	0.5811
	N	34.0000	34.0000	34.0000	34.0000	34.0000	35.0000	34.0000	34.0000	34.0000	35.0000
Org Resource Challenges-Lack of Training	Pearson Correlation	-0.3426	-0.1142	-0.3563	-0.1307	-0.1078	-0.1662	-0.3921	-0.3198	0.0138	0.0212
	Sig. (2-tailed)	0.0473	0.5200	0.0386	0.4614	0.5439	0.3401	0.0218	0.0652	0.9381	0.9037
	N	34.0000	34.0000	34.0000	34.0000	34.0000	35.0000	34.0000	34.0000	34.0000	35.0000
sqrtQ1E3e	Pearson Correlation	-0.2463	-0.3220	-0.2003	-0.3810	-0.0911	-0.2312	-0.2518	-0.1239	-0.2828	-0.1174
	Sig. (2-tailed)	0.1670	0.0677	0.2638	0.0287	0.6143	0.1884	0.1576	0.4922	0.1108	0.5085
	N	33.0000	33.0000	33.0000	33.0000	33.0000	34.0000	33.0000	33.0000	33.0000	34.0000
Org Resource Challenges-Excessive Admin Paperwork	Pearson Correlation	-0.1851	-0.2122	-0.1357	-0.2366	-0.0560	-0.1880	-0.3925	-0.2131	-0.1344	0.0567
	Sig. (2-tailed)	0.2945	0.2284	0.4440	0.1779	0.7529	0.2795	0.0217	0.2262	0.4486	0.7461
	N	34.0000	34.0000	34.0000	34.0000	34.0000	35.0000	34.0000	34.0000	34.0000	35.0000
Org Resource Challenges-Ineffective Technology	Pearson Correlation	-0.0578	-0.0183	-0.3113	-0.2429	-0.1166	-0.2037	-0.3930	-0.3754	-0.0089	0.0123
	Sig. (2-tailed)	0.7453	0.9181	0.0731	0.1663	0.5115	0.2404	0.0215	0.0287	0.9599	0.9442
	N	34.0000	34.0000	34.0000	34.0000	34.0000	35.0000	34.0000	34.0000	34.0000	35.0000
Org Resource Challenges-Ineffective Strategic Focus	Pearson Correlation	-0.1159	0.0093	-0.2705	-0.0434	-0.2037	-0.1511	-0.3373	-0.3108	0.0591	-0.0240
	Sig. (2-tailed)	0.5141	0.9582	0.1218	0.8075	0.2478	0.3864	0.0511	0.0736	0.7397	0.8913
	N	34.0000	34.0000	34.0000	34.0000	34.0000	35.0000	34.0000	34.0000	34.0000	35.0000
Org Resource Challenges-Ineffective Tactical Policy	Pearson Correlation	-0.2554	-0.0599	-0.1713	0.0337	-0.2553	-0.2184	-0.2585	-0.1892	0.0575	0.0280
	Sig. (2-tailed)	0.1449	0.7366	0.3327	0.8500	0.1450	0.2075	0.1399	0.2838	0.7466	0.8732
	N	34.0000	34.0000	34.0000	34.0000	34.0000	35.0000	34.0000	34.0000	34.0000	35.0000
Org Resource Challenges-Lack of Clarity in Duties	Pearson Correlation	-0.2100	-0.0615	-0.3446	0.1039	-0.1218	-0.0638	-0.2173	-0.1660	0.1668	0.0028
	Sig. (2-tailed)	0.2333	0.7297	0.0460	0.5587	0.4927	0.7158	0.2169	0.3480	0.3456	0.9874
	N	34.0000	34.0000	34.0000	34.0000	34.0000	35.0000	34.0000	34.0000	34.0000	35.0000
Org Resource Challenges-Conflict or Lack Comm Leaders and Employees	Pearson Correlation	-0.0700	-0.0816	-0.0431	0.0070	-0.1588	-0.1119	-0.0977	-0.0339	0.0730	-0.0410
	Sig. (2-tailed)	0.6942	0.6464	0.8090	0.9685	0.3698	0.5221	0.5824	0.8491	0.6817	0.8153
	N	34.0000	34.0000	34.0000	34.0000	34.0000	35.0000	34.0000	34.0000	34.0000	35.0000
sqrtQ1E31	Pearson Correlation	-0.2146	-0.2571	-0.2273	0.1828	-0.0749	-0.2212	-0.0937	-0.1064	0.1596	-0.0437
	Sig. (2-tailed)	0.2228	0.1421	0.1961	0.3009	0.6736	0.2015	0.5980	0.5492	0.3674	0.8030
	N	34.0000	34.0000	34.0000	34.0000	34.0000	35.0000	34.0000	34.0000	34.0000	35.0000

Table A6, continued (Row 3, Col 6)

Correlation Matrix, Dependent Variables (Parametric)		sqrtQIIC1c	Perceived Deterrence Domestic Law-TVP	sqrtQIIC1e	sqrtQIID1a	Level Cooperation Domestic Orgs-CSIE	Level Cooperation Domestic Orgs-DWMD	Level Cooperation Domestic Orgs-TVP	Level Cooperation Domestic Orgs-CBP	sqrtQIIF1a	sqrtQIIF1b
sqrtQ1E3a	Pearson Correlation	0.0571	0.1988	0.1558	-0.1416	-0.1553	-0.2637	-0.1839	-0.3699	0.1039	0.0083
	Sig. (2-tailed)	0.7483	0.2596	0.3789	0.4244	0.3804	0.1318	0.2978	0.0313	0.5713	0.9633
	N	34.0000	34.0000	34.0000	34.0000	34.0000	34.0000	34.0000	34.0000	32.0000	33.0000
Org Resource Challenges-Lack of Time	Pearson Correlation	-0.1643	-0.2421	-0.1999	-0.3091	-0.1766	-0.3089	-0.2466	-0.4410	-0.1815	-0.3427
	Sig. (2-tailed)	0.3456	0.1611	0.2496	0.0708	0.3101	0.0709	0.1533	0.0080	0.3202	0.0472
	N	35.0000	35.0000	35.0000	35.0000	35.0000	35.0000	35.0000	35.0000	32.0000	34.0000
Org Resource Challenges-Lack of Knowledge	Pearson Correlation	-0.1289	-0.1397	-0.0826	-0.3537	-0.4078	-0.4448	-0.2323	-0.2361	0.1828	-0.0264
	Sig. (2-tailed)	0.4605	0.4236	0.6372	0.0371	0.0150	0.0074	0.1793	0.1721	0.3167	0.8820
	N	35.0000	35.0000	35.0000	35.0000	35.0000	35.0000	35.0000	35.0000	32.0000	34.0000
Org Resource Challenges-Lack of Training	Pearson Correlation	-0.2015	-0.1769	-0.1079	-0.3828	-0.4665	-0.4764	-0.2813	-0.3095	0.1549	-0.1244
	Sig. (2-tailed)	0.2458	0.3092	0.5372	0.0232	0.0047	0.0038	0.1017	0.0704	0.3974	0.4834
	N	35.0000	35.0000	35.0000	35.0000	35.0000	35.0000	35.0000	35.0000	32.0000	34.0000
sqrtQ1E3e	Pearson Correlation	-0.1531	-0.3281	-0.1530	-0.1077	-0.2576	-0.1964	-0.3635	-0.1248	-0.0059	0.0976
	Sig. (2-tailed)	0.3873	0.0582	0.3877	0.5443	0.1414	0.2657	0.0346	0.4819	0.9747	0.5889
	N	34.0000	34.0000	34.0000	34.0000	34.0000	34.0000	34.0000	34.0000	31.0000	33.0000
Org Resource Challenges-Excessive Admin Paperwork	Pearson Correlation	-0.0730	-0.0947	0.0712	-0.2613	-0.1698	-0.1211	-0.2969	-0.2055	0.0181	-0.0742
	Sig. (2-tailed)	0.6768	0.5885	0.6845	0.1295	0.3295	0.4882	0.0833	0.2363	0.9217	0.6764
	N	35.0000	35.0000	35.0000	35.0000	35.0000	35.0000	35.0000	35.0000	32.0000	34.0000
Org Resource Challenges-Ineffective Technology	Pearson Correlation	-0.1455	-0.1179	-0.0531	-0.3255	-0.3626	-0.4359	-0.2617	-0.4314	-0.1030	-0.0945
	Sig. (2-tailed)	0.4042	0.4999	0.7618	0.0564	0.0323	0.0089	0.1289	0.0097	0.5747	0.5952
	N	35.0000	35.0000	35.0000	35.0000	35.0000	35.0000	35.0000	35.0000	32.0000	34.0000
Org Resource Challenges-Ineffective Strategic Focus	Pearson Correlation	-0.1947	-0.1731	-0.1332	-0.2537	-0.3952	-0.4554	-0.1852	-0.2952	0.0030	-0.0635
	Sig. (2-tailed)	0.2625	0.3200	0.4457	0.1413	0.0188	0.0060	0.2868	0.0851	0.9869	0.7214
	N	35.0000	35.0000	35.0000	35.0000	35.0000	35.0000	35.0000	35.0000	32.0000	34.0000
Org Resource Challenges-Ineffective Tactical Policy	Pearson Correlation	0.0315	0.0064	0.0423	-0.2208	-0.2891	-0.3082	-0.1271	-0.1596	0.0564	-0.0413
	Sig. (2-tailed)	0.8575	0.9708	0.8095	0.2025	0.0922	0.0717	0.4670	0.3598	0.7592	0.8166
	N	35.0000	35.0000	35.0000	35.0000	35.0000	35.0000	35.0000	35.0000	32.0000	34.0000
Org Resource Challenges-Lack of Clarity in Duties	Pearson Correlation	-0.1333	-0.0574	-0.0800	-0.1536	-0.3954	-0.4124	-0.1893	-0.1998	0.1495	0.1132
	Sig. (2-tailed)	0.4451	0.7432	0.6478	0.3784	0.0187	0.0138	0.2760	0.2498	0.4140	0.5240
	N	35.0000	35.0000	35.0000	35.0000	35.0000	35.0000	35.0000	35.0000	32.0000	34.0000
Org Resource Challenges-Conflict or Lack Comm Leaders and Employees	Pearson Correlation	0.0728	0.0405	0.1382	-0.1869	-0.2438	-0.2581	-0.1415	-0.1280	-0.1812	-0.1614
	Sig. (2-tailed)	0.6778	0.8173	0.4286	0.2823	0.1581	0.1345	0.4175	0.4638	0.3211	0.3618
	N	35.0000	35.0000	35.0000	35.0000	35.0000	35.0000	35.0000	35.0000	32.0000	34.0000
sqrtQ1E3l	Pearson Correlation	-0.1463	-0.0578	0.0074	-0.0403	-0.2859	-0.1912	-0.1542	-0.1118	0.0249	-0.1720
	Sig. (2-tailed)	0.4018	0.7417	0.9662	0.8182	0.0960	0.2712	0.3764	0.5227	0.8922	0.3306
	N	35.0000	35.0000	35.0000	35.0000	35.0000	35.0000	35.0000	35.0000	32.0000	34.0000

Table A6, continued (Row 3, Col 7)

Correlation Matrix, Dependent Variables (Parametric)		sqrtQ1IF1c	sqrtQ1IF1d	sqrtQ1IF1e	sqrtQ1IF3a	sqrtQ1IF3b	sqrtQ1IF3c	sqrtQ1IF3d	sqrtQ1IF3e	sqrtQ1IH1a	sqrtQ1IH1b
sqrtQ1E3a	Pearson Correlation	-0.0219	0.1669	0.0338	0.2351	0.1849	0.1040	0.3029	0.2800	0.3580	-0.0423
	Sig. (2-tailed)	0.9035	0.3534	0.8520	0.2029	0.3111	0.5709	0.0919	0.1271	0.0521	0.8211
	N	33.0000	33.0000	33.0000	31.0000	32.0000	32.0000	32.0000	31.0000	30.0000	31.0000
Org Resource Challenges-Lack of Time	Pearson Correlation	-0.2851	-0.0827	-0.2985	-0.0422	-0.0579	-0.1148	0.0942	0.0489	0.0331	-0.2066
	Sig. (2-tailed)	0.1022	0.6420	0.0863	0.8188	0.7490	0.5247	0.6020	0.7906	0.8622	0.2566
	N	34.0000	34.0000	34.0000	32.0000	33.0000	33.0000	33.0000	32.0000	30.0000	32.0000
Org Resource Challenges-Lack of Knowledge	Pearson Correlation	-0.0122	-0.0278	-0.0434	0.2170	-0.0907	-0.1473	0.0033	-0.0534	0.0150	-0.2404
	Sig. (2-tailed)	0.9454	0.8758	0.8077	0.2328	0.6158	0.4134	0.9855	0.7714	0.9373	0.1852
	N	34.0000	34.0000	34.0000	32.0000	33.0000	33.0000	33.0000	32.0000	30.0000	32.0000
Org Resource Challenges-Lack of Training	Pearson Correlation	-0.0925	-0.0631	-0.1092	0.2221	-0.1579	-0.1916	-0.0101	-0.0699	0.0300	-0.2542
	Sig. (2-tailed)	0.6027	0.7230	0.5389	0.2219	0.3802	0.2854	0.9556	0.7038	0.8751	0.1604
	N	34.0000	34.0000	34.0000	32.0000	33.0000	33.0000	33.0000	32.0000	30.0000	32.0000
sqrtQ1E3e	Pearson Correlation	-0.1113	-0.0593	-0.0291	0.0990	0.3142	0.2017	0.2073	0.2104	-0.0761	-0.0309
	Sig. (2-tailed)	0.5375	0.7429	0.8723	0.5962	0.0799	0.2684	0.2549	0.2558	0.6946	0.8690
	N	33.0000	33.0000	33.0000	31.0000	32.0000	32.0000	32.0000	31.0000	29.0000	31.0000
Org Resource Challenges-Excessive Admin Paperwork	Pearson Correlation	-0.1182	0.0207	-0.0996	0.1547	0.1915	0.1194	0.2473	0.2243	0.1248	-0.0828
	Sig. (2-tailed)	0.5056	0.9075	0.5750	0.3979	0.2856	0.5082	0.1652	0.2172	0.5111	0.6521
	N	34.0000	34.0000	34.0000	32.0000	33.0000	33.0000	33.0000	32.0000	30.0000	32.0000
Org Resource Challenges-Ineffective Technology	Pearson Correlation	-0.1798	-0.1182	-0.2780	0.0181	0.0065	-0.0914	-0.0111	-0.0457	-0.1666	-0.0716
	Sig. (2-tailed)	0.3090	0.5057	0.1114	0.9215	0.9713	0.6128	0.9510	0.8037	0.3789	0.6968
	N	34.0000	34.0000	34.0000	32.0000	33.0000	33.0000	33.0000	32.0000	30.0000	32.0000
Org Resource Challenges-Ineffective Strategic Focus	Pearson Correlation	-0.0313	-0.1208	-0.2175	-0.0149	-0.1494	-0.2049	-0.1712	-0.2428	-0.1881	-0.2239
	Sig. (2-tailed)	0.8605	0.4961	0.2165	0.9355	0.4067	0.2527	0.3408	0.1806	0.3195	0.2179
	N	34.0000	34.0000	34.0000	32.0000	33.0000	33.0000	33.0000	32.0000	30.0000	32.0000
Org Resource Challenges-Ineffective Tactical Policy	Pearson Correlation	-0.0606	-0.1634	-0.1491	0.0408	-0.0713	-0.1433	-0.1114	-0.1713	-0.0113	-0.2911
	Sig. (2-tailed)	0.7337	0.3557	0.4001	0.8244	0.6934	0.4264	0.5371	0.3487	0.9526	0.1060
	N	34.0000	34.0000	34.0000	32.0000	33.0000	33.0000	33.0000	32.0000	30.0000	32.0000
Org Resource Challenges-Lack of Clarity in Duties	Pearson Correlation	0.1208	0.0484	-0.0657	0.0856	-0.0518	-0.1022	-0.0818	-0.1365	-0.0500	-0.2275
	Sig. (2-tailed)	0.4962	0.7859	0.7120	0.6414	0.7747	0.5713	0.6507	0.4563	0.7932	0.2105
	N	34.0000	34.0000	34.0000	32.0000	33.0000	33.0000	33.0000	32.0000	30.0000	32.0000
Org Resource Challenges-Conflict or Lack Comm Leaders and Employees	Pearson Correlation	-0.1786	-0.2959	-0.3507	-0.1579	-0.1401	-0.1380	-0.2720	-0.3148	-0.2330	-0.3411
	Sig. (2-tailed)	0.3123	0.0893	0.0420	0.3880	0.4368	0.4438	0.1257	0.0793	0.2153	0.0561
	N	34.0000	34.0000	34.0000	32.0000	33.0000	33.0000	33.0000	32.0000	30.0000	32.0000
sqrtQ1E31	Pearson Correlation	0.0808	-0.0969	-0.2328	0.0611	-0.0917	0.0628	-0.1113	-0.1717	-0.0982	-0.2143
	Sig. (2-tailed)	0.6498	0.5855	0.1851	0.7399	0.6118	0.7286	0.5375	0.3475	0.6058	0.2390
	N	34.0000	34.0000	34.0000	32.0000	33.0000	33.0000	33.0000	32.0000	30.0000	32.0000

Table A6, continued (Row 3, Col 8)

Correlation Matrix, Dependent Variables (Parametric)		sqrtQIIH1c	sqrtQIIH1d	sqrtQIIH1e	sqrtQIIH3a	sqrtQIIH3b	sqrtQIIH3c	sqrtQIIH3d	sqrtQIIH3e	sqrtQIIA1a	sqrtQIIA1b
sqrtQ1E3a	Pearson Correlation	0.1147	0.2068	0.2026	0.2938	-0.0020	0.1196	0.1773	0.0507	0.0342	0.0321
	Sig. (2-tailed)	0.5389	0.2642	0.2829	0.0970	0.9911	0.5074	0.3236	0.7794	0.8503	0.8570
	N	31.0000	31.0000	30.0000	33.0000	33.0000	33.0000	33.0000	33.0000	33.0000	34.0000
Org Resource Challenges-Lack of Time	Pearson Correlation	-0.1002	-0.0312	-0.1359	-0.0769	-0.2469	-0.1272	-0.1567	-0.2548	-0.0162	-0.0835
	Sig. (2-tailed)	0.5916	0.8676	0.4740	0.6707	0.1659	0.4807	0.3838	0.1523	0.9276	0.6336
	N	31.0000	31.0000	30.0000	33.0000	33.0000	33.0000	33.0000	33.0000	34.0000	35.0000
Org Resource Challenges-Lack of Knowledge	Pearson Correlation	0.0377	0.0008	-0.1124	0.1602	-0.0572	0.0831	-0.0073	-0.0352	0.0263	-0.2797
	Sig. (2-tailed)	0.8403	0.9967	0.5543	0.3732	0.7519	0.6456	0.9680	0.8456	0.8828	0.1036
	N	31.0000	31.0000	30.0000	33.0000	33.0000	33.0000	33.0000	33.0000	34.0000	35.0000
Org Resource Challenges-Lack of Training	Pearson Correlation	0.0039	-0.0129	-0.1272	0.1928	-0.0613	0.0732	0.0051	-0.0365	-0.0017	-0.3170
	Sig. (2-tailed)	0.9835	0.9452	0.5029	0.2824	0.7345	0.6858	0.9774	0.8402	0.9925	0.0635
	N	31.0000	31.0000	30.0000	33.0000	33.0000	33.0000	33.0000	33.0000	34.0000	35.0000
sqrtQ1E3e	Pearson Correlation	0.0667	-0.0467	0.0184	0.0569	0.0404	0.0799	0.1056	0.1639	0.0645	0.0298
	Sig. (2-tailed)	0.7263	0.8065	0.9244	0.7571	0.8262	0.6639	0.5652	0.3701	0.7216	0.8673
	N	30.0000	30.0000	29.0000	32.0000	32.0000	32.0000	32.0000	32.0000	33.0000	34.0000
Org Resource Challenges-Excessive Admin Paperwork	Pearson Correlation	0.0575	0.0965	0.1260	0.1426	-0.0256	0.0351	0.1059	0.1202	0.2057	0.1275
	Sig. (2-tailed)	0.7587	0.6057	0.5071	0.4285	0.8876	0.8464	0.5577	0.5051	0.2432	0.4656
	N	31.0000	31.0000	30.0000	33.0000	33.0000	33.0000	33.0000	33.0000	34.0000	35.0000
Org Resource Challenges-Ineffective Technology	Pearson Correlation	0.0372	-0.1228	-0.2584	-0.0159	0.0131	0.1095	-0.0685	-0.1200	-0.0089	0.0746
	Sig. (2-tailed)	0.8424	0.5106	0.1680	0.9302	0.9424	0.5440	0.7050	0.5059	0.9604	0.6700
	N	31.0000	31.0000	30.0000	33.0000	33.0000	33.0000	33.0000	33.0000	34.0000	35.0000
Org Resource Challenges-Ineffective Strategic Focus	Pearson Correlation	-0.0405	-0.1945	-0.3508	-0.0815	-0.1644	-0.0078	-0.1907	-0.2575	0.0761	-0.1040
	Sig. (2-tailed)	0.8286	0.2944	0.0574	0.6523	0.3606	0.9655	0.2878	0.1480	0.6689	0.5522
	N	31.0000	31.0000	30.0000	33.0000	33.0000	33.0000	33.0000	33.0000	34.0000	35.0000
Org Resource Challenges-Ineffective Tactical Policy	Pearson Correlation	-0.0623	-0.1089	-0.1040	0.0959	-0.1575	-0.0297	0.0113	-0.0392	0.1894	-0.0530
	Sig. (2-tailed)	0.7391	0.5599	0.5843	0.5955	0.3813	0.8696	0.9501	0.8285	0.2833	0.7622
	N	31.0000	31.0000	30.0000	33.0000	33.0000	33.0000	33.0000	33.0000	34.0000	35.0000
Org Resource Challenges-Lack of Clarity in Duties	Pearson Correlation	0.0716	-0.0851	-0.2212	0.0518	-0.0838	0.0907	-0.0948	-0.1891	0.1937	-0.1948
	Sig. (2-tailed)	0.7018	0.6488	0.2402	0.7748	0.6429	0.6159	0.5999	0.2920	0.2723	0.2620
	N	31.0000	31.0000	30.0000	33.0000	33.0000	33.0000	33.0000	33.0000	34.0000	35.0000
Org Resource Challenges-Conflict or Lack Comm Leaders and Employees	Pearson Correlation	-0.2299	-0.3350	-0.3020	-0.0302	-0.2300	-0.1855	-0.1098	-0.1310	0.1442	0.0782
	Sig. (2-tailed)	0.2134	0.0655	0.1049	0.8677	0.1979	0.3014	0.5430	0.4675	0.4157	0.6553
	N	31.0000	31.0000	30.0000	33.0000	33.0000	33.0000	33.0000	33.0000	34.0000	35.0000
sqrtQ1E3l	Pearson Correlation	-0.2361	-0.2702	-0.2399	-0.0611	-0.1596	-0.1677	-0.1387	-0.1842	0.1479	-0.1712
	Sig. (2-tailed)	0.2009	0.1415	0.2017	0.7354	0.3750	0.3510	0.4416	0.3047	0.4038	0.3254
	N	31.0000	31.0000	30.0000	33.0000	33.0000	33.0000	33.0000	33.0000	34.0000	35.0000

Table A6, continued (Row 3, Col 9)

Correlation Matrix, Dependent Variables (Parametric)		sqrtQIIIA1c	sqrtQIIIA1d	sqrtQIIIA1e	sqrtQIIID1a	Level Cooperation Domestic Orgs-CNDPS	Level Cooperation Domestic Orgs-CNBC	Level Cooperation Domestic Orgs-CSTP	Level Cooperation Domestic Orgs-TRIPS	sqrtQIIID2a	Level Cooperation International Orgs-CNDPS
sqrtQ1E3a	Pearson Correlation	0.1374	0.1194	-0.0829	0.0230	-0.1200	-0.1800	-0.1702	-0.2506	-0.0594	0.1036
	Sig. (2-tailed)	0.4386	0.5010	0.6413	0.9024	0.5059	0.3163	0.3436	0.1595	0.7426	0.5598
	N	34.0000	34.0000	34.0000	31.0000	33.0000	33.0000	33.0000	33.0000	33.0000	34.0000
Org Resource Challenges-Lack of Time	Pearson Correlation	0.0184	-0.0144	-0.1243	-0.2796	-0.3383	-0.3131	-0.2950	-0.4556	-0.3044	-0.2275
	Sig. (2-tailed)	0.9166	0.9344	0.4767	0.1212	0.0503	0.0714	0.0904	0.0068	0.0801	0.1888
	N	35.0000	35.0000	35.0000	32.0000	34.0000	34.0000	34.0000	34.0000	34.0000	35.0000
Org Resource Challenges-Lack of Knowledge	Pearson Correlation	-0.2263	-0.0268	-0.2772	0.0015	-0.3248	-0.3757	-0.1646	-0.3192	-0.1769	-0.2702
	Sig. (2-tailed)	0.1911	0.8786	0.1069	0.9936	0.0609	0.0285	0.3522	0.0657	0.3168	0.1164
	N	35.0000	35.0000	35.0000	32.0000	34.0000	34.0000	34.0000	34.0000	34.0000	35.0000
Org Resource Challenges-Lack of Training	Pearson Correlation	-0.2731	-0.0901	-0.3359	-0.0421	-0.3530	-0.4226	-0.1937	-0.3354	-0.2034	-0.2894
	Sig. (2-tailed)	0.1124	0.6066	0.0485	0.8190	0.0406	0.0128	0.2724	0.0525	0.2486	0.0917
	N	35.0000	35.0000	35.0000	32.0000	34.0000	34.0000	34.0000	34.0000	34.0000	35.0000
sqrtQ1E3e	Pearson Correlation	0.1285	-0.0141	0.0582	0.0959	-0.0810	-0.0355	-0.0343	0.0295	-0.0190	-0.0860
	Sig. (2-tailed)	0.4688	0.9370	0.7438	0.6079	0.6541	0.8446	0.8497	0.8705	0.9164	0.6287
	N	34.0000	34.0000	34.0000	31.0000	33.0000	33.0000	33.0000	33.0000	33.0000	34.0000
Org Resource Challenges-Excessive Admin Paperwork	Pearson Correlation	0.2022	0.1224	0.0930	0.0279	-0.1288	-0.1819	-0.0498	-0.1475	-0.0482	-0.0530
	Sig. (2-tailed)	0.2441	0.4838	0.5951	0.8797	0.4677	0.3033	0.7799	0.4051	0.7868	0.7622
	N	35.0000	35.0000	35.0000	32.0000	34.0000	34.0000	34.0000	34.0000	34.0000	35.0000
Org Resource Challenges-Ineffective Technology	Pearson Correlation	0.1545	0.1285	-0.1611	-0.1393	-0.1680	-0.2951	-0.1450	-0.2648	-0.1784	-0.1089
	Sig. (2-tailed)	0.3754	0.4620	0.3552	0.4469	0.3424	0.0902	0.4133	0.1301	0.3128	0.5333
	N	35.0000	35.0000	35.0000	32.0000	34.0000	34.0000	34.0000	34.0000	34.0000	35.0000
Org Resource Challenges-Ineffective Strategic Focus	Pearson Correlation	0.0208	0.0143	-0.2920	-0.1005	-0.2940	-0.2771	-0.1540	-0.2889	-0.1595	-0.2729
	Sig. (2-tailed)	0.9058	0.9352	0.0888	0.5842	0.0915	0.1126	0.3846	0.0975	0.3676	0.1127
	N	35.0000	35.0000	35.0000	32.0000	34.0000	34.0000	34.0000	34.0000	34.0000	35.0000
Org Resource Challenges-Ineffective Tactical Policy	Pearson Correlation	0.0520	0.1151	-0.1516	0.1123	-0.1628	-0.1912	-0.0689	-0.1827	-0.1374	-0.2079
	Sig. (2-tailed)	0.7667	0.5103	0.3846	0.5406	0.3577	0.2786	0.6984	0.3011	0.4386	0.2306
	N	35.0000	35.0000	35.0000	32.0000	34.0000	34.0000	34.0000	34.0000	34.0000	35.0000
Org Resource Challenges-Lack of Clarity in Duties	Pearson Correlation	-0.0508	0.0448	-0.2749	0.0586	-0.2796	-0.2877	-0.2099	-0.2803	-0.0313	-0.1810
	Sig. (2-tailed)	0.7718	0.7984	0.1100	0.7501	0.1093	0.0989	0.2334	0.1083	0.8605	0.2982
	N	35.0000	35.0000	35.0000	32.0000	34.0000	34.0000	34.0000	34.0000	34.0000	35.0000
Org Resource Challenges-Conflict or Lack Comm Leaders and Employees	Pearson Correlation	0.1867	0.1597	-0.0643	0.0196	-0.0942	-0.1349	-0.1179	-0.1270	-0.1959	-0.1156
	Sig. (2-tailed)	0.2828	0.3594	0.7135	0.9153	0.5962	0.4469	0.5066	0.4741	0.2667	0.5086
	N	35.0000	35.0000	35.0000	32.0000	34.0000	34.0000	34.0000	34.0000	34.0000	35.0000
sqrtQ1E3l	Pearson Correlation	-0.0484	-0.2347	-0.2254	0.1302	-0.1171	-0.0328	-0.0436	-0.0632	0.0422	-0.2323
	Sig. (2-tailed)	0.7826	0.1747	0.1930	0.4774	0.5095	0.8541	0.8068	0.7224	0.8125	0.1792
	N	35.0000	35.0000	35.0000	32.0000	34.0000	34.0000	34.0000	34.0000	34.0000	35.0000

Table A6, continued (Row 3, Col 10)

Correlation Matrix, Dependent Variables (Parametric)		Level Cooperation International Orgs-CNBC	Level Cooperation International Orgs-CSTP	sqrtQIIID2e	sqrtQIVA1	sqrtQIVA2	sqrtQIVA3	sqrtQIVA5	sqrtQIVA7	sqrtQIVA8	Political Ideology
sqrtQ1E3a	Pearson Correlation	0.0984	-0.0030	-0.0716	0.2920	0.3555	0.2967	0.0015	-0.0107	-0.1731	0.0560
	Sig. (2-tailed)	0.5798	0.9867	0.6874	0.0938	0.0391	0.0936	0.9932	0.9523	0.3277	0.7609
	N	34.0000	34.0000	34.0000	34.0000	34.0000	33.0000	33.0000	34.0000	34.0000	32.0000
Org Resource Challenges-Lack of Time	Pearson Correlation	-0.2063	-0.2480	-0.3042	0.0029	0.1769	-0.0517	0.0635	-0.0614	0.2567	-0.0784
	Sig. (2-tailed)	0.2345	0.1509	0.0756	0.9870	0.3093	0.7716	0.7212	0.7262	0.1366	0.6644
	N	35.0000	35.0000	35.0000	35.0000	35.0000	34.0000	34.0000	35.0000	35.0000	33.0000
Org Resource Challenges-Lack of Knowledge	Pearson Correlation	-0.2763	-0.1889	-0.2873	0.2136	0.1306	0.1567	-0.1624	0.0765	-0.0302	-0.1021
	Sig. (2-tailed)	0.1081	0.2772	0.0942	0.2180	0.4546	0.3763	0.3588	0.6621	0.8634	0.5717
	N	35.0000	35.0000	35.0000	35.0000	35.0000	34.0000	34.0000	35.0000	35.0000	33.0000
Org Resource Challenges-Lack of Training	Pearson Correlation	-0.3140	-0.2335	-0.3437	0.1882	0.1844	0.1301	-0.2116	0.0666	-0.0590	-0.0800
	Sig. (2-tailed)	0.0662	0.1771	0.0432	0.2789	0.2890	0.4633	0.2296	0.7036	0.7364	0.6581
	N	35.0000	35.0000	35.0000	35.0000	35.0000	34.0000	34.0000	35.0000	35.0000	33.0000
sqrtQ1E3e	Pearson Correlation	-0.0732	-0.0943	0.0318	0.0981	0.0666	0.2704	-0.1671	-0.0981	-0.0177	0.1183
	Sig. (2-tailed)	0.6808	0.5959	0.8582	0.5809	0.7082	0.1280	0.3526	0.5811	0.9211	0.5189
	N	34.0000	34.0000	34.0000	34.0000	34.0000	33.0000	33.0000	34.0000	34.0000	32.0000
Org Resource Challenges-Excessive Admin Paperwork	Pearson Correlation	-0.0612	-0.0943	-0.0615	0.0572	0.1212	0.2113	-0.0822	-0.0328	-0.2230	-0.0690
	Sig. (2-tailed)	0.7269	0.5899	0.7255	0.7441	0.4880	0.2303	0.6440	0.8516	0.1979	0.7030
	N	35.0000	35.0000	35.0000	35.0000	35.0000	34.0000	34.0000	35.0000	35.0000	33.0000
Org Resource Challenges-Ineffective Technology	Pearson Correlation	-0.1526	-0.1341	-0.2585	0.2358	0.1196	0.1978	-0.1445	-0.0430	-0.2447	-0.0409
	Sig. (2-tailed)	0.3814	0.4424	0.1337	0.1726	0.4939	0.2622	0.4148	0.8064	0.1566	0.8211
	N	35.0000	35.0000	35.0000	35.0000	35.0000	34.0000	34.0000	35.0000	35.0000	33.0000
Org Resource Challenges-Ineffective Strategic Focus	Pearson Correlation	-0.2741	-0.2184	-0.3170	0.3248	0.1723	0.1703	-0.1517	0.0874	-0.2093	-0.0088
	Sig. (2-tailed)	0.1111	0.2074	0.0635	0.0569	0.3222	0.3355	0.3919	0.6176	0.2276	0.9611
	N	35.0000	35.0000	35.0000	35.0000	35.0000	34.0000	34.0000	35.0000	35.0000	33.0000
Org Resource Challenges-Ineffective Tactical Policy	Pearson Correlation	-0.2227	-0.1647	-0.2417	0.2058	0.1873	0.2609	-0.0647	0.0278	-0.2141	-0.0584
	Sig. (2-tailed)	0.1984	0.3443	0.1619	0.2357	0.2814	0.1362	0.7163	0.8740	0.2168	0.7470
	N	35.0000	35.0000	35.0000	35.0000	35.0000	34.0000	34.0000	35.0000	35.0000	33.0000
Org Resource Challenges-Lack of Clarity in Duties	Pearson Correlation	-0.1936	-0.1137	-0.2185	0.2975	0.1487	0.2110	-0.0922	-0.0212	-0.2333	0.0609
	Sig. (2-tailed)	0.2650	0.5155	0.2074	0.0826	0.3939	0.2310	0.6041	0.9037	0.1774	0.7362
	N	35.0000	35.0000	35.0000	35.0000	35.0000	34.0000	34.0000	35.0000	35.0000	33.0000
Org Resource Challenges-Conflict or Lack Comm Leaders and Employees	Pearson Correlation	-0.1167	-0.1419	-0.1800	0.1614	0.1363	0.2148	-0.1561	0.0376	-0.2012	0.0000
	Sig. (2-tailed)	0.5043	0.4161	0.3007	0.3544	0.4349	0.2226	0.3780	0.8300	0.2465	1.0000
	N	35.0000	35.0000	35.0000	35.0000	35.0000	34.0000	34.0000	35.0000	35.0000	33.0000
sqrtQ1E3l	Pearson Correlation	-0.2091	-0.2572	-0.1945	0.1144	0.1141	0.1633	0.1102	0.1971	-0.1516	-0.0489
	Sig. (2-tailed)	0.2279	0.1357	0.2630	0.5127	0.5141	0.3562	0.5349	0.2565	0.3845	0.7870
	N	35.0000	35.0000	35.0000	35.0000	35.0000	34.0000	34.0000	35.0000	35.0000	33.0000

Table A6, continued (Row 4, Col 1)

Correlation Matrix, Dependent Variables (Parametric)		Importance of Smuggling-Endangered Species	reflectsqrtQ1A1b	reflectsqrtQ1A1c	reflectsqrtQ1A1d	reflectsqrtQ1A1e	sqrtQ1B1a	Knowledge of Smuggling-Narcotics	Knowledge of Smuggling-Weapons	Knowledge of Smuggling-Humans	Knowledge of Smuggling-Contraband
Org Resource Challenges-Conflict or Lack Comm International Orgs	Pearson Correlation	0.0261	-0.3126	-0.3248	-0.0833	0.0119	0.0776	0.1324	-0.1213	0.0368	-0.1600
	Sig. (2-tailed)	0.8818	0.0675	0.0570	0.6341	0.9457	0.6577	0.4484	0.4878	0.8337	0.3587
	N	35.0000	35.0000	35.0000	35.0000	35.0000	35.0000	35.0000	35.0000	35.0000	35.0000
Org Resource Challenges-Conflict or Lack Comm Domestic Orgs	Pearson Correlation	0.0753	-0.3260	-0.2974	-0.1055	0.0191	0.0426	0.1116	-0.1315	-0.0734	-0.1675
	Sig. (2-tailed)	0.6674	0.0560	0.0827	0.5464	0.9131	0.8080	0.5233	0.4513	0.6753	0.3362
	N	35.0000	35.0000	35.0000	35.0000	35.0000	35.0000	35.0000	35.0000	35.0000	35.0000
sqrtQIIA1a	Pearson Correlation	0.0714	0.3292	0.1555	0.1382	-0.1336	0.5077	0.0948	0.2332	0.0326	0.4173
	Sig. (2-tailed)	0.6836	0.0535	0.3724	0.4284	0.4440	0.0018	0.5879	0.1776	0.8525	0.0126
	N	35.0000	35.0000	35.0000	35.0000	35.0000	35.0000	35.0000	35.0000	35.0000	35.0000
Knowledge of Domestic Law-CSIE	Pearson Correlation	-0.0032	-0.2346	0.0142	0.0931	-0.1776	0.0953	0.6809	0.5161	0.1554	0.3006
	Sig. (2-tailed)	0.9852	0.1750	0.9356	0.5947	0.3073	0.5859	0.0000	0.0015	0.3726	0.0793
	N	35.0000	35.0000	35.0000	35.0000	35.0000	35.0000	35.0000	35.0000	35.0000	35.0000
Knowledge of Domestic Law-DWMD	Pearson Correlation	-0.2227	-0.1107	0.0084	0.0954	-0.1624	0.0299	0.5787	0.6878	0.3185	0.4673
	Sig. (2-tailed)	0.1984	0.5268	0.9620	0.5856	0.3512	0.8644	0.0003	0.0000	0.0622	0.0047
	N	35.0000	35.0000	35.0000	35.0000	35.0000	35.0000	35.0000	35.0000	35.0000	35.0000
Knowledge of Domestic Law-TVP	Pearson Correlation	-0.2041	-0.1045	-0.0642	-0.0603	-0.0460	0.1391	0.5195	0.4150	0.5869	0.4621
	Sig. (2-tailed)	0.2396	0.5503	0.7141	0.7308	0.7932	0.4256	0.0014	0.0132	0.0002	0.0052
	N	35.0000	35.0000	35.0000	35.0000	35.0000	35.0000	35.0000	35.0000	35.0000	35.0000
Knowledge of Domestic Law-CBP	Pearson Correlation	-0.1039	0.1069	0.2938	0.1321	-0.2579	0.0992	0.2628	0.5338	0.1776	0.6159
	Sig. (2-tailed)	0.5527	0.5409	0.0867	0.4494	0.1347	0.5707	0.1273	0.0010	0.3074	0.0001
	N	35.0000	35.0000	35.0000	35.0000	35.0000	35.0000	35.0000	35.0000	35.0000	35.0000
sqrtQIIB1a	Pearson Correlation	0.1444	0.2197	-0.0267	0.1104	-0.1642	0.5266	0.0615	0.2414	0.0641	0.2397
	Sig. (2-tailed)	0.4078	0.2047	0.8791	0.5279	0.3460	0.0012	0.7258	0.1623	0.7145	0.1655
	N	35.0000	35.0000	35.0000	35.0000	35.0000	35.0000	35.0000	35.0000	35.0000	35.0000
Perceived Effectiveness Domestic Govt Support-CSIE	Pearson Correlation	-0.3171	-0.2167	-0.1550	-0.0148	-0.4207	-0.0525	0.3300	0.4299	0.1815	0.3448
	Sig. (2-tailed)	0.0634	0.2111	0.3740	0.9327	0.0119	0.7644	0.0529	0.0099	0.2966	0.0425
	N	35.0000	35.0000	35.0000	35.0000	35.0000	35.0000	35.0000	35.0000	35.0000	35.0000
Perceived Effectiveness Domestic Govt Support-DWMD	Pearson Correlation	-0.0909	-0.2119	-0.2500	0.0844	-0.2755	-0.0257	0.3662	0.3848	0.2580	0.3453
	Sig. (2-tailed)	0.5979	0.2148	0.1414	0.6246	0.1039	0.8818	0.0281	0.0205	0.1287	0.0392
	N	36.0000	36.0000	36.0000	36.0000	36.0000	36.0000	36.0000	36.0000	36.0000	36.0000
Perceived Effectiveness Domestic Govt SupportTVP	Pearson Correlation	-0.1500	0.1203	0.0406	0.3279	-0.0776	0.0809	0.0810	0.4147	0.1463	0.3833
	Sig. (2-tailed)	0.3899	0.4912	0.8168	0.0545	0.6576	0.6440	0.6435	0.0133	0.4016	0.0230
	N	35.0000	35.0000	35.0000	35.0000	35.0000	35.0000	35.0000	35.0000	35.0000	35.0000
Perceived Effectiveness Domestic Govt Support-CBP	Pearson Correlation	-0.0849	0.1503	0.1898	0.3699	-0.2319	0.0167	-0.0566	0.2175	-0.0915	0.2676
	Sig. (2-tailed)	0.6276	0.3886	0.2747	0.0287	0.1801	0.9242	0.7468	0.2094	0.6011	0.1202
	N	35.0000	35.0000	35.0000	35.0000	35.0000	35.0000	35.0000	35.0000	35.0000	35.0000

Table A6, continued (Row 4, Col 2)

Correlation Matrix, Dependent Variables (Parametric)		sqrtQIE1a	Personal Resource Challenges-Lack of Time	Personal Resource Challenges-Lack of Knowledge	Personal Resource Challenges-Lack of Training	sqrtQIE1e	Personal Resource Challenges-Excessive Admin Paperwork	Personal Resource Challenges-Ineffective Technology	Personal Resource Challenges-Ineffective Strategic Focus	Personal Resource Challenges-Ineffective Tactical Policy	Personal Resource Challenges-Lack of Clarity in Duties
Org Resource Challenges-Conflict or Lack Comm International Orgs	Pearson Correlation	0.2378	0.3700	0.7712	0.7224	0.3387	0.3204	0.5919	0.6129	0.5677	0.5515
	Sig. (2-tailed)	0.1756	0.0287	0.0000	0.0000	0.0465	0.0606	0.0002	0.0001	0.0004	0.0006
	N	34.0000	35.0000	35.0000	35.0000	35.0000	35.0000	35.0000	35.0000	35.0000	35.0000
Org Resource Challenges-Conflict or Lack Comm Domestic Orgs	Pearson Correlation	0.2694	0.3163	0.7446	0.6898	0.3704	0.3419	0.6206	0.6329	0.5770	0.5381
	Sig. (2-tailed)	0.1234	0.0641	0.0000	0.0000	0.0285	0.0444	0.0001	0.0000	0.0003	0.0009
	N	34.0000	35.0000	35.0000	35.0000	35.0000	35.0000	35.0000	35.0000	35.0000	35.0000
sqrtQIIA1a	Pearson Correlation	0.1149	0.1779	0.1297	0.1362	0.1985	0.1231	-0.0890	0.1663	0.0529	0.1278
	Sig. (2-tailed)	0.5176	0.3066	0.4579	0.4354	0.2530	0.4810	0.6113	0.3398	0.7627	0.4645
	N	34.0000	35.0000	35.0000	35.0000	35.0000	35.0000	35.0000	35.0000	35.0000	35.0000
Knowledge of Domestic Law-CSIE	Pearson Correlation	-0.0396	-0.1054	-0.1119	-0.2222	0.0135	0.1304	0.1874	-0.2240	-0.2112	-0.2785
	Sig. (2-tailed)	0.8241	0.5467	0.5223	0.1996	0.9384	0.4553	0.2811	0.1958	0.2234	0.1053
	N	34.0000	35.0000	35.0000	35.0000	35.0000	35.0000	35.0000	35.0000	35.0000	35.0000
Knowledge of Domestic Law-DWMD	Pearson Correlation	-0.2166	-0.0797	-0.1684	-0.2745	-0.0123	0.0638	0.0578	-0.3036	-0.2200	-0.2676
	Sig. (2-tailed)	0.2186	0.6491	0.3335	0.1105	0.9439	0.7156	0.7415	0.0762	0.2040	0.1201
	N	34.0000	35.0000	35.0000	35.0000	35.0000	35.0000	35.0000	35.0000	35.0000	35.0000
Knowledge of Domestic Law-TVP	Pearson Correlation	-0.1300	-0.0226	0.0131	-0.0242	-0.0726	0.1009	0.0814	-0.0651	-0.0220	0.0909
	Sig. (2-tailed)	0.4636	0.8976	0.9404	0.8901	0.6784	0.5642	0.6421	0.7100	0.9003	0.6036
	N	34.0000	35.0000	35.0000	35.0000	35.0000	35.0000	35.0000	35.0000	35.0000	35.0000
Knowledge of Domestic Law-CBP	Pearson Correlation	-0.1190	0.0886	-0.1704	-0.2953	0.1008	0.0404	-0.1367	-0.2731	-0.2471	-0.1374
	Sig. (2-tailed)	0.5028	0.6129	0.3279	0.0850	0.5644	0.8177	0.4337	0.1125	0.1525	0.4314
	N	34.0000	35.0000	35.0000	35.0000	35.0000	35.0000	35.0000	35.0000	35.0000	35.0000
sqrtQIIB1a	Pearson Correlation	-0.0595	-0.0992	-0.0207	0.0772	0.0554	0.2519	-0.0869	0.1213	0.0551	0.1344
	Sig. (2-tailed)	0.7381	0.5709	0.9061	0.6595	0.7519	0.1444	0.6196	0.4875	0.7534	0.4414
	N	34.0000	35.0000	35.0000	35.0000	35.0000	35.0000	35.0000	35.0000	35.0000	35.0000
Perceived Effectiveness Domestic Govt Support-CSIE	Pearson Correlation	-0.2248	-0.1528	-0.1588	-0.1195	0.0380	0.0177	-0.0620	-0.2103	-0.2880	-0.3218
	Sig. (2-tailed)	0.2013	0.3809	0.3621	0.4940	0.8286	0.9198	0.7234	0.2252	0.0934	0.0594
	N	34.0000	35.0000	35.0000	35.0000	35.0000	35.0000	35.0000	35.0000	35.0000	35.0000
Perceived Effectiveness Domestic Govt Support-DWMD	Pearson Correlation	-0.2630	-0.0369	-0.0216	-0.0557	0.0232	-0.0175	-0.1884	-0.2085	-0.2482	-0.2057
	Sig. (2-tailed)	0.1269	0.8306	0.9006	0.7468	0.8930	0.9193	0.2711	0.2223	0.1444	0.2287
	N	35.0000	36.0000	36.0000	36.0000	36.0000	36.0000	36.0000	36.0000	36.0000	36.0000
Perceived Effectiveness Domestic Govt SupportTVP	Pearson Correlation	-0.2881	-0.0628	-0.2723	-0.2538	-0.0384	0.0173	-0.4288	-0.3213	-0.2887	-0.2773
	Sig. (2-tailed)	0.0985	0.7200	0.1136	0.1413	0.8265	0.9212	0.0102	0.0598	0.0926	0.1069
	N	34.0000	35.0000	35.0000	35.0000	35.0000	35.0000	35.0000	35.0000	35.0000	35.0000
Perceived Effectiveness Domestic Govt Support-CBP	Pearson Correlation	-0.1696	-0.0502	-0.1568	-0.1208	-0.0354	-0.0679	-0.3476	-0.2878	-0.3012	-0.2312
	Sig. (2-tailed)	0.3377	0.7744	0.3684	0.4895	0.8402	0.6981	0.0408	0.0936	0.0787	0.1815
	N	34.0000	35.0000	35.0000	35.0000	35.0000	35.0000	35.0000	35.0000	35.0000	35.0000

Table A6, continued (Row 4, Col 3)

Correlation Matrix, Dependent Variables (Parametric)		Personal Resource Challenges-Conflict or Lack Comm Leaders and Employees	sqrtQIE1l	Personal Resource Challenges-Conflict or Lack Comm International Orgs	Personal Resource Challenges-Conflict or Lack Comm Domestic Orgs	sqrtQIE3a	Org Resource Challenges-Lack of Time	Org Resource Challenges-Lack of Knowledge	Org Resource Challenges-Lack of Training	sqrtQIE3e	Org Resource Challenges-Excessive Admin Paperwork
Org Resource Challenges-Conflict or Lack Comm International Orgs	Pearson Correlation	0.4527	0.3371	0.5283	0.6075	0.3658	0.4475	0.7932	0.7846	0.3551	0.4667
	Sig. (2-tailed)	0.0063	0.0477	0.0011	0.0001	0.0334	0.0070	0.0000	0.0000	0.0393	0.0047
	N	35.0000	35.0000	35.0000	35.0000	34.0000	35.0000	35.0000	35.0000	34.0000	35.0000
Org Resource Challenges-Conflict or Lack Comm Domestic Orgs	Pearson Correlation	0.5411	0.4099	0.4958	0.6459	0.3306	0.3240	0.7503	0.7474	0.3623	0.4788
	Sig. (2-tailed)	0.0008	0.0145	0.0025	0.0000	0.0562	0.0576	0.0000	0.0000	0.0352	0.0036
	N	35.0000	35.0000	35.0000	35.0000	34.0000	35.0000	35.0000	35.0000	34.0000	35.0000
sqrtQIIA1a	Pearson Correlation	0.0748	0.0207	0.2155	0.1088	0.0390	-0.0461	-0.0605	-0.0674	-0.0472	0.1397
	Sig. (2-tailed)	0.6692	0.9059	0.2137	0.5340	0.8295	0.7956	0.7341	0.7050	0.7942	0.4306
	N	35.0000	35.0000	35.0000	35.0000	33.0000	34.0000	34.0000	34.0000	33.0000	34.0000
Knowledge of Domestic Law-CSIE	Pearson Correlation	-0.1977	0.0244	0.0457	-0.1031	-0.0192	0.0654	-0.2321	-0.2196	-0.0513	0.0040
	Sig. (2-tailed)	0.2549	0.8893	0.7945	0.5558	0.9157	0.7133	0.1865	0.2120	0.7766	0.9821
	N	35.0000	35.0000	35.0000	35.0000	33.0000	34.0000	34.0000	34.0000	33.0000	34.0000
Knowledge of Domestic Law-DWMD	Pearson Correlation	-0.2397	-0.1690	-0.0794	-0.2276	-0.0303	0.0926	-0.3174	-0.3426	-0.2463	-0.1851
	Sig. (2-tailed)	0.1655	0.3317	0.6502	0.1885	0.8672	0.6023	0.0674	0.0473	0.1670	0.2945
	N	35.0000	35.0000	35.0000	35.0000	33.0000	34.0000	34.0000	34.0000	33.0000	34.0000
Knowledge of Domestic Law-TVP	Pearson Correlation	-0.1073	-0.2804	0.1555	0.0439	-0.0886	0.0988	-0.0808	-0.1142	-0.3220	-0.2122
	Sig. (2-tailed)	0.5394	0.1028	0.3723	0.8024	0.6241	0.5783	0.6494	0.5200	0.0677	0.2284
	N	35.0000	35.0000	35.0000	35.0000	33.0000	34.0000	34.0000	34.0000	33.0000	34.0000
Knowledge of Domestic Law-CBP	Pearson Correlation	-0.1200	-0.1781	0.0366	-0.0862	-0.1843	-0.1136	-0.3351	-0.3563	-0.2003	-0.1357
	Sig. (2-tailed)	0.4922	0.3061	0.8345	0.6226	0.3046	0.5224	0.0527	0.0386	0.2638	0.4440
	N	35.0000	35.0000	35.0000	35.0000	33.0000	34.0000	34.0000	34.0000	33.0000	34.0000
sqrtQIIB1a	Pearson Correlation	0.0178	0.2308	0.1476	0.0080	-0.2277	-0.4854	-0.1021	-0.1307	-0.3810	-0.2366
	Sig. (2-tailed)	0.9193	0.1822	0.3973	0.9636	0.1953	0.0036	0.5656	0.4614	0.0287	0.1779
	N	35.0000	35.0000	35.0000	35.0000	34.0000	34.0000	34.0000	34.0000	33.0000	34.0000
Perceived Effectiveness Domestic Govt Support-CSIE	Pearson Correlation	-0.3135	-0.0598	-0.0264	-0.2122	-0.0836	-0.1392	-0.0383	-0.1078	-0.0911	-0.0560
	Sig. (2-tailed)	0.0666	0.7329	0.8804	0.2211	0.6435	0.4324	0.8297	0.5439	0.6143	0.7529
	N	35.0000	35.0000	35.0000	35.0000	33.0000	34.0000	34.0000	34.0000	33.0000	34.0000
Perceived Effectiveness Domestic Govt Support-DWMD	Pearson Correlation	-0.2352	-0.1697	0.0064	-0.1523	-0.1092	-0.1100	-0.0571	-0.1662	-0.2312	-0.1880
	Sig. (2-tailed)	0.1673	0.3223	0.9706	0.3751	0.5387	0.5294	0.7444	0.3401	0.1884	0.2795
	N	36.0000	36.0000	36.0000	36.0000	34.0000	35.0000	35.0000	35.0000	34.0000	35.0000
Perceived Effectiveness Domestic Govt SupportTVP	Pearson Correlation	-0.2338	-0.0749	-0.0629	-0.1881	-0.3786	-0.4992	-0.3467	-0.3921	-0.2518	-0.3925
	Sig. (2-tailed)	0.1764	0.6688	0.7195	0.2793	0.0272	0.0027	0.0446	0.0218	0.1576	0.0217
	N	35.0000	35.0000	35.0000	35.0000	34.0000	34.0000	34.0000	34.0000	33.0000	34.0000
Perceived Effectiveness Domestic Govt Support-CBP	Pearson Correlation	-0.2236	-0.1061	-0.0719	-0.2038	-0.3451	-0.5349	-0.2541	-0.3198	-0.1239	-0.2131
	Sig. (2-tailed)	0.1966	0.5440	0.6815	0.2402	0.0456	0.0011	0.1470	0.0652	0.4922	0.2262
	N	35.0000	35.0000	35.0000	35.0000	34.0000	34.0000	34.0000	34.0000	33.0000	34.0000

Table A6, continued (Row 4, Col 4)

Correlation Matrix, Dependent Variables (Parametric)		Org Resource Challenges-Ineffective Technology	Org Resource Challenges-Ineffective Strategic Focus	Org Resource Challenges-Ineffective Tactical Policy	Org Resource Challenges-Lack of Clarity in Duties	Org Resource Challenges-Conflict or Lack Comm Leaders and Employees	sqrtQ1E31	Org Resource Challenges-Conflict or Lack Comm International Orgs	Org Resource Challenges-Conflict or Lack Comm Domestic Orgs	sqrtQIIA1a	Knowledge of Domestic Law-CSIE
Org Resource Challenges-Conflict or Lack Comm International Orgs	Pearson Correlation	0.6756	0.7970	0.7400	0.8647	0.5766	0.4079	1.0000	0.9504	-0.0484	0.0659
	Sig. (2-tailed)	0.0000	0.0000	0.0000	0.0000	0.0003	0.0150	.	0.0000	0.7859	0.7110
	N	35.0000	35.0000	35.0000	35.0000	35.0000	35.0000	35.0000	35.0000	34.0000	34.0000
Org Resource Challenges-Conflict or Lack Comm Domestic Orgs	Pearson Correlation	0.7328	0.8421	0.7592	0.9029	0.6412	0.4448	0.9504	1.0000	-0.0196	0.0912
	Sig. (2-tailed)	0.0000	0.0000	0.0000	0.0000	0.0000	0.0074	0.0000	.	0.9124	0.6079
	N	35.0000	35.0000	35.0000	35.0000	35.0000	35.0000	35.0000	35.0000	34.0000	34.0000
sqrtQIIA1a	Pearson Correlation	-0.1555	-0.0550	0.0757	0.0103	-0.0102	0.0510	-0.0484	-0.0196	1.0000	0.0672
	Sig. (2-tailed)	0.3798	0.7574	0.6703	0.9539	0.9542	0.7743	0.7859	0.9124	.	0.7015
	N	34.0000	34.0000	34.0000	34.0000	34.0000	34.0000	34.0000	34.0000	35.0000	35.0000
Knowledge of Domestic Law-CSIE	Pearson Correlation	0.1273	-0.0390	-0.1634	-0.1033	0.0233	-0.0101	0.0659	0.0912	0.0672	1.0000
	Sig. (2-tailed)	0.4731	0.8266	0.3557	0.5610	0.8959	0.9546	0.7110	0.6079	0.7015	.
	N	34.0000	34.0000	34.0000	34.0000	34.0000	34.0000	34.0000	34.0000	35.0000	35.0000
Knowledge of Domestic Law-DWMD	Pearson Correlation	-0.0578	-0.1159	-0.2554	-0.2100	-0.0700	-0.2146	-0.0527	-0.0657	0.1034	0.8361
	Sig. (2-tailed)	0.7453	0.5141	0.1449	0.2333	0.6942	0.2228	0.7670	0.7119	0.5544	0.0000
	N	34.0000	34.0000	34.0000	34.0000	34.0000	34.0000	34.0000	34.0000	35.0000	35.0000
Knowledge of Domestic Law-TVP	Pearson Correlation	-0.0183	0.0093	-0.0599	-0.0615	-0.0816	-0.2571	0.0544	-0.0513	0.1196	0.5001
	Sig. (2-tailed)	0.9181	0.9582	0.7366	0.7297	0.6464	0.1421	0.7598	0.7732	0.4938	0.0022
	N	34.0000	34.0000	34.0000	34.0000	34.0000	34.0000	34.0000	34.0000	35.0000	35.0000
Knowledge of Domestic Law-CBP	Pearson Correlation	-0.3113	-0.2705	-0.1713	-0.3446	-0.0431	-0.2273	-0.3112	-0.2803	0.3849	0.4842
	Sig. (2-tailed)	0.0731	0.1218	0.3327	0.0460	0.8090	0.1961	0.0732	0.1084	0.0224	0.0032
	N	34.0000	34.0000	34.0000	34.0000	34.0000	34.0000	34.0000	34.0000	35.0000	35.0000
sqrtQIIB1a	Pearson Correlation	-0.2429	-0.0434	0.0337	0.1039	0.0070	0.1828	0.0091	0.0388	0.4329	-0.0768
	Sig. (2-tailed)	0.1663	0.8075	0.8500	0.5587	0.9685	0.3009	0.9594	0.8277	0.0105	0.6662
	N	34.0000	34.0000	34.0000	34.0000	34.0000	34.0000	34.0000	34.0000	34.0000	34.0000
Perceived Effectiveness Domestic Govt Support-CSIE	Pearson Correlation	-0.1166	-0.2037	-0.2553	-0.1218	-0.1588	-0.0749	-0.0232	0.0025	0.1110	0.4760
	Sig. (2-tailed)	0.5115	0.2478	0.1450	0.4927	0.3698	0.6736	0.8962	0.9889	0.5319	0.0044
	N	34.0000	34.0000	34.0000	34.0000	34.0000	34.0000	34.0000	34.0000	34.0000	34.0000
Perceived Effectiveness Domestic Govt Support-DWMD	Pearson Correlation	-0.2037	-0.1511	-0.2184	-0.0638	-0.1119	-0.2212	-0.0006	0.0339	0.1865	0.4127
	Sig. (2-tailed)	0.2404	0.3864	0.2075	0.7158	0.5221	0.2015	0.9973	0.8466	0.2834	0.0137
	N	35.0000	35.0000	35.0000	35.0000	35.0000	35.0000	35.0000	35.0000	35.0000	35.0000
Perceived Effectiveness Domestic Govt SupportTVP	Pearson Correlation	-0.3930	-0.3373	-0.2585	-0.2173	-0.0977	-0.0937	-0.2462	-0.1797	0.2766	0.1491
	Sig. (2-tailed)	0.0215	0.0511	0.1399	0.2169	0.5824	0.5980	0.1605	0.3092	0.1133	0.4000
	N	34.0000	34.0000	34.0000	34.0000	34.0000	34.0000	34.0000	34.0000	34.0000	34.0000
Perceived Effectiveness Domestic Govt Support-CBP	Pearson Correlation	-0.3754	-0.3108	-0.1892	-0.1660	-0.0339	-0.1064	-0.2808	-0.1840	0.2318	0.0592
	Sig. (2-tailed)	0.0287	0.0736	0.2838	0.3480	0.8491	0.5492	0.1077	0.2977	0.1871	0.7394
	N	34.0000	34.0000	34.0000	34.0000	34.0000	34.0000	34.0000	34.0000	34.0000	34.0000

Table A6, continued (Row 4, Col 5)

Correlation Matrix, Dependent Variables (Parametric)		Knowledge of Domestic Law-DWMD	Knowledge of Domestic Law-TVP	Knowledge of Domestic Law-CBP	sqrtQIIB1a	Perceived Effectiveness Domestic Govt Support-CSIE	Perceived Effectiveness Domestic Govt Support-DWMD	Perceived Effectiveness Domestic Govt SupportTVP	Perceived Effectiveness Domestic Govt Support-CBP	sqrtQIIC1a	Perceived Deterrence Domestic Law-CSIE
Org Resource Challenges-Conflict or Lack Comm International Orgs	Pearson Correlation	-0.0527	0.0544	-0.3112	0.0091	-0.0232	-0.0006	-0.2462	-0.2808	0.0780	0.0612
	Sig. (2-tailed)	0.7670	0.7598	0.0732	0.9594	0.8962	0.9973	0.1605	0.1077	0.6609	0.7268
	N	34.0000	34.0000	34.0000	34.0000	34.0000	35.0000	34.0000	34.0000	34.0000	35.0000
Org Resource Challenges-Conflict or Lack Comm Domestic Orgs	Pearson Correlation	-0.0657	-0.0513	-0.2803	0.0388	0.0025	0.0339	-0.1797	-0.1840	0.0915	0.0529
	Sig. (2-tailed)	0.7119	0.7732	0.1084	0.8277	0.9889	0.8466	0.3092	0.2977	0.6070	0.7629
	N	34.0000	34.0000	34.0000	34.0000	34.0000	35.0000	34.0000	34.0000	34.0000	35.0000
sqrtQIIA1a	Pearson Correlation	0.1034	0.1196	0.3849	0.4329	0.1110	0.1865	0.2766	0.2318	0.3777	0.2693
	Sig. (2-tailed)	0.5544	0.4938	0.0224	0.0105	0.5319	0.2834	0.1133	0.1871	0.0276	0.1178
	N	35.0000	35.0000	35.0000	34.0000	34.0000	35.0000	34.0000	34.0000	34.0000	35.0000
Knowledge of Domestic Law-CSIE	Pearson Correlation	0.8361	0.5001	0.4842	-0.0768	0.4760	0.4127	0.1491	0.0592	-0.0535	0.3304
	Sig. (2-tailed)	0.0000	0.0022	0.0032	0.6662	0.0044	0.0137	0.4000	0.7394	0.7639	0.0525
	N	35.0000	35.0000	35.0000	34.0000	34.0000	35.0000	34.0000	34.0000	34.0000	35.0000
Knowledge of Domestic Law-DWMD	Pearson Correlation	1.0000	0.6149	0.6576	-0.0045	0.5128	0.5351	0.3011	0.1858	-0.0096	0.3523
	Sig. (2-tailed)	.	0.0001	0.0000	0.9798	0.0019	0.0009	0.0836	0.2927	0.9569	0.0380
	N	35.0000	35.0000	35.0000	34.0000	34.0000	35.0000	34.0000	34.0000	34.0000	35.0000
Knowledge of Domestic Law-TVP	Pearson Correlation	0.6149	1.0000	0.4377	0.0463	0.2243	0.3008	0.1171	-0.0998	0.1023	0.4352
	Sig. (2-tailed)	0.0001	.	0.0086	0.7950	0.2022	0.0791	0.5096	0.5743	0.5648	0.0090
	N	35.0000	35.0000	35.0000	34.0000	34.0000	35.0000	34.0000	34.0000	34.0000	35.0000
Knowledge of Domestic Law-CBP	Pearson Correlation	0.6576	0.4377	1.0000	0.0776	0.3110	0.3072	0.3580	0.3949	-0.0457	0.3438
	Sig. (2-tailed)	0.0000	0.0086	.	0.6625	0.0734	0.0726	0.0376	0.0208	0.7974	0.0431
	N	35.0000	35.0000	35.0000	34.0000	34.0000	35.0000	34.0000	34.0000	34.0000	35.0000
sqrtQIIB1a	Pearson Correlation	-0.0045	0.0463	0.0776	1.0000	0.1981	0.2450	0.5349	0.4394	0.5519	0.2215
	Sig. (2-tailed)	0.9798	0.7950	0.6625	.	0.2614	0.1560	0.0009	0.0083	0.0006	0.2010
	N	34.0000	34.0000	34.0000	35.0000	34.0000	35.0000	35.0000	35.0000	35.0000	35.0000
Perceived Effectiveness Domestic Govt Support-CSIE	Pearson Correlation	0.5128	0.2243	0.3110	0.1981	1.0000	0.8018	0.5968	0.5640	0.2129	0.6609
	Sig. (2-tailed)	0.0019	0.2022	0.0734	0.2614	.	0.0000	0.0002	0.0005	0.2268	0.0000
	N	34.0000	34.0000	34.0000	34.0000	35.0000	35.0000	34.0000	34.0000	34.0000	35.0000
Perceived Effectiveness Domestic Govt Support-DWMD	Pearson Correlation	0.5351	0.3008	0.3072	0.2450	0.8018	1.0000	0.6983	0.5910	0.2437	0.4928
	Sig. (2-tailed)	0.0009	0.0791	0.0726	0.1560	0.0000	.	0.0000	0.0002	0.1582	0.0023
	N	35.0000	35.0000	35.0000	35.0000	35.0000	36.0000	35.0000	35.0000	35.0000	36.0000
Perceived Effectiveness Domestic Govt SupportTVP	Pearson Correlation	0.3011	0.1171	0.3580	0.5349	0.5968	0.6983	1.0000	0.7929	0.2897	0.2899
	Sig. (2-tailed)	0.0836	0.5096	0.0376	0.0009	0.0002	0.0000	.	0.0000	0.0913	0.0911
	N	34.0000	34.0000	34.0000	35.0000	34.0000	35.0000	35.0000	35.0000	35.0000	35.0000
Perceived Effectiveness Domestic Govt Support-CBP	Pearson Correlation	0.1858	-0.0998	0.3949	0.4394	0.5640	0.5910	0.7929	1.0000	0.1306	0.2298
	Sig. (2-tailed)	0.2927	0.5743	0.0208	0.0083	0.0005	0.0002	0.0000	.	0.4547	0.1841
	N	34.0000	34.0000	34.0000	35.0000	34.0000	35.0000	35.0000	35.0000	35.0000	35.0000

Table A6, continued (Row 4, Col 6)

Correlation Matrix, Dependent Variables (Parametric)		sqrtQIIC1c	Perceived Deterrence Domestic Law-TVP	sqrtQIIC1e	sqrtQIID1a	Level Cooperation Domestic Orgs-CSIE	Level Cooperation Domestic Orgs-DWMD	Level Cooperation Domestic Orgs-TVP	Level Cooperation Domestic Orgs-CBP	sqrtQIIF1a	sqrtQIIF1b
Org Resource Challenges-Conflict or Lack Comm International Orgs	Pearson Correlation	-0.1086	-0.0952	-0.1293	-0.2087	-0.2421	-0.2142	-0.1411	-0.3103	0.2453	0.1317
	Sig. (2-tailed)	0.5345	0.5864	0.4592	0.2288	0.1611	0.2167	0.4189	0.0696	0.1761	0.4579
	N	35.0000	35.0000	35.0000	35.0000	35.0000	35.0000	35.0000	35.0000	32.0000	34.0000
Org Resource Challenges-Conflict or Lack Comm Domestic Orgs	Pearson Correlation	-0.0982	-0.0902	-0.1094	-0.1867	-0.3064	-0.2303	-0.2087	-0.2817	0.2229	0.1558
	Sig. (2-tailed)	0.5745	0.6063	0.5317	0.2829	0.0735	0.1832	0.2289	0.1011	0.2200	0.3788
	N	35.0000	35.0000	35.0000	35.0000	35.0000	35.0000	35.0000	35.0000	32.0000	34.0000
sqrtQIIA1a	Pearson Correlation	0.2928	0.2645	0.2577	0.4524	0.1923	0.1286	0.2592	0.2915	0.1780	-0.0639
	Sig. (2-tailed)	0.0878	0.1247	0.1351	0.0064	0.2684	0.4614	0.1327	0.0893	0.3381	0.7240
	N	35.0000	35.0000	35.0000	35.0000	35.0000	35.0000	35.0000	35.0000	31.0000	33.0000
Knowledge of Domestic Law-CSIE	Pearson Correlation	0.2505	0.1647	0.2162	0.1169	0.5579	0.4830	0.3219	0.1046	-0.2989	-0.0421
	Sig. (2-tailed)	0.1467	0.3443	0.2123	0.5037	0.0005	0.0033	0.0593	0.5499	0.1023	0.8160
	N	35.0000	35.0000	35.0000	35.0000	35.0000	35.0000	35.0000	35.0000	31.0000	33.0000
Knowledge of Domestic Law-DWMD	Pearson Correlation	0.3738	0.2844	0.3080	0.1547	0.6238	0.5291	0.3785	0.2306	-0.2428	-0.0730
	Sig. (2-tailed)	0.0270	0.0978	0.0719	0.3750	0.0001	0.0011	0.0250	0.1826	0.1881	0.6864
	N	35.0000	35.0000	35.0000	35.0000	35.0000	35.0000	35.0000	35.0000	31.0000	33.0000
Knowledge of Domestic Law-TVP	Pearson Correlation	0.4417	0.3312	0.2329	-0.0231	0.4269	0.2014	0.5066	0.0260	-0.3960	-0.2999
	Sig. (2-tailed)	0.0079	0.0519	0.1781	0.8952	0.0105	0.2461	0.0019	0.8821	0.0274	0.0899
	N	35.0000	35.0000	35.0000	35.0000	35.0000	35.0000	35.0000	35.0000	31.0000	33.0000
Knowledge of Domestic Law-CBP	Pearson Correlation	0.4388	0.2772	0.3716	0.3023	0.4855	0.4690	0.3910	0.5621	-0.2627	-0.2365
	Sig. (2-tailed)	0.0084	0.1069	0.0279	0.0775	0.0031	0.0045	0.0202	0.0004	0.1533	0.1852
	N	35.0000	35.0000	35.0000	35.0000	35.0000	35.0000	35.0000	35.0000	31.0000	33.0000
sqrtQIIB1a	Pearson Correlation	0.1356	0.3730	0.2197	0.5693	0.1905	0.2899	0.4428	0.4588	0.3319	0.1682
	Sig. (2-tailed)	0.4375	0.0273	0.2048	0.0004	0.2729	0.0911	0.0077	0.0056	0.0635	0.3493
	N	35.0000	35.0000	35.0000	35.0000	35.0000	35.0000	35.0000	35.0000	32.0000	33.0000
Perceived Effectiveness Domestic Govt Support-CSIE	Pearson Correlation	0.4546	0.4309	0.4639	0.0661	0.3851	0.4537	0.1976	0.2287	0.0749	0.1145
	Sig. (2-tailed)	0.0061	0.0098	0.0050	0.7061	0.0223	0.0062	0.2553	0.1864	0.6889	0.5259
	N	35.0000	35.0000	35.0000	35.0000	35.0000	35.0000	35.0000	35.0000	31.0000	33.0000
Perceived Effectiveness Domestic Govt Support-DWMD	Pearson Correlation	0.5614	0.4388	0.4160	0.1470	0.3983	0.4759	0.2861	0.1858	0.0368	0.2107
	Sig. (2-tailed)	0.0004	0.0074	0.0116	0.3922	0.0161	0.0033	0.0907	0.2780	0.8415	0.2316
	N	36.0000	36.0000	36.0000	36.0000	36.0000	36.0000	36.0000	36.0000	32.0000	34.0000
Perceived Effectiveness Domestic Govt SupportTVP	Pearson Correlation	0.5105	0.4286	0.3648	0.4573	0.2551	0.4948	0.2783	0.4224	0.0961	0.2948
	Sig. (2-tailed)	0.0017	0.0102	0.0312	0.0057	0.1392	0.0025	0.1055	0.0115	0.6010	0.0958
	N	35.0000	35.0000	35.0000	35.0000	35.0000	35.0000	35.0000	35.0000	32.0000	33.0000
Perceived Effectiveness Domestic Govt Support-CBP	Pearson Correlation	0.3629	0.2293	0.3390	0.3960	0.2410	0.4631	0.2235	0.6599	0.0448	0.2786
	Sig. (2-tailed)	0.0322	0.1851	0.0463	0.0185	0.1631	0.0051	0.1968	0.0000	0.8077	0.1164
	N	35.0000	35.0000	35.0000	35.0000	35.0000	35.0000	35.0000	35.0000	32.0000	33.0000

Table A6, continued (Row 4, Col 7)

Correlation Matrix, Dependent Variables (Parametric)		sqrtQIIF1c	sqrtQIIF1d	sqrtQIIF1e	sqrtQIIF3a	sqrtQIIF3b	sqrtQIIF3c	sqrtQIIF3d	sqrtQIIF3e	sqrtQIIH1a	sqrtQIIH1b
Org Resource Challenges-Conflict or Lack Comm International Orgs	Pearson Correlation	0.1528	0.1233	-0.0310	0.1081	-0.0190	-0.0441	-0.0271	-0.0745	0.0730	-0.1373
	Sig. (2-tailed)	0.3884	0.4871	0.8616	0.5558	0.9165	0.8073	0.8812	0.6854	0.7013	0.4536
	N	34.0000	34.0000	34.0000	32.0000	33.0000	33.0000	33.0000	32.0000	30.0000	32.0000
Org Resource Challenges-Conflict or Lack Comm Domestic Orgs	Pearson Correlation	0.1172	0.0962	-0.0495	0.1069	-0.0066	-0.0392	-0.0468	-0.0917	0.0195	-0.1104
	Sig. (2-tailed)	0.5092	0.5882	0.7811	0.5604	0.9711	0.8284	0.7959	0.6176	0.9185	0.5474
	N	34.0000	34.0000	34.0000	32.0000	33.0000	33.0000	33.0000	32.0000	30.0000	32.0000
sqrtQIIA1a	Pearson Correlation	0.1953	0.1907	0.1443	0.0910	-0.0026	0.1361	0.1300	0.1002	0.0933	-0.2110
	Sig. (2-tailed)	0.2761	0.2879	0.4232	0.6265	0.9887	0.4576	0.4782	0.5918	0.6239	0.2465
	N	33.0000	33.0000	33.0000	31.0000	32.0000	32.0000	32.0000	31.0000	30.0000	32.0000
Knowledge of Domestic Law-CSIE	Pearson Correlation	-0.0100	-0.0919	-0.2454	-0.2978	0.0450	0.1313	-0.1426	-0.0982	-0.1712	0.0731
	Sig. (2-tailed)	0.9559	0.6109	0.1687	0.1037	0.8069	0.4738	0.4362	0.5991	0.3658	0.6911
	N	33.0000	33.0000	33.0000	31.0000	32.0000	32.0000	32.0000	31.0000	30.0000	32.0000
Knowledge of Domestic Law-DWMD	Pearson Correlation	0.0213	-0.0683	-0.1448	-0.2318	0.0067	0.0908	-0.0922	-0.0454	-0.0465	0.0936
	Sig. (2-tailed)	0.9063	0.7057	0.4216	0.2096	0.9710	0.6213	0.6158	0.8085	0.8072	0.6102
	N	33.0000	33.0000	33.0000	31.0000	32.0000	32.0000	32.0000	31.0000	30.0000	32.0000
Knowledge of Domestic Law-TVP	Pearson Correlation	-0.0331	-0.3194	-0.3811	-0.4208	-0.2607	-0.1598	-0.3818	-0.3747	-0.2117	-0.0478
	Sig. (2-tailed)	0.8548	0.0700	0.0287	0.0184	0.1495	0.3824	0.0311	0.0378	0.2615	0.7949
	N	33.0000	33.0000	33.0000	31.0000	32.0000	32.0000	32.0000	31.0000	30.0000	32.0000
Knowledge of Domestic Law-CBP	Pearson Correlation	-0.1394	-0.2384	-0.0992	-0.2024	-0.1504	-0.0577	-0.1521	-0.0974	-0.1059	-0.1474
	Sig. (2-tailed)	0.4393	0.1815	0.5827	0.2748	0.4113	0.7536	0.4061	0.6022	0.5774	0.4207
	N	33.0000	33.0000	33.0000	31.0000	32.0000	32.0000	32.0000	31.0000	30.0000	32.0000
sqrtQIIB1a	Pearson Correlation	0.4370	0.2256	0.2721	0.2538	-0.0370	0.1288	0.0064	0.0077	0.1795	-0.1257
	Sig. (2-tailed)	0.0110	0.2068	0.1255	0.1683	0.8408	0.4825	0.9721	0.9674	0.3338	0.4930
	N	33.0000	33.0000	33.0000	31.0000	32.0000	32.0000	32.0000	31.0000	31.0000	32.0000
Perceived Effectiveness Domestic Govt Support-CSIE	Pearson Correlation	0.1969	0.1917	0.1385	0.0846	0.1371	0.2411	0.1298	0.2186	0.0686	0.1714
	Sig. (2-tailed)	0.2721	0.2851	0.4420	0.6509	0.4543	0.1837	0.4790	0.2374	0.7187	0.3484
	N	33.0000	33.0000	33.0000	31.0000	32.0000	32.0000	32.0000	31.0000	30.0000	32.0000
Perceived Effectiveness Domestic Govt Support-DWMD	Pearson Correlation	0.1804	0.1308	0.0380	-0.0322	0.1420	0.2355	-0.0237	0.0333	0.0897	0.1302
	Sig. (2-tailed)	0.3073	0.4608	0.8310	0.8609	0.4304	0.1871	0.8957	0.8563	0.6312	0.4703
	N	34.0000	34.0000	34.0000	32.0000	33.0000	33.0000	33.0000	32.0000	31.0000	33.0000
Perceived Effectiveness Domestic Govt SupportTVP	Pearson Correlation	0.2762	0.0781	0.1525	0.1084	0.2329	0.3610	0.0264	0.0967	0.0847	0.1798
	Sig. (2-tailed)	0.1197	0.6657	0.3970	0.5618	0.1995	0.0424	0.8858	0.6046	0.6504	0.3248
	N	33.0000	33.0000	33.0000	31.0000	32.0000	32.0000	32.0000	31.0000	31.0000	32.0000
Perceived Effectiveness Domestic Govt Support-CBP	Pearson Correlation	0.2424	0.0450	0.1999	0.0538	0.2318	0.3369	0.0325	0.1324	0.0333	0.1542
	Sig. (2-tailed)	0.1741	0.8035	0.2647	0.7739	0.2018	0.0594	0.8599	0.4776	0.8590	0.3996
	N	33.0000	33.0000	33.0000	31.0000	32.0000	32.0000	32.0000	31.0000	31.0000	32.0000

Table A6, continued (Row 4, Col 8)

Correlation Matrix, Dependent Variables (Parametric)		sqrtQIIIH1c	sqrtQIIIH1d	sqrtQIIIH1e	sqrtQIIIH3a	sqrtQIIIH3b	sqrtQIIIH3c	PtHIIIQabs	sqrtQIIIH3e	sqrtQIIIA1a	sqrtQIIIA1b
Org Resource Challenges-Conflict or Lack Comm International Orgs	Pearson Correlation	0.1343	-0.0203	-0.1464	0.1575	0.0560	0.2028	-0.0149	-0.1282	0.0915	-0.2006
	Sig. (2-tailed)	0.4715	0.9137	0.4402	0.3814	0.7571	0.2576	0.9343	0.4770	0.6069	0.2480
	N	31.0000	31.0000	30.0000	33.0000	33.0000	33.0000	33.0000	33.0000	34.0000	35.0000
Org Resource Challenges-Conflict or Lack Comm Domestic Orgs	Pearson Correlation	0.1352	-0.0535	-0.1769	0.1793	0.0743	0.2141	0.0084	-0.0901	0.0784	-0.1661
	Sig. (2-tailed)	0.4685	0.7749	0.3496	0.3180	0.6809	0.2316	0.9629	0.6181	0.6594	0.3401
	N	31.0000	31.0000	30.0000	33.0000	33.0000	33.0000	33.0000	33.0000	34.0000	35.0000
sqrtQIIA1a	Pearson Correlation	-0.1778	-0.0218	0.0465	0.0193	-0.2080	-0.1876	-0.0740	-0.0809	0.6590	0.1279
	Sig. (2-tailed)	0.3385	0.9074	0.8070	0.9151	0.2455	0.2958	0.6823	0.6544	0.0000	0.4639
	N	31.0000	31.0000	30.0000	33.0000	33.0000	33.0000	33.0000	33.0000	34.0000	35.0000
Knowledge of Domestic Law-CSIE	Pearson Correlation	-0.0405	-0.2165	-0.2761	-0.1459	0.0339	0.0086	-0.1387	-0.2131	-0.0793	0.3803
	Sig. (2-tailed)	0.8288	0.2421	0.1398	0.4180	0.8513	0.9621	0.4416	0.2337	0.6557	0.0242
	N	31.0000	31.0000	30.0000	33.0000	33.0000	33.0000	33.0000	33.0000	34.0000	35.0000
Knowledge of Domestic Law-DWMD	Pearson Correlation	-0.0044	-0.0586	-0.1283	-0.1299	0.0058	-0.0144	-0.1081	-0.1729	-0.0986	0.3092
	Sig. (2-tailed)	0.9813	0.7540	0.4994	0.4712	0.9746	0.9366	0.5493	0.3359	0.5790	0.0707
	N	31.0000	31.0000	30.0000	33.0000	33.0000	33.0000	33.0000	33.0000	34.0000	35.0000
Knowledge of Domestic Law-TVP	Pearson Correlation	-0.0641	-0.1677	-0.3042	-0.3558	-0.1177	-0.0806	-0.2696	-0.3563	0.0263	0.2589
	Sig. (2-tailed)	0.7318	0.3672	0.1022	0.0422	0.5140	0.6556	0.1292	0.0419	0.8827	0.1331
	N	31.0000	31.0000	30.0000	33.0000	33.0000	33.0000	33.0000	33.0000	34.0000	35.0000
Knowledge of Domestic Law-CBP	Pearson Correlation	-0.2061	-0.0797	-0.0096	-0.0812	-0.2433	-0.2486	-0.0398	-0.0119	0.0994	0.1914
	Sig. (2-tailed)	0.2661	0.6700	0.9597	0.6531	0.1725	0.1630	0.8260	0.9476	0.5760	0.2707
	N	31.0000	31.0000	30.0000	33.0000	33.0000	33.0000	33.0000	33.0000	34.0000	35.0000
sqrtQIIB1a	Pearson Correlation	-0.0293	0.0257	0.0574	0.1174	-0.0546	-0.0153	-0.0298	-0.0830	0.4835	-0.0555
	Sig. (2-tailed)	0.8737	0.8891	0.7589	0.5084	0.7591	0.9317	0.8671	0.6407	0.0038	0.7517
	N	32.0000	32.0000	31.0000	34.0000	34.0000	34.0000	34.0000	34.0000	34.0000	35.0000
Perceived Effectiveness Domestic Govt Support-CSIE	Pearson Correlation	0.1514	0.1866	0.0964	0.0895	0.2417	0.2037	0.1533	0.1342	-0.0695	0.0196
	Sig. (2-tailed)	0.4161	0.3148	0.6124	0.6203	0.1754	0.2554	0.3942	0.4566	0.6959	0.9111
	N	31.0000	31.0000	30.0000	33.0000	33.0000	33.0000	33.0000	33.0000	34.0000	35.0000
Perceived Effectiveness Domestic Govt Support-DWMD	Pearson Correlation	0.1885	0.0873	-0.0004	0.0860	0.1414	0.1527	0.0579	-0.0009	0.0358	0.1176
	Sig. (2-tailed)	0.3015	0.6346	0.9984	0.6285	0.4249	0.3886	0.7448	0.9959	0.8383	0.4946
	N	32.0000	32.0000	31.0000	34.0000	34.0000	34.0000	34.0000	34.0000	35.0000	36.0000
Perceived Effectiveness Domestic Govt SupportTVP	Pearson Correlation	0.2016	0.0999	0.0867	0.2009	0.2686	0.2557	0.2526	0.2093	0.1463	0.0687
	Sig. (2-tailed)	0.2684	0.5864	0.6428	0.2545	0.1245	0.1444	0.1495	0.2348	0.4090	0.6951
	N	32.0000	32.0000	31.0000	34.0000	34.0000	34.0000	34.0000	34.0000	34.0000	35.0000
Perceived Effectiveness Domestic Govt Support-CBP	Pearson Correlation	0.2406	0.1523	0.2515	0.1265	0.1784	0.1483	0.1568	0.2280	0.1107	0.0435
	Sig. (2-tailed)	0.1847	0.4053	0.1722	0.4760	0.3127	0.4025	0.3758	0.1946	0.5333	0.8039
	N	32.0000	32.0000	31.0000	34.0000	34.0000	34.0000	34.0000	34.0000	34.0000	35.0000

Table A6, continued (Row 4, Col 9)

Correlation Matrix, Dependent Variables (Parametric)		sqrtQIIA1c	sqrtQIIA1d	sqrtQIIA1e	sqrtQIIID1a	Level Cooperation Domestic Orgs–CNDPS	Level Cooperation Domestic Orgs–CNBC	Level Cooperation Domestic Orgs–CSTP	Level Cooperation Domestic Orgs–TRIPS	sqrtQIIID2a	Level Cooperation International Orgs–CNDPS
Org Resource Challenges-Conflict or Lack Comm International Orgs	Pearson Correlation	-0.0822	-0.0833	-0.2899	0.0245	-0.2336	-0.2472	-0.1951	-0.3522	-0.0468	-0.1102
	Sig. (2-tailed)	0.6388	0.6342	0.0912	0.8939	0.1837	0.1586	0.2688	0.0411	0.7927	0.5287
	N	35.0000	35.0000	35.0000	32.0000	34.0000	34.0000	34.0000	34.0000	34.0000	35.0000
Org Resource Challenges-Conflict or Lack Comm Domestic Orgs	Pearson Correlation	-0.0312	-0.0846	-0.2436	-0.0121	-0.2207	-0.2111	-0.2121	-0.2948	-0.0631	-0.0994
	Sig. (2-tailed)	0.8589	0.6289	0.1585	0.9477	0.2098	0.2307	0.2284	0.0905	0.7230	0.5698
	N	35.0000	35.0000	35.0000	32.0000	34.0000	34.0000	34.0000	34.0000	34.0000	35.0000
sqrtQIIA1a	Pearson Correlation	0.1830	0.2485	0.3637	0.2503	0.0416	0.1799	0.1731	0.1626	0.3801	0.0431
	Sig. (2-tailed)	0.2926	0.1499	0.0317	0.1670	0.8152	0.3086	0.3276	0.3581	0.0266	0.8059
	N	35.0000	35.0000	35.0000	32.0000	34.0000	34.0000	34.0000	34.0000	34.0000	35.0000
Knowledge of Domestic Law-CSIE	Pearson Correlation	0.4524	0.0719	0.0763	-0.1148	0.2483	0.2263	0.0270	0.0105	-0.0543	0.2693
	Sig. (2-tailed)	0.0064	0.6814	0.6631	0.5317	0.1567	0.1980	0.8796	0.9529	0.7602	0.1177
	N	35.0000	35.0000	35.0000	32.0000	34.0000	34.0000	34.0000	34.0000	34.0000	35.0000
Knowledge of Domestic Law-DWMD	Pearson Correlation	0.4340	0.1111	0.1761	-0.1301	0.1409	0.2464	-0.0296	-0.0050	-0.1039	0.1853
	Sig. (2-tailed)	0.0092	0.5250	0.3117	0.4778	0.4268	0.1601	0.8680	0.9776	0.5586	0.2867
	N	35.0000	35.0000	35.0000	32.0000	34.0000	34.0000	34.0000	34.0000	34.0000	35.0000
Knowledge of Domestic Law-TVP	Pearson Correlation	0.3175	0.3321	-0.0099	0.0739	0.1655	0.1167	0.2619	-0.0368	0.0341	0.0978
	Sig. (2-tailed)	0.0631	0.0513	0.9550	0.6879	0.3497	0.5112	0.1346	0.8365	0.8481	0.5762
	N	35.0000	35.0000	35.0000	32.0000	34.0000	34.0000	34.0000	34.0000	34.0000	35.0000
Knowledge of Domestic Law-CBP	Pearson Correlation	0.3293	0.2041	0.4573	0.1138	0.1424	0.3494	0.1388	0.3325	-0.0834	0.0795
	Sig. (2-tailed)	0.0534	0.2396	0.0057	0.5352	0.4216	0.0428	0.4338	0.0547	0.6392	0.6497
	N	35.0000	35.0000	35.0000	32.0000	34.0000	34.0000	34.0000	34.0000	34.0000	35.0000
sqrtQIIB1a	Pearson Correlation	0.0273	0.0725	0.1114	0.5321	0.2194	0.3162	0.2759	0.3309	0.5017	0.1186
	Sig. (2-tailed)	0.8761	0.6791	0.5242	0.0017	0.2125	0.0685	0.1143	0.0560	0.0025	0.4973
	N	35.0000	35.0000	35.0000	32.0000	34.0000	34.0000	34.0000	34.0000	34.0000	35.0000
Perceived Effectiveness Domestic Govt Support-CSIE	Pearson Correlation	0.0674	0.0462	0.1435	0.0973	0.2778	0.2639	0.1422	0.1933	0.2241	0.3412
	Sig. (2-tailed)	0.7007	0.7924	0.4107	0.5964	0.1116	0.1316	0.4223	0.2733	0.2026	0.0449
	N	35.0000	35.0000	35.0000	32.0000	34.0000	34.0000	34.0000	34.0000	34.0000	35.0000
Perceived Effectiveness Domestic Govt Support-DWMD	Pearson Correlation	0.1689	0.1085	0.1543	-0.0121	0.2359	0.2289	0.0429	0.0362	0.1288	0.3312
	Sig. (2-tailed)	0.3248	0.5288	0.3688	0.9467	0.1724	0.1859	0.8065	0.8363	0.4607	0.0485
	N	36.0000	36.0000	36.0000	33.0000	35.0000	35.0000	35.0000	35.0000	35.0000	36.0000
Perceived Effectiveness Domestic Govt SupportTVP	Pearson Correlation	0.1978	0.1271	0.2987	0.3436	0.3660	0.5023	0.2435	0.4655	0.3036	0.2826
	Sig. (2-tailed)	0.2546	0.4668	0.0814	0.0542	0.0333	0.0025	0.1652	0.0055	0.0809	0.1000
	N	35.0000	35.0000	35.0000	32.0000	34.0000	34.0000	34.0000	34.0000	34.0000	35.0000
Perceived Effectiveness Domestic Govt Support-CBP	Pearson Correlation	0.1071	0.0802	0.3721	0.4333	0.3414	0.4270	0.2176	0.5794	0.3121	0.3800
	Sig. (2-tailed)	0.5401	0.6472	0.0277	0.0132	0.0481	0.0118	0.2164	0.0003	0.0723	0.0244
	N	35.0000	35.0000	35.0000	32.0000	34.0000	34.0000	34.0000	34.0000	34.0000	35.0000

Table A6, continued (Row 4, Col 10)

Correlation Matrix, Dependent Variables (Parametric)		Level Cooperation International Orgs-CNBC	Level Cooperation International Orgs-CSTP	sqrtQIID2e	sqrtQIVA1	sqrtQIVA2	sqrtQIVA3	sqrtQIVA5	sqrtQIVA7	sqrtQIVA8	Political Ideology
Org Resource Challenges-Conflict or Lack Comm International Orgs	Pearson Correlation	-0.1208	-0.0355	-0.1904	0.3519	0.2023	0.1834	0.1253	-0.2223	-0.0648	0.0373
	Sig. (2-tailed)	0.4895	0.8395	0.2734	0.0382	0.2438	0.2991	0.4803	0.1992	0.7114	0.8365
	N	35.0000	35.0000	35.0000	35.0000	35.0000	34.0000	34.0000	35.0000	35.0000	33.0000
Org Resource Challenges-Conflict or Lack Comm Domestic Orgs	Pearson Correlation	-0.1121	-0.0277	-0.1476	0.3555	0.1494	0.1617	0.0593	-0.0972	-0.2430	0.0842
	Sig. (2-tailed)	0.5216	0.8744	0.3974	0.0361	0.3917	0.3608	0.7389	0.5786	0.1595	0.6414
	N	35.0000	35.0000	35.0000	35.0000	35.0000	34.0000	34.0000	35.0000	35.0000	33.0000
sqrtQIIA1a	Pearson Correlation	0.0968	0.2430	0.1620	-0.1899	-0.0509	-0.2144	-0.0193	0.1354	-0.1746	0.2663
	Sig. (2-tailed)	0.5802	0.1596	0.3525	0.2746	0.7714	0.2233	0.9150	0.4381	0.3233	0.1406
	N	35.0000	35.0000	35.0000	35.0000	35.0000	34.0000	33.0000	35.0000	34.0000	32.0000
Knowledge of Domestic Law-CSIE	Pearson Correlation	0.2882	0.1645	0.1353	0.0265	-0.0986	-0.1775	0.2925	-0.1068	0.0432	0.0819
	Sig. (2-tailed)	0.0932	0.3450	0.4382	0.8798	0.5730	0.3152	0.0986	0.5414	0.8083	0.6557
	N	35.0000	35.0000	35.0000	35.0000	35.0000	34.0000	33.0000	35.0000	34.0000	32.0000
Knowledge of Domestic Law-DWMD	Pearson Correlation	0.2562	0.1028	0.1436	0.0686	-0.0248	-0.1084	0.2711	-0.0749	0.1244	0.2899
	Sig. (2-tailed)	0.1374	0.5569	0.4105	0.6955	0.8877	0.5418	0.1271	0.6689	0.4832	0.1076
	N	35.0000	35.0000	35.0000	35.0000	35.0000	34.0000	33.0000	35.0000	34.0000	32.0000
Knowledge of Domestic Law-TVP	Pearson Correlation	0.0945	0.1248	-0.0195	0.0473	-0.0414	-0.0617	0.2011	-0.0363	0.3014	0.0322
	Sig. (2-tailed)	0.5894	0.4750	0.9117	0.7873	0.8133	0.7290	0.2619	0.8360	0.0832	0.8611
	N	35.0000	35.0000	35.0000	35.0000	35.0000	34.0000	33.0000	35.0000	34.0000	32.0000
Knowledge of Domestic Law-CBP	Pearson Correlation	0.1476	0.0430	0.2240	-0.1427	-0.0942	-0.1213	0.0556	0.1172	0.2077	0.1375
	Sig. (2-tailed)	0.3974	0.8064	0.1958	0.4134	0.5902	0.4943	0.7588	0.5026	0.2385	0.4529
	N	35.0000	35.0000	35.0000	35.0000	35.0000	34.0000	33.0000	35.0000	34.0000	32.0000
sqrtQIIB1a	Pearson Correlation	0.1411	0.2387	0.1285	0.0551	-0.0629	0.1252	0.0988	-0.0153	-0.1597	0.1598
	Sig. (2-tailed)	0.4188	0.1673	0.4621	0.7531	0.7195	0.4804	0.5844	0.9305	0.3671	0.3823
	N	35.0000	35.0000	35.0000	35.0000	35.0000	34.0000	33.0000	35.0000	34.0000	32.0000
Perceived Effectiveness Domestic Govt Support-CSIE	Pearson Correlation	0.3494	0.3083	0.3184	0.1562	-0.0927	0.0444	0.2648	-0.0239	-0.1045	0.2282
	Sig. (2-tailed)	0.0396	0.0715	0.0623	0.3702	0.5964	0.8030	0.1364	0.8916	0.5563	0.2090
	N	35.0000	35.0000	35.0000	35.0000	35.0000	34.0000	33.0000	35.0000	34.0000	32.0000
Perceived Effectiveness Domestic Govt Support-DWMD	Pearson Correlation	0.3500	0.3999	0.2809	0.1258	-0.0618	-0.0688	0.1586	0.0427	-0.0391	0.3143
	Sig. (2-tailed)	0.0364	0.0157	0.0971	0.4646	0.7202	0.6947	0.3703	0.8049	0.8237	0.0748
	N	36.0000	36.0000	36.0000	36.0000	36.0000	35.0000	34.0000	36.0000	35.0000	33.0000
Perceived Effectiveness Domestic Govt SupportTVP	Pearson Correlation	0.3103	0.4354	0.4060	0.0130	-0.1006	0.0903	0.1183	-0.0332	-0.0354	0.4093
	Sig. (2-tailed)	0.0697	0.0089	0.0155	0.9411	0.5651	0.6115	0.5119	0.8498	0.8425	0.0200
	N	35.0000	35.0000	35.0000	35.0000	35.0000	34.0000	33.0000	35.0000	34.0000	32.0000
Perceived Effectiveness Domestic Govt Support-CBP	Pearson Correlation	0.3790	0.3948	0.5288	-0.0315	-0.1118	0.0378	-0.0183	-0.0270	-0.1465	0.4199
	Sig. (2-tailed)	0.0248	0.0189	0.0011	0.8576	0.5224	0.8318	0.9194	0.8775	0.4082	0.0167
	N	35.0000	35.0000	35.0000	35.0000	35.0000	34.0000	33.0000	35.0000	34.0000	32.0000

Correlation Matrix, Dependent Variables (Parametric)		Importance of Smuggling-Endangered Species	reflectsqrtQ1A1b	reflectsqrtQ1A1c	reflectsqrtQ1A1d	reflectsqrtQ1A1e	sqrtQ1B1a	Knowledge of Smuggling-Narcotics	Knowledge of Smuggling-Weapons	Knowledge of Smuggling-Humans	Knowledge of Smuggling-Contraband
sqrtQIIC1a	Pearson Correlation	0.0838	0.0825	-0.0479	-0.0846	-0.1418	0.3969	0.1620	0.1631	0.1132	0.2242
	Sig. (2-tailed)	0.6323	0.6374	0.7848	0.6288	0.4164	0.0182	0.3525	0.3492	0.5172	0.1955
	N	35.0000	35.0000	35.0000	35.0000	35.0000	35.0000	35.0000	35.0000	35.0000	35.0000
Perceived Deterrence Domestic Law-CSIE	Pearson Correlation	-0.2341	-0.1871	-0.0832	-0.3257	-0.3539	0.1588	0.3838	0.3848	0.2830	0.3749
	Sig. (2-tailed)	0.1693	0.2746	0.6295	0.0526	0.0342	0.3550	0.0208	0.0205	0.0944	0.0243
	N	36.0000	36.0000	36.0000	36.0000	36.0000	36.0000	36.0000	36.0000	36.0000	36.0000
sqrtQIIC1c	Pearson Correlation	-0.1238	-0.1524	-0.0944	-0.0979	-0.1055	0.0353	0.4694	0.4439	0.2701	0.4805
	Sig. (2-tailed)	0.4718	0.3747	0.5838	0.5701	0.5404	0.8381	0.0039	0.0067	0.1111	0.0030
	N	36.0000	36.0000	36.0000	36.0000	36.0000	36.0000	36.0000	36.0000	36.0000	36.0000
Perceived Deterrence Domestic Law-TVP	Pearson Correlation	-0.1109	-0.1102	-0.1419	-0.2716	-0.0945	0.0993	0.3394	0.4604	0.1878	0.2528
	Sig. (2-tailed)	0.5197	0.5221	0.4089	0.1090	0.5835	0.5645	0.0429	0.0047	0.2728	0.1368
	N	36.0000	36.0000	36.0000	36.0000	36.0000	36.0000	36.0000	36.0000	36.0000	36.0000
sqrtQIIC1e	Pearson Correlation	-0.2413	-0.0459	0.0556	-0.1219	-0.1092	-0.0364	0.2517	0.3294	-0.0107	0.1780
	Sig. (2-tailed)	0.1563	0.7905	0.7473	0.4788	0.5259	0.8332	0.1386	0.0498	0.9505	0.2989
	N	36.0000	36.0000	36.0000	36.0000	36.0000	36.0000	36.0000	36.0000	36.0000	36.0000
sqrtQIID1a	Pearson Correlation	0.2661	0.2364	0.1976	0.2932	-0.1569	0.6200	0.0729	0.4288	0.0309	0.3750
	Sig. (2-tailed)	0.1167	0.1650	0.2480	0.0826	0.3609	0.0001	0.6725	0.0091	0.8582	0.0242
	N	36.0000	36.0000	36.0000	36.0000	36.0000	36.0000	36.0000	36.0000	36.0000	36.0000
Level Cooperation Domestic Orgs-CSIE	Pearson Correlation	-0.0291	-0.1636	0.0149	0.1377	-0.2225	0.2881	0.5092	0.5158	0.2726	0.3252
	Sig. (2-tailed)	0.8662	0.3404	0.9312	0.4231	0.1922	0.0884	0.0015	0.0013	0.1078	0.0530
	N	36.0000	36.0000	36.0000	36.0000	36.0000	36.0000	36.0000	36.0000	36.0000	36.0000
Level Cooperation Domestic Orgs-DWMD	Pearson Correlation	0.0626	-0.1263	0.0214	0.1513	-0.3094	0.1094	0.3940	0.4225	0.1807	0.3303
	Sig. (2-tailed)	0.7167	0.4630	0.9013	0.3783	0.0663	0.5255	0.0174	0.0103	0.2915	0.0491
	N	36.0000	36.0000	36.0000	36.0000	36.0000	36.0000	36.0000	36.0000	36.0000	36.0000
Level Cooperation Domestic Orgs-TVP	Pearson Correlation	0.1330	-0.1268	-0.0633	0.0183	-0.3146	0.4848	0.4552	0.4073	0.4165	0.4434
	Sig. (2-tailed)	0.4393	0.4612	0.7139	0.9154	0.0617	0.0027	0.0053	0.0137	0.0115	0.0068
	N	36.0000	36.0000	36.0000	36.0000	36.0000	36.0000	36.0000	36.0000	36.0000	36.0000
Level Cooperation Domestic Orgs-CBP	Pearson Correlation	0.0417	0.0764	0.1665	0.2144	-0.3942	0.2573	-0.0049	0.3248	-0.0180	0.3882
	Sig. (2-tailed)	0.8092	0.6578	0.3317	0.2091	0.0174	0.1297	0.9774	0.0532	0.9168	0.0193
	N	36.0000	36.0000	36.0000	36.0000	36.0000	36.0000	36.0000	36.0000	36.0000	36.0000
sqrtQIIF1a	Pearson Correlation	0.0504	0.0604	-0.1249	-0.1993	-0.0240	0.1235	-0.1043	-0.0699	0.1561	-0.0844
	Sig. (2-tailed)	0.7840	0.7427	0.4957	0.2741	0.8965	0.5005	0.5701	0.7038	0.3935	0.6462
	N	32.0000	32.0000	32.0000	32.0000	32.0000	32.0000	32.0000	32.0000	32.0000	32.0000
sqrtQIIF1b	Pearson Correlation	0.0934	-0.1690	-0.1418	0.0424	0.0298	-0.0133	-0.0588	-0.0020	0.1541	-0.1481
	Sig. (2-tailed)	0.5992	0.3392	0.4236	0.8117	0.8673	0.9406	0.7410	0.9909	0.3843	0.4032
	N	34.0000	34.0000	34.0000	34.0000	34.0000	34.0000	34.0000	34.0000	34.0000	34.0000

Table A6, continued (Row 5, Col 2)

Correlation Matrix, Dependent Variables (Parametric)		sqrtQIE1a	Personal Resource Challenges- Lack of Time	Personal Resource Challenges- Lack of Knowledge	Personal Resource Challenges- Lack of Training	sqrtQIE1e	Personal Resource Challenges- Excessive Admin Paperwork	Personal Resource Challenges- Ineffective Technology	Personal Resource Challenges- Ineffective Strategic Focus	Personal Resource Challenges- Ineffective Tactical Policy	Personal Resource Challenges- Lack of Clarity in Duties
sqrtQIIC1a	Pearson Correlation	-0.1783	-0.0112	-0.0097	0.1033	-0.0232	0.1834	-0.0074	0.0771	0.0662	0.1138
	Sig. (2-tailed)	0.3131	0.9489	0.9560	0.5550	0.8946	0.2917	0.9665	0.6599	0.7055	0.5151
	N	34.0000	35.0000	35.0000	35.0000	35.0000	35.0000	35.0000	35.0000	35.0000	35.0000
Perceived Deterrence Domestic Law- CSIE	Pearson Correlation	-0.0002	0.0226	-0.0349	-0.0367	0.2299	0.2142	0.0418	0.0674	-0.0343	0.0701
	Sig. (2-tailed)	0.9993	0.8959	0.8397	0.8315	0.1773	0.2097	0.8088	0.6961	0.8424	0.6847
	N	35.0000	36.0000	36.0000	36.0000	36.0000	36.0000	36.0000	36.0000	36.0000	36.0000
sqrtQIIC1c	Pearson Correlation	-0.1764	0.1106	-0.1669	-0.2088	0.0587	0.1684	-0.2577	-0.1948	-0.1335	0.0130
	Sig. (2-tailed)	0.3108	0.5207	0.3307	0.2216	0.7339	0.3262	0.1292	0.2549	0.4377	0.9399
	N	35.0000	36.0000	36.0000	36.0000	36.0000	36.0000	36.0000	36.0000	36.0000	36.0000
Perceived Deterrence Domestic Law- TVP	Pearson Correlation	-0.1158	-0.1264	-0.2495	-0.1770	0.0541	0.1810	-0.1782	-0.1036	-0.0706	-0.0110
	Sig. (2-tailed)	0.5076	0.4625	0.1422	0.3017	0.7540	0.2909	0.2984	0.5478	0.6824	0.9490
	N	35.0000	36.0000	36.0000	36.0000	36.0000	36.0000	36.0000	36.0000	36.0000	36.0000
sqrtQIIC1e	Pearson Correlation	-0.0258	0.0506	-0.1759	-0.1284	0.0138	0.1871	-0.1381	-0.1071	-0.0541	0.0157
	Sig. (2-tailed)	0.8832	0.7696	0.3048	0.4554	0.9362	0.2746	0.4219	0.5340	0.7539	0.9275
	N	35.0000	36.0000	36.0000	36.0000	36.0000	36.0000	36.0000	36.0000	36.0000	36.0000
sqrtQIID1a	Pearson Correlation	-0.0357	-0.0498	-0.1174	-0.1545	0.2266	0.1332	-0.1490	-0.0144	-0.0835	-0.0795
	Sig. (2-tailed)	0.8388	0.7728	0.4955	0.3682	0.1839	0.4387	0.3857	0.9337	0.6284	0.6447
	N	35.0000	36.0000	36.0000	36.0000	36.0000	36.0000	36.0000	36.0000	36.0000	36.0000
Level Cooperation Domestic Orgs- CSIE	Pearson Correlation	-0.3267	-0.0671	-0.3195	-0.3802	-0.0320	0.0093	-0.2315	-0.3394	-0.3240	-0.2536
	Sig. (2-tailed)	0.0554	0.6976	0.0575	0.0222	0.8528	0.9570	0.1743	0.0429	0.0539	0.1357
	N	35.0000	36.0000	36.0000	36.0000	36.0000	36.0000	36.0000	36.0000	36.0000	36.0000
Level Cooperation Domestic Orgs- DWMD	Pearson Correlation	-0.3174	-0.0939	-0.3120	-0.3942	-0.0340	0.1753	-0.3228	-0.4186	-0.3391	-0.2787
	Sig. (2-tailed)	0.0632	0.5860	0.0639	0.0174	0.8439	0.3065	0.0548	0.0111	0.0430	0.0997
	N	35.0000	36.0000	36.0000	36.0000	36.0000	36.0000	36.0000	36.0000	36.0000	36.0000
Level Cooperation Domestic Orgs- TVP	Pearson Correlation	-0.2215	0.0638	-0.1253	-0.2011	0.0283	0.0584	-0.1657	-0.1068	-0.1520	0.0556
	Sig. (2-tailed)	0.2010	0.7115	0.4667	0.2396	0.8701	0.7350	0.3342	0.5354	0.3760	0.7476
	N	35.0000	36.0000	36.0000	36.0000	36.0000	36.0000	36.0000	36.0000	36.0000	36.0000
Level Cooperation Domestic Orgs- CBP	Pearson Correlation	-0.1697	-0.0404	-0.1085	-0.1170	0.0558	-0.0042	-0.1672	-0.0882	-0.1525	-0.0516
	Sig. (2-tailed)	0.3297	0.8149	0.5287	0.4968	0.7467	0.9804	0.3296	0.6088	0.3747	0.7651
	N	35.0000	36.0000	36.0000	36.0000	36.0000	36.0000	36.0000	36.0000	36.0000	36.0000
sqrtQIIF1a	Pearson Correlation	-0.2070	-0.1109	0.1083	0.1907	0.0661	-0.1616	-0.0084	0.1466	0.0448	0.0846
	Sig. (2-tailed)	0.2638	0.5457	0.5553	0.2959	0.7192	0.3770	0.9637	0.4234	0.8078	0.6455
	N	31.0000	32.0000	32.0000	32.0000	32.0000	32.0000	32.0000	32.0000	32.0000	32.0000
sqrtQIIF1b	Pearson Correlation	-0.0962	-0.2253	-0.0091	0.0057	0.0388	-0.2565	-0.1464	0.0246	-0.0462	-0.0926
	Sig. (2-tailed)	0.5943	0.2001	0.9594	0.9744	0.8277	0.1430	0.4087	0.8902	0.7952	0.6025
	N	33.0000	34.0000	34.0000	34.0000	34.0000	34.0000	34.0000	34.0000	34.0000	34.0000

Table A6, continued (Row 5, Col 3)

Correlation Matrix, Dependent Variables (Parametric)		Personal Resource Challenges-Conflict or Lack Comm Leaders and Employees	sqrtQ1E1l	Personal Resource Challenges-Conflict or Lack Comm International Orgs	Personal Resource Challenges-Conflict or Lack Comm Domestic Orgs	sqrtQ1E3a	Org Resource Challenges-Lack of Time	Org Resource Challenges-Lack of Knowledge	Org Resource Challenges-Lack of Training	sqrtQ1E3e	Org Resource Challenges-Excessive Admin Paperwork
sqrtQIIC1a	Pearson Correlation	0.0073	0.0877	0.1672	-0.0003	-0.0268	-0.2993	0.0181	0.0138	-0.2828	-0.1344
	Sig. (2-tailed)	0.9669	0.6164	0.3371	0.9986	0.8805	0.0855	0.9191	0.9381	0.1108	0.4486
	N	35.0000	35.0000	35.0000	35.0000	34.0000	34.0000	34.0000	34.0000	33.0000	34.0000
Perceived Deterrence Domestic Law-CSIE	Pearson Correlation	-0.0032	-0.0424	0.2196	0.1395	0.1820	-0.0318	0.0966	0.0212	-0.1174	0.0567
	Sig. (2-tailed)	0.9852	0.8060	0.1982	0.4172	0.3028	0.8562	0.5811	0.9037	0.5085	0.7461
	N	36.0000	36.0000	36.0000	36.0000	34.0000	35.0000	35.0000	35.0000	34.0000	35.0000
sqrtQIIC1c	Pearson Correlation	-0.0270	-0.1768	0.2174	0.1262	0.0571	-0.1643	-0.1289	-0.2015	-0.1531	-0.0730
	Sig. (2-tailed)	0.8759	0.3023	0.2029	0.4633	0.7483	0.3456	0.4605	0.2458	0.3873	0.6768
	N	36.0000	36.0000	36.0000	36.0000	34.0000	35.0000	35.0000	35.0000	34.0000	35.0000
Perceived Deterrence Domestic Law-TVP	Pearson Correlation	-0.0760	-0.1162	0.1404	0.0092	0.1988	-0.2421	-0.1397	-0.1769	-0.3281	-0.0947
	Sig. (2-tailed)	0.6595	0.4997	0.4140	0.9574	0.2596	0.1611	0.4236	0.3092	0.0582	0.5885
	N	36.0000	36.0000	36.0000	36.0000	34.0000	35.0000	35.0000	35.0000	34.0000	35.0000
sqrtQIIC1e	Pearson Correlation	-0.0229	-0.0757	0.1757	0.0275	0.1558	-0.1999	-0.0826	-0.1079	-0.1530	0.0712
	Sig. (2-tailed)	0.8946	0.6608	0.3054	0.8735	0.3789	0.2496	0.6372	0.5372	0.3877	0.6845
	N	36.0000	36.0000	36.0000	36.0000	34.0000	35.0000	35.0000	35.0000	34.0000	35.0000
sqrtQIID1a	Pearson Correlation	-0.1120	0.0549	-0.1358	-0.1864	-0.1416	-0.3091	-0.3537	-0.3828	-0.1077	-0.2613
	Sig. (2-tailed)	0.5157	0.7504	0.4298	0.2764	0.4244	0.0708	0.0371	0.0232	0.5443	0.1295
	N	36.0000	36.0000	36.0000	36.0000	34.0000	35.0000	35.0000	35.0000	34.0000	35.0000
Level Cooperation Domestic Orgs-CSIE	Pearson Correlation	-0.3763	-0.2268	-0.1725	-0.3066	-0.1553	-0.1766	-0.4078	-0.4665	-0.2576	-0.1698
	Sig. (2-tailed)	0.0237	0.1835	0.3143	0.0689	0.3804	0.3101	0.0150	0.0047	0.1414	0.3295
	N	36.0000	36.0000	36.0000	36.0000	34.0000	35.0000	35.0000	35.0000	34.0000	35.0000
Level Cooperation Domestic Orgs-DWMD	Pearson Correlation	-0.3806	-0.0638	-0.1342	-0.2523	-0.2637	-0.3089	-0.4448	-0.4764	-0.1964	-0.1211
	Sig. (2-tailed)	0.0220	0.7115	0.4350	0.1377	0.1318	0.0709	0.0074	0.0038	0.2657	0.4882
	N	36.0000	36.0000	36.0000	36.0000	34.0000	35.0000	35.0000	35.0000	34.0000	35.0000
Level Cooperation Domestic Orgs-TVP	Pearson Correlation	-0.1813	-0.0832	0.0026	-0.0655	-0.1839	-0.2466	-0.2323	-0.2813	-0.3635	-0.2969
	Sig. (2-tailed)	0.2899	0.6294	0.9881	0.7043	0.2978	0.1533	0.1793	0.1017	0.0346	0.0833
	N	36.0000	36.0000	36.0000	36.0000	34.0000	35.0000	35.0000	35.0000	34.0000	35.0000
Level Cooperation Domestic Orgs-CBP	Pearson Correlation	-0.1645	-0.0522	-0.1031	-0.2033	-0.3699	-0.4410	-0.2361	-0.3095	-0.1248	-0.2055
	Sig. (2-tailed)	0.3377	0.7623	0.5496	0.2344	0.0313	0.0080	0.1721	0.0704	0.4819	0.2363
	N	36.0000	36.0000	36.0000	36.0000	34.0000	35.0000	35.0000	35.0000	34.0000	35.0000
sqrtQIIF1a	Pearson Correlation	-0.0455	0.0422	-0.1438	-0.0994	0.1039	-0.1815	0.1828	0.1549	-0.0059	0.0181
	Sig. (2-tailed)	0.8047	0.8187	0.4323	0.5883	0.5713	0.3202	0.3167	0.3974	0.9747	0.9217
	N	32.0000	32.0000	32.0000	32.0000	32.0000	32.0000	32.0000	32.0000	31.0000	32.0000
sqrtQIIF1b	Pearson Correlation	-0.1292	-0.1154	-0.3227	-0.2261	0.0083	-0.3427	-0.0264	-0.1244	0.0976	-0.0742
	Sig. (2-tailed)	0.4665	0.5157	0.0627	0.1986	0.9633	0.0472	0.8820	0.4834	0.5889	0.6764
	N	34.0000	34.0000	34.0000	34.0000	33.0000	34.0000	34.0000	34.0000	33.0000	34.0000

Table A6, continued (Row 5, Col 4)

Correlation Matrix, Dependent Variables (Parametric)		Org Resource Challenges-Ineffective Technology	Org Resource Challenges-Ineffective Strategic Focus	Org Resource Challenges-Ineffective Tactical Policy	Org Resource Challenges-Lack of Clarity in Duties	Org Resource Challenges-Conflict or Lack Comm Leaders and Employees	sqrtQIE3I	Org Resource Challenges-Conflict or Lack Comm International Orgs	Org Resource Challenges-Conflict or Lack Comm Domestic Orgs	sqrtQIIA1a	Knowledge of Domestic Law-CSIE
sqrtQIIC1a	Pearson Correlation	-0.0089	0.0591	0.0575	0.1668	0.0730	0.1596	0.0780	0.0915	0.3777	-0.0535
	Sig. (2-tailed)	0.9599	0.7397	0.7466	0.3456	0.6817	0.3674	0.6609	0.6070	0.0276	0.7639
	N	34.0000	34.0000	34.0000	34.0000	34.0000	34.0000	34.0000	34.0000	34.0000	34.0000
Perceived Deterrence Domestic Law-CSIE	Pearson Correlation	0.0123	-0.0240	0.0280	0.0028	-0.0410	-0.0437	0.0612	0.0529	0.2693	0.3304
	Sig. (2-tailed)	0.9442	0.8913	0.8732	0.9874	0.8153	0.8030	0.7268	0.7629	0.1178	0.0525
	N	35.0000	35.0000	35.0000	35.0000	35.0000	35.0000	35.0000	35.0000	35.0000	35.0000
sqrtQIIC1c	Pearson Correlation	-0.1455	-0.1947	0.0315	-0.1333	0.0728	-0.1463	-0.1086	-0.0982	0.2928	0.2505
	Sig. (2-tailed)	0.4042	0.2625	0.8575	0.4451	0.6778	0.4018	0.5345	0.5745	0.0878	0.1467
	N	35.0000	35.0000	35.0000	35.0000	35.0000	35.0000	35.0000	35.0000	35.0000	35.0000
Perceived Deterrence Domestic Law-TVP	Pearson Correlation	-0.1179	-0.1731	0.0064	-0.0574	0.0405	-0.0578	-0.0952	-0.0902	0.2645	0.1647
	Sig. (2-tailed)	0.4999	0.3200	0.9708	0.7432	0.8173	0.7417	0.5864	0.6063	0.1247	0.3443
	N	35.0000	35.0000	35.0000	35.0000	35.0000	35.0000	35.0000	35.0000	35.0000	35.0000
sqrtQIIC1e	Pearson Correlation	-0.0531	-0.1332	0.0423	-0.0800	0.1382	0.0074	-0.1293	-0.1094	0.2577	0.2162
	Sig. (2-tailed)	0.7618	0.4457	0.8095	0.6478	0.4286	0.9662	0.4592	0.5317	0.1351	0.2123
	N	35.0000	35.0000	35.0000	35.0000	35.0000	35.0000	35.0000	35.0000	35.0000	35.0000
sqrtQIID1a	Pearson Correlation	-0.3255	-0.2537	-0.2208	-0.1536	-0.1869	-0.0403	-0.2087	-0.1867	0.4524	0.1169
	Sig. (2-tailed)	0.0564	0.1413	0.2025	0.3784	0.2823	0.8182	0.2288	0.2829	0.0064	0.5037
	N	35.0000	35.0000	35.0000	35.0000	35.0000	35.0000	35.0000	35.0000	35.0000	35.0000
Level Cooperation Domestic Orgs-CSIE	Pearson Correlation	-0.3626	-0.3952	-0.2891	-0.3954	-0.2438	-0.2859	-0.2421	-0.3064	0.1923	0.5579
	Sig. (2-tailed)	0.0323	0.0188	0.0922	0.0187	0.1581	0.0960	0.1611	0.0735	0.2684	0.0005
	N	35.0000	35.0000	35.0000	35.0000	35.0000	35.0000	35.0000	35.0000	35.0000	35.0000
Level Cooperation Domestic Orgs-DWMD	Pearson Correlation	-0.4359	-0.4554	-0.3082	-0.4124	-0.2581	-0.1912	-0.2142	-0.2303	0.1286	0.4830
	Sig. (2-tailed)	0.0089	0.0060	0.0717	0.0138	0.1345	0.2712	0.2167	0.1832	0.4614	0.0033
	N	35.0000	35.0000	35.0000	35.0000	35.0000	35.0000	35.0000	35.0000	35.0000	35.0000
Level Cooperation Domestic Orgs-TVP	Pearson Correlation	-0.2617	-0.1852	-0.1271	-0.1893	-0.1415	-0.1542	-0.1411	-0.2087	0.2592	0.3219
	Sig. (2-tailed)	0.1289	0.2868	0.4670	0.2760	0.4175	0.3764	0.4189	0.2289	0.1327	0.0593
	N	35.0000	35.0000	35.0000	35.0000	35.0000	35.0000	35.0000	35.0000	35.0000	35.0000
Level Cooperation Domestic Orgs-CBP	Pearson Correlation	-0.4314	-0.2952	-0.1596	-0.1998	-0.1280	-0.1118	-0.3103	-0.2817	0.2915	0.1046
	Sig. (2-tailed)	0.0097	0.0851	0.3598	0.2498	0.4638	0.5227	0.0696	0.1011	0.0893	0.5499
	N	35.0000	35.0000	35.0000	35.0000	35.0000	35.0000	35.0000	35.0000	35.0000	35.0000
sqrtQIIF1a	Pearson Correlation	-0.1030	0.0030	0.0564	0.1495	-0.1812	0.0249	0.2453	0.2229	0.1780	-0.2989
	Sig. (2-tailed)	0.5747	0.9869	0.7592	0.4140	0.3211	0.8922	0.1761	0.2200	0.3381	0.1023
	N	32.0000	32.0000	32.0000	32.0000	32.0000	32.0000	32.0000	32.0000	31.0000	31.0000
sqrtQIIF1b	Pearson Correlation	-0.0945	-0.0635	-0.0413	0.1132	-0.1614	-0.1720	0.1317	0.1558	-0.0639	-0.0421
	Sig. (2-tailed)	0.5952	0.7214	0.8166	0.5240	0.3618	0.3306	0.4579	0.3788	0.7240	0.8160
	N	34.0000	34.0000	34.0000	34.0000	34.0000	34.0000	34.0000	34.0000	33.0000	33.0000

Table A6, continued (Row 5, Col 5)

Correlation Matrix, Dependent Variables (Parametric)		Knowledge of Domestic Law-DWMD	Knowledge of Domestic Law-TVP	Knowledge of Domestic Law-CBP	sqrtQIIB1a	Perceived Effectiveness Domestic Govt Support-CSIE	Perceived Effectiveness Domestic Govt Support-DWMD	Perceived Effectiveness Domestic Govt SupportTVP	Perceived Effectiveness Domestic Govt Support-CBP	sqrtQIIC1a	Perceived Deterrence Domestic Law-CSIE
sqrtQIIC1a	Pearson Correlation	-0.0096	0.1023	-0.0457	0.5519	0.2129	0.2437	0.2897	0.1306	1.0000	0.3947
	Sig. (2-tailed)	0.9569	0.5648	0.7974	0.0006	0.2268	0.1582	0.0913	0.4547	.	0.0190
	N	34.0000	34.0000	34.0000	35.0000	34.0000	35.0000	35.0000	35.0000	35.0000	35.0000
Perceived Deterrence Domestic Law-CSIE	Pearson Correlation	0.3523	0.4352	0.3438	0.2215	0.6609	0.4928	0.2899	0.2298	0.3947	1.0000
	Sig. (2-tailed)	0.0380	0.0090	0.0431	0.2010	0.0000	0.0023	0.0911	0.1841	0.0190	.
	N	35.0000	35.0000	35.0000	35.0000	35.0000	36.0000	35.0000	35.0000	35.0000	36.0000
sqrtQIIC1c	Pearson Correlation	0.3738	0.4417	0.4388	0.1356	0.4546	0.5614	0.5105	0.3629	0.4218	0.7070
	Sig. (2-tailed)	0.0270	0.0079	0.0084	0.4375	0.0061	0.0004	0.0017	0.0322	0.0116	0.0000
	N	35.0000	35.0000	35.0000	35.0000	35.0000	36.0000	35.0000	35.0000	35.0000	36.0000
Perceived Deterrence Domestic Law-TVP	Pearson Correlation	0.2844	0.3312	0.2772	0.3730	0.4309	0.4388	0.4286	0.2293	0.6887	0.7158
	Sig. (2-tailed)	0.0978	0.0519	0.1069	0.0273	0.0098	0.0074	0.0102	0.1851	0.0000	0.0000
	N	35.0000	35.0000	35.0000	35.0000	35.0000	36.0000	35.0000	35.0000	35.0000	36.0000
sqrtQIIC1e	Pearson Correlation	0.3080	0.2329	0.3716	0.2197	0.4639	0.4160	0.3648	0.3390	0.6295	0.7057
	Sig. (2-tailed)	0.0719	0.1781	0.0279	0.2048	0.0050	0.0116	0.0312	0.0463	0.0001	0.0000
	N	35.0000	35.0000	35.0000	35.0000	35.0000	36.0000	35.0000	35.0000	35.0000	36.0000
sqrtQIID1a	Pearson Correlation	0.1547	-0.0231	0.3023	0.5693	0.0661	0.1470	0.4573	0.3960	0.2706	0.1456
	Sig. (2-tailed)	0.3750	0.8952	0.0775	0.0004	0.7061	0.3922	0.0057	0.0185	0.1159	0.3968
	N	35.0000	35.0000	35.0000	35.0000	35.0000	36.0000	35.0000	35.0000	35.0000	36.0000
Level Cooperation Domestic Orgs-CSIE	Pearson Correlation	0.6238	0.4269	0.4855	0.1905	0.3851	0.3983	0.2551	0.2410	0.1892	0.4140
	Sig. (2-tailed)	0.0001	0.0105	0.0031	0.2729	0.0223	0.0161	0.1392	0.1631	0.2764	0.0121
	N	35.0000	35.0000	35.0000	35.0000	35.0000	36.0000	35.0000	35.0000	35.0000	36.0000
Level Cooperation Domestic Orgs-DWMD	Pearson Correlation	0.5291	0.2014	0.4690	0.2899	0.4537	0.4759	0.4948	0.4631	0.0624	0.2772
	Sig. (2-tailed)	0.0011	0.2461	0.0045	0.0911	0.0062	0.0033	0.0025	0.0051	0.7218	0.1017
	N	35.0000	35.0000	35.0000	35.0000	35.0000	36.0000	35.0000	35.0000	35.0000	36.0000
Level Cooperation Domestic Orgs-TVP	Pearson Correlation	0.3785	0.5066	0.3910	0.4428	0.1976	0.2861	0.2783	0.2235	0.3114	0.4821
	Sig. (2-tailed)	0.0250	0.0019	0.0202	0.0077	0.2553	0.0907	0.1055	0.1968	0.0686	0.0029
	N	35.0000	35.0000	35.0000	35.0000	35.0000	36.0000	35.0000	35.0000	35.0000	36.0000
Level Cooperation Domestic Orgs-CBP	Pearson Correlation	0.2306	0.0260	0.5621	0.4588	0.2287	0.1858	0.4224	0.6599	0.1347	0.1970
	Sig. (2-tailed)	0.1826	0.8821	0.0004	0.0056	0.1864	0.2780	0.0115	0.0000	0.4403	0.2495
	N	35.0000	35.0000	35.0000	35.0000	35.0000	36.0000	35.0000	35.0000	35.0000	36.0000
sqrtQIIF1a	Pearson Correlation	-0.2428	-0.3960	-0.2627	0.3319	0.0749	0.0368	0.0961	0.0448	0.3509	0.0198
	Sig. (2-tailed)	0.1881	0.0274	0.1533	0.0635	0.6889	0.8415	0.6010	0.8077	0.0490	0.9143
	N	31.0000	31.0000	31.0000	32.0000	31.0000	32.0000	32.0000	32.0000	32.0000	32.0000
sqrtQIIF1b	Pearson Correlation	-0.0730	-0.2999	-0.2365	0.1682	0.1145	0.2107	0.2948	0.2786	0.0264	-0.0600
	Sig. (2-tailed)	0.6864	0.0899	0.1852	0.3493	0.5259	0.2316	0.0958	0.1164	0.8841	0.7359
	N	33.0000	33.0000	33.0000	33.0000	33.0000	34.0000	33.0000	33.0000	33.0000	34.0000

Table A6, continued (Row 5, Col 6)

Correlation Matrix, Dependent Variables (Parametric)		sqrtQIIC1c	Perceived Deterrence Domestic Law-TVP	sqrtQIIC1e	sqrtQIID1a	Level Cooperation Domestic Orgs-CSIE	Level Cooperation Domestic Orgs-DWMD	Level Cooperation Domestic Orgs-TVP	Level Cooperation Domestic Orgs-CBP	sqrtQIIF1a	sqrtQIIF1b
sqrtQIIC1a	Pearson Correlation	0.4218	0.6887	0.6295	0.2706	0.1892	0.0624	0.3114	0.1347	0.3509	0.0264
	Sig. (2-tailed)	0.0116	0.0000	0.0001	0.1159	0.2764	0.7218	0.0686	0.4403	0.0490	0.8841
	N	35.0000	35.0000	35.0000	35.0000	35.0000	35.0000	35.0000	35.0000	32.0000	33.0000
Perceived Deterrence Domestic Law-CSIE	Pearson Correlation	0.7070	0.7158	0.7057	0.1456	0.4140	0.2772	0.4821	0.1970	0.0198	-0.0600
	Sig. (2-tailed)	0.0000	0.0000	0.0000	0.3968	0.0121	0.1017	0.0029	0.2495	0.9143	0.7359
	N	36.0000	36.0000	36.0000	36.0000	36.0000	36.0000	36.0000	36.0000	32.0000	34.0000
sqrtQIIC1c	Pearson Correlation	1.0000	0.7854	0.7500	0.1421	0.4954	0.4056	0.5049	0.1962	-0.1034	-0.0933
	Sig. (2-tailed)	.	0.0000	0.0000	0.4083	0.0021	0.0141	0.0017	0.2515	0.5733	0.5996
	N	36.0000	36.0000	36.0000	36.0000	36.0000	36.0000	36.0000	36.0000	32.0000	34.0000
Perceived Deterrence Domestic Law-TVP	Pearson Correlation	0.7854	1.0000	0.8881	0.1721	0.4002	0.2645	0.3961	0.1353	0.1572	0.0273
	Sig. (2-tailed)	0.0000	.	0.0000	0.3154	0.0156	0.1191	0.0168	0.4312	0.3902	0.8782
	N	36.0000	36.0000	36.0000	36.0000	36.0000	36.0000	36.0000	36.0000	32.0000	34.0000
sqrtQIIC1e	Pearson Correlation	0.7500	0.8881	1.0000	0.1015	0.4195	0.2573	0.3373	0.2347	0.0279	-0.0544
	Sig. (2-tailed)	0.0000	0.0000	.	0.5559	0.0109	0.1298	0.0442	0.1683	0.8797	0.7597
	N	36.0000	36.0000	36.0000	36.0000	36.0000	36.0000	36.0000	36.0000	32.0000	34.0000
sqrtQIID1a	Pearson Correlation	0.1421	0.1721	0.1015	1.0000	0.3596	0.3998	0.4744	0.7020	0.1672	0.3170
	Sig. (2-tailed)	0.4083	0.3154	0.5559	.	0.0312	0.0157	0.0035	0.0000	0.3603	0.0677
	N	36.0000	36.0000	36.0000	36.0000	36.0000	36.0000	36.0000	36.0000	32.0000	34.0000
Level Cooperation Domestic Orgs-CSIE	Pearson Correlation	0.4954	0.4002	0.4195	0.3596	1.0000	0.7912	0.7777	0.4620	-0.0303	0.0519
	Sig. (2-tailed)	0.0021	0.0156	0.0109	0.0312	.	0.0000	0.0000	0.0046	0.8691	0.7706
	N	36.0000	36.0000	36.0000	36.0000	36.0000	36.0000	36.0000	36.0000	32.0000	34.0000
Level Cooperation Domestic Orgs-DWMD	Pearson Correlation	0.4056	0.2645	0.2573	0.3998	0.7912	1.0000	0.6143	0.5201	0.1342	0.2091
	Sig. (2-tailed)	0.0141	0.1191	0.1298	0.0157	0.0000	.	0.0001	0.0012	0.4640	0.2353
	N	36.0000	36.0000	36.0000	36.0000	36.0000	36.0000	36.0000	36.0000	32.0000	34.0000
Level Cooperation Domestic Orgs-TVP	Pearson Correlation	0.5049	0.3961	0.3373	0.4744	0.7777	0.6143	1.0000	0.5351	-0.0326	-0.0090
	Sig. (2-tailed)	0.0017	0.0168	0.0442	0.0035	0.0000	0.0001	.	0.0008	0.8595	0.9596
	N	36.0000	36.0000	36.0000	36.0000	36.0000	36.0000	36.0000	36.0000	32.0000	34.0000
Level Cooperation Domestic Orgs-CBP	Pearson Correlation	0.1962	0.1353	0.2347	0.7020	0.4620	0.5201	0.5351	1.0000	0.0996	0.2217
	Sig. (2-tailed)	0.2515	0.4312	0.1683	0.0000	0.0046	0.0012	0.0008	.	0.5875	0.2076
	N	36.0000	36.0000	36.0000	36.0000	36.0000	36.0000	36.0000	36.0000	32.0000	34.0000
sqrtQIIF1a	Pearson Correlation	-0.1034	0.1572	0.0279	0.1672	-0.0303	0.1342	-0.0326	0.0996	1.0000	0.6732
	Sig. (2-tailed)	0.5733	0.3902	0.8797	0.3603	0.8691	0.4640	0.8595	0.5875	.	0.0000
	N	32.0000	32.0000	32.0000	32.0000	32.0000	32.0000	32.0000	32.0000	32.0000	32.0000
sqrtQIIF1b	Pearson Correlation	-0.0933	0.0273	-0.0544	0.3170	0.0519	0.2091	-0.0090	0.2217	0.6732	1.0000
	Sig. (2-tailed)	0.5996	0.8782	0.7597	0.0677	0.7706	0.2353	0.9596	0.2076	0.0000	.
	N	34.0000	34.0000	34.0000	34.0000	34.0000	34.0000	34.0000	34.0000	32.0000	34.0000

Table A6, continued (Row 5, Col 7)

Correlation Matrix, Dependent Variables (Parametric)		sqrtQIIF1c	sqrtQIIF1d	sqrtQIIF1e	sqrtQIIF3a	sqrtQIIF3b	sqrtQIIF3c	sqrtQIIF3d	sqrtQIIF3e	sqrtQIIH1a	sqrtQIIH1b
sqrtQIIC1a	Pearson Correlation	0.2551	0.2542	0.1100	0.3098	-0.0409	0.0593	0.1240	0.0757	0.1888	-0.0139
	Sig. (2-tailed)	0.1518	0.1534	0.5421	0.0899	0.8240	0.7470	0.4989	0.6858	0.3092	0.9398
	N	33.0000	33.0000	33.0000	31.0000	32.0000	32.0000	32.0000	31.0000	31.0000	32.0000
Perceived Deterrence Domestic Law-CSIE	Pearson Correlation	0.1852	0.0788	-0.0102	0.0847	0.1217	0.1817	0.1424	0.1474	0.0694	0.0275
	Sig. (2-tailed)	0.2943	0.6579	0.9544	0.6447	0.4998	0.3115	0.4293	0.4207	0.7105	0.8792
	N	34.0000	34.0000	34.0000	32.0000	33.0000	33.0000	33.0000	32.0000	31.0000	33.0000
sqrtQIIC1c	Pearson Correlation	-0.0618	-0.1706	-0.1906	-0.0578	0.1047	0.1401	-0.0225	-0.0104	0.0856	0.0662
	Sig. (2-tailed)	0.7283	0.3346	0.2803	0.7532	0.5621	0.4368	0.9013	0.9550	0.6472	0.7144
	N	34.0000	34.0000	34.0000	32.0000	33.0000	33.0000	33.0000	32.0000	31.0000	33.0000
Perceived Deterrence Domestic Law-TVP	Pearson Correlation	0.1614	0.1366	0.0367	0.2510	0.1619	0.2002	0.2154	0.1954	0.3536	0.1334
	Sig. (2-tailed)	0.3619	0.4413	0.8366	0.1658	0.3682	0.2640	0.2287	0.2838	0.0510	0.4593
	N	34.0000	34.0000	34.0000	32.0000	33.0000	33.0000	33.0000	32.0000	31.0000	33.0000
sqrtQIIC1e	Pearson Correlation	0.0422	0.0323	-0.0428	0.2035	0.1719	0.1889	0.2193	0.2129	0.2107	0.0879
	Sig. (2-tailed)	0.8127	0.8560	0.8101	0.2639	0.3388	0.2925	0.2202	0.2421	0.2552	0.6268
	N	34.0000	34.0000	34.0000	32.0000	33.0000	33.0000	33.0000	32.0000	31.0000	33.0000
sqrtQIID1a	Pearson Correlation	0.3935	0.2463	0.2367	0.1514	0.2960	0.3434	0.1798	0.1733	0.0271	-0.0230
	Sig. (2-tailed)	0.0213	0.1603	0.1777	0.4082	0.0944	0.0504	0.3168	0.3429	0.8850	0.8991
	N	34.0000	34.0000	34.0000	32.0000	33.0000	33.0000	33.0000	32.0000	31.0000	33.0000
Level Cooperation Domestic Orgs-CSIE	Pearson Correlation	0.0824	0.1099	0.0496	-0.0021	0.1672	0.1936	0.1428	0.1879	0.1796	0.1240
	Sig. (2-tailed)	0.6433	0.5360	0.7807	0.9908	0.3523	0.2804	0.4280	0.3032	0.3337	0.4919
	N	34.0000	34.0000	34.0000	32.0000	33.0000	33.0000	33.0000	32.0000	31.0000	33.0000
Level Cooperation Domestic Orgs-DWMD	Pearson Correlation	0.1670	0.2001	0.1165	0.0533	0.2021	0.2325	0.1237	0.1631	0.2930	0.2362
	Sig. (2-tailed)	0.3453	0.2566	0.5116	0.7718	0.2593	0.1930	0.4929	0.3724	0.1097	0.1857
	N	34.0000	34.0000	34.0000	32.0000	33.0000	33.0000	33.0000	32.0000	31.0000	33.0000
Level Cooperation Domestic Orgs-TVP	Pearson Correlation	0.1665	0.0086	-0.0644	-0.0222	-0.0028	0.0634	-0.0628	-0.0794	0.0420	-0.0692
	Sig. (2-tailed)	0.3467	0.9616	0.7174	0.9041	0.9876	0.7261	0.7286	0.6659	0.8225	0.7020
	N	34.0000	34.0000	34.0000	32.0000	33.0000	33.0000	33.0000	32.0000	31.0000	33.0000
Level Cooperation Domestic Orgs-CBP	Pearson Correlation	0.2978	0.0796	0.2376	0.1342	0.1548	0.1909	0.0819	0.1017	-0.0078	-0.0200
	Sig. (2-tailed)	0.0872	0.6544	0.1760	0.4640	0.3898	0.2872	0.6503	0.5797	0.9668	0.9120
	N	34.0000	34.0000	34.0000	32.0000	33.0000	33.0000	33.0000	32.0000	31.0000	33.0000
sqrtQIIF1a	Pearson Correlation	0.5796	0.7533	0.8848	0.8285	0.4214	0.3478	0.6597	0.6210	0.7871	0.4942
	Sig. (2-tailed)	0.0005	0.0000	0.0000	0.0000	0.0182	0.0552	0.0001	0.0002	0.0000	0.0055
	N	32.0000	32.0000	32.0000	31.0000	31.0000	31.0000	31.0000	31.0000	30.0000	30.0000
sqrtQIIF1b	Pearson Correlation	0.7245	0.6788	0.7336	0.5764	0.7665	0.6453	0.5768	0.5788	0.5120	0.6379
	Sig. (2-tailed)	0.0000	0.0000	0.0000	0.0006	0.0000	0.0000	0.0001	0.0004	0.0005	0.0038	0.0001
	N	34.0000	34.0000	34.0000	32.0000	33.0000	33.0000	33.0000	32.0000	30.0000	32.0000

Correlation Matrix, Dependent Variables (Parametric)		sqrtQIIIH1c	sqrtQIIIH1d	sqrtQIIIH1e	sqrtQIIIH3a	sqrtQIIIH3b	sqrtQIIIH3c	sqrtQIIIH3d	sqrtQIIIH3e	sqrtQIIIA1a	sqrtQIIIA1b
sqrtQIIC1a	Pearson Correlation	-0.0588	0.0945	0.0260	0.1436	0.0039	-0.0174	0.0510	-0.0092	0.3917	0.0541
	Sig. (2-tailed)	0.7491	0.6070	0.8897	0.4179	0.9825	0.9223	0.7744	0.9590	0.0220	0.7578
	N	32.0000	32.0000	31.0000	34.0000	34.0000	34.0000	34.0000	34.0000	34.0000	35.0000
Perceived Deterrence Domestic Law-CSIE	Pearson Correlation	0.0193	0.1494	0.0663	0.0412	0.0701	0.1075	0.1420	0.0257	0.1148	0.1423
	Sig. (2-tailed)	0.9164	0.4144	0.7229	0.8170	0.6935	0.5453	0.4232	0.8853	0.5114	0.4077
	N	32.0000	32.0000	31.0000	34.0000	34.0000	34.0000	34.0000	34.0000	35.0000	36.0000
sqrtQIIC1c	Pearson Correlation	0.0170	0.0809	0.1001	0.1208	0.0877	0.0608	0.2231	0.1479	0.1131	0.3808
	Sig. (2-tailed)	0.9264	0.6596	0.5923	0.4960	0.6219	0.7326	0.2047	0.4040	0.5177	0.0219
	N	32.0000	32.0000	31.0000	34.0000	34.0000	34.0000	34.0000	34.0000	35.0000	36.0000
Perceived Deterrence Domestic Law-TVP	Pearson Correlation	0.0798	0.2586	0.2142	0.3111	0.1568	0.1510	0.3306	0.1842	0.1576	0.2260
	Sig. (2-tailed)	0.6640	0.1530	0.2473	0.0733	0.3759	0.3940	0.0562	0.2971	0.3660	0.1850
	N	32.0000	32.0000	31.0000	34.0000	34.0000	34.0000	34.0000	34.0000	35.0000	36.0000
sqrtQIIC1e	Pearson Correlation	-0.0001	0.1787	0.1866	0.2111	0.0767	0.0350	0.2468	0.1727	0.1061	0.2386
	Sig. (2-tailed)	0.9994	0.3278	0.3149	0.2308	0.6662	0.8441	0.1594	0.3288	0.5441	0.1611
	N	32.0000	32.0000	31.0000	34.0000	34.0000	34.0000	34.0000	34.0000	35.0000	36.0000
sqrtQIID1a	Pearson Correlation	0.0076	-0.0686	-0.0324	0.0094	-0.0666	-0.0122	-0.0624	-0.1582	0.4921	-0.0045
	Sig. (2-tailed)	0.9673	0.7090	0.8626	0.9577	0.7081	0.9454	0.7259	0.3714	0.0027	0.9794
	N	32.0000	32.0000	31.0000	34.0000	34.0000	34.0000	34.0000	34.0000	35.0000	36.0000
Level Cooperation Domestic Orgs-CSIE	Pearson Correlation	0.0213	0.1323	0.1161	0.0319	-0.0020	-0.0246	0.0971	0.0194	0.1822	0.3594
	Sig. (2-tailed)	0.9079	0.4705	0.5339	0.8581	0.9910	0.8903	0.5850	0.9133	0.2949	0.0314
	N	32.0000	32.0000	31.0000	34.0000	34.0000	34.0000	34.0000	34.0000	35.0000	36.0000
Level Cooperation Domestic Orgs-DWMD	Pearson Correlation	0.2443	0.2878	0.2620	0.1892	0.1949	0.1845	0.2698	0.1941	0.1739	0.2141
	Sig. (2-tailed)	0.1778	0.1102	0.1544	0.2839	0.2692	0.2963	0.1228	0.2715	0.3177	0.2098
	N	32.0000	32.0000	31.0000	34.0000	34.0000	34.0000	34.0000	34.0000	35.0000	36.0000
Level Cooperation Domestic Orgs-TVP	Pearson Correlation	-0.0376	0.0027	-0.0678	-0.0689	-0.1476	-0.0801	-0.0294	-0.1602	0.3406	0.1873
	Sig. (2-tailed)	0.8383	0.9882	0.7172	0.6988	0.4047	0.6527	0.8689	0.3655	0.0453	0.2741
	N	32.0000	32.0000	31.0000	34.0000	34.0000	34.0000	34.0000	34.0000	35.0000	36.0000
Level Cooperation Domestic Orgs-CBP	Pearson Correlation	0.0601	0.0722	0.1311	0.0001	-0.0710	-0.0528	-0.0016	0.0240	0.2939	-0.0578
	Sig. (2-tailed)	0.7437	0.6946	0.4821	0.9996	0.6898	0.7670	0.9927	0.8928	0.0866	0.7378
	N	32.0000	32.0000	31.0000	34.0000	34.0000	34.0000	34.0000	34.0000	35.0000	36.0000
sqrtQIIF1a	Pearson Correlation	0.5548	0.7332	0.7178	0.7082	0.5702	0.5733	0.6263	0.6210	0.1595	-0.2604
	Sig. (2-tailed)	0.0015	0.0000	0.0000	0.0000	0.0007	0.0006	0.0001	0.0001	0.3914	0.1501
	N	30.0000	30.0000	30.0000	32.0000	32.0000	32.0000	32.0000	32.0000	31.0000	32.0000
sqrtQIIF1b	Pearson Correlation	0.7696	0.5478	0.4943	0.5305	0.6961	0.7451	0.5343	0.4745	0.0123	-0.0590
	Sig. (2-tailed)	0.0000	0.0014	0.0055	0.0015	0.0000	0.0000	0.0014	0.0053	0.9459	0.7403
	N	31.0000	31.0000	30.0000	33.0000	33.0000	33.0000	33.0000	33.0000	33.0000	34.0000

Table A6, continued (Row 5, Col 9)

Correlation Matrix, Dependent Variables (Parametric)		sqrtQIIA1c	sqrtQIIA1d	sqrtQIIA1e	sqrtQIIID1a	Level Cooperation Domestic Orgs-CNDPS	Level Cooperation Domestic Orgs-CNBC	Level Cooperation Domestic Orgs-CSTP	Level Cooperation Domestic Orgs-TRIPS	sqrtQIID2a	Level Cooperation International Orgs-CNDPS
sqrtQIIC1a	Pearson Correlation	0.0046	0.1755	-0.0018	0.2122	0.2049	0.1394	0.2250	0.0476	0.4904	0.0787
	Sig. (2-tailed)	0.9790	0.3132	0.9917	0.2437	0.2450	0.4319	0.2007	0.7890	0.0032	0.6532
	N	35.0000	35.0000	35.0000	32.0000	34.0000	34.0000	34.0000	34.0000	34.0000	35.0000
Perceived Deterrence Domestic Law-CSIE	Pearson Correlation	0.2017	0.3117	0.1198	0.3401	0.5149	0.3926	0.4720	0.3427	0.3647	0.4576
	Sig. (2-tailed)	0.2382	0.0642	0.4865	0.0528	0.0015	0.0197	0.0042	0.0439	0.0312	0.0050
	N	36.0000	36.0000	36.0000	33.0000	35.0000	35.0000	35.0000	35.0000	35.0000	36.0000
sqrtQIIC1c	Pearson Correlation	0.3712	0.4705	0.3193	0.2408	0.5659	0.4120	0.4143	0.2866	0.1651	0.4182
	Sig. (2-tailed)	0.0258	0.0038	0.0577	0.1771	0.0004	0.0139	0.0134	0.0951	0.3432	0.0111
	N	36.0000	36.0000	36.0000	33.0000	35.0000	35.0000	35.0000	35.0000	35.0000	36.0000
Perceived Deterrence Domestic Law-TVP	Pearson Correlation	0.2599	0.3727	0.1159	0.2690	0.4611	0.3707	0.3336	0.2052	0.3332	0.3940
	Sig. (2-tailed)	0.1258	0.0252	0.5007	0.1301	0.0053	0.0284	0.0502	0.2371	0.0504	0.0174
	N	36.0000	36.0000	36.0000	33.0000	35.0000	35.0000	35.0000	35.0000	35.0000	36.0000
sqrtQIIC1e	Pearson Correlation	0.2426	0.2825	0.1462	0.1855	0.4708	0.3322	0.3138	0.2598	0.2442	0.3400
	Sig. (2-tailed)	0.1540	0.0950	0.3949	0.3015	0.0043	0.0512	0.0664	0.1318	0.1574	0.0425
	N	36.0000	36.0000	36.0000	33.0000	35.0000	35.0000	35.0000	35.0000	35.0000	36.0000
sqrtQIID1a	Pearson Correlation	0.2147	0.0503	0.2763	0.4991	0.2806	0.5210	0.2009	0.5555	0.5936	0.3070
	Sig. (2-tailed)	0.2087	0.7707	0.1029	0.0031	0.1026	0.0013	0.2473	0.0005	0.0002	0.0686
	N	36.0000	36.0000	36.0000	33.0000	35.0000	35.0000	35.0000	35.0000	35.0000	36.0000
Level Cooperation Domestic Orgs-CSIE	Pearson Correlation	0.3425	0.2440	0.2423	0.1915	0.5766	0.4744	0.4123	0.2704	0.2898	0.4537
	Sig. (2-tailed)	0.0409	0.1515	0.1546	0.2858	0.0003	0.0040	0.0139	0.1162	0.0913	0.0054
	N	36.0000	36.0000	36.0000	33.0000	35.0000	35.0000	35.0000	35.0000	35.0000	36.0000
Level Cooperation Domestic Orgs-DWMD	Pearson Correlation	0.2766	0.0821	0.3109	0.2390	0.4849	0.4952	0.3257	0.3519	0.2354	0.4372
	Sig. (2-tailed)	0.1025	0.6342	0.0649	0.1804	0.0032	0.0025	0.0562	0.0381	0.1735	0.0077
	N	36.0000	36.0000	36.0000	33.0000	35.0000	35.0000	35.0000	35.0000	35.0000	36.0000
Level Cooperation Domestic Orgs-TVP	Pearson Correlation	0.2122	0.3122	0.1111	0.4288	0.6054	0.4910	0.5899	0.4028	0.3361	0.3733
	Sig. (2-tailed)	0.2140	0.0638	0.5190	0.0128	0.0001	0.0027	0.0002	0.0164	0.0484	0.0249
	N	36.0000	36.0000	36.0000	33.0000	35.0000	35.0000	35.0000	35.0000	35.0000	36.0000
Level Cooperation Domestic Orgs-CBP	Pearson Correlation	0.0853	0.0620	0.3090	0.4754	0.2277	0.4178	0.2129	0.5841	0.3215	0.1751
	Sig. (2-tailed)	0.6209	0.7192	0.0667	0.0052	0.1884	0.0125	0.2195	0.0002	0.0597	0.3069
	N	36.0000	36.0000	36.0000	33.0000	35.0000	35.0000	35.0000	35.0000	35.0000	36.0000
sqrtQIIF1a	Pearson Correlation	-0.3081	-0.2370	-0.0338	0.2053	-0.0610	0.1003	-0.0060	-0.0102	0.3038	-0.0310
	Sig. (2-tailed)	0.0863	0.1916	0.8543	0.2764	0.7446	0.5915	0.9744	0.9566	0.0966	0.8662
	N	32.0000	32.0000	32.0000	30.0000	31.0000	31.0000	31.0000	31.0000	31.0000	32.0000
sqrtQIIF1b	Pearson Correlation	0.0163	-0.1305	-0.0017	0.2206	0.1343	0.2765	-0.0108	0.1857	0.2751	0.1960
	Sig. (2-tailed)	0.9273	0.4620	0.9922	0.2250	0.4562	0.1194	0.9524	0.3007	0.1212	0.2665
	N	34.0000	34.0000	34.0000	32.0000	33.0000	33.0000	33.0000	33.0000	33.0000	34.0000

Table A6, continued (Row 5, Col 10)

Correlation Matrix, Dependent Variables (Parametric)		Level Cooperation International Orgs-CNBC	Level Cooperation International Orgs-CSTP	sqrtQIIID2e	sqrtQIVA1	sqrtQIVA2	sqrtQIVA3	sqrtQIVA5	sqrtQIVA7	sqrtQIVA8	Political Ideology
sqrtQIIC1a	Pearson Correlation	0.1115	0.2480	0.0831	0.1876	0.0378	0.1429	-0.1010	0.1827	0.0216	0.2361
	Sig. (2-tailed)	0.5236	0.1509	0.6350	0.2804	0.8294	0.4200	0.5759	0.2936	0.9033	0.1933
	N	35.0000	35.0000	35.0000	35.0000	35.0000	34.0000	33.0000	35.0000	34.0000	32.0000
Perceived Deterrence Domestic Law-CSIE	Pearson Correlation	0.4223	0.4518	0.3324	0.2983	0.0382	0.1987	0.3658	0.1860	0.0146	0.1464
	Sig. (2-tailed)	0.0103	0.0057	0.0476	0.0772	0.8248	0.2526	0.0334	0.2774	0.9339	0.4161
	N	36.0000	36.0000	36.0000	36.0000	36.0000	35.0000	34.0000	36.0000	35.0000	33.0000
sqrtQIIC1c	Pearson Correlation	0.3910	0.4833	0.3326	0.1508	0.0199	0.1412	0.2188	0.1353	0.0876	0.2418
	Sig. (2-tailed)	0.0184	0.0028	0.0475	0.3799	0.9083	0.4184	0.2137	0.4313	0.6167	0.1752
	N	36.0000	36.0000	36.0000	36.0000	36.0000	35.0000	34.0000	36.0000	35.0000	33.0000
Perceived Deterrence Domestic Law-TVP	Pearson Correlation	0.4290	0.4344	0.2971	0.1551	0.0073	0.2144	0.2415	0.1855	-0.0115	0.1152
	Sig. (2-tailed)	0.0090	0.0081	0.0785	0.3663	0.9665	0.2161	0.1688	0.2788	0.9476	0.5233
	N	36.0000	36.0000	36.0000	36.0000	36.0000	35.0000	34.0000	36.0000	35.0000	33.0000
sqrtQIIC1e	Pearson Correlation	0.3660	0.3482	0.2789	0.0644	-0.0168	0.1352	0.0767	0.2336	0.0314	0.1854
	Sig. (2-tailed)	0.0281	0.0374	0.0995	0.7089	0.9227	0.4387	0.6664	0.1704	0.8580	0.3016
	N	36.0000	36.0000	36.0000	36.0000	36.0000	35.0000	34.0000	36.0000	35.0000	33.0000
sqrtQIID1a	Pearson Correlation	0.3896	0.3778	0.5037	0.1145	0.1167	0.1560	0.1165	-0.1753	0.0904	0.4608
	Sig. (2-tailed)	0.0188	0.0231	0.0017	0.5063	0.4977	0.3707	0.5116	0.3065	0.6055	0.0070
	N	36.0000	36.0000	36.0000	36.0000	36.0000	35.0000	34.0000	36.0000	35.0000	33.0000
Level Cooperation Domestic Orgs-CSIE	Pearson Correlation	0.4986	0.3942	0.3621	-0.0166	-0.0436	-0.0670	0.3660	-0.1921	0.0446	0.1078
	Sig. (2-tailed)	0.0020	0.0174	0.0300	0.9236	0.8008	0.7021	0.0333	0.2618	0.7993	0.5503
	N	36.0000	36.0000	36.0000	36.0000	36.0000	35.0000	34.0000	36.0000	35.0000	33.0000
Level Cooperation Domestic Orgs-DWMD	Pearson Correlation	0.4416	0.3629	0.4183	0.0281	-0.0079	-0.0168	0.3984	-0.2136	0.0309	0.1871
	Sig. (2-tailed)	0.0070	0.0296	0.0111	0.8708	0.9636	0.9238	0.0196	0.2110	0.8601	0.2972
	N	36.0000	36.0000	36.0000	36.0000	36.0000	35.0000	34.0000	36.0000	35.0000	33.0000
Level Cooperation Domestic Orgs-TVP	Pearson Correlation	0.3532	0.3892	0.2200	0.0224	0.0079	-0.0141	0.3035	-0.0707	0.0867	0.0611
	Sig. (2-tailed)	0.0346	0.0190	0.1973	0.8967	0.9637	0.9361	0.0810	0.6818	0.6206	0.7357
	N	36.0000	36.0000	36.0000	36.0000	36.0000	35.0000	34.0000	36.0000	35.0000	33.0000
Level Cooperation Domestic Orgs-CBP	Pearson Correlation	0.2419	0.1522	0.4283	-0.0467	0.0137	0.0940	0.0006	-0.0284	0.0727	0.3480
	Sig. (2-tailed)	0.1553	0.3755	0.0092	0.7866	0.9367	0.5911	0.9973	0.8692	0.6780	0.0472
	N	36.0000	36.0000	36.0000	36.0000	36.0000	35.0000	34.0000	36.0000	35.0000	33.0000
sqrtQIIF1a	Pearson Correlation	0.0546	0.1186	0.1090	0.1736	0.0936	0.2097	0.1776	0.0042	-0.2700	0.1344
	Sig. (2-tailed)	0.7666	0.5181	0.5527	0.3421	0.6104	0.2575	0.3391	0.9818	0.1350	0.4788
	N	32.0000	32.0000	32.0000	32.0000	32.0000	31.0000	31.0000	32.0000	32.0000	30.0000
sqrtQIIF1b	Pearson Correlation	0.2685	0.3540	0.3607	0.2036	0.0815	0.2987	0.2395	-0.1961	-0.2826	0.2361
	Sig. (2-tailed)	0.1247	0.0400	0.0361	0.2481	0.6470	0.0913	0.1794	0.2662	0.1054	0.1933
	N	34.0000	34.0000	34.0000	34.0000	34.0000	33.0000	33.0000	34.0000	34.0000	32.0000

Table A6, continued (Row 6, Col 1)

Correlation Matrix, Dependent Variables (Parametric)		Importance of Smuggling-Endangered Species	reflectsqrtQIA1b	reflectsqrtQIA1c	reflectsqrtQIA1d	reflectsqrtQIA1e	sqrtQIB1a	Knowledge of Smuggling-Narcotics	Knowledge of Smuggling-Weapons	Knowledge of Smuggling-Humans	Knowledge of Smuggling-Contraband
sqrtQIIF1c	Pearson Correlation	0.0165	-0.1062	-0.1201	-0.0528	-0.3576	0.2251	-0.0835	0.1940	0.2198	0.1269
	Sig. (2-tailed)	0.9260	0.5502	0.4986	0.7668	0.0379	0.2006	0.6387	0.2717	0.2116	0.4746
	N	34.0000	34.0000	34.0000	34.0000	34.0000	34.0000	34.0000	34.0000	34.0000	34.0000
sqrtQIIF1d	Pearson Correlation	0.0284	-0.1074	-0.1416	-0.1716	-0.3022	0.1861	-0.1039	0.0901	0.2118	-0.0415
	Sig. (2-tailed)	0.8732	0.5454	0.4245	0.3318	0.0824	0.2920	0.5587	0.6124	0.2291	0.8155
	N	34.0000	34.0000	34.0000	34.0000	34.0000	34.0000	34.0000	34.0000	34.0000	34.0000
sqrtQIIF1e	Pearson Correlation	-0.0537	0.1569	0.0686	-0.1147	-0.0120	0.1549	-0.1528	0.0153	0.1843	-0.0458
	Sig. (2-tailed)	0.7628	0.3756	0.6998	0.5182	0.9462	0.3818	0.3883	0.9317	0.2967	0.7971
	N	34.0000	34.0000	34.0000	34.0000	34.0000	34.0000	34.0000	34.0000	34.0000	34.0000
sqrtQIIF3a	Pearson Correlation	-0.2414	-0.0647	-0.1281	-0.1500	0.0052	-0.0668	-0.1191	0.0330	0.0503	-0.1160
	Sig. (2-tailed)	0.1832	0.7248	0.4848	0.4124	0.9776	0.7166	0.5162	0.8576	0.7844	0.5271
	N	32.0000	32.0000	32.0000	32.0000	32.0000	32.0000	32.0000	32.0000	32.0000	32.0000
sqrtQIIF3b	Pearson Correlation	-0.2512	-0.1102	0.0011	0.1236	0.1371	-0.1502	0.0091	0.1041	0.1032	-0.0951
	Sig. (2-tailed)	0.1584	0.5417	0.9953	0.4930	0.4467	0.4040	0.9600	0.5642	0.5677	0.5985
	N	33.0000	33.0000	33.0000	33.0000	33.0000	33.0000	33.0000	33.0000	33.0000	33.0000
sqrtQIIF3c	Pearson Correlation	-0.2383	-0.0034	0.0398	0.1548	-0.0259	-0.0322	0.0473	0.2319	0.1408	0.0989
	Sig. (2-tailed)	0.1817	0.9849	0.8261	0.3898	0.8863	0.8587	0.7939	0.1940	0.4345	0.5840
	N	33.0000	33.0000	33.0000	33.0000	33.0000	33.0000	33.0000	33.0000	33.0000	33.0000
sqrtQIIF3d	Pearson Correlation	-0.3544	-0.0148	0.0272	-0.0797	0.0467	-0.0703	-0.0908	0.0772	0.1034	-0.1229
	Sig. (2-tailed)	0.0430	0.9348	0.8804	0.6594	0.7962	0.6975	0.6152	0.6693	0.5669	0.4957
	N	33.0000	33.0000	33.0000	33.0000	33.0000	33.0000	33.0000	33.0000	33.0000	33.0000
sqrtQIIF3e	Pearson Correlation	-0.3864	0.0348	0.1298	0.0007	0.0663	-0.0543	-0.0659	0.1019	0.1169	-0.0991
	Sig. (2-tailed)	0.0289	0.8502	0.4790	0.9971	0.7185	0.7678	0.7202	0.5788	0.5239	0.5894
	N	32.0000	32.0000	32.0000	32.0000	32.0000	32.0000	32.0000	32.0000	32.0000	32.0000
sqrtQIIH1a	Pearson Correlation	-0.1081	-0.0970	-0.1550	-0.2176	0.0715	-0.0600	0.0786	0.1345	0.0682	-0.1638
	Sig. (2-tailed)	0.5628	0.6036	0.4051	0.2397	0.7024	0.7487	0.6741	0.4708	0.7156	0.3787
	N	31.0000	31.0000	31.0000	31.0000	31.0000	31.0000	31.0000	31.0000	31.0000	31.0000
sqrtQIIH1b	Pearson Correlation	-0.2764	0.0090	0.1046	0.0467	0.2733	-0.2608	0.0491	0.0259	0.1668	-0.1180
	Sig. (2-tailed)	0.1195	0.9606	0.5624	0.7965	0.1238	0.1427	0.7860	0.8864	0.3535	0.5130
	N	33.0000	33.0000	33.0000	33.0000	33.0000	33.0000	33.0000	33.0000	33.0000	33.0000
sqrtQIIH1c	Pearson Correlation	-0.2027	-0.1862	-0.0804	0.0113	0.0988	-0.2745	-0.0001	-0.0341	0.1997	-0.1555
	Sig. (2-tailed)	0.2659	0.3075	0.6616	0.9510	0.5906	0.1285	0.9996	0.8531	0.2733	0.3954
	N	32.0000	32.0000	32.0000	32.0000	32.0000	32.0000	32.0000	32.0000	32.0000	32.0000
sqrtQIIH1d	Pearson Correlation	-0.3250	-0.0960	-0.0028	-0.1859	-0.0266	-0.1833	-0.0615	0.0282	0.2083	-0.1024
	Sig. (2-tailed)	0.0696	0.6013	0.9878	0.3083	0.8851	0.3152	0.7382	0.8782	0.2526	0.5772
	N	32.0000	32.0000	32.0000	32.0000	32.0000	32.0000	32.0000	32.0000	32.0000	32.0000

Table A6, continued (Row 6, Col 2)

Correlation Matrix, Dependent Variables (Parametric)		sqrtQIIE1a	Personal Resource Challenges-Lack of Time	Personal Resource Challenges-Lack of Knowledge	Personal Resource Challenges-Lack of Training	sqrtQIIE1e	Personal Resource Challenges-Excessive Admin Paperwork	Personal Resource Challenges-Ineffective Technology	Personal Resource Challenges-Ineffective Strategic Focus	Personal Resource Challenges-Ineffective Tactical Policy	Personal Resource Challenges-Lack of Clarity in Duties
sqrtQIIF1c	Pearson Correlation	-0.0437	-0.2986	0.0427	0.1015	0.0927	-0.0410	-0.1622	0.1301	-0.0279	-0.0274
	Sig. (2-tailed)	0.8092	0.0863	0.8104	0.5680	0.6020	0.8178	0.3595	0.4635	0.8753	0.8778
	N	33.0000	34.0000	34.0000	34.0000	34.0000	34.0000	34.0000	34.0000	34.0000	34.0000
sqrtQIIF1d	Pearson Correlation	-0.0732	-0.1764	-0.0585	0.0279	0.0833	-0.1363	-0.1558	0.0206	-0.0811	-0.1833
	Sig. (2-tailed)	0.6856	0.3182	0.7422	0.8756	0.6396	0.4423	0.3788	0.9078	0.6484	0.2995
	N	33.0000	34.0000	34.0000	34.0000	34.0000	34.0000	34.0000	34.0000	34.0000	34.0000
sqrtQIIF1e	Pearson Correlation	-0.2009	-0.1978	-0.1075	-0.0027	0.0729	-0.3311	-0.1023	0.0108	-0.0942	-0.1149
	Sig. (2-tailed)	0.2622	0.2622	0.5451	0.9878	0.6822	0.0558	0.5649	0.9515	0.5963	0.5174
	N	33.0000	34.0000	34.0000	34.0000	34.0000	34.0000	34.0000	34.0000	34.0000	34.0000
sqrtQIIF3a	Pearson Correlation	-0.0570	0.0787	0.1141	0.1976	0.0805	-0.1245	0.0750	0.1669	0.0477	0.0840
	Sig. (2-tailed)	0.7608	0.6686	0.5341	0.2784	0.6612	0.4972	0.6834	0.3611	0.7956	0.6476
	N	31.0000	32.0000	32.0000	32.0000	32.0000	32.0000	32.0000	32.0000	32.0000	32.0000
sqrtQIIF3b	Pearson Correlation	0.1746	0.0032	-0.0232	-0.0366	0.1213	-0.0371	-0.1372	0.0401	-0.0116	-0.1195
	Sig. (2-tailed)	0.3393	0.9858	0.8979	0.8397	0.5011	0.8378	0.4466	0.8247	0.9488	0.5077
	N	32.0000	33.0000	33.0000	33.0000	33.0000	33.0000	33.0000	33.0000	33.0000	33.0000
sqrtQIIF3c	Pearson Correlation	0.1386	-0.0273	-0.0038	-0.0206	0.2117	0.0921	-0.1400	0.0107	-0.0994	-0.1611
	Sig. (2-tailed)	0.4493	0.8802	0.9835	0.9094	0.2368	0.6104	0.4372	0.9528	0.5819	0.3704
	N	32.0000	33.0000	33.0000	33.0000	33.0000	33.0000	33.0000	33.0000	33.0000	33.0000
sqrtQIIF3d	Pearson Correlation	0.0894	0.0682	-0.0373	0.0343	0.0945	-0.1067	-0.0575	0.0652	-0.0059	-0.1174
	Sig. (2-tailed)	0.6266	0.7060	0.8368	0.8496	0.6008	0.5546	0.7506	0.7184	0.9739	0.5154
	N	32.0000	33.0000	33.0000	33.0000	33.0000	33.0000	33.0000	33.0000	33.0000	33.0000
sqrtQIIF3e	Pearson Correlation	0.0932	0.0585	-0.0989	-0.0256	0.0923	-0.1303	-0.0434	-0.0002	-0.0514	-0.1774
	Sig. (2-tailed)	0.6181	0.7504	0.5903	0.8893	0.6155	0.4772	0.8136	0.9992	0.7799	0.3315
	N	31.0000	32.0000	32.0000	32.0000	32.0000	32.0000	32.0000	32.0000	32.0000	32.0000
sqrtQIIH1a	Pearson Correlation	-0.1399	-0.0793	-0.0276	0.0682	-0.0718	-0.1560	-0.1413	-0.0698	-0.1009	-0.0227
	Sig. (2-tailed)	0.4611	0.6713	0.8830	0.7154	0.7010	0.4019	0.4483	0.7093	0.5893	0.9033
	N	30.0000	31.0000	31.0000	31.0000	31.0000	31.0000	31.0000	31.0000	31.0000	31.0000
sqrtQIIH1b	Pearson Correlation	-0.1329	-0.3969	-0.1980	-0.1366	-0.2252	-0.2115	-0.1802	-0.2101	-0.2229	-0.2694
	Sig. (2-tailed)	0.4685	0.0222	0.2694	0.4485	0.2077	0.2374	0.3155	0.2406	0.2125	0.1295
	N	32.0000	33.0000	33.0000	33.0000	33.0000	33.0000	33.0000	33.0000	33.0000	33.0000
sqrtQIIH1c	Pearson Correlation	-0.0513	-0.1848	0.0821	0.1364	-0.1211	-0.1947	-0.0530	-0.0487	-0.0750	-0.0687
	Sig. (2-tailed)	0.7839	0.3112	0.6552	0.4567	0.5091	0.2856	0.7734	0.7911	0.6834	0.7086
	N	31.0000	32.0000	32.0000	32.0000	32.0000	32.0000	32.0000	32.0000	32.0000	32.0000
sqrtQIIH1d	Pearson Correlation	-0.1180	-0.1055	-0.0850	0.0330	-0.1269	-0.2166	-0.1520	-0.0923	-0.0966	-0.0852
	Sig. (2-tailed)	0.5274	0.5654	0.6439	0.8578	0.4889	0.2337	0.4061	0.6155	0.5988	0.6429
	N	31.0000	32.0000	32.0000	32.0000	32.0000	32.0000	32.0000	32.0000	32.0000	32.0000

Table A6, continued (Row 6, Col 3)

Correlation Matrix, Dependent Variables (Parametric)		Personal Resource Challenges-Conflict or Lack Comm Leaders and Employees	sqrtQIE1l	Personal Resource Challenges-Conflict or Lack Comm International Orgs	Personal Resource Challenges-Conflict or Lack Comm Domestic Orgs	sqrtQIE3a	Org Resource Challenges-Lack of Time	Org Resource Challenges-Lack of Knowledge	Org Resource Challenges-Lack of Training	sqrtQIE3e	Org Resource Challenges-Excessive Admin Paperwork
sqrtQIIF1c	Pearson Correlation	-0.1723	0.0713	-0.0674	-0.2200	-0.0219	-0.2851	-0.0122	-0.0925	-0.1113	-0.1182
	Sig. (2-tailed)	0.3297	0.6888	0.7050	0.2113	0.9035	0.1022	0.9454	0.6027	0.5375	0.5056
	N	34.0000	34.0000	34.0000	34.0000	33.0000	34.0000	34.0000	34.0000	33.0000	34.0000
sqrtQIIF1d	Pearson Correlation	-0.2909	-0.0724	-0.2852	-0.3097	0.1669	-0.0827	-0.0278	-0.0631	-0.0593	0.0207
	Sig. (2-tailed)	0.0951	0.6839	0.1021	0.0747	0.3534	0.6420	0.8758	0.7230	0.7429	0.9075
	N	34.0000	34.0000	34.0000	34.0000	33.0000	34.0000	34.0000	34.0000	33.0000	34.0000
sqrtQIIF1e	Pearson Correlation	-0.1789	-0.2049	-0.3538	-0.3158	0.0338	-0.2985	-0.0434	-0.1092	-0.0291	-0.0996
	Sig. (2-tailed)	0.3114	0.2449	0.0401	0.0689	0.8520	0.0863	0.8077	0.5389	0.8723	0.5750
	N	34.0000	34.0000	34.0000	34.0000	33.0000	34.0000	34.0000	34.0000	33.0000	34.0000
sqrtQIIF3a	Pearson Correlation	-0.0331	0.0475	-0.2485	-0.0629	0.2351	-0.0422	0.2170	0.2221	0.0990	0.1547
	Sig. (2-tailed)	0.8574	0.7962	0.1703	0.7324	0.2029	0.8188	0.2328	0.2219	0.5962	0.3979
	N	32.0000	32.0000	32.0000	32.0000	31.0000	32.0000	32.0000	32.0000	31.0000	32.0000
sqrtQIIF3b	Pearson Correlation	-0.0592	-0.0390	-0.2527	-0.1287	0.1849	-0.0579	-0.0907	-0.1579	0.3142	0.1915
	Sig. (2-tailed)	0.7436	0.8295	0.1559	0.4752	0.3111	0.7490	0.6158	0.3802	0.0799	0.2856
	N	33.0000	33.0000	33.0000	33.0000	32.0000	33.0000	33.0000	33.0000	32.0000	33.0000
sqrtQIIF3c	Pearson Correlation	-0.1344	0.0830	-0.0719	-0.1530	0.1040	-0.1148	-0.1473	-0.1916	0.2017	0.1194
	Sig. (2-tailed)	0.4557	0.6461	0.6909	0.3954	0.5709	0.5247	0.4134	0.2854	0.2684	0.5082
	N	33.0000	33.0000	33.0000	33.0000	32.0000	33.0000	33.0000	33.0000	32.0000	33.0000
sqrtQIIF3d	Pearson Correlation	-0.1288	-0.0956	-0.3422	-0.1822	0.3029	0.0942	0.0033	-0.0101	0.2073	0.2473
	Sig. (2-tailed)	0.4750	0.5965	0.0513	0.3103	0.0919	0.6020	0.9855	0.9556	0.2549	0.1652
	N	33.0000	33.0000	33.0000	33.0000	32.0000	33.0000	33.0000	33.0000	32.0000	33.0000
sqrtQIIF3e	Pearson Correlation	-0.1714	-0.1490	-0.3818	-0.2323	0.2800	0.0489	-0.0534	-0.0699	0.2104	0.2243
	Sig. (2-tailed)	0.3483	0.4156	0.0311	0.2008	0.1271	0.7906	0.7714	0.7038	0.2558	0.2172
	N	32.0000	32.0000	32.0000	32.0000	31.0000	32.0000	32.0000	32.0000	31.0000	32.0000
sqrtQIIH1a	Pearson Correlation	-0.1973	-0.1591	-0.2561	-0.1179	0.3580	0.0331	0.0150	0.0300	-0.0761	0.1248
	Sig. (2-tailed)	0.2875	0.3926	0.1643	0.5276	0.0521	0.8622	0.9373	0.8751	0.6946	0.5111
	N	31.0000	31.0000	31.0000	31.0000	30.0000	30.0000	30.0000	30.0000	29.0000	30.0000
sqrtQIIH1b	Pearson Correlation	-0.2543	-0.1984	-0.4468	-0.3552	-0.0423	-0.2066	-0.2404	-0.2542	-0.0309	-0.0828
	Sig. (2-tailed)	0.1532	0.2684	0.0091	0.0425	0.8211	0.2566	0.1852	0.1604	0.8690	0.6521
	N	33.0000	33.0000	33.0000	33.0000	31.0000	32.0000	32.0000	32.0000	31.0000	32.0000
sqrtQIIH1c	Pearson Correlation	-0.2072	-0.2524	-0.3581	-0.1514	0.1147	-0.1002	0.0377	0.0039	0.0667	0.0575
	Sig. (2-tailed)	0.2552	0.1635	0.0442	0.4081	0.5389	0.5916	0.8403	0.9835	0.7263	0.7587
	N	32.0000	32.0000	32.0000	32.0000	31.0000	31.0000	31.0000	31.0000	30.0000	31.0000
sqrtQIIH1d	Pearson Correlation	-0.2420	-0.2989	-0.3934	-0.1940	0.2068	-0.0312	0.0008	-0.0129	-0.0467	0.0965
	Sig. (2-tailed)	0.1821	0.0966	0.0259	0.2874	0.2642	0.8676	0.9967	0.9452	0.8065	0.6057
	N	32.0000	32.0000	32.0000	32.0000	31.0000	31.0000	31.0000	31.0000	30.0000	31.0000

Table A6, continued (Row 6, Col 4)

Correlation Matrix, Dependent Variables (Parametric)		Org Resource Challenges-Ineffective Technology	Org Resource Challenges-Ineffective Strategic Focus	Org Resource Challenges-Ineffective Tactical Policy	Org Resource Challenges-Lack of Clarity in Duties	Org Resource Challenges-Conflict or Lack Comm Leaders and Employees	sqrtQIE31	Org Resource Challenges-Conflict or Lack Comm International Orgs	Org Resource Challenges-Conflict or Lack Comm Domestic Orgs	sqrtQIIA1a	Knowledge of Domestic Law-CSIE
sqrtQIIF1c	Pearson Correlation	-0.1798	-0.0313	-0.0606	0.1208	-0.1786	0.0808	0.1528	0.1172	0.1953	-0.0100
	Sig. (2-tailed)	0.3090	0.8605	0.7337	0.4962	0.3123	0.6498	0.3884	0.5092	0.2761	0.9559
	N	34.0000	34.0000	34.0000	34.0000	34.0000	34.0000	34.0000	34.0000	33.0000	33.0000
sqrtQIIF1d	Pearson Correlation	-0.1182	-0.1208	-0.1634	0.0484	-0.2959	-0.0969	0.1233	0.0962	0.1907	-0.0919
	Sig. (2-tailed)	0.5057	0.4961	0.3557	0.7859	0.0893	0.5855	0.4871	0.5882	0.2879	0.6109
	N	34.0000	34.0000	34.0000	34.0000	34.0000	34.0000	34.0000	34.0000	33.0000	33.0000
sqrtQIIF1e	Pearson Correlation	-0.2780	-0.2175	-0.1491	-0.0657	-0.3507	-0.2328	-0.0310	-0.0495	0.1443	-0.2454
	Sig. (2-tailed)	0.1114	0.2165	0.4001	0.7120	0.0420	0.1851	0.8616	0.7811	0.4232	0.1687
	N	34.0000	34.0000	34.0000	34.0000	34.0000	34.0000	34.0000	34.0000	33.0000	33.0000
sqrtQIIF3a	Pearson Correlation	0.0181	-0.0149	0.0408	0.0856	-0.1579	0.0611	0.1081	0.1069	0.0910	-0.2978
	Sig. (2-tailed)	0.9215	0.9355	0.8244	0.6414	0.3880	0.7399	0.5558	0.5604	0.6265	0.1037
	N	32.0000	32.0000	32.0000	32.0000	32.0000	32.0000	32.0000	32.0000	31.0000	31.0000
sqrtQIIF3b	Pearson Correlation	0.0065	-0.1494	-0.0713	-0.0518	-0.1401	-0.0917	-0.0190	-0.0066	-0.0026	0.0450
	Sig. (2-tailed)	0.9713	0.4067	0.6934	0.7747	0.4368	0.6118	0.9165	0.9711	0.9887	0.8069
	N	33.0000	33.0000	33.0000	33.0000	33.0000	33.0000	33.0000	33.0000	32.0000	32.0000
sqrtQIIF3c	Pearson Correlation	-0.0914	-0.2049	-0.1433	-0.1022	-0.1380	0.0628	-0.0441	-0.0392	0.1361	0.1313
	Sig. (2-tailed)	0.6128	0.2527	0.4264	0.5713	0.4438	0.7286	0.8073	0.8284	0.4576	0.4738
	N	33.0000	33.0000	33.0000	33.0000	33.0000	33.0000	33.0000	33.0000	32.0000	32.0000
sqrtQIIF3d	Pearson Correlation	-0.0111	-0.1712	-0.1114	-0.0818	-0.2720	-0.1113	-0.0271	-0.0468	0.1300	-0.1426
	Sig. (2-tailed)	0.9510	0.3408	0.5371	0.6507	0.1257	0.5375	0.8812	0.7959	0.4782	0.4362
	N	33.0000	33.0000	33.0000	33.0000	33.0000	33.0000	33.0000	33.0000	32.0000	32.0000
sqrtQIIF3e	Pearson Correlation	-0.0457	-0.2428	-0.1713	-0.1365	-0.3148	-0.1717	-0.0745	-0.0917	0.1002	-0.0982
	Sig. (2-tailed)	0.8037	0.1806	0.3487	0.4563	0.0793	0.3475	0.6854	0.6176	0.5918	0.5991
	N	32.0000	32.0000	32.0000	32.0000	32.0000	32.0000	32.0000	32.0000	31.0000	31.0000
sqrtQIIH1a	Pearson Correlation	-0.1666	-0.1881	-0.0113	-0.0500	-0.2330	-0.0982	0.0730	0.0195	0.0933	-0.1712
	Sig. (2-tailed)	0.3789	0.3195	0.9526	0.7932	0.2153	0.6058	0.7013	0.9185	0.6239	0.3658
	N	30.0000	30.0000	30.0000	30.0000	30.0000	30.0000	30.0000	30.0000	30.0000	30.0000
sqrtQIIH1b	Pearson Correlation	-0.0716	-0.2239	-0.2911	-0.2275	-0.3411	-0.2143	-0.1373	-0.1104	-0.2110	0.0731
	Sig. (2-tailed)	0.6968	0.2179	0.1060	0.2105	0.0561	0.2390	0.4536	0.5474	0.2465	0.6911
	N	32.0000	32.0000	32.0000	32.0000	32.0000	32.0000	32.0000	32.0000	32.0000	32.0000
sqrtQIIH1c	Pearson Correlation	0.0372	-0.0405	-0.0623	0.0716	-0.2299	-0.2361	0.1343	0.1352	-0.1778	-0.0405
	Sig. (2-tailed)	0.8424	0.8286	0.7391	0.7018	0.2134	0.2009	0.4715	0.4685	0.3385	0.8288
	N	31.0000	31.0000	31.0000	31.0000	31.0000	31.0000	31.0000	31.0000	31.0000	31.0000
sqrtQIIH1d	Pearson Correlation	-0.1228	-0.1945	-0.1089	-0.0851	-0.3350	-0.2702	-0.0203	-0.0535	-0.0218	-0.2165
	Sig. (2-tailed)	0.5106	0.2944	0.5599	0.6488	0.0655	0.1415	0.9137	0.7749	0.9074	0.2421
	N	31.0000	31.0000	31.0000	31.0000	31.0000	31.0000	31.0000	31.0000	31.0000	31.0000

Table A6, continued (Row 6, Col 5)

Correlation Matrix, Dependent Variables (Parametric)		Knowledge of Domestic Law-DWMD	Knowledge of Domestic Law-TVP	Knowledge of Domestic Law-CBP	sqrtQIIB1a	Perceived Effectiveness Domestic Govt Support-CSIE	Perceived Effectiveness Domestic Govt Support-DWMD	Perceived Effectiveness Domestic Govt SupportTVP	Perceived Effectiveness Domestic Govt Support-CBP	sqrtQIIC1a	Perceived Deterrence Domestic Law-CSIE
sqrtQIIF1c	Pearson Correlation	0.0213	-0.0331	-0.1394	0.4370	0.1969	0.1804	0.2762	0.2424	0.2551	0.1852
	Sig. (2-tailed)	0.9063	0.8548	0.4393	0.0110	0.2721	0.3073	0.1197	0.1741	0.1518	0.2943
	N	33.0000	33.0000	33.0000	33.0000	33.0000	34.0000	33.0000	33.0000	33.0000	34.0000
sqrtQIIF1d	Pearson Correlation	-0.0683	-0.3194	-0.2384	0.2256	0.1917	0.1308	0.0781	0.0450	0.2542	0.0788
	Sig. (2-tailed)	0.7057	0.0700	0.1815	0.2068	0.2851	0.4608	0.6657	0.8035	0.1534	0.6579
	N	33.0000	33.0000	33.0000	33.0000	33.0000	34.0000	33.0000	33.0000	33.0000	34.0000
sqrtQIIF1e	Pearson Correlation	-0.1448	-0.3811	-0.0992	0.2721	0.1385	0.0380	0.1525	0.1999	0.1100	-0.0102
	Sig. (2-tailed)	0.4216	0.0287	0.5827	0.1255	0.4420	0.8310	0.3970	0.2647	0.5421	0.9544
	N	33.0000	33.0000	33.0000	33.0000	33.0000	34.0000	33.0000	33.0000	33.0000	34.0000
sqrtQIIF3a	Pearson Correlation	-0.2318	-0.4208	-0.2024	0.2538	0.0846	-0.0322	0.1084	0.0538	0.3098	0.0847
	Sig. (2-tailed)	0.2096	0.0184	0.2748	0.1683	0.6509	0.8609	0.5618	0.7739	0.0899	0.6447
	N	31.0000	31.0000	31.0000	31.0000	31.0000	32.0000	31.0000	31.0000	31.0000	32.0000
sqrtQIIF3b	Pearson Correlation	0.0067	-0.2607	-0.1504	-0.0370	0.1371	0.1420	0.2329	0.2318	-0.0409	0.1217
	Sig. (2-tailed)	0.9710	0.1495	0.4113	0.8408	0.4543	0.4304	0.1995	0.2018	0.8240	0.4998
	N	32.0000	32.0000	32.0000	32.0000	32.0000	33.0000	32.0000	32.0000	32.0000	33.0000
sqrtQIIF3c	Pearson Correlation	0.0908	-0.1598	-0.0577	0.1288	0.2411	0.2355	0.3610	0.3369	0.0593	0.1817
	Sig. (2-tailed)	0.6213	0.3824	0.7536	0.4825	0.1837	0.1871	0.0424	0.0594	0.7470	0.3115
	N	32.0000	32.0000	32.0000	32.0000	32.0000	33.0000	32.0000	32.0000	32.0000	33.0000
sqrtQIIF3d	Pearson Correlation	-0.0922	-0.3818	-0.1521	0.0064	0.1298	-0.0237	0.0264	0.0325	0.1240	0.1424
	Sig. (2-tailed)	0.6158	0.0311	0.4061	0.9721	0.4790	0.8957	0.8858	0.8599	0.4989	0.4293
	N	32.0000	32.0000	32.0000	32.0000	32.0000	33.0000	32.0000	32.0000	32.0000	33.0000
sqrtQIIF3e	Pearson Correlation	-0.0454	-0.3747	-0.0974	0.0077	0.2186	0.0333	0.0967	0.1324	0.0757	0.1474
	Sig. (2-tailed)	0.8085	0.0378	0.6022	0.9674	0.2374	0.8563	0.6046	0.4776	0.6858	0.4207
	N	31.0000	31.0000	31.0000	31.0000	31.0000	32.0000	31.0000	31.0000	31.0000	32.0000
sqrtQIIH1a	Pearson Correlation	-0.0465	-0.2117	-0.1059	0.1795	0.0686	0.0897	0.0847	0.0333	0.1888	0.0694
	Sig. (2-tailed)	0.8072	0.2615	0.5774	0.3338	0.7187	0.6312	0.6504	0.8590	0.3092	0.7105
	N	30.0000	30.0000	30.0000	31.0000	30.0000	31.0000	31.0000	31.0000	31.0000	31.0000
sqrtQIIH1b	Pearson Correlation	0.0936	-0.0478	-0.1474	-0.1257	0.1714	0.1302	0.1798	0.1542	-0.0139	0.0275
	Sig. (2-tailed)	0.6102	0.7949	0.4207	0.4930	0.3484	0.4703	0.3248	0.3996	0.9398	0.8792
	N	32.0000	32.0000	32.0000	32.0000	32.0000	33.0000	32.0000	32.0000	32.0000	33.0000
sqrtQIIH1c	Pearson Correlation	-0.0044	-0.0641	-0.2061	-0.0293	0.1514	0.1885	0.2016	0.2406	-0.0588	0.0193
	Sig. (2-tailed)	0.9813	0.7318	0.2661	0.8737	0.4161	0.3015	0.2684	0.1847	0.7491	0.9164
	N	31.0000	31.0000	31.0000	32.0000	31.0000	32.0000	32.0000	32.0000	32.0000	32.0000
sqrtQIIH1d	Pearson Correlation	-0.0586	-0.1677	-0.0797	0.0257	0.1866	0.0873	0.0999	0.1523	0.0945	0.1494
	Sig. (2-tailed)	0.7540	0.3672	0.6700	0.8891	0.3148	0.6346	0.5864	0.4053	0.6070	0.4144
	N	31.0000	31.0000	31.0000	32.0000	31.0000	32.0000	32.0000	32.0000	32.0000	32.0000

Correlation Matrix, Dependent Variables (Parametric)		sqrtQIIC1c	Perceived Deterrence Domestic Law-TVP	sqrtQIIC1e	sqrtQIID1a	Level Cooperation Domestic Orgs-CSIE	Level Cooperation Domestic Orgs-DWMD	Level Cooperation Domestic Orgs-TVP	Level Cooperation Domestic Orgs-CBP	sqrtQIIF1a	sqrtQIIF1b
sqrtQIIF1c	Pearson Correlation	-0.0618	0.1614	0.0422	0.3935	0.0824	0.1670	0.1665	0.2978	0.5796	0.7245
	Sig. (2-tailed)	0.7283	0.3619	0.8127	0.0213	0.6433	0.3453	0.3467	0.0872	0.0005	0.0000
	N	34.0000	34.0000	34.0000	34.0000	34.0000	34.0000	34.0000	34.0000	32.0000	34.0000
sqrtQIIF1d	Pearson Correlation	-0.1706	0.1366	0.0323	0.2463	0.1099	0.2001	0.0086	0.0796	0.7533	0.6788
	Sig. (2-tailed)	0.3346	0.4413	0.8560	0.1603	0.5360	0.2566	0.9616	0.6544	0.0000	0.0000
	N	34.0000	34.0000	34.0000	34.0000	34.0000	34.0000	34.0000	34.0000	32.0000	34.0000
sqrtQIIF1e	Pearson Correlation	-0.1906	0.0367	-0.0428	0.2367	0.0496	0.1165	-0.0644	0.2376	0.8848	0.7336
	Sig. (2-tailed)	0.2803	0.8366	0.8101	0.1777	0.7807	0.5116	0.7174	0.1760	0.0000	0.0000
	N	34.0000	34.0000	34.0000	34.0000	34.0000	34.0000	34.0000	34.0000	32.0000	34.0000
sqrtQIIF3a	Pearson Correlation	-0.0578	0.2510	0.2035	0.1514	-0.0021	0.0533	-0.0222	0.1342	0.8285	0.5764
	Sig. (2-tailed)	0.7532	0.1658	0.2639	0.4082	0.9908	0.7718	0.9041	0.4640	0.0000	0.0006
	N	32.0000	32.0000	32.0000	32.0000	32.0000	32.0000	32.0000	32.0000	31.0000	32.0000
sqrtQIIF3b	Pearson Correlation	0.1047	0.1619	0.1719	0.2960	0.1672	0.2021	-0.0028	0.1548	0.4214	0.7665
	Sig. (2-tailed)	0.5621	0.3682	0.3388	0.0944	0.3523	0.2593	0.9876	0.3898	0.0182	0.0000
	N	33.0000	33.0000	33.0000	33.0000	33.0000	33.0000	33.0000	33.0000	31.0000	33.0000
sqrtQIIF3c	Pearson Correlation	0.1401	0.2002	0.1889	0.3434	0.1936	0.2325	0.0634	0.1909	0.3478	0.6453
	Sig. (2-tailed)	0.4368	0.2640	0.2925	0.0504	0.2804	0.1930	0.7261	0.2872	0.0552	0.0001
	N	33.0000	33.0000	33.0000	33.0000	33.0000	33.0000	33.0000	33.0000	31.0000	33.0000
sqrtQIIF3d	Pearson Correlation	-0.0225	0.2154	0.2193	0.1798	0.1428	0.1237	-0.0628	0.0819	0.6597	0.5768
	Sig. (2-tailed)	0.9013	0.2287	0.2202	0.3168	0.4280	0.4929	0.7286	0.6503	0.0001	0.0004
	N	33.0000	33.0000	33.0000	33.0000	33.0000	33.0000	33.0000	33.0000	31.0000	33.0000
sqrtQIIF3e	Pearson Correlation	-0.0104	0.1954	0.2129	0.1733	0.1879	0.1631	-0.0794	0.1017	0.6210	0.5788
	Sig. (2-tailed)	0.9550	0.2838	0.2421	0.3429	0.3032	0.3724	0.6659	0.5797	0.0002	0.0005
	N	32.0000	32.0000	32.0000	32.0000	32.0000	32.0000	32.0000	32.0000	31.0000	32.0000
sqrtQIIH1a	Pearson Correlation	0.0856	0.3536	0.2107	0.0271	0.1796	0.2930	0.0420	-0.0078	0.7871	0.5120
	Sig. (2-tailed)	0.6472	0.0510	0.2552	0.8850	0.3337	0.1097	0.8225	0.9668	0.0000	0.0038
	N	31.0000	31.0000	31.0000	31.0000	31.0000	31.0000	31.0000	31.0000	30.0000	30.0000
sqrtQIIH1b	Pearson Correlation	0.0662	0.1334	0.0879	-0.0230	0.1240	0.2362	-0.0692	-0.0200	0.4942	0.6379
	Sig. (2-tailed)	0.7144	0.4593	0.6268	0.8991	0.4919	0.1857	0.7020	0.9120	0.0055	0.0001
	N	33.0000	33.0000	33.0000	33.0000	33.0000	33.0000	33.0000	33.0000	30.0000	32.0000
sqrtQIIH1c	Pearson Correlation	0.0170	0.0798	-0.0001	0.0076	0.0213	0.2443	-0.0376	0.0601	0.5548	0.7696
	Sig. (2-tailed)	0.9264	0.6640	0.9994	0.9673	0.9079	0.1778	0.8383	0.7437	0.0015	0.0000
	N	32.0000	32.0000	32.0000	32.0000	32.0000	32.0000	32.0000	32.0000	30.0000	31.0000
sqrtQIIH1d	Pearson Correlation	0.0809	0.2586	0.1787	-0.0686	0.1323	0.2878	0.0027	0.0722	0.7332	0.5478
	Sig. (2-tailed)	0.6596	0.1530	0.3278	0.7090	0.4705	0.1102	0.9882	0.6946	0.0000	0.0014
	N	32.0000	32.0000	32.0000	32.0000	32.0000	32.0000	32.0000	32.0000	30.0000	31.0000

Table A6, continued (Row 6, Col 7)

Correlation Matrix, Dependent Variables (Parametric)		sqrtQIIF1c	sqrtQIIF1d	sqrtQIIF1e	sqrtQIIF3a	sqrtQIIF3b	sqrtQIIF3c	sqrtQIIF3d	sqrtQIIF3e	sqrtQIIH1a	sqrtQIIH1b
sqrtQIIF1c	Pearson Correlation	1.0000	0.7313	0.5797	0.4657	0.5591	0.6764	0.4465	0.4105	0.3897	0.4268
	Sig. (2-tailed)	.	0.0000	0.0003	0.0072	0.0007	0.0000	0.0092	0.0196	0.0333	0.0149
	N	34.0000	34.0000	34.0000	32.0000	33.0000	33.0000	33.0000	32.0000	30.0000	32.0000
sqrtQIIF1d	Pearson Correlation	0.7313	1.0000	0.7169	0.6807	0.5486	0.5190	0.7523	0.7255	0.6509	0.3596
	Sig. (2-tailed)	0.0000	.	0.0000	0.0000	0.0009	0.0020	0.0000	0.0000	0.0001	0.0433
	N	34.0000	34.0000	34.0000	32.0000	33.0000	33.0000	33.0000	32.0000	30.0000	32.0000
sqrtQIIF1e	Pearson Correlation	0.5797	0.7169	1.0000	0.7289	0.4745	0.3973	0.6643	0.7251	0.6841	0.4701
	Sig. (2-tailed)	0.0003	0.0000	.	0.0000	0.0053	0.0220	0.0000	0.0000	0.0000	0.0066
	N	34.0000	34.0000	34.0000	32.0000	33.0000	33.0000	33.0000	32.0000	30.0000	32.0000
sqrtQIIF3a	Pearson Correlation	0.4657	0.6807	0.7289	1.0000	0.5968	0.5129	0.8531	0.8036	0.8695	0.5237
	Sig. (2-tailed)	0.0072	0.0000	0.0000	.	0.0003	0.0027	0.0000	0.0000	0.0000	0.0030
	N	32.0000	32.0000	32.0000	32.0000	32.0000	32.0000	32.0000	32.0000	29.0000	30.0000
sqrtQIIF3b	Pearson Correlation	0.5591	0.5486	0.4745	0.5968	1.0000	0.9043	0.8000	0.7986	0.5377	0.7351
	Sig. (2-tailed)	0.0007	0.0009	0.0053	0.0003	.	0.0000	0.0000	0.0000	0.0026	0.0000
	N	33.0000	33.0000	33.0000	32.0000	33.0000	33.0000	33.0000	32.0000	29.0000	31.0000
sqrtQIIF3c	Pearson Correlation	0.6764	0.5190	0.3973	0.5129	0.9043	1.0000	0.6771	0.6858	0.4429	0.6575
	Sig. (2-tailed)	0.0000	0.0020	0.0220	0.0027	0.0000	.	0.0000	0.0000	0.0161	0.0001
	N	33.0000	33.0000	33.0000	32.0000	33.0000	33.0000	33.0000	32.0000	29.0000	31.0000
sqrtQIIF3d	Pearson Correlation	0.4465	0.7523	0.6643	0.8531	0.8000	0.6771	1.0000	0.9817	0.8011	0.5959
	Sig. (2-tailed)	0.0092	0.0000	0.0000	0.0000	0.0000	0.0000	.	0.0000	0.0000	0.0004
	N	33.0000	33.0000	33.0000	32.0000	33.0000	33.0000	33.0000	32.0000	29.0000	31.0000
sqrtQIIF3e	Pearson Correlation	0.4105	0.7255	0.7251	0.8036	0.7986	0.6858	0.9817	1.0000	0.7575	0.6179
	Sig. (2-tailed)	0.0196	0.0000	0.0000	0.0000	0.0000	0.0000	0.0000	.	0.0000	0.0003
	N	32.0000	32.0000	32.0000	32.0000	32.0000	32.0000	32.0000	32.0000	29.0000	30.0000
sqrtQIIH1a	Pearson Correlation	0.3897	0.6509	0.6841	0.8695	0.5377	0.4429	0.8011	0.7575	1.0000	0.5635
	Sig. (2-tailed)	0.0333	0.0001	0.0000	0.0000	0.0026	0.0161	0.0000	0.0000	.	0.0010
	N	30.0000	30.0000	30.0000	29.0000	29.0000	29.0000	29.0000	29.0000	31.0000	31.0000
sqrtQIIH1b	Pearson Correlation	0.4268	0.3596	0.4701	0.5237	0.7351	0.6575	0.5959	0.6179	0.5635	1.0000
	Sig. (2-tailed)	0.0149	0.0433	0.0066	0.0030	0.0000	0.0001	0.0004	0.0003	0.0010	.
	N	32.0000	32.0000	32.0000	30.0000	31.0000	31.0000	31.0000	30.0000	31.0000	33.0000
sqrtQIIH1c	Pearson Correlation	0.5651	0.4941	0.5140	0.6182	0.7857	0.6880	0.6316	0.6371	0.6477	0.8623
	Sig. (2-tailed)	0.0009	0.0047	0.0031	0.0004	0.0000	0.0000	0.0002	0.0002	0.0001	0.0000
	N	31.0000	31.0000	31.0000	29.0000	30.0000	30.0000	30.0000	29.0000	31.0000	32.0000
sqrtQIIH1d	Pearson Correlation	0.4198	0.6397	0.7036	0.8025	0.5823	0.4611	0.8117	0.8170	0.8656	0.7164
	Sig. (2-tailed)	0.0187	0.0001	0.0000	0.0000	0.0007	0.0103	0.0000	0.0000	0.0000	0.0000
	N	31.0000	31.0000	31.0000	29.0000	30.0000	30.0000	30.0000	29.0000	31.0000	32.0000

Table A6, continued (Row 6, Col 8)

Correlation Matrix, Dependent Variables (Parametric)		sqrtQIIH1c	sqrtQIIH1d	sqrtQIIH1e	sqrtQIIH3a	sqrtQIIH3b	sqrtQIIH3c	sqrtQIIH3d	sqrtQIIH3e	sqrtQIIIA1a	sqrtQIIIA1b
sqrtQIIF1c	Pearson Correlation	0.5651	0.4198	0.2940	0.2630	0.4814	0.5506	0.2574	0.1324	0.2282	-0.1073
	Sig. (2-tailed)	0.0009	0.0187	0.1148	0.1392	0.0046	0.0009	0.1481	0.4625	0.2015	0.5459
	N	31.0000	31.0000	30.0000	33.0000	33.0000	33.0000	33.0000	33.0000	33.0000	34.0000
sqrtQIIF1d	Pearson Correlation	0.4941	0.6397	0.5099	0.4935	0.4272	0.4932	0.4714	0.3442	0.3475	-0.1862
	Sig. (2-tailed)	0.0047	0.0001	0.0040	0.0035	0.0132	0.0035	0.0056	0.0498	0.0475	0.2916
	N	31.0000	31.0000	30.0000	33.0000	33.0000	33.0000	33.0000	33.0000	33.0000	34.0000
sqrtQIIF1e	Pearson Correlation	0.5140	0.7036	0.7828	0.5765	0.5366	0.5155	0.5662	0.6302	0.0369	-0.2143
	Sig. (2-tailed)	0.0031	0.0000	0.0000	0.0004	0.0013	0.0021	0.0006	0.0001	0.8384	0.2236
	N	31.0000	31.0000	30.0000	33.0000	33.0000	33.0000	33.0000	33.0000	33.0000	34.0000
sqrtQIIF3a	Pearson Correlation	0.6182	0.8025	0.7226	0.8414	0.5591	0.6354	0.7640	0.6940	0.0369	-0.2298
	Sig. (2-tailed)	0.0004	0.0000	0.0000	0.0000	0.0011	0.0001	0.0000	0.0000	0.8440	0.2058
	N	29.0000	29.0000	29.0000	31.0000	31.0000	31.0000	31.0000	31.0000	31.0000	32.0000
sqrtQIIF3b	Pearson Correlation	0.7857	0.5823	0.5732	0.5160	0.7108	0.7434	0.6066	0.5249	0.0173	0.2334
	Sig. (2-tailed)	0.0000	0.0007	0.0012	0.0025	0.0000	0.0000	0.0002	0.0020	0.9252	0.1912
	N	30.0000	30.0000	29.0000	32.0000	32.0000	32.0000	32.0000	32.0000	32.0000	33.0000
sqrtQIIF3c	Pearson Correlation	0.6880	0.4611	0.4521	0.4233	0.6323	0.6439	0.4735	0.4059	0.0867	0.2856
	Sig. (2-tailed)	0.0000	0.0103	0.0138	0.0158	0.0001	0.0001	0.0062	0.0212	0.6371	0.1071
	N	30.0000	30.0000	29.0000	32.0000	32.0000	32.0000	32.0000	32.0000	32.0000	33.0000
sqrtQIIF3d	Pearson Correlation	0.6316	0.8117	0.7800	0.6789	0.5801	0.6169	0.7237	0.6489	0.1116	-0.0151
	Sig. (2-tailed)	0.0002	0.0000	0.0000	0.0000	0.0005	0.0002	0.0000	0.0001	0.5432	0.9337
	N	30.0000	30.0000	29.0000	32.0000	32.0000	32.0000	32.0000	32.0000	32.0000	33.0000
sqrtQIIF3e	Pearson Correlation	0.6371	0.8170	0.8132	0.6569	0.6032	0.6209	0.7275	0.6992	0.0707	0.0478
	Sig. (2-tailed)	0.0002	0.0000	0.0000	0.0001	0.0003	0.0002	0.0000	0.0000	0.7056	0.7951
	N	29.0000	29.0000	29.0000	31.0000	31.0000	31.0000	31.0000	31.0000	31.0000	32.0000
sqrtQIIH1a	Pearson Correlation	0.6477	0.8656	0.8161	0.8866	0.5679	0.6450	0.8188	0.6878	-0.0251	-0.1300
	Sig. (2-tailed)	0.0001	0.0000	0.0000	0.0000	0.0009	0.0001	0.0000	0.0000	0.8951	0.4858
	N	31.0000	31.0000	31.0000	31.0000	31.0000	31.0000	31.0000	31.0000	30.0000	31.0000
sqrtQIIH1b	Pearson Correlation	0.8623	0.7164	0.6404	0.5014	0.9492	0.8736	0.6697	0.6697	-0.3571	0.1708
	Sig. (2-tailed)	0.0000	0.0000	0.0001	0.0035	0.0000	0.0000	0.0000	0.0000	0.0448	0.3420
	N	32.0000	32.0000	31.0000	32.0000	32.0000	32.0000	32.0000	32.0000	32.0000	33.0000
sqrtQIIH1c	Pearson Correlation	1.0000	0.8049	0.6353	0.6101	0.8754	0.9709	0.7089	0.6169	-0.1949	0.0105
	Sig. (2-tailed)	.	0.0000	0.0001	0.0002	0.0000	0.0000	0.0000	0.0002	0.2934	0.9543
	N	32.0000	32.0000	31.0000	32.0000	32.0000	32.0000	32.0000	32.0000	31.0000	32.0000
sqrtQIIH1d	Pearson Correlation	0.8049	1.0000	0.8696	0.7497	0.7198	0.7897	0.8697	0.7940	-0.0654	-0.0886
	Sig. (2-tailed)	0.0000	.	0.0000	0.0000	0.0000	0.0000	0.0000	0.0000	0.7265	0.6297
	N	32.0000	32.0000	31.0000	32.0000	32.0000	32.0000	32.0000	32.0000	31.0000	32.0000

Table A6, continued (Row 6, Col 9)

Correlation Matrix, Dependent Variables (Parametric)		sqrtQIIIA1c	sqrtQIIIA1d	sqrtQIIIA1e	sqrtQIIID1a	Level Cooperation Domestic Orgs-CNDPS	Level Cooperation Domestic Orgs-CNBC	Level Cooperation Domestic Orgs-CSTP	Level Cooperation Domestic Orgs-TRIPS	sqrtQIIID2a	Level Cooperation International Orgs-CNDPS
sqrtQIIF1c	Pearson Correlation	0.0488	-0.0392	-0.0602	0.4435	0.1011	0.3299	0.1786	0.2511	0.5201	0.1855
	Sig. (2-tailed)	0.7841	0.8259	0.7351	0.0110	0.5758	0.0608	0.3199	0.1587	0.0019	0.2934
	N	34.0000	34.0000	34.0000	32.0000	33.0000	33.0000	33.0000	33.0000	33.0000	34.0000
sqrtQIIF1d	Pearson Correlation	-0.0947	-0.0314	0.0150	0.2604	0.0871	0.2153	0.0672	0.0566	0.4447	0.1989
	Sig. (2-tailed)	0.5944	0.8599	0.9327	0.1500	0.6299	0.2288	0.7103	0.7544	0.0095	0.2594
	N	34.0000	34.0000	34.0000	32.0000	33.0000	33.0000	33.0000	33.0000	33.0000	34.0000
sqrtQIIF1e	Pearson Correlation	-0.2657	-0.1991	0.0981	0.2121	-0.0502	0.1230	-0.0398	0.1207	0.2564	-0.0087
	Sig. (2-tailed)	0.1288	0.2589	0.5810	0.2440	0.7813	0.4951	0.8258	0.5034	0.1498	0.9610
	N	34.0000	34.0000	34.0000	32.0000	33.0000	33.0000	33.0000	33.0000	33.0000	34.0000
sqrtQIIF3a	Pearson Correlation	-0.1798	-0.1325	-0.0454	0.3182	0.0867	0.2661	0.1688	0.1825	0.2906	-0.0217
	Sig. (2-tailed)	0.3249	0.4699	0.8051	0.0865	0.6428	0.1480	0.3640	0.3258	0.1128	0.9062
	N	32.0000	32.0000	32.0000	30.0000	31.0000	31.0000	31.0000	31.0000	31.0000	32.0000
sqrtQIIF3b	Pearson Correlation	0.3223	0.1035	0.2106	0.3040	0.3808	0.4816	0.2133	0.3763	0.4033	0.4067
	Sig. (2-tailed)	0.0673	0.5664	0.2393	0.0964	0.0315	0.0053	0.2412	0.0338	0.0221	0.0188
	N	33.0000	33.0000	33.0000	31.0000	32.0000	32.0000	32.0000	32.0000	32.0000	33.0000
sqrtQIIF3c	Pearson Correlation	0.3829	0.1528	0.2647	0.3853	0.3658	0.5200	0.2908	0.4083	0.5036	0.4391
	Sig. (2-tailed)	0.0279	0.3960	0.1366	0.0323	0.0395	0.0023	0.1064	0.0204	0.0033	0.0106
	N	33.0000	33.0000	33.0000	31.0000	32.0000	32.0000	32.0000	32.0000	32.0000	33.0000
sqrtQIIF3d	Pearson Correlation	0.0305	0.0265	0.1542	0.2708	0.2297	0.3456	0.1853	0.2402	0.3891	0.2233
	Sig. (2-tailed)	0.8661	0.8835	0.3915	0.1406	0.2060	0.0527	0.3099	0.1855	0.0277	0.2116
	N	33.0000	33.0000	33.0000	31.0000	32.0000	32.0000	32.0000	32.0000	32.0000	33.0000
sqrtQIIF3e	Pearson Correlation	0.0673	0.0400	0.2479	0.2642	0.2515	0.3374	0.1772	0.2662	0.3926	0.2580
	Sig. (2-tailed)	0.7146	0.8277	0.1713	0.1583	0.1723	0.0635	0.3401	0.1477	0.0289	0.1539
	N	32.0000	32.0000	32.0000	30.0000	31.0000	31.0000	31.0000	31.0000	31.0000	32.0000
sqrtQIIH1a	Pearson Correlation	-0.1069	-0.1186	-0.0656	0.3384	0.1763	0.3406	0.1787	0.0870	0.2735	0.1755
	Sig. (2-tailed)	0.5672	0.5252	0.7258	0.0726	0.3513	0.0655	0.3448	0.6475	0.1436	0.3451
	N	31.0000	31.0000	31.0000	29.0000	30.0000	30.0000	30.0000	30.0000	30.0000	31.0000
sqrtQIIH1b	Pearson Correlation	0.1289	-0.0993	0.0559	0.1287	0.2798	0.4085	0.2376	0.2795	0.2978	0.3326
	Sig. (2-tailed)	0.4747	0.5825	0.7572	0.4901	0.1210	0.0203	0.1904	0.1213	0.0979	0.0586
	N	33.0000	33.0000	33.0000	31.0000	32.0000	32.0000	32.0000	32.0000	32.0000	33.0000
sqrtQIIH1c	Pearson Correlation	0.0961	-0.0148	-0.0148	0.3094	0.2055	0.3510	0.2264	0.2817	0.3123	0.3441
	Sig. (2-tailed)	0.6009	0.9359	0.9361	0.0962	0.2675	0.0528	0.2207	0.1247	0.0871	0.0538
	N	32.0000	32.0000	32.0000	30.0000	31.0000	31.0000	31.0000	31.0000	31.0000	32.0000
sqrtQIIH1d	Pearson Correlation	-0.0641	0.0261	0.0853	0.3239	0.2069	0.3231	0.2829	0.2414	0.2975	0.2385
	Sig. (2-tailed)	0.7273	0.8873	0.6425	0.0808	0.2642	0.0762	0.1231	0.1908	0.1041	0.1886
	N	32.0000	32.0000	32.0000	30.0000	31.0000	31.0000	31.0000	31.0000	31.0000	32.0000

Table A6, continued (Row 6, Col 10)

Correlation Matrix, Dependent Variables (Parametric)		Level Cooperation International Orgs-CNBC	Level Cooperation International Orgs-CSTP	sqrtQIIID2e	sqrtQIVA1	sqrtQIVA2	sqrtQIVA3	sqrtQIVA5	sqrtQIVA7	sqrtQIVA8	Political Ideology
sqrtQIIF1c	Pearson Correlation	0.2705	0.3665	0.3880	0.3371	0.1761	0.3641	0.4104	-0.0459	-0.1944	0.2775
	Sig. (2-tailed)	0.1218	0.0330	0.0234	0.0512	0.3192	0.0373	0.0177	0.7964	0.2706	0.1242
	N	34.0000	34.0000	34.0000	34.0000	34.0000	33.0000	33.0000	34.0000	34.0000	32.0000
sqrtQIIF1d	Pearson Correlation	0.2750	0.3306	0.2890	0.1211	0.0531	0.1787	0.3166	-0.1818	-0.2812	0.2006
	Sig. (2-tailed)	0.1154	0.0562	0.0974	0.4950	0.7657	0.3198	0.0726	0.3034	0.1072	0.2709
	N	34.0000	34.0000	34.0000	34.0000	34.0000	33.0000	33.0000	34.0000	34.0000	32.0000
sqrtQIIF1e	Pearson Correlation	0.0801	0.0958	0.1683	0.0991	0.0508	0.2001	0.1539	-0.0809	-0.2682	0.1522
	Sig. (2-tailed)	0.6525	0.5900	0.3414	0.5770	0.7754	0.2643	0.3925	0.6491	0.1252	0.4058
	N	34.0000	34.0000	34.0000	34.0000	34.0000	33.0000	33.0000	34.0000	34.0000	32.0000
sqrtQIIF3a	Pearson Correlation	0.1006	0.1558	0.1522	0.0535	0.0241	0.3517	0.1114	0.0366	-0.2630	0.0779
	Sig. (2-tailed)	0.5840	0.3946	0.4056	0.7710	0.8958	0.0523	0.5506	0.8425	0.1458	0.6826
	N	32.0000	32.0000	32.0000	32.0000	32.0000	31.0000	31.0000	32.0000	32.0000	30.0000
sqrtQIIF3b	Pearson Correlation	0.4854	0.5636	0.5579	0.1137	0.0626	0.4703	0.3467	-0.2480	-0.2199	0.2636
	Sig. (2-tailed)	0.0042	0.0006	0.0007	0.5287	0.7294	0.0066	0.0519	0.1641	0.2189	0.1519
	N	33.0000	33.0000	33.0000	33.0000	33.0000	32.0000	32.0000	33.0000	33.0000	31.0000
sqrtQIIF3c	Pearson Correlation	0.5242	0.6369	0.6178	0.1636	0.1178	0.4902	0.3564	-0.1760	-0.1814	0.3096
	Sig. (2-tailed)	0.0017	0.0001	0.0001	0.3628	0.5139	0.0044	0.0453	0.3273	0.3123	0.0901
	N	33.0000	33.0000	33.0000	33.0000	33.0000	32.0000	32.0000	33.0000	33.0000	31.0000
sqrtQIIF3d	Pearson Correlation	0.3272	0.3511	0.3574	-0.0107	-0.0033	0.3475	0.2840	-0.1771	-0.2564	0.1763
	Sig. (2-tailed)	0.0631	0.0451	0.0412	0.9529	0.9853	0.0513	0.1152	0.3242	0.1498	0.3428
	N	33.0000	33.0000	33.0000	33.0000	33.0000	32.0000	32.0000	33.0000	33.0000	31.0000
sqrtQIIF3e	Pearson Correlation	0.3460	0.3644	0.3926	0.0292	0.0070	0.3792	0.2612	-0.1990	-0.2412	0.2026
	Sig. (2-tailed)	0.0524	0.0403	0.0262	0.8738	0.9698	0.0354	0.1559	0.2748	0.1836	0.2830
	N	32.0000	32.0000	32.0000	32.0000	32.0000	31.0000	31.0000	32.0000	32.0000	30.0000
sqrtQIIH1a	Pearson Correlation	0.2923	0.2228	0.2138	0.0160	0.0259	0.1566	0.3603	-0.0264	-0.2494	0.0261
	Sig. (2-tailed)	0.1105	0.2284	0.2482	0.9319	0.8901	0.4084	0.0548	0.8880	0.1839	0.8953
	N	31.0000	31.0000	31.0000	31.0000	31.0000	30.0000	29.0000	31.0000	30.0000	28.0000
sqrtQIIH1b	Pearson Correlation	0.4241	0.3613	0.4736	0.1020	0.0479	0.1802	0.3797	-0.0114	-0.2635	0.1321
	Sig. (2-tailed)	0.0139	0.0388	0.0054	0.5723	0.7911	0.3237	0.0351	0.9497	0.1451	0.4864
	N	33.0000	33.0000	33.0000	33.0000	33.0000	32.0000	31.0000	33.0000	32.0000	30.0000
sqrtQIIH1c	Pearson Correlation	0.3949	0.4161	0.4864	0.1657	0.0824	0.2596	0.3078	-0.1064	-0.2441	0.1971
	Sig. (2-tailed)	0.0253	0.0179	0.0048	0.3647	0.6538	0.1584	0.0980	0.5621	0.1857	0.3054
	N	32.0000	32.0000	32.0000	32.0000	32.0000	31.0000	30.0000	32.0000	31.0000	29.0000
sqrtQIIH1d	Pearson Correlation	0.3012	0.2656	0.3513	0.0801	0.0561	0.2312	0.3320	0.0077	-0.2446	0.1049
	Sig. (2-tailed)	0.0938	0.1418	0.0487	0.6630	0.7604	0.2107	0.0730	0.9666	0.1848	0.5881
	N	32.0000	32.0000	32.0000	32.0000	32.0000	31.0000	30.0000	32.0000	31.0000	29.0000

Table A6, continued (Row 7, Col 1)

Correlation Matrix, Dependent Variables (Parametric)		Importance of Smuggling-Endangered Species	reflectsqrtQ1A1b	reflectsqrtQ1A1c	reflectsqrtQ1A1d	reflectsqrtQ1A1e	sqrtQ1B1a	Knowledge of Smuggling-Narcotics	Knowledge of Smuggling-Weapons	Knowledge of Smuggling-Humans	Knowledge of Smuggling-Contraband
sqrtQIIH1e	Pearson Correlation	-0.2381	0.1926	0.1787	-0.1453	0.1380	-0.1340	-0.0256	-0.0302	0.1067	-0.0722
	Sig. (2-tailed)	0.1971	0.2993	0.3360	0.4356	0.4592	0.4724	0.8912	0.8719	0.5678	0.6997
	N	31.0000	31.0000	31.0000	31.0000	31.0000	31.0000	31.0000	31.0000	31.0000	31.0000
sqrtQIIH3a	Pearson Correlation	-0.0493	-0.1360	-0.1850	-0.1860	0.1135	-0.1723	0.0632	0.1058	-0.0003	-0.1491
	Sig. (2-tailed)	0.7820	0.4430	0.2949	0.2922	0.5227	0.3299	0.7225	0.5514	0.9989	0.3999
	N	34.0000	34.0000	34.0000	34.0000	34.0000	34.0000	34.0000	34.0000	34.0000	34.0000
sqrtQIIH3b	Pearson Correlation	-0.2851	-0.0175	0.0051	-0.0495	0.2423	-0.2976	0.0665	0.0136	0.1945	-0.1162
	Sig. (2-tailed)	0.1022	0.9217	0.9772	0.7812	0.1673	0.0874	0.7087	0.9391	0.2704	0.5128
	N	34.0000	34.0000	34.0000	34.0000	34.0000	34.0000	34.0000	34.0000	34.0000	34.0000
sqrtQIIH3c	Pearson Correlation	-0.2406	-0.2103	-0.1055	-0.0621	0.1325	-0.2605	0.0367	0.0256	0.2078	-0.1528
	Sig. (2-tailed)	0.1704	0.2324	0.5525	0.7272	0.4551	0.1367	0.8366	0.8858	0.2384	0.3884
	N	34.0000	34.0000	34.0000	34.0000	34.0000	34.0000	34.0000	34.0000	34.0000	34.0000
sqrtQIIH3d	Pearson Correlation	-0.2563	-0.1407	-0.0472	-0.1862	0.1279	-0.2476	0.0117	0.1006	0.1212	-0.1184
	Sig. (2-tailed)	0.1434	0.4275	0.7910	0.2917	0.4710	0.1580	0.9478	0.5713	0.4949	0.5048
	N	34.0000	34.0000	34.0000	34.0000	34.0000	34.0000	34.0000	34.0000	34.0000	34.0000
sqrtQIIH3e	Pearson Correlation	-0.3019	0.0943	0.0969	-0.1238	0.2300	-0.3064	-0.0274	-0.0306	0.1222	-0.0652
	Sig. (2-tailed)	0.0827	0.5956	0.5858	0.4853	0.1907	0.0780	0.8775	0.8637	0.4911	0.7141
	N	34.0000	34.0000	34.0000	34.0000	34.0000	34.0000	34.0000	34.0000	34.0000	34.0000
sqrtQIIIA1a	Pearson Correlation	0.1539	0.1940	0.0303	0.1534	-0.2490	0.5686	0.0614	0.1530	0.2038	0.3504
	Sig. (2-tailed)	0.3774	0.2642	0.8627	0.3788	0.1492	0.0004	0.7262	0.3804	0.2403	0.0390
	N	35.0000	35.0000	35.0000	35.0000	35.0000	35.0000	35.0000	35.0000	35.0000	35.0000
sqrtQIIIA1b	Pearson Correlation	-0.0319	0.0782	0.1695	0.1824	0.1344	0.0163	0.4628	0.2114	0.2662	0.3009
	Sig. (2-tailed)	0.8535	0.6503	0.3229	0.2870	0.4346	0.9248	0.0045	0.2159	0.1166	0.0745
	N	36.0000	36.0000	36.0000	36.0000	36.0000	36.0000	36.0000	36.0000	36.0000	36.0000
sqrtQIIIA1c	Pearson Correlation	-0.1127	-0.0579	0.0782	0.2523	0.0069	0.0481	0.4045	0.4489	0.2159	0.3780
	Sig. (2-tailed)	0.5128	0.7373	0.6503	0.1377	0.9683	0.7807	0.0144	0.0060	0.2061	0.0230
	N	36.0000	36.0000	36.0000	36.0000	36.0000	36.0000	36.0000	36.0000	36.0000	36.0000
sqrtQIIIA1d	Pearson Correlation	-0.1182	-0.0618	-0.0557	-0.0240	-0.1092	0.1280	0.3222	0.2949	0.4759	0.4396
	Sig. (2-tailed)	0.4923	0.7201	0.7470	0.8894	0.5260	0.4570	0.0553	0.0808	0.0033	0.0073
	N	36.0000	36.0000	36.0000	36.0000	36.0000	36.0000	36.0000	36.0000	36.0000	36.0000
sqrtQIIIA1e	Pearson Correlation	-0.1398	0.3553	0.3276	0.2496	-0.0503	0.1387	0.1691	0.2459	0.2935	0.5612
	Sig. (2-tailed)	0.4159	0.0335	0.0511	0.1421	0.7708	0.4197	0.3241	0.1483	0.0823	0.0004
	N	36.0000	36.0000	36.0000	36.0000	36.0000	36.0000	36.0000	36.0000	36.0000	36.0000
sqrtQIIID1a	Pearson Correlation	-0.0834	0.0701	0.1064	0.0308	-0.1836	0.4138	0.1939	0.3706	0.1707	0.3408
	Sig. (2-tailed)	0.6445	0.6984	0.5557	0.8648	0.3065	0.0167	0.2797	0.0337	0.3422	0.0523
	N	33.0000	33.0000	33.0000	33.0000	33.0000	33.0000	33.0000	33.0000	33.0000	33.0000

Table A6, continued (Row 7, Col 2)

Correlation Matrix, Dependent Variables (Parametric)		sqrtQIE1a	Personal Resource Challenges-Lack of Time	Personal Resource Challenges-Lack of Knowledge	Personal Resource Challenges-Lack of Training	sqrtQIE1e	Personal Resource Challenges-Excessive Admin Paperwork	Personal Resource Challenges-Ineffective Technology	Personal Resource Challenges-Ineffective Strategic Focus	Personal Resource Challenges-Ineffective Tactical Policy	Personal Resource Challenges-Lack of Clarity in Duties
sqrtQIIH1e	Pearson Correlation	-0.0339	-0.0919	-0.1499	-0.0387	-0.1392	-0.1780	-0.2013	-0.1590	-0.1189	-0.0667
	Sig. (2-tailed)	0.8590	0.6229	0.4210	0.8362	0.4552	0.3380	0.2775	0.3929	0.5240	0.7214
	N	30.0000	31.0000	31.0000	31.0000	31.0000	31.0000	31.0000	31.0000	31.0000	31.0000
sqrtQIIH3a	Pearson Correlation	-0.1628	0.0323	0.0573	0.1218	0.0438	-0.1361	-0.0141	-0.0841	-0.1267	-0.0320
	Sig. (2-tailed)	0.3654	0.8563	0.7478	0.4926	0.8058	0.4427	0.9371	0.6362	0.4753	0.8575
	N	33.0000	34.0000	34.0000	34.0000	34.0000	34.0000	34.0000	34.0000	34.0000	34.0000
sqrtQIIH3b	Pearson Correlation	-0.1273	-0.3235	-0.1203	-0.0259	-0.1685	-0.1377	-0.0797	-0.1749	-0.1559	-0.2148
	Sig. (2-tailed)	0.4803	0.0620	0.4978	0.8845	0.3409	0.4374	0.6541	0.3226	0.3785	0.2225
	N	33.0000	34.0000	34.0000	34.0000	34.0000	34.0000	34.0000	34.0000	34.0000	34.0000
sqrtQIIH3c	Pearson Correlation	-0.0821	-0.1906	0.0261	0.0917	-0.0905	-0.1565	-0.0039	-0.0566	-0.0755	-0.1023
	Sig. (2-tailed)	0.6495	0.2802	0.8837	0.6059	0.6107	0.3768	0.9827	0.7505	0.6711	0.5646
	N	33.0000	34.0000	34.0000	34.0000	34.0000	34.0000	34.0000	34.0000	34.0000	34.0000
sqrtQIIH3d	Pearson Correlation	-0.1608	-0.0051	-0.1690	-0.0896	0.0060	-0.1547	-0.1921	-0.1473	-0.1363	-0.1130
	Sig. (2-tailed)	0.3713	0.9770	0.3393	0.6144	0.9732	0.3822	0.2765	0.4059	0.4422	0.5245
	N	33.0000	34.0000	34.0000	34.0000	34.0000	34.0000	34.0000	34.0000	34.0000	34.0000
sqrtQIIH3e	Pearson Correlation	-0.1548	-0.0089	-0.1839	-0.0900	-0.0226	-0.1709	-0.1572	-0.1766	-0.1435	-0.1166
	Sig. (2-tailed)	0.3898	0.9600	0.2978	0.6128	0.8991	0.3340	0.3745	0.3177	0.4181	0.5114
	N	33.0000	34.0000	34.0000	34.0000	34.0000	34.0000	34.0000	34.0000	34.0000	34.0000
sqrtQIIIA1a	Pearson Correlation	0.3282	0.3114	0.1295	0.1581	0.2187	0.3565	-0.0354	0.3285	0.3383	0.3095
	Sig. (2-tailed)	0.0581	0.0686	0.4584	0.3642	0.2069	0.0356	0.8399	0.0540	0.0468	0.0704
	N	34.0000	35.0000	35.0000	35.0000	35.0000	35.0000	35.0000	35.0000	35.0000	35.0000
sqrtQIIIA1b	Pearson Correlation	0.2881	0.0694	-0.1696	-0.2311	-0.0790	0.2407	0.0213	-0.1415	0.0382	-0.0093
	Sig. (2-tailed)	0.0933	0.6877	0.3227	0.1750	0.6468	0.1573	0.9020	0.4103	0.8250	0.9569
	N	35.0000	36.0000	36.0000	36.0000	36.0000	36.0000	36.0000	36.0000	36.0000	36.0000
sqrtQIIIA1c	Pearson Correlation	0.3869	0.1221	-0.1149	-0.1980	0.1071	0.3647	0.0335	-0.0162	0.1323	0.0524
	Sig. (2-tailed)	0.0217	0.4779	0.5044	0.2471	0.5340	0.0288	0.8461	0.9254	0.4418	0.7615
	N	35.0000	36.0000	36.0000	36.0000	36.0000	36.0000	36.0000	36.0000	36.0000	36.0000
sqrtQIIIA1d	Pearson Correlation	0.2685	0.2363	-0.0342	-0.0110	0.1396	0.2381	0.0131	0.0718	0.1710	0.1479
	Sig. (2-tailed)	0.1188	0.1653	0.8430	0.9493	0.4166	0.1620	0.9398	0.6775	0.3186	0.3892
	N	35.0000	36.0000	36.0000	36.0000	36.0000	36.0000	36.0000	36.0000	36.0000	36.0000
sqrtQIIIA1e	Pearson Correlation	0.2605	0.1714	-0.1854	-0.2242	0.0952	0.2494	-0.1226	-0.1359	-0.0048	-0.0612
	Sig. (2-tailed)	0.1307	0.3175	0.2790	0.1888	0.5809	0.1424	0.4762	0.4294	0.9778	0.7228
	N	35.0000	36.0000	36.0000	36.0000	36.0000	36.0000	36.0000	36.0000	36.0000	36.0000
sqrtQIIID1a	Pearson Correlation	-0.0079	0.1206	0.0284	0.1815	0.2646	0.2109	-0.1934	0.0917	-0.0591	0.1341
	Sig. (2-tailed)	0.9652	0.5039	0.8754	0.3122	0.1367	0.2387	0.2809	0.6117	0.7439	0.4568
	N	33.0000	33.0000	33.0000	33.0000	33.0000	33.0000	33.0000	33.0000	33.0000	33.0000

Correlation Matrix, Dependent Variables (Parametric)		Personal Resource Challenges-Conflict or Lack Comm Leaders and Employees	sqrtQIE11	Personal Resource Challenges-Conflict or Lack Comm International Orgs	Personal Resource Challenges-Conflict or Lack Comm Domestic Orgs	sqrtQIE3a	Org Resource Challenges-Lack of Time	Org Resource Challenges-Lack of Knowledge	Org Resource Challenges-Lack of Training	sqrtQIE3e	Org Resource Challenges-Excessive Admin Paperwork
sqrtQIIH1e	Pearson Correlation	-0.1481	-0.2417	-0.2447	-0.1619	0.2026	-0.1359	-0.1124	-0.1272	0.0184	0.1260
	Sig. (2-tailed)	0.4265	0.1902	0.1845	0.3842	0.2829	0.4740	0.5543	0.5029	0.9244	0.5071
	N	31.0000	31.0000	31.0000	31.0000	30.0000	30.0000	30.0000	30.0000	29.0000	30.0000
sqrtQIIH3a	Pearson Correlation	-0.1224	-0.1231	-0.1401	0.0276	0.2938	-0.0769	0.1602	0.1928	0.0569	0.1426
	Sig. (2-tailed)	0.4906	0.4881	0.4295	0.8769	0.0970	0.6707	0.3732	0.2824	0.7571	0.4285
	N	34.0000	34.0000	34.0000	34.0000	33.0000	33.0000	33.0000	33.0000	32.0000	33.0000
sqrtQIIH3b	Pearson Correlation	-0.2159	-0.1713	-0.2608	-0.2020	-0.0020	-0.2469	-0.0572	-0.0613	0.0404	-0.0256
	Sig. (2-tailed)	0.2200	0.3327	0.1363	0.2518	0.9911	0.1659	0.7519	0.7345	0.8262	0.8876
	N	34.0000	34.0000	34.0000	34.0000	33.0000	33.0000	33.0000	33.0000	32.0000	33.0000
sqrtQIIH3c	Pearson Correlation	-0.1763	-0.1942	-0.2933	-0.0826	0.1196	-0.1272	0.0831	0.0732	0.0799	0.0351
	Sig. (2-tailed)	0.3186	0.2710	0.0922	0.6422	0.5074	0.4807	0.6456	0.6858	0.6639	0.8464
	N	34.0000	34.0000	34.0000	34.0000	33.0000	33.0000	33.0000	33.0000	32.0000	33.0000
sqrtQIIH3d	Pearson Correlation	-0.1437	-0.1863	-0.2497	-0.0254	0.1773	-0.1567	-0.0073	0.0051	0.1056	0.1059
	Sig. (2-tailed)	0.4175	0.2915	0.1544	0.8868	0.3236	0.3838	0.9680	0.9774	0.5652	0.5577
	N	34.0000	34.0000	34.0000	34.0000	33.0000	33.0000	33.0000	33.0000	32.0000	33.0000
sqrtQIIH3e	Pearson Correlation	-0.0984	-0.1976	-0.2169	-0.0713	0.0507	-0.2548	-0.0352	-0.0365	0.1639	0.1202
	Sig. (2-tailed)	0.5800	0.2627	0.2179	0.6887	0.7794	0.1523	0.8456	0.8402	0.3701	0.5051
	N	34.0000	34.0000	34.0000	34.0000	33.0000	33.0000	33.0000	33.0000	32.0000	33.0000
sqrtQIIIA1a	Pearson Correlation	0.2006	0.2261	0.2839	0.2088	0.0342	-0.0162	0.0263	-0.0017	0.0645	0.2057
	Sig. (2-tailed)	0.2479	0.1915	0.0984	0.2287	0.8503	0.9276	0.8828	0.9925	0.7216	0.2432
	N	35.0000	35.0000	35.0000	35.0000	33.0000	34.0000	34.0000	34.0000	33.0000	34.0000
sqrtQIIIA1b	Pearson Correlation	0.1294	-0.0278	0.1332	0.0700	0.0321	-0.0835	-0.2797	-0.3170	0.0298	0.1275
	Sig. (2-tailed)	0.4521	0.8719	0.4388	0.6850	0.8570	0.6336	0.1036	0.0635	0.8673	0.4656
	N	36.0000	36.0000	36.0000	36.0000	34.0000	35.0000	35.0000	35.0000	34.0000	35.0000
sqrtQIIIA1c	Pearson Correlation	0.1660	0.0690	0.0944	0.1161	0.1374	0.0184	-0.2263	-0.2731	0.1285	0.2022
	Sig. (2-tailed)	0.3334	0.6893	0.5840	0.5001	0.4386	0.9166	0.1911	0.1124	0.4688	0.2441
	N	36.0000	36.0000	36.0000	36.0000	34.0000	35.0000	35.0000	35.0000	34.0000	35.0000
sqrtQIIIA1d	Pearson Correlation	0.1161	-0.1745	0.2105	0.2141	0.1194	-0.0144	-0.0268	-0.0901	-0.0141	0.1224
	Sig. (2-tailed)	0.5002	0.3088	0.2179	0.2099	0.5010	0.9344	0.8786	0.6066	0.9370	0.4838
	N	36.0000	36.0000	36.0000	36.0000	34.0000	35.0000	35.0000	35.0000	34.0000	35.0000
sqrtQIIIA1e	Pearson Correlation	0.0572	-0.0507	0.0680	-0.0306	-0.0829	-0.1243	-0.2772	-0.3359	0.0582	0.0930
	Sig. (2-tailed)	0.7403	0.7689	0.6937	0.8595	0.6413	0.4767	0.1069	0.0485	0.7438	0.5951
	N	36.0000	36.0000	36.0000	36.0000	34.0000	35.0000	35.0000	35.0000	34.0000	35.0000
sqrtQIIID1a	Pearson Correlation	-0.1135	-0.0093	0.0776	0.0771	0.0230	-0.2796	0.0015	-0.0421	0.0959	0.0279
	Sig. (2-tailed)	0.5296	0.9590	0.6677	0.6697	0.9024	0.1212	0.9936	0.8190	0.6079	0.8797
	N	33.0000	33.0000	33.0000	33.0000	31.0000	32.0000	32.0000	32.0000	31.0000	32.0000

Table A6, continued (Row 7, Col 4)

Correlation Matrix, Dependent Variables (Parametric)		Org Resource Challenges-Ineffective Technology	Org Resource Challenges-Ineffective Strategic Focus	Org Resource Challenges-Ineffective Tactical Policy	Org Resource Challenges-Lack of Clarity in Duties	Org Resource Challenges-Conflict or Lack Comm Leaders and Employees	sqrtQ1E31	Org Resource Challenges-Conflict or Lack Comm International Orgs	Org Resource Challenges-Conflict or Lack Comm Domestic Orgs	sqrtQIIA1a	Knowledge of Domestic Law-CSIE
sqrtQIIH1e	Pearson Correlation	-0.2584	-0.3508	-0.1040	-0.2212	-0.3020	-0.2399	-0.1464	-0.1769	0.0465	-0.2761
	Sig. (2-tailed)	0.1680	0.0574	0.5843	0.2402	0.1049	0.2017	0.4402	0.3496	0.8070	0.1398
	N	30.0000	30.0000	30.0000	30.0000	30.0000	30.0000	30.0000	30.0000	30.0000	30.0000
sqrtQIIH3a	Pearson Correlation	-0.0159	-0.0815	0.0959	0.0518	-0.0302	-0.0611	0.1575	0.1793	0.0193	-0.1459
	Sig. (2-tailed)	0.9302	0.6523	0.5955	0.7748	0.8677	0.7354	0.3814	0.3180	0.9151	0.4180
	N	33.0000	33.0000	33.0000	33.0000	33.0000	33.0000	33.0000	33.0000	33.0000	33.0000
sqrtQIIH3b	Pearson Correlation	0.0131	-0.1644	-0.1575	-0.0838	-0.2300	-0.1596	0.0560	0.0743	-0.2080	0.0339
	Sig. (2-tailed)	0.9424	0.3606	0.3813	0.6429	0.1979	0.3750	0.7571	0.6809	0.2455	0.8513
	N	33.0000	33.0000	33.0000	33.0000	33.0000	33.0000	33.0000	33.0000	33.0000	33.0000
sqrtQIIH3c	Pearson Correlation	0.1095	-0.0078	-0.0297	0.0907	-0.1855	-0.1677	0.2028	0.2141	-0.1876	0.0086
	Sig. (2-tailed)	0.5440	0.9655	0.8696	0.6159	0.3014	0.3510	0.2576	0.2316	0.2958	0.9621
	N	33.0000	33.0000	33.0000	33.0000	33.0000	33.0000	33.0000	33.0000	33.0000	33.0000
sqrtQIIH3d	Pearson Correlation	-0.0685	-0.1907	0.0113	-0.0948	-0.1098	-0.1387	-0.0149	0.0084	-0.0740	-0.1387
	Sig. (2-tailed)	0.7050	0.2878	0.9501	0.5999	0.5430	0.4416	0.9343	0.9629	0.6823	0.4416
	N	33.0000	33.0000	33.0000	33.0000	33.0000	33.0000	33.0000	33.0000	33.0000	33.0000
sqrtQIIH3e	Pearson Correlation	-0.1200	-0.2575	-0.0392	-0.1891	-0.1310	-0.1842	-0.1282	-0.0901	-0.0809	-0.2131
	Sig. (2-tailed)	0.5059	0.1480	0.8285	0.2920	0.4675	0.3047	0.4770	0.6181	0.6544	0.2337
	N	33.0000	33.0000	33.0000	33.0000	33.0000	33.0000	33.0000	33.0000	33.0000	33.0000
sqrtQIIIA1a	Pearson Correlation	-0.0089	0.0761	0.1894	0.1937	0.1442	0.1479	0.0915	0.0784	0.6590	-0.0793
	Sig. (2-tailed)	0.9604	0.6689	0.2833	0.2723	0.4157	0.4038	0.6069	0.6594	0.0000	0.6557
	N	34.0000	34.0000	34.0000	34.0000	34.0000	34.0000	34.0000	34.0000	34.0000	34.0000
sqrtQIIIA1b	Pearson Correlation	0.0746	-0.1040	-0.0530	-0.1948	0.0782	-0.1712	-0.2006	-0.1661	0.1279	0.3803
	Sig. (2-tailed)	0.6700	0.5522	0.7622	0.2620	0.6553	0.3254	0.2480	0.3401	0.4639	0.0242
	N	35.0000	35.0000	35.0000	35.0000	35.0000	35.0000	35.0000	35.0000	35.0000	35.0000
sqrtQIIIA1c	Pearson Correlation	0.1545	0.0208	0.0520	-0.0508	0.1867	-0.0484	-0.0822	-0.0312	0.1830	0.4524
	Sig. (2-tailed)	0.3754	0.9058	0.7667	0.7718	0.2828	0.7826	0.6388	0.8589	0.2926	0.0064
	N	35.0000	35.0000	35.0000	35.0000	35.0000	35.0000	35.0000	35.0000	35.0000	35.0000
sqrtQIIIA1d	Pearson Correlation	0.1285	0.0143	0.1151	0.0448	0.1597	-0.2347	-0.0833	-0.0846	0.2485	0.0719
	Sig. (2-tailed)	0.4620	0.9352	0.5103	0.7984	0.3594	0.1747	0.6342	0.6289	0.1499	0.6814
	N	35.0000	35.0000	35.0000	35.0000	35.0000	35.0000	35.0000	35.0000	35.0000	35.0000
sqrtQIIIA1e	Pearson Correlation	-0.1611	-0.2920	-0.1516	-0.2749	-0.0643	-0.2254	-0.2899	-0.2436	0.3637	0.0763
	Sig. (2-tailed)	0.3552	0.0888	0.3846	0.1100	0.7135	0.1930	0.0912	0.1585	0.0317	0.6631
	N	35.0000	35.0000	35.0000	35.0000	35.0000	35.0000	35.0000	35.0000	35.0000	35.0000
sqrtQIIID1a	Pearson Correlation	-0.1393	-0.1005	0.1123	0.0586	0.0196	0.1302	0.0245	-0.0121	0.2503	-0.1148
	Sig. (2-tailed)	0.4469	0.5842	0.5406	0.7501	0.9153	0.4774	0.8939	0.9477	0.1670	0.5317
	N	32.0000	32.0000	32.0000	32.0000	32.0000	32.0000	32.0000	32.0000	32.0000	32.0000

Table A6, continued (Row 7, Col 5)

Correlation Matrix, Dependent Variables (Parametric)		Knowledge of Domestic Law-DWMD	Knowledge of Domestic Law-TVP	Knowledge of Domestic Law-CBP	sqrtQIIB1a	Perceived Effectiveness Domestic Govt Support-CSIE	Perceived Effectiveness Domestic Govt Support-DWMD	Perceived Effectiveness Domestic Govt SupportTVP	Perceived Effectiveness Domestic Govt Support-CBP	sqrtQIIC1a	Perceived Deterrence Domestic Law-CSIE
sqrtQIIH1e	Pearson Correlation	-0.1283	-0.3042	-0.0096	0.0574	0.0964	-0.0004	0.0867	0.2515	0.0260	0.0663
	Sig. (2-tailed)	0.4994	0.1022	0.9597	0.7589	0.6124	0.9984	0.6428	0.1722	0.8897	0.7229
	N	30.0000	30.0000	30.0000	31.0000	30.0000	31.0000	31.0000	31.0000	31.0000	31.0000
sqrtQIIH3a	Pearson Correlation	-0.1299	-0.3558	-0.0812	0.1174	0.0895	0.0860	0.2009	0.1265	0.1436	0.0412
	Sig. (2-tailed)	0.4712	0.0422	0.6531	0.5084	0.6203	0.6285	0.2545	0.4760	0.4179	0.8170
	N	33.0000	33.0000	33.0000	34.0000	33.0000	34.0000	34.0000	34.0000	34.0000	34.0000
sqrtQIIH3b	Pearson Correlation	0.0058	-0.1177	-0.2433	-0.0546	0.2417	0.1414	0.2686	0.1784	0.0039	0.0701
	Sig. (2-tailed)	0.9746	0.5140	0.1725	0.7591	0.1754	0.4249	0.1245	0.3127	0.9825	0.6935
	N	33.0000	33.0000	33.0000	34.0000	33.0000	34.0000	34.0000	34.0000	34.0000	34.0000
sqrtQIIH3c	Pearson Correlation	-0.0144	-0.0806	-0.2486	-0.0153	0.2037	0.1527	0.2557	0.1483	-0.0174	0.1075
	Sig. (2-tailed)	0.9366	0.6556	0.1630	0.9317	0.2554	0.3886	0.1444	0.4025	0.9223	0.5453
	N	33.0000	33.0000	33.0000	34.0000	33.0000	34.0000	34.0000	34.0000	34.0000	34.0000
sqrtQIIH3d	Pearson Correlation	-0.1081	-0.2696	-0.0398	-0.0298	0.1533	0.0579	0.2526	0.1568	0.0510	0.1420
	Sig. (2-tailed)	0.5493	0.1292	0.8260	0.8671	0.3942	0.7448	0.1495	0.3758	0.7744	0.4232
	N	33.0000	33.0000	33.0000	34.0000	33.0000	34.0000	34.0000	34.0000	34.0000	34.0000
sqrtQIIH3e	Pearson Correlation	-0.1729	-0.3563	-0.0119	-0.0830	0.1342	-0.0009	0.2093	0.2280	-0.0092	0.0257
	Sig. (2-tailed)	0.3359	0.0419	0.9476	0.6407	0.4566	0.9959	0.2348	0.1946	0.9590	0.8853
	N	33.0000	33.0000	33.0000	34.0000	33.0000	34.0000	34.0000	34.0000	34.0000	34.0000
sqrtQIIIA1a	Pearson Correlation	-0.0986	0.0263	0.0994	0.4835	-0.0695	0.0358	0.1463	0.1107	0.3917	0.1148
	Sig. (2-tailed)	0.5790	0.8827	0.5760	0.0038	0.6959	0.8383	0.4090	0.5333	0.0220	0.5114
	N	34.0000	34.0000	34.0000	34.0000	34.0000	35.0000	34.0000	34.0000	34.0000	35.0000
sqrtQIIIA1b	Pearson Correlation	0.3092	0.2589	0.1914	-0.0555	0.0196	0.1176	0.0687	0.0435	0.0541	0.1423
	Sig. (2-tailed)	0.0707	0.1331	0.2707	0.7517	0.9111	0.4946	0.6951	0.8039	0.7578	0.4077
	N	35.0000	35.0000	35.0000	35.0000	35.0000	36.0000	35.0000	35.0000	35.0000	36.0000
sqrtQIIIA1c	Pearson Correlation	0.4340	0.3175	0.3293	0.0273	0.0674	0.1689	0.1978	0.1071	0.0046	0.2017
	Sig. (2-tailed)	0.0092	0.0631	0.0534	0.8761	0.7007	0.3248	0.2546	0.5401	0.9790	0.2382
	N	35.0000	35.0000	35.0000	35.0000	35.0000	36.0000	35.0000	35.0000	35.0000	36.0000
sqrtQIIIA1d	Pearson Correlation	0.1111	0.3321	0.2041	0.0725	0.0462	0.1085	0.1271	0.0802	0.1755	0.3117
	Sig. (2-tailed)	0.5250	0.0513	0.2396	0.6791	0.7924	0.5288	0.4668	0.6472	0.3132	0.0642
	N	35.0000	35.0000	35.0000	35.0000	35.0000	36.0000	35.0000	35.0000	35.0000	36.0000
sqrtQIIIA1e	Pearson Correlation	0.1761	-0.0099	0.4573	0.1114	0.1435	0.1543	0.2987	0.3721	-0.0018	0.1198
	Sig. (2-tailed)	0.3117	0.9550	0.0057	0.5242	0.4107	0.3688	0.0814	0.0277	0.9917	0.4865
	N	35.0000	35.0000	35.0000	35.0000	35.0000	36.0000	35.0000	35.0000	35.0000	36.0000
sqrtQIIID1a	Pearson Correlation	-0.1301	0.0739	0.1138	0.5321	0.0973	-0.0121	0.3436	0.4333	0.2122	0.3401
	Sig. (2-tailed)	0.4778	0.6879	0.5352	0.0017	0.5964	0.9467	0.0542	0.0132	0.2437	0.0528
	N	32.0000	32.0000	32.0000	32.0000	32.0000	33.0000	32.0000	32.0000	32.0000	33.0000

Correlation Matrix, Dependent Variables (Parametric)		sqrtQIIC1c	Perceived Deterrence Domestic Law-TVP	sqrtQIIC1e	sqrtQIID1a	Level Cooperation Domestic Orgs-CSIE	Level Cooperation Domestic Orgs-DWMD	Level Cooperation Domestic Orgs-TVP	Level Cooperation Domestic Orgs-CBP	sqrtQIIF1a	sqrtQIIF1b
sqrtQIIH1e	Pearson Correlation	0.1001	0.2142	0.1866	-0.0324	0.1161	0.2620	-0.0678	0.1311	0.7178	0.4943
	Sig. (2-tailed)	0.5923	0.2473	0.3149	0.8626	0.5339	0.1544	0.7172	0.4821	0.0000	0.0055
	N	31.0000	31.0000	31.0000	31.0000	31.0000	31.0000	31.0000	31.0000	30.0000	30.0000
sqrtQIIH3a	Pearson Correlation	0.1208	0.3111	0.2111	0.0094	0.0319	0.1892	-0.0689	0.0001	0.7082	0.5305
	Sig. (2-tailed)	0.4960	0.0733	0.2308	0.9577	0.8581	0.2839	0.6988	0.9996	0.0000	0.0015
	N	34.0000	34.0000	34.0000	34.0000	34.0000	34.0000	34.0000	34.0000	32.0000	33.0000
sqrtQIIH3b	Pearson Correlation	0.0877	0.1568	0.0767	-0.0666	-0.0020	0.1949	-0.1476	-0.0710	0.5702	0.6961
	Sig. (2-tailed)	0.6219	0.3759	0.6662	0.7081	0.9910	0.2692	0.4047	0.6898	0.0007	0.0000
	N	34.0000	34.0000	34.0000	34.0000	34.0000	34.0000	34.0000	34.0000	32.0000	33.0000
sqrtQIIH3c	Pearson Correlation	0.0608	0.1510	0.0350	-0.0122	-0.0246	0.1845	-0.0801	-0.0528	0.5733	0.7451
	Sig. (2-tailed)	0.7326	0.3940	0.8441	0.9454	0.8903	0.2963	0.6527	0.7670	0.0006	0.0000
	N	34.0000	34.0000	34.0000	34.0000	34.0000	34.0000	34.0000	34.0000	32.0000	33.0000
sqrtQIIH3d	Pearson Correlation	0.2231	0.3306	0.2468	-0.0624	0.0971	0.2698	-0.0294	-0.0016	0.6263	0.5343
	Sig. (2-tailed)	0.2047	0.0562	0.1594	0.7259	0.5850	0.1228	0.8689	0.9927	0.0001	0.0014
	N	34.0000	34.0000	34.0000	34.0000	34.0000	34.0000	34.0000	34.0000	32.0000	33.0000
sqrtQIIH3e	Pearson Correlation	0.1479	0.1842	0.1727	-0.1582	0.0194	0.1941	-0.1602	0.0240	0.6210	0.4745
	Sig. (2-tailed)	0.4040	0.2971	0.3288	0.3714	0.9133	0.2715	0.3655	0.8928	0.0001	0.0053
	N	34.0000	34.0000	34.0000	34.0000	34.0000	34.0000	34.0000	34.0000	32.0000	33.0000
sqrtQIIIA1a	Pearson Correlation	0.1131	0.1576	0.1061	0.4921	0.1822	0.1739	0.3406	0.2939	0.1595	0.0123
	Sig. (2-tailed)	0.5177	0.3660	0.5441	0.0027	0.2949	0.3177	0.0453	0.0866	0.3914	0.9459
	N	35.0000	35.0000	35.0000	35.0000	35.0000	35.0000	35.0000	35.0000	31.0000	33.0000
sqrtQIIIA1b	Pearson Correlation	0.3808	0.2260	0.2386	-0.0045	0.3594	0.2141	0.1873	-0.0578	-0.2604	-0.0590
	Sig. (2-tailed)	0.0219	0.1850	0.1611	0.9794	0.0314	0.2098	0.2741	0.7378	0.1501	0.7403
	N	36.0000	36.0000	36.0000	36.0000	36.0000	36.0000	36.0000	36.0000	32.0000	34.0000
sqrtQIIIA1c	Pearson Correlation	0.3712	0.2599	0.2426	0.2147	0.3425	0.2766	0.2122	0.0853	-0.3081	0.0163
	Sig. (2-tailed)	0.0258	0.1258	0.1540	0.2087	0.0409	0.1025	0.2140	0.6209	0.0863	0.9273
	N	36.0000	36.0000	36.0000	36.0000	36.0000	36.0000	36.0000	36.0000	32.0000	34.0000
sqrtQIIIA1d	Pearson Correlation	0.4705	0.3727	0.2825	0.0503	0.2440	0.0821	0.3122	0.0620	-0.2370	-0.1305
	Sig. (2-tailed)	0.0038	0.0252	0.0950	0.7707	0.1515	0.6342	0.0638	0.7192	0.1916	0.4620
	N	36.0000	36.0000	36.0000	36.0000	36.0000	36.0000	36.0000	36.0000	32.0000	34.0000
sqrtQIIIA1e	Pearson Correlation	0.3193	0.1159	0.1462	0.2763	0.2423	0.3109	0.1111	0.3090	-0.0338	-0.0017
	Sig. (2-tailed)	0.0577	0.5007	0.3949	0.1029	0.1546	0.0649	0.5190	0.0667	0.8543	0.9922
	N	36.0000	36.0000	36.0000	36.0000	36.0000	36.0000	36.0000	36.0000	32.0000	34.0000
sqrtQIIID1a	Pearson Correlation	0.2408	0.2690	0.1855	0.4991	0.1915	0.2390	0.4288	0.4754	0.2053	0.2206
	Sig. (2-tailed)	0.1771	0.1301	0.3015	0.0031	0.2858	0.1804	0.0128	0.0052	0.2764	0.2250
	N	33.0000	33.0000	33.0000	33.0000	33.0000	33.0000	33.0000	33.0000	30.0000	32.0000

Table A6, continued (Row 7, Col 7)

Correlation Matrix, Dependent Variables (Parametric)		sqrtQIIF1c	sqrtQIIF1d	sqrtQIIF1e	sqrtQIIF3a	sqrtQIIF3b	sqrtQIIF3c	sqrtQIIF3d	sqrtQIIF3e	sqrtQIIH1a	sqrtQIIH1b
sqrtQIIH1e	Pearson Correlation	0.2940	0.5099	0.7828	0.7226	0.5732	0.4521	0.7800	0.8132	0.8161	0.6404
	Sig. (2-tailed)	0.1148	0.0040	0.0000	0.0000	0.0012	0.0138	0.0000	0.0000	0.0000	0.0001
	N	30.0000	30.0000	30.0000	29.0000	29.0000	29.0000	29.0000	29.0000	31.0000	31.0000
sqrtQIIH3a	Pearson Correlation	0.2630	0.4935	0.5765	0.8414	0.5160	0.4233	0.6789	0.6569	0.8866	0.5014
	Sig. (2-tailed)	0.1392	0.0035	0.0004	0.0000	0.0025	0.0158	0.0000	0.0001	0.0000	0.0035
	N	33.0000	33.0000	33.0000	31.0000	32.0000	32.0000	32.0000	31.0000	31.0000	32.0000
sqrtQIIH3b	Pearson Correlation	0.4814	0.4272	0.5366	0.5591	0.7108	0.6323	0.5801	0.6032	0.5679	0.9492
	Sig. (2-tailed)	0.0046	0.0132	0.0013	0.0011	0.0000	0.0001	0.0005	0.0003	0.0009	0.0000
	N	33.0000	33.0000	33.0000	31.0000	32.0000	32.0000	32.0000	31.0000	31.0000	32.0000
sqrtQIIH3c	Pearson Correlation	0.5506	0.4932	0.5155	0.6354	0.7434	0.6439	0.6169	0.6209	0.6450	0.8736
	Sig. (2-tailed)	0.0009	0.0035	0.0021	0.0001	0.0000	0.0001	0.0002	0.0002	0.0001	0.0000
	N	33.0000	33.0000	33.0000	31.0000	32.0000	32.0000	32.0000	31.0000	31.0000	32.0000
sqrtQIIH3d	Pearson Correlation	0.2574	0.4714	0.5662	0.7640	0.6066	0.4735	0.7237	0.7275	0.8188	0.6697
	Sig. (2-tailed)	0.1481	0.0056	0.0006	0.0000	0.0002	0.0062	0.0000	0.0000	0.0000	0.0000
	N	33.0000	33.0000	33.0000	31.0000	32.0000	32.0000	32.0000	31.0000	31.0000	32.0000
sqrtQIIH3e	Pearson Correlation	0.1324	0.3442	0.6302	0.6940	0.5249	0.4059	0.6489	0.6992	0.6878	0.6697
	Sig. (2-tailed)	0.4625	0.0498	0.0001	0.0000	0.0020	0.0212	0.0001	0.0000	0.0000	0.0000
	N	33.0000	33.0000	33.0000	31.0000	32.0000	32.0000	32.0000	31.0000	31.0000	32.0000
sqrtQIIIA1a	Pearson Correlation	0.2282	0.3475	0.0369	0.0369	0.0173	0.0867	0.1116	0.0707	-0.0251	-0.3571
	Sig. (2-tailed)	0.2015	0.0475	0.8384	0.8440	0.9252	0.6371	0.5432	0.7056	0.8951	0.0448
	N	33.0000	33.0000	33.0000	31.0000	32.0000	32.0000	32.0000	31.0000	30.0000	32.0000
sqrtQIIIA1b	Pearson Correlation	-0.1073	-0.1862	-0.2143	-0.2298	0.2334	0.2856	-0.0151	0.0478	-0.1300	0.1708
	Sig. (2-tailed)	0.5459	0.2916	0.2236	0.2058	0.1912	0.1071	0.9337	0.7951	0.4858	0.3420
	N	34.0000	34.0000	34.0000	32.0000	33.0000	33.0000	33.0000	32.0000	31.0000	33.0000
sqrtQIIIA1c	Pearson Correlation	0.0488	-0.0947	-0.2657	-0.1798	0.3223	0.3829	0.0305	0.0673	-0.1069	0.1289
	Sig. (2-tailed)	0.7841	0.5944	0.1288	0.3249	0.0673	0.0279	0.8661	0.7146	0.5672	0.4747
	N	34.0000	34.0000	34.0000	32.0000	33.0000	33.0000	33.0000	32.0000	31.0000	33.0000
sqrtQIIIA1d	Pearson Correlation	-0.0392	-0.0314	-0.1991	-0.1325	0.1035	0.1528	0.0265	0.0400	-0.1186	-0.0993
	Sig. (2-tailed)	0.8259	0.8599	0.2589	0.4699	0.5664	0.3960	0.8835	0.8277	0.5252	0.5825
	N	34.0000	34.0000	34.0000	32.0000	33.0000	33.0000	33.0000	32.0000	31.0000	33.0000
sqrtQIIIA1e	Pearson Correlation	-0.0602	0.0150	0.0981	-0.0454	0.2106	0.2647	0.1542	0.2479	-0.0656	0.0559
	Sig. (2-tailed)	0.7351	0.9327	0.5810	0.8051	0.2393	0.1366	0.3915	0.1713	0.7258	0.7572
	N	34.0000	34.0000	34.0000	32.0000	33.0000	33.0000	33.0000	32.0000	31.0000	33.0000
sqrtQIIID1a	Pearson Correlation	0.4435	0.2604	0.2121	0.3182	0.3040	0.3853	0.2708	0.2642	0.3384	0.1287
	Sig. (2-tailed)	0.0110	0.1500	0.2440	0.0865	0.0964	0.0323	0.1406	0.1583	0.0726	0.4901
	N	32.0000	32.0000	32.0000	30.0000	31.0000	31.0000	31.0000	30.0000	29.0000	31.0000

Table A6, continued (Row 7, Col 8)

Correlation Matrix, Dependent Variables (Parametric)		sqrtQIIH1c	sqrtQIIH1d	sqrtQIIH1e	sqrtQIIH3a	sqrtQIIH3b	sqrtQIIH3c	sqrtQIIH3d	sqrtQIIH3e	sqrtQIIIA1a	sqrtQIIIA1b
sqrtQIIH1e	Pearson Correlation	0.6353	0.8696	1.0000	0.7125	0.6618	0.6001	0.7868	0.8589	-0.0741	0.0419
	Sig. (2-tailed)	0.0001	0.0000	.	0.0000	0.0001	0.0004	0.0000	0.0000	0.6970	0.8230
	N	31.0000	31.0000	31.0000	31.0000	31.0000	31.0000	31.0000	31.0000	30.0000	31.0000
sqrtQIIH3a	Pearson Correlation	0.6101	0.7497	0.7125	1.0000	0.6130	0.6788	0.8916	0.7986	-0.0604	-0.0652
	Sig. (2-tailed)	0.0002	0.0000	0.0000	.	0.0001	0.0000	0.0000	0.0000	0.7386	0.7142
	N	32.0000	32.0000	31.0000	34.0000	34.0000	34.0000	34.0000	34.0000	33.0000	34.0000
sqrtQIIH3b	Pearson Correlation	0.8754	0.7198	0.6618	0.6130	1.0000	0.9254	0.7391	0.7418	-0.2741	0.1475
	Sig. (2-tailed)	0.0000	0.0000	0.0001	0.0001	.	0.0000	0.0000	0.0000	0.1227	0.4051
	N	32.0000	32.0000	31.0000	34.0000	34.0000	34.0000	34.0000	34.0000	33.0000	34.0000
sqrtQIIH3c	Pearson Correlation	0.9709	0.7897	0.6001	0.6788	0.9254	1.0000	0.7810	0.6712	-0.2059	0.0407
	Sig. (2-tailed)	0.0000	0.0000	0.0004	0.0000	0.0000	.	0.0000	0.0000	0.2502	0.8193
	N	32.0000	32.0000	31.0000	34.0000	34.0000	34.0000	34.0000	34.0000	33.0000	34.0000
sqrtQIIH3d	Pearson Correlation	0.7089	0.8697	0.7868	0.8916	0.7391	0.7810	1.0000	0.9142	-0.0964	0.0350
	Sig. (2-tailed)	0.0000	0.0000	0.0000	0.0000	0.0000	0.0000	.	0.0000	0.5935	0.8442
	N	32.0000	32.0000	31.0000	34.0000	34.0000	34.0000	34.0000	34.0000	33.0000	34.0000
sqrtQIIH3e	Pearson Correlation	0.6169	0.7940	0.8589	0.7986	0.7418	0.6712	0.9142	1.0000	-0.1520	0.1237
	Sig. (2-tailed)	0.0002	0.0000	0.0000	0.0000	0.0000	0.0000	0.0000	.	0.3984	0.4857
	N	32.0000	32.0000	31.0000	34.0000	34.0000	34.0000	34.0000	34.0000	33.0000	34.0000
sqrtQIIIA1a	Pearson Correlation	-0.1949	-0.0654	-0.0741	-0.0604	-0.2741	-0.2059	-0.0964	-0.1520	1.0000	0.2259
	Sig. (2-tailed)	0.2934	0.7265	0.6970	0.7386	0.1227	0.2502	0.5935	0.3984	.	0.1919
	N	31.0000	31.0000	30.0000	33.0000	33.0000	33.0000	33.0000	33.0000	35.0000	35.0000
sqrtQIIIA1b	Pearson Correlation	0.0105	-0.0886	0.0419	-0.0652	0.1475	0.0407	0.0350	0.1237	0.2259	1.0000
	Sig. (2-tailed)	0.9543	0.6297	0.8230	0.7142	0.4051	0.8193	0.8442	0.4857	0.1919	.
	N	32.0000	32.0000	31.0000	34.0000	34.0000	34.0000	34.0000	34.0000	35.0000	36.0000
sqrtQIIIA1c	Pearson Correlation	0.0961	-0.0641	-0.0855	-0.0204	0.1099	0.1363	0.0782	0.0256	0.3507	0.8490
	Sig. (2-tailed)	0.6009	0.7273	0.6474	0.9090	0.5360	0.4420	0.6603	0.8858	0.0389	0.0000
	N	32.0000	32.0000	31.0000	34.0000	34.0000	34.0000	34.0000	34.0000	35.0000	36.0000
sqrtQIIIA1d	Pearson Correlation	-0.0148	0.0261	-0.0285	0.0002	-0.0091	0.0272	0.1255	0.1069	0.5148	0.6948
	Sig. (2-tailed)	0.9359	0.8873	0.8788	0.9990	0.9594	0.8786	0.4794	0.5475	0.0016	0.0000
	N	32.0000	32.0000	31.0000	34.0000	34.0000	34.0000	34.0000	34.0000	35.0000	36.0000
sqrtQIIIA1e	Pearson Correlation	-0.0148	0.0853	0.2824	0.0318	0.0986	-0.0189	0.1446	0.3204	0.4789	0.6515
	Sig. (2-tailed)	0.9361	0.6425	0.1237	0.8584	0.5792	0.9153	0.4146	0.0647	0.0036	0.0000
	N	32.0000	32.0000	31.0000	34.0000	34.0000	34.0000	34.0000	34.0000	35.0000	36.0000
sqrtQIIID1a	Pearson Correlation	0.3094	0.3239	0.3147	0.3058	0.1909	0.2906	0.3321	0.2186	0.3686	-0.0887
	Sig. (2-tailed)	0.0962	0.0808	0.0964	0.0888	0.2952	0.1066	0.0633	0.2294	0.0379	0.6235
	N	30.0000	30.0000	29.0000	32.0000	32.0000	32.0000	32.0000	32.0000	32.0000	33.0000

Table A6, continued (Row 7, Col 9)

Correlation Matrix, Dependent Variables (Parametric)		sqrtQIIIA1c	sqrtQIIIA1d	sqrtQIIIA1e	sqrtQIIID1a	Level Cooperation Domestic Orgs-CNDPS	Level Cooperation Domestic Orgs-CNBC	Level Cooperation Domestic Orgs-CSTP	Level Cooperation Domestic Orgs-TRIPS	sqrtQIIID2a	Level Cooperation International Orgs-CNDPS
sqrtQIIH1e	Pearson Correlation	-0.0855	-0.0285	0.2824	0.3147	0.1952	0.2686	0.1647	0.2562	0.2060	0.2287
	Sig. (2-tailed)	0.6474	0.8788	0.1237	0.0964	0.3014	0.1512	0.3844	0.1717	0.2747	0.2159
	N	31.0000	31.0000	31.0000	29.0000	30.0000	30.0000	30.0000	30.0000	30.0000	31.0000
sqrtQIIH3a	Pearson Correlation	-0.0204	0.0002	0.0318	0.3058	0.2213	0.3407	0.1701	0.1917	0.1149	0.1964
	Sig. (2-tailed)	0.9090	0.9990	0.8584	0.0888	0.2159	0.0524	0.3439	0.2852	0.5244	0.2657
	N	34.0000	34.0000	34.0000	32.0000	33.0000	33.0000	33.0000	33.0000	33.0000	34.0000
sqrtQIIH3b	Pearson Correlation	0.1099	-0.0091	0.0986	0.1909	0.2514	0.3091	0.1712	0.2375	0.2231	0.3192
	Sig. (2-tailed)	0.5360	0.9594	0.5792	0.2952	0.1581	0.0801	0.3408	0.1833	0.2121	0.0658
	N	34.0000	34.0000	34.0000	32.0000	33.0000	33.0000	33.0000	33.0000	33.0000	34.0000
sqrtQIIH3c	Pearson Correlation	0.1363	0.0272	-0.0189	0.2906	0.2606	0.3617	0.2459	0.2791	0.2606	0.3171
	Sig. (2-tailed)	0.4420	0.8786	0.9153	0.1066	0.1430	0.0386	0.1678	0.1158	0.1430	0.0677
	N	34.0000	34.0000	34.0000	32.0000	33.0000	33.0000	33.0000	33.0000	33.0000	34.0000
sqrtQIIH3d	Pearson Correlation	0.0782	0.1255	0.1446	0.3321	0.3865	0.4591	0.3474	0.3436	0.1569	0.2830
	Sig. (2-tailed)	0.6603	0.4794	0.4146	0.0633	0.0263	0.0072	0.0476	0.0503	0.3831	0.1048
	N	34.0000	34.0000	34.0000	32.0000	33.0000	33.0000	33.0000	33.0000	33.0000	34.0000
sqrtQIIH3e	Pearson Correlation	0.0256	0.1069	0.3204	0.2186	0.2565	0.3025	0.2382	0.2872	0.0475	0.1744
	Sig. (2-tailed)	0.8858	0.5475	0.0647	0.2294	0.1496	0.0871	0.1820	0.1051	0.7929	0.3238
	N	34.0000	34.0000	34.0000	32.0000	33.0000	33.0000	33.0000	33.0000	33.0000	34.0000
sqrtQIIIA1a	Pearson Correlation	0.3507	0.5148	0.4789	0.3686	0.1688	0.1747	0.2413	0.1641	0.4457	0.1327
	Sig. (2-tailed)	0.0389	0.0016	0.0036	0.0379	0.3399	0.3232	0.1692	0.3537	0.0082	0.4474
	N	35.0000	35.0000	35.0000	32.0000	34.0000	34.0000	34.0000	34.0000	34.0000	35.0000
sqrtQIIIA1b	Pearson Correlation	0.8490	0.6948	0.6515	-0.0887	0.3611	0.1456	0.2324	0.0813	0.0042	0.3385
	Sig. (2-tailed)	0.0000	0.0000	0.0000	0.6235	0.0331	0.4041	0.1791	0.6425	0.9810	0.0435
	N	36.0000	36.0000	36.0000	33.0000	35.0000	35.0000	35.0000	35.0000	35.0000	36.0000
sqrtQIIIA1c	Pearson Correlation	1.0000	0.7061	0.6206	0.1355	0.3847	0.3799	0.3031	0.2621	0.1217	0.3611
	Sig. (2-tailed)	.	0.0000	0.0001	0.4522	0.0225	0.0244	0.0768	0.1282	0.4862	0.0305
	N	36.0000	36.0000	36.0000	33.0000	35.0000	35.0000	35.0000	35.0000	35.0000	36.0000
sqrtQIIIA1d	Pearson Correlation	0.7061	1.0000	0.6351	0.2733	0.3798	0.1910	0.4205	0.2136	0.1578	0.3697
	Sig. (2-tailed)	0.0000	.	0.0000	0.1238	0.0244	0.2718	0.0119	0.2180	0.3651	0.0265
	N	36.0000	36.0000	36.0000	33.0000	35.0000	35.0000	35.0000	35.0000	35.0000	36.0000
sqrtQIIIA1e	Pearson Correlation	0.6206	0.6351	1.0000	0.1785	0.2279	0.2346	0.1730	0.3145	0.1320	0.2666
	Sig. (2-tailed)	0.0001	0.0000	.	0.3202	0.1880	0.1750	0.3203	0.0657	0.4499	0.1159
	N	36.0000	36.0000	36.0000	33.0000	35.0000	35.0000	35.0000	35.0000	35.0000	36.0000
sqrtQIIID1a	Pearson Correlation	0.1355	0.2733	0.1785	1.0000	0.6244	0.7451	0.7309	0.8610	0.6773	0.4875
	Sig. (2-tailed)	0.4522	0.1238	0.3202	.	0.0001	0.0000	0.0000	0.0000	0.0000	0.0040
	N	33.0000	33.0000	33.0000	33.0000	33.0000	33.0000	33.0000	33.0000	33.0000	33.0000

Table A6, continued (Row 7, Col 10)

Correlation Matrix, Dependent Variables (Parametric)		Level Cooperation International Orgs-CNBC	Level Cooperation International Orgs-CSTP	sqrtQIIID2e	sqrtQIVA1	sqrtQIVA2	sqrtQIVA3	sqrtQIVA5	sqrtQIVA7	sqrtQIVA8	Political Ideology
sqrtQIIH1e	Pearson Correlation	0.2694	0.2167	0.3099	-0.0097	0.0371	0.2499	0.2606	-0.0777	-0.2274	0.1074
	Sig. (2-tailed)	0.1427	0.2416	0.0898	0.9588	0.8429	0.1829	0.1721	0.6780	0.2268	0.5864
	N	31.0000	31.0000	31.0000	31.0000	31.0000	30.0000	29.0000	31.0000	30.0000	28.0000
sqrtQIIH3a	Pearson Correlation	0.2917	0.3070	0.2616	0.0443	0.0329	0.2085	0.1032	-0.0003	-0.2805	0.0473
	Sig. (2-tailed)	0.0941	0.0774	0.1351	0.8035	0.8535	0.2442	0.5742	0.9986	0.1139	0.8004
	N	34.0000	34.0000	34.0000	34.0000	34.0000	33.0000	32.0000	34.0000	33.0000	31.0000
sqrtQIIH3b	Pearson Correlation	0.3596	0.4034	0.4203	0.1762	0.0884	0.2821	0.3122	-0.0973	-0.2809	0.2016
	Sig. (2-tailed)	0.0367	0.0180	0.0133	0.3188	0.6193	0.1117	0.0819	0.5840	0.1133	0.2767
	N	34.0000	34.0000	34.0000	34.0000	34.0000	33.0000	32.0000	34.0000	33.0000	31.0000
sqrtQIIH3c	Pearson Correlation	0.3551	0.4368	0.4287	0.2587	0.1112	0.3266	0.3255	-0.0759	-0.2665	0.1985
	Sig. (2-tailed)	0.0393	0.0098	0.0114	0.1396	0.5311	0.0636	0.0691	0.6695	0.1338	0.2843
	N	34.0000	34.0000	34.0000	34.0000	34.0000	33.0000	32.0000	34.0000	33.0000	31.0000
sqrtQIIH3d	Pearson Correlation	0.3395	0.3652	0.3657	0.0605	0.0392	0.2759	0.2533	0.0446	-0.2701	0.0586
	Sig. (2-tailed)	0.0495	0.0337	0.0334	0.7340	0.8259	0.1201	0.1619	0.8023	0.1285	0.7540
	N	34.0000	34.0000	34.0000	34.0000	34.0000	33.0000	32.0000	34.0000	33.0000	31.0000
sqrtQIIH3e	Pearson Correlation	0.2175	0.2460	0.2936	-0.0270	0.0141	0.2502	0.0530	0.0377	-0.2608	0.0391
	Sig. (2-tailed)	0.2165	0.1608	0.0919	0.8794	0.9371	0.1603	0.7731	0.8325	0.1427	0.8344
	N	34.0000	34.0000	34.0000	34.0000	34.0000	33.0000	32.0000	34.0000	33.0000	31.0000
sqrtQIIIA1a	Pearson Correlation	0.1273	0.2966	0.1620	-0.0305	0.1332	0.1338	-0.1075	-0.1239	-0.1046	0.2577
	Sig. (2-tailed)	0.4660	0.0836	0.3525	0.8618	0.4456	0.4505	0.5515	0.4782	0.5559	0.1545
	N	35.0000	35.0000	35.0000	35.0000	35.0000	34.0000	33.0000	35.0000	34.0000	32.0000
sqrtQIIIA1b	Pearson Correlation	0.2883	0.3935	0.2210	0.1503	0.1325	0.2814	-0.0871	-0.0378	-0.0375	0.0529
	Sig. (2-tailed)	0.0882	0.0176	0.1953	0.3817	0.4412	0.1015	0.6241	0.8268	0.8308	0.7698
	N	36.0000	36.0000	36.0000	36.0000	36.0000	35.0000	34.0000	36.0000	35.0000	33.0000
sqrtQIIIA1c	Pearson Correlation	0.3753	0.4306	0.3836	0.2397	0.2001	0.3763	0.0113	-0.0143	-0.0063	0.2063
	Sig. (2-tailed)	0.0241	0.0087	0.0209	0.1591	0.2421	0.0259	0.9496	0.9342	0.9714	0.2495
	N	36.0000	36.0000	36.0000	36.0000	36.0000	35.0000	34.0000	36.0000	35.0000	33.0000
sqrtQIIIA1d	Pearson Correlation	0.3133	0.4785	0.2707	0.0857	0.1293	0.3482	-0.1313	-0.0541	-0.0047	0.0506
	Sig. (2-tailed)	0.0628	0.0032	0.1102	0.6190	0.4522	0.0404	0.4593	0.7538	0.9785	0.7798
	N	36.0000	36.0000	36.0000	36.0000	36.0000	35.0000	34.0000	36.0000	35.0000	33.0000
sqrtQIIIA1e	Pearson Correlation	0.2476	0.3484	0.3784	0.0085	0.1471	0.2982	-0.1273	-0.1297	0.0381	0.2530
	Sig. (2-tailed)	0.1454	0.0373	0.0229	0.9607	0.3918	0.0819	0.4732	0.4509	0.8280	0.1554
	N	36.0000	36.0000	36.0000	36.0000	36.0000	35.0000	34.0000	36.0000	35.0000	33.0000
sqrtQIIID1a	Pearson Correlation	0.5190	0.5302	0.5762	0.0581	-0.0825	0.2669	0.2827	-0.1366	0.0378	0.2165
	Sig. (2-tailed)	0.0020	0.0015	0.0004	0.7480	0.6479	0.1397	0.1233	0.4485	0.8375	0.2420
	N	33.0000	33.0000	33.0000	33.0000	33.0000	32.0000	31.0000	33.0000	32.0000	31.0000

Table A6, continued (Row 8, Col 1)

Correlation Matrix, Dependent Variables (Parametric)		Importance of Smuggling-Endangered Species	reflectsqrtQ1A1b	reflectsqrtQ1A1c	reflectsqrtQ1A1d	reflectsqrtQ1A1e	sqrtQ1B1a	Knowledge of Smuggling-Narcotics	Knowledge of Smuggling-Weapons	Knowledge of Smuggling-Humans	Knowledge of Smuggling-Contraband
Level Cooperation Domestic Orgs-CNDPS	Pearson Correlation	-0.0518	-0.0744	0.1564	0.1160	-0.0204	0.2400	0.3670	0.2723	0.1638	0.1460
	Sig. (2-tailed)	0.7677	0.6711	0.3696	0.5069	0.9072	0.1649	0.0301	0.1136	0.3471	0.4028
	N	35.0000	35.0000	35.0000	35.0000	35.0000	35.0000	35.0000	35.0000	35.0000	35.0000
Level Cooperation Domestic Orgs-CNBC	Pearson Correlation	-0.1244	0.0249	0.1364	0.1835	-0.0434	0.2866	0.2308	0.4812	0.1396	0.3090
	Sig. (2-tailed)	0.4764	0.8870	0.4348	0.2913	0.8045	0.0951	0.1821	0.0034	0.4239	0.0709
	N	35.0000	35.0000	35.0000	35.0000	35.0000	35.0000	35.0000	35.0000	35.0000	35.0000
Level Cooperation Domestic Orgs-CSTP	Pearson Correlation	-0.1646	0.0051	0.1535	0.0920	-0.0947	0.2611	0.2171	0.2043	0.2787	0.2677
	Sig. (2-tailed)	0.3448	0.9767	0.3786	0.5993	0.5886	0.1298	0.2103	0.2391	0.1050	0.1200
	N	35.0000	35.0000	35.0000	35.0000	35.0000	35.0000	35.0000	35.0000	35.0000	35.0000
Level Cooperation Domestic Orgs-TRIPS	Pearson Correlation	-0.1113	0.1878	0.3916	0.2575	-0.0987	0.2429	-0.0035	0.2767	0.0033	0.2737
	Sig. (2-tailed)	0.5246	0.2800	0.0200	0.1353	0.5725	0.1597	0.9839	0.1075	0.9852	0.1117
	N	35.0000	35.0000	35.0000	35.0000	35.0000	35.0000	35.0000	35.0000	35.0000	35.0000
sqrtQIIID2a	Pearson Correlation	0.0214	0.2075	0.2276	0.1701	-0.0940	0.5361	-0.0078	0.2198	0.1284	0.1527
	Sig. (2-tailed)	0.9028	0.2317	0.1886	0.3285	0.5913	0.0009	0.9646	0.2044	0.4625	0.3810
	N	35.0000	35.0000	35.0000	35.0000	35.0000	35.0000	35.0000	35.0000	35.0000	35.0000
Level Cooperation International Orgs-CNDPS	Pearson Correlation	0.1124	0.0021	0.1330	0.0575	-0.0534	0.1694	0.2711	0.2907	0.1288	0.0678
	Sig. (2-tailed)	0.5139	0.9902	0.4393	0.7391	0.7571	0.3233	0.1098	0.0855	0.4541	0.6944
	N	36.0000	36.0000	36.0000	36.0000	36.0000	36.0000	36.0000	36.0000	36.0000	36.0000
Level Cooperation International Orgs-CNBC	Pearson Correlation	0.0449	0.0023	0.0860	0.1102	-0.0231	0.1797	0.2604	0.4227	0.1151	0.1025
	Sig. (2-tailed)	0.7949	0.9895	0.6180	0.5222	0.8936	0.2943	0.1251	0.0102	0.5040	0.5518
	N	36.0000	36.0000	36.0000	36.0000	36.0000	36.0000	36.0000	36.0000	36.0000	36.0000
Level Cooperation International Orgs-CSTP	Pearson Correlation	0.0549	0.0373	0.0793	0.1459	-0.0056	0.2332	0.2177	0.2247	0.2938	0.1867
	Sig. (2-tailed)	0.7504	0.8292	0.6459	0.3959	0.9740	0.1710	0.2021	0.1876	0.0820	0.2757
	N	36.0000	36.0000	36.0000	36.0000	36.0000	36.0000	36.0000	36.0000	36.0000	36.0000
sqrtQIIID2e	Pearson Correlation	-0.0110	0.0624	0.2157	0.2396	-0.1143	0.1194	0.0106	0.3393	0.0382	0.1958
	Sig. (2-tailed)	0.9491	0.7177	0.2065	0.1593	0.5070	0.4880	0.9511	0.0429	0.8247	0.2524
	N	36.0000	36.0000	36.0000	36.0000	36.0000	36.0000	36.0000	36.0000	36.0000	36.0000
sqrtQIVA1	Pearson Correlation	0.1272	-0.1992	0.0037	-0.1471	-0.2422	0.1477	0.0975	0.1958	0.1268	0.1346
	Sig. (2-tailed)	0.4597	0.2442	0.9827	0.3919	0.1546	0.3899	0.5715	0.2525	0.4610	0.4339
	N	36.0000	36.0000	36.0000	36.0000	36.0000	36.0000	36.0000	36.0000	36.0000	36.0000
sqrtQIVA2	Pearson Correlation	0.1038	0.0760	-0.0544	-0.2229	-0.0831	0.1831	-0.1039	0.0264	0.0276	0.0214
	Sig. (2-tailed)	0.5471	0.6595	0.7528	0.1914	0.6301	0.2852	0.5464	0.8784	0.8732	0.9013
	N	36.0000	36.0000	36.0000	36.0000	36.0000	36.0000	36.0000	36.0000	36.0000	36.0000
sqrtQIVA3	Pearson Correlation	-0.2036	-0.0784	-0.0162	-0.1433	-0.0897	-0.0036	0.0204	0.1837	0.2654	0.1990
	Sig. (2-tailed)	0.2408	0.6545	0.9265	0.4115	0.6085	0.9835	0.9073	0.2908	0.1234	0.2517
	N	35.0000	35.0000	35.0000	35.0000	35.0000	35.0000	35.0000	35.0000	35.0000	35.0000

Table A6, continued (Row 8, Col 2)

Correlation Matrix, Dependent Variables (Parametric)		sqrtQ1E1a	Personal Resource Challenges- Lack of Time	Personal Resource Challenges- Lack of Knowledge	Personal Resource Challenges- Lack of Training	sqrtQ1E1e	Personal Resource Challenges- Excessive Admin Paperwork	Personal Resource Challenges- Ineffective Technology	Personal Resource Challenges- Ineffective Strategic Focus	Personal Resource Challenges- Ineffective Tactical Policy	Personal Resource Challenges- Lack of Clarity in Duties
Level Cooperation Domestic Orgs-CNDPS	Pearson Correlation	-0.1191	0.0242	-0.3494	-0.3143	-0.0257	0.0392	-0.3843	-0.2957	-0.3184	-0.1994
	Sig. (2-tailed)	0.4956	0.8903	0.0397	0.0660	0.8833	0.8230	0.0227	0.0845	0.0623	0.2509
	N	35.0000	35.0000	35.0000	35.0000	35.0000	35.0000	35.0000	35.0000	35.0000	35.0000
Level Cooperation Domestic Orgs-CNBC	Pearson Correlation	-0.1925	-0.0511	-0.3097	-0.2839	0.1179	0.0146	-0.4478	-0.2249	-0.3398	-0.2423
	Sig. (2-tailed)	0.2680	0.7705	0.0702	0.0984	0.4998	0.9334	0.0070	0.1940	0.0458	0.1608
	N	35.0000	35.0000	35.0000	35.0000	35.0000	35.0000	35.0000	35.0000	35.0000	35.0000
Level Cooperation Domestic Orgs-CSTP	Pearson Correlation	-0.1203	0.1117	-0.1833	-0.1215	0.0768	0.0791	-0.3132	-0.1131	-0.2203	-0.0036
	Sig. (2-tailed)	0.4912	0.5231	0.2919	0.4870	0.6610	0.6514	0.0669	0.5179	0.2034	0.9835
	N	35.0000	35.0000	35.0000	35.0000	35.0000	35.0000	35.0000	35.0000	35.0000	35.0000
Level Cooperation Domestic Orgs-TRIPS	Pearson Correlation	-0.0535	0.0041	-0.2496	-0.1957	0.1020	0.0394	-0.3367	-0.1968	-0.2806	-0.1610
	Sig. (2-tailed)	0.7601	0.9813	0.1481	0.2598	0.5600	0.8221	0.0479	0.2572	0.1025	0.3556
	N	35.0000	35.0000	35.0000	35.0000	35.0000	35.0000	35.0000	35.0000	35.0000	35.0000
sqrtQIIID2a	Pearson Correlation	-0.0563	-0.1385	-0.0454	0.0772	0.2775	0.1931	-0.1671	0.0834	-0.0788	-0.0609
	Sig. (2-tailed)	0.7519	0.4277	0.7956	0.6593	0.1066	0.2663	0.3375	0.6337	0.6526	0.7280
	N	34.0000	35.0000	35.0000	35.0000	35.0000	35.0000	35.0000	35.0000	35.0000	35.0000
Level Cooperation International Orgs-CNDPS	Pearson Correlation	-0.0521	-0.1679	-0.1854	-0.1642	0.2058	0.1350	-0.1814	-0.2790	-0.3088	-0.2645
	Sig. (2-tailed)	0.7663	0.3277	0.2791	0.3386	0.2285	0.4324	0.2896	0.0994	0.0669	0.1190
	N	35.0000	36.0000	36.0000	36.0000	36.0000	36.0000	36.0000	36.0000	36.0000	36.0000
Level Cooperation International Orgs-CNBC	Pearson Correlation	-0.1166	-0.2175	-0.1852	-0.1489	0.2551	0.0927	-0.2226	-0.2551	-0.3368	-0.3009
	Sig. (2-tailed)	0.5047	0.2026	0.2795	0.3860	0.1333	0.5908	0.1918	0.1332	0.0446	0.0745
	N	35.0000	36.0000	36.0000	36.0000	36.0000	36.0000	36.0000	36.0000	36.0000	36.0000
Level Cooperation International Orgs-CSTP	Pearson Correlation	-0.0751	-0.0209	-0.0530	-0.0524	0.1915	0.0969	-0.2263	-0.1966	-0.2681	-0.1977
	Sig. (2-tailed)	0.6679	0.9038	0.7586	0.7616	0.2632	0.5738	0.1844	0.2504	0.1139	0.2477
	N	35.0000	36.0000	36.0000	36.0000	36.0000	36.0000	36.0000	36.0000	36.0000	36.0000
sqrtQIIID2e	Pearson Correlation	-0.1284	-0.2123	-0.1736	-0.1508	0.2529	0.0811	-0.2817	-0.2426	-0.3346	-0.3052
	Sig. (2-tailed)	0.4624	0.2138	0.3114	0.3800	0.1366	0.6380	0.0960	0.1540	0.0461	0.0702
	N	35.0000	36.0000	36.0000	36.0000	36.0000	36.0000	36.0000	36.0000	36.0000	36.0000
sqrtQIVA1	Pearson Correlation	0.0884	0.0179	0.2114	0.1371	0.2619	0.3080	0.3243	0.2088	0.2928	0.2937
	Sig. (2-tailed)	0.6135	0.9176	0.2158	0.4251	0.1228	0.0676	0.0537	0.2216	0.0831	0.0821
	N	35.0000	36.0000	36.0000	36.0000	36.0000	36.0000	36.0000	36.0000	36.0000	36.0000
sqrtQIVA2	Pearson Correlation	0.2392	0.0627	0.1892	0.0768	0.2009	0.2318	0.2996	0.2963	0.4052	0.2994
	Sig. (2-tailed)	0.1663	0.7164	0.2690	0.6560	0.2400	0.1738	0.0758	0.0794	0.0142	0.0761
	N	35.0000	36.0000	36.0000	36.0000	36.0000	36.0000	36.0000	36.0000	36.0000	36.0000
sqrtQIVA3	Pearson Correlation	0.3484	0.1729	0.1521	0.1250	0.2528	0.4174	0.2555	0.3183	0.4473	0.3700
	Sig. (2-tailed)	0.0435	0.3206	0.3830	0.4742	0.1428	0.0126	0.1385	0.0624	0.0071	0.0287
	N	34.0000	35.0000	35.0000	35.0000	35.0000	35.0000	35.0000	35.0000	35.0000	35.0000

Table A6, continued (Row 8, Col 3)

Correlation Matrix, Dependent Variables (Parametric)		Personal Resource Challenges-Conflict or Lack Comm Leaders and Employees	sqrtQ1E1I	Personal Resource Challenges-Conflict or Lack Comm International Orgs	Personal Resource Challenges-Conflict or Lack Comm Domestic Orgs	sqrtQ1E3a	Org Resource Challenges-Lack of Time	Org Resource Challenges-Lack of Knowledge	Org Resource Challenges-Lack of Training	sqrtQ1E3e	Org Resource Challenges-Excessive Admin Paperwork
Level Cooperation Domestic Orgs-CNDPS	Pearson Correlation	-0.2432	-0.1364	-0.1258	-0.0970	-0.1200	-0.3383	-0.3248	-0.3530	-0.0810	-0.1288
	Sig. (2-tailed)	0.1592	0.4346	0.4716	0.5793	0.5059	0.0503	0.0609	0.0406	0.6541	0.4677
	N	35.0000	35.0000	35.0000	35.0000	33.0000	34.0000	34.0000	34.0000	33.0000	34.0000
Level Cooperation Domestic Orgs-CNBC	Pearson Correlation	-0.2412	-0.0657	-0.2421	-0.2036	-0.1800	-0.3131	-0.3757	-0.4226	-0.0355	-0.1819
	Sig. (2-tailed)	0.1628	0.7077	0.1611	0.2409	0.3163	0.0714	0.0285	0.0128	0.8446	0.3033
	N	35.0000	35.0000	35.0000	35.0000	33.0000	34.0000	34.0000	34.0000	33.0000	34.0000
Level Cooperation Domestic Orgs-CSTP	Pearson Correlation	-0.1756	-0.1034	-0.0921	-0.0198	-0.1702	-0.2950	-0.1646	-0.1937	-0.0343	-0.0498
	Sig. (2-tailed)	0.3128	0.5545	0.5988	0.9102	0.3436	0.0904	0.3522	0.2724	0.8497	0.7799
	N	35.0000	35.0000	35.0000	35.0000	33.0000	34.0000	34.0000	34.0000	33.0000	34.0000
Level Cooperation Domestic Orgs-TRIPS	Pearson Correlation	-0.1849	-0.0830	-0.1925	-0.1262	-0.2506	-0.4556	-0.3192	-0.3354	0.0295	-0.1475
	Sig. (2-tailed)	0.2877	0.6355	0.2678	0.4701	0.1595	0.0068	0.0657	0.0525	0.8705	0.4051
	N	35.0000	35.0000	35.0000	35.0000	33.0000	34.0000	34.0000	34.0000	33.0000	34.0000
sqrtQIIID2a	Pearson Correlation	-0.2003	0.0048	-0.0771	-0.1538	-0.0594	-0.3044	-0.1769	-0.2034	-0.0190	-0.0482
	Sig. (2-tailed)	0.2487	0.9781	0.6596	0.3778	0.7426	0.0801	0.3168	0.2486	0.9164	0.7868
	N	35.0000	35.0000	35.0000	35.0000	33.0000	34.0000	34.0000	34.0000	33.0000	34.0000
Level Cooperation International Orgs-CNDPS	Pearson Correlation	-0.3302	-0.2251	-0.0630	-0.1353	0.1036	-0.2275	-0.2702	-0.2894	-0.0860	-0.0530
	Sig. (2-tailed)	0.0492	0.1868	0.7150	0.4315	0.5598	0.1888	0.1164	0.0917	0.6287	0.7622
	N	36.0000	36.0000	36.0000	36.0000	34.0000	35.0000	35.0000	35.0000	34.0000	35.0000
Level Cooperation International Orgs-CNBC	Pearson Correlation	-0.3636	-0.2286	-0.1384	-0.2322	0.0984	-0.2063	-0.2763	-0.3140	-0.0732	-0.0612
	Sig. (2-tailed)	0.0293	0.1799	0.4207	0.1729	0.5798	0.2345	0.1081	0.0662	0.6808	0.7269
	N	36.0000	36.0000	36.0000	36.0000	34.0000	35.0000	35.0000	35.0000	34.0000	35.0000
Level Cooperation International Orgs-CSTP	Pearson Correlation	-0.2689	-0.2462	-0.0166	-0.0763	-0.0030	-0.2480	-0.1889	-0.2335	-0.0943	-0.0943
	Sig. (2-tailed)	0.1128	0.1477	0.9236	0.6582	0.9867	0.1509	0.2772	0.1771	0.5959	0.5899
	N	36.0000	36.0000	36.0000	36.0000	34.0000	35.0000	35.0000	35.0000	34.0000	35.0000
sqrtQIIID2e	Pearson Correlation	-0.3400	-0.2096	-0.1955	-0.2643	-0.0716	-0.3042	-0.2873	-0.3437	0.0318	-0.0615
	Sig. (2-tailed)	0.0425	0.2199	0.2531	0.1193	0.6874	0.0756	0.0942	0.0432	0.8582	0.7255
	N	36.0000	36.0000	36.0000	36.0000	34.0000	35.0000	35.0000	35.0000	34.0000	35.0000
sqrtQIVA1	Pearson Correlation	0.2933	0.2187	0.1870	0.2684	0.2920	0.0029	0.2136	0.1882	0.0981	0.0572
	Sig. (2-tailed)	0.0825	0.2001	0.2749	0.1134	0.0938	0.9870	0.2180	0.2789	0.5809	0.7441
	N	36.0000	36.0000	36.0000	36.0000	34.0000	35.0000	35.0000	35.0000	34.0000	35.0000
sqrtQIVA2	Pearson Correlation	0.3287	0.2301	0.2393	0.2483	0.3555	0.1769	0.1306	0.1844	0.0666	0.1212
	Sig. (2-tailed)	0.0503	0.1770	0.1599	0.1443	0.0391	0.3093	0.4546	0.2890	0.7082	0.4880
	N	36.0000	36.0000	36.0000	36.0000	34.0000	35.0000	35.0000	35.0000	34.0000	35.0000
sqrtQIVA3	Pearson Correlation	0.4069	0.3031	0.2714	0.3473	0.2967	-0.0517	0.1567	0.1301	0.2704	0.2113
	Sig. (2-tailed)	0.0153	0.0767	0.1148	0.0409	0.0936	0.7716	0.3763	0.4633	0.1280	0.2303
	N	35.0000	35.0000	35.0000	35.0000	33.0000	34.0000	34.0000	34.0000	33.0000	34.0000

Table A6, continued (Row 8, Col 4)

Correlation Matrix, Dependent Variables (Parametric)		Org Resource Challenges-Ineffective Technology	Org Resource Challenges-Ineffective Strategic Focus	Org Resource Challenges-Ineffective Tactical Policy	Org Resource Challenges-Lack of Clarity in Duties	Org Resource Challenges-Conflict or Lack Comm Leaders and Employees	sqrtQ1E3l	Org Resource Challenges-Conflict or Lack Comm International Orgs	Org Resource Challenges-Conflict or Lack Comm Domestic Orgs	sqrtQIIA1a	Knowledge of Domestic Law-CSIE
Level Cooperation Domestic Orgs-CNDPS	Pearson Correlation	-0.1680	-0.2940	-0.1628	-0.2796	-0.0942	-0.1171	-0.2336	-0.2207	0.0416	0.2483
	Sig. (2-tailed)	0.3424	0.0915	0.3577	0.1093	0.5962	0.5095	0.1837	0.2098	0.8152	0.1567
	N	34.0000	34.0000	34.0000	34.0000	34.0000	34.0000	34.0000	34.0000	34.0000	34.0000
Level Cooperation Domestic Orgs-CNBC	Pearson Correlation	-0.2951	-0.2771	-0.1912	-0.2877	-0.1349	-0.0328	-0.2472	-0.2111	0.1799	0.2263
	Sig. (2-tailed)	0.0902	0.1126	0.2786	0.0989	0.4469	0.8541	0.1586	0.2307	0.3086	0.1980
	N	34.0000	34.0000	34.0000	34.0000	34.0000	34.0000	34.0000	34.0000	34.0000	34.0000
Level Cooperation Domestic Orgs-CSTP	Pearson Correlation	-0.1450	-0.1540	-0.0689	-0.2099	-0.1179	-0.0436	-0.1951	-0.2121	0.1731	0.0270
	Sig. (2-tailed)	0.4133	0.3846	0.6984	0.2334	0.5066	0.8068	0.2688	0.2284	0.3276	0.8796
	N	34.0000	34.0000	34.0000	34.0000	34.0000	34.0000	34.0000	34.0000	34.0000	34.0000
Level Cooperation Domestic Orgs-TRIPS	Pearson Correlation	-0.2648	-0.2889	-0.1827	-0.2803	-0.1270	-0.0632	-0.3522	-0.2948	0.1626	0.0105
	Sig. (2-tailed)	0.1301	0.0975	0.3011	0.1083	0.4741	0.7224	0.0411	0.0905	0.3581	0.9529
	N	34.0000	34.0000	34.0000	34.0000	34.0000	34.0000	34.0000	34.0000	34.0000	34.0000
sqrtQIIID2a	Pearson Correlation	-0.1784	-0.1595	-0.1374	-0.0313	-0.1959	0.0422	-0.0468	-0.0631	0.3801	-0.0543
	Sig. (2-tailed)	0.3128	0.3676	0.4386	0.8605	0.2667	0.8125	0.7927	0.7230	0.0266	0.7602
	N	34.0000	34.0000	34.0000	34.0000	34.0000	34.0000	34.0000	34.0000	34.0000	34.0000
Level Cooperation International Orgs-CNDPS	Pearson Correlation	-0.1089	-0.2729	-0.2079	-0.1810	-0.1156	-0.2323	-0.1102	-0.0994	0.0431	0.2693
	Sig. (2-tailed)	0.5333	0.1127	0.2306	0.2982	0.5086	0.1792	0.5287	0.5698	0.8059	0.1177
	N	35.0000	35.0000	35.0000	35.0000	35.0000	35.0000	35.0000	35.0000	35.0000	35.0000
Level Cooperation International Orgs-CNBC	Pearson Correlation	-0.1526	-0.2741	-0.2227	-0.1936	-0.1167	-0.2091	-0.1208	-0.1121	0.0968	0.2882
	Sig. (2-tailed)	0.3814	0.1111	0.1984	0.2650	0.5043	0.2279	0.4895	0.5216	0.5802	0.0932
	N	35.0000	35.0000	35.0000	35.0000	35.0000	35.0000	35.0000	35.0000	35.0000	35.0000
Level Cooperation International Orgs-CSTP	Pearson Correlation	-0.1341	-0.2184	-0.1647	-0.1137	-0.1419	-0.2572	-0.0355	-0.0277	0.2430	0.1645
	Sig. (2-tailed)	0.4424	0.2074	0.3443	0.5155	0.4161	0.1357	0.8395	0.8744	0.1596	0.3450
	N	35.0000	35.0000	35.0000	35.0000	35.0000	35.0000	35.0000	35.0000	35.0000	35.0000
sqrtQIIID2e	Pearson Correlation	-0.2585	-0.3170	-0.2417	-0.2185	-0.1800	-0.1945	-0.1904	-0.1476	0.1620	0.1353
	Sig. (2-tailed)	0.1337	0.0635	0.1619	0.2074	0.3007	0.2630	0.2734	0.3974	0.3525	0.4382
	N	35.0000	35.0000	35.0000	35.0000	35.0000	35.0000	35.0000	35.0000	35.0000	35.0000
sqrtQIVA1	Pearson Correlation	0.2358	0.3248	0.2058	0.2975	0.1614	0.1144	0.3519	0.3555	-0.1899	0.0265
	Sig. (2-tailed)	0.1726	0.0569	0.2357	0.0826	0.3544	0.5127	0.0382	0.0361	0.2746	0.8798
	N	35.0000	35.0000	35.0000	35.0000	35.0000	35.0000	35.0000	35.0000	35.0000	35.0000
sqrtQIVA2	Pearson Correlation	0.1196	0.1723	0.1873	0.1487	0.1363	0.1141	0.2023	0.1494	-0.0509	-0.0986
	Sig. (2-tailed)	0.4939	0.3222	0.2814	0.3939	0.4349	0.5141	0.2438	0.3917	0.7714	0.5730
	N	35.0000	35.0000	35.0000	35.0000	35.0000	35.0000	35.0000	35.0000	35.0000	35.0000
sqrtQIVA3	Pearson Correlation	0.1978	0.1703	0.2609	0.2110	0.2148	0.1633	0.1834	0.1617	-0.2144	-0.1775
	Sig. (2-tailed)	0.2622	0.3355	0.1362	0.2310	0.2226	0.3562	0.2991	0.3608	0.2233	0.3152
	N	34.0000	34.0000	34.0000	34.0000	34.0000	34.0000	34.0000	34.0000	34.0000	34.0000

Table A6, continued (Row 8, Col 5)

Correlation Matrix, Dependent Variables (Parametric)		Knowledge of Domestic Law-DWMD	Knowledge of Domestic Law-TVP	Knowledge of Domestic Law-CBP	sqrtQIIB1a	Perceived Effectiveness Domestic Govt Support-CSIE	Perceived Effectiveness Domestic Govt Support-DWMD	Perceived Effectiveness Domestic Govt Support TVP	Perceived Effectiveness Domestic Govt Support-CBP	sqrtQIIC1a	Perceived Deterrence Domestic Law-CSIE
Level Cooperation Domestic Orgs-CNDPS	Pearson Correlation	0.1409	0.1655	0.1424	0.2194	0.2778	0.2359	0.3660	0.3414	0.2049	0.5149
	Sig. (2-tailed)	0.4268	0.3497	0.4216	0.2125	0.1116	0.1724	0.0333	0.0481	0.2450	0.0015
	N	34.0000	34.0000	34.0000	34.0000	34.0000	35.0000	34.0000	34.0000	34.0000	35.0000
Level Cooperation Domestic Orgs-CNBC	Pearson Correlation	0.2464	0.1167	0.3494	0.3162	0.2639	0.2289	0.5023	0.4270	0.1394	0.3926
	Sig. (2-tailed)	0.1601	0.5112	0.0428	0.0685	0.1316	0.1859	0.0025	0.0118	0.4319	0.0197
	N	34.0000	34.0000	34.0000	34.0000	34.0000	35.0000	34.0000	34.0000	34.0000	35.0000
Level Cooperation Domestic Orgs-CSTP	Pearson Correlation	-0.0296	0.2619	0.1388	0.2759	0.1422	0.0429	0.2435	0.2176	0.2250	0.4720
	Sig. (2-tailed)	0.8680	0.1346	0.4338	0.1143	0.4223	0.8065	0.1652	0.2164	0.2007	0.0042
	N	34.0000	34.0000	34.0000	34.0000	34.0000	35.0000	34.0000	34.0000	34.0000	35.0000
Level Cooperation Domestic Orgs-TRIPS	Pearson Correlation	-0.0050	-0.0368	0.3325	0.3309	0.1933	0.0362	0.4655	0.5794	0.0476	0.3427
	Sig. (2-tailed)	0.9776	0.8365	0.0547	0.0560	0.2733	0.8363	0.0055	0.0003	0.7890	0.0439
	N	34.0000	34.0000	34.0000	34.0000	34.0000	35.0000	34.0000	34.0000	34.0000	35.0000
sqrtQIIID2a	Pearson Correlation	-0.1039	0.0341	-0.0834	0.5017	0.2241	0.1288	0.3036	0.3121	0.4904	0.3647
	Sig. (2-tailed)	0.5586	0.8481	0.6392	0.0025	0.2026	0.4607	0.0809	0.0723	0.0032	0.0312
	N	34.0000	34.0000	34.0000	34.0000	34.0000	35.0000	34.0000	34.0000	34.0000	35.0000
Level Cooperation International Orgs-CNDPS	Pearson Correlation	0.1853	0.0978	0.0795	0.1186	0.3412	0.3312	0.2826	0.3800	0.0787	0.4576
	Sig. (2-tailed)	0.2867	0.5762	0.6497	0.4973	0.0449	0.0485	0.1000	0.0244	0.6532	0.0050
	N	35.0000	35.0000	35.0000	35.0000	35.0000	36.0000	35.0000	35.0000	35.0000	36.0000
Level Cooperation International Orgs-CNBC	Pearson Correlation	0.2562	0.0945	0.1476	0.1411	0.3494	0.3500	0.3103	0.3790	0.1115	0.4223
	Sig. (2-tailed)	0.1374	0.5894	0.3974	0.4188	0.0396	0.0364	0.0697	0.0248	0.5236	0.0103
	N	35.0000	35.0000	35.0000	35.0000	35.0000	36.0000	35.0000	35.0000	35.0000	36.0000
Level Cooperation International Orgs-CSTP	Pearson Correlation	0.1028	0.1248	0.0430	0.2387	0.3083	0.3999	0.4354	0.3948	0.2480	0.4518
	Sig. (2-tailed)	0.5569	0.4750	0.8064	0.1673	0.0715	0.0157	0.0089	0.0189	0.1509	0.0057
	N	35.0000	35.0000	35.0000	35.0000	35.0000	36.0000	35.0000	35.0000	35.0000	36.0000
sqrtQIIID2e	Pearson Correlation	0.1436	-0.0195	0.2240	0.1285	0.3184	0.2809	0.4060	0.5288	0.0831	0.3324
	Sig. (2-tailed)	0.4105	0.9117	0.1958	0.4621	0.0623	0.0971	0.0155	0.0011	0.6350	0.0476
	N	35.0000	35.0000	35.0000	35.0000	35.0000	36.0000	35.0000	35.0000	35.0000	36.0000
sqrtQIVA1	Pearson Correlation	0.0686	0.0473	-0.1427	0.0551	0.1562	0.1258	0.0130	-0.0315	0.1876	0.2983
	Sig. (2-tailed)	0.6955	0.7873	0.4134	0.7531	0.3702	0.4646	0.9411	0.8576	0.2804	0.0772
	N	35.0000	35.0000	35.0000	35.0000	35.0000	36.0000	35.0000	35.0000	35.0000	36.0000
sqrtQIVA2	Pearson Correlation	-0.0248	-0.0414	-0.0942	-0.0629	-0.0927	-0.0618	-0.1006	-0.1118	0.0378	0.0382
	Sig. (2-tailed)	0.8877	0.8133	0.5902	0.7195	0.5964	0.7202	0.5651	0.5224	0.8294	0.8248
	N	35.0000	35.0000	35.0000	35.0000	35.0000	36.0000	35.0000	35.0000	35.0000	36.0000
sqrtQIVA3	Pearson Correlation	-0.1084	-0.0617	-0.1213	0.1252	0.0444	-0.0688	0.0903	0.0378	0.1429	0.1987
	Sig. (2-tailed)	0.5418	0.7290	0.4943	0.4804	0.8030	0.6947	0.6115	0.8318	0.4200	0.2526
	N	34.0000	34.0000	34.0000	34.0000	34.0000	35.0000	34.0000	34.0000	34.0000	35.0000

Correlation Matrix, Dependent Variables (Parametric)		sqrtQIIC1c	Perceived Deterrence Domestic Law-TVP	sqrtQIIC1e	sqrtQIID1a	Level Cooperation Domestic Orgs-CSIE	Level Cooperation Domestic Orgs-DWMD	Level Cooperation Domestic Orgs-TVP	Level Cooperation Domestic Orgs-CBP	sqrtQIIF1a	sqrtQIIF1b
Level Cooperation Domestic Orgs-CNDPS	Pearson Correlation	0.5659	0.4611	0.4708	0.2806	0.5766	0.4849	0.6054	0.2277	-0.0610	0.1343
	Sig. (2-tailed)	0.0004	0.0053	0.0043	0.1026	0.0003	0.0032	0.0001	0.1884	0.7446	0.4562
	N	35.0000	35.0000	35.0000	35.0000	35.0000	35.0000	35.0000	35.0000	31.0000	33.0000
Level Cooperation Domestic Orgs-CNBC	Pearson Correlation	0.4120	0.3707	0.3322	0.5210	0.4744	0.4952	0.4910	0.4178	0.1003	0.2765
	Sig. (2-tailed)	0.0139	0.0284	0.0512	0.0013	0.0040	0.0025	0.0027	0.0125	0.5915	0.1194
	N	35.0000	35.0000	35.0000	35.0000	35.0000	35.0000	35.0000	35.0000	31.0000	33.0000
Level Cooperation Domestic Orgs-CSTP	Pearson Correlation	0.4143	0.3336	0.3138	0.2009	0.4123	0.3257	0.5899	0.2129	-0.0060	-0.0108
	Sig. (2-tailed)	0.0134	0.0502	0.0664	0.2473	0.0139	0.0562	0.0002	0.2195	0.9744	0.9524
	N	35.0000	35.0000	35.0000	35.0000	35.0000	35.0000	35.0000	35.0000	31.0000	33.0000
Level Cooperation Domestic Orgs-TRIPS	Pearson Correlation	0.2866	0.2052	0.2598	0.5555	0.2704	0.3519	0.4028	0.5841	-0.0102	0.1857
	Sig. (2-tailed)	0.0951	0.2371	0.1318	0.0005	0.1162	0.0381	0.0164	0.0002	0.9566	0.3007
	N	35.0000	35.0000	35.0000	35.0000	35.0000	35.0000	35.0000	35.0000	31.0000	33.0000
sqrtQIIID2a	Pearson Correlation	0.1651	0.3332	0.2442	0.5936	0.2898	0.2354	0.3361	0.3215	0.3038	0.2751
	Sig. (2-tailed)	0.3432	0.0504	0.1574	0.0002	0.0913	0.1735	0.0484	0.0597	0.0966	0.1212
	N	35.0000	35.0000	35.0000	35.0000	35.0000	35.0000	35.0000	35.0000	31.0000	33.0000
Level Cooperation International Orgs-CNDPS	Pearson Correlation	0.4182	0.3940	0.3400	0.3070	0.4537	0.4372	0.3733	0.1751	-0.0310	0.1960
	Sig. (2-tailed)	0.0111	0.0174	0.0425	0.0686	0.0054	0.0077	0.0249	0.3069	0.8662	0.2665
	N	36.0000	36.0000	36.0000	36.0000	36.0000	36.0000	36.0000	36.0000	32.0000	34.0000
Level Cooperation International Orgs-CNBC	Pearson Correlation	0.3910	0.4290	0.3660	0.3896	0.4986	0.4416	0.3532	0.2419	0.0546	0.2685
	Sig. (2-tailed)	0.0184	0.0090	0.0281	0.0188	0.0020	0.0070	0.0346	0.1553	0.7666	0.1247
	N	36.0000	36.0000	36.0000	36.0000	36.0000	36.0000	36.0000	36.0000	32.0000	34.0000
Level Cooperation International Orgs-CSTP	Pearson Correlation	0.4833	0.4344	0.3482	0.3778	0.3942	0.3629	0.3892	0.1522	0.1186	0.3540
	Sig. (2-tailed)	0.0028	0.0081	0.0374	0.0231	0.0174	0.0296	0.0190	0.3755	0.5181	0.0400
	N	36.0000	36.0000	36.0000	36.0000	36.0000	36.0000	36.0000	36.0000	32.0000	34.0000
sqrtQIIID2e	Pearson Correlation	0.3326	0.2971	0.2789	0.5037	0.3621	0.4183	0.2200	0.4283	0.1090	0.3607
	Sig. (2-tailed)	0.0475	0.0785	0.0995	0.0017	0.0300	0.0111	0.1973	0.0092	0.5527	0.0361
	N	36.0000	36.0000	36.0000	36.0000	36.0000	36.0000	36.0000	36.0000	32.0000	34.0000
sqrtQIVA1	Pearson Correlation	0.1508	0.1551	0.0644	0.1145	-0.0166	0.0281	0.0224	-0.0467	0.1736	0.2036
	Sig. (2-tailed)	0.3799	0.3663	0.7089	0.5063	0.9236	0.8708	0.8967	0.7866	0.3421	0.2481
	N	36.0000	36.0000	36.0000	36.0000	36.0000	36.0000	36.0000	36.0000	32.0000	34.0000
sqrtQIVA2	Pearson Correlation	0.0199	0.0073	-0.0168	0.1167	-0.0436	-0.0079	0.0079	0.0137	0.0936	0.0815
	Sig. (2-tailed)	0.9083	0.9665	0.9227	0.4977	0.8008	0.9636	0.9637	0.9367	0.6104	0.6470
	N	36.0000	36.0000	36.0000	36.0000	36.0000	36.0000	36.0000	36.0000	32.0000	34.0000
sqrtQIVA3	Pearson Correlation	0.1412	0.2144	0.1352	0.1560	-0.0670	-0.0168	-0.0141	0.0940	0.2097	0.2987
	Sig. (2-tailed)	0.4184	0.2161	0.4387	0.3707	0.7021	0.9238	0.9361	0.5911	0.2575	0.0913
	N	35.0000	35.0000	35.0000	35.0000	35.0000	35.0000	35.0000	35.0000	31.0000	33.0000

Table A6, continued (Row 8, Col 7)

Correlation Matrix, Dependent Variables (Parametric)		sqrtQIIIF1c	sqrtQIIIF1d	sqrtQIIIF1e	sqrtQIIIF3a	sqrtQIIIF3b	sqrtQIIIF3c	sqrtQIIIF3d	sqrtQIIIF3e	sqrtQIIIH1a	sqrtQIIIH1b
Level Cooperation Domestic Orgs-CNDPS	Pearson Correlation	0.1011	0.0871	-0.0502	0.0867	0.3808	0.3658	0.2297	0.2515	0.1763	0.2798
	Sig. (2-tailed)	0.5758	0.6299	0.7813	0.6428	0.0315	0.0395	0.2060	0.1723	0.3513	0.1210
	N	33.0000	33.0000	33.0000	31.0000	32.0000	32.0000	32.0000	31.0000	30.0000	32.0000
Level Cooperation Domestic Orgs-CNBC	Pearson Correlation	0.3299	0.2153	0.1230	0.2661	0.4816	0.5200	0.3456	0.3374	0.3406	0.4085
	Sig. (2-tailed)	0.0608	0.2288	0.4951	0.1480	0.0053	0.0023	0.0527	0.0635	0.0655	0.0203
	N	33.0000	33.0000	33.0000	31.0000	32.0000	32.0000	32.0000	31.0000	30.0000	32.0000
Level Cooperation Domestic Orgs-CSTP	Pearson Correlation	0.1786	0.0672	-0.0398	0.1688	0.2133	0.2908	0.1853	0.1772	0.1787	0.2376
	Sig. (2-tailed)	0.3199	0.7103	0.8258	0.3640	0.2412	0.1064	0.3099	0.3401	0.3448	0.1904
	N	33.0000	33.0000	33.0000	31.0000	32.0000	32.0000	32.0000	31.0000	30.0000	32.0000
Level Cooperation Domestic Orgs-TRIPS	Pearson Correlation	0.2511	0.0566	0.1207	0.1825	0.3763	0.4083	0.2402	0.2662	0.0870	0.2795
	Sig. (2-tailed)	0.1587	0.7544	0.5034	0.3258	0.0338	0.0204	0.1855	0.1477	0.6475	0.1213
	N	33.0000	33.0000	33.0000	31.0000	32.0000	32.0000	32.0000	31.0000	30.0000	32.0000
sqrtQIIID2a	Pearson Correlation	0.5201	0.4447	0.2564	0.2906	0.4033	0.5036	0.3891	0.3926	0.2735	0.2978
	Sig. (2-tailed)	0.0019	0.0095	0.1498	0.1128	0.0221	0.0033	0.0277	0.0289	0.1436	0.0979
	N	33.0000	33.0000	33.0000	31.0000	32.0000	32.0000	32.0000	31.0000	30.0000	32.0000
Level Cooperation International Orgs-CNDPS	Pearson Correlation	0.1855	0.1989	-0.0087	-0.0217	0.4067	0.4391	0.2233	0.2580	0.1755	0.3326
	Sig. (2-tailed)	0.2934	0.2594	0.9610	0.9062	0.0188	0.0106	0.2116	0.1539	0.3451	0.0586
	N	34.0000	34.0000	34.0000	32.0000	33.0000	33.0000	33.0000	32.0000	31.0000	33.0000
Level Cooperation International Orgs-CNBC	Pearson Correlation	0.2705	0.2750	0.0801	0.1006	0.4854	0.5242	0.3272	0.3460	0.2923	0.4241
	Sig. (2-tailed)	0.1218	0.1154	0.6525	0.5840	0.0042	0.0017	0.0631	0.0524	0.1105	0.0139
	N	34.0000	34.0000	34.0000	32.0000	33.0000	33.0000	33.0000	32.0000	31.0000	33.0000
Level Cooperation International Orgs-CSTP	Pearson Correlation	0.3665	0.3306	0.0958	0.1558	0.5636	0.6369	0.3511	0.3644	0.2228	0.3613
	Sig. (2-tailed)	0.0330	0.0562	0.5900	0.3946	0.0006	0.0001	0.0451	0.0403	0.2284	0.0388
	N	34.0000	34.0000	34.0000	32.0000	33.0000	33.0000	33.0000	32.0000	31.0000	33.0000
sqrtQIIID2e	Pearson Correlation	0.3880	0.2890	0.1683	0.1522	0.5579	0.6178	0.3574	0.3926	0.2138	0.4736
	Sig. (2-tailed)	0.0234	0.0974	0.3414	0.4056	0.0007	0.0001	0.0412	0.0262	0.2482	0.0054
	N	34.0000	34.0000	34.0000	32.0000	33.0000	33.0000	33.0000	32.0000	31.0000	33.0000
sqrtQIVA1	Pearson Correlation	0.3371	0.1211	0.0991	0.0535	0.1137	0.1636	-0.0107	0.0292	0.0160	0.1020
	Sig. (2-tailed)	0.0512	0.4950	0.5770	0.7710	0.5287	0.3628	0.9529	0.8738	0.9319	0.5723
	N	34.0000	34.0000	34.0000	32.0000	33.0000	33.0000	33.0000	32.0000	31.0000	33.0000
sqrtQIVA2	Pearson Correlation	0.1761	0.0531	0.0508	0.0241	0.0626	0.1178	-0.0033	0.0070	0.0259	0.0479
	Sig. (2-tailed)	0.3192	0.7657	0.7754	0.8958	0.7294	0.5139	0.9853	0.9698	0.8901	0.7911
	N	34.0000	34.0000	34.0000	32.0000	33.0000	33.0000	33.0000	32.0000	31.0000	33.0000
sqrtQIVA3	Pearson Correlation	0.3641	0.1787	0.2001	0.3517	0.4703	0.4902	0.3475	0.3792	0.1566	0.1802
	Sig. (2-tailed)	0.0373	0.3198	0.2643	0.0523	0.0066	0.0044	0.0513	0.0354	0.4084	0.3237
	N	33.0000	33.0000	33.0000	31.0000	32.0000	32.0000	32.0000	31.0000	30.0000	32.0000

Table A6, continued (Row 8, Col 8)

Correlation Matrix, Dependent Variables (Parametric)		sqrtQIIH1c	sqrtQIIH1d	sqrtQIIH1e	sqrtQIIH3a	sqrtQIIH3b	sqrtQIIH3c	sqrtQIIH3d	sqrtQIIH3e	sqrtQIIIA1a	sqrtQIIIA1b
Level Cooperation Domestic Orgs-CNDPS	Pearson Correlation	0.2055	0.2069	0.1952	0.2213	0.2514	0.2606	0.3865	0.2565	0.1688	0.3611
	Sig. (2-tailed)	0.2675	0.2642	0.3014	0.2159	0.1581	0.1430	0.0263	0.1496	0.3399	0.0331
	N	31.0000	31.0000	30.0000	33.0000	33.0000	33.0000	33.0000	33.0000	34.0000	35.0000
Level Cooperation Domestic Orgs-CNBC	Pearson Correlation	0.3510	0.3231	0.2686	0.3407	0.3091	0.3617	0.4591	0.3025	0.1747	0.1456
	Sig. (2-tailed)	0.0528	0.0762	0.1512	0.0524	0.0801	0.0386	0.0072	0.0871	0.3232	0.4041
	N	31.0000	31.0000	30.0000	33.0000	33.0000	33.0000	33.0000	33.0000	34.0000	35.0000
Level Cooperation Domestic Orgs-CSTP	Pearson Correlation	0.2264	0.2829	0.1647	0.1701	0.1712	0.2459	0.3474	0.2382	0.2413	0.2324
	Sig. (2-tailed)	0.2207	0.1231	0.3844	0.3439	0.3408	0.1678	0.0476	0.1820	0.1692	0.1791
	N	31.0000	31.0000	30.0000	33.0000	33.0000	33.0000	33.0000	33.0000	34.0000	35.0000
Level Cooperation Domestic Orgs-TRIPS	Pearson Correlation	0.2817	0.2414	0.2562	0.1917	0.2375	0.2791	0.3436	0.2872	0.1641	0.0813
	Sig. (2-tailed)	0.1247	0.1908	0.1717	0.2852	0.1833	0.1158	0.0503	0.1051	0.3537	0.6425
	N	31.0000	31.0000	30.0000	33.0000	33.0000	33.0000	33.0000	33.0000	34.0000	35.0000
sqrtQIIID2a	Pearson Correlation	0.3123	0.2975	0.2060	0.1149	0.2231	0.2606	0.1569	0.0475	0.4457	0.0042
	Sig. (2-tailed)	0.0871	0.1041	0.2747	0.5244	0.2121	0.1430	0.3831	0.7929	0.0082	0.9810
	N	31.0000	31.0000	30.0000	33.0000	33.0000	33.0000	33.0000	33.0000	34.0000	35.0000
Level Cooperation International Orgs-CNDPS	Pearson Correlation	0.3441	0.2385	0.2287	0.1964	0.3192	0.3171	0.2830	0.1744	0.1327	0.3385
	Sig. (2-tailed)	0.0538	0.1886	0.2159	0.2657	0.0658	0.0677	0.1048	0.3238	0.4474	0.0435
	N	32.0000	32.0000	31.0000	34.0000	34.0000	34.0000	34.0000	34.0000	35.0000	36.0000
Level Cooperation International Orgs-CNBC	Pearson Correlation	0.3949	0.3012	0.2694	0.2917	0.3596	0.3551	0.3395	0.2175	0.1273	0.2883
	Sig. (2-tailed)	0.0253	0.0938	0.1427	0.0941	0.0367	0.0393	0.0495	0.2165	0.4660	0.0882
	N	32.0000	32.0000	31.0000	34.0000	34.0000	34.0000	34.0000	34.0000	35.0000	36.0000
Level Cooperation International Orgs-CSTP	Pearson Correlation	0.4161	0.2656	0.2167	0.3070	0.4034	0.4368	0.3652	0.2460	0.2966	0.3935
	Sig. (2-tailed)	0.0179	0.1418	0.2416	0.0774	0.0180	0.0098	0.0337	0.1608	0.0836	0.0176
	N	32.0000	32.0000	31.0000	34.0000	34.0000	34.0000	34.0000	34.0000	35.0000	36.0000
sqrtQIIID2e	Pearson Correlation	0.4864	0.3513	0.3099	0.2616	0.4203	0.4287	0.3657	0.2936	0.1620	0.2210
	Sig. (2-tailed)	0.0048	0.0487	0.0898	0.1351	0.0133	0.0114	0.0334	0.0919	0.3525	0.1953
	N	32.0000	32.0000	31.0000	34.0000	34.0000	34.0000	34.0000	34.0000	35.0000	36.0000
sqrtQIVA1	Pearson Correlation	0.1657	0.0801	-0.0097	0.0443	0.1762	0.2587	0.0605	-0.0270	-0.0305	0.1503
	Sig. (2-tailed)	0.3647	0.6630	0.9588	0.8035	0.3188	0.1396	0.7340	0.8794	0.8618	0.3817
	N	32.0000	32.0000	31.0000	34.0000	34.0000	34.0000	34.0000	34.0000	35.0000	36.0000
sqrtQIVA2	Pearson Correlation	0.0824	0.0561	0.0371	0.0329	0.0884	0.1112	0.0392	0.0141	0.1332	0.1325
	Sig. (2-tailed)	0.6538	0.7604	0.8429	0.8535	0.6193	0.5311	0.8259	0.9371	0.4456	0.4412
	N	32.0000	32.0000	31.0000	34.0000	34.0000	34.0000	34.0000	34.0000	35.0000	36.0000
sqrtQIVA3	Pearson Correlation	0.2596	0.2312	0.2499	0.2085	0.2821	0.3266	0.2759	0.2502	0.1338	0.2814
	Sig. (2-tailed)	0.1584	0.2107	0.1829	0.2442	0.1117	0.0636	0.1201	0.1603	0.4505	0.1015
	N	31.0000	31.0000	30.0000	33.0000	33.0000	33.0000	33.0000	33.0000	34.0000	35.0000

Table A6, continued (Row 8, Col 9)

Correlation Matrix, Dependent Variables (Parametric)		sqrtQIIIA1c	sqrtQIIIA1d	sqrtQIIIA1e	sqrtQIIID1a	Level Cooperation Domestic Orgs-CNDPS	Level Cooperation Domestic Orgs-CNBC	Level Cooperation Domestic Orgs-CSTP	Level Cooperation Domestic Orgs-TRIPS	sqrtQIIID2a	Level Cooperation International Orgs-CNDPS
Level Cooperation Domestic Orgs-CNDPS	Pearson Correlation	0.3847	0.3798	0.2279	0.6244	1.0000	0.8026	0.8367	0.7218	0.5215	0.7429
	Sig. (2-tailed)	0.0225	0.0244	0.1880	0.0001	.	0.0000	0.0000	0.0000	0.0016	0.0000
	N	35.0000	35.0000	35.0000	33.0000	35.0000	35.0000	35.0000	35.0000	34.0000	35.0000
Level Cooperation Domestic Orgs-CNBC	Pearson Correlation	0.3799	0.1910	0.2346	0.7451	0.8026	1.0000	0.7652	0.8388	0.5921	0.5740
	Sig. (2-tailed)	0.0244	0.2718	0.1750	0.0000	0.0000	.	0.0000	0.0000	0.0002	0.0003
	N	35.0000	35.0000	35.0000	33.0000	35.0000	35.0000	35.0000	35.0000	34.0000	35.0000
Level Cooperation Domestic Orgs-CSTP	Pearson Correlation	0.3031	0.4205	0.1730	0.7309	0.8367	0.7652	1.0000	0.7454	0.5839	0.5336
	Sig. (2-tailed)	0.0768	0.0119	0.3203	0.0000	0.0000	0.0000	.	0.0000	0.0003	0.0010
	N	35.0000	35.0000	35.0000	33.0000	35.0000	35.0000	35.0000	35.0000	34.0000	35.0000
Level Cooperation Domestic Orgs-TRIPS	Pearson Correlation	0.2621	0.2136	0.3145	0.8610	0.7218	0.8388	0.7454	1.0000	0.6301	0.5652
	Sig. (2-tailed)	0.1282	0.2180	0.0657	0.0000	0.0000	0.0000	0.0000	.	0.0001	0.0004
	N	35.0000	35.0000	35.0000	33.0000	35.0000	35.0000	35.0000	35.0000	34.0000	35.0000
sqrtQIIID2a	Pearson Correlation	0.1217	0.1578	0.1320	0.6773	0.5215	0.5921	0.5839	0.6301	1.0000	0.6279
	Sig. (2-tailed)	0.4862	0.3651	0.4499	0.0000	0.0016	0.0002	0.0003	0.0001	.	0.0001
	N	35.0000	35.0000	35.0000	33.0000	34.0000	34.0000	34.0000	34.0000	35.0000	35.0000
Level Cooperation International Orgs-CNDPS	Pearson Correlation	0.3611	0.3697	0.2666	0.4875	0.7429	0.5740	0.5336	0.5652	0.6279	1.0000
	Sig. (2-tailed)	0.0305	0.0265	0.1159	0.0040	0.0000	0.0003	0.0010	0.0004	0.0001	.
	N	36.0000	36.0000	36.0000	33.0000	35.0000	35.0000	35.0000	35.0000	35.0000	36.0000
Level Cooperation International Orgs-CNBC	Pearson Correlation	0.3753	0.3133	0.2476	0.5190	0.7025	0.6777	0.5202	0.5840	0.6703	0.9533
	Sig. (2-tailed)	0.0241	0.0628	0.1454	0.0020	0.0000	0.0000	0.0014	0.0002	0.0000	0.0000
	N	36.0000	36.0000	36.0000	33.0000	35.0000	35.0000	35.0000	35.0000	35.0000	36.0000
Level Cooperation International Orgs-CSTP	Pearson Correlation	0.4306	0.4785	0.3484	0.5302	0.7276	0.6264	0.6078	0.5612	0.6914	0.8766
	Sig. (2-tailed)	0.0087	0.0032	0.0373	0.0015	0.0000	0.0001	0.0001	0.0005	0.0000	0.0000
	N	36.0000	36.0000	36.0000	33.0000	35.0000	35.0000	35.0000	35.0000	35.0000	36.0000
sqrtQIIID2e	Pearson Correlation	0.3836	0.2707	0.3784	0.5762	0.5567	0.6783	0.4824	0.6977	0.7477	0.8155
	Sig. (2-tailed)	0.0209	0.1102	0.0229	0.0004	0.0005	0.0000	0.0033	0.0000	0.0000	0.0000
	N	36.0000	36.0000	36.0000	33.0000	35.0000	35.0000	35.0000	35.0000	35.0000	36.0000
sqrtQIVA1	Pearson Correlation	0.2397	0.0857	0.0085	0.0581	0.0086	-0.0119	-0.0012	0.0231	0.1966	0.1894
	Sig. (2-tailed)	0.1591	0.6190	0.9607	0.7480	0.9607	0.9460	0.9943	0.8954	0.2577	0.2685
	N	36.0000	36.0000	36.0000	33.0000	35.0000	35.0000	35.0000	35.0000	35.0000	36.0000
sqrtQIVA2	Pearson Correlation	0.2001	0.1293	0.1471	-0.0825	-0.1697	-0.1323	-0.1856	-0.1187	-0.0114	-0.0352
	Sig. (2-tailed)	0.2421	0.4522	0.3918	0.6479	0.3297	0.4488	0.2858	0.4972	0.9483	0.8386
	N	36.0000	36.0000	36.0000	33.0000	35.0000	35.0000	35.0000	35.0000	35.0000	36.0000
sqrtQIVA3	Pearson Correlation	0.3763	0.3482	0.2982	0.2669	0.0685	0.1054	0.0864	0.1817	0.2231	0.1060
	Sig. (2-tailed)	0.0259	0.0404	0.0819	0.1397	0.7003	0.5531	0.6269	0.3039	0.2047	0.5445
	N	35.0000	35.0000	35.0000	32.0000	34.0000	34.0000	34.0000	34.0000	34.0000	35.0000

Table A6, continued (Row 8, Col 10)

Correlation Matrix, Dependent Variables (Parametric)		Level Cooperation International Orgs-CNBC	Level Cooperation International Orgs-CSTP	sqrtQIIID2e	sqrtQIVA1	sqrtQIVA2	sqrtQIVA3	sqrtQIVA5	sqrtQIVA7	sqrtQIVA8	Political Ideology
Level Cooperation Domestic Orgs-CNDPS	Pearson Correlation	0.7025	0.7276	0.5567	0.0086	-0.1697	0.0685	0.3836	-0.0858	-0.0429	0.0741
	Sig. (2-tailed)	0.0000	0.0000	0.0005	0.9607	0.3297	0.7003	0.0276	0.6240	0.8094	0.6821
	N	35.0000	35.0000	35.0000	35.0000	35.0000	34.0000	33.0000	35.0000	34.0000	33.0000
Level Cooperation Domestic Orgs-CNBC	Pearson Correlation	0.6777	0.6264	0.6783	-0.0119	-0.1323	0.1054	0.4469	-0.0358	-0.0303	0.1898
	Sig. (2-tailed)	0.0000	0.0001	0.0000	0.9460	0.4488	0.5531	0.0091	0.8381	0.8650	0.2901
	N	35.0000	35.0000	35.0000	35.0000	35.0000	34.0000	33.0000	35.0000	34.0000	33.0000
Level Cooperation Domestic Orgs-CSTP	Pearson Correlation	0.5202	0.6078	0.4824	-0.0012	-0.1856	0.0864	0.2712	0.0676	-0.0118	-0.0347
	Sig. (2-tailed)	0.0014	0.0001	0.0033	0.9943	0.2858	0.6269	0.1269	0.6997	0.9471	0.8479
	N	35.0000	35.0000	35.0000	35.0000	35.0000	34.0000	33.0000	35.0000	34.0000	33.0000
Level Cooperation Domestic Orgs-TRIPS	Pearson Correlation	0.5840	0.5612	0.6977	0.0231	-0.1187	0.1817	0.1971	-0.0335	-0.0056	0.2431
	Sig. (2-tailed)	0.0002	0.0005	0.0000	0.8954	0.4972	0.3039	0.2716	0.8485	0.9749	0.1728
	N	35.0000	35.0000	35.0000	35.0000	35.0000	34.0000	33.0000	35.0000	34.0000	33.0000
sqrtQIIID2a	Pearson Correlation	0.6703	0.6914	0.7477	0.1966	-0.0114	0.2231	0.2822	-0.1921	-0.0879	0.3376
	Sig. (2-tailed)	0.0000	0.0000	0.0000	0.2577	0.9483	0.2047	0.1115	0.2689	0.6211	0.0588
	N	35.0000	35.0000	35.0000	35.0000	35.0000	34.0000	33.0000	35.0000	34.0000	32.0000
Level Cooperation International Orgs-CNDPS	Pearson Correlation	0.9533	0.8766	0.8155	0.1894	-0.0352	0.1060	0.3539	-0.2484	-0.1162	0.2327
	Sig. (2-tailed)	0.0000	0.0000	0.0000	0.2685	0.8386	0.5445	0.0400	0.1441	0.5061	0.1925
	N	36.0000	36.0000	36.0000	36.0000	36.0000	35.0000	34.0000	36.0000	35.0000	33.0000
Level Cooperation International Orgs-CNBC	Pearson Correlation	1.0000	0.8595	0.8809	0.1438	-0.0574	0.0931	0.3854	-0.2283	-0.1323	0.2434
	Sig. (2-tailed)	.	0.0000	0.0000	0.4026	0.7393	0.5947	0.0244	0.1805	0.4485	0.1723
	N	36.0000	36.0000	36.0000	36.0000	36.0000	35.0000	34.0000	36.0000	35.0000	33.0000
Level Cooperation International Orgs-CSTP	Pearson Correlation	0.8595	1.0000	0.8018	0.1731	-0.0246	0.2020	0.2961	-0.2587	-0.1031	0.2934
	Sig. (2-tailed)	0.0000	.	0.0000	0.3128	0.8869	0.2446	0.0890	0.1276	0.5554	0.0974
	N	36.0000	36.0000	36.0000	36.0000	36.0000	35.0000	34.0000	36.0000	35.0000	33.0000
sqrtQIIID2e	Pearson Correlation	0.8809	0.8018	1.0000	0.2164	0.0058	0.2163	0.2794	-0.1450	-0.0616	0.3916
	Sig. (2-tailed)	0.0000	0.0000	.	0.2050	0.9734	0.2120	0.1096	0.3986	0.7254	0.0242
	N	36.0000	36.0000	36.0000	36.0000	36.0000	35.0000	34.0000	36.0000	35.0000	33.0000
sqrtQIVA1	Pearson Correlation	0.1438	0.1731	0.2164	1.0000	0.5700	0.6709	0.0655	0.0921	0.0066	0.4036
	Sig. (2-tailed)	0.4026	0.3128	0.2050	.	0.0003	0.0000	0.7130	0.5932	0.9698	0.0198
	N	36.0000	36.0000	36.0000	36.0000	36.0000	35.0000	34.0000	36.0000	35.0000	33.0000
sqrtQIVA2	Pearson Correlation	-0.0574	-0.0246	0.0058	0.5700	1.0000	0.5323	-0.0997	-0.0019	-0.0312	0.3057
	Sig. (2-tailed)	0.7393	0.8869	0.9734	0.0003	.	0.0010	0.5748	0.9913	0.8587	0.0836
	N	36.0000	36.0000	36.0000	36.0000	36.0000	35.0000	34.0000	36.0000	35.0000	33.0000
sqrtQIVA3	Pearson Correlation	0.0931	0.2020	0.2163	0.6709	0.5323	1.0000	0.0292	-0.1935	0.0019	0.2858
	Sig. (2-tailed)	0.5947	0.2446	0.2120	0.0000	0.0010	.	0.8717	0.2654	0.9917	0.1128
	N	35.0000	35.0000	35.0000	35.0000	35.0000	35.0000	33.0000	35.0000	34.0000	32.0000

Table A6, continued (Row 9, Col 1)

Correlation Matrix, Dependent Variables (Parametric)		Importance of Smuggling-Endangered Species	reflectsqrtQIA1b	reflectsqrtQIA1c	reflectsqrtQIA1d	reflectsqrtQIA1e	sqrtQIB1a	Knowledge of Smuggling-Narcotics	Knowledge of Smuggling-Weapons	Knowledge of Smuggling-Humans	Knowledge of Smuggling-Contraband
sqrtQIVA5	Pearson Correlation	-0.1126	-0.3136	-0.1166	-0.0908	-0.1674	0.1451	0.1769	0.2895	0.1668	0.0464
	Sig. (2-tailed)	0.5259	0.0709	0.5114	0.6095	0.3440	0.4129	0.3169	0.0968	0.3458	0.7946
	N	34.0000	34.0000	34.0000	34.0000	34.0000	34.0000	34.0000	34.0000	34.0000	34.0000
sqrtQIVA7	Pearson Correlation	-0.0287	-0.0640	0.0205	-0.2604	-0.1845	-0.1589	-0.1265	-0.0129	-0.2391	0.0134
	Sig. (2-tailed)	0.8680	0.7108	0.9057	0.1250	0.2813	0.3545	0.4621	0.9406	0.1602	0.9384
	N	36.0000	36.0000	36.0000	36.0000	36.0000	36.0000	36.0000	36.0000	36.0000	36.0000
sqrtQIVA8	Pearson Correlation	-0.0400	0.1170	0.1854	0.1977	-0.0653	0.0121	0.0783	0.0283	0.1825	0.2487
	Sig. (2-tailed)	0.8195	0.5031	0.2864	0.2548	0.7093	0.9450	0.6548	0.8720	0.2939	0.1497
	N	35.0000	35.0000	35.0000	35.0000	35.0000	35.0000	35.0000	35.0000	35.0000	35.0000
Political Ideology	Pearson Correlation	-0.1693	0.3071	0.2647	0.1013	0.0011	0.1583	0.0522	0.3089	0.0541	0.2656
	Sig. (2-tailed)	0.3464	0.0821	0.1366	0.5750	0.9951	0.3789	0.7729	0.0802	0.7649	0.1352
	N	33.0000	33.0000	33.0000	33.0000	33.0000	33.0000	33.0000	33.0000	33.0000	33.0000

Table A6, continued (Row 9, Col 2)

Correlation Matrix, Dependent Variables (Parametric)		sqrtQ1E1a	Personal Resource Challenges-Lack of Time	Personal Resource Challenges-Lack of Knowledge	Personal Resource Challenges-Lack of Training	sqrtQ1E1e	Personal Resource Challenges-Excessive Admin Paperwork	Personal Resource Challenges-Ineffective Technology	Personal Resource Challenges-Ineffective Strategic Focus	Personal Resource Challenges-Ineffective Tactical Policy	Personal Resource Challenges-Lack of Clarity in Duties
sqrtQIVA5	Pearson Correlation	-0.0613	-0.3000	-0.2011	-0.2275	0.0274	0.0237	-0.3674	-0.0811	-0.1987	-0.2636
	Sig. (2-tailed)	0.7347	0.0847	0.2541	0.1957	0.8780	0.8939	0.0325	0.6486	0.2599	0.1320
	N	33.0000	34.0000	34.0000	34.0000	34.0000	34.0000	34.0000	34.0000	34.0000	34.0000
sqrtQIVA7	Pearson Correlation	-0.0508	-0.0716	-0.0987	-0.0693	-0.0159	-0.0877	-0.0528	0.0901	-0.0004	0.1326
	Sig. (2-tailed)	0.7719	0.6782	0.5670	0.6881	0.9268	0.6111	0.7597	0.6014	0.9983	0.4406
	N	35.0000	36.0000	36.0000	36.0000	36.0000	36.0000	36.0000	36.0000	36.0000	36.0000
sqrtQIVA8	Pearson Correlation	-0.1871	0.2606	-0.0474	-0.0792	-0.1426	0.0388	-0.1169	-0.2959	-0.2056	-0.1085
	Sig. (2-tailed)	0.2894	0.1305	0.7868	0.6510	0.4139	0.8251	0.5037	0.0843	0.2361	0.5350
	N	34.0000	35.0000	35.0000	35.0000	35.0000	35.0000	35.0000	35.0000	35.0000	35.0000
Political Ideology	Pearson Correlation	-0.1008	0.1789	0.1173	0.1329	0.1533	0.2197	0.1397	0.0123	0.1382	0.0998
	Sig. (2-tailed)	0.5767	0.3193	0.5155	0.4610	0.3945	0.2192	0.4381	0.9460	0.4431	0.5805
	N	33.0000	33.0000	33.0000	33.0000	33.0000	33.0000	33.0000	33.0000	33.0000	33.0000

Table A6, continued (Row 9, Col 3)

Correlation Matrix, Dependent Variables (Parametric)		Personal Resource Challenges-Conflict or Lack Comm Leaders and Employees	sqrtQIE11	Personal Resource Challenges-Conflict or Lack Comm International Orgs	Personal Resource Challenges-Conflict or Lack Comm Domestic Orgs	sqrtQIE3a	Org Resource Challenges-Lack of Time	Org Resource Challenges-Lack of Knowledge	Org Resource Challenges-Lack of Training	sqrtQIE3e	Org Resource Challenges-Excessive Admin Paperwork
sqrtQIVA5	Pearson Correlation	-0.2154	0.0993	-0.0521	-0.1372	0.0015	0.0635	-0.1624	-0.2116	-0.1671	-0.0822
	Sig. (2-tailed)	0.2212	0.5762	0.7700	0.4391	0.9932	0.7212	0.3588	0.2296	0.3526	0.6440
	N	34.0000	34.0000	34.0000	34.0000	33.0000	34.0000	34.0000	34.0000	33.0000	34.0000
sqrtQIVA7	Pearson Correlation	0.1726	0.1235	-0.0101	0.0575	-0.0107	-0.0614	0.0765	0.0666	-0.0981	-0.0328
	Sig. (2-tailed)	0.3140	0.4729	0.9535	0.7392	0.9523	0.7262	0.6621	0.7036	0.5811	0.8516
	N	36.0000	36.0000	36.0000	36.0000	34.0000	35.0000	35.0000	35.0000	34.0000	35.0000
sqrtQIVA8	Pearson Correlation	-0.2587	-0.2521	0.0640	-0.1378	-0.1731	0.2567	-0.0302	-0.0590	-0.0177	-0.2230
	Sig. (2-tailed)	0.1335	0.1440	0.7150	0.4300	0.3277	0.1366	0.8634	0.7364	0.9211	0.1979
	N	35.0000	35.0000	35.0000	35.0000	34.0000	35.0000	35.0000	35.0000	34.0000	35.0000
Political Ideology	Pearson Correlation	0.0549	-0.0632	0.0389	0.0614	0.0560	-0.0784	-0.1021	-0.0800	0.1183	-0.0690
	Sig. (2-tailed)	0.7615	0.7268	0.8299	0.7343	0.7609	0.6644	0.5717	0.6581	0.5189	0.7030
	N	33.0000	33.0000	33.0000	33.0000	32.0000	33.0000	33.0000	33.0000	32.0000	33.0000

Table A6, continued (Row 9, Col 4)

Correlation Matrix, Dependent Variables (Parametric)		Org Resource Challenges-Ineffective Technology	Org Resource Challenges-Ineffective Strategic Focus	Org Resource Challenges-Ineffective Tactical Policy	Org Resource Challenges-Lack of Clarity in Duties	Org Resource Challenges-Conflict or Lack Comm Leaders and Employees	sqrtQIE31	Org Resource Challenges-Conflict or Lack Comm International Orgs	Org Resource Challenges-Conflict or Lack Comm Domestic Orgs	sqrtQIIA1a	Knowledge of Domestic Law-CSIE
sqrtQIVA5	Pearson Correlation	-0.1445	-0.1517	-0.0647	-0.0922	-0.1561	0.1102	0.1253	0.0593	-0.0193	0.2925
	Sig. (2-tailed)	0.4148	0.3919	0.7163	0.6041	0.3780	0.5349	0.4803	0.7389	0.9150	0.0986
	N	34.0000	34.0000	34.0000	34.0000	34.0000	34.0000	34.0000	34.0000	33.0000	33.0000
sqrtQIVA7	Pearson Correlation	-0.0430	0.0874	0.0278	-0.0212	0.0376	0.1971	-0.2223	-0.0972	0.1354	-0.1068
	Sig. (2-tailed)	0.8064	0.6176	0.8740	0.9037	0.8300	0.2565	0.1992	0.5786	0.4381	0.5414
	N	35.0000	35.0000	35.0000	35.0000	35.0000	35.0000	35.0000	35.0000	35.0000	35.0000
sqrtQIVA8	Pearson Correlation	-0.2447	-0.2093	-0.2141	-0.2333	-0.2012	-0.1516	-0.0648	-0.2430	-0.1746	0.0432
	Sig. (2-tailed)	0.1566	0.2276	0.2168	0.1774	0.2465	0.3845	0.7114	0.1595	0.3233	0.8083
	N	35.0000	35.0000	35.0000	35.0000	35.0000	35.0000	35.0000	35.0000	34.0000	34.0000
Political Ideology	Pearson Correlation	-0.0409	-0.0088	-0.0584	0.0609	0.0000	-0.0489	0.0373	0.0842	0.2663	0.0819
	Sig. (2-tailed)	0.8211	0.9611	0.7470	0.7362	1.0000	0.7870	0.8365	0.6414	0.1406	0.6557
	N	33.0000	33.0000	33.0000	33.0000	33.0000	33.0000	33.0000	33.0000	32.0000	32.0000

Table A6, continued (Row 9, Col 5)

Correlation Matrix, Dependent Variables (Parametric)		Knowledge of Domestic Law-DWMD	Knowledge of Domestic Law-TVP	Knowledge of Domestic Law-CBP	sqrtQIIB1a	Perceived Effectiveness Domestic Govt Support-CSIE	Perceived Effectiveness Domestic Govt Support-DWMD	Perceived Effectiveness Domestic Govt SupportTVP	Perceived Effectiveness Domestic Govt Support-CBP	sqrtQIIC1a	Perceived Deterrence Domestic Law-CSIE
sqrtQIVA5	Pearson Correlation	0.2711	0.2011	0.0556	0.0988	0.2648	0.1586	0.1183	-0.0183	-0.1010	0.3658
	Sig. (2-tailed)	0.1271	0.2619	0.7588	0.5844	0.1364	0.3703	0.5119	0.9194	0.5759	0.0334
	N	33.0000	33.0000	33.0000	33.0000	33.0000	34.0000	33.0000	33.0000	33.0000	34.0000
sqrtQIVA7	Pearson Correlation	-0.0749	-0.0363	0.1172	-0.0153	-0.0239	0.0427	-0.0332	-0.0270	0.1827	0.1860
	Sig. (2-tailed)	0.6689	0.8360	0.5026	0.9305	0.8916	0.8049	0.8498	0.8775	0.2936	0.2774
	N	35.0000	35.0000	35.0000	35.0000	35.0000	36.0000	35.0000	35.0000	35.0000	36.0000
sqrtQIVA8	Pearson Correlation	0.1244	0.3014	0.2077	-0.1597	-0.1045	-0.0391	-0.0354	-0.1465	0.0216	0.0146
	Sig. (2-tailed)	0.4832	0.0832	0.2385	0.3671	0.5563	0.8237	0.8425	0.4082	0.9033	0.9339
	N	34.0000	34.0000	34.0000	34.0000	34.0000	35.0000	34.0000	34.0000	34.0000	35.0000
Political Ideology	Pearson Correlation	0.2899	0.0322	0.1375	0.1598	0.2282	0.3143	0.4093	0.4199	0.2361	0.1464
	Sig. (2-tailed)	0.1076	0.8611	0.4529	0.3823	0.2090	0.0748	0.0200	0.0167	0.1933	0.4161
	N	32.0000	32.0000	32.0000	32.0000	32.0000	33.0000	32.0000	32.0000	32.0000	33.0000

Table A6, continued (Row 9, Col 6)

Correlation Matrix, Dependent Variables (Parametric)		sqrtQIIC1c	Perceived Deterrence Domestic Law-TVP	sqrtQIIC1e	sqrtQIID1a	Level Cooperation Domestic Orgs-CSIE	Level Cooperation Domestic Orgs-DWMD	Level Cooperation Domestic Orgs-TVP	Level Cooperation Domestic Orgs-CBP	sqrtQIIF1a	sqrtQIIF1b
sqrtQIVA5	Pearson Correlation	0.2188	0.2415	0.0767	0.1165	0.3660	0.3984	0.3035	0.0006	0.1776	0.2395
	Sig. (2-tailed)	0.2137	0.1688	0.6664	0.5116	0.0333	0.0196	0.0810	0.9973	0.3391	0.1794
	N	34.0000	34.0000	34.0000	34.0000	34.0000	34.0000	34.0000	34.0000	31.0000	33.0000
sqrtQIVA7	Pearson Correlation	0.1353	0.1855	0.2336	-0.1753	-0.1921	-0.2136	-0.0707	-0.0284	0.0042	-0.1961
	Sig. (2-tailed)	0.4313	0.2788	0.1704	0.3065	0.2618	0.2110	0.6818	0.8692	0.9818	0.2662
	N	36.0000	36.0000	36.0000	36.0000	36.0000	36.0000	36.0000	36.0000	32.0000	34.0000
sqrtQIVA8	Pearson Correlation	0.0876	-0.0115	0.0314	0.0904	0.0446	0.0309	0.0867	0.0727	-0.2700	-0.2826
	Sig. (2-tailed)	0.6167	0.9476	0.8580	0.6055	0.7993	0.8601	0.6206	0.6780	0.1350	0.1054
	N	35.0000	35.0000	35.0000	35.0000	35.0000	35.0000	35.0000	35.0000	32.0000	34.0000
Political Ideology	Pearson Correlation	0.2418	0.1152	0.1854	0.4608	0.1078	0.1871	0.0611	0.3480	0.1344	0.2361
	Sig. (2-tailed)	0.1752	0.5233	0.3016	0.0070	0.5503	0.2972	0.7357	0.0472	0.4788	0.1933
	N	33.0000	33.0000	33.0000	33.0000	33.0000	33.0000	33.0000	33.0000	30.0000	32.0000

Table A6, continued (Row 9, Col 7)

Correlation Matrix, Dependent Variables (Parametric)		sqrtQIIF1c	sqrtQIIF1d	sqrtQIIF1e	sqrtQIIF3a	sqrtQIIF3b	sqrtQIIF3c	sqrtQIIF3d	sqrtQIIF3e	sqrtQIIH1a	sqrtQIIH1b
sqrtQIVA5	Pearson Correlation	0.4104	0.3166	0.1539	0.1114	0.3467	0.3564	0.2840	0.2612	0.3603	0.3797
	Sig. (2-tailed)	0.0177	0.0726	0.3925	0.5506	0.0519	0.0453	0.1152	0.1559	0.0548	0.0351
	N	33.0000	33.0000	33.0000	31.0000	32.0000	32.0000	32.0000	31.0000	29.0000	31.0000
sqrtQIVA7	Pearson Correlation	-0.0459	-0.1818	-0.0809	0.0366	-0.2480	-0.1760	-0.1771	-0.1990	-0.0264	-0.0114
	Sig. (2-tailed)	0.7964	0.3034	0.6491	0.8425	0.1641	0.3273	0.3242	0.2748	0.8880	0.9497
	N	34.0000	34.0000	34.0000	32.0000	33.0000	33.0000	33.0000	32.0000	31.0000	33.0000
sqrtQIVA8	Pearson Correlation	-0.1944	-0.2812	-0.2682	-0.2630	-0.2199	-0.1814	-0.2564	-0.2412	-0.2494	-0.2635
	Sig. (2-tailed)	0.2706	0.1072	0.1252	0.1458	0.2189	0.3123	0.1498	0.1836	0.1839	0.1451
	N	34.0000	34.0000	34.0000	32.0000	33.0000	33.0000	33.0000	32.0000	30.0000	32.0000
Political Ideology	Pearson Correlation	0.2775	0.2006	0.1522	0.0779	0.2636	0.3096	0.1763	0.2026	0.0261	0.1321
	Sig. (2-tailed)	0.1242	0.2709	0.4058	0.6826	0.1519	0.0901	0.3428	0.2830	0.8953	0.4864
	N	32.0000	32.0000	32.0000	30.0000	31.0000	31.0000	31.0000	30.0000	28.0000	30.0000

Table A6, continued (Row 9, Col 8)

Correlation Matrix, Dependent Variables (Parametric)		sqrtQIIH1c	sqrtQIIH1d	sqrtQIIH1e	sqrtQIIH3a	sqrtQIIH3b	sqrtQIIH3c	sqrtQIIH3d	sqrtQIIH3e	sqrtQIIIA1a	sqrtQIIIA1b
sqrtQIVA5	Pearson Correlation	0.3078	0.3320	0.2606	0.1032	0.3122	0.3255	0.2533	0.0530	-0.1075	-0.0871
	Sig. (2-tailed)	0.0980	0.0730	0.1721	0.5742	0.0819	0.0691	0.1619	0.7731	0.5515	0.6241
	N	30.0000	30.0000	29.0000	32.0000	32.0000	32.0000	32.0000	32.0000	33.0000	34.0000
sqrtQIVA7	Pearson Correlation	-0.1064	0.0077	-0.0777	-0.0003	-0.0973	-0.0759	0.0446	0.0377	-0.1239	-0.0378
	Sig. (2-tailed)	0.5621	0.9666	0.6780	0.9986	0.5840	0.6695	0.8023	0.8325	0.4782	0.8268
	N	32.0000	32.0000	31.0000	34.0000	34.0000	34.0000	34.0000	34.0000	35.0000	36.0000
sqrtQIVA8	Pearson Correlation	-0.2441	-0.2446	-0.2274	-0.2805	-0.2809	-0.2665	-0.2701	-0.2608	-0.1046	-0.0375
	Sig. (2-tailed)	0.1857	0.1848	0.2268	0.1139	0.1133	0.1338	0.1285	0.1427	0.5559	0.8308
	N	31.0000	31.0000	30.0000	33.0000	33.0000	33.0000	33.0000	33.0000	34.0000	35.0000
Political Ideology	Pearson Correlation	0.1971	0.1049	0.1074	0.0473	0.2016	0.1985	0.0586	0.0391	0.2577	0.0529
	Sig. (2-tailed)	0.3054	0.5881	0.5864	0.8004	0.2767	0.2843	0.7540	0.8344	0.1545	0.7698
	N	29.0000	29.0000	28.0000	31.0000	31.0000	31.0000	31.0000	31.0000	32.0000	33.0000

Table A6, continued (Row 9, Col 9)

Correlation Matrix, Dependent Variables (Parametric)		sqrtQIIIA1c	sqrtQIIIA1d	sqrtQIIIA1e	sqrtQIIID1a	Level Cooperation Domestic Orgs-CNDPS	Level Cooperation Domestic Orgs-CNBC	Level Cooperation Domestic Orgs-CSTP	Level Cooperation Domestic Orgs-TRIPS	sqrtQIIID2a	Level Cooperation International Orgs-CNDPS
sqrtQIVA5	Pearson Correlation	0.0113	-0.1313	-0.1273	0.2827	0.3836	0.4469	0.2712	0.1971	0.2822	0.3539
	Sig. (2-tailed)	0.9496	0.4593	0.4732	0.1233	0.0276	0.0091	0.1269	0.2716	0.1115	0.0400
	N	34.0000	34.0000	34.0000	31.0000	33.0000	33.0000	33.0000	33.0000	33.0000	34.0000
sqrtQIVA7	Pearson Correlation	-0.0143	-0.0541	-0.1297	-0.1366	-0.0858	-0.0358	0.0676	-0.0335	-0.1921	-0.2484
	Sig. (2-tailed)	0.9342	0.7538	0.4509	0.4485	0.6240	0.8381	0.6997	0.8485	0.2689	0.1441
	N	36.0000	36.0000	36.0000	33.0000	35.0000	35.0000	35.0000	35.0000	35.0000	36.0000
sqrtQIVA8	Pearson Correlation	-0.0063	-0.0047	0.0381	0.0378	-0.0429	-0.0303	-0.0118	-0.0056	-0.0879	-0.1162
	Sig. (2-tailed)	0.9714	0.9785	0.8280	0.8375	0.8094	0.8650	0.9471	0.9749	0.6211	0.5061
	N	35.0000	35.0000	35.0000	32.0000	34.0000	34.0000	34.0000	34.0000	34.0000	35.0000
Political Ideology	Pearson Correlation	0.2063	0.0506	0.2530	0.2165	0.0741	0.1898	-0.0347	0.2431	0.3376	0.2327
	Sig. (2-tailed)	0.2495	0.7798	0.1554	0.2420	0.6821	0.2901	0.8479	0.1728	0.0588	0.1925
	N	33.0000	33.0000	33.0000	31.0000	33.0000	33.0000	33.0000	33.0000	32.0000	33.0000

Table A6, continued (Row 9, Col 10)

Correlation Matrix, Dependent Variables (Parametric)		Level Cooperation International Orgs-CNBC	Level Cooperation International Orgs-CSTP	sqrtQIIID2e	sqrtQIVA1	sqrtQIVA2	sqrtQIVA3	sqrtQIVA5	sqrtQIVA7	sqrtQIVA8	Political Ideology
sqrtQIVA5	Pearson Correlation	0.3854	0.2961	0.2794	0.0655	-0.0997	0.0292	1.0000	-0.2149	-0.1246	-0.1715
	Sig. (2-tailed)	0.0244	0.0890	0.1096	0.7130	0.5748	0.8717	.	0.2223	0.4828	0.3480
	N	34.0000	34.0000	34.0000	34.0000	34.0000	33.0000	34.0000	34.0000	34.0000	32.0000
sqrtQIVA7	Pearson Correlation	-0.2283	-0.2587	-0.1450	0.0921	-0.0019	-0.1935	-0.2149	1.0000	-0.0698	-0.0214
	Sig. (2-tailed)	0.1805	0.1276	0.3986	0.5932	0.9913	0.2654	0.2223	.	0.6904	0.9059
	N	36.0000	36.0000	36.0000	36.0000	36.0000	35.0000	34.0000	36.0000	35.0000	33.0000
sqrtQIVA8	Pearson Correlation	-0.1323	-0.1031	-0.0616	0.0066	-0.0312	0.0019	-0.1246	-0.0698	1.0000	0.0146
	Sig. (2-tailed)	0.4485	0.5554	0.7254	0.9698	0.8587	0.9917	0.4828	0.6904	.	0.9356
	N	35.0000	35.0000	35.0000	35.0000	35.0000	34.0000	34.0000	35.0000	35.0000	33.0000
Political Ideology	Pearson Correlation	0.2434	0.2934	0.3916	0.4036	0.3057	0.2858	-0.1715	-0.0214	0.0146	1.0000
	Sig. (2-tailed)	0.1723	0.0974	0.0242	0.0198	0.0836	0.1128	0.3480	0.9059	0.9356	.
	N	33.0000	33.0000	33.0000	33.0000	33.0000	32.0000	32.0000	33.0000	33.0000	33.0000

Appendix 7: Correlation Matrix – International Variables (Parametric)

Table A7 is broken down into the following 72 sub-tables, arranged in a matrix of 8 rows and 9 columns:

Row 1 Col 1	Row 1 Col 2	Row 1 Col 3	Row 1 Col 4	Row 1 Col 5	Row 1 Col 6	Row 1 Col 7	Row 1 Col 8	Row 1 Col 9
Row 2 Col 1	Row 2 Col 2	Row 2 Col 3	Row 2 Col 4	Row 2 Col 5	Row 2 Col 6	Row 2 Col 7	Row 2 Col 8	Row 2 Col 9
Row 3 Col 1	Row 3 Col 2	Row 3 Col 3	Row 3 Col 4	Row 3 Col 5	Row 3 Col 6	Row 3 Col 7	Row 3 Col 8	Row 3 Col 9
Row 4 Col 1	Row 4 Col 2	Row 4 Col 3	Row 4 Col 4	Row 4 Col 5	Row 4 Col 6	Row 4 Col 7	Row 4 Col 8	Row 4 Col 9
Row 5 Col 1	Row 5 Col 2	Row 5 Col 3	Row 5 Col 4	Row 5 Col 5	Row 5 Col 6	Row 5 Col 7	Row 5 Col 8	Row 5 Col 9
Row 6 Col 1	Row 6 Col 2	Row 6 Col 3	Row 6 Col 4	Row 6 Col 5	Row 6 Col 6	Row 6 Col 7	Row 6 Col 8	Row 6 Col 9
Row 7 Col 1	Row 7 Col 2	Row 7 Col 3	Row 7 Col 4	Row 7 Col 5	Row 7 Col 6	Row 7 Col 7	Row 7 Col 8	Row 7 Col 9
Row 8 Col 1	Row 8 Col 2	Row 8 Col 3	Row 8 Col 4	Row 8 Col 5	Row 8 Col 6	Row 8 Col 7	Row 8 Col 8	Row 8 Col 9

To promote accuracy and legibility, all tables are presented in their original printing.

Table A7. Correlation Matrix – International Variables (Parametric) (Row 1, Col 1)

Correlation Matrix, International Variables (Parametric)		Importance of Smuggling-Endangered Species	reflectsqrtQ1A1b	reflectsqrtQ1A1c	reflectsqrtQ1A1d	reflectsqrtQ1A1e	sqrtQ1B1a	Knowledge of Smuggling-Narcotics	Knowledge of Smuggling-Weapons	Knowledge of Smuggling-Humans	Knowledge of Smuggling-Contraband
Importance of Smuggling-Endangered Species	Pearson Correlation	1.0000	-0.0784	-0.0965	-0.0759	-0.1760	0.4053	0.0395	-0.1727	-0.1831	-0.0867
	Sig. (2-tailed)	.	0.6496	0.5757	0.6598	0.3047	0.0142	0.8193	0.3137	0.2852	0.6150
	N	36.0000	36.0000	36.0000	36.0000	36.0000	36.0000	36.0000	36.0000	36.0000	36.0000
reflectsqrtQ1A1b	Pearson Correlation	-0.0784	1.0000	0.6310	0.2015	0.4542	0.2640	-0.2259	-0.1211	0.0181	0.0993
	Sig. (2-tailed)	0.6496	.	0.0000	0.2386	0.0054	0.1198	0.1852	0.4818	0.9165	0.5647
	N	36.0000	36.0000	36.0000	36.0000	36.0000	36.0000	36.0000	36.0000	36.0000	36.0000
reflectsqrtQ1A1c	Pearson Correlation	-0.0965	0.6310	1.0000	0.4053	0.1972	0.2011	-0.2008	-0.1053	-0.0978	0.0536
	Sig. (2-tailed)	0.5757	0.0000	.	0.0142	0.2489	0.2397	0.2403	0.5409	0.5703	0.7560
	N	36.0000	36.0000	36.0000	36.0000	36.0000	36.0000	36.0000	36.0000	36.0000	36.0000
reflectsqrtQ1A1d	Pearson Correlation	-0.0759	0.2015	0.4053	1.0000	0.1431	0.1065	-0.1408	0.0206	-0.1564	0.0659
	Sig. (2-tailed)	0.6598	0.2386	0.0142	.	0.4052	0.5366	0.4126	0.9050	0.3622	0.7024
	N	36.0000	36.0000	36.0000	36.0000	36.0000	36.0000	36.0000	36.0000	36.0000	36.0000
reflectsqrtQ1A1e	Pearson Correlation	-0.1760	0.4542	0.1972	0.1431	1.0000	-0.1598	-0.0782	-0.2644	-0.0633	-0.4163
	Sig. (2-tailed)	0.3047	0.0054	0.2489	0.4052	.	0.3520	0.6505	0.1192	0.7136	0.0115
	N	36.0000	36.0000	36.0000	36.0000	36.0000	36.0000	36.0000	36.0000	36.0000	36.0000
sqrtQ1B1a	Pearson Correlation	0.4053	0.2640	0.2011	0.1065	-0.1598	1.0000	0.2037	0.2523	0.2008	0.3338
	Sig. (2-tailed)	0.0142	0.1198	0.2397	0.5366	0.3520	.	0.2335	0.1376	0.2402	0.0466
	N	36.0000	36.0000	36.0000	36.0000	36.0000	36.0000	36.0000	36.0000	36.0000	36.0000
Knowledge of Smuggling-Narcotics	Pearson Correlation	0.0395	-0.2259	-0.2008	-0.1408	-0.0782	0.2037	1.0000	0.5816	0.4286	0.5001
	Sig. (2-tailed)	0.8193	0.1852	0.2403	0.4126	0.6505	0.2335	.	0.0002	0.0091	0.0019
	N	36.0000	36.0000	36.0000	36.0000	36.0000	36.0000	36.0000	36.0000	36.0000	36.0000
Knowledge of Smuggling-Weapons	Pearson Correlation	-0.1727	-0.1211	-0.1053	0.0206	-0.2644	0.2523	0.5816	1.0000	0.3046	0.6419
	Sig. (2-tailed)	0.3137	0.4818	0.5409	0.9050	0.1192	0.1376	0.0002	.	0.0708	0.0000
	N	36.0000	36.0000	36.0000	36.0000	36.0000	36.0000	36.0000	36.0000	36.0000	36.0000
Knowledge of Smuggling-Humans	Pearson Correlation	-0.1831	0.0181	-0.0978	-0.1564	-0.0633	0.2008	0.4286	0.3046	1.0000	0.5803
	Sig. (2-tailed)	0.2852	0.9165	0.5703	0.3622	0.7136	0.2402	0.0091	0.0708	.	0.0002
	N	36.0000	36.0000	36.0000	36.0000	36.0000	36.0000	36.0000	36.0000	36.0000	36.0000
Knowledge of Smuggling-Contraband	Pearson Correlation	-0.0867	0.0993	0.0536	0.0659	-0.4163	0.3338	0.5001	0.6419	0.5803	1.0000
	Sig. (2-tailed)	0.6150	0.5647	0.7560	0.7024	0.0115	0.0466	0.0019	0.0000	0.0002	.
	N	36.0000	36.0000	36.0000	36.0000	36.0000	36.0000	36.0000	36.0000	36.0000	36.0000
sqrtQ1E1a	Pearson Correlation	-0.0786	0.0433	0.1506	0.0706	0.0150	0.0094	-0.0175	-0.0949	-0.1211	-0.0438
	Sig. (2-tailed)	0.6535	0.8050	0.3879	0.6871	0.9319	0.9572	0.9206	0.5878	0.4883	0.8029
	N	35.0000	35.0000	35.0000	35.0000	35.0000	35.0000	35.0000	35.0000	35.0000	35.0000

Table A7, continued (Row 1, Col 2)

Correlation Matrix, International Variables (Parametric)		sqrtQ1E1a	Personal Resource Challenges-Lack of Time	Personal Resource Challenges-Lack of Knowledge	Personal Resource Challenges-Lack of Training	sqrtQ1E1e	Personal Resource Challenges-Excessive Admin Paperwork	Personal Resource Challenges-Ineffective Technology	Personal Resource Challenges-Ineffective Strategic Focus	Personal Resource Challenges-Ineffective Tactical Policy	Personal Resource Challenges-Lack of Clarity in Duties
Importance of Smuggling-Endangered Species	Pearson Correlation	-0.0786	-0.2521	-0.0060	-0.1118	0.0017	-0.1143	-0.0332	-0.1285	-0.1699	-0.0555
	Sig. (2-tailed)	0.6535	0.1380	0.9725	0.5161	0.9923	0.5070	0.8474	0.4550	0.3218	0.7476
	N	35.0000	36.0000	36.0000	36.0000	36.0000	36.0000	36.0000	36.0000	36.0000	36.0000
reflectsqrtQ1A1b	Pearson Correlation	0.0433	0.0491	-0.1074	-0.0574	0.0673	0.1222	-0.0507	-0.0880	-0.0058	-0.0091
	Sig. (2-tailed)	0.8050	0.7762	0.5329	0.7396	0.6965	0.4777	0.7692	0.6099	0.9732	0.9579
	N	35.0000	36.0000	36.0000	36.0000	36.0000	36.0000	36.0000	36.0000	36.0000	36.0000
reflectsqrtQ1A1c	Pearson Correlation	0.1506	0.1354	-0.1398	-0.1409	-0.0870	0.0631	-0.0964	-0.2280	-0.0994	-0.1168
	Sig. (2-tailed)	0.3879	0.4311	0.4162	0.4125	0.6141	0.7148	0.5758	0.1811	0.5643	0.4976
	N	35.0000	36.0000	36.0000	36.0000	36.0000	36.0000	36.0000	36.0000	36.0000	36.0000
reflectsqrtQ1A1d	Pearson Correlation	0.0706	0.1898	0.0012	-0.0396	-0.1839	-0.0777	-0.2668	-0.2106	-0.1638	-0.1988
	Sig. (2-tailed)	0.6871	0.2676	0.9945	0.8186	0.2829	0.6526	0.1157	0.2177	0.3397	0.2451
	N	35.0000	36.0000	36.0000	36.0000	36.0000	36.0000	36.0000	36.0000	36.0000	36.0000
reflectsqrtQ1A1e	Pearson Correlation	0.0150	0.0699	0.0140	0.0473	0.0016	-0.0052	0.0638	0.0616	0.1821	0.1008
	Sig. (2-tailed)	0.9319	0.6854	0.9356	0.7840	0.9928	0.9760	0.7115	0.7211	0.2879	0.5587
	N	35.0000	36.0000	36.0000	36.0000	36.0000	36.0000	36.0000	36.0000	36.0000	36.0000
sqrtQ1B1a	Pearson Correlation	0.0094	0.0171	0.0056	0.0112	0.2065	0.0536	0.0157	0.1585	0.0430	0.0533
	Sig. (2-tailed)	0.9572	0.9213	0.9743	0.9483	0.2270	0.7560	0.9276	0.3558	0.8033	0.7575
	N	35.0000	36.0000	36.0000	36.0000	36.0000	36.0000	36.0000	36.0000	36.0000	36.0000
Knowledge of Smuggling-Narcotics	Pearson Correlation	-0.0175	0.1009	-0.0019	-0.0190	0.0853	0.2558	0.2258	-0.0792	-0.0393	0.0626
	Sig. (2-tailed)	0.9206	0.5582	0.9911	0.9126	0.6208	0.1320	0.1854	0.6460	0.8202	0.7166
	N	35.0000	36.0000	36.0000	36.0000	36.0000	36.0000	36.0000	36.0000	36.0000	36.0000
Knowledge of Smuggling-Weapons	Pearson Correlation	-0.0949	-0.0720	-0.2415	-0.2339	0.2980	0.2285	-0.0585	-0.1197	-0.1135	-0.1099
	Sig. (2-tailed)	0.5878	0.6766	0.1560	0.1698	0.0775	0.1802	0.7349	0.4868	0.5097	0.5235
	N	35.0000	36.0000	36.0000	36.0000	36.0000	36.0000	36.0000	36.0000	36.0000	36.0000
Knowledge of Smuggling-Humans	Pearson Correlation	-0.1211	0.1074	0.0093	-0.0248	0.0830	-0.0120	0.0177	-0.0164	0.0170	0.0758
	Sig. (2-tailed)	0.4883	0.5331	0.9572	0.8859	0.6301	0.9445	0.9184	0.9245	0.9215	0.6605
	N	35.0000	36.0000	36.0000	36.0000	36.0000	36.0000	36.0000	36.0000	36.0000	36.0000
Knowledge of Smuggling-Contraband	Pearson Correlation	-0.0438	0.1384	-0.0687	-0.1326	0.1690	0.2170	-0.0706	-0.1110	-0.1189	0.0121
	Sig. (2-tailed)	0.8029	0.4207	0.6905	0.4409	0.3243	0.2037	0.6824	0.5192	0.4899	0.9442
	N	35.0000	36.0000	36.0000	36.0000	36.0000	36.0000	36.0000	36.0000	36.0000	36.0000
sqrtQ1E1a	Pearson Correlation	1.0000	0.3118	0.3342	0.2759	0.1914	0.4520	0.3708	0.5510	0.6237	0.5042
	Sig. (2-tailed)	.	0.0683	0.0497	0.1087	0.2708	0.0064	0.0283	0.0006	0.0001	0.0020
	N	35.0000	35.0000	35.0000	35.0000	35.0000	35.0000	35.0000	35.0000	35.0000	35.0000

Table A7, continued (Row 1, Col 3)

Correlation Matrix, International Variables (Parametric)		Personal Resource Challenges-Conflict or Lack Comm Leaders and Employees	sqrtQ1E1l	Personal Resource Challenges-Conflict or Lack Comm International Orgs	Personal Resource Challenges-Conflict or Lack Comm Domestic Orgs	sqrtQ1E3a	Org Resource Challenges-Lack of Time	Org Resource Challenges-Lack of Knowledge	Org Resource Challenges-Lack of Training	sqrtQ1E3e	Org Resource Challenges-Excessive Admin Paperwork
Importance of Smuggling-Endangered Species	Pearson Correlation	-0.0670	0.0461	0.0229	-0.0208	0.0133	-0.2552	-0.1379	-0.1090	-0.2357	-0.2130
	Sig. (2-tailed)	0.6979	0.7894	0.8946	0.9041	0.9404	0.1390	0.4295	0.5331	0.1795	0.2193
	N	36.0000	36.0000	36.0000	36.0000	34.0000	35.0000	35.0000	35.0000	34.0000	35.0000
reflectsqrtQ1A1b	Pearson Correlation	0.0368	-0.0333	0.0465	-0.1078	-0.1596	-0.1996	-0.3436	-0.2567	-0.0838	-0.1647
	Sig. (2-tailed)	0.8314	0.8470	0.7876	0.5314	0.3674	0.2502	0.0433	0.1366	0.6376	0.3445
	N	36.0000	36.0000	36.0000	36.0000	34.0000	35.0000	35.0000	35.0000	34.0000	35.0000
reflectsqrtQ1A1c	Pearson Correlation	-0.0162	-0.0776	-0.0535	-0.0861	-0.2365	-0.1862	-0.3719	-0.2689	-0.0101	-0.0928
	Sig. (2-tailed)	0.9253	0.6528	0.7567	0.6178	0.1782	0.2843	0.0278	0.1184	0.9550	0.5960
	N	36.0000	36.0000	36.0000	36.0000	34.0000	35.0000	35.0000	35.0000	34.0000	35.0000
reflectsqrtQ1A1d	Pearson Correlation	-0.1624	0.0044	-0.1854	-0.2570	-0.3896	-0.0401	-0.1642	-0.1838	0.1432	-0.0628
	Sig. (2-tailed)	0.3439	0.9796	0.2789	0.1303	0.0227	0.8190	0.3458	0.2906	0.4192	0.7202
	N	36.0000	36.0000	36.0000	36.0000	34.0000	35.0000	35.0000	35.0000	34.0000	35.0000
reflectsqrtQ1A1e	Pearson Correlation	0.2367	-0.1415	-0.0606	0.1232	0.0326	0.0005	-0.0840	-0.0341	0.1655	0.0211
	Sig. (2-tailed)	0.1646	0.4104	0.7254	0.4741	0.8548	0.9978	0.6316	0.8458	0.3496	0.9040
	N	36.0000	36.0000	36.0000	36.0000	34.0000	35.0000	35.0000	35.0000	34.0000	35.0000
sqrtQ1B1a	Pearson Correlation	0.0124	0.0984	0.0694	-0.0188	-0.0214	-0.1127	-0.1504	-0.1441	-0.2154	-0.2287
	Sig. (2-tailed)	0.9427	0.5681	0.6876	0.9131	0.9043	0.5192	0.3884	0.4090	0.2211	0.1863
	N	36.0000	36.0000	36.0000	36.0000	34.0000	35.0000	35.0000	35.0000	34.0000	35.0000
Knowledge of Smuggling-Narcotics	Pearson Correlation	-0.0357	-0.0247	0.1843	0.1111	0.2403	0.0762	-0.0412	-0.0791	0.0355	0.1035
	Sig. (2-tailed)	0.8364	0.8862	0.2818	0.5187	0.1711	0.6634	0.8141	0.6516	0.8419	0.5540
	N	36.0000	36.0000	36.0000	36.0000	34.0000	35.0000	35.0000	35.0000	34.0000	35.0000
Knowledge of Smuggling-Weapons	Pearson Correlation	-0.1635	0.0217	-0.0188	-0.1551	0.2145	-0.0246	-0.2739	-0.3116	-0.0703	-0.0973
	Sig. (2-tailed)	0.3406	0.9001	0.9134	0.3663	0.2232	0.8886	0.1114	0.0684	0.6926	0.5783
	N	36.0000	36.0000	36.0000	36.0000	34.0000	35.0000	35.0000	35.0000	34.0000	35.0000
Knowledge of Smuggling-Humans	Pearson Correlation	-0.0869	-0.2842	-0.0105	-0.0370	-0.0719	0.0081	-0.0646	-0.1464	-0.2233	-0.2894
	Sig. (2-tailed)	0.6142	0.0930	0.9517	0.8303	0.6860	0.9632	0.7124	0.4014	0.2043	0.0917
	N	36.0000	36.0000	36.0000	36.0000	34.0000	35.0000	35.0000	35.0000	34.0000	35.0000
Knowledge of Smuggling-Contraband	Pearson Correlation	-0.0616	0.0032	0.1416	-0.0556	-0.1157	-0.0850	-0.1819	-0.2547	-0.1197	-0.1697
	Sig. (2-tailed)	0.7213	0.9854	0.4100	0.7474	0.5145	0.6275	0.2956	0.1398	0.5001	0.3299
	N	36.0000	36.0000	36.0000	36.0000	34.0000	35.0000	35.0000	35.0000	34.0000	35.0000
sqrtQ1E1a	Pearson Correlation	0.5982	0.5175	0.3957	0.4968	0.5355	0.3713	0.2971	0.3371	0.4286	0.6521
	Sig. (2-tailed)	0.0001	0.0015	0.0186	0.0024	0.0013	0.0306	0.0879	0.0512	0.0128	0.0000
	N	35.0000	35.0000	35.0000	35.0000	33.0000	34.0000	34.0000	34.0000	33.0000	34.0000

Table A7, continued (Row 1, Col 4)

Correlation Matrix, International Variables (Parametric)		Org Resource Challenges-Ineffective Technology	Org Resource Challenges-Ineffective Strategic Focus	Org Resource Challenges-Ineffective Tactical Policy	Org Resource Challenges-Lack of Clarity in Duties	Org Resource Challenges-Conflict or Lack Comm Leaders and Employees	sqrtQ1E3l	Org Resource Challenges-Conflict or Lack Comm International Orgs	Org Resource Challenges-Conflict or Lack Comm Domestic Orgs	sqrtQIAIa	Knowledge of Domestic Law-CSIE
Importance of Smuggling-Endangered Species	Pearson Correlation	-0.1288	-0.0368	-0.0218	0.0492	-0.0220	-0.0396	0.0261	0.0753	0.0714	-0.0032
	Sig. (2-tailed)	0.4609	0.8339	0.9009	0.7792	0.9000	0.8214	0.8818	0.6674	0.6836	0.9852
	N	35.0000	35.0000	35.0000	35.0000	35.0000	35.0000	35.0000	35.0000	35.0000	35.0000
reflectsqrtQ1A1b	Pearson Correlation	-0.2495	-0.2400	-0.2306	-0.3141	-0.1516	-0.0530	-0.3126	-0.3260	0.3292	-0.2346
	Sig. (2-tailed)	0.1483	0.1649	0.1827	0.0661	0.3846	0.7622	0.0675	0.0560	0.0535	0.1750
	N	35.0000	35.0000	35.0000	35.0000	35.0000	35.0000	35.0000	35.0000	35.0000	35.0000
reflectsqrtQ1A1c	Pearson Correlation	-0.1343	-0.2113	-0.2437	-0.3196	-0.1189	-0.0769	-0.3248	-0.2974	0.1555	0.0142
	Sig. (2-tailed)	0.4419	0.2231	0.1584	0.0613	0.4961	0.6604	0.0570	0.0827	0.3724	0.9356
	N	35.0000	35.0000	35.0000	35.0000	35.0000	35.0000	35.0000	35.0000	35.0000	35.0000
reflectsqrtQ1A1d	Pearson Correlation	-0.0683	-0.0591	-0.1340	-0.1009	0.0441	0.0348	-0.0833	-0.1055	0.1382	0.0931
	Sig. (2-tailed)	0.6967	0.7359	0.4429	0.5642	0.8016	0.8425	0.6341	0.5464	0.4284	0.5947
	N	35.0000	35.0000	35.0000	35.0000	35.0000	35.0000	35.0000	35.0000	35.0000	35.0000
reflectsqrtQ1A1e	Pearson Correlation	0.1518	0.0927	0.1423	0.0087	0.1340	-0.1052	0.0119	0.0191	-0.1336	-0.1776
	Sig. (2-tailed)	0.3840	0.5964	0.4147	0.9603	0.4430	0.5474	0.9457	0.9131	0.4440	0.3073
	N	35.0000	35.0000	35.0000	35.0000	35.0000	35.0000	35.0000	35.0000	35.0000	35.0000
sqrtQ1B1a	Pearson Correlation	-0.0945	0.0266	-0.0108	0.0917	-0.0517	0.0804	0.0776	0.0426	0.5077	0.0953
	Sig. (2-tailed)	0.5894	0.8796	0.9507	0.6001	0.7678	0.6460	0.6577	0.8080	0.0018	0.5859
	N	35.0000	35.0000	35.0000	35.0000	35.0000	35.0000	35.0000	35.0000	35.0000	35.0000
Knowledge of Smuggling-Narcotics	Pearson Correlation	0.2007	0.0133	0.0210	0.0127	0.0840	-0.0488	0.1324	0.1116	0.0948	0.6809
	Sig. (2-tailed)	0.2477	0.9398	0.9048	0.9422	0.6316	0.7808	0.4484	0.5233	0.5879	0.0000
	N	35.0000	35.0000	35.0000	35.0000	35.0000	35.0000	35.0000	35.0000	35.0000	35.0000
Knowledge of Smuggling-Weapons	Pearson Correlation	-0.0701	-0.1614	-0.1416	-0.1453	0.0522	0.0348	-0.1213	-0.1315	0.2332	0.5161
	Sig. (2-tailed)	0.6890	0.3543	0.4172	0.4050	0.7657	0.8428	0.4878	0.4513	0.1776	0.0015
	N	35.0000	35.0000	35.0000	35.0000	35.0000	35.0000	35.0000	35.0000	35.0000	35.0000
Knowledge of Smuggling-Humans	Pearson Correlation	-0.0244	-0.0382	-0.1871	-0.0797	-0.2450	-0.4343	0.0368	-0.0734	0.0326	0.1554
	Sig. (2-tailed)	0.8893	0.8277	0.2818	0.6492	0.1560	0.0091	0.8337	0.6753	0.8525	0.3726
	N	35.0000	35.0000	35.0000	35.0000	35.0000	35.0000	35.0000	35.0000	35.0000	35.0000
Knowledge of Smuggling-Contraband	Pearson Correlation	-0.1510	-0.1665	-0.1946	-0.1955	-0.0940	-0.0865	-0.1600	-0.1675	0.4173	0.3006
	Sig. (2-tailed)	0.3867	0.3390	0.2626	0.2604	0.5912	0.6213	0.3587	0.3362	0.0126	0.0793
	N	35.0000	35.0000	35.0000	35.0000	35.0000	35.0000	35.0000	35.0000	35.0000	35.0000
sqrtQ1E1a	Pearson Correlation	0.5895	0.3989	0.4226	0.3674	0.4307	0.4065	0.2378	0.2694	0.1149	-0.0396
	Sig. (2-tailed)	0.0002	0.0194	0.0128	0.0326	0.0110	0.0171	0.1756	0.1234	0.5176	0.8241
	N	34.0000	34.0000	34.0000	34.0000	34.0000	34.0000	34.0000	34.0000	34.0000	34.0000

Table A7, continued (Row 1, Col 5)

Correlation Matrix, International Variables (Parametric)		Knowledge of Domestic Law-DWMD	Knowledge of Domestic Law-TVP	Knowledge of Domestic Law-CBP	sqrtQIID1a	Level Cooperation Domestic Orgs-CSIE	Level Cooperation Domestic Orgs-DWMD	Level Cooperation Domestic Orgs-TVP	Level Cooperation Domestic Orgs-CBP	sqrtQIIIA1a	sqrtQIIIA1b
Importance of Smuggling-Endangered Species	Pearson Correlation	-0.2227	-0.2041	-0.1039	0.2661	-0.0291	0.0626	0.1330	0.0417	0.1539	-0.0319
	Sig. (2-tailed)	0.1984	0.2396	0.5527	0.1167	0.8662	0.7167	0.4393	0.8092	0.3774	0.8535
	N	35.0000	35.0000	35.0000	36.0000	36.0000	36.0000	36.0000	36.0000	35.0000	36.0000
reflectsqrtQ1A1b	Pearson Correlation	-0.1107	-0.1045	0.1069	0.2364	-0.1636	-0.1263	-0.1268	0.0764	0.1940	0.0782
	Sig. (2-tailed)	0.5268	0.5503	0.5409	0.1650	0.3404	0.4630	0.4612	0.6578	0.2642	0.6503
	N	35.0000	35.0000	35.0000	36.0000	36.0000	36.0000	36.0000	36.0000	35.0000	36.0000
reflectsqrtQ1A1c	Pearson Correlation	0.0084	-0.0642	0.2938	0.1976	0.0149	0.0214	-0.0633	0.1665	0.0303	0.1695
	Sig. (2-tailed)	0.9620	0.7141	0.0867	0.2480	0.9312	0.9013	0.7139	0.3317	0.8627	0.3229
	N	35.0000	35.0000	35.0000	36.0000	36.0000	36.0000	36.0000	36.0000	35.0000	36.0000
reflectsqrtQ1A1d	Pearson Correlation	0.0954	-0.0603	0.1321	0.2932	0.1377	0.1513	0.0183	0.2144	0.1534	0.1824
	Sig. (2-tailed)	0.5856	0.7308	0.4494	0.0826	0.4231	0.3783	0.9154	0.2091	0.3788	0.2870
	N	35.0000	35.0000	35.0000	36.0000	36.0000	36.0000	36.0000	36.0000	35.0000	36.0000
reflectsqrtQ1A1e	Pearson Correlation	-0.1624	-0.0460	-0.2579	-0.1569	-0.2225	-0.3094	-0.3146	-0.3942	-0.2490	0.1344
	Sig. (2-tailed)	0.3512	0.7932	0.1347	0.3609	0.1922	0.0663	0.0617	0.0174	0.1492	0.4346
	N	35.0000	35.0000	35.0000	36.0000	36.0000	36.0000	36.0000	36.0000	35.0000	36.0000
sqrtQ1B1a	Pearson Correlation	0.0299	0.1391	0.0992	0.6200	0.2881	0.1094	0.4848	0.2573	0.5686	0.0163
	Sig. (2-tailed)	0.8644	0.4256	0.5707	0.0001	0.0884	0.5255	0.0027	0.1297	0.0004	0.9248
	N	35.0000	35.0000	35.0000	36.0000	36.0000	36.0000	36.0000	36.0000	35.0000	36.0000
Knowledge of Smuggling-Narcotics	Pearson Correlation	0.5787	0.5195	0.2628	0.0729	0.5092	0.3940	0.4552	-0.0049	0.0614	0.4628
	Sig. (2-tailed)	0.0003	0.0014	0.1273	0.6725	0.0015	0.0174	0.0053	0.9774	0.7262	0.0045
	N	35.0000	35.0000	35.0000	36.0000	36.0000	36.0000	36.0000	36.0000	35.0000	36.0000
Knowledge of Smuggling-Weapons	Pearson Correlation	0.6878	0.4150	0.5338	0.4288	0.5158	0.4225	0.4073	0.3248	0.1530	0.2114
	Sig. (2-tailed)	0.0000	0.0132	0.0010	0.0091	0.0013	0.0103	0.0137	0.0532	0.3804	0.2159
	N	35.0000	35.0000	35.0000	36.0000	36.0000	36.0000	36.0000	36.0000	35.0000	36.0000
Knowledge of Smuggling-Humans	Pearson Correlation	0.3185	0.5869	0.1776	0.0309	0.2726	0.1807	0.4165	-0.0180	0.2038	0.2662
	Sig. (2-tailed)	0.0622	0.0002	0.3074	0.8582	0.1078	0.2915	0.0115	0.9168	0.2403	0.1166
	N	35.0000	35.0000	35.0000	36.0000	36.0000	36.0000	36.0000	36.0000	35.0000	36.0000
Knowledge of Smuggling-Contraband	Pearson Correlation	0.4673	0.4621	0.6159	0.3750	0.3252	0.3303	0.4434	0.3882	0.3504	0.3009
	Sig. (2-tailed)	0.0047	0.0052	0.0001	0.0242	0.0530	0.0491	0.0068	0.0193	0.0390	0.0745
	N	35.0000	35.0000	35.0000	36.0000	36.0000	36.0000	36.0000	36.0000	35.0000	36.0000
sqrtQ1E1a	Pearson Correlation	-0.2166	-0.1300	-0.1190	-0.0357	-0.3267	-0.3174	-0.2215	-0.1697	0.3282	0.2881
	Sig. (2-tailed)	0.2186	0.4636	0.5028	0.8388	0.0554	0.0632	0.2010	0.3297	0.0581	0.0933
	N	34.0000	34.0000	34.0000	35.0000	35.0000	35.0000	35.0000	35.0000	34.0000	35.0000

Table A7, continued (Row 1, Col 6)

Correlation Matrix, International Variables (Parametric)		sqrtQIIIA1c	sqrtQIIIA1d	sqrtQIIIA1e	sqrtQIIID1a	Level Cooperation Domestic Orgs-CNDPS	Level Cooperation Domestic Orgs-CNBC	Level Cooperation Domestic Orgs-CSTP	Level Cooperation Domestic Orgs-TRIPS	sqrtQIIID2a	Level Cooperation International Orgs-CNDPS
Importance of Smuggling-Endangered Species	Pearson Correlation	-0.1127	-0.1182	-0.1398	-0.0834	-0.0518	-0.1244	-0.1646	-0.1113	0.0214	0.1124
	Sig. (2-tailed)	0.5128	0.4923	0.4159	0.6445	0.7677	0.4764	0.3448	0.5246	0.9028	0.5139
	N	36.0000	36.0000	36.0000	33.0000	35.0000	35.0000	35.0000	35.0000	35.0000	36.0000
reflectsqrtQ1A1b	Pearson Correlation	-0.0579	-0.0618	0.3553	0.0701	-0.0744	0.0249	0.0051	0.1878	0.2075	0.0021
	Sig. (2-tailed)	0.7373	0.7201	0.0335	0.6984	0.6711	0.8870	0.9767	0.2800	0.2317	0.9902
	N	36.0000	36.0000	36.0000	33.0000	35.0000	35.0000	35.0000	35.0000	35.0000	36.0000
reflectsqrtQ1A1c	Pearson Correlation	0.0782	-0.0557	0.3276	0.1064	0.1564	0.1364	0.1535	0.3916	0.2276	0.1330
	Sig. (2-tailed)	0.6503	0.7470	0.0511	0.5557	0.3696	0.4348	0.3786	0.0200	0.1886	0.4393
	N	36.0000	36.0000	36.0000	33.0000	35.0000	35.0000	35.0000	35.0000	35.0000	36.0000
reflectsqrtQ1A1d	Pearson Correlation	0.2523	-0.0240	0.2496	0.0308	0.1160	0.1835	0.0920	0.2575	0.1701	0.0575
	Sig. (2-tailed)	0.1377	0.8894	0.1421	0.8648	0.5069	0.2913	0.5993	0.1353	0.3285	0.7391
	N	36.0000	36.0000	36.0000	33.0000	35.0000	35.0000	35.0000	35.0000	35.0000	36.0000
reflectsqrtQ1A1e	Pearson Correlation	0.0069	-0.1092	-0.0503	-0.1836	-0.0204	-0.0434	-0.0947	-0.0987	-0.0940	-0.0534
	Sig. (2-tailed)	0.9683	0.5260	0.7708	0.3065	0.9072	0.8045	0.5886	0.5725	0.5913	0.7571
	N	36.0000	36.0000	36.0000	33.0000	35.0000	35.0000	35.0000	35.0000	35.0000	36.0000
sqrtQ1B1a	Pearson Correlation	0.0481	0.1280	0.1387	0.4138	0.2400	0.2866	0.2611	0.2429	0.5361	0.1694
	Sig. (2-tailed)	0.7807	0.4570	0.4197	0.0167	0.1649	0.0951	0.1298	0.1597	0.0009	0.3233
	N	36.0000	36.0000	36.0000	33.0000	35.0000	35.0000	35.0000	35.0000	35.0000	36.0000
Knowledge of Smuggling-Narcotics	Pearson Correlation	0.4045	0.3222	0.1691	0.1939	0.3670	0.2308	0.2171	-0.0035	-0.0078	0.2711
	Sig. (2-tailed)	0.0144	0.0553	0.3241	0.2797	0.0301	0.1821	0.2103	0.9839	0.9646	0.1098
	N	36.0000	36.0000	36.0000	33.0000	35.0000	35.0000	35.0000	35.0000	35.0000	36.0000
Knowledge of Smuggling-Weapons	Pearson Correlation	0.4489	0.2949	0.2459	0.3706	0.2723	0.4812	0.2043	0.2767	0.2198	0.2907
	Sig. (2-tailed)	0.0060	0.0808	0.1483	0.0337	0.1136	0.0034	0.2391	0.1075	0.2044	0.0855
	N	36.0000	36.0000	36.0000	33.0000	35.0000	35.0000	35.0000	35.0000	35.0000	36.0000
Knowledge of Smuggling-Humans	Pearson Correlation	0.2159	0.4759	0.2935	0.1707	0.1638	0.1396	0.2787	0.0033	0.1284	0.1288
	Sig. (2-tailed)	0.2061	0.0033	0.0823	0.3422	0.3471	0.4239	0.1050	0.9852	0.4625	0.4541
	N	36.0000	36.0000	36.0000	33.0000	35.0000	35.0000	35.0000	35.0000	35.0000	36.0000
Knowledge of Smuggling-Contraband	Pearson Correlation	0.3780	0.4396	0.5612	0.3408	0.1460	0.3090	0.2677	0.2737	0.1527	0.0678
	Sig. (2-tailed)	0.0230	0.0073	0.0004	0.0523	0.4028	0.0709	0.1200	0.1117	0.3810	0.6944
	N	36.0000	36.0000	36.0000	33.0000	35.0000	35.0000	35.0000	35.0000	35.0000	36.0000
sqrtQ1E1a	Pearson Correlation	0.3869	0.2685	0.2605	-0.0079	-0.1191	-0.1925	-0.1203	-0.0535	-0.0563	-0.0521
	Sig. (2-tailed)	0.0217	0.1188	0.1307	0.9652	0.4956	0.2680	0.4912	0.7601	0.7519	0.7663
	N	35.0000	35.0000	35.0000	33.0000	35.0000	35.0000	35.0000	35.0000	34.0000	35.0000

Table A7, continued (Row 1, Col 7)

Correlation Matrix, International Variables (Parametric)		Level Cooperation International Orgs- CNBC	Level Cooperation International Orgs- CSTP	sqrtQIIID2e	sqrtQIVA1	sqrtQIVA2	sqrtQIVA3	sqrtQIVA5	sqrtQIVA7	sqrtQIVA8	Political Ideology
Importance of Smuggling-Endangered Species	Pearson Correlation	0.0449	0.0549	-0.0110	0.1272	0.1038	-0.2036	-0.1126	-0.0287	-0.0400	-0.1693
	Sig. (2-tailed)	0.7949	0.7504	0.9491	0.4597	0.5471	0.2408	0.5259	0.8680	0.8195	0.3464
	N	36.0000	36.0000	36.0000	36.0000	36.0000	35.0000	34.0000	36.0000	35.0000	33.0000
reflectsqrtQ1A1b	Pearson Correlation	0.0023	0.0373	0.0624	-0.1992	0.0760	-0.0784	-0.3136	-0.0640	0.1170	0.3071
	Sig. (2-tailed)	0.9895	0.8292	0.7177	0.2442	0.6595	0.6545	0.0709	0.7108	0.5031	0.0821
	N	36.0000	36.0000	36.0000	36.0000	36.0000	35.0000	34.0000	36.0000	35.0000	33.0000
reflectsqrtQ1A1c	Pearson Correlation	0.0860	0.0793	0.2157	0.0037	-0.0544	-0.0162	-0.1166	0.0205	0.1854	0.2647
	Sig. (2-tailed)	0.6180	0.6459	0.2065	0.9827	0.7528	0.9265	0.5114	0.9057	0.2864	0.1366
	N	36.0000	36.0000	36.0000	36.0000	36.0000	35.0000	34.0000	36.0000	35.0000	33.0000
reflectsqrtQ1A1d	Pearson Correlation	0.1102	0.1459	0.2396	-0.1471	-0.2229	-0.1433	-0.0908	-0.2604	0.1977	0.1013
	Sig. (2-tailed)	0.5222	0.3959	0.1593	0.3919	0.1914	0.4115	0.6095	0.1250	0.2548	0.5750
	N	36.0000	36.0000	36.0000	36.0000	36.0000	35.0000	34.0000	36.0000	35.0000	33.0000
reflectsqrtQ1A1e	Pearson Correlation	-0.0231	-0.0056	-0.1143	-0.2422	-0.0831	-0.0897	-0.1674	-0.1845	-0.0653	0.0011
	Sig. (2-tailed)	0.8936	0.9740	0.5070	0.1546	0.6301	0.6085	0.3440	0.2813	0.7093	0.9951
	N	36.0000	36.0000	36.0000	36.0000	36.0000	35.0000	34.0000	36.0000	35.0000	33.0000
sqrtQ1B1a	Pearson Correlation	0.1797	0.2332	0.1194	0.1477	0.1831	-0.0036	0.1451	-0.1589	0.0121	0.1583
	Sig. (2-tailed)	0.2943	0.1710	0.4880	0.3899	0.2852	0.9835	0.4129	0.3545	0.9450	0.3789
	N	36.0000	36.0000	36.0000	36.0000	36.0000	35.0000	34.0000	36.0000	35.0000	33.0000
Knowledge of Smuggling-Narcotics	Pearson Correlation	0.2604	0.2177	0.0106	0.0975	-0.1039	0.0204	0.1769	-0.1265	0.0783	0.0522
	Sig. (2-tailed)	0.1251	0.2021	0.9511	0.5715	0.5464	0.9073	0.3169	0.4621	0.6548	0.7729
	N	36.0000	36.0000	36.0000	36.0000	36.0000	35.0000	34.0000	36.0000	35.0000	33.0000
Knowledge of Smuggling-Weapons	Pearson Correlation	0.4227	0.2247	0.3393	0.1958	0.0264	0.1837	0.2895	-0.0129	0.0283	0.3089
	Sig. (2-tailed)	0.0102	0.1876	0.0429	0.2525	0.8784	0.2908	0.0968	0.9406	0.8720	0.0802
	N	36.0000	36.0000	36.0000	36.0000	36.0000	35.0000	34.0000	36.0000	35.0000	33.0000
Knowledge of Smuggling-Humans	Pearson Correlation	0.1151	0.2938	0.0382	0.1268	0.0276	0.2654	0.1668	-0.2391	0.1825	0.0541
	Sig. (2-tailed)	0.5040	0.0820	0.8247	0.4610	0.8732	0.1234	0.3458	0.1602	0.2939	0.7649
	N	36.0000	36.0000	36.0000	36.0000	36.0000	35.0000	34.0000	36.0000	35.0000	33.0000
Knowledge of Smuggling-Contraband	Pearson Correlation	0.1025	0.1867	0.1958	0.1346	0.0214	0.1990	0.0464	0.0134	0.2487	0.2656
	Sig. (2-tailed)	0.5518	0.2757	0.2524	0.4339	0.9013	0.2517	0.7946	0.9384	0.1497	0.1352
	N	36.0000	36.0000	36.0000	36.0000	36.0000	35.0000	34.0000	36.0000	35.0000	33.0000
sqrtQ1E1a	Pearson Correlation	-0.1166	-0.0751	-0.1284	0.0884	0.2392	0.3484	-0.0613	-0.0508	-0.1871	-0.1008
	Sig. (2-tailed)	0.5047	0.6679	0.4624	0.6135	0.1663	0.0435	0.7347	0.7719	0.2894	0.5767
	N	35.0000	35.0000	35.0000	35.0000	35.0000	34.0000	33.0000	35.0000	34.0000	33.0000

Table A7, continued (Row 1, Col 8)

Correlation Matrix, International Variables (Parametric)		sqrtQIIIB1a	sqrtQIIIB1b	sqrtQIIIB1c	sqrtQIIIB1d	sqrtQIIIB1e	sqrtQIIIB2a	Perceived Effectiveness Domestic Govt Support-CNDPS	Perceived Effectiveness Domestic Govt Support-CNBC	Perceived Effectiveness Domestic Govt Support-CSTP	Perceived Effectiveness Domestic Govt Support-TRIPS
Importance of Smuggling-Endangered Species	Pearson Correlation	-0.0064	-0.2026	-0.1399	-0.1844	-0.1375	0.0635	-0.1400	-0.1490	-0.1739	-0.1067
	Sig. (2-tailed)	0.9707	0.2431	0.4228	0.2889	0.4309	0.7170	0.4155	0.3930	0.3177	0.5418
	N	35.0000	35.0000	35.0000	35.0000	35.0000	35.0000	36.0000	35.0000	35.0000	35.0000
reflectsqrtQ1A1b	Pearson Correlation	-0.0953	-0.0939	-0.1566	0.1203	0.2347	-0.0980	-0.2238	-0.1267	-0.1105	0.2468
	Sig. (2-tailed)	0.5861	0.5916	0.3690	0.4913	0.1747	0.5752	0.1895	0.4683	0.5275	0.1530
	N	35.0000	35.0000	35.0000	35.0000	35.0000	35.0000	36.0000	35.0000	35.0000	35.0000
reflectsqrtQ1A1c	Pearson Correlation	-0.2405	-0.0183	-0.1390	0.0633	0.0805	-0.2608	-0.1688	-0.1742	-0.1375	0.0546
	Sig. (2-tailed)	0.1640	0.9171	0.4259	0.7179	0.6458	0.1302	0.3251	0.3169	0.4308	0.7554
	N	35.0000	35.0000	35.0000	35.0000	35.0000	35.0000	36.0000	35.0000	35.0000	35.0000
reflectsqrtQ1A1d	Pearson Correlation	0.0748	0.0756	0.0127	0.3355	0.0279	-0.0043	-0.0924	-0.0036	0.0211	-0.0489
	Sig. (2-tailed)	0.6693	0.6662	0.9425	0.0488	0.8734	0.9806	0.5921	0.9838	0.9042	0.7801
	N	35.0000	35.0000	35.0000	35.0000	35.0000	35.0000	36.0000	35.0000	35.0000	35.0000
reflectsqrtQ1A1e	Pearson Correlation	-0.1673	-0.1348	-0.1235	-0.1088	-0.0004	0.0880	-0.0269	0.0691	0.0792	0.1141
	Sig. (2-tailed)	0.3368	0.4401	0.4797	0.5340	0.9980	0.6151	0.8762	0.6933	0.6511	0.5139
	N	35.0000	35.0000	35.0000	35.0000	35.0000	35.0000	36.0000	35.0000	35.0000	35.0000
sqrtQ1B1a	Pearson Correlation	0.0681	-0.0359	0.0250	0.0906	-0.0557	0.1703	-0.1663	-0.0192	-0.0832	-0.1506
	Sig. (2-tailed)	0.6975	0.8376	0.8865	0.6047	0.7504	0.3279	0.3324	0.9128	0.6345	0.3878
	N	35.0000	35.0000	35.0000	35.0000	35.0000	35.0000	36.0000	35.0000	35.0000	35.0000
Knowledge of Smuggling-Narcotics	Pearson Correlation	-0.1725	0.0272	0.1208	0.1077	-0.1535	-0.0971	0.1388	0.1538	-0.0643	-0.1250
	Sig. (2-tailed)	0.3218	0.8767	0.4893	0.5380	0.3787	0.5789	0.4195	0.3778	0.7136	0.4744
	N	35.0000	35.0000	35.0000	35.0000	35.0000	35.0000	36.0000	35.0000	35.0000	35.0000
Knowledge of Smuggling-Weapons	Pearson Correlation	-0.0706	0.2148	0.1422	0.4559	-0.1759	-0.1032	0.0372	0.1431	-0.0915	-0.0492
	Sig. (2-tailed)	0.6870	0.2153	0.4153	0.0059	0.3121	0.5551	0.8294	0.4121	0.6011	0.7790
	N	35.0000	35.0000	35.0000	35.0000	35.0000	35.0000	36.0000	35.0000	35.0000	35.0000
Knowledge of Smuggling-Humans	Pearson Correlation	0.1040	0.1398	0.2626	0.1624	0.1760	0.0728	0.1104	0.2286	0.2052	0.0019
	Sig. (2-tailed)	0.5521	0.4231	0.1275	0.3514	0.3119	0.6776	0.5215	0.1865	0.2371	0.9914
	N	35.0000	35.0000	35.0000	35.0000	35.0000	35.0000	36.0000	35.0000	35.0000	35.0000
Knowledge of Smuggling-Contraband	Pearson Correlation	0.0096	0.0816	0.0814	0.4283	0.1273	-0.1897	-0.1968	-0.1430	-0.1544	-0.0110
	Sig. (2-tailed)	0.9563	0.6412	0.6421	0.0103	0.4662	0.2749	0.2501	0.4124	0.3759	0.9499
	N	35.0000	35.0000	35.0000	35.0000	35.0000	35.0000	36.0000	35.0000	35.0000	35.0000
sqrtQ1E1a	Pearson Correlation	-0.2349	-0.2137	-0.2595	-0.2588	-0.1575	-0.2875	-0.1912	-0.1564	-0.1366	-0.2977
	Sig. (2-tailed)	0.1811	0.2249	0.1384	0.1394	0.3737	0.0993	0.2712	0.3771	0.4411	0.0873
	N	34.0000	34.0000	34.0000	34.0000	34.0000	34.0000	35.0000	34.0000	34.0000	34.0000

Table A7, continued (Row 1, Col 9)

Correlation Matrix, International Variables (Parametric)		sqrtQIIIC1a	sqrtQIIIC1b	sqrtQIIIC1c	sqrtQIIIC1d	sqrtQIIIC1e
Importance of Smuggling-Endangered Species	Pearson Correlation	-0.0130	-0.1800	-0.1525	-0.1876	-0.2288
	Sig. (2-tailed)	0.9419	0.3008	0.3893	0.2880	0.1930
	N	34.0000	35.0000	34.0000	34.0000	34.0000
reflectsqrtQ1A1b	Pearson Correlation	0.0318	-0.0176	-0.0339	0.0861	0.0816
	Sig. (2-tailed)	0.8582	0.9199	0.8490	0.6281	0.6463
	N	34.0000	35.0000	34.0000	34.0000	34.0000
reflectsqrtQ1A1c	Pearson Correlation	-0.0482	0.0683	-0.0370	0.1095	0.1691
	Sig. (2-tailed)	0.7867	0.6968	0.8356	0.5376	0.3391
	N	34.0000	35.0000	34.0000	34.0000	34.0000
reflectsqrtQ1A1d	Pearson Correlation	-0.1489	-0.0639	-0.0869	-0.0435	0.0131
	Sig. (2-tailed)	0.4006	0.7152	0.6249	0.8072	0.9413
	N	34.0000	35.0000	34.0000	34.0000	34.0000
reflectsqrtQ1A1e	Pearson Correlation	-0.2777	-0.2819	-0.2016	-0.2844	-0.2906
	Sig. (2-tailed)	0.1118	0.1009	0.2528	0.1031	0.0954
	N	34.0000	35.0000	34.0000	34.0000	34.0000
sqrtQ1B1a	Pearson Correlation	0.2686	0.1986	0.2744	0.2154	0.1255
	Sig. (2-tailed)	0.1245	0.2528	0.1163	0.2211	0.4795
	N	34.0000	35.0000	34.0000	34.0000	34.0000
Knowledge of Smuggling-Narcotics	Pearson Correlation	-0.1304	0.0605	0.1023	-0.1387	-0.1891
	Sig. (2-tailed)	0.4625	0.7297	0.5650	0.4340	0.2840
	N	34.0000	35.0000	34.0000	34.0000	34.0000
Knowledge of Smuggling-Weapons	Pearson Correlation	-0.0255	0.1466	0.1886	0.0749	0.0148
	Sig. (2-tailed)	0.8863	0.4006	0.2855	0.6737	0.9337
	N	34.0000	35.0000	34.0000	34.0000	34.0000
Knowledge of Smuggling-Humans	Pearson Correlation	0.1806	0.1650	0.2258	0.1630	0.1067
	Sig. (2-tailed)	0.3069	0.3436	0.1991	0.3570	0.5481
	N	34.0000	35.0000	34.0000	34.0000	34.0000
Knowledge of Smuggling-Contraband	Pearson Correlation	0.1805	0.1186	0.0909	0.1928	0.1510
	Sig. (2-tailed)	0.3069	0.4974	0.6090	0.2745	0.3941
	N	34.0000	35.0000	34.0000	34.0000	34.0000
sqrtQ1E1a	Pearson Correlation	-0.1274	-0.1727	-0.2354	-0.1428	-0.1289
	Sig. (2-tailed)	0.4729	0.3212	0.1802	0.4205	0.4675
	N	34.0000	35.0000	34.0000	34.0000	34.0000

Table A7, continued (Row 2, Col 1)

Correlation Matrix, International Variables (Parametric)		Importance of Smuggling-Endangered Species	reflectsqrtQ1A1b	reflectsqrtQ1A1c	reflectsqrtQ1A1d	reflectsqrtQ1A1e	sqrtQ1B1a	Knowledge of Smuggling-Narcotics	Knowledge of Smuggling-Weapons	Knowledge of Smuggling-Humans	Knowledge of Smuggling-Contraband
Personal Resource Challenges-Lack of Time	Pearson Correlation	-0.2521	0.0491	0.1354	0.1898	0.0699	0.0171	0.1009	-0.0720	0.1074	0.1384
	Sig. (2-tailed)	0.1380	0.7762	0.4311	0.2676	0.6854	0.9213	0.5582	0.6766	0.5331	0.4207
	N	36.0000	36.0000	36.0000	36.0000	36.0000	36.0000	36.0000	36.0000	36.0000	36.0000
Personal Resource Challenges-Lack of Knowledge	Pearson Correlation	-0.0060	-0.1074	-0.1398	0.0012	0.0140	0.0056	-0.0019	-0.2415	0.0093	-0.0687
	Sig. (2-tailed)	0.9725	0.5329	0.4162	0.9945	0.9356	0.9743	0.9911	0.1560	0.9572	0.6905
	N	36.0000	36.0000	36.0000	36.0000	36.0000	36.0000	36.0000	36.0000	36.0000	36.0000
Personal Resource Challenges-Lack of Training	Pearson Correlation	-0.1118	-0.0574	-0.1409	-0.0396	0.0473	0.0112	-0.0190	-0.2339	-0.0248	-0.1326
	Sig. (2-tailed)	0.5161	0.7396	0.4125	0.8186	0.7840	0.9483	0.9126	0.1698	0.8859	0.4409
	N	36.0000	36.0000	36.0000	36.0000	36.0000	36.0000	36.0000	36.0000	36.0000	36.0000
sqrtQ1E1e	Pearson Correlation	0.0017	0.0673	-0.0870	-0.1839	0.0016	0.2065	0.0853	0.2980	0.0830	0.1690
	Sig. (2-tailed)	0.9923	0.6965	0.6141	0.2829	0.9928	0.2270	0.6208	0.0775	0.6301	0.3243
	N	36.0000	36.0000	36.0000	36.0000	36.0000	36.0000	36.0000	36.0000	36.0000	36.0000
Personal Resource Challenges-Excessive Admin Paperwork	Pearson Correlation	-0.1143	0.1222	0.0631	-0.0777	-0.0052	0.0536	0.2558	0.2285	-0.0120	0.2170
	Sig. (2-tailed)	0.5070	0.4777	0.7148	0.6526	0.9760	0.7560	0.1320	0.1802	0.9445	0.2037
	N	36.0000	36.0000	36.0000	36.0000	36.0000	36.0000	36.0000	36.0000	36.0000	36.0000
Personal Resource Challenges-Ineffective Technology	Pearson Correlation	-0.0332	-0.0507	-0.0964	-0.2668	0.0638	0.0157	0.2258	-0.0585	0.0177	-0.0706
	Sig. (2-tailed)	0.8474	0.7692	0.5758	0.1157	0.7115	0.9276	0.1854	0.7349	0.9184	0.6824
	N	36.0000	36.0000	36.0000	36.0000	36.0000	36.0000	36.0000	36.0000	36.0000	36.0000
Personal Resource Challenges-Ineffective Strategic Focus	Pearson Correlation	-0.1285	-0.0880	-0.2280	-0.2106	0.0616	0.1585	-0.0792	-0.1197	-0.0164	-0.1110
	Sig. (2-tailed)	0.4550	0.6099	0.1811	0.2177	0.7211	0.3558	0.6460	0.4868	0.9245	0.5192
	N	36.0000	36.0000	36.0000	36.0000	36.0000	36.0000	36.0000	36.0000	36.0000	36.0000
Personal Resource Challenges-Ineffective Tactical Policy	Pearson Correlation	-0.1699	-0.0058	-0.0994	-0.1638	0.1821	0.0430	-0.0393	-0.1135	0.0170	-0.1189
	Sig. (2-tailed)	0.3218	0.9732	0.5643	0.3397	0.2879	0.8033	0.8202	0.5097	0.9215	0.4899
	N	36.0000	36.0000	36.0000	36.0000	36.0000	36.0000	36.0000	36.0000	36.0000	36.0000
Personal Resource Challenges-Lack of Clarity in Duties	Pearson Correlation	-0.0555	-0.0091	-0.1168	-0.1988	0.1008	0.0533	0.0626	-0.1099	0.0758	0.0121
	Sig. (2-tailed)	0.7476	0.9579	0.4976	0.2451	0.5587	0.7575	0.7166	0.5235	0.6605	0.9442
	N	36.0000	36.0000	36.0000	36.0000	36.0000	36.0000	36.0000	36.0000	36.0000	36.0000
Personal Resource Challenges-Conflict or Lack Comm Leaders and Employees	Pearson Correlation	-0.0670	0.0368	-0.0162	-0.1624	0.2367	0.0124	-0.0357	-0.1635	-0.0869	-0.0616
	Sig. (2-tailed)	0.6979	0.8314	0.9253	0.3439	0.1646	0.9427	0.8364	0.3406	0.6142	0.7213
	N	36.0000	36.0000	36.0000	36.0000	36.0000	36.0000	36.0000	36.0000	36.0000	36.0000
sqrtQ1E1l	Pearson Correlation	0.0461	-0.0333	-0.0776	0.0044	-0.1415	0.0984	-0.0247	0.0217	-0.2842	0.0032
	Sig. (2-tailed)	0.7894	0.8470	0.6528	0.9796	0.4104	0.5681	0.8862	0.9001	0.0930	0.9854
	N	36.0000	36.0000	36.0000	36.0000	36.0000	36.0000	36.0000	36.0000	36.0000	36.0000

Table A7, continued (Row 2, Col 2)

Correlation Matrix, International Variables (Parametric)		sqrtQ1E1a	Personal Resource Challenges–Lack of Time	Personal Resource Challenges–Lack of Knowledge	Personal Resource Challenges–Lack of Training	sqrtQ1E1e	Personal Resource Challenges–Excessive Admin Paperwork	Personal Resource Challenges–Ineffective Technology	Personal Resource Challenges–Ineffective Strategic Focus	Personal Resource Challenges–Ineffective Tactical Policy	Personal Resource Challenges–Lack of Clarity in Duties
Personal Resource Challenges-Lack of Time	Pearson Correlation	0.3118	1.0000	0.5812	0.4861	0.3338	0.3445	0.2844	0.4073	0.4851	0.5687
	Sig. (2-tailed)	0.0683	.	0.0002	0.0027	0.0466	0.0396	0.0927	0.0137	0.0027	0.0003
	N	35.0000	36.0000	36.0000	36.0000	36.0000	36.0000	36.0000	36.0000	36.0000	36.0000
Personal Resource Challenges-Lack of Knowledge	Pearson Correlation	0.3342	0.5812	1.0000	0.9275	0.3493	0.3018	0.6239	0.6827	0.5897	0.6849
	Sig. (2-tailed)	0.0497	0.0002	.	0.0000	0.0368	0.0736	0.0000	0.0000	0.0002	0.0000
	N	35.0000	36.0000	36.0000	36.0000	36.0000	36.0000	36.0000	36.0000	36.0000	36.0000
Personal Resource Challenges-Lack of Training	Pearson Correlation	0.2759	0.4861	0.9275	1.0000	0.2734	0.2702	0.5769	0.6850	0.5761	0.6457
	Sig. (2-tailed)	0.1087	0.0027	0.0000	.	0.1066	0.1110	0.0002	0.0000	0.0002	0.0000
	N	35.0000	36.0000	36.0000	36.0000	36.0000	36.0000	36.0000	36.0000	36.0000	36.0000
sqrtQ1E1e	Pearson Correlation	0.1914	0.3338	0.3493	0.2734	1.0000	0.5245	0.3197	0.5547	0.4222	0.4292
	Sig. (2-tailed)	0.2708	0.0466	0.0368	0.1066	.	0.0010	0.0574	0.0004	0.0103	0.0090
	N	35.0000	36.0000	36.0000	36.0000	36.0000	36.0000	36.0000	36.0000	36.0000	36.0000
Personal Resource Challenges-Excessive Admin Paperwork	Pearson Correlation	0.4520	0.3445	0.3018	0.2702	0.5245	1.0000	0.3484	0.4345	0.5723	0.5320
	Sig. (2-tailed)	0.0064	0.0396	0.0736	0.1110	0.0010	.	0.0373	0.0081	0.0003	0.0008
	N	35.0000	36.0000	36.0000	36.0000	36.0000	36.0000	36.0000	36.0000	36.0000	36.0000
Personal Resource Challenges-Ineffective Technology	Pearson Correlation	0.3708	0.2844	0.6239	0.5769	0.3197	0.3484	1.0000	0.5567	0.5629	0.5197
	Sig. (2-tailed)	0.0283	0.0927	0.0000	0.0002	0.0574	0.0373	.	0.0004	0.0004	0.0012
	N	35.0000	36.0000	36.0000	36.0000	36.0000	36.0000	36.0000	36.0000	36.0000	36.0000
Personal Resource Challenges-Ineffective Strategic Focus	Pearson Correlation	0.5510	0.4073	0.6827	0.6850	0.5547	0.4345	0.5567	1.0000	0.8897	0.8164
	Sig. (2-tailed)	0.0006	0.0137	0.0000	0.0000	0.0004	0.0081	0.0004	.	0.0000	0.0000
	N	35.0000	36.0000	36.0000	36.0000	36.0000	36.0000	36.0000	36.0000	36.0000	36.0000
Personal Resource Challenges-Ineffective Tactical Policy	Pearson Correlation	0.6237	0.4851	0.5897	0.5761	0.4222	0.5723	0.5629	0.8897	1.0000	0.8650
	Sig. (2-tailed)	0.0001	0.0027	0.0002	0.0002	0.0103	0.0003	0.0004	0.0000	.	0.0000
	N	35.0000	36.0000	36.0000	36.0000	36.0000	36.0000	36.0000	36.0000	36.0000	36.0000
Personal Resource Challenges-Lack of Clarity in Duties	Pearson Correlation	0.5042	0.5687	0.6849	0.6457	0.4292	0.5320	0.5197	0.8164	0.8650	1.0000
	Sig. (2-tailed)	0.0020	0.0003	0.0000	0.0000	0.0090	0.0008	0.0012	0.0000	0.0000	.
	N	35.0000	36.0000	36.0000	36.0000	36.0000	36.0000	36.0000	36.0000	36.0000	36.0000
Personal Resource Challenges-Conflict or Lack Comm Leaders and Employees	Pearson Correlation	0.5982	0.4964	0.5447	0.4604	0.4211	0.5114	0.4778	0.8107	0.8852	0.8299
	Sig. (2-tailed)	0.0001	0.0021	0.0006	0.0047	0.0105	0.0014	0.0032	0.0000	0.0000	0.0000
	N	35.0000	36.0000	36.0000	36.0000	36.0000	36.0000	36.0000	36.0000	36.0000	36.0000
sqrtQ1E1l	Pearson Correlation	0.5175	0.1927	0.2645	0.1879	0.3410	0.5958	0.2670	0.5559	0.5402	0.4613
	Sig. (2-tailed)	0.0015	0.2602	0.1190	0.2724	0.0418	0.0001	0.1154	0.0004	0.0007	0.0046
	N	35.0000	36.0000	36.0000	36.0000	36.0000	36.0000	36.0000	36.0000	36.0000	36.0000

Table A7, continued (Row 2, Col 3)

Correlation Matrix, International Variables (Parametric)		Personal Resource Challenges-Conflict or Lack Comm Leaders and Employees	sqrtQ1E1l	Personal Resource Challenges-Conflict or Lack Comm International Orgs	Personal Resource Challenges-Conflict or Lack Comm Domestic Orgs	sqrtQ1E3a	Org Resource Challenges-Lack of Time	Org Resource Challenges-Lack of Knowledge	Org Resource Challenges-Lack of Training	sqrtQ1E3e	Org Resource Challenges-Excessive Admin Paperwork
Personal Resource Challenges-Lack of Time	Pearson Correlation	0.4964	0.1927	0.4594	0.6319	0.2228	0.4499	0.4761	0.4834	0.5283	0.4741
	Sig. (2-tailed)	0.0021	0.2602	0.0048	0.0000	0.2053	0.0067	0.0038	0.0033	0.0013	0.0040
	N	36.0000	36.0000	36.0000	36.0000	34.0000	35.0000	35.0000	35.0000	34.0000	35.0000
Personal Resource Challenges-Lack of Knowledge	Pearson Correlation	0.5447	0.2645	0.5736	0.6835	0.2711	0.4688	0.8329	0.8367	0.3772	0.5046
	Sig. (2-tailed)	0.0006	0.1190	0.0003	0.0000	0.1210	0.0045	0.0000	0.0000	0.0279	0.0020
	N	36.0000	36.0000	36.0000	36.0000	34.0000	35.0000	35.0000	35.0000	34.0000	35.0000
Personal Resource Challenges-Lack of Training	Pearson Correlation	0.4604	0.1879	0.5330	0.6132	0.2455	0.3864	0.8421	0.8394	0.3616	0.4976
	Sig. (2-tailed)	0.0047	0.2724	0.0008	0.0001	0.1617	0.0219	0.0000	0.0000	0.0356	0.0024
	N	36.0000	36.0000	36.0000	36.0000	34.0000	35.0000	35.0000	35.0000	34.0000	35.0000
sqrtQ1E1e	Pearson Correlation	0.4211	0.3410	0.3925	0.4321	0.4098	0.0904	0.2760	0.2369	0.4965	0.4340
	Sig. (2-tailed)	0.0105	0.0418	0.0179	0.0085	0.0161	0.6053	0.1085	0.1707	0.0028	0.0092
	N	36.0000	36.0000	36.0000	36.0000	34.0000	35.0000	35.0000	35.0000	34.0000	35.0000
Personal Resource Challenges-Excessive Admin Paperwork	Pearson Correlation	0.5114	0.5958	0.6658	0.5785	0.2648	0.0679	0.1780	0.2168	0.3455	0.5589
	Sig. (2-tailed)	0.0014	0.0001	0.0000	0.0002	0.1302	0.6983	0.3064	0.2110	0.0454	0.0005
	N	36.0000	36.0000	36.0000	36.0000	34.0000	35.0000	35.0000	35.0000	34.0000	35.0000
Personal Resource Challenges-Ineffective Technology	Pearson Correlation	0.4778	0.2670	0.3591	0.5291	0.4635	0.3841	0.5886	0.6681	0.3066	0.4503
	Sig. (2-tailed)	0.0032	0.1154	0.0315	0.0009	0.0058	0.0227	0.0002	0.0000	0.0778	0.0066
	N	36.0000	36.0000	36.0000	36.0000	34.0000	35.0000	35.0000	35.0000	34.0000	35.0000
Personal Resource Challenges-Ineffective Strategic Focus	Pearson Correlation	0.8107	0.5559	0.5279	0.7125	0.3866	0.3242	0.7021	0.6671	0.5175	0.6065
	Sig. (2-tailed)	0.0000	0.0004	0.0009	0.0000	0.0239	0.0575	0.0000	0.0000	0.0017	0.0001
	N	36.0000	36.0000	36.0000	36.0000	34.0000	35.0000	35.0000	35.0000	34.0000	35.0000
Personal Resource Challenges-Ineffective Tactical Policy	Pearson Correlation	0.8852	0.5402	0.5658	0.7745	0.4224	0.3104	0.5752	0.5784	0.5213	0.6251
	Sig. (2-tailed)	0.0000	0.0007	0.0003	0.0000	0.0128	0.0696	0.0003	0.0003	0.0016	0.0001
	N	36.0000	36.0000	36.0000	36.0000	34.0000	35.0000	35.0000	35.0000	34.0000	35.0000
Personal Resource Challenges-Lack of Clarity in Duties	Pearson Correlation	0.8299	0.4613	0.6280	0.8215	0.4139	0.2282	0.6555	0.6437	0.4520	0.5833
	Sig. (2-tailed)	0.0000	0.0046	0.0000	0.0000	0.0150	0.1873	0.0000	0.0000	0.0073	0.0002
	N	36.0000	36.0000	36.0000	36.0000	34.0000	35.0000	35.0000	35.0000	34.0000	35.0000
Personal Resource Challenges-Conflict or Lack Comm Leaders and Employees	Pearson Correlation	1.0000	0.6103	0.5973	0.8361	0.3253	0.2036	0.5026	0.4964	0.4955	0.5537
	Sig. (2-tailed)	.	0.0001	0.0001	0.0000	0.0605	0.2408	0.0021	0.0024	0.0029	0.0006
	N	36.0000	36.0000	36.0000	36.0000	34.0000	35.0000	35.0000	35.0000	34.0000	35.0000
sqrtQ1E1l	Pearson Correlation	0.6103	1.0000	0.5245	0.4760	0.1459	0.0786	0.2653	0.3241	0.4006	0.4504
	Sig. (2-tailed)	0.0001	.	0.0010	0.0033	0.4103	0.6537	0.1235	0.0575	0.0189	0.0066
	N	36.0000	36.0000	36.0000	36.0000	34.0000	35.0000	35.0000	35.0000	34.0000	35.0000

Table A7, continued (Row 2, Col 4)

Correlation Matrix, International Variables (Parametric)		Org Resource Challenges-Ineffective Technology	Org Resource Challenges-Ineffective Strategic Focus	Org Resource Challenges-Ineffective Tactical Policy	Org Resource Challenges-Lack of Clarity in Duties	Org Resource Challenges-Conflict or Lack Comm Leaders and Employees	sqrtQ1E3l	Org Resource Challenges-Conflict or Lack Comm International Orgs	Org Resource Challenges-Conflict or Lack Comm Domestic Orgs	sqrtQ1A1a	Knowledge of Domestic Law-CSIE
Personal Resource Challenges-Lack of Time	Pearson Correlation	0.3837	0.4444	0.5063	0.3689	0.4729	0.2147	0.3700	0.3163	0.1779	-0.1054
	Sig. (2-tailed)	0.0229	0.0075	0.0019	0.0292	0.0041	0.2155	0.0287	0.0641	0.3066	0.5467
	N	35.0000	35.0000	35.0000	35.0000	35.0000	35.0000	35.0000	35.0000	35.0000	35.0000
Personal Resource Challenges-Lack of Knowledge	Pearson Correlation	0.5715	0.7606	0.6627	0.7468	0.5058	0.2868	0.7712	0.7446	0.1297	-0.1119
	Sig. (2-tailed)	0.0003	0.0000	0.0000	0.0000	0.0019	0.0948	0.0000	0.0000	0.4579	0.5223
	N	35.0000	35.0000	35.0000	35.0000	35.0000	35.0000	35.0000	35.0000	35.0000	35.0000
Personal Resource Challenges-Lack of Training	Pearson Correlation	0.5343	0.7089	0.6414	0.7607	0.4702	0.2943	0.7224	0.6898	0.1362	-0.2222
	Sig. (2-tailed)	0.0009	0.0000	0.0000	0.0000	0.0044	0.0862	0.0000	0.0000	0.4354	0.1996
	N	35.0000	35.0000	35.0000	35.0000	35.0000	35.0000	35.0000	35.0000	35.0000	35.0000
sqrtQ1E1e	Pearson Correlation	0.3100	0.3791	0.4666	0.3853	0.4733	0.3287	0.3387	0.3704	0.1985	0.0135
	Sig. (2-tailed)	0.0699	0.0247	0.0047	0.0223	0.0041	0.0539	0.0465	0.0285	0.2530	0.9384
	N	35.0000	35.0000	35.0000	35.0000	35.0000	35.0000	35.0000	35.0000	35.0000	35.0000
Personal Resource Challenges-Excessive Admin Paperwork	Pearson Correlation	0.3545	0.3099	0.4462	0.2944	0.5096	0.5204	0.3204	0.3419	0.1231	0.1304
	Sig. (2-tailed)	0.0367	0.0700	0.0072	0.0860	0.0018	0.0014	0.0606	0.0444	0.4810	0.4553
	N	35.0000	35.0000	35.0000	35.0000	35.0000	35.0000	35.0000	35.0000	35.0000	35.0000
Personal Resource Challenges-Ineffective Technology	Pearson Correlation	0.7341	0.6454	0.4557	0.5999	0.3705	0.2168	0.5919	0.6206	-0.0890	0.1874
	Sig. (2-tailed)	0.0000	0.0000	0.0059	0.0001	0.0285	0.2108	0.0002	0.0001	0.6113	0.2811
	N	35.0000	35.0000	35.0000	35.0000	35.0000	35.0000	35.0000	35.0000	35.0000	35.0000
Personal Resource Challenges-Ineffective Strategic Focus	Pearson Correlation	0.6251	0.7928	0.7917	0.7915	0.6182	0.5372	0.6129	0.6329	0.1663	-0.2240
	Sig. (2-tailed)	0.0001	0.0000	0.0000	0.0000	0.0001	0.0009	0.0001	0.0000	0.3398	0.1958
	N	35.0000	35.0000	35.0000	35.0000	35.0000	35.0000	35.0000	35.0000	35.0000	35.0000
Personal Resource Challenges-Ineffective Tactical Policy	Pearson Correlation	0.6686	0.7660	0.8024	0.7397	0.6952	0.4737	0.5677	0.5770	0.0529	-0.2112
	Sig. (2-tailed)	0.0000	0.0000	0.0000	0.0000	0.0000	0.0040	0.0004	0.0003	0.7627	0.2234
	N	35.0000	35.0000	35.0000	35.0000	35.0000	35.0000	35.0000	35.0000	35.0000	35.0000
Personal Resource Challenges-Lack of Clarity in Duties	Pearson Correlation	0.5461	0.7172	0.8184	0.6774	0.6451	0.4299	0.5515	0.5381	0.1278	-0.2785
	Sig. (2-tailed)	0.0007	0.0000	0.0000	0.0000	0.0000	0.0100	0.0006	0.0009	0.4645	0.1053
	N	35.0000	35.0000	35.0000	35.0000	35.0000	35.0000	35.0000	35.0000	35.0000	35.0000
Personal Resource Challenges-Conflict or Lack Comm Leaders and Employees	Pearson Correlation	0.6035	0.7479	0.8003	0.6391	0.7390	0.5035	0.4527	0.5411	0.0748	-0.1977
	Sig. (2-tailed)	0.0001	0.0000	0.0000	0.0000	0.0000	0.0020	0.0063	0.0008	0.6692	0.2549
	N	35.0000	35.0000	35.0000	35.0000	35.0000	35.0000	35.0000	35.0000	35.0000	35.0000
sqrtQ1E1l	Pearson Correlation	0.4102	0.4507	0.4718	0.3910	0.5790	0.9287	0.3371	0.4099	0.0207	0.0244
	Sig. (2-tailed)	0.0144	0.0066	0.0042	0.0202	0.0003	0.0000	0.0477	0.0145	0.9059	0.8893
	N	35.0000	35.0000	35.0000	35.0000	35.0000	35.0000	35.0000	35.0000	35.0000	35.0000

Table A7, continued (Row 2, Col 5)

Correlation Matrix, International Variables (Parametric)		Knowledge of Domestic Law-DWMD	Knowledge of Domestic Law-TVP	Knowledge of Domestic Law-CBP	sqrtQIID1a	Level Cooperation Domestic Orgs-CSIE	Level Cooperation Domestic Orgs-DWMD	Level Cooperation Domestic Orgs-TVP	Level Cooperation Domestic Orgs-CBP	sqrtQIIIA1a	sqrtQIIIA1b
Personal Resource Challenges-Lack of Time	Pearson Correlation	-0.0797	-0.0226	0.0886	-0.0498	-0.0671	-0.0939	0.0638	-0.0404	0.3114	0.0694
	Sig. (2-tailed)	0.6491	0.8976	0.6129	0.7728	0.6976	0.5860	0.7115	0.8149	0.0686	0.6877
	N	35.0000	35.0000	35.0000	36.0000	36.0000	36.0000	36.0000	36.0000	35.0000	36.0000
Personal Resource Challenges-Lack of Knowledge	Pearson Correlation	-0.1684	0.0131	-0.1704	-0.1174	-0.3195	-0.3120	-0.1253	-0.1085	0.1295	-0.1696
	Sig. (2-tailed)	0.3335	0.9404	0.3279	0.4955	0.0575	0.0639	0.4667	0.5287	0.4584	0.3227
	N	35.0000	35.0000	35.0000	36.0000	36.0000	36.0000	36.0000	36.0000	35.0000	36.0000
Personal Resource Challenges-Lack of Training	Pearson Correlation	-0.2745	-0.0242	-0.2953	-0.1545	-0.3802	-0.3942	-0.2011	-0.1170	0.1581	-0.2311
	Sig. (2-tailed)	0.1105	0.8901	0.0850	0.3682	0.0222	0.0174	0.2396	0.4968	0.3642	0.1750
	N	35.0000	35.0000	35.0000	36.0000	36.0000	36.0000	36.0000	36.0000	35.0000	36.0000
sqrtQ1E1e	Pearson Correlation	-0.0123	-0.0726	0.1008	0.2266	-0.0320	-0.0340	0.0283	0.0558	0.2187	-0.0790
	Sig. (2-tailed)	0.9439	0.6784	0.5644	0.1839	0.8528	0.8439	0.8701	0.7467	0.2069	0.6468
	N	35.0000	35.0000	35.0000	36.0000	36.0000	36.0000	36.0000	36.0000	35.0000	36.0000
Personal Resource Challenges-Excessive Admin Paperwork	Pearson Correlation	0.0638	0.1009	0.0404	0.1332	0.0093	0.1753	0.0584	-0.0042	0.3565	0.2407
	Sig. (2-tailed)	0.7156	0.5642	0.8177	0.4387	0.9570	0.3065	0.7350	0.9804	0.0356	0.1573
	N	35.0000	35.0000	35.0000	36.0000	36.0000	36.0000	36.0000	36.0000	35.0000	36.0000
Personal Resource Challenges-Ineffective Technology	Pearson Correlation	0.0578	0.0814	-0.1367	-0.1490	-0.2315	-0.3228	-0.1657	-0.1672	-0.0354	0.0213
	Sig. (2-tailed)	0.7415	0.6421	0.4337	0.3857	0.1743	0.0548	0.3342	0.3296	0.8399	0.9020
	N	35.0000	35.0000	35.0000	36.0000	36.0000	36.0000	36.0000	36.0000	35.0000	36.0000
Personal Resource Challenges-Ineffective Strategic Focus	Pearson Correlation	-0.3036	-0.0651	-0.2731	-0.0144	-0.3394	-0.4186	-0.1068	-0.0882	0.3285	-0.1415
	Sig. (2-tailed)	0.0762	0.7100	0.1125	0.9337	0.0429	0.0111	0.5354	0.6088	0.0540	0.4103
	N	35.0000	35.0000	35.0000	36.0000	36.0000	36.0000	36.0000	36.0000	35.0000	36.0000
Personal Resource Challenges-Ineffective Tactical Policy	Pearson Correlation	-0.2200	-0.0220	-0.2471	-0.0835	-0.3240	-0.3391	-0.1520	-0.1525	0.3383	0.0382
	Sig. (2-tailed)	0.2040	0.9003	0.1525	0.6284	0.0539	0.0430	0.3760	0.3747	0.0468	0.8250
	N	35.0000	35.0000	35.0000	36.0000	36.0000	36.0000	36.0000	36.0000	35.0000	36.0000
Personal Resource Challenges-Lack of Clarity in Duties	Pearson Correlation	-0.2676	0.0909	-0.1374	-0.0795	-0.2536	-0.2787	0.0556	-0.0516	0.3095	-0.0093
	Sig. (2-tailed)	0.1201	0.6036	0.4314	0.6447	0.1357	0.0997	0.7476	0.7651	0.0704	0.9569
	N	35.0000	35.0000	35.0000	36.0000	36.0000	36.0000	36.0000	36.0000	35.0000	36.0000
Personal Resource Challenges-Conflict or Lack Comm Leaders and Employees	Pearson Correlation	-0.2397	-0.1073	-0.1200	-0.1120	-0.3763	-0.3806	-0.1813	-0.1645	0.2006	0.1294
	Sig. (2-tailed)	0.1655	0.5394	0.4922	0.5157	0.0237	0.0220	0.2899	0.3377	0.2479	0.4521
	N	35.0000	35.0000	35.0000	36.0000	36.0000	36.0000	36.0000	36.0000	35.0000	36.0000
sqrtQ1E1l	Pearson Correlation	-0.1690	-0.2804	-0.1781	0.0549	-0.2268	-0.0638	-0.0832	-0.0522	0.2261	-0.0278
	Sig. (2-tailed)	0.3317	0.1028	0.3061	0.7504	0.1835	0.7115	0.6294	0.7623	0.1915	0.8719
	N	35.0000	35.0000	35.0000	36.0000	36.0000	36.0000	36.0000	36.0000	35.0000	36.0000

Table A7, continued (Row 2, Col 6)

Correlation Matrix, International Variables (Parametric)		sqrtQIIIA1c	sqrtQIIIA1d	sqrtQIIIA1e	sqrtQIIID1a	Level Cooperation Domestic Orgs-CNDPS	Level Cooperation Domestic Orgs-CNBC	Level Cooperation Domestic Orgs-CSTP	Level Cooperation Domestic Orgs-TRIPS	sqrtQIIID2a	Level Cooperation International Orgs-CNDPS
Personal Resource Challenges-Lack of Time	Pearson Correlation	0.1221	0.2363	0.1714	0.1206	0.0242	-0.0511	0.1117	0.0041	-0.1385	-0.1679
	Sig. (2-tailed)	0.4779	0.1653	0.3175	0.5039	0.8903	0.7705	0.5231	0.9813	0.4277	0.3277
	N	36.0000	36.0000	36.0000	33.0000	35.0000	35.0000	35.0000	35.0000	35.0000	36.0000
Personal Resource Challenges-Lack of Knowledge	Pearson Correlation	-0.1149	-0.0342	-0.1854	0.0284	-0.3494	-0.3097	-0.1833	-0.2496	-0.0454	-0.1854
	Sig. (2-tailed)	0.5044	0.8430	0.2790	0.8754	0.0397	0.0702	0.2919	0.1481	0.7956	0.2791
	N	36.0000	36.0000	36.0000	33.0000	35.0000	35.0000	35.0000	35.0000	35.0000	36.0000
Personal Resource Challenges-Lack of Training	Pearson Correlation	-0.1980	-0.0110	-0.2242	0.1815	-0.3143	-0.2839	-0.1215	-0.1957	0.0772	-0.1642
	Sig. (2-tailed)	0.2471	0.9493	0.1888	0.3122	0.0660	0.0984	0.4870	0.2598	0.6593	0.3386
	N	36.0000	36.0000	36.0000	33.0000	35.0000	35.0000	35.0000	35.0000	35.0000	36.0000
sqrtQ1E1e	Pearson Correlation	0.1071	0.1396	0.0952	0.2646	-0.0257	0.1179	0.0768	0.1020	0.2775	0.2058
	Sig. (2-tailed)	0.5340	0.4166	0.5809	0.1367	0.8833	0.4998	0.6610	0.5600	0.1066	0.2285
	N	36.0000	36.0000	36.0000	33.0000	35.0000	35.0000	35.0000	35.0000	35.0000	36.0000
Personal Resource Challenges-Excessive Admin Paperwork	Pearson Correlation	0.3647	0.2381	0.2494	0.2109	0.0392	0.0146	0.0791	0.0394	0.1931	0.1350
	Sig. (2-tailed)	0.0288	0.1620	0.1424	0.2387	0.8230	0.9334	0.6514	0.8221	0.2663	0.4324
	N	36.0000	36.0000	36.0000	33.0000	35.0000	35.0000	35.0000	35.0000	35.0000	36.0000
Personal Resource Challenges-Ineffective Technology	Pearson Correlation	0.0335	0.0131	-0.1226	-0.1934	-0.3843	-0.4478	-0.3132	-0.3367	-0.1671	-0.1814
	Sig. (2-tailed)	0.8461	0.9398	0.4762	0.2809	0.0227	0.0070	0.0669	0.0479	0.3375	0.2896
	N	36.0000	36.0000	36.0000	33.0000	35.0000	35.0000	35.0000	35.0000	35.0000	36.0000
Personal Resource Challenges-Ineffective Strategic Focus	Pearson Correlation	-0.0162	0.0718	-0.1359	0.0917	-0.2957	-0.2249	-0.1131	-0.1968	0.0834	-0.2790
	Sig. (2-tailed)	0.9254	0.6775	0.4294	0.6117	0.0845	0.1940	0.5179	0.2572	0.6337	0.0994
	N	36.0000	36.0000	36.0000	33.0000	35.0000	35.0000	35.0000	35.0000	35.0000	36.0000
Personal Resource Challenges-Ineffective Tactical Policy	Pearson Correlation	0.1323	0.1710	-0.0048	-0.0591	-0.3184	-0.3398	-0.2203	-0.2806	-0.0788	-0.3088
	Sig. (2-tailed)	0.4418	0.3186	0.9778	0.7439	0.0623	0.0458	0.2034	0.1025	0.6526	0.0669
	N	36.0000	36.0000	36.0000	33.0000	35.0000	35.0000	35.0000	35.0000	35.0000	36.0000
Personal Resource Challenges-Lack of Clarity in Duties	Pearson Correlation	0.0524	0.1479	-0.0612	0.1341	-0.1994	-0.2423	-0.0036	-0.1610	-0.0609	-0.2645
	Sig. (2-tailed)	0.7615	0.3892	0.7228	0.4568	0.2509	0.1608	0.9835	0.3556	0.7280	0.1190
	N	36.0000	36.0000	36.0000	33.0000	35.0000	35.0000	35.0000	35.0000	35.0000	36.0000
Personal Resource Challenges-Conflict or Lack Comm Leaders and Employees	Pearson Correlation	0.1660	0.1161	0.0572	-0.1135	-0.2432	-0.2412	-0.1756	-0.1849	-0.2003	-0.3302
	Sig. (2-tailed)	0.3334	0.5002	0.7403	0.5296	0.1592	0.1628	0.3128	0.2877	0.2487	0.0492
	N	36.0000	36.0000	36.0000	33.0000	35.0000	35.0000	35.0000	35.0000	35.0000	36.0000
sqrtQ1E11	Pearson Correlation	0.0690	-0.1745	-0.0507	-0.0093	-0.1364	-0.0657	-0.1034	-0.0830	0.0048	-0.2251
	Sig. (2-tailed)	0.6893	0.3088	0.7689	0.9590	0.4346	0.7077	0.5545	0.6355	0.9781	0.1868
	N	36.0000	36.0000	36.0000	33.0000	35.0000	35.0000	35.0000	35.0000	35.0000	36.0000

Table A7, continued (Row 2, Col 7)

Correlation Matrix, International Variables (Parametric)		Level Cooperation International Orgs- CNBC	Level Cooperation International Orgs- CSTP	sqrtQIIID2e	sqrtQIVA1	sqrtQIVA2	sqrtQIVA3	sqrtQIVA5	sqrtQIVA7	sqrtQIVA8	Political Ideology
Personal Resource Challenges- Lack of Time	Pearson Correlation	-0.2175	-0.0209	-0.2123	0.0179	0.0627	0.1729	-0.3000	-0.0716	0.2606	0.1789
	Sig. (2-tailed)	0.2026	0.9038	0.2138	0.9176	0.7164	0.3206	0.0847	0.6782	0.1305	0.3193
	N	36.0000	36.0000	36.0000	36.0000	36.0000	35.0000	34.0000	36.0000	35.0000	33.0000
Personal Resource Challenges- Lack of Knowledge	Pearson Correlation	-0.1852	-0.0530	-0.1736	0.2114	0.1892	0.1521	-0.2011	-0.0987	-0.0474	0.1173
	Sig. (2-tailed)	0.2795	0.7586	0.3114	0.2158	0.2690	0.3830	0.2541	0.5670	0.7868	0.5155
	N	36.0000	36.0000	36.0000	36.0000	36.0000	35.0000	34.0000	36.0000	35.0000	33.0000
Personal Resource Challenges- Lack of Training	Pearson Correlation	-0.1489	-0.0524	-0.1508	0.1371	0.0768	0.1250	-0.2275	-0.0693	-0.0792	0.1329
	Sig. (2-tailed)	0.3860	0.7616	0.3800	0.4251	0.6560	0.4742	0.1957	0.6881	0.6510	0.4610
	N	36.0000	36.0000	36.0000	36.0000	36.0000	35.0000	34.0000	36.0000	35.0000	33.0000
sqrtQ1E1e	Pearson Correlation	0.2551	0.1915	0.2529	0.2619	0.2009	0.2528	0.0274	-0.0159	-0.1426	0.1533
	Sig. (2-tailed)	0.1333	0.2632	0.1366	0.1228	0.2400	0.1428	0.8780	0.9268	0.4139	0.3945
	N	36.0000	36.0000	36.0000	36.0000	36.0000	35.0000	34.0000	36.0000	35.0000	33.0000
Personal Resource Challenges- Excessive Admin Paperwork	Pearson Correlation	0.0927	0.0969	0.0811	0.3080	0.2318	0.4174	0.0237	-0.0877	0.0388	0.2197
	Sig. (2-tailed)	0.5908	0.5738	0.6380	0.0676	0.1738	0.0126	0.8939	0.6111	0.8251	0.2192
	N	36.0000	36.0000	36.0000	36.0000	36.0000	35.0000	34.0000	36.0000	35.0000	33.0000
Personal Resource Challenges- Ineffective Technology	Pearson Correlation	-0.2226	-0.2263	-0.2817	0.3243	0.2996	0.2555	-0.3674	-0.0528	-0.1169	0.1397
	Sig. (2-tailed)	0.1918	0.1844	0.0960	0.0537	0.0758	0.1385	0.0325	0.7597	0.5037	0.4381
	N	36.0000	36.0000	36.0000	36.0000	36.0000	35.0000	34.0000	36.0000	35.0000	33.0000
Personal Resource Challenges- Ineffective Strategic Focus	Pearson Correlation	-0.2551	-0.1966	-0.2426	0.2088	0.2963	0.3183	-0.0811	0.0901	-0.2959	0.0123
	Sig. (2-tailed)	0.1332	0.2504	0.1540	0.2216	0.0794	0.0624	0.6486	0.6014	0.0843	0.9460
	N	36.0000	36.0000	36.0000	36.0000	36.0000	35.0000	34.0000	36.0000	35.0000	33.0000
Personal Resource Challenges- Ineffective Tactical Policy	Pearson Correlation	-0.3368	-0.2681	-0.3346	0.2928	0.4052	0.4473	-0.1987	-0.0004	-0.2056	0.1382
	Sig. (2-tailed)	0.0446	0.1139	0.0461	0.0831	0.0142	0.0071	0.2599	0.9983	0.2361	0.4431
	N	36.0000	36.0000	36.0000	36.0000	36.0000	35.0000	34.0000	36.0000	35.0000	33.0000
Personal Resource Challenges- Lack of Clarity in Duties	Pearson Correlation	-0.3009	-0.1977	-0.3052	0.2937	0.2994	0.3700	-0.2636	0.1326	-0.1085	0.0998
	Sig. (2-tailed)	0.0745	0.2477	0.0702	0.0821	0.0761	0.0287	0.1320	0.4406	0.5350	0.5805
	N	36.0000	36.0000	36.0000	36.0000	36.0000	35.0000	34.0000	36.0000	35.0000	33.0000
Personal Resource Challenges- Conflict or Lack Comm Leaders and Employees	Pearson Correlation	-0.3636	-0.2689	-0.3400	0.2933	0.3287	0.4069	-0.2154	0.1726	-0.2587	0.0549
	Sig. (2-tailed)	0.0293	0.1128	0.0425	0.0825	0.0503	0.0153	0.2212	0.3140	0.1335	0.7615
	N	36.0000	36.0000	36.0000	36.0000	36.0000	35.0000	34.0000	36.0000	35.0000	33.0000
sqrtQ1E1l	Pearson Correlation	-0.2286	-0.2462	-0.2096	0.2187	0.2301	0.3031	0.0993	0.1235	-0.2521	-0.0632
	Sig. (2-tailed)	0.1799	0.1477	0.2199	0.2001	0.1770	0.0767	0.5762	0.4729	0.1440	0.7268
	N	36.0000	36.0000	36.0000	36.0000	36.0000	35.0000	34.0000	36.0000	35.0000	33.0000

Table A7, continued (Row 2, Col 8)

Correlation Matrix, International Variables (Parametric)		sqrtQIIIB1a	sqrtQIIIB1b	sqrtQIIIB1c	sqrtQIIIB1d	sqrtQIIIB1e	sqrtQIIIB2a	Perceived Effectiveness Domestic Govt Support-CNDPS	Perceived Effectiveness Domestic Govt Support-CNBC	Perceived Effectiveness Domestic Govt Support-CSTP	Perceived Effectiveness Domestic Govt Support-TRIPS
Personal Resource Challenges-Lack of Time	Pearson Correlation	-0.0956	-0.2154	-0.1101	-0.0530	-0.1510	0.0062	-0.0700	-0.0091	0.0651	-0.3510
	Sig. (2-tailed)	0.5850	0.2139	0.5290	0.7623	0.3866	0.9719	0.6849	0.9587	0.7104	0.0387
	N	35.0000	35.0000	35.0000	35.0000	35.0000	35.0000	36.0000	35.0000	35.0000	35.0000
Personal Resource Challenges-Lack of Knowledge	Pearson Correlation	0.2034	-0.0827	0.0931	-0.2529	0.0737	0.1504	-0.1352	0.0324	0.0864	-0.2624
	Sig. (2-tailed)	0.2413	0.6366	0.5948	0.1427	0.6740	0.3884	0.4316	0.8534	0.6215	0.1278
	N	35.0000	35.0000	35.0000	35.0000	35.0000	35.0000	36.0000	35.0000	35.0000	35.0000
Personal Resource Challenges-Lack of Training	Pearson Correlation	0.3054	0.0084	0.1671	-0.2368	0.1633	0.2613	-0.0590	0.1201	0.1846	-0.1527
	Sig. (2-tailed)	0.0744	0.9619	0.3372	0.1708	0.3486	0.1295	0.7324	0.4918	0.2884	0.3813
	N	35.0000	35.0000	35.0000	35.0000	35.0000	35.0000	36.0000	35.0000	35.0000	35.0000
sqrtQ1E1e	Pearson Correlation	-0.0309	-0.1206	-0.0900	-0.0121	-0.1018	0.0297	-0.2124	-0.0477	-0.1587	-0.1752
	Sig. (2-tailed)	0.8601	0.4903	0.6072	0.9450	0.5608	0.8654	0.2137	0.7857	0.3624	0.3141
	N	35.0000	35.0000	35.0000	35.0000	35.0000	35.0000	36.0000	35.0000	35.0000	35.0000
Personal Resource Challenges-Excessive Admin Paperwork	Pearson Correlation	-0.0115	0.0496	-0.0073	0.0842	0.0038	-0.0745	-0.1055	-0.1486	-0.1759	-0.0981
	Sig. (2-tailed)	0.9479	0.7772	0.9670	0.6304	0.9825	0.6707	0.5403	0.3943	0.3121	0.5751
	N	35.0000	35.0000	35.0000	35.0000	35.0000	35.0000	36.0000	35.0000	35.0000	35.0000
Personal Resource Challenges-Ineffective Technology	Pearson Correlation	-0.1319	-0.2363	-0.1399	-0.4103	-0.1608	-0.2308	-0.2806	-0.2593	-0.3074	-0.4159
	Sig. (2-tailed)	0.4501	0.1717	0.4228	0.0144	0.3560	0.1823	0.0974	0.1325	0.0725	0.0130
	N	35.0000	35.0000	35.0000	35.0000	35.0000	35.0000	36.0000	35.0000	35.0000	35.0000
Personal Resource Challenges-Ineffective Strategic Focus	Pearson Correlation	0.0853	-0.1917	-0.1101	-0.3056	-0.0425	0.0858	-0.2536	-0.1277	-0.0767	-0.3050
	Sig. (2-tailed)	0.6263	0.2700	0.5288	0.0742	0.8085	0.6243	0.1356	0.4648	0.6616	0.0748
	N	35.0000	35.0000	35.0000	35.0000	35.0000	35.0000	36.0000	35.0000	35.0000	35.0000
Personal Resource Challenges-Ineffective Tactical Policy	Pearson Correlation	-0.0370	-0.1551	-0.1324	-0.2738	-0.0525	-0.0236	-0.1759	-0.1634	-0.0979	-0.2758
	Sig. (2-tailed)	0.8328	0.3737	0.4485	0.1115	0.7643	0.8931	0.3047	0.3483	0.5756	0.1088
	N	35.0000	35.0000	35.0000	35.0000	35.0000	35.0000	36.0000	35.0000	35.0000	35.0000
Personal Resource Challenges-Lack of Clarity in Duties	Pearson Correlation	-0.0098	-0.2370	-0.1041	-0.2881	-0.0701	0.0245	-0.2140	-0.0981	-0.0273	-0.3199
	Sig. (2-tailed)	0.9555	0.1704	0.5517	0.0933	0.6892	0.8887	0.2102	0.5749	0.8762	0.0610
	N	35.0000	35.0000	35.0000	35.0000	35.0000	35.0000	36.0000	35.0000	35.0000	35.0000
Personal Resource Challenges-Conflict or Lack Comm Leaders and Employees	Pearson Correlation	-0.1040	-0.2256	-0.1972	-0.2288	-0.0133	-0.0914	-0.2336	-0.2435	-0.1599	-0.1964
	Sig. (2-tailed)	0.5520	0.1925	0.2561	0.1861	0.9397	0.6015	0.1703	0.1586	0.3588	0.2582
	N	35.0000	35.0000	35.0000	35.0000	35.0000	35.0000	36.0000	35.0000	35.0000	35.0000
sqrtQ1E11	Pearson Correlation	0.0079	-0.1511	-0.2570	-0.0268	-0.1266	-0.1545	-0.3019	-0.3558	-0.3583	-0.2201
	Sig. (2-tailed)	0.9641	0.3864	0.1362	0.8784	0.4687	0.3755	0.0735	0.0359	0.0346	0.2040
	N	35.0000	35.0000	35.0000	35.0000	35.0000	35.0000	36.0000	35.0000	35.0000	35.0000

Table A7, continued (Row 2, Col 9)

Correlation Matrix, International Variables (Parametric)		sqrtQIIIC1a	sqrtQIIIC1b	sqrtQIIIC1c	sqrtQIIIC1d	sqrtQIIIC1e
Personal Resource Challenges-Lack of Time	Pearson Correlation	-0.0227	-0.1933	-0.2392	-0.1474	-0.1336
	Sig. (2-tailed)	0.8984	0.2659	0.1730	0.4054	0.4511
	N	34.0000	35.0000	34.0000	34.0000	34.0000
Personal Resource Challenges-Lack of Knowledge	Pearson Correlation	0.1436	-0.1942	-0.1883	-0.0882	-0.1212
	Sig. (2-tailed)	0.4178	0.2635	0.2861	0.6198	0.4949
	N	34.0000	35.0000	34.0000	34.0000	34.0000
Personal Resource Challenges-Lack of Training	Pearson Correlation	0.2489	-0.1335	-0.0929	-0.0110	-0.0391
	Sig. (2-tailed)	0.1557	0.4446	0.6012	0.9509	0.8263
	N	34.0000	35.0000	34.0000	34.0000	34.0000
sqrtQ1E1e	Pearson Correlation	-0.0011	-0.0670	-0.1292	-0.0682	-0.0948
	Sig. (2-tailed)	0.9951	0.7022	0.4664	0.7015	0.5939
	N	34.0000	35.0000	34.0000	34.0000	34.0000
Personal Resource Challenges-Excessive Admin Paperwork	Pearson Correlation	0.0863	0.0710	-0.0352	0.0703	0.0453
	Sig. (2-tailed)	0.6274	0.6851	0.8432	0.6927	0.7992
	N	34.0000	35.0000	34.0000	34.0000	34.0000
Personal Resource Challenges-Ineffective Technology	Pearson Correlation	0.0601	-0.1989	-0.2150	-0.1691	-0.1778
	Sig. (2-tailed)	0.7357	0.2520	0.2220	0.3391	0.3144
	N	34.0000	35.0000	34.0000	34.0000	34.0000
Personal Resource Challenges-Ineffective Strategic Focus	Pearson Correlation	0.1613	-0.1192	-0.1036	-0.0263	-0.0441
	Sig. (2-tailed)	0.3622	0.4952	0.5597	0.8824	0.8043
	N	34.0000	35.0000	34.0000	34.0000	34.0000
Personal Resource Challenges-Ineffective Tactical Policy	Pearson Correlation	0.0791	-0.1536	-0.1582	-0.0663	-0.0602
	Sig. (2-tailed)	0.6564	0.3784	0.3716	0.7097	0.7352
	N	34.0000	35.0000	34.0000	34.0000	34.0000
Personal Resource Challenges-Lack of Clarity in Duties	Pearson Correlation	0.1031	-0.2089	-0.1724	-0.0819	-0.0985
	Sig. (2-tailed)	0.5619	0.2285	0.3295	0.6452	0.5795
	N	34.0000	35.0000	34.0000	34.0000	34.0000
Personal Resource Challenges-Conflict or Lack Comm Leaders and Employees	Pearson Correlation	0.0448	-0.1851	-0.2172	-0.0987	-0.0891
	Sig. (2-tailed)	0.8012	0.2871	0.2173	0.5788	0.6165
	N	34.0000	35.0000	34.0000	34.0000	34.0000
sqrtQ1E1l	Pearson Correlation	0.0890	0.0138	-0.1029	0.0099	-0.0275
	Sig. (2-tailed)	0.6167	0.9375	0.5627	0.9558	0.8771
	N	34.0000	35.0000	34.0000	34.0000	34.0000

Table A7, continued (Row 3, Col 1)

Correlation Matrix, International Variables (Parametric)		Importance of Smuggling-Endangered Species	reflectsqrtQ1A1b	reflectsqrtQ1A1c	reflectsqrtQ1A1d	reflectsqrtQ1A1e	sqrtQ1B1a	Knowledge of Smuggling-Narcotics	Knowledge of Smuggling-Weapons	Knowledge of Smuggling-Humans	Knowledge of Smuggling-Contraband
Personal Resource Challenges-Conflict or Lack Comm International Orgs	Pearson Correlation	0.0229	0.0465	-0.0535	-0.1854	-0.0606	0.0694	0.1843	-0.0188	-0.0105	0.1416
	Sig. (2-tailed)	0.8946	0.7876	0.7567	0.2789	0.7254	0.6876	0.2818	0.9134	0.9517	0.4100
	N	36.0000	36.0000	36.0000	36.0000	36.0000	36.0000	36.0000	36.0000	36.0000	36.0000
Personal Resource Challenges-Conflict or Lack Comm Domestic Orgs	Pearson Correlation	-0.0208	-0.1078	-0.0861	-0.2570	0.1232	-0.0188	0.1111	-0.1551	-0.0370	-0.0556
	Sig. (2-tailed)	0.9041	0.5314	0.6178	0.1303	0.4741	0.9131	0.5187	0.3663	0.8303	0.7474
	N	36.0000	36.0000	36.0000	36.0000	36.0000	36.0000	36.0000	36.0000	36.0000	36.0000
sqrtQ1E3a	Pearson Correlation	0.0133	-0.1596	-0.2365	-0.3896	0.0326	-0.0214	0.2403	0.2145	-0.0719	-0.1157
	Sig. (2-tailed)	0.9404	0.3674	0.1782	0.0227	0.8548	0.9043	0.1711	0.2232	0.6860	0.5145
	N	34.0000	34.0000	34.0000	34.0000	34.0000	34.0000	34.0000	34.0000	34.0000	34.0000
Org Resource Challenges-Lack of Time	Pearson Correlation	-0.2552	-0.1996	-0.1862	-0.0401	0.0005	-0.1127	0.0762	-0.0246	0.0081	-0.0850
	Sig. (2-tailed)	0.1390	0.2502	0.2843	0.8190	0.9978	0.5192	0.6634	0.8886	0.9632	0.6275
	N	35.0000	35.0000	35.0000	35.0000	35.0000	35.0000	35.0000	35.0000	35.0000	35.0000
Org Resource Challenges-Lack of Knowledge	Pearson Correlation	-0.1379	-0.3436	-0.3719	-0.1642	-0.0840	-0.1504	-0.0412	-0.2739	-0.0646	-0.1819
	Sig. (2-tailed)	0.4295	0.0433	0.0278	0.3458	0.6316	0.3884	0.8141	0.1114	0.7124	0.2956
	N	35.0000	35.0000	35.0000	35.0000	35.0000	35.0000	35.0000	35.0000	35.0000	35.0000
Org Resource Challenges-Lack of Training	Pearson Correlation	-0.1090	-0.2567	-0.2689	-0.1838	-0.0341	-0.1441	-0.0791	-0.3116	-0.1464	-0.2547
	Sig. (2-tailed)	0.5331	0.1366	0.1184	0.2906	0.8458	0.4090	0.6516	0.0684	0.4014	0.1398
	N	35.0000	35.0000	35.0000	35.0000	35.0000	35.0000	35.0000	35.0000	35.0000	35.0000
sqrtQ1E3e	Pearson Correlation	-0.2357	-0.0838	-0.0101	0.1432	0.1655	-0.2154	0.0355	-0.0703	-0.2233	-0.1197
	Sig. (2-tailed)	0.1795	0.6376	0.9550	0.4192	0.3496	0.2211	0.8419	0.6926	0.2043	0.5001
	N	34.0000	34.0000	34.0000	34.0000	34.0000	34.0000	34.0000	34.0000	34.0000	34.0000
Org Resource Challenges-Excessive Admin Paperwork	Pearson Correlation	-0.2130	-0.1647	-0.0928	-0.0628	0.0211	-0.2287	0.1035	-0.0973	-0.2894	-0.1697
	Sig. (2-tailed)	0.2193	0.3445	0.5960	0.7202	0.9040	0.1863	0.5540	0.5783	0.0917	0.3299
	N	35.0000	35.0000	35.0000	35.0000	35.0000	35.0000	35.0000	35.0000	35.0000	35.0000
Org Resource Challenges-Ineffective Technology	Pearson Correlation	-0.1288	-0.2495	-0.1343	-0.0683	0.1518	-0.0945	0.2007	-0.0701	-0.0244	-0.1510
	Sig. (2-tailed)	0.4609	0.1483	0.4419	0.6967	0.3840	0.5894	0.2477	0.6890	0.8893	0.3867
	N	35.0000	35.0000	35.0000	35.0000	35.0000	35.0000	35.0000	35.0000	35.0000	35.0000
Org Resource Challenges-Ineffective Strategic Focus	Pearson Correlation	-0.0368	-0.2400	-0.2113	-0.0591	0.0927	0.0266	0.0133	-0.1614	-0.0382	-0.1665
	Sig. (2-tailed)	0.8339	0.1649	0.2231	0.7359	0.5964	0.8796	0.9398	0.3543	0.8277	0.3390
	N	35.0000	35.0000	35.0000	35.0000	35.0000	35.0000	35.0000	35.0000	35.0000	35.0000
Org Resource Challenges-Ineffective Tactical Policy	Pearson Correlation	-0.0218	-0.2306	-0.2437	-0.1340	0.1423	-0.0108	0.0210	-0.1416	-0.1871	-0.1946
	Sig. (2-tailed)	0.9009	0.1827	0.1584	0.4429	0.4147	0.9507	0.9048	0.4172	0.2818	0.2626
	N	35.0000	35.0000	35.0000	35.0000	35.0000	35.0000	35.0000	35.0000	35.0000	35.0000

Table A7, continued (Row 3, Col 2)

Correlation Matrix, International Variables (Parametric)		sqrtQ1E1a	Personal Resource Challenges-Lack of Time	Personal Resource Challenges-Lack of Knowledge	Personal Resource Challenges-Lack of Training	sqrtQ1E1e	Personal Resource Challenges-Excessive Admin Paperwork	Personal Resource Challenges-Ineffective Technology	Personal Resource Challenges-Ineffective Strategic Focus	Personal Resource Challenges-Ineffective Tactical Policy	Personal Resource Challenges-Lack of Clarity in Duties
Personal Resource Challenges-Conflict or Lack Comm International Orgs	Pearson Correlation	0.3957	0.4594	0.5736	0.5330	0.3925	0.6658	0.3591	0.5279	0.5658	0.6280
	Sig. (2-tailed)	0.0186	0.0048	0.0003	0.0008	0.0179	0.0000	0.0315	0.0009	0.0003	0.0000
	N	35.0000	36.0000	36.0000	36.0000	36.0000	36.0000	36.0000	36.0000	36.0000	36.0000
Personal Resource Challenges-Conflict or Lack Comm Domestic Orgs	Pearson Correlation	0.4968	0.6319	0.6835	0.6132	0.4321	0.5785	0.5291	0.7125	0.7745	0.8215
	Sig. (2-tailed)	0.0024	0.0000	0.0000	0.0001	0.0085	0.0002	0.0009	0.0000	0.0000	0.0000
	N	35.0000	36.0000	36.0000	36.0000	36.0000	36.0000	36.0000	36.0000	36.0000	36.0000
sqrtQ1E3a	Pearson Correlation	0.5355	0.2228	0.2711	0.2455	0.4098	0.2648	0.4635	0.3866	0.4224	0.4139
	Sig. (2-tailed)	0.0013	0.2053	0.1210	0.1617	0.0161	0.1302	0.0058	0.0239	0.0128	0.0150
	N	33.0000	34.0000	34.0000	34.0000	34.0000	34.0000	34.0000	34.0000	34.0000	34.0000
Org Resource Challenges-Lack of Time	Pearson Correlation	0.3713	0.4499	0.4688	0.3864	0.0904	0.0679	0.3841	0.3242	0.3104	0.2282
	Sig. (2-tailed)	0.0306	0.0067	0.0045	0.0219	0.6053	0.6983	0.0227	0.0575	0.0696	0.1873
	N	34.0000	35.0000	35.0000	35.0000	35.0000	35.0000	35.0000	35.0000	35.0000	35.0000
Org Resource Challenges-Lack of Knowledge	Pearson Correlation	0.2971	0.4761	0.8329	0.8421	0.2760	0.1780	0.5886	0.7021	0.5752	0.6555
	Sig. (2-tailed)	0.0879	0.0038	0.0000	0.0000	0.1085	0.3064	0.0002	0.0000	0.0003	0.0000
	N	34.0000	35.0000	35.0000	35.0000	35.0000	35.0000	35.0000	35.0000	35.0000	35.0000
Org Resource Challenges-Lack of Training	Pearson Correlation	0.3371	0.4834	0.8367	0.8394	0.2369	0.2168	0.6681	0.6671	0.5784	0.6437
	Sig. (2-tailed)	0.0512	0.0033	0.0000	0.0000	0.1707	0.2110	0.0000	0.0000	0.0003	0.0000
	N	34.0000	35.0000	35.0000	35.0000	35.0000	35.0000	35.0000	35.0000	35.0000	35.0000
sqrtQ1E3e	Pearson Correlation	0.4286	0.5283	0.3772	0.3616	0.4965	0.3455	0.3066	0.5175	0.5213	0.4520
	Sig. (2-tailed)	0.0128	0.0013	0.0279	0.0356	0.0028	0.0454	0.0778	0.0017	0.0016	0.0073
	N	33.0000	34.0000	34.0000	34.0000	34.0000	34.0000	34.0000	34.0000	34.0000	34.0000
Org Resource Challenges-Excessive Admin Paperwork	Pearson Correlation	0.6521	0.4741	0.5046	0.4976	0.4340	0.5589	0.4503	0.6065	0.6251	0.5833
	Sig. (2-tailed)	0.0000	0.0040	0.0020	0.0024	0.0092	0.0005	0.0066	0.0001	0.0001	0.0002
	N	34.0000	35.0000	35.0000	35.0000	35.0000	35.0000	35.0000	35.0000	35.0000	35.0000
Org Resource Challenges-Ineffective Technology	Pearson Correlation	0.5895	0.3837	0.5715	0.5343	0.3100	0.3545	0.7341	0.6251	0.6686	0.5461
	Sig. (2-tailed)	0.0002	0.0229	0.0003	0.0009	0.0699	0.0367	0.0000	0.0001	0.0000	0.0007
	N	34.0000	35.0000	35.0000	35.0000	35.0000	35.0000	35.0000	35.0000	35.0000	35.0000
Org Resource Challenges-Ineffective Strategic Focus	Pearson Correlation	0.3989	0.4444	0.7606	0.7089	0.3791	0.3099	0.6454	0.7928	0.7660	0.7172
	Sig. (2-tailed)	0.0194	0.0075	0.0000	0.0000	0.0247	0.0700	0.0000	0.0000	0.0000	0.0000
	N	34.0000	35.0000	35.0000	35.0000	35.0000	35.0000	35.0000	35.0000	35.0000	35.0000
Org Resource Challenges-Ineffective Tactical Policy	Pearson Correlation	0.4226	0.5063	0.6627	0.6414	0.4666	0.4462	0.4557	0.7917	0.8024	0.8184
	Sig. (2-tailed)	0.0128	0.0019	0.0000	0.0000	0.0047	0.0072	0.0059	0.0000	0.0000	0.0000
	N	34.0000	35.0000	35.0000	35.0000	35.0000	35.0000	35.0000	35.0000	35.0000	35.0000

Table A7, continued (Row 3, Col 3)

Correlation Matrix, International Variables (Parametric)		Personal Resource Challenges-Conflict or Lack Comm Leaders and Employees	sqrtQ1E11	Personal Resource Challenges-Conflict or Lack Comm International Orgs	Personal Resource Challenges-Conflict or Lack Comm Domestic Orgs	sqrtQ1E3a	Org Resource Challenges-Lack of Time	Org Resource Challenges-Lack of Knowledge	Org Resource Challenges-Lack of Training	sqrtQ1E3e	Org Resource Challenges-Excessive Admin Paperwork
Personal Resource Challenges-Conflict or Lack Comm International Orgs	Pearson Correlation	0.5973	0.5245	1.0000	0.7869	0.2008	0.1757	0.5045	0.5332	0.2910	0.4796
	Sig. (2-tailed)	0.0001	0.0010	.	0.0000	0.2548	0.3127	0.0020	0.0010	0.0950	0.0036
	N	36.0000	36.0000	36.0000	36.0000	34.0000	35.0000	35.0000	35.0000	34.0000	35.0000
Personal Resource Challenges-Conflict or Lack Comm Domestic Orgs	Pearson Correlation	0.8361	0.4760	0.7869	1.0000	0.3785	0.2783	0.6298	0.6691	0.4769	0.6087
	Sig. (2-tailed)	0.0000	0.0033	0.0000	.	0.0273	0.1055	0.0001	0.0000	0.0043	0.0001
	N	36.0000	36.0000	36.0000	36.0000	34.0000	35.0000	35.0000	35.0000	34.0000	35.0000
sqrtQ1E3a	Pearson Correlation	0.3253	0.1459	0.2008	0.3785	1.0000	0.5117	0.3452	0.3915	0.3655	0.5827
	Sig. (2-tailed)	0.0605	0.4103	0.2548	0.0273	.	0.0020	0.0455	0.0220	0.0365	0.0003
	N	34.0000	34.0000	34.0000	34.0000	34.0000	34.0000	34.0000	34.0000	33.0000	34.0000
Org Resource Challenges-Lack of Time	Pearson Correlation	0.2036	0.0786	0.1757	0.2783	0.5117	1.0000	0.5157	0.5404	0.3159	0.4224
	Sig. (2-tailed)	0.2408	0.6537	0.3127	0.1055	0.0020	.	0.0015	0.0008	0.0688	0.0115
	N	35.0000	35.0000	35.0000	35.0000	34.0000	35.0000	35.0000	35.0000	34.0000	35.0000
Org Resource Challenges-Lack of Knowledge	Pearson Correlation	0.5026	0.2653	0.5045	0.6298	0.3452	0.5157	1.0000	0.9587	0.4325	0.5495
	Sig. (2-tailed)	0.0021	0.1235	0.0020	0.0001	0.0455	0.0015	.	0.0000	0.0106	0.0006
	N	35.0000	35.0000	35.0000	35.0000	34.0000	35.0000	35.0000	35.0000	34.0000	35.0000
Org Resource Challenges-Lack of Training	Pearson Correlation	0.4964	0.3241	0.5332	0.6691	0.3915	0.5404	0.9587	1.0000	0.4030	0.5554
	Sig. (2-tailed)	0.0024	0.0575	0.0010	0.0000	0.0220	0.0008	0.0000	.	0.0181	0.0005
	N	35.0000	35.0000	35.0000	35.0000	34.0000	35.0000	35.0000	35.0000	34.0000	35.0000
sqrtQ1E3e	Pearson Correlation	0.4955	0.4006	0.2910	0.4769	0.3655	0.3159	0.4325	0.4030	1.0000	0.7700
	Sig. (2-tailed)	0.0029	0.0189	0.0950	0.0043	0.0365	0.0688	0.0106	0.0181	.	0.0000
	N	34.0000	34.0000	34.0000	34.0000	33.0000	34.0000	34.0000	34.0000	34.0000	34.0000
Org Resource Challenges-Excessive Admin Paperwork	Pearson Correlation	0.5537	0.4504	0.4796	0.6087	0.5827	0.4224	0.5495	0.5554	0.7700	1.0000
	Sig. (2-tailed)	0.0006	0.0066	0.0036	0.0001	0.0003	0.0115	0.0006	0.0005	0.0000	.
	N	35.0000	35.0000	35.0000	35.0000	34.0000	35.0000	35.0000	35.0000	34.0000	35.0000
Org Resource Challenges-Ineffective Technology	Pearson Correlation	0.6035	0.4102	0.3417	0.5933	0.5270	0.4404	0.6191	0.6693	0.4891	0.5929
	Sig. (2-tailed)	0.0001	0.0144	0.0446	0.0002	0.0014	0.0081	0.0001	0.0000	0.0033	0.0002
	N	35.0000	35.0000	35.0000	35.0000	34.0000	35.0000	35.0000	35.0000	34.0000	35.0000
Org Resource Challenges-Ineffective Strategic Focus	Pearson Correlation	0.7479	0.4507	0.4554	0.6978	0.3169	0.3804	0.7509	0.7401	0.4064	0.4743
	Sig. (2-tailed)	0.0000	0.0066	0.0060	0.0000	0.0678	0.0242	0.0000	0.0000	0.0171	0.0040
	N	35.0000	35.0000	35.0000	35.0000	34.0000	35.0000	35.0000	35.0000	34.0000	35.0000
Org Resource Challenges-Ineffective Tactical Policy	Pearson Correlation	0.8003	0.4718	0.6704	0.8536	0.3936	0.2420	0.7079	0.6817	0.5428	0.6589
	Sig. (2-tailed)	0.0000	0.0042	0.0000	0.0000	0.0213	0.1614	0.0000	0.0000	0.0009	0.0000
	N	35.0000	35.0000	35.0000	35.0000	34.0000	35.0000	35.0000	35.0000	34.0000	35.0000

Table A7, continued (Row 3, Col 4)

Correlation Matrix, International Variables (Parametric)		Org Resource Challenges-Ineffective Technology	Org Resource Challenges-Ineffective Strategic Focus	Org Resource Challenges-Ineffective Tactical Policy	Org Resource Challenges-Lack of Clarity in Duties	Org Resource Challenges-Conflict or Lack Comm Leaders and Employees	sqrtQ1E3l	Org Resource Challenges-Conflict or Lack Comm International Orgs	Org Resource Challenges-Conflict or Lack Comm Domestic Orgs	sqrtQ1IA1a	Knowledge of Domestic Law-CSIE
Personal Resource Challenges-Conflict or Lack Comm International Orgs	Pearson Correlation	0.3417	0.4554	0.6704	0.5006	0.6766	0.5669	0.5283	0.4958	0.2155	0.0457
	Sig. (2-tailed)	0.0446	0.0060	0.0000	0.0022	0.0000	0.0004	0.0011	0.0025	0.2137	0.7945
	N	35.0000	35.0000	35.0000	35.0000	35.0000	35.0000	35.0000	35.0000	35.0000	35.0000
Personal Resource Challenges-Conflict or Lack Comm Domestic Orgs	Pearson Correlation	0.5933	0.6978	0.8536	0.6819	0.7312	0.4613	0.6075	0.6459	0.1088	-0.1031
	Sig. (2-tailed)	0.0002	0.0000	0.0000	0.0000	0.0000	0.0053	0.0001	0.0000	0.5340	0.5558
	N	35.0000	35.0000	35.0000	35.0000	35.0000	35.0000	35.0000	35.0000	35.0000	35.0000
sqrtQ1E3a	Pearson Correlation	0.5270	0.3169	0.3936	0.3625	0.2974	0.1722	0.3658	0.3306	0.0390	-0.0192
	Sig. (2-tailed)	0.0014	0.0678	0.0213	0.0351	0.0876	0.3302	0.0334	0.0562	0.8295	0.9157
	N	34.0000	34.0000	34.0000	34.0000	34.0000	34.0000	34.0000	34.0000	33.0000	33.0000
Org Resource Challenges-Lack of Time	Pearson Correlation	0.4404	0.3804	0.2420	0.2906	0.1354	0.1338	0.4475	0.3240	-0.0461	0.0654
	Sig. (2-tailed)	0.0081	0.0242	0.1614	0.0904	0.4381	0.4436	0.0070	0.0576	0.7956	0.7133
	N	35.0000	35.0000	35.0000	35.0000	35.0000	35.0000	35.0000	35.0000	34.0000	34.0000
Org Resource Challenges-Lack of Knowledge	Pearson Correlation	0.6191	0.7509	0.7079	0.7829	0.5025	0.3496	0.7932	0.7503	-0.0605	-0.2321
	Sig. (2-tailed)	0.0001	0.0000	0.0000	0.0000	0.0021	0.0395	0.0000	0.0000	0.7341	0.1865
	N	35.0000	35.0000	35.0000	35.0000	35.0000	35.0000	35.0000	35.0000	34.0000	34.0000
Org Resource Challenges-Lack of Training	Pearson Correlation	0.6693	0.7401	0.6817	0.7546	0.5110	0.4188	0.7846	0.7474	-0.0674	-0.2196
	Sig. (2-tailed)	0.0000	0.0000	0.0000	0.0000	0.0017	0.0123	0.0000	0.0000	0.7050	0.2120
	N	35.0000	35.0000	35.0000	35.0000	35.0000	35.0000	35.0000	35.0000	34.0000	34.0000
sqrtQ1E3e	Pearson Correlation	0.4891	0.4064	0.5428	0.3878	0.5015	0.4392	0.3551	0.3623	-0.0472	-0.0513
	Sig. (2-tailed)	0.0033	0.0171	0.0009	0.0234	0.0025	0.0094	0.0393	0.0352	0.7942	0.7766
	N	34.0000	34.0000	34.0000	34.0000	34.0000	34.0000	34.0000	34.0000	33.0000	33.0000
Org Resource Challenges-Excessive Admin Paperwork	Pearson Correlation	0.5929	0.4743	0.6589	0.4762	0.5461	0.4573	0.4667	0.4788	0.1397	0.0040
	Sig. (2-tailed)	0.0002	0.0040	0.0000	0.0038	0.0007	0.0057	0.0047	0.0036	0.4306	0.9821
	N	35.0000	35.0000	35.0000	35.0000	35.0000	35.0000	35.0000	35.0000	34.0000	34.0000
Org Resource Challenges-Ineffective Technology	Pearson Correlation	1.0000	0.8327	0.6391	0.7585	0.6652	0.4128	0.6756	0.7328	-0.1555	0.1273
	Sig. (2-tailed)	.	0.0000	0.0000	0.0000	0.0000	0.0137	0.0000	0.0000	0.3798	0.4731
	N	35.0000	35.0000	35.0000	35.0000	35.0000	35.0000	35.0000	35.0000	34.0000	34.0000
Org Resource Challenges-Ineffective Strategic Focus	Pearson Correlation	0.8327	1.0000	0.8061	0.9043	0.7485	0.4589	0.7970	0.8421	-0.0550	-0.0390
	Sig. (2-tailed)	0.0000	.	0.0000	0.0000	0.0000	0.0056	0.0000	0.0000	0.7574	0.8266
	N	35.0000	35.0000	35.0000	35.0000	35.0000	35.0000	35.0000	35.0000	34.0000	34.0000
Org Resource Challenges-Ineffective Tactical Policy	Pearson Correlation	0.6391	0.8061	1.0000	0.8464	0.8618	0.5439	0.7400	0.7592	0.0757	-0.1634
	Sig. (2-tailed)	0.0000	0.0000	.	0.0000	0.0000	0.0007	0.0000	0.0000	0.6703	0.3557
	N	35.0000	35.0000	35.0000	35.0000	35.0000	35.0000	35.0000	35.0000	34.0000	34.0000

Table A7, continued (Row 3, Col 5)

Correlation Matrix, International Variables (Parametric)		Knowledge of Domestic Law-DWMD	Knowledge of Domestic Law-TVP	Knowledge of Domestic Law-CBP	sqrtQIID1a	Level Cooperation Domestic Orgs-CSIE	Level Cooperation Domestic Orgs-DWMD	Level Cooperation Domestic Orgs-TVP	Level Cooperation Domestic Orgs-CBP	sqrtQIIIA1a	sqrtQIIIA1b
Personal Resource Challenges-Conflict or Lack Comm International Orgs	Pearson Correlation	-0.0794	0.1555	0.0366	-0.1358	-0.1725	-0.1342	0.0026	-0.1031	0.2839	0.1332
	Sig. (2-tailed)	0.6502	0.3723	0.8345	0.4298	0.3143	0.4350	0.9881	0.5496	0.0984	0.4388
	N	35.0000	35.0000	35.0000	36.0000	36.0000	36.0000	36.0000	36.0000	35.0000	36.0000
Personal Resource Challenges-Conflict or Lack Comm Domestic Orgs	Pearson Correlation	-0.2276	0.0439	-0.0862	-0.1864	-0.3066	-0.2523	-0.0655	-0.2033	0.2088	0.0700
	Sig. (2-tailed)	0.1885	0.8024	0.6226	0.2764	0.0689	0.1377	0.7043	0.2344	0.2287	0.6850
	N	35.0000	35.0000	35.0000	36.0000	36.0000	36.0000	36.0000	36.0000	35.0000	36.0000
sqrtQ1E3a	Pearson Correlation	-0.0303	-0.0886	-0.1843	-0.1416	-0.1553	-0.2637	-0.1839	-0.3699	0.0342	0.0321
	Sig. (2-tailed)	0.8672	0.6241	0.3046	0.4244	0.3804	0.1318	0.2978	0.0313	0.8503	0.8570
	N	33.0000	33.0000	33.0000	34.0000	34.0000	34.0000	34.0000	34.0000	33.0000	34.0000
Org Resource Challenges-Lack of Time	Pearson Correlation	0.0926	0.0988	-0.1136	-0.3091	-0.1766	-0.3089	-0.2466	-0.4410	-0.0162	-0.0835
	Sig. (2-tailed)	0.6023	0.5783	0.5224	0.0708	0.3101	0.0709	0.1533	0.0080	0.9276	0.6336
	N	34.0000	34.0000	34.0000	35.0000	35.0000	35.0000	35.0000	35.0000	34.0000	35.0000
Org Resource Challenges-Lack of Knowledge	Pearson Correlation	-0.3174	-0.0808	-0.3351	-0.3537	-0.4078	-0.4448	-0.2323	-0.2361	0.0263	-0.2797
	Sig. (2-tailed)	0.0674	0.6494	0.0527	0.0371	0.0150	0.0074	0.1793	0.1721	0.8828	0.1036
	N	34.0000	34.0000	34.0000	35.0000	35.0000	35.0000	35.0000	35.0000	34.0000	35.0000
Org Resource Challenges-Lack of Training	Pearson Correlation	-0.3426	-0.1142	-0.3563	-0.3828	-0.4665	-0.4764	-0.2813	-0.3095	-0.0017	-0.3170
	Sig. (2-tailed)	0.0473	0.5200	0.0386	0.0232	0.0047	0.0038	0.1017	0.0704	0.9925	0.0635
	N	34.0000	34.0000	34.0000	35.0000	35.0000	35.0000	35.0000	35.0000	34.0000	35.0000
sqrtQ1E3e	Pearson Correlation	-0.2463	-0.3220	-0.2003	-0.1077	-0.2576	-0.1964	-0.3635	-0.1248	0.0645	0.0298
	Sig. (2-tailed)	0.1670	0.0677	0.2638	0.5443	0.1414	0.2657	0.0346	0.4819	0.7216	0.8673
	N	33.0000	33.0000	33.0000	34.0000	34.0000	34.0000	34.0000	34.0000	33.0000	34.0000
Org Resource Challenges-Excessive Admin Paperwork	Pearson Correlation	-0.1851	-0.2122	-0.1357	-0.2613	-0.1698	-0.1211	-0.2969	-0.2055	0.2057	0.1275
	Sig. (2-tailed)	0.2945	0.2284	0.4440	0.1295	0.3295	0.4882	0.0833	0.2363	0.2432	0.4656
	N	34.0000	34.0000	34.0000	35.0000	35.0000	35.0000	35.0000	35.0000	34.0000	35.0000
Org Resource Challenges-Ineffective Technology	Pearson Correlation	-0.0578	-0.0183	-0.3113	-0.3255	-0.3626	-0.4359	-0.2617	-0.4314	-0.0089	0.0746
	Sig. (2-tailed)	0.7453	0.9181	0.0731	0.0564	0.0323	0.0089	0.1289	0.0097	0.9604	0.6700
	N	34.0000	34.0000	34.0000	35.0000	35.0000	35.0000	35.0000	35.0000	34.0000	35.0000
Org Resource Challenges-Ineffective Strategic Focus	Pearson Correlation	-0.1159	0.0093	-0.2705	-0.2537	-0.3952	-0.4554	-0.1852	-0.2952	0.0761	-0.1040
	Sig. (2-tailed)	0.5141	0.9582	0.1218	0.1413	0.0188	0.0060	0.2868	0.0851	0.6689	0.5522
	N	34.0000	34.0000	34.0000	35.0000	35.0000	35.0000	35.0000	35.0000	34.0000	35.0000
Org Resource Challenges-Ineffective Tactical Policy	Pearson Correlation	-0.2554	-0.0599	-0.1713	-0.2208	-0.2891	-0.3082	-0.1271	-0.1596	0.1894	-0.0530
	Sig. (2-tailed)	0.1449	0.7366	0.3327	0.2025	0.0922	0.0717	0.4670	0.3598	0.2833	0.7622
	N	34.0000	34.0000	34.0000	35.0000	35.0000	35.0000	35.0000	35.0000	34.0000	35.0000

Table A7, continued (Row 3, Col 6)

Correlation Matrix, International Variables (Parametric)		sqrtQIIIA1c	sqrtQIIIA1d	sqrtQIIIA1e	sqrtQIIID1a	Level Cooperation Domestic Orgs-CNDPS	Level Cooperation Domestic Orgs-CNBC	Level Cooperation Domestic Orgs-CSTP	Level Cooperation Domestic Orgs-TRIPS	sqrtQIIID2a	Level Cooperation International Orgs-CNDPS
Personal Resource Challenges-Conflict or Lack Comm International Orgs	Pearson Correlation	0.0944	0.2105	0.0680	0.0776	-0.1258	-0.2421	-0.0921	-0.1925	-0.0771	-0.0630
	Sig. (2-tailed)	0.5840	0.2179	0.6937	0.6677	0.4716	0.1611	0.5988	0.2678	0.6596	0.7150
	N	36.0000	36.0000	36.0000	33.0000	35.0000	35.0000	35.0000	35.0000	35.0000	36.0000
Personal Resource Challenges-Conflict or Lack Comm Domestic Orgs	Pearson Correlation	0.1161	0.2141	-0.0306	0.0771	-0.0970	-0.2036	-0.0198	-0.1262	-0.1538	-0.1353
	Sig. (2-tailed)	0.5001	0.2099	0.8595	0.6697	0.5793	0.2409	0.9102	0.4701	0.3778	0.4315
	N	36.0000	36.0000	36.0000	33.0000	35.0000	35.0000	35.0000	35.0000	35.0000	36.0000
sqrtQ1E3a	Pearson Correlation	0.1374	0.1194	-0.0829	0.0230	-0.1200	-0.1800	-0.1702	-0.2506	-0.0594	0.1036
	Sig. (2-tailed)	0.4386	0.5010	0.6413	0.9024	0.5059	0.3163	0.3436	0.1595	0.7426	0.5598
	N	34.0000	34.0000	34.0000	31.0000	33.0000	33.0000	33.0000	33.0000	33.0000	34.0000
Org Resource Challenges-Lack of Time	Pearson Correlation	0.0184	-0.0144	-0.1243	-0.2796	-0.3383	-0.3131	-0.2950	-0.4556	-0.3044	-0.2275
	Sig. (2-tailed)	0.9166	0.9344	0.4767	0.1212	0.0503	0.0714	0.0904	0.0068	0.0801	0.1888
	N	35.0000	35.0000	35.0000	32.0000	34.0000	34.0000	34.0000	34.0000	34.0000	35.0000
Org Resource Challenges-Lack of Knowledge	Pearson Correlation	-0.2263	-0.0268	-0.2772	0.0015	-0.3248	-0.3757	-0.1646	-0.3192	-0.1769	-0.2702
	Sig. (2-tailed)	0.1911	0.8786	0.1069	0.9936	0.0609	0.0285	0.3522	0.0657	0.3168	0.1164
	N	35.0000	35.0000	35.0000	32.0000	34.0000	34.0000	34.0000	34.0000	34.0000	35.0000
Org Resource Challenges-Lack of Training	Pearson Correlation	-0.2731	-0.0901	-0.3359	-0.0421	-0.3530	-0.4226	-0.1937	-0.3354	-0.2034	-0.2894
	Sig. (2-tailed)	0.1124	0.6066	0.0485	0.8190	0.0406	0.0128	0.2724	0.0525	0.2486	0.0917
	N	35.0000	35.0000	35.0000	32.0000	34.0000	34.0000	34.0000	34.0000	34.0000	35.0000
sqrtQ1E3e	Pearson Correlation	0.1285	-0.0141	0.0582	0.0959	-0.0810	-0.0355	-0.0343	0.0295	-0.0190	-0.0860
	Sig. (2-tailed)	0.4688	0.9370	0.7438	0.6079	0.6541	0.8446	0.8497	0.8705	0.9164	0.6287
	N	34.0000	34.0000	34.0000	31.0000	33.0000	33.0000	33.0000	33.0000	33.0000	34.0000
Org Resource Challenges-Excessive Admin Paperwork	Pearson Correlation	0.2022	0.1224	0.0930	0.0279	-0.1288	-0.1819	-0.0498	-0.1475	-0.0482	-0.0530
	Sig. (2-tailed)	0.2441	0.4838	0.5951	0.8797	0.4677	0.3033	0.7799	0.4051	0.7868	0.7622
	N	35.0000	35.0000	35.0000	32.0000	34.0000	34.0000	34.0000	34.0000	34.0000	35.0000
Org Resource Challenges-Ineffective Technology	Pearson Correlation	0.1545	0.1285	-0.1611	-0.1393	-0.1680	-0.2951	-0.1450	-0.2648	-0.1784	-0.1089
	Sig. (2-tailed)	0.3754	0.4620	0.3552	0.4469	0.3424	0.0902	0.4133	0.1301	0.3128	0.5333
	N	35.0000	35.0000	35.0000	32.0000	34.0000	34.0000	34.0000	34.0000	34.0000	35.0000
Org Resource Challenges-Ineffective Strategic Focus	Pearson Correlation	0.0208	0.0143	-0.2920	-0.1005	-0.2940	-0.2771	-0.1540	-0.2889	-0.1595	-0.2729
	Sig. (2-tailed)	0.9058	0.9352	0.0888	0.5842	0.0915	0.1126	0.3846	0.0975	0.3676	0.1127
	N	35.0000	35.0000	35.0000	32.0000	34.0000	34.0000	34.0000	34.0000	34.0000	35.0000
Org Resource Challenges-Ineffective Tactical Policy	Pearson Correlation	0.0520	0.1151	-0.1516	0.1123	-0.1628	-0.1912	-0.0689	-0.1827	-0.1374	-0.2079
	Sig. (2-tailed)	0.7667	0.5103	0.3846	0.5406	0.3577	0.2786	0.6984	0.3011	0.4386	0.2306
	N	35.0000	35.0000	35.0000	32.0000	34.0000	34.0000	34.0000	34.0000	34.0000	35.0000

Table A7, continued (Row 3, Col 7)

Correlation Matrix, International Variables (Parametric)		Level Cooperation International Orgs-CNBC	Level Cooperation International Orgs-CSTP	sqrtQIIID2e	sqrtQIVA1	sqrtQIVA2	sqrtQIVA3	sqrtQIVA5	sqrtQIVA7	sqrtQIVA8	Political Ideology
Personal Resource Challenges-Conflict or Lack Comm International Orgs	Pearson Correlation	-0.1384	-0.0166	-0.1955	0.1870	0.2393	0.2714	-0.0521	-0.0101	0.0640	0.0389
	Sig. (2-tailed)	0.4207	0.9236	0.2531	0.2749	0.1599	0.1148	0.7700	0.9535	0.7150	0.8299
	N	36.0000	36.0000	36.0000	36.0000	36.0000	35.0000	34.0000	36.0000	35.0000	33.0000
Personal Resource Challenges-Conflict or Lack Comm Domestic Orgs	Pearson Correlation	-0.2322	-0.0763	-0.2643	0.2684	0.2483	0.3473	-0.1372	0.0575	-0.1378	0.0614
	Sig. (2-tailed)	0.1729	0.6582	0.1193	0.1134	0.1443	0.0409	0.4391	0.7392	0.4300	0.7343
	N	36.0000	36.0000	36.0000	36.0000	36.0000	35.0000	34.0000	36.0000	35.0000	33.0000
sqrtQ1E3a	Pearson Correlation	0.0984	-0.0030	-0.0716	0.2920	0.3555	0.2967	0.0015	-0.0107	-0.1731	0.0560
	Sig. (2-tailed)	0.5798	0.9867	0.6874	0.0938	0.0391	0.0936	0.9932	0.9523	0.3277	0.7609
	N	34.0000	34.0000	34.0000	34.0000	34.0000	33.0000	33.0000	34.0000	34.0000	32.0000
Org Resource Challenges-Lack of Time	Pearson Correlation	-0.2063	-0.2480	-0.3042	0.0029	0.1769	-0.0517	0.0635	-0.0614	0.2567	-0.0784
	Sig. (2-tailed)	0.2345	0.1509	0.0756	0.9870	0.3093	0.7716	0.7212	0.7262	0.1366	0.6644
	N	35.0000	35.0000	35.0000	35.0000	35.0000	34.0000	34.0000	35.0000	35.0000	33.0000
Org Resource Challenges-Lack of Knowledge	Pearson Correlation	-0.2763	-0.1889	-0.2873	0.2136	0.1306	0.1567	-0.1624	0.0765	-0.0302	-0.1021
	Sig. (2-tailed)	0.1081	0.2772	0.0942	0.2180	0.4546	0.3763	0.3588	0.6621	0.8634	0.5717
	N	35.0000	35.0000	35.0000	35.0000	35.0000	34.0000	34.0000	35.0000	35.0000	33.0000
Org Resource Challenges-Lack of Training	Pearson Correlation	-0.3140	-0.2335	-0.3437	0.1882	0.1844	0.1301	-0.2116	0.0666	-0.0590	-0.0800
	Sig. (2-tailed)	0.0662	0.1771	0.0432	0.2789	0.2890	0.4633	0.2296	0.7036	0.7364	0.6581
	N	35.0000	35.0000	35.0000	35.0000	35.0000	34.0000	34.0000	35.0000	35.0000	33.0000
sqrtQ1E3e	Pearson Correlation	-0.0732	-0.0943	0.0318	0.0981	0.0666	0.2704	-0.1671	-0.0981	-0.0177	0.1183
	Sig. (2-tailed)	0.6808	0.5959	0.8582	0.5809	0.7082	0.1280	0.3526	0.5811	0.9211	0.5189
	N	34.0000	34.0000	34.0000	34.0000	34.0000	33.0000	33.0000	34.0000	34.0000	32.0000
Org Resource Challenges-Excessive Admin Paperwork	Pearson Correlation	-0.0612	-0.0943	-0.0615	0.0572	0.1212	0.2113	-0.0822	-0.0328	-0.2230	-0.0690
	Sig. (2-tailed)	0.7269	0.5899	0.7255	0.7441	0.4880	0.2303	0.6440	0.8516	0.1979	0.7030
	N	35.0000	35.0000	35.0000	35.0000	35.0000	34.0000	34.0000	35.0000	35.0000	33.0000
Org Resource Challenges-Ineffective Technology	Pearson Correlation	-0.1526	-0.1341	-0.2585	0.2358	0.1196	0.1978	-0.1445	-0.0430	-0.2447	-0.0409
	Sig. (2-tailed)	0.3814	0.4424	0.1337	0.1726	0.4939	0.2622	0.4148	0.8064	0.1566	0.8211
	N	35.0000	35.0000	35.0000	35.0000	35.0000	34.0000	34.0000	35.0000	35.0000	33.0000
Org Resource Challenges-Ineffective Strategic Focus	Pearson Correlation	-0.2741	-0.2184	-0.3170	0.3248	0.1723	0.1703	-0.1517	0.0874	-0.2093	-0.0088
	Sig. (2-tailed)	0.1111	0.2074	0.0635	0.0569	0.3222	0.3355	0.3919	0.6176	0.2276	0.9611
	N	35.0000	35.0000	35.0000	35.0000	35.0000	34.0000	34.0000	35.0000	35.0000	33.0000
Org Resource Challenges-Ineffective Tactical Policy	Pearson Correlation	-0.2227	-0.1647	-0.2417	0.2058	0.1873	0.2609	-0.0647	0.0278	-0.2141	-0.0584
	Sig. (2-tailed)	0.1984	0.3443	0.1619	0.2357	0.2814	0.1362	0.7163	0.8740	0.2168	0.7470
	N	35.0000	35.0000	35.0000	35.0000	35.0000	34.0000	34.0000	35.0000	35.0000	33.0000

Table A7, continued (Row 3, Col 8)

Correlation Matrix, International Variables (Parametric)		sqrtQIIIB1a	sqrtQIIIB1b	sqrtQIIIB1c	sqrtQIIIB1d	sqrtQIIIB1e	sqrtQIIIB2a	Perceived Effectiveness Domestic Govt Support-CNDPS	Perceived Effectiveness Domestic Govt Support-CNBC	Perceived Effectiveness Domestic Govt Support-CSTP	Perceived Effectiveness Domestic Govt Support-TRIPS
Personal Resource Challenges-Conflict or Lack Comm International Orgs	Pearson Correlation	0.0969	-0.0059	0.1059	-0.0239	0.1707	0.0143	-0.0332	-0.0437	0.0061	-0.0147
	Sig. (2-tailed)	0.5796	0.9731	0.5449	0.8917	0.3268	0.9352	0.8475	0.8032	0.9725	0.9332
	N	35.0000	35.0000	35.0000	35.0000	35.0000	35.0000	36.0000	35.0000	35.0000	35.0000
Personal Resource Challenges-Conflict or Lack Comm Domestic Orgs	Pearson Correlation	-0.0293	-0.1643	-0.0594	-0.1830	-0.0412	0.0406	-0.0816	-0.0825	0.0094	-0.2366
	Sig. (2-tailed)	0.8671	0.3457	0.7348	0.2927	0.8142	0.8167	0.6362	0.6376	0.9571	0.1712
	N	35.0000	35.0000	35.0000	35.0000	35.0000	35.0000	36.0000	35.0000	35.0000	35.0000
sqrtQ1E3a	Pearson Correlation	-0.2950	-0.2137	-0.1631	-0.3862	-0.4157	-0.0814	0.0519	0.1264	-0.0265	-0.3064
	Sig. (2-tailed)	0.0903	0.2249	0.3568	0.0241	0.0145	0.6472	0.7708	0.4764	0.8818	0.0780
	N	34.0000	34.0000	34.0000	34.0000	34.0000	34.0000	34.0000	34.0000	34.0000	34.0000
Org Resource Challenges-Lack of Time	Pearson Correlation	-0.3238	-0.3496	-0.2681	-0.4731	-0.4350	-0.2053	-0.0762	-0.0086	-0.1177	-0.4033
	Sig. (2-tailed)	0.0617	0.0427	0.1253	0.0047	0.0101	0.2442	0.6635	0.9616	0.5073	0.0180
	N	34.0000	34.0000	34.0000	34.0000	34.0000	34.0000	35.0000	34.0000	34.0000	34.0000
Org Resource Challenges-Lack of Knowledge	Pearson Correlation	0.2335	-0.0496	0.1261	-0.3492	0.0666	0.1962	-0.0103	0.0951	0.1774	-0.1934
	Sig. (2-tailed)	0.1838	0.7807	0.4773	0.0429	0.7081	0.2661	0.9530	0.5926	0.3156	0.2732
	N	34.0000	34.0000	34.0000	34.0000	34.0000	34.0000	35.0000	34.0000	34.0000	34.0000
Org Resource Challenges-Lack of Training	Pearson Correlation	0.1683	-0.1123	0.0400	-0.3882	-0.0282	0.1238	-0.0907	0.0106	0.0964	-0.2887
	Sig. (2-tailed)	0.3413	0.5272	0.8221	0.0233	0.8743	0.4854	0.6045	0.9526	0.5875	0.0977
	N	34.0000	34.0000	34.0000	34.0000	34.0000	34.0000	35.0000	34.0000	34.0000	34.0000
sqrtQ1E3e	Pearson Correlation	-0.2437	-0.2697	-0.3545	-0.2357	-0.2222	-0.1391	-0.1881	-0.2252	-0.1995	-0.2178
	Sig. (2-tailed)	0.1717	0.1291	0.0429	0.1867	0.2140	0.4400	0.2867	0.2077	0.2657	0.2234
	N	33.0000	33.0000	33.0000	33.0000	33.0000	33.0000	34.0000	33.0000	33.0000	33.0000
Org Resource Challenges-Excessive Admin Paperwork	Pearson Correlation	-0.2578	-0.2462	-0.2551	-0.3611	-0.2810	-0.1720	-0.0829	-0.1254	-0.1523	-0.3237
	Sig. (2-tailed)	0.1410	0.1604	0.1454	0.0359	0.1075	0.3306	0.6359	0.4799	0.3898	0.0618
	N	34.0000	34.0000	34.0000	34.0000	34.0000	34.0000	35.0000	34.0000	34.0000	34.0000
Org Resource Challenges-Ineffective Technology	Pearson Correlation	-0.0493	-0.1009	-0.0495	-0.3719	-0.1349	-0.1102	-0.1216	-0.0894	-0.0826	-0.4039
	Sig. (2-tailed)	0.7819	0.5704	0.7811	0.0303	0.4469	0.5351	0.4865	0.6153	0.6425	0.0179
	N	34.0000	34.0000	34.0000	34.0000	34.0000	34.0000	35.0000	34.0000	34.0000	34.0000
Org Resource Challenges-Ineffective Strategic Focus	Pearson Correlation	0.1769	-0.0510	0.0676	-0.3289	0.0191	0.1170	-0.1063	-0.0245	0.0094	-0.3116
	Sig. (2-tailed)	0.3169	0.7747	0.7040	0.0575	0.9148	0.5100	0.5435	0.8907	0.9580	0.0728
	N	34.0000	34.0000	34.0000	34.0000	34.0000	34.0000	35.0000	34.0000	34.0000	34.0000
Org Resource Challenges-Ineffective Tactical Policy	Pearson Correlation	0.0713	-0.0928	0.0108	-0.2646	-0.0281	0.1517	-0.0316	-0.0081	0.0558	-0.2169
	Sig. (2-tailed)	0.6887	0.6016	0.9517	0.1305	0.8745	0.3917	0.8570	0.9638	0.7540	0.2178
	N	34.0000	34.0000	34.0000	34.0000	34.0000	34.0000	35.0000	34.0000	34.0000	34.0000

347

Table A7, continued (Row 3, Col 9)

Correlation Matrix, International Variables (Parametric)		sqrtQIIIC1a	sqrtQIIIC1b	sqrtQIIIC1c	sqrtQIIIC1d	sqrtQIIIC1e
Personal Resource Challenges-Conflict or Lack Comm International Orgs	Pearson Correlation	0.1652	-0.0285	-0.0537	0.0106	-0.0186
	Sig. (2-tailed)	0.3504	0.8710	0.7631	0.9526	0.9167
	N	34.0000	35.0000	34.0000	34.0000	34.0000
Personal Resource Challenges-Conflict or Lack Comm Domestic Orgs	Pearson Correlation	0.0992	-0.1505	-0.1993	-0.0862	-0.1104
	Sig. (2-tailed)	0.5767	0.3883	0.2584	0.6278	0.5341
	N	34.0000	35.0000	34.0000	34.0000	34.0000
sqrtQ1E3a	Pearson Correlation	-0.1657	-0.2059	-0.1578	-0.2465	-0.3178
	Sig. (2-tailed)	0.3567	0.2503	0.3804	0.1668	0.0715
	N	33.0000	33.0000	33.0000	33.0000	33.0000
Org Resource Challenges-Lack of Time	Pearson Correlation	-0.3343	-0.3432	-0.3385	-0.3835	-0.4523
	Sig. (2-tailed)	0.0572	0.0469	0.0540	0.0276	0.0082
	N	33.0000	34.0000	33.0000	33.0000	33.0000
Org Resource Challenges-Lack of Knowledge	Pearson Correlation	0.1838	-0.1343	-0.1171	-0.0609	-0.0694
	Sig. (2-tailed)	0.3060	0.4489	0.5165	0.7365	0.7011
	N	33.0000	34.0000	33.0000	33.0000	33.0000
Org Resource Challenges-Lack of Training	Pearson Correlation	0.1669	-0.1932	-0.1836	-0.1057	-0.1328
	Sig. (2-tailed)	0.3531	0.2736	0.3065	0.5581	0.4614
	N	33.0000	34.0000	33.0000	33.0000	33.0000
sqrtQ1E3e	Pearson Correlation	-0.3023	-0.2822	-0.4482	-0.3229	-0.2711
	Sig. (2-tailed)	0.0927	0.1116	0.0101	0.0715	0.1334
	N	32.0000	33.0000	32.0000	32.0000	32.0000
Org Resource Challenges-Excessive Admin Paperwork	Pearson Correlation	-0.1881	-0.1751	-0.2797	-0.2230	-0.2009
	Sig. (2-tailed)	0.2944	0.3219	0.1149	0.2122	0.2622
	N	33.0000	34.0000	33.0000	33.0000	33.0000
Org Resource Challenges-Ineffective Technology	Pearson Correlation	0.0267	-0.1899	-0.1943	-0.1590	-0.1737
	Sig. (2-tailed)	0.8828	0.2820	0.2786	0.3768	0.3335
	N	33.0000	34.0000	33.0000	33.0000	33.0000
Org Resource Challenges-Ineffective Strategic Focus	Pearson Correlation	0.2110	-0.1182	-0.0957	-0.0160	-0.0507
	Sig. (2-tailed)	0.2385	0.5056	0.5961	0.9295	0.7792
	N	33.0000	34.0000	33.0000	33.0000	33.0000
Org Resource Challenges-Ineffective Tactical Policy	Pearson Correlation	0.1542	-0.1002	-0.0906	-0.0142	-0.0390
	Sig. (2-tailed)	0.3916	0.5731	0.6163	0.9374	0.8294
	N	33.0000	34.0000	33.0000	33.0000	33.0000

Table A7, continued (Row 4, Col 1)

Correlation Matrix, International Variables (Parametric)		Importance of Smuggling-Endangered Species	reflectsqrtQIA1b	reflectsqrtQIA1c	reflectsqrtQIA1d	reflectsqrtQIA1e	sqrtQIB1a	Knowledge of Smuggling-Narcotics	Knowledge of Smuggling-Weapons	Knowledge of Smuggling-Humans	Knowledge of Smuggling-Contraband
Org Resource Challenges-Lack of Clarity in Duties	Pearson Correlation	0.0492	-0.3141	-0.3196	-0.1009	0.0087	0.0917	0.0127	-0.1453	-0.0797	-0.1955
	Sig. (2-tailed)	0.7792	0.0661	0.0613	0.5642	0.9603	0.6001	0.9422	0.4050	0.6492	0.2604
	N	35.0000	35.0000	35.0000	35.0000	35.0000	35.0000	35.0000	35.0000	35.0000	35.0000
Org Resource Challenges-Conflict or Lack Comm Leaders and Employees	Pearson Correlation	-0.0220	-0.1516	-0.1189	0.0441	0.1340	-0.0517	0.0840	0.0522	-0.2450	-0.0940
	Sig. (2-tailed)	0.9000	0.3846	0.4961	0.8016	0.4430	0.7678	0.6316	0.7657	0.1560	0.5912
	N	35.0000	35.0000	35.0000	35.0000	35.0000	35.0000	35.0000	35.0000	35.0000	35.0000
sqrtQ1E31	Pearson Correlation	-0.0396	-0.0530	-0.0769	0.0348	-0.1052	0.0804	-0.0488	0.0348	-0.4343	-0.0865
	Sig. (2-tailed)	0.8214	0.7622	0.6604	0.8425	0.5474	0.6460	0.7808	0.8428	0.0091	0.6213
	N	35.0000	35.0000	35.0000	35.0000	35.0000	35.0000	35.0000	35.0000	35.0000	35.0000
Org Resource Challenges-Conflict or Lack Comm International Orgs	Pearson Correlation	0.0261	-0.3126	-0.3248	-0.0833	0.0119	0.0776	0.1324	-0.1213	0.0368	-0.1600
	Sig. (2-tailed)	0.8818	0.0675	0.0570	0.6341	0.9457	0.6577	0.4484	0.4878	0.8337	0.3587
	N	35.0000	35.0000	35.0000	35.0000	35.0000	35.0000	35.0000	35.0000	35.0000	35.0000
Org Resource Challenges-Conflict or Lack Comm Domestic Orgs	Pearson Correlation	0.0753	-0.3260	-0.2974	-0.1055	0.0191	0.0426	0.1116	-0.1315	-0.0734	-0.1675
	Sig. (2-tailed)	0.6674	0.0560	0.0827	0.5464	0.9131	0.8080	0.5233	0.4513	0.6753	0.3362
	N	35.0000	35.0000	35.0000	35.0000	35.0000	35.0000	35.0000	35.0000	35.0000	35.0000
sqrtQIIA1a	Pearson Correlation	0.0714	0.3292	0.1555	0.1382	-0.1336	0.5077	0.0948	0.2332	0.0326	0.4173
	Sig. (2-tailed)	0.6836	0.0535	0.3724	0.4284	0.4440	0.0018	0.5879	0.1776	0.8525	0.0126
	N	35.0000	35.0000	35.0000	35.0000	35.0000	35.0000	35.0000	35.0000	35.0000	35.0000
Knowledge of Domestic Law-CSIE	Pearson Correlation	-0.0032	-0.2346	0.0142	0.0931	-0.1776	0.0953	0.6809	0.5161	0.1554	0.3006
	Sig. (2-tailed)	0.9852	0.1750	0.9356	0.5947	0.3073	0.5859	0.0000	0.0015	0.3726	0.0793
	N	35.0000	35.0000	35.0000	35.0000	35.0000	35.0000	35.0000	35.0000	35.0000	35.0000
Knowledge of Domestic Law-DWMD	Pearson Correlation	-0.2227	-0.1107	0.0084	0.0954	-0.1624	0.0299	0.5787	0.6878	0.3185	0.4673
	Sig. (2-tailed)	0.1984	0.5268	0.9620	0.5856	0.3512	0.8644	0.0003	0.0000	0.0622	0.0047
	N	35.0000	35.0000	35.0000	35.0000	35.0000	35.0000	35.0000	35.0000	35.0000	35.0000
Knowledge of Domestic Law-TVP	Pearson Correlation	-0.2041	-0.1045	-0.0642	-0.0603	-0.0460	0.1391	0.5195	0.4150	0.5869	0.4621
	Sig. (2-tailed)	0.2396	0.5503	0.7141	0.7308	0.7932	0.4256	0.0014	0.0132	0.0002	0.0052
	N	35.0000	35.0000	35.0000	35.0000	35.0000	35.0000	35.0000	35.0000	35.0000	35.0000
Knowledge of Domestic Law-CBP	Pearson Correlation	-0.1039	0.1069	0.2938	0.1321	-0.2579	0.0992	0.2628	0.5338	0.1776	0.6159
	Sig. (2-tailed)	0.5527	0.5409	0.0867	0.4494	0.1347	0.5707	0.1273	0.0010	0.3074	0.0001
	N	35.0000	35.0000	35.0000	35.0000	35.0000	35.0000	35.0000	35.0000	35.0000	35.0000
sqrtQIID1a	Pearson Correlation	0.2661	0.2364	0.1976	0.2932	-0.1569	0.6200	0.0729	0.4288	0.0309	0.3750
	Sig. (2-tailed)	0.1167	0.1650	0.2480	0.0826	0.3609	0.0001	0.6725	0.0091	0.8582	0.0242
	N	36.0000	36.0000	36.0000	36.0000	36.0000	36.0000	36.0000	36.0000	36.0000	36.0000

Table A7, continued (Row 4, Col 2)

Correlation Matrix, International Variables (Parametric)		sqrtQ1E1a	Personal Resource Challenges-Lack of Time	Personal Resource Challenges-Lack of Knowledge	Personal Resource Challenges-Lack of Training	sqrtQ1E1e	Personal Resource Challenges-Excessive Admin Paperwork	Personal Resource Challenges-Ineffective Technology	Personal Resource Challenges-Ineffective Strategic Focus	Personal Resource Challenges-Ineffective Tactical Policy	Personal Resource Challenges-Lack of Clarity in Duties
Org Resource Challenges-Lack of Clarity in Duties	Pearson Correlation	0.3674	0.3689	0.7468	0.7607	0.3853	0.2944	0.5999	0.7915	0.7397	0.6774
	Sig. (2-tailed)	0.0326	0.0292	0.0000	0.0000	0.0223	0.0860	0.0001	0.0000	0.0000	0.0000
	N	34.0000	35.0000	35.0000	35.0000	35.0000	35.0000	35.0000	35.0000	35.0000	35.0000
Org Resource Challenges-Conflict or Lack Comm Leaders and Employees	Pearson Correlation	0.4307	0.4729	0.5058	0.4702	0.4733	0.5096	0.3705	0.6182	0.6952	0.6451
	Sig. (2-tailed)	0.0110	0.0041	0.0019	0.0044	0.0041	0.0018	0.0285	0.0001	0.0000	0.0000
	N	34.0000	35.0000	35.0000	35.0000	35.0000	35.0000	35.0000	35.0000	35.0000	35.0000
sqrtQ1E31	Pearson Correlation	0.4065	0.2147	0.2868	0.2943	0.3287	0.5204	0.2168	0.5372	0.4737	0.4299
	Sig. (2-tailed)	0.0171	0.2155	0.0948	0.0862	0.0539	0.0014	0.2108	0.0009	0.0040	0.0100
	N	34.0000	35.0000	35.0000	35.0000	35.0000	35.0000	35.0000	35.0000	35.0000	35.0000
Org Resource Challenges-Conflict or Lack Comm International Orgs	Pearson Correlation	0.2378	0.3700	0.7712	0.7224	0.3387	0.3204	0.5919	0.6129	0.5677	0.5515
	Sig. (2-tailed)	0.1756	0.0287	0.0000	0.0000	0.0465	0.0606	0.0002	0.0001	0.0004	0.0006
	N	34.0000	35.0000	35.0000	35.0000	35.0000	35.0000	35.0000	35.0000	35.0000	35.0000
Org Resource Challenges-Conflict or Lack Comm Domestic Orgs	Pearson Correlation	0.2694	0.3163	0.7446	0.6898	0.3704	0.3419	0.6206	0.6329	0.5770	0.5381
	Sig. (2-tailed)	0.1234	0.0641	0.0000	0.0000	0.0285	0.0444	0.0001	0.0000	0.0003	0.0009
	N	34.0000	35.0000	35.0000	35.0000	35.0000	35.0000	35.0000	35.0000	35.0000	35.0000
sqrtQIIA1a	Pearson Correlation	0.1149	0.1779	0.1297	0.1362	0.1985	0.1231	-0.0890	0.1663	0.0529	0.1278
	Sig. (2-tailed)	0.5176	0.3066	0.4579	0.4354	0.2530	0.4810	0.6113	0.3398	0.7627	0.4645
	N	34.0000	35.0000	35.0000	35.0000	35.0000	35.0000	35.0000	35.0000	35.0000	35.0000
Knowledge of Domestic Law-CSIE	Pearson Correlation	-0.0396	-0.1054	-0.1119	-0.2222	0.0135	0.1304	0.1874	-0.2240	-0.2112	-0.2785
	Sig. (2-tailed)	0.8241	0.5467	0.5223	0.1996	0.9384	0.4553	0.2811	0.1958	0.2234	0.1053
	N	34.0000	35.0000	35.0000	35.0000	35.0000	35.0000	35.0000	35.0000	35.0000	35.0000
Knowledge of Domestic Law-DWMD	Pearson Correlation	-0.2166	-0.0797	-0.1684	-0.2745	-0.0123	0.0638	0.0578	-0.3036	-0.2200	-0.2676
	Sig. (2-tailed)	0.2186	0.6491	0.3335	0.1105	0.9439	0.7156	0.7415	0.0762	0.2040	0.1201
	N	34.0000	35.0000	35.0000	35.0000	35.0000	35.0000	35.0000	35.0000	35.0000	35.0000
Knowledge of Domestic Law-TVP	Pearson Correlation	-0.1300	-0.0226	0.0131	-0.0242	-0.0726	0.1009	0.0814	-0.0651	-0.0220	0.0909
	Sig. (2-tailed)	0.4636	0.8976	0.9404	0.8901	0.6784	0.5642	0.6421	0.7100	0.9003	0.6036
	N	34.0000	35.0000	35.0000	35.0000	35.0000	35.0000	35.0000	35.0000	35.0000	35.0000
Knowledge of Domestic Law-CBP	Pearson Correlation	-0.1190	0.0886	-0.1704	-0.2953	0.1008	0.0404	-0.1367	-0.2731	-0.2471	-0.1374
	Sig. (2-tailed)	0.5028	0.6129	0.3279	0.0850	0.5644	0.8177	0.4337	0.1125	0.1525	0.4314
	N	34.0000	35.0000	35.0000	35.0000	35.0000	35.0000	35.0000	35.0000	35.0000	35.0000
sqrtQIID1a	Pearson Correlation	-0.0357	-0.0498	-0.1174	-0.1545	0.2266	0.1332	-0.1490	-0.0144	-0.0835	-0.0795
	Sig. (2-tailed)	0.8388	0.7728	0.4955	0.3682	0.1839	0.4387	0.3857	0.9337	0.6284	0.6447
	N	35.0000	36.0000	36.0000	36.0000	36.0000	36.0000	36.0000	36.0000	36.0000	36.0000

Correlation Matrix, International Variables (Parametric)		Personal Resource Challenges–Conflict or Lack Comm Leaders and Employees	sqrtQ1E1l	Personal Resource Challenges–Conflict or Lack Comm International Orgs	Personal Resource Challenges–Conflict or Lack Comm Domestic Orgs	sqrtQ1E3a	Org Resource Challenges–Lack of Time	Org Resource Challenges–Lack of Knowledge	Org Resource Challenges–Lack of Training	sqrtQ1E3e	Org Resource Challenges–Excessive Admin Paperwork
Org Resource Challenges-Lack of Clarity in Duties	Pearson Correlation	0.6391	0.3910	0.5006	0.6819	0.3625	0.2906	0.7829	0.7546	0.3878	0.4762
	Sig. (2-tailed)	0.0000	0.0202	0.0022	0.0000	0.0351	0.0904	0.0000	0.0000	0.0234	0.0038
	N	35.0000	35.0000	35.0000	35.0000	34.0000	35.0000	35.0000	35.0000	34.0000	35.0000
Org Resource Challenges-Conflict or Lack Comm Leaders and Employees	Pearson Correlation	0.7390	0.5790	0.6766	0.7312	0.2974	0.1354	0.5025	0.5110	0.5015	0.5461
	Sig. (2-tailed)	0.0000	0.0003	0.0000	0.0000	0.0876	0.4381	0.0021	0.0017	0.0025	0.0007
	N	35.0000	35.0000	35.0000	35.0000	34.0000	35.0000	35.0000	35.0000	34.0000	35.0000
sqrtQ1E3l	Pearson Correlation	0.5035	0.9287	0.5669	0.4613	0.1722	0.1338	0.3496	0.4188	0.4392	0.4573
	Sig. (2-tailed)	0.0020	0.0000	0.0004	0.0053	0.3302	0.4436	0.0395	0.0123	0.0094	0.0057
	N	35.0000	35.0000	35.0000	35.0000	34.0000	35.0000	35.0000	35.0000	34.0000	35.0000
Org Resource Challenges-Conflict or Lack Comm International Orgs	Pearson Correlation	0.4527	0.3371	0.5283	0.6075	0.3658	0.4475	0.7932	0.7846	0.3551	0.4667
	Sig. (2-tailed)	0.0063	0.0477	0.0011	0.0001	0.0334	0.0070	0.0000	0.0000	0.0393	0.0047
	N	35.0000	35.0000	35.0000	35.0000	34.0000	35.0000	35.0000	35.0000	34.0000	35.0000
Org Resource Challenges-Conflict or Lack Comm Domestic Orgs	Pearson Correlation	0.5411	0.4099	0.4958	0.6459	0.3306	0.3240	0.7503	0.7474	0.3623	0.4788
	Sig. (2-tailed)	0.0008	0.0145	0.0025	0.0000	0.0562	0.0576	0.0000	0.0000	0.0352	0.0036
	N	35.0000	35.0000	35.0000	35.0000	34.0000	35.0000	35.0000	35.0000	34.0000	35.0000
sqrtQIIA1a	Pearson Correlation	0.0748	0.0207	0.2155	0.1088	0.0390	-0.0461	-0.0605	-0.0674	-0.0472	0.1397
	Sig. (2-tailed)	0.6692	0.9059	0.2137	0.5340	0.8295	0.7956	0.7341	0.7050	0.7942	0.4306
	N	35.0000	35.0000	35.0000	35.0000	33.0000	34.0000	34.0000	34.0000	33.0000	34.0000
Knowledge of Domestic Law-CSIE	Pearson Correlation	-0.1977	0.0244	0.0457	-0.1031	-0.0192	0.0654	-0.2321	-0.2196	-0.0513	0.0040
	Sig. (2-tailed)	0.2549	0.8893	0.7945	0.5558	0.9157	0.7133	0.1865	0.2120	0.7766	0.9821
	N	35.0000	35.0000	35.0000	35.0000	33.0000	34.0000	34.0000	34.0000	33.0000	34.0000
Knowledge of Domestic Law-DWMD	Pearson Correlation	-0.2397	-0.1690	-0.0794	-0.2276	-0.0303	0.0926	-0.3174	-0.3426	-0.2463	-0.1851
	Sig. (2-tailed)	0.1655	0.3317	0.6502	0.1885	0.8672	0.6023	0.0674	0.0473	0.1670	0.2945
	N	35.0000	35.0000	35.0000	35.0000	33.0000	34.0000	34.0000	34.0000	33.0000	34.0000
Knowledge of Domestic Law-TVP	Pearson Correlation	-0.1073	-0.2804	0.1555	0.0439	-0.0886	0.0988	-0.0808	-0.1142	-0.3220	-0.2122
	Sig. (2-tailed)	0.5394	0.1028	0.3723	0.8024	0.6241	0.5783	0.6494	0.5200	0.0677	0.2284
	N	35.0000	35.0000	35.0000	35.0000	33.0000	34.0000	34.0000	34.0000	33.0000	34.0000
Knowledge of Domestic Law-CBP	Pearson Correlation	-0.1200	-0.1781	0.0366	-0.0862	-0.1843	-0.1136	-0.3351	-0.3563	-0.2003	-0.1357
	Sig. (2-tailed)	0.4922	0.3061	0.8345	0.6226	0.3046	0.5224	0.0527	0.0386	0.2638	0.4440
	N	35.0000	35.0000	35.0000	35.0000	33.0000	34.0000	34.0000	34.0000	33.0000	34.0000
sqrtQIID1a	Pearson Correlation	-0.1120	0.0549	-0.1358	-0.1864	-0.1416	-0.3091	-0.3537	-0.3828	-0.1077	-0.2613
	Sig. (2-tailed)	0.5157	0.7504	0.4298	0.2764	0.4244	0.0708	0.0371	0.0232	0.5443	0.1295
	N	36.0000	36.0000	36.0000	36.0000	34.0000	35.0000	35.0000	35.0000	34.0000	35.0000

Table A7, continued (Row 4, Col 4)

Correlation Matrix, International Variables (Parametric)		Org Resource Challenges-Ineffective Technology	Org Resource Challenges-Ineffective Strategic Focus	Org Resource Challenges-Ineffective Tactical Policy	Org Resource Challenges-Lack of Clarity in Duties	Org Resource Challenges-Conflict or Lack Comm Leaders and Employees	sqrtQ1E31	Org Resource Challenges-Conflict or Lack Comm International Orgs	Org Resource Challenges-Conflict or Lack Comm Domestic Orgs	sqrtQIIA1a	Knowledge of Domestic Law-CSIE
Org Resource Challenges-Lack of Clarity in Duties	Pearson Correlation	0.7585	0.9043	0.8464	1.0000	0.7352	0.4632	0.8647	0.9029	0.0103	-0.1033
	Sig. (2-tailed)	0.0000	0.0000	0.0000	.	0.0000	0.0051	0.0000	0.0000	0.9539	0.5610
	N	35.0000	35.0000	35.0000	35.0000	35.0000	35.0000	35.0000	35.0000	34.0000	34.0000
Org Resource Challenges-Conflict or Lack Comm Leaders and Employees	Pearson Correlation	0.6652	0.7485	0.8618	0.7352	1.0000	0.6403	0.5766	0.6412	-0.0102	0.0233
	Sig. (2-tailed)	0.0000	0.0000	0.0000	0.0000	.	0.0000	0.0003	0.0000	0.9542	0.8959
	N	35.0000	35.0000	35.0000	35.0000	35.0000	35.0000	35.0000	35.0000	34.0000	34.0000
sqrtQ1E31	Pearson Correlation	0.4128	0.4589	0.5439	0.4632	0.6403	1.0000	0.4079	0.4448	0.0510	-0.0101
	Sig. (2-tailed)	0.0137	0.0056	0.0007	0.0051	0.0000	.	0.0150	0.0074	0.7743	0.9546
	N	35.0000	35.0000	35.0000	35.0000	35.0000	35.0000	35.0000	35.0000	34.0000	34.0000
Org Resource Challenges-Conflict or Lack Comm International Orgs	Pearson Correlation	0.6756	0.7970	0.7400	0.8647	0.5766	0.4079	1.0000	0.9504	-0.0484	0.0659
	Sig. (2-tailed)	0.0000	0.0000	0.0000	0.0000	0.0003	0.0150	.	0.0000	0.7859	0.7110
	N	35.0000	35.0000	35.0000	35.0000	35.0000	35.0000	35.0000	35.0000	34.0000	34.0000
Org Resource Challenges-Conflict or Lack Comm Domestic Orgs	Pearson Correlation	0.7328	0.8421	0.7592	0.9029	0.6412	0.4448	0.9504	1.0000	-0.0196	0.0912
	Sig. (2-tailed)	0.0000	0.0000	0.0000	0.0000	0.0000	0.0074	0.0000	.	0.9124	0.6079
	N	35.0000	35.0000	35.0000	35.0000	35.0000	35.0000	35.0000	35.0000	34.0000	34.0000
sqrtQIIA1a	Pearson Correlation	-0.1555	-0.0550	0.0757	0.0103	-0.0102	0.0510	-0.0484	-0.0196	1.0000	0.0672
	Sig. (2-tailed)	0.3798	0.7574	0.6703	0.9539	0.9542	0.7743	0.7859	0.9124	.	0.7015
	N	34.0000	34.0000	34.0000	34.0000	34.0000	34.0000	34.0000	34.0000	35.0000	35.0000
Knowledge of Domestic Law-CSIE	Pearson Correlation	0.1273	-0.0390	-0.1634	-0.1033	0.0233	-0.0101	0.0659	0.0912	0.0672	1.0000
	Sig. (2-tailed)	0.4731	0.8266	0.3557	0.5610	0.8959	0.9546	0.7110	0.6079	0.7015	.
	N	34.0000	34.0000	34.0000	34.0000	34.0000	34.0000	34.0000	34.0000	35.0000	35.0000
Knowledge of Domestic Law-DWMD	Pearson Correlation	-0.0578	-0.1159	-0.2554	-0.2100	-0.0700	-0.2146	-0.0527	-0.0657	0.1034	0.8361
	Sig. (2-tailed)	0.7453	0.5141	0.1449	0.2333	0.6942	0.2228	0.7670	0.7119	0.5544	0.0000
	N	34.0000	34.0000	34.0000	34.0000	34.0000	34.0000	34.0000	34.0000	35.0000	35.0000
Knowledge of Domestic Law-TVP	Pearson Correlation	-0.0183	0.0093	-0.0599	-0.0615	-0.0816	-0.2571	0.0544	-0.0513	0.1196	0.5001
	Sig. (2-tailed)	0.9181	0.9582	0.7366	0.7297	0.6464	0.1421	0.7598	0.7732	0.4938	0.0022
	N	34.0000	34.0000	34.0000	34.0000	34.0000	34.0000	34.0000	34.0000	35.0000	35.0000
Knowledge of Domestic Law-CBP	Pearson Correlation	-0.3113	-0.2705	-0.1713	-0.3446	-0.0431	-0.2273	-0.3112	-0.2803	0.3849	0.4842
	Sig. (2-tailed)	0.0731	0.1218	0.3327	0.0460	0.8090	0.1961	0.0732	0.1084	0.0224	0.0032
	N	34.0000	34.0000	34.0000	34.0000	34.0000	34.0000	34.0000	34.0000	35.0000	35.0000
sqrtQIID1a	Pearson Correlation	-0.3255	-0.2537	-0.2208	-0.1536	-0.1869	-0.0403	-0.2087	-0.1867	0.4524	0.1169
	Sig. (2-tailed)	0.0564	0.1413	0.2025	0.3784	0.2823	0.8182	0.2288	0.2829	0.0064	0.5037
	N	35.0000	35.0000	35.0000	35.0000	35.0000	35.0000	35.0000	35.0000	35.0000	35.0000

Table A7, continued (Row 4, Col 5)

Correlation Matrix, International Variables (Parametric)		Knowledge of Domestic Law-DWMD	Knowledge of Domestic Law-TVP	Knowledge of Domestic Law-CBP	sqrtQIID1a	Level Cooperation Domestic Orgs-CSIE	Level Cooperation Domestic Orgs-DWMD	Level Cooperation Domestic Orgs-TVP	Level Cooperation Domestic Orgs-CBP	sqrtQIIIA1a	sqrtQIIIA1b
Org Resource Challenges-Lack of Clarity in Duties	Pearson Correlation	-0.2100	-0.0615	-0.3446	-0.1536	-0.3954	-0.4124	-0.1893	-0.1998	0.1937	-0.1948
	Sig. (2-tailed)	0.2333	0.7297	0.0460	0.3784	0.0187	0.0138	0.2760	0.2498	0.2723	0.2620
	N	34.0000	34.0000	34.0000	35.0000	35.0000	35.0000	35.0000	35.0000	34.0000	35.0000
Org Resource Challenges-Conflict or Lack Comm Leaders and Employees	Pearson Correlation	-0.0700	-0.0816	-0.0431	-0.1869	-0.2438	-0.2581	-0.1415	-0.1280	0.1442	0.0782
	Sig. (2-tailed)	0.6942	0.6464	0.8090	0.2823	0.1581	0.1345	0.4175	0.4638	0.4157	0.6553
	N	34.0000	34.0000	34.0000	35.0000	35.0000	35.0000	35.0000	35.0000	34.0000	35.0000
sqrtQ1E31	Pearson Correlation	-0.2146	-0.2571	-0.2273	-0.0403	-0.2859	-0.1912	-0.1542	-0.1118	0.1479	-0.1712
	Sig. (2-tailed)	0.2228	0.1421	0.1961	0.8182	0.0960	0.2712	0.3764	0.5227	0.4038	0.3254
	N	34.0000	34.0000	34.0000	35.0000	35.0000	35.0000	35.0000	35.0000	34.0000	35.0000
Org Resource Challenges-Conflict or Lack Comm International Orgs	Pearson Correlation	-0.0527	0.0544	-0.3112	-0.2087	-0.2421	-0.2142	-0.1411	-0.3103	0.0915	-0.2006
	Sig. (2-tailed)	0.7670	0.7598	0.0732	0.2288	0.1611	0.2167	0.4189	0.0696	0.6069	0.2480
	N	34.0000	34.0000	34.0000	35.0000	35.0000	35.0000	35.0000	35.0000	34.0000	35.0000
Org Resource Challenges-Conflict or Lack Comm Domestic Orgs	Pearson Correlation	-0.0657	-0.0513	-0.2803	-0.1867	-0.3064	-0.2303	-0.2087	-0.2817	0.0784	-0.1661
	Sig. (2-tailed)	0.7119	0.7732	0.1084	0.2829	0.0735	0.1832	0.2289	0.1011	0.6594	0.3401
	N	34.0000	34.0000	34.0000	35.0000	35.0000	35.0000	35.0000	35.0000	34.0000	35.0000
sqrtQIIA1a	Pearson Correlation	0.1034	0.1196	0.3849	0.4524	0.1923	0.1286	0.2592	0.2915	0.6590	0.1279
	Sig. (2-tailed)	0.5544	0.4938	0.0224	0.0064	0.2684	0.4614	0.1327	0.0893	0.0000	0.4639
	N	35.0000	35.0000	35.0000	35.0000	35.0000	35.0000	35.0000	35.0000	34.0000	35.0000
Knowledge of Domestic Law-CSIE	Pearson Correlation	0.8361	0.5001	0.4842	0.1169	0.5579	0.4830	0.3219	0.1046	-0.0793	0.3803
	Sig. (2-tailed)	0.0000	0.0022	0.0032	0.5037	0.0005	0.0033	0.0593	0.5499	0.6557	0.0242
	N	35.0000	35.0000	35.0000	35.0000	35.0000	35.0000	35.0000	35.0000	34.0000	35.0000
Knowledge of Domestic Law-DWMD	Pearson Correlation	1.0000	0.6149	0.6576	0.1547	0.6238	0.5291	0.3785	0.2306	-0.0986	0.3092
	Sig. (2-tailed)	.	0.0001	0.0000	0.3750	0.0001	0.0011	0.0250	0.1826	0.5790	0.0707
	N	35.0000	35.0000	35.0000	35.0000	35.0000	35.0000	35.0000	35.0000	34.0000	35.0000
Knowledge of Domestic Law-TVP	Pearson Correlation	0.6149	1.0000	0.4377	-0.0231	0.4269	0.2014	0.5066	0.0260	0.0263	0.2589
	Sig. (2-tailed)	0.0001	.	0.0086	0.8952	0.0105	0.2461	0.0019	0.8821	0.8827	0.1331
	N	35.0000	35.0000	35.0000	35.0000	35.0000	35.0000	35.0000	35.0000	34.0000	35.0000
Knowledge of Domestic Law-CBP	Pearson Correlation	0.6576	0.4377	1.0000	0.3023	0.4855	0.4690	0.3910	0.5621	0.0994	0.1914
	Sig. (2-tailed)	0.0000	0.0086	.	0.0775	0.0031	0.0045	0.0202	0.0004	0.5760	0.2707
	N	35.0000	35.0000	35.0000	35.0000	35.0000	35.0000	35.0000	35.0000	34.0000	35.0000
sqrtQIID1a	Pearson Correlation	0.1547	-0.0231	0.3023	1.0000	0.3596	0.3998	0.4744	0.7020	0.4921	-0.0045
	Sig. (2-tailed)	0.3750	0.8952	0.0775	.	0.0312	0.0157	0.0035	0.0000	0.0027	0.9794
	N	35.0000	35.0000	35.0000	36.0000	36.0000	36.0000	36.0000	36.0000	35.0000	36.0000

Table A7, continued (Row 4, Col 6)

Correlation Matrix, International Variables (Parametric)		sqrtQIIA1c	sqrtQIIA1d	sqrtQIIA1e	sqrtQIID1a	Level Cooperation Domestic Orgs-CNDPS	Level Cooperation Domestic Orgs-CNBC	Level Cooperation Domestic Orgs-CSTP	Level Cooperation Domestic Orgs-TRIPS	sqrtQIID2a	Level Cooperation International Orgs-CNDPS
Org Resource Challenges-Lack of Clarity in Duties	Pearson Correlation	-0.0508	0.0448	-0.2749	0.0586	-0.2796	-0.2877	-0.2099	-0.2803	-0.0313	-0.1810
	Sig. (2-tailed)	0.7718	0.7984	0.1100	0.7501	0.1093	0.0989	0.2334	0.1083	0.8605	0.2982
	N	35.0000	35.0000	35.0000	32.0000	34.0000	34.0000	34.0000	34.0000	34.0000	35.0000
Org Resource Challenges-Conflict or Lack Comm Leaders and Employees	Pearson Correlation	0.1867	0.1597	-0.0643	0.0196	-0.0942	-0.1349	-0.1179	-0.1270	-0.1959	-0.1156
	Sig. (2-tailed)	0.2828	0.3594	0.7135	0.9153	0.5962	0.4469	0.5066	0.4741	0.2667	0.5086
	N	35.0000	35.0000	35.0000	32.0000	34.0000	34.0000	34.0000	34.0000	34.0000	35.0000
sqrtQ1E31	Pearson Correlation	-0.0484	-0.2347	-0.2254	0.1302	-0.1171	-0.0328	-0.0436	-0.0632	0.0422	-0.2323
	Sig. (2-tailed)	0.7826	0.1747	0.1930	0.4774	0.5095	0.8541	0.8068	0.7224	0.8125	0.1792
	N	35.0000	35.0000	35.0000	32.0000	34.0000	34.0000	34.0000	34.0000	34.0000	35.0000
Org Resource Challenges-Conflict or Lack Comm International Orgs	Pearson Correlation	-0.0822	-0.0833	-0.2899	0.0245	-0.2336	-0.2472	-0.1951	-0.3522	-0.0468	-0.1102
	Sig. (2-tailed)	0.6388	0.6342	0.0912	0.8939	0.1837	0.1586	0.2688	0.0411	0.7927	0.5287
	N	35.0000	35.0000	35.0000	32.0000	34.0000	34.0000	34.0000	34.0000	34.0000	35.0000
Org Resource Challenges-Conflict or Lack Comm Domestic Orgs	Pearson Correlation	-0.0312	-0.0846	-0.2436	-0.0121	-0.2207	-0.2111	-0.2121	-0.2948	-0.0631	-0.0994
	Sig. (2-tailed)	0.8589	0.6289	0.1585	0.9477	0.2098	0.2307	0.2284	0.0905	0.7230	0.5698
	N	35.0000	35.0000	35.0000	32.0000	34.0000	34.0000	34.0000	34.0000	34.0000	35.0000
sqrtQIIA1a	Pearson Correlation	0.1830	0.2485	0.3637	0.2503	0.0416	0.1799	0.1731	0.1626	0.3801	0.0431
	Sig. (2-tailed)	0.2926	0.1499	0.0317	0.1670	0.8152	0.3086	0.3276	0.3581	0.0266	0.8059
	N	35.0000	35.0000	35.0000	32.0000	34.0000	34.0000	34.0000	34.0000	34.0000	35.0000
Knowledge of Domestic Law-CSIE	Pearson Correlation	0.4524	0.0719	0.0763	-0.1148	0.2483	0.2263	0.0270	0.0105	-0.0543	0.2693
	Sig. (2-tailed)	0.0064	0.6814	0.6631	0.5317	0.1567	0.1980	0.8796	0.9529	0.7602	0.1177
	N	35.0000	35.0000	35.0000	32.0000	34.0000	34.0000	34.0000	34.0000	34.0000	35.0000
Knowledge of Domestic Law-DWMD	Pearson Correlation	0.4340	0.1111	0.1761	-0.1301	0.1409	0.2464	-0.0296	-0.0050	-0.1039	0.1853
	Sig. (2-tailed)	0.0092	0.5250	0.3117	0.4778	0.4268	0.1601	0.8680	0.9776	0.5586	0.2867
	N	35.0000	35.0000	35.0000	32.0000	34.0000	34.0000	34.0000	34.0000	34.0000	35.0000
Knowledge of Domestic Law-TVP	Pearson Correlation	0.3175	0.3321	-0.0099	0.0739	0.1655	0.1167	0.2619	-0.0368	0.0341	0.0978
	Sig. (2-tailed)	0.0631	0.0513	0.9550	0.6879	0.3497	0.5112	0.1346	0.8365	0.8481	0.5762
	N	35.0000	35.0000	35.0000	32.0000	34.0000	34.0000	34.0000	34.0000	34.0000	35.0000
Knowledge of Domestic Law-CBP	Pearson Correlation	0.3293	0.2041	0.4573	0.1138	0.1424	0.3494	0.1388	0.3325	-0.0834	0.0795
	Sig. (2-tailed)	0.0534	0.2396	0.0057	0.5352	0.4216	0.0428	0.4338	0.0547	0.6392	0.6497
	N	35.0000	35.0000	35.0000	32.0000	34.0000	34.0000	34.0000	34.0000	34.0000	35.0000
sqrtQIID1a	Pearson Correlation	0.2147	0.0503	0.2763	0.4991	0.2806	0.5210	0.2009	0.5555	0.5936	0.3070
	Sig. (2-tailed)	0.2087	0.7707	0.1029	0.0031	0.1026	0.0013	0.2473	0.0005	0.0002	0.0686
	N	36.0000	36.0000	36.0000	33.0000	35.0000	35.0000	35.0000	35.0000	35.0000	36.0000

Table A7, continued (Row 4, Col 7)

Correlation Matrix, International Variables (Parametric)		Level Cooperation International Orgs- CNBC	Level Cooperation International Orgs- CSTP	sqrtQIID2e	sqrtQIVA1	sqrtQIVA2	sqrtQIVA3	sqrtQIVA5	sqrtQIVA7	sqrtQIVA8	Political Ideology
Org Resource Challenges- Lack of Clarity in Duties	Pearson Correlation	-0.1936	-0.1137	-0.2185	0.2975	0.1487	0.2110	-0.0922	-0.0212	-0.2333	0.0609
	Sig. (2-tailed)	0.2650	0.5155	0.2074	0.0826	0.3939	0.2310	0.6041	0.9037	0.1774	0.7362
	N	35.0000	35.0000	35.0000	35.0000	35.0000	34.0000	34.0000	35.0000	35.0000	33.0000
Org Resource Challenges- Conflict or Lack Comm Leaders and Employees	Pearson Correlation	-0.1167	-0.1419	-0.1800	0.1614	0.1363	0.2148	-0.1561	0.0376	-0.2012	0.0000
	Sig. (2-tailed)	0.5043	0.4161	0.3007	0.3544	0.4349	0.2226	0.3780	0.8300	0.2465	1.0000
	N	35.0000	35.0000	35.0000	35.0000	35.0000	34.0000	34.0000	35.0000	35.0000	33.0000
sqrtQ1E3l	Pearson Correlation	-0.2091	-0.2572	-0.1945	0.1144	0.1141	0.1633	0.1102	0.1971	-0.1516	-0.0489
	Sig. (2-tailed)	0.2279	0.1357	0.2630	0.5127	0.5141	0.3562	0.5349	0.2565	0.3845	0.7870
	N	35.0000	35.0000	35.0000	35.0000	35.0000	34.0000	34.0000	35.0000	35.0000	33.0000
Org Resource Challenges- Conflict or Lack Comm International Orgs	Pearson Correlation	-0.1208	-0.0355	-0.1904	0.3519	0.2023	0.1834	0.1253	-0.2223	-0.0648	0.0373
	Sig. (2-tailed)	0.4895	0.8395	0.2734	0.0382	0.2438	0.2991	0.4803	0.1992	0.7114	0.8365
	N	35.0000	35.0000	35.0000	35.0000	35.0000	34.0000	34.0000	35.0000	35.0000	33.0000
Org Resource Challenges- Conflict or Lack Comm Domestic Orgs	Pearson Correlation	-0.1121	-0.0277	-0.1476	0.3555	0.1494	0.1617	0.0593	-0.0972	-0.2430	0.0842
	Sig. (2-tailed)	0.5216	0.8744	0.3974	0.0361	0.3917	0.3608	0.7389	0.5786	0.1595	0.6414
	N	35.0000	35.0000	35.0000	35.0000	35.0000	34.0000	34.0000	35.0000	35.0000	33.0000
sqrtQIIA1a	Pearson Correlation	0.0968	0.2430	0.1620	-0.1899	-0.0509	-0.2144	-0.0193	0.1354	-0.1746	0.2663
	Sig. (2-tailed)	0.5802	0.1596	0.3525	0.2746	0.7714	0.2233	0.9150	0.4381	0.3233	0.1406
	N	35.0000	35.0000	35.0000	35.0000	35.0000	34.0000	33.0000	35.0000	34.0000	32.0000
Knowledge of Domestic Law- CSIE	Pearson Correlation	0.2882	0.1645	0.1353	0.0265	-0.0986	-0.1775	0.2925	-0.1068	0.0432	0.0819
	Sig. (2-tailed)	0.0932	0.3450	0.4382	0.8798	0.5730	0.3152	0.0986	0.5414	0.8083	0.6557
	N	35.0000	35.0000	35.0000	35.0000	35.0000	34.0000	33.0000	35.0000	34.0000	32.0000
Knowledge of Domestic Law- DWMD	Pearson Correlation	0.2562	0.1028	0.1436	0.0686	-0.0248	-0.1084	0.2711	-0.0749	0.1244	0.2899
	Sig. (2-tailed)	0.1374	0.5569	0.4105	0.6955	0.8877	0.5418	0.1271	0.6689	0.4832	0.1076
	N	35.0000	35.0000	35.0000	35.0000	35.0000	34.0000	33.0000	35.0000	34.0000	32.0000
Knowledge of Domestic Law- TVP	Pearson Correlation	0.0945	0.1248	-0.0195	0.0473	-0.0414	-0.0617	0.2011	-0.0363	0.3014	0.0322
	Sig. (2-tailed)	0.5894	0.4750	0.9117	0.7873	0.8133	0.7290	0.2619	0.8360	0.0832	0.8611
	N	35.0000	35.0000	35.0000	35.0000	35.0000	34.0000	33.0000	35.0000	34.0000	32.0000
Knowledge of Domestic Law- CBP	Pearson Correlation	0.1476	0.0430	0.2240	-0.1427	-0.0942	-0.1213	0.0556	0.1172	0.2077	0.1375
	Sig. (2-tailed)	0.3974	0.8064	0.1958	0.4134	0.5902	0.4943	0.7588	0.5026	0.2385	0.4529
	N	35.0000	35.0000	35.0000	35.0000	35.0000	34.0000	33.0000	35.0000	34.0000	32.0000
sqrtQIID1a	Pearson Correlation	0.3896	0.3778	0.5037	0.1145	0.1167	0.1560	0.1165	-0.1753	0.0904	0.4608
	Sig. (2-tailed)	0.0188	0.0231	0.0017	0.5063	0.4977	0.3707	0.5116	0.3065	0.6055	0.0070
	N	36.0000	36.0000	36.0000	36.0000	36.0000	35.0000	34.0000	36.0000	35.0000	33.0000

Table A7, continued (Row 4, Col 8)

Correlation Matrix, International Variables (Parametric)		sqrtQIIIB1a	sqrtQIIIB1b	sqrtQIIIB1c	sqrtQIIIB1d	sqrtQIIIB1e	sqrtQIIIB2a	Perceived Effectiveness Domestic Govt Support-CNDPS	Perceived Effectiveness Domestic Govt Support-CNBC	Perceived Effectiveness Domestic Govt Support-CSTP	Perceived Effectiveness Domestic Govt Support-TRIPS
Org Resource Challenges-Lack of Clarity in Duties	Pearson Correlation	0.3327	0.0813	0.1920	-0.2197	0.0979	0.3006	0.0163	0.0677	0.1315	-0.2121
	Sig. (2-tailed)	0.0545	0.6477	0.2767	0.2118	0.5819	0.0841	0.9259	0.7037	0.4586	0.2285
	N	34.0000	34.0000	34.0000	34.0000	34.0000	34.0000	35.0000	34.0000	34.0000	34.0000
Org Resource Challenges-Conflict or Lack Comm Leaders and Employees	Pearson Correlation	0.0754	0.0064	0.0358	-0.0850	0.0186	0.0223	-0.0426	-0.0429	-0.0296	-0.1714
	Sig. (2-tailed)	0.6715	0.9713	0.8409	0.6326	0.9170	0.9002	0.8079	0.8097	0.8680	0.3325
	N	34.0000	34.0000	34.0000	34.0000	34.0000	34.0000	35.0000	34.0000	34.0000	34.0000
sqrtQ1E3l	Pearson Correlation	0.0932	-0.1091	-0.1849	-0.0527	-0.1333	-0.0406	-0.2661	-0.2775	-0.2669	-0.2123
	Sig. (2-tailed)	0.6002	0.5389	0.2951	0.7673	0.4523	0.8198	0.1223	0.1120	0.1270	0.2280
	N	34.0000	34.0000	34.0000	34.0000	34.0000	34.0000	35.0000	34.0000	34.0000	34.0000
Org Resource Challenges-Conflict or Lack Comm International Orgs	Pearson Correlation	0.2832	0.1308	0.2590	-0.2290	0.0608	0.3056	0.1232	0.1663	0.1619	-0.1664
	Sig. (2-tailed)	0.1045	0.4611	0.1391	0.1926	0.7328	0.0788	0.4807	0.3474	0.3603	0.3469
	N	34.0000	34.0000	34.0000	34.0000	34.0000	34.0000	35.0000	34.0000	34.0000	34.0000
Org Resource Challenges-Conflict or Lack Comm Domestic Orgs	Pearson Correlation	0.3080	0.1546	0.2420	-0.1671	0.0971	0.2810	0.0813	0.0729	0.0951	-0.1498
	Sig. (2-tailed)	0.0763	0.3825	0.1679	0.3448	0.5848	0.1074	0.6426	0.6820	0.5925	0.3977
	N	34.0000	34.0000	34.0000	34.0000	34.0000	34.0000	35.0000	34.0000	34.0000	34.0000
sqrtQIIA1a	Pearson Correlation	0.0247	-0.0648	-0.0003	0.2744	-0.0187	0.0859	-0.1132	-0.0123	0.0350	-0.0527
	Sig. (2-tailed)	0.8897	0.7158	0.9985	0.1163	0.9165	0.6289	0.5175	0.9448	0.8441	0.7674
	N	34.0000	34.0000	34.0000	34.0000	34.0000	34.0000	35.0000	34.0000	34.0000	34.0000
Knowledge of Domestic Law-CSIE	Pearson Correlation	-0.1568	0.1600	0.1399	0.1966	-0.1450	-0.2168	0.1569	0.0572	-0.1782	-0.0990
	Sig. (2-tailed)	0.3758	0.3661	0.4301	0.2651	0.4132	0.2182	0.3682	0.7480	0.3134	0.5775
	N	34.0000	34.0000	34.0000	34.0000	34.0000	34.0000	35.0000	34.0000	34.0000	34.0000
Knowledge of Domestic Law-DWMD	Pearson Correlation	-0.1206	0.2547	0.2321	0.3377	-0.0499	-0.1875	0.2273	0.1671	-0.0809	0.0247
	Sig. (2-tailed)	0.4970	0.1461	0.1865	0.0508	0.7792	0.2884	0.1890	0.3449	0.6494	0.8899
	N	34.0000	34.0000	34.0000	34.0000	34.0000	34.0000	35.0000	34.0000	34.0000	34.0000
Knowledge of Domestic Law-TVP	Pearson Correlation	-0.0057	0.1065	0.2695	0.1316	-0.0001	-0.0108	0.0865	0.1800	0.0953	-0.1032
	Sig. (2-tailed)	0.9743	0.5489	0.1232	0.4583	0.9997	0.9518	0.6212	0.3082	0.5921	0.5613
	N	34.0000	34.0000	34.0000	34.0000	34.0000	34.0000	35.0000	34.0000	34.0000	34.0000
Knowledge of Domestic Law-CBP	Pearson Correlation	-0.2156	0.0538	0.0025	0.3787	-0.0424	-0.2641	-0.0420	-0.0507	-0.1559	0.0099
	Sig. (2-tailed)	0.2207	0.7625	0.9889	0.0272	0.8119	0.1312	0.8105	0.7758	0.3785	0.9556
	N	34.0000	34.0000	34.0000	34.0000	34.0000	34.0000	35.0000	34.0000	34.0000	34.0000
sqrtQIID1a	Pearson Correlation	0.1642	0.1981	0.0815	0.4622	0.0588	0.2048	-0.1007	0.0232	0.0226	0.0926
	Sig. (2-tailed)	0.3458	0.2540	0.6415	0.0052	0.7372	0.2379	0.5589	0.8948	0.8976	0.5967
	N	35.0000	35.0000	35.0000	35.0000	35.0000	35.0000	36.0000	35.0000	35.0000	35.0000

Table A7, continued (Row 4, Col 9)

Correlation Matrix, International Variables (Parametric)		sqrtQIIIC1a	sqrtQIIIC1b	sqrtQIIIC1c	sqrtQIIIC1d	sqrtQIIIC1e
Org Resource Challenges-Lack of Clarity in Duties	Pearson Correlation	0.3285	-0.0233	0.0148	0.0927	0.0415
	Sig. (2-tailed)	0.0620	0.8961	0.9350	0.6078	0.8187
	N	33.0000	34.0000	33.0000	33.0000	33.0000
Org Resource Challenges-Conflict or Lack Comm Leaders and Employees	Pearson Correlation	0.0814	-0.1401	-0.1366	-0.0755	-0.0712
	Sig. (2-tailed)	0.6526	0.4295	0.4484	0.6764	0.6938
	N	33.0000	34.0000	33.0000	33.0000	33.0000
sqrtQ1E31	Pearson Correlation	0.1503	-0.0049	-0.0698	0.0361	-0.0295
	Sig. (2-tailed)	0.4037	0.9779	0.6995	0.8420	0.8704
	N	33.0000	34.0000	33.0000	33.0000	33.0000
Org Resource Challenges-Conflict or Lack Comm International Orgs	Pearson Correlation	0.2394	0.0697	0.0573	0.0872	-0.0110
	Sig. (2-tailed)	0.1796	0.6952	0.7514	0.6293	0.9517
	N	33.0000	34.0000	33.0000	33.0000	33.0000
Org Resource Challenges-Conflict or Lack Comm Domestic Orgs	Pearson Correlation	0.2852	0.0777	0.0412	0.1203	0.0296
	Sig. (2-tailed)	0.1077	0.6621	0.8198	0.5050	0.8703
	N	33.0000	34.0000	33.0000	33.0000	33.0000
sqrtQIIA1a	Pearson Correlation	0.2077	0.0923	0.1583	0.1952	0.1391
	Sig. (2-tailed)	0.2460	0.6036	0.3790	0.2762	0.4402
	N	33.0000	34.0000	33.0000	33.0000	33.0000
Knowledge of Domestic Law-CSIE	Pearson Correlation	-0.2020	0.2064	0.1450	-0.0198	-0.0354
	Sig. (2-tailed)	0.2596	0.2416	0.4209	0.9129	0.8450
	N	33.0000	34.0000	33.0000	33.0000	33.0000
Knowledge of Domestic Law-DWMD	Pearson Correlation	-0.1522	0.2612	0.2506	0.1034	0.0802
	Sig. (2-tailed)	0.3977	0.1357	0.1595	0.5669	0.6573
	N	33.0000	34.0000	33.0000	33.0000	33.0000
Knowledge of Domestic Law-TVP	Pearson Correlation	-0.0323	0.0634	0.1953	0.0621	-0.0023
	Sig. (2-tailed)	0.8583	0.7217	0.2762	0.7312	0.9898
	N	33.0000	34.0000	33.0000	33.0000	33.0000
Knowledge of Domestic Law-CBP	Pearson Correlation	-0.0883	0.1344	0.0791	0.1447	0.1648
	Sig. (2-tailed)	0.6250	0.4486	0.6619	0.4216	0.3594
	N	33.0000	34.0000	33.0000	33.0000	33.0000
sqrtQIID1a	Pearson Correlation	0.1755	0.2461	0.2282	0.2866	0.2789
	Sig. (2-tailed)	0.3208	0.1540	0.1943	0.1003	0.1102
	N	34.0000	35.0000	34.0000	34.0000	34.0000

Table A7, continued (Row 5, Col 1)

Correlation Matrix, International Variables (Parametric)		Importance of Smuggling-Endangered Species	reflectsqrtQ1A1b	reflectsqrtQ1A1c	reflectsqrtQ1A1d	reflectsqrtQ1A1e	sqrtQ1B1a	Knowledge of Smuggling-Narcotics	Knowledge of Smuggling-Weapons	Knowledge of Smuggling-Humans	Knowledge of Smuggling-Contraband
Level Cooperation Domestic Orgs-CSIE	Pearson Correlation	-0.0291	-0.1636	0.0149	0.1377	-0.2225	0.2881	0.5092	0.5158	0.2726	0.3252
	Sig. (2-tailed)	0.8662	0.3404	0.9312	0.4231	0.1922	0.0884	0.0015	0.0013	0.1078	0.0530
	N	36.0000	36.0000	36.0000	36.0000	36.0000	36.0000	36.0000	36.0000	36.0000	36.0000
Level Cooperation Domestic Orgs-DWMD	Pearson Correlation	0.0626	-0.1263	0.0214	0.1513	-0.3094	0.1094	0.3940	0.4225	0.1807	0.3303
	Sig. (2-tailed)	0.7167	0.4630	0.9013	0.3783	0.0663	0.5255	0.0174	0.0103	0.2915	0.0491
	N	36.0000	36.0000	36.0000	36.0000	36.0000	36.0000	36.0000	36.0000	36.0000	36.0000
Level Cooperation Domestic Orgs-TVP	Pearson Correlation	0.1330	-0.1268	-0.0633	0.0183	-0.3146	0.4848	0.4552	0.4073	0.4165	0.4434
	Sig. (2-tailed)	0.4393	0.4612	0.7139	0.9154	0.0617	0.0027	0.0053	0.0137	0.0115	0.0068
	N	36.0000	36.0000	36.0000	36.0000	36.0000	36.0000	36.0000	36.0000	36.0000	36.0000
Level Cooperation Domestic Orgs-CBP	Pearson Correlation	0.0417	0.0764	0.1665	0.2144	-0.3942	0.2573	-0.0049	0.3248	-0.0180	0.3882
	Sig. (2-tailed)	0.8092	0.6578	0.3317	0.2091	0.0174	0.1297	0.9774	0.0532	0.9168	0.0193
	N	36.0000	36.0000	36.0000	36.0000	36.0000	36.0000	36.0000	36.0000	36.0000	36.0000
sqrtQIIIA1a	Pearson Correlation	0.1539	0.1940	0.0303	0.1534	-0.2490	0.5686	0.0614	0.1530	0.2038	0.3504
	Sig. (2-tailed)	0.3774	0.2642	0.8627	0.3788	0.1492	0.0004	0.7262	0.3804	0.2403	0.0390
	N	35.0000	35.0000	35.0000	35.0000	35.0000	35.0000	35.0000	35.0000	35.0000	35.0000
sqrtQIIIA1b	Pearson Correlation	-0.0319	0.0782	0.1695	0.1824	0.1344	0.0163	0.4628	0.2114	0.2662	0.3009
	Sig. (2-tailed)	0.8535	0.6503	0.3229	0.2870	0.4346	0.9248	0.0045	0.2159	0.1166	0.0745
	N	36.0000	36.0000	36.0000	36.0000	36.0000	36.0000	36.0000	36.0000	36.0000	36.0000
sqrtQIIIA1c	Pearson Correlation	-0.1127	-0.0579	0.0782	0.2523	0.0069	0.0481	0.4045	0.4489	0.2159	0.3780
	Sig. (2-tailed)	0.5128	0.7373	0.6503	0.1377	0.9683	0.7807	0.0144	0.0060	0.2061	0.0230
	N	36.0000	36.0000	36.0000	36.0000	36.0000	36.0000	36.0000	36.0000	36.0000	36.0000
sqrtQIIIA1d	Pearson Correlation	-0.1182	-0.0618	-0.0557	-0.0240	-0.1092	0.1280	0.3222	0.2949	0.4759	0.4396
	Sig. (2-tailed)	0.4923	0.7201	0.7470	0.8894	0.5260	0.4570	0.0553	0.0808	0.0033	0.0073
	N	36.0000	36.0000	36.0000	36.0000	36.0000	36.0000	36.0000	36.0000	36.0000	36.0000
sqrtQIIIA1e	Pearson Correlation	-0.1398	0.3553	0.3276	0.2496	-0.0503	0.1387	0.1691	0.2459	0.2935	0.5612
	Sig. (2-tailed)	0.4159	0.0335	0.0511	0.1421	0.7708	0.4197	0.3241	0.1483	0.0823	0.0004
	N	36.0000	36.0000	36.0000	36.0000	36.0000	36.0000	36.0000	36.0000	36.0000	36.0000
sqrtQIIID1a	Pearson Correlation	-0.0834	0.0701	0.1064	0.0308	-0.1836	0.4138	0.1939	0.3706	0.1707	0.3408
	Sig. (2-tailed)	0.6445	0.6984	0.5557	0.8648	0.3065	0.0167	0.2797	0.0337	0.3422	0.0523
	N	33.0000	33.0000	33.0000	33.0000	33.0000	33.0000	33.0000	33.0000	33.0000	33.0000
Level Cooperation Domestic Orgs-CNDPS	Pearson Correlation	-0.0518	-0.0744	0.1564	0.1160	-0.0204	0.2400	0.3670	0.2723	0.1638	0.1460
	Sig. (2-tailed)	0.7677	0.6711	0.3696	0.5069	0.9072	0.1649	0.0301	0.1136	0.3471	0.4028
	N	35.0000	35.0000	35.0000	35.0000	35.0000	35.0000	35.0000	35.0000	35.0000	35.0000

Table A7, continued (Row 5, Col 2)

Correlation Matrix, International Variables (Parametric)		sqrtQ1E1a	Personal Resource Challenges-Lack of Time	Personal Resource Challenges-Lack of Knowledge	Personal Resource Challenges-Lack of Training	sqrtQ1E1e	Personal Resource Challenges-Excessive Admin Paperwork	Personal Resource Challenges-Ineffective Technology	Personal Resource Challenges-Ineffective Strategic Focus	Personal Resource Challenges-Ineffective Tactical Policy	Personal Resource Challenges-Lack of Clarity in Duties
Level Cooperation Domestic Orgs-CSIE	Pearson Correlation	-0.3267	-0.0671	-0.3195	-0.3802	-0.0320	0.0093	-0.2315	-0.3394	-0.3240	-0.2536
	Sig. (2-tailed)	0.0554	0.6976	0.0575	0.0222	0.8528	0.9570	0.1743	0.0429	0.0539	0.1357
	N	35.0000	36.0000	36.0000	36.0000	36.0000	36.0000	36.0000	36.0000	36.0000	36.0000
Level Cooperation Domestic Orgs-DWMD	Pearson Correlation	-0.3174	-0.0939	-0.3120	-0.3942	-0.0340	0.1753	-0.3228	-0.4186	-0.3391	-0.2787
	Sig. (2-tailed)	0.0632	0.5860	0.0639	0.0174	0.8439	0.3065	0.0548	0.0111	0.0430	0.0997
	N	35.0000	36.0000	36.0000	36.0000	36.0000	36.0000	36.0000	36.0000	36.0000	36.0000
Level Cooperation Domestic Orgs-TVP	Pearson Correlation	-0.2215	0.0638	-0.1253	-0.2011	0.0283	0.0584	-0.1657	-0.1068	-0.1520	0.0556
	Sig. (2-tailed)	0.2010	0.7115	0.4667	0.2396	0.8701	0.7350	0.3342	0.5354	0.3760	0.7476
	N	35.0000	36.0000	36.0000	36.0000	36.0000	36.0000	36.0000	36.0000	36.0000	36.0000
Level Cooperation Domestic Orgs-CBP	Pearson Correlation	-0.1697	-0.0404	-0.1085	-0.1170	0.0558	-0.0042	-0.1672	-0.0882	-0.1525	-0.0516
	Sig. (2-tailed)	0.3297	0.8149	0.5287	0.4968	0.7467	0.9804	0.3296	0.6088	0.3747	0.7651
	N	35.0000	36.0000	36.0000	36.0000	36.0000	36.0000	36.0000	36.0000	36.0000	36.0000
sqrtQIIIA1a	Pearson Correlation	0.3282	0.3114	0.1295	0.1581	0.2187	0.3565	-0.0354	0.3285	0.3383	0.3095
	Sig. (2-tailed)	0.0581	0.0686	0.4584	0.3642	0.2069	0.0356	0.8399	0.0540	0.0468	0.0704
	N	34.0000	35.0000	35.0000	35.0000	35.0000	35.0000	35.0000	35.0000	35.0000	35.0000
sqrtQIIIA1b	Pearson Correlation	0.2881	0.0694	-0.1696	-0.2311	-0.0790	0.2407	0.0213	-0.1415	0.0382	-0.0093
	Sig. (2-tailed)	0.0933	0.6877	0.3227	0.1750	0.6468	0.1573	0.9020	0.4103	0.8250	0.9569
	N	35.0000	36.0000	36.0000	36.0000	36.0000	36.0000	36.0000	36.0000	36.0000	36.0000
sqrtQIIIA1c	Pearson Correlation	0.3869	0.1221	-0.1149	-0.1980	0.1071	0.3647	0.0335	-0.0162	0.1323	0.0524
	Sig. (2-tailed)	0.0217	0.4779	0.5044	0.2471	0.5340	0.0288	0.8461	0.9254	0.4418	0.7615
	N	35.0000	36.0000	36.0000	36.0000	36.0000	36.0000	36.0000	36.0000	36.0000	36.0000
sqrtQIIIA1d	Pearson Correlation	0.2685	0.2363	-0.0342	-0.0110	0.1396	0.2381	0.0131	0.0718	0.1710	0.1479
	Sig. (2-tailed)	0.1188	0.1653	0.8430	0.9493	0.4166	0.1620	0.9398	0.6775	0.3186	0.3892
	N	35.0000	36.0000	36.0000	36.0000	36.0000	36.0000	36.0000	36.0000	36.0000	36.0000
sqrtQIIIA1e	Pearson Correlation	0.2605	0.1714	-0.1854	-0.2242	0.0952	0.2494	-0.1226	-0.1359	-0.0048	-0.0612
	Sig. (2-tailed)	0.1307	0.3175	0.2790	0.1888	0.5809	0.1424	0.4762	0.4294	0.9778	0.7228
	N	35.0000	36.0000	36.0000	36.0000	36.0000	36.0000	36.0000	36.0000	36.0000	36.0000
sqrtQIIID1a	Pearson Correlation	-0.0079	0.1206	0.0284	0.1815	0.2646	0.2109	-0.1934	0.0917	-0.0591	0.1341
	Sig. (2-tailed)	0.9652	0.5039	0.8754	0.3122	0.1367	0.2387	0.2809	0.6117	0.7439	0.4568
	N	33.0000	33.0000	33.0000	33.0000	33.0000	33.0000	33.0000	33.0000	33.0000	33.0000
Level Cooperation Domestic Orgs-CNDPS	Pearson Correlation	-0.1191	0.0242	-0.3494	-0.3143	-0.0257	0.0392	-0.3843	-0.2957	-0.3184	-0.1994
	Sig. (2-tailed)	0.4956	0.8903	0.0397	0.0660	0.8833	0.8230	0.0227	0.0845	0.0623	0.2509
	N	35.0000	35.0000	35.0000	35.0000	35.0000	35.0000	35.0000	35.0000	35.0000	35.0000

Table A7, continued (Row 5, Col 3)

Correlation Matrix, International Variables (Parametric)		Personal Resource Challenges-Conflict or Lack Comm Leaders and Employees	sqrtQ1E11	Personal Resource Challenges-Conflict or Lack Comm International Orgs	Personal Resource Challenges-Conflict or Lack Comm Domestic Orgs	sqrtQ1E3a	Org Resource Challenges-Lack of Time	Org Resource Challenges-Lack of Knowledge	Org Resource Challenges-Lack of Training	sqrtQ1E3e	Org Resource Challenges-Excessive Admin Paperwork
Level Cooperation Domestic Orgs-CSIE	Pearson Correlation	-0.3763	-0.2268	-0.1725	-0.3066	-0.1553	-0.1766	-0.4078	-0.4665	-0.2576	-0.1698
	Sig. (2-tailed)	0.0237	0.1835	0.3143	0.0689	0.3804	0.3101	0.0150	0.0047	0.1414	0.3295
	N	36.0000	36.0000	36.0000	36.0000	34.0000	35.0000	35.0000	35.0000	34.0000	35.0000
Level Cooperation Domestic Orgs-DWMD	Pearson Correlation	-0.3806	-0.0638	-0.1342	-0.2523	-0.2637	-0.3089	-0.4448	-0.4764	-0.1964	-0.1211
	Sig. (2-tailed)	0.0220	0.7115	0.4350	0.1377	0.1318	0.0709	0.0074	0.0038	0.2657	0.4882
	N	36.0000	36.0000	36.0000	36.0000	34.0000	35.0000	35.0000	35.0000	34.0000	35.0000
Level Cooperation Domestic Orgs-TVP	Pearson Correlation	-0.1813	-0.0832	0.0026	-0.0655	-0.1839	-0.2466	-0.2323	-0.2813	-0.3635	-0.2969
	Sig. (2-tailed)	0.2899	0.6294	0.9881	0.7043	0.2978	0.1533	0.1793	0.1017	0.0346	0.0833
	N	36.0000	36.0000	36.0000	36.0000	34.0000	35.0000	35.0000	35.0000	34.0000	35.0000
Level Cooperation Domestic Orgs-CBP	Pearson Correlation	-0.1645	-0.0522	-0.1031	-0.2033	-0.3699	-0.4410	-0.2361	-0.3095	-0.1248	-0.2055
	Sig. (2-tailed)	0.3377	0.7623	0.5496	0.2344	0.0313	0.0080	0.1721	0.0704	0.4819	0.2363
	N	36.0000	36.0000	36.0000	36.0000	34.0000	35.0000	35.0000	35.0000	34.0000	35.0000
sqrtQIIIA1a	Pearson Correlation	0.2006	0.2261	0.2839	0.2088	0.0342	-0.0162	0.0263	-0.0017	0.0645	0.2057
	Sig. (2-tailed)	0.2479	0.1915	0.0984	0.2287	0.8503	0.9276	0.8828	0.9925	0.7216	0.2432
	N	35.0000	35.0000	35.0000	35.0000	33.0000	34.0000	34.0000	34.0000	33.0000	34.0000
sqrtQIIIA1b	Pearson Correlation	0.1294	-0.0278	0.1332	0.0700	0.0321	-0.0835	-0.2797	-0.3170	0.0298	0.1275
	Sig. (2-tailed)	0.4521	0.8719	0.4388	0.6850	0.8570	0.6336	0.1036	0.0635	0.8673	0.4656
	N	36.0000	36.0000	36.0000	36.0000	34.0000	35.0000	35.0000	35.0000	34.0000	35.0000
sqrtQIIIA1c	Pearson Correlation	0.1660	0.0690	0.0944	0.1161	0.1374	0.0184	-0.2263	-0.2731	0.1285	0.2022
	Sig. (2-tailed)	0.3334	0.6893	0.5840	0.5001	0.4386	0.9166	0.1911	0.1124	0.4688	0.2441
	N	36.0000	36.0000	36.0000	36.0000	34.0000	35.0000	35.0000	35.0000	34.0000	35.0000
sqrtQIIIA1d	Pearson Correlation	0.1161	-0.1745	0.2105	0.2141	0.1194	-0.0144	-0.0268	-0.0901	-0.0141	0.1224
	Sig. (2-tailed)	0.5002	0.3088	0.2179	0.2099	0.5010	0.9344	0.8786	0.6066	0.9370	0.4838
	N	36.0000	36.0000	36.0000	36.0000	34.0000	35.0000	35.0000	35.0000	34.0000	35.0000
sqrtQIIIA1e	Pearson Correlation	0.0572	-0.0507	0.0680	-0.0306	-0.0829	-0.1243	-0.2772	-0.3359	0.0582	0.0930
	Sig. (2-tailed)	0.7403	0.7689	0.6937	0.8595	0.6413	0.4767	0.1069	0.0485	0.7438	0.5951
	N	36.0000	36.0000	36.0000	36.0000	34.0000	35.0000	35.0000	35.0000	34.0000	35.0000
sqrtQIIID1a	Pearson Correlation	-0.1135	-0.0093	0.0776	0.0771	0.0230	-0.2796	0.0015	-0.0421	0.0959	0.0279
	Sig. (2-tailed)	0.5296	0.9590	0.6677	0.6697	0.9024	0.1212	0.9936	0.8190	0.6079	0.8797
	N	33.0000	33.0000	33.0000	33.0000	31.0000	32.0000	32.0000	32.0000	31.0000	32.0000
Level Cooperation Domestic Orgs-CNDPS	Pearson Correlation	-0.2432	-0.1364	-0.1258	-0.0970	-0.1200	-0.3383	-0.3248	-0.3530	-0.0810	-0.1288
	Sig. (2-tailed)	0.1592	0.4346	0.4716	0.5793	0.5059	0.0503	0.0609	0.0406	0.6541	0.4677
	N	35.0000	35.0000	35.0000	35.0000	33.0000	34.0000	34.0000	34.0000	33.0000	34.0000

Table A7, continued (Row 5, Col 4)

Correlation Matrix, International Variables (Parametric)		Org Resource Challenges-Ineffective Technology	Org Resource Challenges-Ineffective Strategic Focus	Org Resource Challenges-Ineffective Tactical Policy	Org Resource Challenges-Lack of Clarity in Duties	Org Resource Challenges-Conflict or Lack Comm Leaders and Employees	sqrtQ1E31	Org Resource Challenges-Conflict or Lack Comm International Orgs	Org Resource Challenges-Conflict or Lack Comm Domestic Orgs	sqrtQIIIA1a	Knowledge of Domestic Law-CSIE
Level Cooperation Domestic Orgs-CSIE	Pearson Correlation	-0.3626	-0.3952	-0.2891	-0.3954	-0.2438	-0.2859	-0.2421	-0.3064	0.1923	0.5579
	Sig. (2-tailed)	0.0323	0.0188	0.0922	0.0187	0.1581	0.0960	0.1611	0.0735	0.2684	0.0005
	N	35.0000	35.0000	35.0000	35.0000	35.0000	35.0000	35.0000	35.0000	35.0000	35.0000
Level Cooperation Domestic Orgs-DWMD	Pearson Correlation	-0.4359	-0.4554	-0.3082	-0.4124	-0.2581	-0.1912	-0.2142	-0.2303	0.1286	0.4830
	Sig. (2-tailed)	0.0089	0.0060	0.0717	0.0138	0.1345	0.2712	0.2167	0.1832	0.4614	0.0033
	N	35.0000	35.0000	35.0000	35.0000	35.0000	35.0000	35.0000	35.0000	35.0000	35.0000
Level Cooperation Domestic Orgs-TVP	Pearson Correlation	-0.2617	-0.1852	-0.1271	-0.1893	-0.1415	-0.1542	-0.1411	-0.2087	0.2592	0.3219
	Sig. (2-tailed)	0.1289	0.2868	0.4670	0.2760	0.4175	0.3764	0.4189	0.2289	0.1327	0.0593
	N	35.0000	35.0000	35.0000	35.0000	35.0000	35.0000	35.0000	35.0000	35.0000	35.0000
Level Cooperation Domestic Orgs-CBP	Pearson Correlation	-0.4314	-0.2952	-0.1596	-0.1998	-0.1280	-0.1118	-0.3103	-0.2817	0.2915	0.1046
	Sig. (2-tailed)	0.0097	0.0851	0.3598	0.2498	0.4638	0.5227	0.0696	0.1011	0.0893	0.5499
	N	35.0000	35.0000	35.0000	35.0000	35.0000	35.0000	35.0000	35.0000	35.0000	35.0000
sqrtQIIIA1a	Pearson Correlation	-0.0089	0.0761	0.1894	0.1937	0.1442	0.1479	0.0915	0.0784	0.6590	-0.0793
	Sig. (2-tailed)	0.9604	0.6689	0.2833	0.2723	0.4157	0.4038	0.6069	0.6594	0.0000	0.6557
	N	34.0000	34.0000	34.0000	34.0000	34.0000	34.0000	34.0000	34.0000	34.0000	34.0000
sqrtQIIIA1b	Pearson Correlation	0.0746	-0.1040	-0.0530	-0.1948	0.0782	-0.1712	-0.2006	-0.1661	0.1279	0.3803
	Sig. (2-tailed)	0.6700	0.5522	0.7622	0.2620	0.6553	0.3254	0.2480	0.3401	0.4639	0.0242
	N	35.0000	35.0000	35.0000	35.0000	35.0000	35.0000	35.0000	35.0000	35.0000	35.0000
sqrtQIIIA1c	Pearson Correlation	0.1545	0.0208	0.0520	-0.0508	0.1867	-0.0484	-0.0822	-0.0312	0.1830	0.4524
	Sig. (2-tailed)	0.3754	0.9058	0.7667	0.7718	0.2828	0.7826	0.6388	0.8589	0.2926	0.0064
	N	35.0000	35.0000	35.0000	35.0000	35.0000	35.0000	35.0000	35.0000	35.0000	35.0000
sqrtQIIIA1d	Pearson Correlation	0.1285	0.0143	0.1151	0.0448	0.1597	-0.2347	-0.0833	-0.0846	0.2485	0.0719
	Sig. (2-tailed)	0.4620	0.9352	0.5103	0.7984	0.3594	0.1747	0.6342	0.6289	0.1499	0.6814
	N	35.0000	35.0000	35.0000	35.0000	35.0000	35.0000	35.0000	35.0000	35.0000	35.0000
sqrtQIIIA1e	Pearson Correlation	-0.1611	-0.2920	-0.1516	-0.2749	-0.0643	-0.2254	-0.2899	-0.2436	0.3637	0.0763
	Sig. (2-tailed)	0.3552	0.0888	0.3846	0.1100	0.7135	0.1930	0.0912	0.1585	0.0317	0.6631
	N	35.0000	35.0000	35.0000	35.0000	35.0000	35.0000	35.0000	35.0000	35.0000	35.0000
sqrtQIIID1a	Pearson Correlation	-0.1393	-0.1005	0.1123	0.0586	0.0196	0.1302	0.0245	-0.0121	0.2503	-0.1148
	Sig. (2-tailed)	0.4469	0.5842	0.5406	0.7501	0.9153	0.4774	0.8939	0.9477	0.1670	0.5317
	N	32.0000	32.0000	32.0000	32.0000	32.0000	32.0000	32.0000	32.0000	32.0000	32.0000
Level Cooperation Domestic Orgs-CNDPS	Pearson Correlation	-0.1680	-0.2940	-0.1628	-0.2796	-0.0942	-0.1171	-0.2336	-0.2207	0.0416	0.2483
	Sig. (2-tailed)	0.3424	0.0915	0.3577	0.1093	0.5962	0.5095	0.1837	0.2098	0.8152	0.1567
	N	34.0000	34.0000	34.0000	34.0000	34.0000	34.0000	34.0000	34.0000	34.0000	34.0000

Table A7, continued (Row 5, Col 5)

Correlation Matrix, International Variables (Parametric)		Knowledge of Domestic Law-DWMD	Knowledge of Domestic Law-TVP	Knowledge of Domestic Law-CBP	sqrtQIID1a	Level Cooperation Domestic Orgs-CSIE	Level Cooperation Domestic Orgs-DWMD	Level Cooperation Domestic Orgs-TVP	Level Cooperation Domestic Orgs-CBP	sqrtQIIIA1a	sqrtQIIIA1b
Level Cooperation Domestic Orgs-CSIE	Pearson Correlation	0.6238	0.4269	0.4855	0.3596	1.0000	0.7912	0.7777	0.4620	0.1822	0.3594
	Sig. (2-tailed)	0.0001	0.0105	0.0031	0.0312	.	0.0000	0.0000	0.0046	0.2949	0.0314
	N	35.0000	35.0000	35.0000	36.0000	36.0000	36.0000	36.0000	36.0000	35.0000	36.0000
Level Cooperation Domestic Orgs-DWMD	Pearson Correlation	0.5291	0.2014	0.4690	0.3998	0.7912	1.0000	0.6143	0.5201	0.1739	0.2141
	Sig. (2-tailed)	0.0011	0.2461	0.0045	0.0157	0.0000	.	0.0001	0.0012	0.3177	0.2098
	N	35.0000	35.0000	35.0000	36.0000	36.0000	36.0000	36.0000	36.0000	35.0000	36.0000
Level Cooperation Domestic Orgs-TVP	Pearson Correlation	0.3785	0.5066	0.3910	0.4744	0.7777	0.6143	1.0000	0.5351	0.3406	0.1873
	Sig. (2-tailed)	0.0250	0.0019	0.0202	0.0035	0.0000	0.0001	.	0.0008	0.0453	0.2741
	N	35.0000	35.0000	35.0000	36.0000	36.0000	36.0000	36.0000	36.0000	35.0000	36.0000
Level Cooperation Domestic Orgs-CBP	Pearson Correlation	0.2306	0.0260	0.5621	0.7020	0.4620	0.5201	0.5351	1.0000	0.2939	-0.0578
	Sig. (2-tailed)	0.1826	0.8821	0.0004	0.0000	0.0046	0.0012	0.0008	.	0.0866	0.7378
	N	35.0000	35.0000	35.0000	36.0000	36.0000	36.0000	36.0000	36.0000	35.0000	36.0000
sqrtQIIIA1a	Pearson Correlation	-0.0986	0.0263	0.0994	0.4921	0.1822	0.1739	0.3406	0.2939	1.0000	0.2259
	Sig. (2-tailed)	0.5790	0.8827	0.5760	0.0027	0.2949	0.3177	0.0453	0.0866	.	0.1919
	N	34.0000	34.0000	34.0000	35.0000	35.0000	35.0000	35.0000	35.0000	35.0000	35.0000
sqrtQIIIA1b	Pearson Correlation	0.3092	0.2589	0.1914	-0.0045	0.3594	0.2141	0.1873	-0.0578	0.2259	1.0000
	Sig. (2-tailed)	0.0707	0.1331	0.2707	0.9794	0.0314	0.2098	0.2741	0.7378	0.1919	.
	N	35.0000	35.0000	35.0000	36.0000	36.0000	36.0000	36.0000	36.0000	35.0000	36.0000
sqrtQIIIA1c	Pearson Correlation	0.4340	0.3175	0.3293	0.2147	0.3425	0.2766	0.2122	0.0853	0.3507	0.8490
	Sig. (2-tailed)	0.0092	0.0631	0.0534	0.2087	0.0409	0.1025	0.2140	0.6209	0.0389	0.0000
	N	35.0000	35.0000	35.0000	36.0000	36.0000	36.0000	36.0000	36.0000	35.0000	36.0000
sqrtQIIIA1d	Pearson Correlation	0.1111	0.3321	0.2041	0.0503	0.2440	0.0821	0.3122	0.0620	0.5148	0.6948
	Sig. (2-tailed)	0.5250	0.0513	0.2396	0.7707	0.1515	0.6342	0.0638	0.7192	0.0016	0.0000
	N	35.0000	35.0000	35.0000	36.0000	36.0000	36.0000	36.0000	36.0000	35.0000	36.0000
sqrtQIIIA1e	Pearson Correlation	0.1761	-0.0099	0.4573	0.2763	0.2423	0.3109	0.1111	0.3090	0.4789	0.6515
	Sig. (2-tailed)	0.3117	0.9550	0.0057	0.1029	0.1546	0.0649	0.5190	0.0667	0.0036	0.0000
	N	35.0000	35.0000	35.0000	36.0000	36.0000	36.0000	36.0000	36.0000	35.0000	36.0000
sqrtQIIID1a	Pearson Correlation	-0.1301	0.0739	0.1138	0.4991	0.1915	0.2390	0.4288	0.4754	0.3686	-0.0887
	Sig. (2-tailed)	0.4778	0.6879	0.5352	0.0031	0.2858	0.1804	0.0128	0.0052	0.0379	0.6235
	N	32.0000	32.0000	32.0000	33.0000	33.0000	33.0000	33.0000	33.0000	32.0000	33.0000
Level Cooperation Domestic Orgs-CNDPS	Pearson Correlation	0.1409	0.1655	0.1424	0.2806	0.5766	0.4849	0.6054	0.2277	0.1688	0.3611
	Sig. (2-tailed)	0.4268	0.3497	0.4216	0.1026	0.0003	0.0032	0.0001	0.1884	0.3399	0.0331
	N	34.0000	34.0000	34.0000	35.0000	35.0000	35.0000	35.0000	35.0000	34.0000	35.0000

Table A7, continued (Row 5, Col 6)

Correlation Matrix, International Variables (Parametric)		sqrtQIIIA1c	sqrtQIIIA1d	sqrtQIIIA1e	sqrtQIIID1a	Level Cooperation Domestic Orgs-CNDPS	Level Cooperation Domestic Orgs-CNBC	Level Cooperation Domestic Orgs-CSTP	Level Cooperation Domestic Orgs-TRIPS	sqrtQIIID2a	Level Cooperation International Orgs-CNDPS
Level Cooperation Domestic Orgs-CSIE	Pearson Correlation	0.3425	0.2440	0.2423	0.1915	0.5766	0.4744	0.4123	0.2704	0.2898	0.4537
	Sig. (2-tailed)	0.0409	0.1515	0.1546	0.2858	0.0003	0.0040	0.0139	0.1162	0.0913	0.0054
	N	36.0000	36.0000	36.0000	33.0000	35.0000	35.0000	35.0000	35.0000	35.0000	36.0000
Level Cooperation Domestic Orgs-DWMD	Pearson Correlation	0.2766	0.0821	0.3109	0.2390	0.4849	0.4952	0.3257	0.3519	0.2354	0.4372
	Sig. (2-tailed)	0.1025	0.6342	0.0649	0.1804	0.0032	0.0025	0.0562	0.0381	0.1735	0.0077
	N	36.0000	36.0000	36.0000	33.0000	35.0000	35.0000	35.0000	35.0000	35.0000	36.0000
Level Cooperation Domestic Orgs-TVP	Pearson Correlation	0.2122	0.3122	0.1111	0.4288	0.6054	0.4910	0.5899	0.4028	0.3361	0.3733
	Sig. (2-tailed)	0.2140	0.0638	0.5190	0.0128	0.0001	0.0027	0.0002	0.0164	0.0484	0.0249
	N	36.0000	36.0000	36.0000	33.0000	35.0000	35.0000	35.0000	35.0000	35.0000	36.0000
Level Cooperation Domestic Orgs-CBP	Pearson Correlation	0.0853	0.0620	0.3090	0.4754	0.2277	0.4178	0.2129	0.5841	0.3215	0.1751
	Sig. (2-tailed)	0.6209	0.7192	0.0667	0.0052	0.1884	0.0125	0.2195	0.0002	0.0597	0.3069
	N	36.0000	36.0000	36.0000	33.0000	35.0000	35.0000	35.0000	35.0000	35.0000	36.0000
sqrtQIIIA1a	Pearson Correlation	0.3507	0.5148	0.4789	0.3686	0.1688	0.1747	0.2413	0.1641	0.4457	0.1327
	Sig. (2-tailed)	0.0389	0.0016	0.0036	0.0379	0.3399	0.3232	0.1692	0.3537	0.0082	0.4474
	N	35.0000	35.0000	35.0000	32.0000	34.0000	34.0000	34.0000	34.0000	34.0000	35.0000
sqrtQIIIA1b	Pearson Correlation	0.8490	0.6948	0.6515	-0.0887	0.3611	0.1456	0.2324	0.0813	0.0042	0.3385
	Sig. (2-tailed)	0.0000	0.0000	0.0000	0.6235	0.0331	0.4041	0.1791	0.6425	0.9810	0.0435
	N	36.0000	36.0000	36.0000	33.0000	35.0000	35.0000	35.0000	35.0000	35.0000	36.0000
sqrtQIIIA1c	Pearson Correlation	1.0000	0.7061	0.6206	0.1355	0.3847	0.3799	0.3031	0.2621	0.1217	0.3611
	Sig. (2-tailed)	.	0.0000	0.0001	0.4522	0.0225	0.0244	0.0768	0.1282	0.4862	0.0305
	N	36.0000	36.0000	36.0000	33.0000	35.0000	35.0000	35.0000	35.0000	35.0000	36.0000
sqrtQIIIA1d	Pearson Correlation	0.7061	1.0000	0.6351	0.2733	0.3798	0.1910	0.4205	0.2136	0.1578	0.3697
	Sig. (2-tailed)	0.0000	.	0.0000	0.1238	0.0244	0.2718	0.0119	0.2180	0.3651	0.0265
	N	36.0000	36.0000	36.0000	33.0000	35.0000	35.0000	35.0000	35.0000	35.0000	36.0000
sqrtQIIIA1e	Pearson Correlation	0.6206	0.6351	1.0000	0.1785	0.2279	0.2346	0.1730	0.3145	0.1320	0.2666
	Sig. (2-tailed)	0.0001	0.0000	.	0.3202	0.1880	0.1750	0.3203	0.0657	0.4499	0.1159
	N	36.0000	36.0000	36.0000	33.0000	35.0000	35.0000	35.0000	35.0000	35.0000	36.0000
sqrtQIIID1a	Pearson Correlation	0.1355	0.2733	0.1785	1.0000	0.6244	0.7451	0.7309	0.8610	0.6773	0.4875
	Sig. (2-tailed)	0.4522	0.1238	0.3202	.	0.0001	0.0000	0.0000	0.0000	0.0000	0.0040
	N	33.0000	33.0000	33.0000	33.0000	33.0000	33.0000	33.0000	33.0000	33.0000	33.0000
Level Cooperation Domestic Orgs-CNDPS	Pearson Correlation	0.3847	0.3798	0.2279	0.6244	1.0000	0.8026	0.8367	0.7218	0.5215	0.7429
	Sig. (2-tailed)	0.0225	0.0244	0.1880	0.0001	.	0.0000	0.0000	0.0000	0.0016	0.0000
	N	35.0000	35.0000	35.0000	33.0000	35.0000	35.0000	35.0000	35.0000	34.0000	35.0000

Table A7, continued (Row 5, Col 7)

Correlation Matrix, International Variables (Parametric)		Level Cooperation International Orgs-CNBC	Level Cooperation International Orgs-CSTP	sqrtQIIID2e	sqrtQIVA1	sqrtQIVA2	sqrtQIVA3	sqrtQIVA5	sqrtQIVA7	sqrtQIVA8	Political Ideology
Level Cooperation Domestic Orgs-CSIE	Pearson Correlation	0.4986	0.3942	0.3621	-0.0166	-0.0436	-0.0670	0.3660	-0.1921	0.0446	0.1078
	Sig. (2-tailed)	0.0020	0.0174	0.0300	0.9236	0.8008	0.7021	0.0333	0.2618	0.7993	0.5503
	N	36.0000	36.0000	36.0000	36.0000	36.0000	35.0000	34.0000	36.0000	35.0000	33.0000
Level Cooperation Domestic Orgs-DWMD	Pearson Correlation	0.4416	0.3629	0.4183	0.0281	-0.0079	-0.0168	0.3984	-0.2136	0.0309	0.1871
	Sig. (2-tailed)	0.0070	0.0296	0.0111	0.8708	0.9636	0.9238	0.0196	0.2110	0.8601	0.2972
	N	36.0000	36.0000	36.0000	36.0000	36.0000	35.0000	34.0000	36.0000	35.0000	33.0000
Level Cooperation Domestic Orgs-TVP	Pearson Correlation	0.3532	0.3892	0.2200	0.0224	0.0079	-0.0141	0.3035	-0.0707	0.0867	0.0611
	Sig. (2-tailed)	0.0346	0.0190	0.1973	0.8967	0.9637	0.9361	0.0810	0.6818	0.6206	0.7357
	N	36.0000	36.0000	36.0000	36.0000	36.0000	35.0000	34.0000	36.0000	35.0000	33.0000
Level Cooperation Domestic Orgs-CBP	Pearson Correlation	0.2419	0.1522	0.4283	-0.0467	0.0137	0.0940	0.0006	-0.0284	0.0727	0.3480
	Sig. (2-tailed)	0.1553	0.3755	0.0092	0.7866	0.9367	0.5911	0.9973	0.8692	0.6780	0.0472
	N	36.0000	36.0000	36.0000	36.0000	36.0000	35.0000	34.0000	36.0000	35.0000	33.0000
sqrtQIIIA1a	Pearson Correlation	0.1273	0.2966	0.1620	-0.0305	0.1332	0.1338	-0.1075	-0.1239	-0.1046	0.2577
	Sig. (2-tailed)	0.4660	0.0836	0.3525	0.8618	0.4456	0.4505	0.5515	0.4782	0.5559	0.1545
	N	35.0000	35.0000	35.0000	35.0000	35.0000	34.0000	33.0000	35.0000	34.0000	32.0000
sqrtQIIIA1b	Pearson Correlation	0.2883	0.3935	0.2210	0.1503	0.1325	0.2814	-0.0871	-0.0378	-0.0375	0.0529
	Sig. (2-tailed)	0.0882	0.0176	0.1953	0.3817	0.4412	0.1015	0.6241	0.8268	0.8308	0.7698
	N	36.0000	36.0000	36.0000	36.0000	36.0000	35.0000	34.0000	36.0000	35.0000	33.0000
sqrtQIIIA1c	Pearson Correlation	0.3753	0.4306	0.3836	0.2397	0.2001	0.3763	0.0113	-0.0143	-0.0063	0.2063
	Sig. (2-tailed)	0.0241	0.0087	0.0209	0.1591	0.2421	0.0259	0.9496	0.9342	0.9714	0.2495
	N	36.0000	36.0000	36.0000	36.0000	36.0000	35.0000	34.0000	36.0000	35.0000	33.0000
sqrtQIIIA1d	Pearson Correlation	0.3133	0.4785	0.2707	0.0857	0.1293	0.3482	-0.1313	-0.0541	-0.0047	0.0506
	Sig. (2-tailed)	0.0628	0.0032	0.1102	0.6190	0.4522	0.0404	0.4593	0.7538	0.9785	0.7798
	N	36.0000	36.0000	36.0000	36.0000	36.0000	35.0000	34.0000	36.0000	35.0000	33.0000
sqrtQIIIA1e	Pearson Correlation	0.2476	0.3484	0.3784	0.0085	0.1471	0.2982	-0.1273	-0.1297	0.0381	0.2530
	Sig. (2-tailed)	0.1454	0.0373	0.0229	0.9607	0.3918	0.0819	0.4732	0.4509	0.8280	0.1554
	N	36.0000	36.0000	36.0000	36.0000	36.0000	35.0000	34.0000	36.0000	35.0000	33.0000
sqrtQIIID1a	Pearson Correlation	0.5190	0.5302	0.5762	0.0581	-0.0825	0.2669	0.2827	-0.1366	0.0378	0.2165
	Sig. (2-tailed)	0.0020	0.0015	0.0004	0.7480	0.6479	0.1397	0.1233	0.4485	0.8375	0.2420
	N	33.0000	33.0000	33.0000	33.0000	33.0000	32.0000	31.0000	33.0000	32.0000	31.0000
Level Cooperation Domestic Orgs-CNDPS	Pearson Correlation	0.7025	0.7276	0.5567	0.0086	-0.1697	0.0685	0.3836	-0.0858	-0.0429	0.0741
	Sig. (2-tailed)	0.0000	0.0000	0.0005	0.9607	0.3297	0.7003	0.0276	0.6240	0.8094	0.6821
	N	35.0000	35.0000	35.0000	35.0000	35.0000	34.0000	33.0000	35.0000	34.0000	33.0000

Table A7, continued (Row 5, Col 8)

Correlation Matrix, International Variables (Parametric)		sqrtQIIIB1a	sqrtQIIIB1b	sqrtQIIIB1c	sqrtQIIIB1d	sqrtQIIIB1e	sqrtQIIIB2a	Perceived Effectiveness Domestic Govt Support-CNDPS	Perceived Effectiveness Domestic Govt Support-CNBC	Perceived Effectiveness Domestic Govt Support-CSTP	Perceived Effectiveness Domestic Govt Support-TRIPS
Level Cooperation Domestic Orgs-CSIE	Pearson Correlation	-0.1373	0.1711	0.2136	0.2584	-0.1565	-0.0136	0.2940	0.2628	0.0732	-0.0167
	Sig. (2-tailed)	0.4315	0.3258	0.2179	0.1339	0.3694	0.9382	0.0817	0.1271	0.6760	0.9240
	N	35.0000	35.0000	35.0000	35.0000	35.0000	35.0000	36.0000	35.0000	35.0000	35.0000
Level Cooperation Domestic Orgs-DWMD	Pearson Correlation	0.0172	0.3376	0.2338	0.5121	0.0070	0.0614	0.3304	0.2299	0.0664	0.1741
	Sig. (2-tailed)	0.9221	0.0473	0.1764	0.0017	0.9684	0.7259	0.0490	0.1840	0.7045	0.3172
	N	35.0000	35.0000	35.0000	35.0000	35.0000	35.0000	36.0000	35.0000	35.0000	35.0000
Level Cooperation Domestic Orgs-TVP	Pearson Correlation	0.0777	0.1300	0.2622	0.2625	-0.0204	0.1299	0.1501	0.2681	0.1924	-0.0877
	Sig. (2-tailed)	0.6573	0.4566	0.1281	0.1276	0.9075	0.4570	0.3824	0.1195	0.2682	0.6165
	N	35.0000	35.0000	35.0000	35.0000	35.0000	35.0000	36.0000	35.0000	35.0000	35.0000
Level Cooperation Domestic Orgs-CBP	Pearson Correlation	0.1536	0.2426	0.1368	0.4177	0.2302	0.0198	-0.0320	-0.0107	0.0123	0.1787
	Sig. (2-tailed)	0.3784	0.1603	0.4334	0.0125	0.1834	0.9103	0.8530	0.9512	0.9443	0.3043
	N	35.0000	35.0000	35.0000	35.0000	35.0000	35.0000	36.0000	35.0000	35.0000	35.0000
sqrtQIIIA1a	Pearson Correlation	0.1480	0.0277	0.0397	0.1457	-0.0020	0.1665	-0.0081	0.0002	0.0866	-0.1267
	Sig. (2-tailed)	0.4036	0.8765	0.8238	0.4111	0.9910	0.3466	0.9631	0.9991	0.6261	0.4753
	N	34.0000	34.0000	34.0000	34.0000	34.0000	34.0000	35.0000	34.0000	34.0000	34.0000
sqrtQIIIA1b	Pearson Correlation	-0.2197	0.0289	0.0850	0.0740	0.0353	-0.2977	0.1148	0.0020	-0.0391	0.0128
	Sig. (2-tailed)	0.2047	0.8689	0.6274	0.6727	0.8407	0.0824	0.5048	0.9910	0.8236	0.9418
	N	35.0000	35.0000	35.0000	35.0000	35.0000	35.0000	36.0000	35.0000	35.0000	35.0000
sqrtQIIIA1c	Pearson Correlation	-0.0906	0.1552	0.1381	0.2132	-0.0432	-0.1840	0.1046	0.0359	-0.0149	-0.0767
	Sig. (2-tailed)	0.6045	0.3733	0.4288	0.2189	0.8055	0.2900	0.5439	0.8376	0.9322	0.6616
	N	35.0000	35.0000	35.0000	35.0000	35.0000	35.0000	36.0000	35.0000	35.0000	35.0000
sqrtQIIIA1d	Pearson Correlation	0.0221	0.1203	0.2295	0.1222	0.1111	-0.0513	0.1474	0.1471	0.2077	-0.0486
	Sig. (2-tailed)	0.8996	0.4911	0.1847	0.4845	0.5253	0.7697	0.3911	0.3992	0.2313	0.7816
	N	35.0000	35.0000	35.0000	35.0000	35.0000	35.0000	36.0000	35.0000	35.0000	35.0000
sqrtQIIIA1e	Pearson Correlation	-0.1440	0.0930	0.0052	0.3129	0.2043	-0.2656	-0.0094	-0.1126	-0.0855	0.1779
	Sig. (2-tailed)	0.4093	0.5953	0.9763	0.0672	0.2390	0.1231	0.9568	0.5194	0.6252	0.3065
	N	35.0000	35.0000	35.0000	35.0000	35.0000	35.0000	36.0000	35.0000	35.0000	35.0000
sqrtQIIID1a	Pearson Correlation	0.3557	0.3476	0.3254	0.3420	0.2169	0.4180	0.1142	0.3432	0.3670	0.1490
	Sig. (2-tailed)	0.0457	0.0513	0.0692	0.0554	0.2332	0.0173	0.5268	0.0545	0.0388	0.4158
	N	32.0000	32.0000	32.0000	32.0000	32.0000	32.0000	33.0000	32.0000	32.0000	32.0000
Level Cooperation Domestic Orgs-CNDPS	Pearson Correlation	0.1559	0.4002	0.4193	0.3435	0.1338	0.3119	0.4791	0.4991	0.4630	0.2319
	Sig. (2-tailed)	0.3787	0.0190	0.0136	0.0467	0.4507	0.0726	0.0036	0.0027	0.0058	0.1870
	N	34.0000	34.0000	34.0000	34.0000	34.0000	34.0000	35.0000	34.0000	34.0000	34.0000

Table A7, continued (Row 5, Col 9)

Correlation Matrix, International Variables (Parametric)		sqrtQIIIC1a	sqrtQIIIC1b	sqrtQIIIC1c	sqrtQIIIC1d	sqrtQIIIC1e
Level Cooperation Domestic Orgs-CSIE	Pearson Correlation	-0.1107	0.3696	0.4242	0.1500	0.1731
	Sig. (2-tailed)	0.5331	0.0289	0.0124	0.3972	0.3274
	N	34.0000	35.0000	34.0000	34.0000	34.0000
Level Cooperation Domestic Orgs-DWMD	Pearson Correlation	-0.0364	0.4777	0.3842	0.2883	0.3046
	Sig. (2-tailed)	0.8382	0.0037	0.0249	0.0983	0.0798
	N	34.0000	35.0000	34.0000	34.0000	34.0000
Level Cooperation Domestic Orgs-TVP	Pearson Correlation	0.1560	0.3611	0.4525	0.2792	0.2723
	Sig. (2-tailed)	0.3784	0.0331	0.0072	0.1098	0.1193
	N	34.0000	35.0000	34.0000	34.0000	34.0000
Level Cooperation Domestic Orgs-CBP	Pearson Correlation	0.2050	0.3365	0.2793	0.3933	0.4889
	Sig. (2-tailed)	0.2447	0.0481	0.1097	0.0214	0.0033
	N	34.0000	35.0000	34.0000	34.0000	34.0000
sqrtQIIIA1a	Pearson Correlation	0.3025	0.1548	0.1877	0.2515	0.2017
	Sig. (2-tailed)	0.0871	0.3819	0.2956	0.1579	0.2602
	N	33.0000	34.0000	33.0000	33.0000	33.0000
sqrtQIIIA1b	Pearson Correlation	-0.0562	0.0659	0.0997	-0.0240	0.0218
	Sig. (2-tailed)	0.7522	0.7067	0.5748	0.8929	0.9024
	N	34.0000	35.0000	34.0000	34.0000	34.0000
sqrtQIIIA1c	Pearson Correlation	0.0174	0.1306	0.1179	0.1012	0.0999
	Sig. (2-tailed)	0.9223	0.4547	0.5067	0.5689	0.5742
	N	34.0000	35.0000	34.0000	34.0000	34.0000
sqrtQIIIA1d	Pearson Correlation	0.2362	0.0957	0.1858	0.1545	0.1787
	Sig. (2-tailed)	0.1786	0.5844	0.2929	0.3830	0.3119
	N	34.0000	35.0000	34.0000	34.0000	34.0000
sqrtQIIIA1e	Pearson Correlation	0.0568	0.1706	0.0721	0.1855	0.2334
	Sig. (2-tailed)	0.7495	0.3272	0.6852	0.2935	0.1841
	N	34.0000	35.0000	34.0000	34.0000	34.0000
sqrtQIIID1a	Pearson Correlation	0.4114	0.4041	0.3840	0.4812	0.4420
	Sig. (2-tailed)	0.0193	0.0197	0.0300	0.0053	0.0113
	N	32.0000	33.0000	32.0000	32.0000	32.0000
Level Cooperation Domestic Orgs-CNDPS	Pearson Correlation	0.1404	0.5133	0.5190	0.3622	0.3664
	Sig. (2-tailed)	0.4284	0.0016	0.0017	0.0353	0.0330
	N	34.0000	35.0000	34.0000	34.0000	34.0000

Table A7, continued (Row 6, Col 1)

Correlation Matrix, International Variables (Parametric)		Importance of Smuggling-Endangered Species	reflectsqrtQ1A1b	reflectsqrtQ1A1c	reflectsqrtQ1A1d	reflectsqrtQ1A1e	sqrtQ1B1a	Knowledge of Smuggling-Narcotics	Knowledge of Smuggling-Weapons	Knowledge of Smuggling-Humans	Knowledge of Smuggling-Contraband
Level Cooperation Domestic Orgs-CNBC	Pearson Correlation	-0.1244	0.0249	0.1364	0.1835	-0.0434	0.2866	0.2308	0.4812	0.1396	0.3090
	Sig. (2-tailed)	0.4764	0.8870	0.4348	0.2913	0.8045	0.0951	0.1821	0.0034	0.4239	0.0709
	N	35.0000	35.0000	35.0000	35.0000	35.0000	35.0000	35.0000	35.0000	35.0000	35.0000
Level Cooperation Domestic Orgs-CSTP	Pearson Correlation	-0.1646	0.0051	0.1535	0.0920	-0.0947	0.2611	0.2171	0.2043	0.2787	0.2677
	Sig. (2-tailed)	0.3448	0.9767	0.3786	0.5993	0.5886	0.1298	0.2103	0.2391	0.1050	0.1200
	N	35.0000	35.0000	35.0000	35.0000	35.0000	35.0000	35.0000	35.0000	35.0000	35.0000
Level Cooperation Domestic Orgs-TRIPS	Pearson Correlation	-0.1113	0.1878	0.3916	0.2575	-0.0987	0.2429	-0.0035	0.2767	0.0033	0.2737
	Sig. (2-tailed)	0.5246	0.2800	0.0200	0.1353	0.5725	0.1597	0.9839	0.1075	0.9852	0.1117
	N	35.0000	35.0000	35.0000	35.0000	35.0000	35.0000	35.0000	35.0000	35.0000	35.0000
sqrtQIIID2a	Pearson Correlation	0.0214	0.2075	0.2276	0.1701	-0.0940	0.5361	-0.0078	0.2198	0.1284	0.1527
	Sig. (2-tailed)	0.9028	0.2317	0.1886	0.3285	0.5913	0.0009	0.9646	0.2044	0.4625	0.3810
	N	35.0000	35.0000	35.0000	35.0000	35.0000	35.0000	35.0000	35.0000	35.0000	35.0000
Level Cooperation International Orgs-CNDPS	Pearson Correlation	0.1124	0.0021	0.1330	0.0575	-0.0534	0.1694	0.2711	0.2907	0.1288	0.0678
	Sig. (2-tailed)	0.5139	0.9902	0.4393	0.7391	0.7571	0.3233	0.1098	0.0855	0.4541	0.6944
	N	36.0000	36.0000	36.0000	36.0000	36.0000	36.0000	36.0000	36.0000	36.0000	36.0000
Level Cooperation International Orgs-CNBC	Pearson Correlation	0.0449	0.0023	0.0860	0.1102	-0.0231	0.1797	0.2604	0.4227	0.1151	0.1025
	Sig. (2-tailed)	0.7949	0.9895	0.6180	0.5222	0.8936	0.2943	0.1251	0.0102	0.5040	0.5518
	N	36.0000	36.0000	36.0000	36.0000	36.0000	36.0000	36.0000	36.0000	36.0000	36.0000
Level Cooperation International Orgs-CSTP	Pearson Correlation	0.0549	0.0373	0.0793	0.1459	-0.0056	0.2332	0.2177	0.2247	0.2938	0.1867
	Sig. (2-tailed)	0.7504	0.8292	0.6459	0.3959	0.9740	0.1710	0.2021	0.1876	0.0820	0.2757
	N	36.0000	36.0000	36.0000	36.0000	36.0000	36.0000	36.0000	36.0000	36.0000	36.0000
sqrtQIIID2e	Pearson Correlation	-0.0110	0.0624	0.2157	0.2396	-0.1143	0.1194	0.0106	0.3393	0.0382	0.1958
	Sig. (2-tailed)	0.9491	0.7177	0.2065	0.1593	0.5070	0.4880	0.9511	0.0429	0.8247	0.2524
	N	36.0000	36.0000	36.0000	36.0000	36.0000	36.0000	36.0000	36.0000	36.0000	36.0000
sqrtQIVA1	Pearson Correlation	0.1272	-0.1992	0.0037	-0.1471	-0.2422	0.1477	0.0975	0.1958	0.1268	0.1346
	Sig. (2-tailed)	0.4597	0.2442	0.9827	0.3919	0.1546	0.3899	0.5715	0.2525	0.4610	0.4339
	N	36.0000	36.0000	36.0000	36.0000	36.0000	36.0000	36.0000	36.0000	36.0000	36.0000
sqrtQIVA2	Pearson Correlation	0.1038	0.0760	-0.0544	-0.2229	-0.0831	0.1831	-0.1039	0.0264	0.0276	0.0214
	Sig. (2-tailed)	0.5471	0.6595	0.7528	0.1914	0.6301	0.2852	0.5464	0.8784	0.8732	0.9013
	N	36.0000	36.0000	36.0000	36.0000	36.0000	36.0000	36.0000	36.0000	36.0000	36.0000
sqrtQIVA3	Pearson Correlation	-0.2036	-0.0784	-0.0162	-0.1433	-0.0897	-0.0036	0.0204	0.1837	0.2654	0.1990
	Sig. (2-tailed)	0.2408	0.6545	0.9265	0.4115	0.6085	0.9835	0.9073	0.2908	0.1234	0.2517
	N	35.0000	35.0000	35.0000	35.0000	35.0000	35.0000	35.0000	35.0000	35.0000	35.0000

Table A7, continued (Row 6, Col 2)

Correlation Matrix, International Variables (Parametric)		sqrtQ1E1a	Personal Resource Challenges-Lack of Time	Personal Resource Challenges-Lack of Knowledge	Personal Resource Challenges-Lack of Training	sqrtQ1E1e	Personal Resource Challenges-Excessive Admin Paperwork	Personal Resource Challenges-Ineffective Technology	Personal Resource Challenges-Ineffective Strategic Focus	Personal Resource Challenges-Ineffective Tactical Policy	Personal Resource Challenges-Lack of Clarity in Duties
Level Cooperation Domestic Orgs-CNBC	Pearson Correlation	-0.1925	-0.0511	-0.3097	-0.2839	0.1179	0.0146	-0.4478	-0.2249	-0.3398	-0.2423
	Sig. (2-tailed)	0.2680	0.7705	0.0702	0.0984	0.4998	0.9334	0.0070	0.1940	0.0458	0.1608
	N	35.0000	35.0000	35.0000	35.0000	35.0000	35.0000	35.0000	35.0000	35.0000	35.0000
Level Cooperation Domestic Orgs-CSTP	Pearson Correlation	-0.1203	0.1117	-0.1833	-0.1215	0.0768	0.0791	-0.3132	-0.1131	-0.2203	-0.0036
	Sig. (2-tailed)	0.4912	0.5231	0.2919	0.4870	0.6610	0.6514	0.0669	0.5179	0.2034	0.9835
	N	35.0000	35.0000	35.0000	35.0000	35.0000	35.0000	35.0000	35.0000	35.0000	35.0000
Level Cooperation Domestic Orgs-TRIPS	Pearson Correlation	-0.0535	0.0041	-0.2496	-0.1957	0.1020	0.0394	-0.3367	-0.1968	-0.2806	-0.1610
	Sig. (2-tailed)	0.7601	0.9813	0.1481	0.2598	0.5600	0.8221	0.0479	0.2572	0.1025	0.3556
	N	35.0000	35.0000	35.0000	35.0000	35.0000	35.0000	35.0000	35.0000	35.0000	35.0000
sqrtQIIID2a	Pearson Correlation	-0.0563	-0.1385	-0.0454	0.0772	0.2775	0.1931	-0.1671	0.0834	-0.0788	-0.0609
	Sig. (2-tailed)	0.7519	0.4277	0.7956	0.6593	0.1066	0.2663	0.3375	0.6337	0.6526	0.7280
	N	34.0000	35.0000	35.0000	35.0000	35.0000	35.0000	35.0000	35.0000	35.0000	35.0000
Level Cooperation International Orgs-CNDPS	Pearson Correlation	-0.0521	-0.1679	-0.1854	-0.1642	0.2058	0.1350	-0.1814	-0.2790	-0.3088	-0.2645
	Sig. (2-tailed)	0.7663	0.3277	0.2791	0.3386	0.2285	0.4324	0.2896	0.0994	0.0669	0.1190
	N	35.0000	36.0000	36.0000	36.0000	36.0000	36.0000	36.0000	36.0000	36.0000	36.0000
Level Cooperation International Orgs-CNBC	Pearson Correlation	-0.1166	-0.2175	-0.1852	-0.1489	0.2551	0.0927	-0.2226	-0.2551	-0.3368	-0.3009
	Sig. (2-tailed)	0.5047	0.2026	0.2795	0.3860	0.1333	0.5908	0.1918	0.1332	0.0446	0.0745
	N	35.0000	36.0000	36.0000	36.0000	36.0000	36.0000	36.0000	36.0000	36.0000	36.0000
Level Cooperation International Orgs-CSTP	Pearson Correlation	-0.0751	-0.0209	-0.0530	-0.0524	0.1915	0.0969	-0.2263	-0.1966	-0.2681	-0.1977
	Sig. (2-tailed)	0.6679	0.9038	0.7586	0.7616	0.2632	0.5738	0.1844	0.2504	0.1139	0.2477
	N	35.0000	36.0000	36.0000	36.0000	36.0000	36.0000	36.0000	36.0000	36.0000	36.0000
sqrtQIIID2e	Pearson Correlation	-0.1284	-0.2123	-0.1736	-0.1508	0.2529	0.0811	-0.2817	-0.2426	-0.3346	-0.3052
	Sig. (2-tailed)	0.4624	0.2138	0.3114	0.3800	0.1366	0.6380	0.0960	0.1540	0.0461	0.0702
	N	35.0000	36.0000	36.0000	36.0000	36.0000	36.0000	36.0000	36.0000	36.0000	36.0000
sqrtQIVA1	Pearson Correlation	0.0884	0.0179	0.2114	0.1371	0.2619	0.3080	0.3243	0.2088	0.2928	0.2937
	Sig. (2-tailed)	0.6135	0.9176	0.2158	0.4251	0.1228	0.0676	0.0537	0.2216	0.0831	0.0821
	N	35.0000	36.0000	36.0000	36.0000	36.0000	36.0000	36.0000	36.0000	36.0000	36.0000
sqrtQIVA2	Pearson Correlation	0.2392	0.0627	0.1892	0.0768	0.2009	0.2318	0.2996	0.2963	0.4052	0.2994
	Sig. (2-tailed)	0.1663	0.7164	0.2690	0.6560	0.2400	0.1738	0.0758	0.0794	0.0142	0.0761
	N	35.0000	36.0000	36.0000	36.0000	36.0000	36.0000	36.0000	36.0000	36.0000	36.0000
sqrtQIVA3	Pearson Correlation	0.3484	0.1729	0.1521	0.1250	0.2528	0.4174	0.2555	0.3183	0.4473	0.3700
	Sig. (2-tailed)	0.0435	0.3206	0.3830	0.4742	0.1428	0.0126	0.1385	0.0624	0.0071	0.0287
	N	34.0000	35.0000	35.0000	35.0000	35.0000	35.0000	35.0000	35.0000	35.0000	35.0000

Correlation Matrix, International Variables (Parametric)		Personal Resource Challenges-Conflict or Lack Comm Leaders and Employees	sqrtQ1E1	Personal Resource Challenges-Conflict or Lack Comm International Orgs	Personal Resource Challenges-Conflict or Lack Comm Domestic Orgs	sqrtQ1E3a	Org Resource Challenges-Lack of Time	Org Resource Challenges-Lack of Knowledge	Org Resource Challenges-Lack of Training	sqrtQ1E3e	Org Resource Challenges-Excessive Admin Paperwork
Level Cooperation Domestic Orgs-CNBC	Pearson Correlation	-0.2412	-0.0657	-0.2421	-0.2036	-0.1800	-0.3131	-0.3757	-0.4226	-0.0355	-0.1819
	Sig. (2-tailed)	0.1628	0.7077	0.1611	0.2409	0.3163	0.0714	0.0285	0.0128	0.8446	0.3033
	N	35.0000	35.0000	35.0000	35.0000	33.0000	34.0000	34.0000	34.0000	33.0000	34.0000
Level Cooperation Domestic Orgs-CSTP	Pearson Correlation	-0.1756	-0.1034	-0.0921	-0.0198	-0.1702	-0.2950	-0.1646	-0.1937	-0.0343	-0.0498
	Sig. (2-tailed)	0.3128	0.5545	0.5988	0.9102	0.3436	0.0904	0.3522	0.2724	0.8497	0.7799
	N	35.0000	35.0000	35.0000	35.0000	33.0000	34.0000	34.0000	34.0000	33.0000	34.0000
Level Cooperation Domestic Orgs-TRIPS	Pearson Correlation	-0.1849	-0.0830	-0.1925	-0.1262	-0.2506	-0.4556	-0.3192	-0.3354	0.0295	-0.1475
	Sig. (2-tailed)	0.2877	0.6355	0.2678	0.4701	0.1595	0.0068	0.0657	0.0525	0.8705	0.4051
	N	35.0000	35.0000	35.0000	35.0000	33.0000	34.0000	34.0000	34.0000	33.0000	34.0000
sqrtQIIID2a	Pearson Correlation	-0.2003	0.0048	-0.0771	-0.1538	-0.0594	-0.3044	-0.1769	-0.2034	-0.0190	-0.0482
	Sig. (2-tailed)	0.2487	0.9781	0.6596	0.3778	0.7426	0.0801	0.3168	0.2486	0.9164	0.7868
	N	35.0000	35.0000	35.0000	35.0000	33.0000	34.0000	34.0000	34.0000	33.0000	34.0000
Level Cooperation International Orgs-CNDPS	Pearson Correlation	-0.3302	-0.2251	-0.0630	-0.1353	0.1036	-0.2275	-0.2702	-0.2894	-0.0860	-0.0530
	Sig. (2-tailed)	0.0492	0.1868	0.7150	0.4315	0.5598	0.1888	0.1164	0.0917	0.6287	0.7622
	N	36.0000	36.0000	36.0000	36.0000	34.0000	35.0000	35.0000	35.0000	34.0000	35.0000
Level Cooperation International Orgs-CNBC	Pearson Correlation	-0.3636	-0.2286	-0.1384	-0.2322	0.0984	-0.2063	-0.2763	-0.3140	-0.0732	-0.0612
	Sig. (2-tailed)	0.0293	0.1799	0.4207	0.1729	0.5798	0.2345	0.1081	0.0662	0.6808	0.7269
	N	36.0000	36.0000	36.0000	36.0000	34.0000	35.0000	35.0000	35.0000	34.0000	35.0000
Level Cooperation International Orgs-CSTP	Pearson Correlation	-0.2689	-0.2462	-0.0166	-0.0763	-0.0030	-0.2480	-0.1889	-0.2335	-0.0943	-0.0943
	Sig. (2-tailed)	0.1128	0.1477	0.9236	0.6582	0.9867	0.1509	0.2772	0.1771	0.5959	0.5899
	N	36.0000	36.0000	36.0000	36.0000	34.0000	35.0000	35.0000	35.0000	34.0000	35.0000
sqrtQIIID2e	Pearson Correlation	-0.3400	-0.2096	-0.1955	-0.2643	-0.0716	-0.3042	-0.2873	-0.3437	0.0318	-0.0615
	Sig. (2-tailed)	0.0425	0.2199	0.2531	0.1193	0.6874	0.0756	0.0942	0.0432	0.8582	0.7255
	N	36.0000	36.0000	36.0000	36.0000	34.0000	35.0000	35.0000	35.0000	34.0000	35.0000
sqrtQIVA1	Pearson Correlation	0.2933	0.2187	0.1870	0.2684	0.2920	0.0029	0.2136	0.1882	0.0981	0.0572
	Sig. (2-tailed)	0.0825	0.2001	0.2749	0.1134	0.0938	0.9870	0.2180	0.2789	0.5809	0.7441
	N	36.0000	36.0000	36.0000	36.0000	34.0000	35.0000	35.0000	35.0000	34.0000	35.0000
sqrtQIVA2	Pearson Correlation	0.3287	0.2301	0.2393	0.2483	0.3555	0.1769	0.1306	0.1844	0.0666	0.1212
	Sig. (2-tailed)	0.0503	0.1770	0.1599	0.1443	0.0391	0.3093	0.4546	0.2890	0.7082	0.4880
	N	36.0000	36.0000	36.0000	36.0000	34.0000	35.0000	35.0000	35.0000	34.0000	35.0000
sqrtQIVA3	Pearson Correlation	0.4069	0.3031	0.2714	0.3473	0.2967	-0.0517	0.1567	0.1301	0.2704	0.2113
	Sig. (2-tailed)	0.0153	0.0767	0.1148	0.0409	0.0936	0.7716	0.3763	0.4633	0.1280	0.2303
	N	35.0000	35.0000	35.0000	35.0000	33.0000	34.0000	34.0000	34.0000	33.0000	34.0000

Table A7, continued (Row 6, Col 4)

Correlation Matrix, International Variables (Parametric)		Org Resource Challenges-Ineffective Technology	Org Resource Challenges-Ineffective Strategic Focus	Org Resource Challenges-Ineffective Tactical Policy	Org Resource Challenges-Lack of Clarity in Duties	Org Resource Challenges-Conflict or Lack Comm Leaders and Employees	sqrtQ1E3I	Org Resource Challenges-Conflict or Lack Comm International Orgs	Org Resource Challenges-Conflict or Lack Comm Domestic Orgs	sqrtQIIA1a	Knowledge of Domestic Law-CSIE
Level Cooperation Domestic Orgs-CNBC	Pearson Correlation	-0.2951	-0.2771	-0.1912	-0.2877	-0.1349	-0.0328	-0.2472	-0.2111	0.1799	0.2263
	Sig. (2-tailed)	0.0902	0.1126	0.2786	0.0989	0.4469	0.8541	0.1586	0.2307	0.3086	0.1980
	N	34.0000	34.0000	34.0000	34.0000	34.0000	34.0000	34.0000	34.0000	34.0000	34.0000
Level Cooperation Domestic Orgs-CSTP	Pearson Correlation	-0.1450	-0.1540	-0.0689	-0.2099	-0.1179	-0.0436	-0.1951	-0.2121	0.1731	0.0270
	Sig. (2-tailed)	0.4133	0.3846	0.6984	0.2334	0.5066	0.8068	0.2688	0.2284	0.3276	0.8796
	N	34.0000	34.0000	34.0000	34.0000	34.0000	34.0000	34.0000	34.0000	34.0000	34.0000
Level Cooperation Domestic Orgs-TRIPS	Pearson Correlation	-0.2648	-0.2889	-0.1827	-0.2803	-0.1270	-0.0632	-0.3522	-0.2948	0.1626	0.0105
	Sig. (2-tailed)	0.1301	0.0975	0.3011	0.1083	0.4741	0.7224	0.0411	0.0905	0.3581	0.9529
	N	34.0000	34.0000	34.0000	34.0000	34.0000	34.0000	34.0000	34.0000	34.0000	34.0000
sqrtQIIID2a	Pearson Correlation	-0.1784	-0.1595	-0.1374	-0.0313	-0.1959	0.0422	-0.0468	-0.0631	0.3801	-0.0543
	Sig. (2-tailed)	0.3128	0.3676	0.4386	0.8605	0.2667	0.8125	0.7927	0.7230	0.0266	0.7602
	N	34.0000	34.0000	34.0000	34.0000	34.0000	34.0000	34.0000	34.0000	34.0000	34.0000
Level Cooperation International Orgs-CNDPS	Pearson Correlation	-0.1089	-0.2729	-0.2079	-0.1810	-0.1156	-0.2323	-0.1102	-0.0994	0.0431	0.2693
	Sig. (2-tailed)	0.5333	0.1127	0.2306	0.2982	0.5086	0.1792	0.5287	0.5698	0.8059	0.1177
	N	35.0000	35.0000	35.0000	35.0000	35.0000	35.0000	35.0000	35.0000	35.0000	35.0000
Level Cooperation International Orgs-CNBC	Pearson Correlation	-0.1526	-0.2741	-0.2227	-0.1936	-0.1167	-0.2091	-0.1208	-0.1121	0.0968	0.2882
	Sig. (2-tailed)	0.3814	0.1111	0.1984	0.2650	0.5043	0.2279	0.4895	0.5216	0.5802	0.0932
	N	35.0000	35.0000	35.0000	35.0000	35.0000	35.0000	35.0000	35.0000	35.0000	35.0000
Level Cooperation International Orgs-CSTP	Pearson Correlation	-0.1341	-0.2184	-0.1647	-0.1137	-0.1419	-0.2572	-0.0355	-0.0277	0.2430	0.1645
	Sig. (2-tailed)	0.4424	0.2074	0.3443	0.5155	0.4161	0.1357	0.8395	0.8744	0.1596	0.3450
	N	35.0000	35.0000	35.0000	35.0000	35.0000	35.0000	35.0000	35.0000	35.0000	35.0000
sqrtQIIID2e	Pearson Correlation	-0.2585	-0.3170	-0.2417	-0.2185	-0.1800	-0.1945	-0.1904	-0.1476	0.1620	0.1353
	Sig. (2-tailed)	0.1337	0.0635	0.1619	0.2074	0.3007	0.2630	0.2734	0.3974	0.3525	0.4382
	N	35.0000	35.0000	35.0000	35.0000	35.0000	35.0000	35.0000	35.0000	35.0000	35.0000
sqrtQIVA1	Pearson Correlation	0.2358	0.3248	0.2058	0.2975	0.1614	0.1144	0.3519	0.3555	-0.1899	0.0265
	Sig. (2-tailed)	0.1726	0.0569	0.2357	0.0826	0.3544	0.5127	0.0382	0.0361	0.2746	0.8798
	N	35.0000	35.0000	35.0000	35.0000	35.0000	35.0000	35.0000	35.0000	35.0000	35.0000
sqrtQIVA2	Pearson Correlation	0.1196	0.1723	0.1873	0.1487	0.1363	0.1141	0.2023	0.1494	-0.0509	-0.0986
	Sig. (2-tailed)	0.4939	0.3222	0.2814	0.3939	0.4349	0.5141	0.2438	0.3917	0.7714	0.5730
	N	35.0000	35.0000	35.0000	35.0000	35.0000	35.0000	35.0000	35.0000	35.0000	35.0000
sqrtQIVA3	Pearson Correlation	0.1978	0.1703	0.2609	0.2110	0.2148	0.1633	0.1834	0.1617	-0.2144	-0.1775
	Sig. (2-tailed)	0.2622	0.3355	0.1362	0.2310	0.2226	0.3562	0.2991	0.3608	0.2233	0.3152
	N	34.0000	34.0000	34.0000	34.0000	34.0000	34.0000	34.0000	34.0000	34.0000	34.0000

Table A7, continued (Row 6, Col 5)

Correlation Matrix, International Variables (Parametric)		Knowledge of Domestic Law-DWMD	Knowledge of Domestic Law-TVP	Knowledge of Domestic Law-CBP	sqrtQIID1a	Level Cooperation Domestic Orgs-CSIE	Level Cooperation Domestic Orgs-DWMD	Level Cooperation Domestic Orgs-TVP	Level Cooperation Domestic Orgs-CBP	sqrtQIIIA1a	sqrtQIIIA1b
Level Cooperation Domestic Orgs-CNBC	Pearson Correlation	0.2464	0.1167	0.3494	0.5210	0.4744	0.4952	0.4910	0.4178	0.1747	0.1456
	Sig. (2-tailed)	0.1601	0.5112	0.0428	0.0013	0.0040	0.0025	0.0027	0.0125	0.3232	0.4041
	N	34.0000	34.0000	34.0000	35.0000	35.0000	35.0000	35.0000	35.0000	34.0000	35.0000
Level Cooperation Domestic Orgs-CSTP	Pearson Correlation	-0.0296	0.2619	0.1388	0.2009	0.4123	0.3257	0.5899	0.2129	0.2413	0.2324
	Sig. (2-tailed)	0.8680	0.1346	0.4338	0.2473	0.0139	0.0562	0.0002	0.2195	0.1692	0.1791
	N	34.0000	34.0000	34.0000	35.0000	35.0000	35.0000	35.0000	35.0000	34.0000	35.0000
Level Cooperation Domestic Orgs-TRIPS	Pearson Correlation	-0.0050	-0.0368	0.3325	0.5555	0.2704	0.3519	0.4028	0.5841	0.1641	0.0813
	Sig. (2-tailed)	0.9776	0.8365	0.0547	0.0005	0.1162	0.0381	0.0164	0.0002	0.3537	0.6425
	N	34.0000	34.0000	34.0000	35.0000	35.0000	35.0000	35.0000	35.0000	34.0000	35.0000
sqrtQIIID2a	Pearson Correlation	-0.1039	0.0341	-0.0834	0.5936	0.2898	0.2354	0.3361	0.3215	0.4457	0.0042
	Sig. (2-tailed)	0.5586	0.8481	0.6392	0.0002	0.0913	0.1735	0.0484	0.0597	0.0082	0.9810
	N	34.0000	34.0000	34.0000	35.0000	35.0000	35.0000	35.0000	35.0000	34.0000	35.0000
Level Cooperation International Orgs-CNDPS	Pearson Correlation	0.1853	0.0978	0.0795	0.3070	0.4537	0.4372	0.3733	0.1751	0.1327	0.3385
	Sig. (2-tailed)	0.2867	0.5762	0.6497	0.0686	0.0054	0.0077	0.0249	0.3069	0.4474	0.0435
	N	35.0000	35.0000	35.0000	36.0000	36.0000	36.0000	36.0000	36.0000	35.0000	36.0000
Level Cooperation International Orgs-CNBC	Pearson Correlation	0.2562	0.0945	0.1476	0.3896	0.4986	0.4416	0.3532	0.2419	0.1273	0.2883
	Sig. (2-tailed)	0.1374	0.5894	0.3974	0.0188	0.0020	0.0070	0.0346	0.1553	0.4660	0.0882
	N	35.0000	35.0000	35.0000	36.0000	36.0000	36.0000	36.0000	36.0000	35.0000	36.0000
Level Cooperation International Orgs-CSTP	Pearson Correlation	0.1028	0.1248	0.0430	0.3778	0.3942	0.3629	0.3892	0.1522	0.2966	0.3935
	Sig. (2-tailed)	0.5569	0.4750	0.8064	0.0231	0.0174	0.0296	0.0190	0.3755	0.0836	0.0176
	N	35.0000	35.0000	35.0000	36.0000	36.0000	36.0000	36.0000	36.0000	35.0000	36.0000
sqrtQIIID2e	Pearson Correlation	0.1436	-0.0195	0.2240	0.5037	0.3621	0.4183	0.2200	0.4283	0.1620	0.2210
	Sig. (2-tailed)	0.4105	0.9117	0.1958	0.0017	0.0300	0.0111	0.1973	0.0092	0.3525	0.1953
	N	35.0000	35.0000	35.0000	36.0000	36.0000	36.0000	36.0000	36.0000	35.0000	36.0000
sqrtQIVA1	Pearson Correlation	0.0686	0.0473	-0.1427	0.1145	-0.0166	0.0281	0.0224	-0.0467	-0.0305	0.1503
	Sig. (2-tailed)	0.6955	0.7873	0.4134	0.5063	0.9236	0.8708	0.8967	0.7866	0.8618	0.3817
	N	35.0000	35.0000	35.0000	36.0000	36.0000	36.0000	36.0000	36.0000	35.0000	36.0000
sqrtQIVA2	Pearson Correlation	-0.0248	-0.0414	-0.0942	0.1167	-0.0436	-0.0079	0.0079	0.0137	0.1332	0.1325
	Sig. (2-tailed)	0.8877	0.8133	0.5902	0.4977	0.8008	0.9636	0.9637	0.9367	0.4456	0.4412
	N	35.0000	35.0000	35.0000	36.0000	36.0000	36.0000	36.0000	36.0000	35.0000	36.0000
sqrtQIVA3	Pearson Correlation	-0.1084	-0.0617	-0.1213	0.1560	-0.0670	-0.0168	-0.0141	0.0940	0.1338	0.2814
	Sig. (2-tailed)	0.5418	0.7290	0.4943	0.3707	0.7021	0.9238	0.9361	0.5911	0.4505	0.1015
	N	34.0000	34.0000	34.0000	35.0000	35.0000	35.0000	35.0000	35.0000	34.0000	35.0000

Table A7, continued (Row 6, Col 6)

Correlation Matrix, International Variables (Parametric)		sqrtQIIIA1c	sqrtQIIIA1d	sqrtQIIIA1e	sqrtQIIID1a	Level Cooperation Domestic Orgs-CNDPS	Level Cooperation Domestic Orgs-CNBC	Level Cooperation Domestic Orgs-CSTP	Level Cooperation Domestic Orgs-TRIPS	sqrtQIIID2a	Level Cooperation International Orgs-CNDPS
Level Cooperation Domestic Orgs-CNBC	Pearson Correlation	0.3799	0.1910	0.2346	0.7451	0.8026	1.0000	0.7652	0.8388	0.5921	0.5740
	Sig. (2-tailed)	0.0244	0.2718	0.1750	0.0000	0.0000	.	0.0000	0.0000	0.0002	0.0003
	N	35.0000	35.0000	35.0000	33.0000	35.0000	35.0000	35.0000	35.0000	34.0000	35.0000
Level Cooperation Domestic Orgs-CSTP	Pearson Correlation	0.3031	0.4205	0.1730	0.7309	0.8367	0.7652	1.0000	0.7454	0.5839	0.5336
	Sig. (2-tailed)	0.0768	0.0119	0.3203	0.0000	0.0000	0.0000	.	0.0000	0.0003	0.0010
	N	35.0000	35.0000	35.0000	33.0000	35.0000	35.0000	35.0000	35.0000	34.0000	35.0000
Level Cooperation Domestic Orgs-TRIPS	Pearson Correlation	0.2621	0.2136	0.3145	0.8610	0.7218	0.8388	0.7454	1.0000	0.6301	0.5652
	Sig. (2-tailed)	0.1282	0.2180	0.0657	0.0000	0.0000	0.0000	0.0000	.	0.0001	0.0004
	N	35.0000	35.0000	35.0000	33.0000	35.0000	35.0000	35.0000	35.0000	34.0000	35.0000
sqrtQIIID2a	Pearson Correlation	0.1217	0.1578	0.1320	0.6773	0.5215	0.5921	0.5839	0.6301	1.0000	0.6279
	Sig. (2-tailed)	0.4862	0.3651	0.4499	0.0000	0.0016	0.0002	0.0003	0.0001	.	0.0001
	N	35.0000	35.0000	35.0000	33.0000	34.0000	34.0000	34.0000	34.0000	35.0000	35.0000
Level Cooperation International Orgs-CNDPS	Pearson Correlation	0.3611	0.3697	0.2666	0.4875	0.7429	0.5740	0.5336	0.5652	0.6279	1.0000
	Sig. (2-tailed)	0.0305	0.0265	0.1159	0.0040	0.0000	0.0003	0.0010	0.0004	0.0001	.
	N	36.0000	36.0000	36.0000	33.0000	35.0000	35.0000	35.0000	35.0000	35.0000	36.0000
Level Cooperation International Orgs-CNBC	Pearson Correlation	0.3753	0.3133	0.2476	0.5190	0.7025	0.6777	0.5202	0.5840	0.6703	0.9533
	Sig. (2-tailed)	0.0241	0.0628	0.1454	0.0020	0.0000	0.0000	0.0014	0.0002	0.0000	0.0000
	N	36.0000	36.0000	36.0000	33.0000	35.0000	35.0000	35.0000	35.0000	35.0000	36.0000
Level Cooperation International Orgs-CSTP	Pearson Correlation	0.4306	0.4785	0.3484	0.5302	0.7276	0.6264	0.6078	0.5612	0.6914	0.8766
	Sig. (2-tailed)	0.0087	0.0032	0.0373	0.0015	0.0000	0.0001	0.0001	0.0005	0.0000	0.0000
	N	36.0000	36.0000	36.0000	33.0000	35.0000	35.0000	35.0000	35.0000	35.0000	36.0000
sqrtQIIID2e	Pearson Correlation	0.3836	0.2707	0.3784	0.5762	0.5567	0.6783	0.4824	0.6977	0.7477	0.8155
	Sig. (2-tailed)	0.0209	0.1102	0.0229	0.0004	0.0005	0.0000	0.0033	0.0000	0.0000	0.0000
	N	36.0000	36.0000	36.0000	33.0000	35.0000	35.0000	35.0000	35.0000	35.0000	36.0000
sqrtQIVA1	Pearson Correlation	0.2397	0.0857	0.0085	0.0581	0.0086	-0.0119	-0.0012	0.0231	0.1966	0.1894
	Sig. (2-tailed)	0.1591	0.6190	0.9607	0.7480	0.9607	0.9460	0.9943	0.8954	0.2577	0.2685
	N	36.0000	36.0000	36.0000	33.0000	35.0000	35.0000	35.0000	35.0000	35.0000	36.0000
sqrtQIVA2	Pearson Correlation	0.2001	0.1293	0.1471	-0.0825	-0.1697	-0.1323	-0.1856	-0.1187	-0.0114	-0.0352
	Sig. (2-tailed)	0.2421	0.4522	0.3918	0.6479	0.3297	0.4488	0.2858	0.4972	0.9483	0.8386
	N	36.0000	36.0000	36.0000	33.0000	35.0000	35.0000	35.0000	35.0000	35.0000	36.0000
sqrtQIVA3	Pearson Correlation	0.3763	0.3482	0.2982	0.2669	0.0685	0.1054	0.0864	0.1817	0.2231	0.1060
	Sig. (2-tailed)	0.0259	0.0404	0.0819	0.1397	0.7003	0.5531	0.6269	0.3039	0.2047	0.5445
	N	35.0000	35.0000	35.0000	32.0000	34.0000	34.0000	34.0000	34.0000	34.0000	35.0000

Table A7, continued (Row 6, Col 7)

Correlation Matrix, International Variables (Parametric)		Level Cooperation International Orgs-CNBC	Level Cooperation International Orgs-CSTP	sqrtQIIID2e	sqrtQIVA1	sqrtQIVA2	sqrtQIVA3	sqrtQIVA5	sqrtQIVA7	sqrtQIVA8	Political Ideology
Level Cooperation Domestic Orgs-CNBC	Pearson Correlation	0.6777	0.6264	0.6783	-0.0119	-0.1323	0.1054	0.4469	-0.0358	-0.0303	0.1898
	Sig. (2-tailed)	0.0000	0.0001	0.0000	0.9460	0.4488	0.5531	0.0091	0.8381	0.8650	0.2901
	N	35.0000	35.0000	35.0000	35.0000	35.0000	34.0000	33.0000	35.0000	34.0000	33.0000
Level Cooperation Domestic Orgs-CSTP	Pearson Correlation	0.5202	0.6078	0.4824	-0.0012	-0.1856	0.0864	0.2712	0.0676	-0.0118	-0.0347
	Sig. (2-tailed)	0.0014	0.0001	0.0033	0.9943	0.2858	0.6269	0.1269	0.6997	0.9471	0.8479
	N	35.0000	35.0000	35.0000	35.0000	35.0000	34.0000	33.0000	35.0000	34.0000	33.0000
Level Cooperation Domestic Orgs-TRIPS	Pearson Correlation	0.5840	0.5612	0.6977	0.0231	-0.1187	0.1817	0.1971	-0.0335	-0.0056	0.2431
	Sig. (2-tailed)	0.0002	0.0005	0.0000	0.8954	0.4972	0.3039	0.2716	0.8485	0.9749	0.1728
	N	35.0000	35.0000	35.0000	35.0000	35.0000	34.0000	33.0000	35.0000	34.0000	33.0000
sqrtQIIID2a	Pearson Correlation	0.6703	0.6914	0.7477	0.1966	-0.0114	0.2231	0.2822	-0.1921	-0.0879	0.3376
	Sig. (2-tailed)	0.0000	0.0000	0.0000	0.2577	0.9483	0.2047	0.1115	0.2689	0.6211	0.0588
	N	35.0000	35.0000	35.0000	35.0000	35.0000	34.0000	33.0000	35.0000	34.0000	32.0000
Level Cooperation International Orgs-CNDPS	Pearson Correlation	0.9533	0.8766	0.8155	0.1894	-0.0352	0.1060	0.3539	-0.2484	-0.1162	0.2327
	Sig. (2-tailed)	0.0000	0.0000	0.0000	0.2685	0.8386	0.5445	0.0400	0.1441	0.5061	0.1925
	N	36.0000	36.0000	36.0000	36.0000	36.0000	35.0000	34.0000	36.0000	35.0000	33.0000
Level Cooperation International Orgs-CNBC	Pearson Correlation	1.0000	0.8595	0.8809	0.1438	-0.0574	0.0931	0.3854	-0.2283	-0.1323	0.2434
	Sig. (2-tailed)	.	0.0000	0.0000	0.4026	0.7393	0.5947	0.0244	0.1805	0.4485	0.1723
	N	36.0000	36.0000	36.0000	36.0000	36.0000	35.0000	34.0000	36.0000	35.0000	33.0000
Level Cooperation International Orgs-CSTP	Pearson Correlation	0.8595	1.0000	0.8018	0.1731	-0.0246	0.2020	0.2961	-0.2587	-0.1031	0.2934
	Sig. (2-tailed)	0.0000	.	0.0000	0.3128	0.8869	0.2446	0.0890	0.1276	0.5554	0.0974
	N	36.0000	36.0000	36.0000	36.0000	36.0000	35.0000	34.0000	36.0000	35.0000	33.0000
sqrtQIIID2e	Pearson Correlation	0.8809	0.8018	1.0000	0.2164	0.0058	0.2163	0.2794	-0.1450	-0.0616	0.3916
	Sig. (2-tailed)	0.0000	0.0000	.	0.2050	0.9734	0.2120	0.1096	0.3986	0.7254	0.0242
	N	36.0000	36.0000	36.0000	36.0000	36.0000	35.0000	34.0000	36.0000	35.0000	33.0000
sqrtQIVA1	Pearson Correlation	0.1438	0.1731	0.2164	1.0000	0.5700	0.6709	0.0655	0.0921	0.0066	0.4036
	Sig. (2-tailed)	0.4026	0.3128	0.2050	.	0.0003	0.0000	0.7130	0.5932	0.9698	0.0198
	N	36.0000	36.0000	36.0000	36.0000	36.0000	35.0000	34.0000	36.0000	35.0000	33.0000
sqrtQIVA2	Pearson Correlation	-0.0574	-0.0246	0.0058	0.5700	1.0000	0.5323	-0.0997	-0.0019	-0.0312	0.3057
	Sig. (2-tailed)	0.7393	0.8869	0.9734	0.0003	.	0.0010	0.5748	0.9913	0.8587	0.0836
	N	36.0000	36.0000	36.0000	36.0000	36.0000	35.0000	34.0000	36.0000	35.0000	33.0000
sqrtQIVA3	Pearson Correlation	0.0931	0.2020	0.2163	0.6709	0.5323	1.0000	0.0292	-0.1935	0.0019	0.2858
	Sig. (2-tailed)	0.5947	0.2446	0.2120	0.0000	0.0010	.	0.8717	0.2654	0.9917	0.1128
	N	35.0000	35.0000	35.0000	35.0000	35.0000	35.0000	33.0000	35.0000	34.0000	32.0000

Correlation Matrix, International Variables (Parametric)		sqrtQIIIB1a	sqrtQIIIB1b	sqrtQIIIB1c	sqrtQIIIB1d	sqrtQIIIB1e	sqrtQIIIB2a	Perceived Effectiveness Domestic Govt Support-CNDPS	Perceived Effectiveness Domestic Govt Support-CNBC	Perceived Effectiveness Domestic Govt Support-CSTP	Perceived Effectiveness Domestic Govt Support-TRIPS
Level Cooperation Domestic Orgs-CNBC	Pearson Correlation	0.2587	0.4481	0.3594	0.5053	0.1435	0.3704	0.2959	0.4183	0.3540	0.2732
	Sig. (2-tailed)	0.1396	0.0079	0.0369	0.0023	0.4182	0.0311	0.0844	0.0138	0.0400	0.1180
	N	34.0000	34.0000	34.0000	34.0000	34.0000	34.0000	35.0000	34.0000	34.0000	34.0000
Level Cooperation Domestic Orgs-CSTP	Pearson Correlation	0.1978	0.2144	0.2962	0.2311	0.0865	0.2711	0.1921	0.3409	0.3637	0.0294
	Sig. (2-tailed)	0.2621	0.2234	0.0889	0.1885	0.6265	0.1209	0.2688	0.0485	0.0345	0.8689
	N	34.0000	34.0000	34.0000	34.0000	34.0000	34.0000	35.0000	34.0000	34.0000	34.0000
Level Cooperation Domestic Orgs-TRIPS	Pearson Correlation	0.2126	0.3788	0.2614	0.4608	0.2805	0.2119	0.1305	0.2503	0.2974	0.2889
	Sig. (2-tailed)	0.2273	0.0272	0.1353	0.0061	0.1081	0.2289	0.4549	0.1533	0.0876	0.0976
	N	34.0000	34.0000	34.0000	34.0000	34.0000	34.0000	35.0000	34.0000	34.0000	34.0000
sqrtQIIID2a	Pearson Correlation	0.4195	0.3876	0.3475	0.3129	0.2167	0.5197	0.1652	0.3219	0.3378	0.2198
	Sig. (2-tailed)	0.0135	0.0235	0.0440	0.0716	0.2182	0.0016	0.3429	0.0634	0.0507	0.2118
	N	34.0000	34.0000	34.0000	34.0000	34.0000	34.0000	35.0000	34.0000	34.0000	34.0000
Level Cooperation International Orgs-CNDPS	Pearson Correlation	0.1624	0.4505	0.4534	0.2656	0.2185	0.2670	0.5128	0.5663	0.4353	0.3588
	Sig. (2-tailed)	0.3512	0.0066	0.0062	0.1231	0.2074	0.1210	0.0014	0.0004	0.0090	0.0343
	N	35.0000	35.0000	35.0000	35.0000	35.0000	35.0000	36.0000	35.0000	35.0000	35.0000
Level Cooperation International Orgs-CNBC	Pearson Correlation	0.1984	0.4780	0.4594	0.3022	0.1824	0.3083	0.4738	0.5873	0.4240	0.3588
	Sig. (2-tailed)	0.2532	0.0037	0.0055	0.0777	0.2943	0.0715	0.0035	0.0002	0.0111	0.0343
	N	35.0000	35.0000	35.0000	35.0000	35.0000	35.0000	36.0000	35.0000	35.0000	35.0000
Level Cooperation International Orgs-CSTP	Pearson Correlation	0.3855	0.5216	0.5874	0.4195	0.3356	0.4554	0.4903	0.5798	0.5840	0.3442
	Sig. (2-tailed)	0.0222	0.0013	0.0002	0.0121	0.0488	0.0060	0.0024	0.0003	0.0002	0.0429
	N	35.0000	35.0000	35.0000	35.0000	35.0000	35.0000	36.0000	35.0000	35.0000	35.0000
sqrtQIIID2e	Pearson Correlation	0.2763	0.5079	0.4070	0.4028	0.2909	0.2723	0.2993	0.3613	0.3289	0.4039
	Sig. (2-tailed)	0.1081	0.0018	0.0153	0.0164	0.0900	0.1136	0.0762	0.0329	0.0537	0.0161
	N	35.0000	35.0000	35.0000	35.0000	35.0000	35.0000	36.0000	35.0000	35.0000	35.0000
sqrtQIVA1	Pearson Correlation	0.1782	0.2722	0.2774	0.0196	0.1426	0.0926	0.1125	0.0462	0.0332	0.0644
	Sig. (2-tailed)	0.3058	0.1136	0.1067	0.9112	0.4137	0.5967	0.5135	0.7923	0.8498	0.7133
	N	35.0000	35.0000	35.0000	35.0000	35.0000	35.0000	36.0000	35.0000	35.0000	35.0000
sqrtQIVA2	Pearson Correlation	0.0242	0.0745	0.0593	-0.0905	0.0608	-0.0717	-0.0722	-0.1269	-0.1260	-0.0295
	Sig. (2-tailed)	0.8901	0.6705	0.7351	0.6052	0.7286	0.6824	0.6756	0.4676	0.4709	0.8662
	N	35.0000	35.0000	35.0000	35.0000	35.0000	35.0000	36.0000	35.0000	35.0000	35.0000
sqrtQIVA3	Pearson Correlation	0.1562	0.2499	0.1811	0.1192	0.1856	0.0613	0.0622	0.0050	0.0971	0.0772
	Sig. (2-tailed)	0.3777	0.1540	0.3054	0.5018	0.2933	0.7305	0.7226	0.9778	0.5847	0.6644
	N	34.0000	34.0000	34.0000	34.0000	34.0000	34.0000	35.0000	34.0000	34.0000	34.0000

Correlation Matrix, International Variables (Parametric)		sqrtQIIIC1a	sqrtQIIIC1b	sqrtQIIIC1c	sqrtQIIIC1d	sqrtQIIIC1e
Level Cooperation Domestic Orgs-CNBC	Pearson Correlation	0.2254	0.5154	0.4894	0.4695	0.4147
	Sig. (2-tailed)	0.2000	0.0015	0.0033	0.0051	0.0148
	N	34.0000	35.0000	34.0000	34.0000	34.0000
Level Cooperation Domestic Orgs-CSTP	Pearson Correlation	0.2957	0.4105	0.4361	0.3984	0.3734
	Sig. (2-tailed)	0.0895	0.0143	0.0099	0.0196	0.0296
	N	34.0000	35.0000	34.0000	34.0000	34.0000
Level Cooperation Domestic Orgs-TRIPS	Pearson Correlation	0.2565	0.4502	0.3524	0.4778	0.5183
	Sig. (2-tailed)	0.1431	0.0067	0.0409	0.0043	0.0017
	N	34.0000	35.0000	34.0000	34.0000	34.0000
sqrtQIIID2a	Pearson Correlation	0.4155	0.5007	0.5383	0.5214	0.4913
	Sig. (2-tailed)	0.0162	0.0026	0.0012	0.0019	0.0037
	N	33.0000	34.0000	33.0000	33.0000	33.0000
Level Cooperation International Orgs-CNDPS	Pearson Correlation	0.0632	0.4565	0.4485	0.2979	0.3037
	Sig. (2-tailed)	0.7226	0.0058	0.0078	0.0870	0.0808
	N	34.0000	35.0000	34.0000	34.0000	34.0000
Level Cooperation International Orgs-CNBC	Pearson Correlation	0.0656	0.4414	0.4658	0.2980	0.2853
	Sig. (2-tailed)	0.7123	0.0079	0.0055	0.0870	0.1020
	N	34.0000	35.0000	34.0000	34.0000	34.0000
Level Cooperation International Orgs-CSTP	Pearson Correlation	0.2914	0.4868	0.5196	0.4211	0.3893
	Sig. (2-tailed)	0.0945	0.0030	0.0016	0.0131	0.0229
	N	34.0000	35.0000	34.0000	34.0000	34.0000
sqrtQIIID2e	Pearson Correlation	0.1783	0.4431	0.3962	0.4276	0.4373
	Sig. (2-tailed)	0.3131	0.0077	0.0204	0.0117	0.0097
	N	34.0000	35.0000	34.0000	34.0000	34.0000
sqrtQIVA1	Pearson Correlation	0.2992	0.2639	0.1990	0.2562	0.2434
	Sig. (2-tailed)	0.0856	0.1255	0.2591	0.1436	0.1654
	N	34.0000	35.0000	34.0000	34.0000	34.0000
sqrtQIVA2	Pearson Correlation	0.1420	0.0879	0.0462	0.1140	0.1050
	Sig. (2-tailed)	0.4232	0.6155	0.7953	0.5209	0.5547
	N	34.0000	35.0000	34.0000	34.0000	34.0000
sqrtQIVA3	Pearson Correlation	0.3380	0.2481	0.1772	0.2924	0.3016
	Sig. (2-tailed)	0.0544	0.1571	0.3238	0.0987	0.0880
	N	33.0000	34.0000	33.0000	33.0000	33.0000

Table A7, continued (Row 7, Col 1)

Correlation Matrix, International Variables (Parametric)		Importance of Smuggling-Endangered Species	reflectsqrtQ1A1b	reflectsqrtQ1A1c	reflectsqrtQ1A1d	reflectsqrtQ1A1e	sqrtQ1B1a	Knowledge of Smuggling-Narcotics	Knowledge of Smuggling-Weapons	Knowledge of Smuggling-Humans	Knowledge of Smuggling-Contraband
sqrtQIVA5	Pearson Correlation	-0.1126	-0.3136	-0.1166	-0.0908	-0.1674	0.1451	0.1769	0.2895	0.1668	0.0464
	Sig. (2-tailed)	0.5259	0.0709	0.5114	0.6095	0.3440	0.4129	0.3169	0.0968	0.3458	0.7946
	N	34.0000	34.0000	34.0000	34.0000	34.0000	34.0000	34.0000	34.0000	34.0000	34.0000
sqrtQIVA7	Pearson Correlation	-0.0287	-0.0640	0.0205	-0.2604	-0.1845	-0.1589	-0.1265	-0.0129	-0.2391	0.0134
	Sig. (2-tailed)	0.8680	0.7108	0.9057	0.1250	0.2813	0.3545	0.4621	0.9406	0.1602	0.9384
	N	36.0000	36.0000	36.0000	36.0000	36.0000	36.0000	36.0000	36.0000	36.0000	36.0000
sqrtQIVA8	Pearson Correlation	-0.0400	0.1170	0.1854	0.1977	-0.0653	0.0121	0.0783	0.0283	0.1825	0.2487
	Sig. (2-tailed)	0.8195	0.5031	0.2864	0.2548	0.7093	0.9450	0.6548	0.8720	0.2939	0.1497
	N	35.0000	35.0000	35.0000	35.0000	35.0000	35.0000	35.0000	35.0000	35.0000	35.0000
Political Ideology	Pearson Correlation	-0.1693	0.3071	0.2647	0.1013	0.0011	0.1583	0.0522	0.3089	0.0541	0.2656
	Sig. (2-tailed)	0.3464	0.0821	0.1366	0.5750	0.9951	0.3789	0.7729	0.0802	0.7649	0.1352
	N	33.0000	33.0000	33.0000	33.0000	33.0000	33.0000	33.0000	33.0000	33.0000	33.0000
sqrtQIIIB1a	Pearson Correlation	-0.0064	-0.0953	-0.2405	0.0748	-0.1673	0.0681	-0.1725	-0.0706	0.1040	0.0096
	Sig. (2-tailed)	0.9707	0.5861	0.1640	0.6693	0.3368	0.6975	0.3218	0.6870	0.5521	0.9563
	N	35.0000	35.0000	35.0000	35.0000	35.0000	35.0000	35.0000	35.0000	35.0000	35.0000
sqrtQIIIB1b	Pearson Correlation	-0.2026	-0.0939	-0.0183	0.0756	-0.1348	-0.0359	0.0272	0.2148	0.1398	0.0816
	Sig. (2-tailed)	0.2431	0.5916	0.9171	0.6662	0.4401	0.8376	0.8767	0.2153	0.4231	0.6412
	N	35.0000	35.0000	35.0000	35.0000	35.0000	35.0000	35.0000	35.0000	35.0000	35.0000
sqrtQIIIB1c	Pearson Correlation	-0.1399	-0.1566	-0.1390	0.0127	-0.1235	0.0250	0.1208	0.1422	0.2626	0.0814
	Sig. (2-tailed)	0.4228	0.3690	0.4259	0.9425	0.4797	0.8865	0.4893	0.4153	0.1275	0.6421
	N	35.0000	35.0000	35.0000	35.0000	35.0000	35.0000	35.0000	35.0000	35.0000	35.0000
sqrtQIIIB1d	Pearson Correlation	-0.1844	0.1203	0.0633	0.3355	-0.1088	0.0906	0.1077	0.4559	0.1624	0.4283
	Sig. (2-tailed)	0.2889	0.4913	0.7179	0.0488	0.5340	0.6047	0.5380	0.0059	0.3514	0.0103
	N	35.0000	35.0000	35.0000	35.0000	35.0000	35.0000	35.0000	35.0000	35.0000	35.0000
sqrtQIIIB1e	Pearson Correlation	-0.1375	0.2347	0.0805	0.0279	-0.0004	-0.0557	-0.1535	-0.1759	0.1760	0.1273
	Sig. (2-tailed)	0.4309	0.1747	0.6458	0.8734	0.9980	0.7504	0.3787	0.3121	0.3119	0.4662
	N	35.0000	35.0000	35.0000	35.0000	35.0000	35.0000	35.0000	35.0000	35.0000	35.0000
sqrtQIIIB2a	Pearson Correlation	0.0635	-0.0980	-0.2608	-0.0043	0.0880	0.1703	-0.0971	-0.1032	0.0728	-0.1897
	Sig. (2-tailed)	0.7170	0.5752	0.1302	0.9806	0.6151	0.3279	0.5789	0.5551	0.6776	0.2749
	N	35.0000	35.0000	35.0000	35.0000	35.0000	35.0000	35.0000	35.0000	35.0000	35.0000
Perceived Effectiveness Domestic Govt Support-CNDPS	Pearson Correlation	-0.1400	-0.2238	-0.1688	-0.0924	-0.0269	-0.1663	0.1388	0.0372	0.1104	-0.1968
	Sig. (2-tailed)	0.4155	0.1895	0.3251	0.5921	0.8762	0.3324	0.4195	0.8294	0.5215	0.2501
	N	36.0000	36.0000	36.0000	36.0000	36.0000	36.0000	36.0000	36.0000	36.0000	36.0000

Table A7, continued (Row 7, Col 2)

Correlation Matrix, International Variables (Parametric)		sqrtQ1E1a	Personal Resource Challenges-Lack of Time	Personal Resource Challenges-Lack of Knowledge	Personal Resource Challenges-Lack of Training	sqrtQ1E1e	Personal Resource Challenges-Excessive Admin Paperwork	Personal Resource Challenges-Ineffective Technology	Personal Resource Challenges-Ineffective Strategic Focus	Personal Resource Challenges-Ineffective Tactical Policy	Personal Resource Challenges-Lack of Clarity in Duties
sqrtQIVA5	Pearson Correlation	-0.0613	-0.3000	-0.2011	-0.2275	0.0274	0.0237	-0.3674	-0.0811	-0.1987	-0.2636
	Sig. (2-tailed)	0.7347	0.0847	0.2541	0.1957	0.8780	0.8939	0.0325	0.6486	0.2599	0.1320
	N	33.0000	34.0000	34.0000	34.0000	34.0000	34.0000	34.0000	34.0000	34.0000	34.0000
sqrtQIVA7	Pearson Correlation	-0.0508	-0.0716	-0.0987	-0.0693	-0.0159	-0.0877	-0.0528	0.0901	-0.0004	0.1326
	Sig. (2-tailed)	0.7719	0.6782	0.5670	0.6881	0.9268	0.6111	0.7597	0.6014	0.9983	0.4406
	N	35.0000	36.0000	36.0000	36.0000	36.0000	36.0000	36.0000	36.0000	36.0000	36.0000
sqrtQIVA8	Pearson Correlation	-0.1871	0.2606	-0.0474	-0.0792	-0.1426	0.0388	-0.1169	-0.2959	-0.2056	-0.1085
	Sig. (2-tailed)	0.2894	0.1305	0.7868	0.6510	0.4139	0.8251	0.5037	0.0843	0.2361	0.5350
	N	34.0000	35.0000	35.0000	35.0000	35.0000	35.0000	35.0000	35.0000	35.0000	35.0000
Political Ideology	Pearson Correlation	-0.1008	0.1789	0.1173	0.1329	0.1533	0.2197	0.1397	0.0123	0.1382	0.0998
	Sig. (2-tailed)	0.5767	0.3193	0.5155	0.4610	0.3945	0.2192	0.4381	0.9460	0.4431	0.5805
	N	33.0000	33.0000	33.0000	33.0000	33.0000	33.0000	33.0000	33.0000	33.0000	33.0000
sqrtQIIIB1a	Pearson Correlation	-0.2349	-0.0956	0.2034	0.3054	-0.0309	-0.0115	-0.1319	0.0853	-0.0370	-0.0098
	Sig. (2-tailed)	0.1811	0.5850	0.2413	0.0744	0.8601	0.9479	0.4501	0.6263	0.8328	0.9555
	N	34.0000	35.0000	35.0000	35.0000	35.0000	35.0000	35.0000	35.0000	35.0000	35.0000
sqrtQIIIB1b	Pearson Correlation	-0.2137	-0.2154	-0.0827	0.0084	-0.1206	0.0496	-0.2363	-0.1917	-0.1551	-0.2370
	Sig. (2-tailed)	0.2249	0.2139	0.6366	0.9619	0.4903	0.7772	0.1717	0.2700	0.3737	0.1704
	N	34.0000	35.0000	35.0000	35.0000	35.0000	35.0000	35.0000	35.0000	35.0000	35.0000
sqrtQIIIB1c	Pearson Correlation	-0.2595	-0.1101	0.0931	0.1671	-0.0900	-0.0073	-0.1399	-0.1101	-0.1324	-0.1041
	Sig. (2-tailed)	0.1384	0.5290	0.5948	0.3372	0.6072	0.9670	0.4228	0.5288	0.4485	0.5517
	N	34.0000	35.0000	35.0000	35.0000	35.0000	35.0000	35.0000	35.0000	35.0000	35.0000
sqrtQIIIB1d	Pearson Correlation	-0.2588	-0.0530	-0.2529	-0.2368	-0.0121	0.0842	-0.4103	-0.3056	-0.2738	-0.2881
	Sig. (2-tailed)	0.1394	0.7623	0.1427	0.1708	0.9450	0.6304	0.0144	0.0742	0.1115	0.0933
	N	34.0000	35.0000	35.0000	35.0000	35.0000	35.0000	35.0000	35.0000	35.0000	35.0000
sqrtQIIIB1e	Pearson Correlation	-0.1575	-0.1510	0.0737	0.1633	-0.1018	0.0038	-0.1608	-0.0425	-0.0525	-0.0701
	Sig. (2-tailed)	0.3737	0.3866	0.6740	0.3486	0.5608	0.9825	0.3560	0.8085	0.7643	0.6892
	N	34.0000	35.0000	35.0000	35.0000	35.0000	35.0000	35.0000	35.0000	35.0000	35.0000
sqrtQIIIB2a	Pearson Correlation	-0.2875	0.0062	0.1504	0.2613	0.0297	-0.0745	-0.2308	0.0858	-0.0236	0.0245
	Sig. (2-tailed)	0.0993	0.9719	0.3884	0.1295	0.8654	0.6707	0.1823	0.6243	0.8931	0.8887
	N	34.0000	35.0000	35.0000	35.0000	35.0000	35.0000	35.0000	35.0000	35.0000	35.0000
Perceived Effectiveness Domestic Govt Support-CNDPS	Pearson Correlation	-0.1912	-0.0700	-0.1352	-0.0590	-0.2124	-0.1055	-0.2806	-0.2536	-0.1759	-0.2140
	Sig. (2-tailed)	0.2712	0.6849	0.4316	0.7324	0.2137	0.5403	0.0974	0.1356	0.3047	0.2102
	N	35.0000	36.0000	36.0000	36.0000	36.0000	36.0000	36.0000	36.0000	36.0000	36.0000

Table A7, continued (Row 7, Col 3)

Correlation Matrix, International Variables (Parametric)		Personal Resource Challenges-Conflict or Lack Comm Leaders and Employees	sqrtQ1E1I	Personal Resource Challenges-Conflict or Lack Comm International Orgs	Personal Resource Challenges-Conflict or Lack Comm Domestic Orgs	sqrtQ1E3a	Org Resource Challenges-Lack of Time	Org Resource Challenges-Lack of Knowledge	Org Resource Challenges-Lack of Training	sqrtQ1E3e	Org Resource Challenges-Excessive Admin Paperwork
sqrtQIVA5	Pearson Correlation	-0.2154	0.0993	-0.0521	-0.1372	0.0015	0.0635	-0.1624	-0.2116	-0.1671	-0.0822
	Sig. (2-tailed)	0.2212	0.5762	0.7700	0.4391	0.9932	0.7212	0.3588	0.2296	0.3526	0.6440
	N	34.0000	34.0000	34.0000	34.0000	33.0000	34.0000	34.0000	34.0000	33.0000	34.0000
sqrtQIVA7	Pearson Correlation	0.1726	0.1235	-0.0101	0.0575	-0.0107	-0.0614	0.0765	0.0666	-0.0981	-0.0328
	Sig. (2-tailed)	0.3140	0.4729	0.9535	0.7392	0.9523	0.7262	0.6621	0.7036	0.5811	0.8516
	N	36.0000	36.0000	36.0000	36.0000	34.0000	35.0000	35.0000	35.0000	34.0000	35.0000
sqrtQIVA8	Pearson Correlation	-0.2587	-0.2521	0.0640	-0.1378	-0.1731	0.2567	-0.0302	-0.0590	-0.0177	-0.2230
	Sig. (2-tailed)	0.1335	0.1440	0.7150	0.4300	0.3277	0.1366	0.8634	0.7364	0.9211	0.1979
	N	35.0000	35.0000	35.0000	35.0000	34.0000	35.0000	35.0000	35.0000	34.0000	35.0000
Political Ideology	Pearson Correlation	0.0549	-0.0632	0.0389	0.0614	0.0560	-0.0784	-0.1021	-0.0800	0.1183	-0.0690
	Sig. (2-tailed)	0.7615	0.7268	0.8299	0.7343	0.7609	0.6644	0.5717	0.6581	0.5189	0.7030
	N	33.0000	33.0000	33.0000	33.0000	32.0000	33.0000	33.0000	33.0000	32.0000	33.0000
sqrtQIIIB1a	Pearson Correlation	-0.1040	0.0079	0.0969	-0.0293	-0.2950	-0.3238	0.2335	0.1683	-0.2437	-0.2578
	Sig. (2-tailed)	0.5520	0.9641	0.5796	0.8671	0.0903	0.0617	0.1838	0.3413	0.1717	0.1410
	N	35.0000	35.0000	35.0000	35.0000	34.0000	34.0000	34.0000	34.0000	33.0000	34.0000
sqrtQIIIB1b	Pearson Correlation	-0.2256	-0.1511	-0.0059	-0.1643	-0.2137	-0.3496	-0.0496	-0.1123	-0.2697	-0.2462
	Sig. (2-tailed)	0.1925	0.3864	0.9731	0.3457	0.2249	0.0427	0.7807	0.5272	0.1291	0.1604
	N	35.0000	35.0000	35.0000	35.0000	34.0000	34.0000	34.0000	34.0000	33.0000	34.0000
sqrtQIIIB1c	Pearson Correlation	-0.1972	-0.2570	0.1059	-0.0594	-0.1631	-0.2681	0.1261	0.0400	-0.3545	-0.2551
	Sig. (2-tailed)	0.2561	0.1362	0.5449	0.7348	0.3568	0.1253	0.4773	0.8221	0.0429	0.1454
	N	35.0000	35.0000	35.0000	35.0000	34.0000	34.0000	34.0000	34.0000	33.0000	34.0000
sqrtQIIIB1d	Pearson Correlation	-0.2288	-0.0268	-0.0239	-0.1830	-0.3862	-0.4731	-0.3492	-0.3882	-0.2357	-0.3611
	Sig. (2-tailed)	0.1861	0.8784	0.8917	0.2927	0.0241	0.0047	0.0429	0.0233	0.1867	0.0359
	N	35.0000	35.0000	35.0000	35.0000	34.0000	34.0000	34.0000	34.0000	33.0000	34.0000
sqrtQIIIB1e	Pearson Correlation	-0.0133	-0.1266	0.1707	-0.0412	-0.4157	-0.4350	0.0666	-0.0282	-0.2222	-0.2810
	Sig. (2-tailed)	0.9397	0.4687	0.3268	0.8142	0.0145	0.0101	0.7081	0.8743	0.2140	0.1075
	N	35.0000	35.0000	35.0000	35.0000	34.0000	34.0000	34.0000	34.0000	33.0000	34.0000
sqrtQIIIB2a	Pearson Correlation	-0.0914	-0.1545	0.0143	0.0406	-0.0814	-0.2053	0.1962	0.1238	-0.1391	-0.1720
	Sig. (2-tailed)	0.6015	0.3755	0.9352	0.8167	0.6472	0.2442	0.2661	0.4854	0.4400	0.3306
	N	35.0000	35.0000	35.0000	35.0000	34.0000	34.0000	34.0000	34.0000	33.0000	34.0000
Perceived Effectiveness Domestic Govt Support-CNDPS	Pearson Correlation	-0.2336	-0.3019	-0.0332	-0.0816	0.0519	-0.0762	-0.0103	-0.0907	-0.1881	-0.0829
	Sig. (2-tailed)	0.1703	0.0735	0.8475	0.6362	0.7708	0.6635	0.9530	0.6045	0.2867	0.6359
	N	36.0000	36.0000	36.0000	36.0000	34.0000	35.0000	35.0000	35.0000	34.0000	35.0000

Table A7, continued (Row 7, Col 4)

Correlation Matrix, International Variables (Parametric)		Org Resource Challenges-Ineffective Technology	Org Resource Challenges-Ineffective Strategic Focus	Org Resource Challenges-Ineffective Tactical Policy	Org Resource Challenges-Lack of Clarity in Duties	Org Resource Challenges-Conflict or Lack Comm Leaders and Employees	sqrtQ1E3l	Org Resource Challenges-Conflict or Lack Comm International Orgs	Org Resource Challenges-Conflict or Lack Comm Domestic Orgs	sqrtQIIA1a	Knowledge of Domestic Law-CSIE
sqrtQIVA5	Pearson Correlation	-0.1445	-0.1517	-0.0647	-0.0922	-0.1561	0.1102	0.1253	0.0593	-0.0193	0.2925
	Sig. (2-tailed)	0.4148	0.3919	0.7163	0.6041	0.3780	0.5349	0.4803	0.7389	0.9150	0.0986
	N	34.0000	34.0000	34.0000	34.0000	34.0000	34.0000	34.0000	34.0000	33.0000	33.0000
sqrtQIVA7	Pearson Correlation	-0.0430	0.0874	0.0278	-0.0212	0.0376	0.1971	-0.2223	-0.0972	0.1354	-0.1068
	Sig. (2-tailed)	0.8064	0.6176	0.8740	0.9037	0.8300	0.2565	0.1992	0.5786	0.4381	0.5414
	N	35.0000	35.0000	35.0000	35.0000	35.0000	35.0000	35.0000	35.0000	35.0000	35.0000
sqrtQIVA8	Pearson Correlation	-0.2447	-0.2093	-0.2141	-0.2333	-0.2012	-0.1516	-0.0648	-0.2430	-0.1746	0.0432
	Sig. (2-tailed)	0.1566	0.2276	0.2168	0.1774	0.2465	0.3845	0.7114	0.1595	0.3233	0.8083
	N	35.0000	35.0000	35.0000	35.0000	35.0000	35.0000	35.0000	35.0000	34.0000	34.0000
Political Ideology	Pearson Correlation	-0.0409	-0.0088	-0.0584	0.0609	0.0000	-0.0489	0.0373	0.0842	0.2663	0.0819
	Sig. (2-tailed)	0.8211	0.9611	0.7470	0.7362	1.0000	0.7870	0.8365	0.6414	0.1406	0.6557
	N	33.0000	33.0000	33.0000	33.0000	33.0000	33.0000	33.0000	33.0000	32.0000	32.0000
sqrtQIIIB1a	Pearson Correlation	-0.0493	0.1769	0.0713	0.3327	0.0754	0.0932	0.2832	0.3080	0.0247	-0.1568
	Sig. (2-tailed)	0.7819	0.3169	0.6887	0.0545	0.6715	0.6002	0.1045	0.0763	0.8897	0.3758
	N	34.0000	34.0000	34.0000	34.0000	34.0000	34.0000	34.0000	34.0000	34.0000	34.0000
sqrtQIIIB1b	Pearson Correlation	-0.1009	-0.0510	-0.0928	0.0813	0.0064	-0.1091	0.1308	0.1546	-0.0648	0.1600
	Sig. (2-tailed)	0.5704	0.7747	0.6016	0.6477	0.9713	0.5389	0.4611	0.3825	0.7158	0.3661
	N	34.0000	34.0000	34.0000	34.0000	34.0000	34.0000	34.0000	34.0000	34.0000	34.0000
sqrtQIIIB1c	Pearson Correlation	-0.0495	0.0676	0.0108	0.1920	0.0358	-0.1849	0.2590	0.2420	-0.0003	0.1399
	Sig. (2-tailed)	0.7811	0.7040	0.9517	0.2767	0.8409	0.2951	0.1391	0.1679	0.9985	0.4301
	N	34.0000	34.0000	34.0000	34.0000	34.0000	34.0000	34.0000	34.0000	34.0000	34.0000
sqrtQIIIB1d	Pearson Correlation	-0.3719	-0.3289	-0.2646	-0.2197	-0.0850	-0.0527	-0.2290	-0.1671	0.2744	0.1966
	Sig. (2-tailed)	0.0303	0.0575	0.1305	0.2118	0.6326	0.7673	0.1926	0.3448	0.1163	0.2651
	N	34.0000	34.0000	34.0000	34.0000	34.0000	34.0000	34.0000	34.0000	34.0000	34.0000
sqrtQIIIB1e	Pearson Correlation	-0.1349	0.0191	-0.0281	0.0979	0.0186	-0.1333	0.0608	0.0971	-0.0187	-0.1450
	Sig. (2-tailed)	0.4469	0.9148	0.8745	0.5819	0.9170	0.4523	0.7328	0.5848	0.9165	0.4132
	N	34.0000	34.0000	34.0000	34.0000	34.0000	34.0000	34.0000	34.0000	34.0000	34.0000
sqrtQIIIB2a	Pearson Correlation	-0.1102	0.1170	0.1517	0.3006	0.0223	-0.0406	0.3056	0.2810	0.0859	-0.2168
	Sig. (2-tailed)	0.5351	0.5100	0.3917	0.0841	0.9002	0.8198	0.0788	0.1074	0.6289	0.2182
	N	34.0000	34.0000	34.0000	34.0000	34.0000	34.0000	34.0000	34.0000	34.0000	34.0000
Perceived Effectiveness Domestic Govt Support-CNDPS	Pearson Correlation	-0.1216	-0.1063	-0.0316	0.0163	-0.0426	-0.2661	0.1232	0.0813	-0.1132	0.1569
	Sig. (2-tailed)	0.4865	0.5435	0.8570	0.9259	0.8079	0.1223	0.4807	0.6426	0.5175	0.3682
	N	35.0000	35.0000	35.0000	35.0000	35.0000	35.0000	35.0000	35.0000	35.0000	35.0000

Table A7, continued (Row 7, Col 5)

Correlation Matrix, International Variables (Parametric)		Knowledge of Domestic Law-DWMD	Knowledge of Domestic Law-TVP	Knowledge of Domestic Law-CBP	sqrtQIID1a	Level Cooperation Domestic Orgs-CSIE	Level Cooperation Domestic Orgs-DWMD	Level Cooperation Domestic Orgs-TVP	Level Cooperation Domestic Orgs-CBP	sqrtQIIIA1a	sqrtQIIIA1b
sqrtQIVA5	Pearson Correlation	0.2711	0.2011	0.0556	0.1165	0.3660	0.3984	0.3035	0.0006	-0.1075	-0.0871
	Sig. (2-tailed)	0.1271	0.2619	0.7588	0.5116	0.0333	0.0196	0.0810	0.9973	0.5515	0.6241
	N	33.0000	33.0000	33.0000	34.0000	34.0000	34.0000	34.0000	34.0000	33.0000	34.0000
sqrtQIVA7	Pearson Correlation	-0.0749	-0.0363	0.1172	-0.1753	-0.1921	-0.2136	-0.0707	-0.0284	-0.1239	-0.0378
	Sig. (2-tailed)	0.6689	0.8360	0.5026	0.3065	0.2618	0.2110	0.6818	0.8692	0.4782	0.8268
	N	35.0000	35.0000	35.0000	36.0000	36.0000	36.0000	36.0000	36.0000	35.0000	36.0000
sqrtQIVA8	Pearson Correlation	0.1244	0.3014	0.2077	0.0904	0.0446	0.0309	0.0867	0.0727	-0.1046	-0.0375
	Sig. (2-tailed)	0.4832	0.0832	0.2385	0.6055	0.7993	0.8601	0.6206	0.6780	0.5559	0.8308
	N	34.0000	34.0000	34.0000	35.0000	35.0000	35.0000	35.0000	35.0000	34.0000	35.0000
Political Ideology	Pearson Correlation	0.2899	0.0322	0.1375	0.4608	0.1078	0.1871	0.0611	0.3480	0.2577	0.0529
	Sig. (2-tailed)	0.1076	0.8611	0.4529	0.0070	0.5503	0.2972	0.7357	0.0472	0.1545	0.7698
	N	32.0000	32.0000	32.0000	33.0000	33.0000	33.0000	33.0000	33.0000	32.0000	33.0000
sqrtQIIIB1a	Pearson Correlation	-0.1206	-0.0057	-0.2156	0.1642	-0.1373	0.0172	0.0777	0.1536	0.1480	-0.2197
	Sig. (2-tailed)	0.4970	0.9743	0.2207	0.3458	0.4315	0.9221	0.6573	0.3784	0.4036	0.2047
	N	34.0000	34.0000	34.0000	35.0000	35.0000	35.0000	35.0000	35.0000	34.0000	35.0000
sqrtQIIIB1b	Pearson Correlation	0.2547	0.1065	0.0538	0.1981	0.1711	0.3376	0.1300	0.2426	0.0277	0.0289
	Sig. (2-tailed)	0.1461	0.5489	0.7625	0.2540	0.3258	0.0473	0.4566	0.1603	0.8765	0.8689
	N	34.0000	34.0000	34.0000	35.0000	35.0000	35.0000	35.0000	35.0000	34.0000	35.0000
sqrtQIIIB1c	Pearson Correlation	0.2321	0.2695	0.0025	0.0815	0.2136	0.2338	0.2622	0.1368	0.0397	0.0850
	Sig. (2-tailed)	0.1865	0.1232	0.9889	0.6415	0.2179	0.1764	0.1281	0.4334	0.8238	0.6274
	N	34.0000	34.0000	34.0000	35.0000	35.0000	35.0000	35.0000	35.0000	34.0000	35.0000
sqrtQIIIB1d	Pearson Correlation	0.3377	0.1316	0.3787	0.4622	0.2584	0.5121	0.2625	0.4177	0.1457	0.0740
	Sig. (2-tailed)	0.0508	0.4583	0.0272	0.0052	0.1339	0.0017	0.1276	0.0125	0.4111	0.6727
	N	34.0000	34.0000	34.0000	35.0000	35.0000	35.0000	35.0000	35.0000	34.0000	35.0000
sqrtQIIIB1e	Pearson Correlation	-0.0499	-0.0001	-0.0424	0.0588	-0.1565	0.0070	-0.0204	0.2302	-0.0020	0.0353
	Sig. (2-tailed)	0.7792	0.9997	0.8119	0.7372	0.3694	0.9684	0.9075	0.1834	0.9910	0.8407
	N	34.0000	34.0000	34.0000	35.0000	35.0000	35.0000	35.0000	35.0000	34.0000	35.0000
sqrtQIIIB2a	Pearson Correlation	-0.1875	-0.0108	-0.2641	0.2048	-0.0136	0.0614	0.1299	0.0198	0.1665	-0.2977
	Sig. (2-tailed)	0.2884	0.9518	0.1312	0.2379	0.9382	0.7259	0.4570	0.9103	0.3466	0.0824
	N	34.0000	34.0000	34.0000	35.0000	35.0000	35.0000	35.0000	35.0000	34.0000	35.0000
Perceived Effectiveness Domestic Govt Support-CNDPS	Pearson Correlation	0.2273	0.0865	-0.0420	-0.1007	0.2940	0.3304	0.1501	-0.0320	-0.0081	0.1148
	Sig. (2-tailed)	0.1890	0.6212	0.8105	0.5589	0.0817	0.0490	0.3824	0.8530	0.9631	0.5048
	N	35.0000	35.0000	35.0000	36.0000	36.0000	36.0000	36.0000	36.0000	35.0000	36.0000

Table A7, continued (Row 7, Col 6)

Correlation Matrix, International Variables (Parametric)		sqrtQIIIA1c	sqrtQIIIA1d	sqrtQIIIA1e	sqrtQIIID1a	Level Cooperation Domestic Orgs-CNDPS	Level Cooperation Domestic Orgs-CNBC	Level Cooperation Domestic Orgs-CSTP	Level Cooperation Domestic Orgs-TRIPS	sqrtQIIID2a	Level Cooperation International Orgs-CNDPS
sqrtQIVA5	Pearson Correlation	0.0113	-0.1313	-0.1273	0.2827	0.3836	0.4469	0.2712	0.1971	0.2822	0.3539
	Sig. (2-tailed)	0.9496	0.4593	0.4732	0.1233	0.0276	0.0091	0.1269	0.2716	0.1115	0.0400
	N	34.0000	34.0000	34.0000	31.0000	33.0000	33.0000	33.0000	33.0000	33.0000	34.0000
sqrtQIVA7	Pearson Correlation	-0.0143	-0.0541	-0.1297	-0.1366	-0.0858	-0.0358	0.0676	-0.0335	-0.1921	-0.2484
	Sig. (2-tailed)	0.9342	0.7538	0.4509	0.4485	0.6240	0.8381	0.6997	0.8485	0.2689	0.1441
	N	36.0000	36.0000	36.0000	33.0000	35.0000	35.0000	35.0000	35.0000	35.0000	36.0000
sqrtQIVA8	Pearson Correlation	-0.0063	-0.0047	0.0381	0.0378	-0.0429	-0.0303	-0.0118	-0.0056	-0.0879	-0.1162
	Sig. (2-tailed)	0.9714	0.9785	0.8280	0.8375	0.8094	0.8650	0.9471	0.9749	0.6211	0.5061
	N	35.0000	35.0000	35.0000	32.0000	34.0000	34.0000	34.0000	34.0000	34.0000	35.0000
Political Ideology	Pearson Correlation	0.2063	0.0506	0.2530	0.2165	0.0741	0.1898	-0.0347	0.2431	0.3376	0.2327
	Sig. (2-tailed)	0.2495	0.7798	0.1554	0.2420	0.6821	0.2901	0.8479	0.1728	0.0588	0.1925
	N	33.0000	33.0000	33.0000	31.0000	33.0000	33.0000	33.0000	33.0000	32.0000	33.0000
sqrtQIIIB1a	Pearson Correlation	-0.0906	0.0221	-0.1440	0.3557	0.1559	0.2587	0.1978	0.2126	0.4195	0.1624
	Sig. (2-tailed)	0.6045	0.8996	0.4093	0.0457	0.3787	0.1396	0.2621	0.2273	0.0135	0.3512
	N	35.0000	35.0000	35.0000	32.0000	34.0000	34.0000	34.0000	34.0000	34.0000	35.0000
sqrtQIIIB1b	Pearson Correlation	0.1552	0.1203	0.0930	0.3476	0.4002	0.4481	0.2144	0.3788	0.3876	0.4505
	Sig. (2-tailed)	0.3733	0.4911	0.5953	0.0513	0.0190	0.0079	0.2234	0.0272	0.0235	0.0066
	N	35.0000	35.0000	35.0000	32.0000	34.0000	34.0000	34.0000	34.0000	34.0000	35.0000
sqrtQIIIB1c	Pearson Correlation	0.1381	0.2295	0.0052	0.3254	0.4193	0.3594	0.2962	0.2614	0.3475	0.4534
	Sig. (2-tailed)	0.4288	0.1847	0.9763	0.0692	0.0136	0.0369	0.0889	0.1353	0.0440	0.0062
	N	35.0000	35.0000	35.0000	32.0000	34.0000	34.0000	34.0000	34.0000	34.0000	35.0000
sqrtQIIIB1d	Pearson Correlation	0.2132	0.1222	0.3129	0.3420	0.3435	0.5053	0.2311	0.4608	0.3129	0.2656
	Sig. (2-tailed)	0.2189	0.4845	0.0672	0.0554	0.0467	0.0023	0.1885	0.0061	0.0716	0.1231
	N	35.0000	35.0000	35.0000	32.0000	34.0000	34.0000	34.0000	34.0000	34.0000	35.0000
sqrtQIIIB1e	Pearson Correlation	-0.0432	0.1111	0.2043	0.2169	0.1338	0.1435	0.0865	0.2805	0.2167	0.2185
	Sig. (2-tailed)	0.8055	0.5253	0.2390	0.2332	0.4507	0.4182	0.6265	0.1081	0.2182	0.2074
	N	35.0000	35.0000	35.0000	32.0000	34.0000	34.0000	34.0000	34.0000	34.0000	35.0000
sqrtQIIIB2a	Pearson Correlation	-0.1840	-0.0513	-0.2656	0.4180	0.3119	0.3704	0.2711	0.2119	0.5197	0.2670
	Sig. (2-tailed)	0.2900	0.7697	0.1231	0.0173	0.0726	0.0311	0.1209	0.2289	0.0016	0.1210
	N	35.0000	35.0000	35.0000	32.0000	34.0000	34.0000	34.0000	34.0000	34.0000	35.0000
Perceived Effectiveness Domestic Govt Support-CNDPS	Pearson Correlation	0.1046	0.1474	-0.0094	0.1142	0.4791	0.2959	0.1921	0.1305	0.1652	0.5128
	Sig. (2-tailed)	0.5439	0.3911	0.9568	0.5268	0.0036	0.0844	0.2688	0.4549	0.3429	0.0014
	N	36.0000	36.0000	36.0000	33.0000	35.0000	35.0000	35.0000	35.0000	35.0000	36.0000

Table A7, continued (Row 7, Col 7)

Correlation Matrix, International Variables (Parametric)		Level Cooperation International Orgs-CNBC	Level Cooperation International Orgs-CSTP	sqrtQIIID2e	sqrtQIVA1	sqrtQIVA2	sqrtQIVA3	sqrtQIVA5	sqrtQIVA7	sqrtQIVA8	Political Ideology
sqrtQIVA5	Pearson Correlation	0.3854	0.2961	0.2794	0.0655	-0.0997	0.0292	1.0000	-0.2149	-0.1246	-0.1715
	Sig. (2-tailed)	0.0244	0.0890	0.1096	0.7130	0.5748	0.8717	.	0.2223	0.4828	0.3480
	N	34.0000	34.0000	34.0000	34.0000	34.0000	33.0000	34.0000	34.0000	34.0000	32.0000
sqrtQIVA7	Pearson Correlation	-0.2283	-0.2587	-0.1450	0.0921	-0.0019	-0.1935	-0.2149	1.0000	-0.0698	-0.0214
	Sig. (2-tailed)	0.1805	0.1276	0.3986	0.5932	0.9913	0.2654	0.2223	.	0.6904	0.9059
	N	36.0000	36.0000	36.0000	36.0000	36.0000	35.0000	34.0000	36.0000	35.0000	33.0000
sqrtQIVA8	Pearson Correlation	-0.1323	-0.1031	-0.0616	0.0066	-0.0312	0.0019	-0.1246	-0.0698	1.0000	0.0146
	Sig. (2-tailed)	0.4485	0.5554	0.7254	0.9698	0.8587	0.9917	0.4828	0.6904	.	0.9356
	N	35.0000	35.0000	35.0000	35.0000	35.0000	34.0000	34.0000	35.0000	35.0000	33.0000
Political Ideology	Pearson Correlation	0.2434	0.2934	0.3916	0.4036	0.3057	0.2858	-0.1715	-0.0214	0.0146	1.0000
	Sig. (2-tailed)	0.1723	0.0974	0.0242	0.0198	0.0836	0.1128	0.3480	0.9059	0.9356	.
	N	33.0000	33.0000	33.0000	33.0000	33.0000	32.0000	32.0000	33.0000	33.0000	33.0000
sqrtQIIIB1a	Pearson Correlation	0.1984	0.3855	0.2763	0.1782	0.0242	0.1562	0.0328	0.0335	-0.0231	0.2201
	Sig. (2-tailed)	0.2532	0.0222	0.1081	0.3058	0.8901	0.3777	0.8561	0.8485	0.8969	0.2261
	N	35.0000	35.0000	35.0000	35.0000	35.0000	34.0000	33.0000	35.0000	34.0000	32.0000
sqrtQIIIB1b	Pearson Correlation	0.4780	0.5216	0.5079	0.2722	0.0745	0.2499	0.2991	-0.1257	-0.0308	0.4071
	Sig. (2-tailed)	0.0037	0.0013	0.0018	0.1136	0.6705	0.1540	0.0908	0.4717	0.8626	0.0207
	N	35.0000	35.0000	35.0000	35.0000	35.0000	34.0000	33.0000	35.0000	34.0000	32.0000
sqrtQIIIB1c	Pearson Correlation	0.4594	0.5874	0.4070	0.2774	0.0593	0.1811	0.2419	-0.0801	-0.0099	0.3012
	Sig. (2-tailed)	0.0055	0.0002	0.0153	0.1067	0.7351	0.3054	0.1750	0.6473	0.9556	0.0939
	N	35.0000	35.0000	35.0000	35.0000	35.0000	34.0000	33.0000	35.0000	34.0000	32.0000
sqrtQIIIB1d	Pearson Correlation	0.3022	0.4195	0.4028	0.0196	-0.0905	0.1192	0.1576	-0.0728	-0.0175	0.3948
	Sig. (2-tailed)	0.0777	0.0121	0.0164	0.9112	0.6052	0.5018	0.3811	0.6779	0.9216	0.0253
	N	35.0000	35.0000	35.0000	35.0000	35.0000	34.0000	33.0000	35.0000	34.0000	32.0000
sqrtQIIIB1e	Pearson Correlation	0.1824	0.3356	0.2909	0.1426	0.0608	0.1856	0.0041	-0.0496	0.0029	0.2883
	Sig. (2-tailed)	0.2943	0.0488	0.0900	0.4137	0.7286	0.2933	0.9821	0.7774	0.9871	0.1095
	N	35.0000	35.0000	35.0000	35.0000	35.0000	34.0000	33.0000	35.0000	34.0000	32.0000
sqrtQIIIB2a	Pearson Correlation	0.3083	0.4554	0.2723	0.0926	-0.0717	0.0613	0.1734	-0.1063	0.0146	0.1494
	Sig. (2-tailed)	0.0715	0.0060	0.1136	0.5967	0.6824	0.7305	0.3344	0.5435	0.9346	0.4145
	N	35.0000	35.0000	35.0000	35.0000	35.0000	34.0000	33.0000	35.0000	34.0000	32.0000
Perceived Effectiveness Domestic Govt Support-CNDPS	Pearson Correlation	0.4738	0.4903	0.2993	0.1125	-0.0722	0.0622	0.3514	-0.1471	-0.0184	0.1564
	Sig. (2-tailed)	0.0035	0.0024	0.0762	0.5135	0.6756	0.7226	0.0416	0.3918	0.9166	0.3848
	N	36.0000	36.0000	36.0000	36.0000	36.0000	35.0000	34.0000	36.0000	35.0000	33.0000

Table A7, continued (Row 7, Col 8)

Correlation Matrix, International Variables (Parametric)		sqrtQIIIB1a	sqrtQIIIB1b	sqrtQIIIB1c	sqrtQIIIB1d	sqrtQIIIB1e	sqrtQIIIB2a	Perceived Effectiveness Domestic Govt Support-CNDPS	Perceived Effectiveness Domestic Govt Support-CNBC	Perceived Effectiveness Domestic Govt Support-CSTP	Perceived Effectiveness Domestic Govt Support-TRIPS
sqrtQIVA5	Pearson Correlation	0.0328	0.2991	0.2419	0.1576	0.0041	0.1734	0.3514	0.3829	0.2354	0.2132
	Sig. (2-tailed)	0.8561	0.0908	0.1750	0.3811	0.9821	0.3344	0.0416	0.0279	0.1872	0.2337
	N	33.0000	33.0000	33.0000	33.0000	33.0000	33.0000	34.0000	33.0000	33.0000	33.0000
sqrtQIVA7	Pearson Correlation	0.0335	-0.1257	-0.0801	-0.0728	-0.0496	-0.1063	-0.1471	-0.1731	-0.1295	-0.0469
	Sig. (2-tailed)	0.8485	0.4717	0.6473	0.6779	0.7774	0.5435	0.3918	0.3200	0.4586	0.7891
	N	35.0000	35.0000	35.0000	35.0000	35.0000	35.0000	36.0000	35.0000	35.0000	35.0000
sqrtQIVA8	Pearson Correlation	-0.0231	-0.0308	-0.0099	-0.0175	0.0029	0.0146	-0.0184	-0.0119	0.0174	0.0445
	Sig. (2-tailed)	0.8969	0.8626	0.9556	0.9216	0.9871	0.9346	0.9166	0.9468	0.9221	0.8027
	N	34.0000	34.0000	34.0000	34.0000	34.0000	34.0000	35.0000	34.0000	34.0000	34.0000
Political Ideology	Pearson Correlation	0.2201	0.4071	0.3012	0.3948	0.2883	0.1494	0.1564	0.0496	0.1094	0.2555
	Sig. (2-tailed)	0.2261	0.0207	0.0939	0.0253	0.1095	0.4145	0.3848	0.7875	0.5512	0.1581
	N	32.0000	32.0000	32.0000	32.0000	32.0000	32.0000	33.0000	32.0000	32.0000	32.0000
sqrtQIIIB1a	Pearson Correlation	1.0000	0.7636	0.8062	0.5292	0.7056	0.8056	0.4510	0.4958	0.6488	0.4657
	Sig. (2-tailed)	.	0.0000	0.0000	0.0011	0.0000	0.0000	0.0065	0.0025	0.0000	0.0048
	N	35.0000	35.0000	35.0000	35.0000	35.0000	35.0000	35.0000	35.0000	35.0000	35.0000
sqrtQIIIB1b	Pearson Correlation	0.7636	1.0000	0.9132	0.6349	0.7493	0.6343	0.7499	0.6431	0.7008	0.7017
	Sig. (2-tailed)	0.0000	.	0.0000	0.0000	0.0000	0.0000	0.0000	0.0000	0.0000	0.0000
	N	35.0000	35.0000	35.0000	35.0000	35.0000	35.0000	35.0000	35.0000	35.0000	35.0000
sqrtQIIIB1c	Pearson Correlation	0.8062	0.9132	1.0000	0.5235	0.7334	0.6969	0.7610	0.7462	0.7991	0.5885
	Sig. (2-tailed)	0.0000	0.0000	.	0.0012	0.0000	0.0000	0.0000	0.0000	0.0000	0.0002
	N	35.0000	35.0000	35.0000	35.0000	35.0000	35.0000	35.0000	35.0000	35.0000	35.0000
sqrtQIIIB1d	Pearson Correlation	0.5292	0.6349	0.5235	1.0000	0.4709	0.4086	0.3338	0.3151	0.3586	0.4627
	Sig. (2-tailed)	0.0011	0.0000	0.0012	.	0.0043	0.0148	0.0500	0.0652	0.0344	0.0051
	N	35.0000	35.0000	35.0000	35.0000	35.0000	35.0000	35.0000	35.0000	35.0000	35.0000
sqrtQIIIB1e	Pearson Correlation	0.7056	0.7493	0.7334	0.4709	1.0000	0.4600	0.4526	0.3972	0.5582	0.8042
	Sig. (2-tailed)	0.0000	0.0000	0.0000	0.0043	.	0.0054	0.0063	0.0181	0.0005	0.0000
	N	35.0000	35.0000	35.0000	35.0000	35.0000	35.0000	35.0000	35.0000	35.0000	35.0000
sqrtQIIIB2a	Pearson Correlation	0.8056	0.6343	0.6969	0.4086	0.4600	1.0000	0.6332	0.7003	0.7898	0.4604
	Sig. (2-tailed)	0.0000	0.0000	0.0000	0.0148	0.0054	.	0.0000	0.0000	0.0000	0.0054
	N	35.0000	35.0000	35.0000	35.0000	35.0000	35.0000	35.0000	35.0000	35.0000	35.0000
Perceived Effectiveness Domestic Govt Support-CNDPS	Pearson Correlation	0.4510	0.7499	0.7610	0.3338	0.4526	0.6332	1.0000	0.8873	0.8335	0.6530
	Sig. (2-tailed)	0.0065	0.0000	0.0000	0.0500	0.0063	0.0000	.	0.0000	0.0000	0.0000
	N	35.0000	35.0000	35.0000	35.0000	35.0000	35.0000	36.0000	35.0000	35.0000	35.0000

Table A7, continued (Row 7, Col 9)

Correlation Matrix, International Variables (Parametric)		sqrtQIIIC1a	sqrtQIIIC1b	sqrtQIIIC1c	sqrtQIIIC1d	sqrtQIIIC1e
sqrtQIVA5	Pearson Correlation	-0.0075	0.4989	0.4474	0.3039	0.2187
	Sig. (2-tailed)	0.9676	0.0031	0.0102	0.0908	0.2291
	N	32.0000	33.0000	32.0000	32.0000	32.0000
sqrtQIVA7	Pearson Correlation	0.1880	-0.0425	0.0134	0.0734	0.0788
	Sig. (2-tailed)	0.2870	0.8086	0.9403	0.6800	0.6580
	N	34.0000	35.0000	34.0000	34.0000	34.0000
sqrtQIVA8	Pearson Correlation	-0.0705	-0.0988	-0.1175	-0.0663	-0.0625
	Sig. (2-tailed)	0.6966	0.5781	0.5149	0.7138	0.7296
	N	33.0000	34.0000	33.0000	33.0000	33.0000
Political Ideology	Pearson Correlation	0.2135	0.2477	0.1788	0.3414	0.3245
	Sig. (2-tailed)	0.2408	0.1646	0.3276	0.0559	0.0700
	N	32.0000	33.0000	32.0000	32.0000	32.0000
sqrtQIIIB1a	Pearson Correlation	0.7639	0.5533	0.6067	0.6772	0.6301
	Sig. (2-tailed)	0.0000	0.0007	0.0001	0.0000	0.0001
	N	34.0000	34.0000	34.0000	34.0000	34.0000
sqrtQIIIB1b	Pearson Correlation	0.5705	0.7873	0.7518	0.7584	0.7619
	Sig. (2-tailed)	0.0004	0.0000	0.0000	0.0000	0.0000
	N	34.0000	34.0000	34.0000	34.0000	34.0000
sqrtQIIIB1c	Pearson Correlation	0.6313	0.7282	0.7956	0.7142	0.7007
	Sig. (2-tailed)	0.0001	0.0000	0.0000	0.0000	0.0000
	N	34.0000	34.0000	34.0000	34.0000	34.0000
sqrtQIIIB1d	Pearson Correlation	0.3251	0.4763	0.4219	0.4746	0.4727
	Sig. (2-tailed)	0.0606	0.0044	0.0130	0.0046	0.0048
	N	34.0000	34.0000	34.0000	34.0000	34.0000
sqrtQIIIB1e	Pearson Correlation	0.5667	0.5801	0.5304	0.6505	0.7090
	Sig. (2-tailed)	0.0005	0.0003	0.0013	0.0000	0.0000
	N	34.0000	34.0000	34.0000	34.0000	34.0000
sqrtQIIIB2a	Pearson Correlation	0.5408	0.4957	0.5929	0.5253	0.4501
	Sig. (2-tailed)	0.0010	0.0029	0.0002	0.0014	0.0076
	N	34.0000	34.0000	34.0000	34.0000	34.0000
Perceived Effectiveness Domestic Govt Support-CNDPS	Pearson Correlation	0.2645	0.6657	0.7119	0.5112	0.5163
	Sig. (2-tailed)	0.1306	0.0000	0.0000	0.0020	0.0018
	N	34.0000	35.0000	34.0000	34.0000	34.0000

Table A7, continued (Row 8, Col 1)

Correlation Matrix, International Variables (Parametric)		Importance of Smuggling-Endangered Species	reflectsqrtQ1A1b	reflectsqrtQ1A1c	reflectsqrtQ1A1d	reflectsqrtQ1A1e	sqrtQ1B1a	Knowledge of Smuggling-Narcotics	Knowledge of Smuggling-Weapons	Knowledge of Smuggling-Humans	Knowledge of Smuggling-Contraband
Perceived Effectiveness Domestic Govt Support-CNBC	Pearson Correlation	-0.1490	-0.1267	-0.1742	-0.0036	0.0691	-0.0192	0.1538	0.1431	0.2286	-0.1430
	Sig. (2-tailed)	0.3930	0.4683	0.3169	0.9838	0.6933	0.9128	0.3778	0.4121	0.1865	0.4124
	N	35.0000	35.0000	35.0000	35.0000	35.0000	35.0000	35.0000	35.0000	35.0000	35.0000
Perceived Effectiveness Domestic Govt Support-CSTP	Pearson Correlation	-0.1739	-0.1105	-0.1375	0.0211	0.0792	-0.0832	-0.0643	-0.0915	0.2052	-0.1544
	Sig. (2-tailed)	0.3177	0.5275	0.4308	0.9042	0.6511	0.6345	0.7136	0.6011	0.2371	0.3759
	N	35.0000	35.0000	35.0000	35.0000	35.0000	35.0000	35.0000	35.0000	35.0000	35.0000
Perceived Effectiveness Domestic Govt Support-TRIPS	Pearson Correlation	-0.1067	0.2468	0.0546	-0.0489	0.1141	-0.1506	-0.1250	-0.0492	0.0019	-0.0110
	Sig. (2-tailed)	0.5418	0.1530	0.7554	0.7801	0.5139	0.3878	0.4744	0.7790	0.9914	0.9499
	N	35.0000	35.0000	35.0000	35.0000	35.0000	35.0000	35.0000	35.0000	35.0000	35.0000
sqrtQIIIC1a	Pearson Correlation	-0.0130	0.0318	-0.0482	-0.1489	-0.2777	0.2686	-0.1304	-0.0255	0.1806	0.1805
	Sig. (2-tailed)	0.9419	0.8582	0.7867	0.4006	0.1118	0.1245	0.4625	0.8863	0.3069	0.3069
	N	34.0000	34.0000	34.0000	34.0000	34.0000	34.0000	34.0000	34.0000	34.0000	34.0000
sqrtQIIIC1b	Pearson Correlation	-0.1800	-0.0176	0.0683	-0.0639	-0.2819	0.1986	0.0605	0.1466	0.1650	0.1186
	Sig. (2-tailed)	0.3008	0.9199	0.6968	0.7152	0.1009	0.2528	0.7297	0.4006	0.3436	0.4974
	N	35.0000	35.0000	35.0000	35.0000	35.0000	35.0000	35.0000	35.0000	35.0000	35.0000
sqrtQIIIC1c	Pearson Correlation	-0.1525	-0.0339	-0.0370	-0.0869	-0.2016	0.2744	0.1023	0.1886	0.2258	0.0909
	Sig. (2-tailed)	0.3893	0.8490	0.8356	0.6249	0.2528	0.1163	0.5650	0.2855	0.1991	0.6090
	N	34.0000	34.0000	34.0000	34.0000	34.0000	34.0000	34.0000	34.0000	34.0000	34.0000
sqrtQIIIC1d	Pearson Correlation	-0.1876	0.0861	0.1095	-0.0435	-0.2844	0.2154	-0.1387	0.0749	0.1630	0.1928
	Sig. (2-tailed)	0.2880	0.6281	0.5376	0.8072	0.1031	0.2211	0.4340	0.6737	0.3570	0.2745
	N	34.0000	34.0000	34.0000	34.0000	34.0000	34.0000	34.0000	34.0000	34.0000	34.0000
sqrtQIIIC1e	Pearson Correlation	-0.2288	0.0816	0.1691	0.0131	-0.2906	0.1255	-0.1891	0.0148	0.1067	0.1510
	Sig. (2-tailed)	0.1930	0.6463	0.3391	0.9413	0.0954	0.4795	0.2840	0.9337	0.5481	0.3941
	N	34.0000	34.0000	34.0000	34.0000	34.0000	34.0000	34.0000	34.0000	34.0000	34.0000

Table A7, continued (Row 8, Col 2)

Correlation Matrix, International Variables (Parametric)		sqrtQ1E1a	Personal Resource Challenges-Lack of Time	Personal Resource Challenges-Lack of Knowledge	Personal Resource Challenges-Lack of Training	sqrtQ1E1e	Personal Resource Challenges-Excessive Admin Paperwork	Personal Resource Challenges-Ineffective Technology	Personal Resource Challenges-Ineffective Strategic Focus	Personal Resource Challenges-Ineffective Tactical Policy	Personal Resource Challenges-Lack of Clarity in Duties
Perceived Effectiveness Domestic Govt Support-CNBC	Pearson Correlation	-0.1564	-0.0091	0.0324	0.1201	-0.0477	-0.1486	-0.2593	-0.1277	-0.1634	-0.0981
	Sig. (2-tailed)	0.3771	0.9587	0.8534	0.4918	0.7857	0.3943	0.1325	0.4648	0.3483	0.5749
	N	34.0000	35.0000	35.0000	35.0000	35.0000	35.0000	35.0000	35.0000	35.0000	35.0000
Perceived Effectiveness Domestic Govt Support-CSTP	Pearson Correlation	-0.1366	0.0651	0.0864	0.1846	-0.1587	-0.1759	-0.3074	-0.0767	-0.0979	-0.0273
	Sig. (2-tailed)	0.4411	0.7104	0.6215	0.2884	0.3624	0.3121	0.0725	0.6616	0.5756	0.8762
	N	34.0000	35.0000	35.0000	35.0000	35.0000	35.0000	35.0000	35.0000	35.0000	35.0000
Perceived Effectiveness Domestic Govt Support-TRIPS	Pearson Correlation	-0.2977	-0.3510	-0.2624	-0.1527	-0.1752	-0.0981	-0.4159	-0.3050	-0.2758	-0.3199
	Sig. (2-tailed)	0.0873	0.0387	0.1278	0.3813	0.3141	0.5751	0.0130	0.0748	0.1088	0.0610
	N	34.0000	35.0000	35.0000	35.0000	35.0000	35.0000	35.0000	35.0000	35.0000	35.0000
sqrtQIIIC1a	Pearson Correlation	-0.1274	-0.0227	0.1436	0.2489	-0.0011	0.0863	0.0601	0.1613	0.0791	0.1031
	Sig. (2-tailed)	0.4729	0.8984	0.4178	0.1557	0.9951	0.6274	0.7357	0.3622	0.6564	0.5619
	N	34.0000	34.0000	34.0000	34.0000	34.0000	34.0000	34.0000	34.0000	34.0000	34.0000
sqrtQIIIC1b	Pearson Correlation	-0.1727	-0.1933	-0.1942	-0.1335	-0.0670	0.0710	-0.1989	-0.1192	-0.1536	-0.2089
	Sig. (2-tailed)	0.3212	0.2659	0.2635	0.4446	0.7022	0.6851	0.2520	0.4952	0.3784	0.2285
	N	35.0000	35.0000	35.0000	35.0000	35.0000	35.0000	35.0000	35.0000	35.0000	35.0000
sqrtQIIIC1c	Pearson Correlation	-0.2354	-0.2392	-0.1883	-0.0929	-0.1292	-0.0352	-0.2150	-0.1036	-0.1582	-0.1724
	Sig. (2-tailed)	0.1802	0.1730	0.2861	0.6012	0.4664	0.8432	0.2220	0.5597	0.3716	0.3295
	N	34.0000	34.0000	34.0000	34.0000	34.0000	34.0000	34.0000	34.0000	34.0000	34.0000
sqrtQIIIC1d	Pearson Correlation	-0.1428	-0.1474	-0.0882	-0.0110	-0.0682	0.0703	-0.1691	-0.0263	-0.0663	-0.0819
	Sig. (2-tailed)	0.4205	0.4054	0.6198	0.9509	0.7015	0.6927	0.3391	0.8824	0.7097	0.6452
	N	34.0000	34.0000	34.0000	34.0000	34.0000	34.0000	34.0000	34.0000	34.0000	34.0000
sqrtQIIIC1e	Pearson Correlation	-0.1289	-0.1336	-0.1212	-0.0391	-0.0948	0.0453	-0.1778	-0.0441	-0.0602	-0.0985
	Sig. (2-tailed)	0.4675	0.4511	0.4949	0.8263	0.5939	0.7992	0.3144	0.8043	0.7352	0.5795
	N	34.0000	34.0000	34.0000	34.0000	34.0000	34.0000	34.0000	34.0000	34.0000	34.0000

Table A7, continued (Row 8, Col 3)

Correlation Matrix, International Variables (Parametric)		Personal Resource Challenges-Conflict or Lack Comm Leaders and Employees	sqrtQ1EI1	Personal Resource Challenges-Conflict or Lack Comm International Orgs	Personal Resource Challenges-Conflict or Lack Comm Domestic Orgs	sqrtQ1E3a	Org Resource Challenges-Lack of Time	Org Resource Challenges-Lack of Knowledge	Org Resource Challenges-Lack of Training	sqrtQ1E3e	Org Resource Challenges-Excessive Admin Paperwork
Perceived Effectiveness Domestic Govt Support-CNBC	Pearson Correlation	-0.2435	-0.3558	-0.0437	-0.0825	0.1264	-0.0086	0.0951	0.0106	-0.2252	-0.1254
	Sig. (2-tailed)	0.1586	0.0359	0.8032	0.6376	0.4764	0.9616	0.5926	0.9526	0.2077	0.4799
	N	35.0000	35.0000	35.0000	35.0000	34.0000	34.0000	34.0000	34.0000	33.0000	34.0000
Perceived Effectiveness Domestic Govt Support-CSTP	Pearson Correlation	-0.1599	-0.3583	0.0061	0.0094	-0.0265	-0.1177	0.1774	0.0964	-0.1995	-0.1523
	Sig. (2-tailed)	0.3588	0.0346	0.9725	0.9571	0.8818	0.5073	0.3156	0.5875	0.2657	0.3898
	N	35.0000	35.0000	35.0000	35.0000	34.0000	34.0000	34.0000	34.0000	33.0000	34.0000
Perceived Effectiveness Domestic Govt Support-TRIPS	Pearson Correlation	-0.1964	-0.2201	-0.0147	-0.2366	-0.3064	-0.4033	-0.1934	-0.2887	-0.2178	-0.3237
	Sig. (2-tailed)	0.2582	0.2040	0.9332	0.1712	0.0780	0.0180	0.2732	0.0977	0.2234	0.0618
	N	35.0000	35.0000	35.0000	35.0000	34.0000	34.0000	34.0000	34.0000	33.0000	34.0000
sqrtQIIIC1a	Pearson Correlation	0.0448	0.0890	0.1652	0.0992	-0.1657	-0.3343	0.1838	0.1669	-0.3023	-0.1881
	Sig. (2-tailed)	0.8012	0.6167	0.3504	0.5767	0.3567	0.0572	0.3060	0.3531	0.0927	0.2944
	N	34.0000	34.0000	34.0000	34.0000	33.0000	33.0000	33.0000	33.0000	32.0000	33.0000
sqrtQIIIC1b	Pearson Correlation	-0.1851	0.0138	-0.0285	-0.1505	-0.2059	-0.3432	-0.1343	-0.1932	-0.2822	-0.1751
	Sig. (2-tailed)	0.2871	0.9375	0.8710	0.3883	0.2503	0.0469	0.4489	0.2736	0.1116	0.3219
	N	35.0000	35.0000	35.0000	35.0000	33.0000	34.0000	34.0000	34.0000	33.0000	34.0000
sqrtQIIIC1c	Pearson Correlation	-0.2172	-0.1029	-0.0537	-0.1993	-0.1578	-0.3385	-0.1171	-0.1836	-0.4482	-0.2797
	Sig. (2-tailed)	0.2173	0.5627	0.7631	0.2584	0.3804	0.0540	0.5165	0.3065	0.0101	0.1149
	N	34.0000	34.0000	34.0000	34.0000	33.0000	33.0000	33.0000	33.0000	32.0000	33.0000
sqrtQIIIC1d	Pearson Correlation	-0.0987	0.0099	0.0106	-0.0862	-0.2465	-0.3835	-0.0609	-0.1057	-0.3229	-0.2230
	Sig. (2-tailed)	0.5788	0.9558	0.9526	0.6278	0.1668	0.0276	0.7365	0.5581	0.0715	0.2122
	N	34.0000	34.0000	34.0000	34.0000	33.0000	33.0000	33.0000	33.0000	32.0000	33.0000
sqrtQIIIC1e	Pearson Correlation	-0.0891	-0.0275	-0.0186	-0.1104	-0.3178	-0.4523	-0.0694	-0.1328	-0.2711	-0.2009
	Sig. (2-tailed)	0.6165	0.8771	0.9167	0.5341	0.0715	0.0082	0.7011	0.4614	0.1334	0.2622
	N	34.0000	34.0000	34.0000	34.0000	33.0000	33.0000	33.0000	33.0000	32.0000	33.0000

Table A7, continued (Row 8, Col 4)

Correlation Matrix, International Variables (Parametric)		Org Resource Challenges-Ineffective Technology	Org Resource Challenges-Ineffective Strategic Focus	Org Resource Challenges-Ineffective Tactical Policy	Org Resource Challenges-Lack of Clarity in Duties	Org Resource Challenges-Conflict or Lack Comm Leaders and Employees	sqrtQ1E3I	Org Resource Challenges-Conflict or Lack Comm International Orgs	Org Resource Challenges-Conflict or Lack Comm Domestic Orgs	sqrtQIIA1a	Knowledge of Domestic Law-CSIE
Perceived Effectiveness Domestic Govt Support-CNBC	Pearson Correlation	-0.0894	-0.0245	-0.0081	0.0677	-0.0429	-0.2775	0.1663	0.0729	-0.0123	0.0572
	Sig. (2-tailed)	0.6153	0.8907	0.9638	0.7037	0.8097	0.1120	0.3474	0.6820	0.9448	0.7480
	N	34.0000	34.0000	34.0000	34.0000	34.0000	34.0000	34.0000	34.0000	34.0000	34.0000
Perceived Effectiveness Domestic Govt Support-CSTP	Pearson Correlation	-0.0826	0.0094	0.0558	0.1315	-0.0296	-0.2669	0.1619	0.0951	0.0350	-0.1782
	Sig. (2-tailed)	0.6425	0.9580	0.7540	0.4586	0.8680	0.1270	0.3603	0.5925	0.8441	0.3134
	N	34.0000	34.0000	34.0000	34.0000	34.0000	34.0000	34.0000	34.0000	34.0000	34.0000
Perceived Effectiveness Domestic Govt Support-TRIPS	Pearson Correlation	-0.4039	-0.3116	-0.2169	-0.2121	-0.1714	-0.2123	-0.1664	-0.1498	-0.0527	-0.0990
	Sig. (2-tailed)	0.0179	0.0728	0.2178	0.2285	0.3325	0.2280	0.3469	0.3977	0.7674	0.5775
	N	34.0000	34.0000	34.0000	34.0000	34.0000	34.0000	34.0000	34.0000	34.0000	34.0000
sqrtQIIIC1a	Pearson Correlation	0.0267	0.2110	0.1542	0.3285	0.0814	0.1503	0.2394	0.2852	0.2077	-0.2020
	Sig. (2-tailed)	0.8828	0.2385	0.3916	0.0620	0.6526	0.4037	0.1796	0.1077	0.2460	0.2596
	N	33.0000	33.0000	33.0000	33.0000	33.0000	33.0000	33.0000	33.0000	33.0000	33.0000
sqrtQIIIC1b	Pearson Correlation	-0.1899	-0.1182	-0.1002	-0.0233	-0.1401	-0.0049	0.0697	0.0777	0.0923	0.2064
	Sig. (2-tailed)	0.2820	0.5056	0.5731	0.8961	0.4295	0.9779	0.6952	0.6621	0.6036	0.2416
	N	34.0000	34.0000	34.0000	34.0000	34.0000	34.0000	34.0000	34.0000	34.0000	34.0000
sqrtQIIIC1c	Pearson Correlation	-0.1943	-0.0957	-0.0906	0.0148	-0.1366	-0.0698	0.0573	0.0412	0.1583	0.1450
	Sig. (2-tailed)	0.2786	0.5961	0.6163	0.9350	0.4484	0.6995	0.7514	0.8198	0.3790	0.4209
	N	33.0000	33.0000	33.0000	33.0000	33.0000	33.0000	33.0000	33.0000	33.0000	33.0000
sqrtQIIIC1d	Pearson Correlation	-0.1590	-0.0160	-0.0142	0.0927	-0.0755	0.0361	0.0872	0.1203	0.1952	-0.0198
	Sig. (2-tailed)	0.3768	0.9295	0.9374	0.6078	0.6764	0.8420	0.6293	0.5050	0.2762	0.9129
	N	33.0000	33.0000	33.0000	33.0000	33.0000	33.0000	33.0000	33.0000	33.0000	33.0000
sqrtQIIIC1e	Pearson Correlation	-0.1737	-0.0507	-0.0390	0.0415	-0.0712	-0.0295	-0.0110	0.0296	0.1391	-0.0354
	Sig. (2-tailed)	0.3335	0.7792	0.8294	0.8187	0.6938	0.8704	0.9517	0.8703	0.4402	0.8450
	N	33.0000	33.0000	33.0000	33.0000	33.0000	33.0000	33.0000	33.0000	33.0000	33.0000

Table A7, continued (Row 8, Col 5)

Correlation Matrix, International Variables (Parametric)		Knowledge of Domestic Law-DWMD	Knowledge of Domestic Law-TVP	Knowledge of Domestic Law-CBP	sqrtQIID1a	Level Cooperation Domestic Orgs-CSIE	Level Cooperation Domestic Orgs-DWMD	Level Cooperation Domestic Orgs-TVP	Level Cooperation Domestic Orgs-CBP	sqrtQIIIA1a	sqrtQIIIA1b
Perceived Effectiveness Domestic Govt Support-CNBC	Pearson Correlation	0.1671	0.1800	-0.0507	0.0232	0.2628	0.2299	0.2681	-0.0107	0.0002	0.0020
	Sig. (2-tailed)	0.3449	0.3082	0.7758	0.8948	0.1271	0.1840	0.1195	0.9512	0.9991	0.9910
	N	34.0000	34.0000	34.0000	35.0000	35.0000	35.0000	35.0000	35.0000	34.0000	35.0000
Perceived Effectiveness Domestic Govt Support-CSTP	Pearson Correlation	-0.0809	0.0953	-0.1559	0.0226	0.0732	0.0664	0.1924	0.0123	0.0866	-0.0391
	Sig. (2-tailed)	0.6494	0.5921	0.3785	0.8976	0.6760	0.7045	0.2682	0.9443	0.6261	0.8236
	N	34.0000	34.0000	34.0000	35.0000	35.0000	35.0000	35.0000	35.0000	34.0000	35.0000
Perceived Effectiveness Domestic Govt Support-TRIPS	Pearson Correlation	0.0247	-0.1032	0.0099	0.0926	-0.0167	0.1741	-0.0877	0.1787	-0.1267	0.0128
	Sig. (2-tailed)	0.8899	0.5613	0.9556	0.5967	0.9240	0.3172	0.6165	0.3043	0.4753	0.9418
	N	34.0000	34.0000	34.0000	35.0000	35.0000	35.0000	35.0000	35.0000	34.0000	35.0000
sqrtQIIIC1a	Pearson Correlation	-0.1522	-0.0323	-0.0883	0.1755	-0.1107	-0.0364	0.1560	0.2050	0.3025	-0.0562
	Sig. (2-tailed)	0.3977	0.8583	0.6250	0.3208	0.5331	0.8382	0.3784	0.2447	0.0871	0.7522
	N	33.0000	33.0000	33.0000	34.0000	34.0000	34.0000	34.0000	34.0000	33.0000	34.0000
sqrtQIIIC1b	Pearson Correlation	0.2612	0.0634	0.1344	0.2461	0.3696	0.4777	0.3611	0.3365	0.1548	0.0659
	Sig. (2-tailed)	0.1357	0.7217	0.4486	0.1540	0.0289	0.0037	0.0331	0.0481	0.3819	0.7067
	N	34.0000	34.0000	34.0000	35.0000	35.0000	35.0000	35.0000	35.0000	34.0000	35.0000
sqrtQIIIC1c	Pearson Correlation	0.2506	0.1953	0.0791	0.2282	0.4242	0.3842	0.4525	0.2793	0.1877	0.0997
	Sig. (2-tailed)	0.1595	0.2762	0.6619	0.1943	0.0124	0.0249	0.0072	0.1097	0.2956	0.5748
	N	33.0000	33.0000	33.0000	34.0000	34.0000	34.0000	34.0000	34.0000	33.0000	34.0000
sqrtQIIIC1d	Pearson Correlation	0.1034	0.0621	0.1447	0.2866	0.1500	0.2883	0.2792	0.3933	0.2515	-0.0240
	Sig. (2-tailed)	0.5669	0.7312	0.4216	0.1003	0.3972	0.0983	0.1098	0.0214	0.1579	0.8929
	N	33.0000	33.0000	33.0000	34.0000	34.0000	34.0000	34.0000	34.0000	33.0000	34.0000
sqrtQIIIC1e	Pearson Correlation	0.0802	-0.0023	0.1648	0.2789	0.1731	0.3046	0.2723	0.4889	0.2017	0.0218
	Sig. (2-tailed)	0.6573	0.9898	0.3594	0.1102	0.3274	0.0798	0.1193	0.0033	0.2602	0.9024
	N	33.0000	33.0000	33.0000	34.0000	34.0000	34.0000	34.0000	34.0000	33.0000	34.0000

Table A7, continued (Row 8, Col 6)

Correlation Matrix, International Variables (Parametric)		sqrtQIIIA1c	sqrtQIIIA1d	sqrtQIIIA1e	sqrtQIIID1a	Level Cooperation Domestic Orgs-CNDPS	Level Cooperation Domestic Orgs-CNBC	Level Cooperation Domestic Orgs-CSTP	Level Cooperation Domestic Orgs-TRIPS	sqrtQIIID2a	Level Cooperation International Orgs-CNDPS
Perceived Effectiveness Domestic Govt Support-CNBC	Pearson Correlation	0.0359	0.1471	-0.1126	0.3432	0.4991	0.4183	0.3409	0.2503	0.3219	0.5663
	Sig. (2-tailed)	0.8376	0.3992	0.5194	0.0545	0.0027	0.0138	0.0485	0.1533	0.0634	0.0004
	N	35.0000	35.0000	35.0000	32.0000	34.0000	34.0000	34.0000	34.0000	34.0000	35.0000
Perceived Effectiveness Domestic Govt Support-CSTP	Pearson Correlation	-0.0149	0.2077	-0.0855	0.3670	0.4630	0.3540	0.3637	0.2974	0.3378	0.4353
	Sig. (2-tailed)	0.9322	0.2313	0.6252	0.0388	0.0058	0.0400	0.0345	0.0876	0.0507	0.0090
	N	35.0000	35.0000	35.0000	32.0000	34.0000	34.0000	34.0000	34.0000	34.0000	35.0000
Perceived Effectiveness Domestic Govt Support-TRIPS	Pearson Correlation	-0.0767	-0.0486	0.1779	0.1490	0.2319	0.2732	0.0294	0.2889	0.2198	0.3588
	Sig. (2-tailed)	0.6616	0.7816	0.3065	0.4158	0.1870	0.1180	0.8689	0.0976	0.2118	0.0343
	N	35.0000	35.0000	35.0000	32.0000	34.0000	34.0000	34.0000	34.0000	34.0000	35.0000
sqrtQIIIC1a	Pearson Correlation	0.0174	0.2362	0.0568	0.4114	0.1404	0.2254	0.2957	0.2565	0.4155	0.0632
	Sig. (2-tailed)	0.9223	0.1786	0.7495	0.0193	0.4284	0.2000	0.0895	0.1431	0.0162	0.7226
	N	34.0000	34.0000	34.0000	32.0000	34.0000	34.0000	34.0000	34.0000	33.0000	34.0000
sqrtQIIIC1b	Pearson Correlation	0.1306	0.0957	0.1706	0.4041	0.5133	0.5154	0.4105	0.4502	0.5007	0.4565
	Sig. (2-tailed)	0.4547	0.5844	0.3272	0.0197	0.0016	0.0015	0.0143	0.0067	0.0026	0.0058
	N	35.0000	35.0000	35.0000	33.0000	35.0000	35.0000	35.0000	35.0000	34.0000	35.0000
sqrtQIIIC1c	Pearson Correlation	0.1179	0.1858	0.0721	0.3840	0.5190	0.4894	0.4361	0.3524	0.5383	0.4485
	Sig. (2-tailed)	0.5067	0.2929	0.6852	0.0300	0.0017	0.0033	0.0099	0.0409	0.0012	0.0078
	N	34.0000	34.0000	34.0000	32.0000	34.0000	34.0000	34.0000	34.0000	33.0000	34.0000
sqrtQIIIC1d	Pearson Correlation	0.1012	0.1545	0.1855	0.4812	0.3622	0.4695	0.3984	0.4778	0.5214	0.2979
	Sig. (2-tailed)	0.5689	0.3830	0.2935	0.0053	0.0353	0.0051	0.0196	0.0043	0.0019	0.0870
	N	34.0000	34.0000	34.0000	32.0000	34.0000	34.0000	34.0000	34.0000	33.0000	34.0000
sqrtQIIIC1e	Pearson Correlation	0.0999	0.1787	0.2334	0.4420	0.3664	0.4147	0.3734	0.5183	0.4913	0.3037
	Sig. (2-tailed)	0.5742	0.3119	0.1841	0.0113	0.0330	0.0148	0.0296	0.0017	0.0037	0.0808
	N	34.0000	34.0000	34.0000	32.0000	34.0000	34.0000	34.0000	34.0000	33.0000	34.0000

Table A7, continued (Row 8, Col 7)

Correlation Matrix, International Variables (Parametric)		Level Cooperation International Orgs-CNBC	Level Cooperation International Orgs-CSTP	sqrtQIIID2e	sqrtQIVA1	sqrtQIVA2	sqrtQIVA3	sqrtQIVA5	sqrtQIVA7	sqrtQIVA8	Political Ideology
Perceived Effectiveness Domestic Govt Support-CNBC	Pearson Correlation	0.5873	0.5798	0.3613	0.0462	-0.1269	0.0050	0.3829	-0.1731	-0.0119	0.0496
	Sig. (2-tailed)	0.0002	0.0003	0.0329	0.7923	0.4676	0.9778	0.0279	0.3200	0.9468	0.7875
	N	35.0000	35.0000	35.0000	35.0000	35.0000	34.0000	33.0000	35.0000	34.0000	32.0000
Perceived Effectiveness Domestic Govt Support-CSTP	Pearson Correlation	0.4240	0.5840	0.3289	0.0332	-0.1260	0.0971	0.2354	-0.1295	0.0174	0.1094
	Sig. (2-tailed)	0.0111	0.0002	0.0537	0.8498	0.4709	0.5847	0.1872	0.4586	0.9221	0.5512
	N	35.0000	35.0000	35.0000	35.0000	35.0000	34.0000	33.0000	35.0000	34.0000	32.0000
Perceived Effectiveness Domestic Govt Support-TRIPS	Pearson Correlation	0.3588	0.3442	0.4039	0.0644	-0.0295	0.0772	0.2132	-0.0469	0.0445	0.2555
	Sig. (2-tailed)	0.0343	0.0429	0.0161	0.7133	0.8662	0.6644	0.2337	0.7891	0.8027	0.1581
	N	35.0000	35.0000	35.0000	35.0000	35.0000	34.0000	33.0000	35.0000	34.0000	32.0000
sqrtQIIIC1a	Pearson Correlation	0.0656	0.2914	0.1783	0.2992	0.1420	0.3380	-0.0075	0.1880	-0.0705	0.2135
	Sig. (2-tailed)	0.7123	0.0945	0.3131	0.0856	0.4232	0.0544	0.9676	0.2870	0.6966	0.2408
	N	34.0000	34.0000	34.0000	34.0000	34.0000	33.0000	32.0000	34.0000	33.0000	32.0000
sqrtQIIIC1b	Pearson Correlation	0.4414	0.4868	0.4431	0.2639	0.0879	0.2481	0.4989	-0.0425	-0.0988	0.2477
	Sig. (2-tailed)	0.0079	0.0030	0.0077	0.1255	0.6155	0.1571	0.0031	0.8086	0.5781	0.1646
	N	35.0000	35.0000	35.0000	35.0000	35.0000	34.0000	33.0000	35.0000	34.0000	33.0000
sqrtQIIIC1c	Pearson Correlation	0.4658	0.5196	0.3962	0.1990	0.0462	0.1772	0.4474	0.0134	-0.1175	0.1788
	Sig. (2-tailed)	0.0055	0.0016	0.0204	0.2591	0.7953	0.3238	0.0102	0.9403	0.5149	0.3276
	N	34.0000	34.0000	34.0000	34.0000	34.0000	33.0000	32.0000	34.0000	33.0000	32.0000
sqrtQIIIC1d	Pearson Correlation	0.2980	0.4211	0.4276	0.2562	0.1140	0.2924	0.3039	0.0734	-0.0663	0.3414
	Sig. (2-tailed)	0.0870	0.0131	0.0117	0.1436	0.5209	0.0987	0.0908	0.6800	0.7138	0.0559
	N	34.0000	34.0000	34.0000	34.0000	34.0000	33.0000	32.0000	34.0000	33.0000	32.0000
sqrtQIIIC1e	Pearson Correlation	0.2853	0.3893	0.4373	0.2434	0.1050	0.3016	0.2187	0.0788	-0.0625	0.3245
	Sig. (2-tailed)	0.1020	0.0229	0.0097	0.1654	0.5547	0.0880	0.2291	0.6580	0.7296	0.0700
	N	34.0000	34.0000	34.0000	34.0000	34.0000	33.0000	32.0000	34.0000	33.0000	32.0000

Table A7, continued (Row 8, Col 8)

Correlation Matrix, International Variables (Parametric)		sqrtQIIIB1a	sqrtQIIIB1b	sqrtQIIIB1c	sqrtQIIIB1d	sqrtQIIIB1e	sqrtQIIIB2a	Perceived Effectiveness Domestic Govt Support-CNDPS	Perceived Effectiveness Domestic Govt Support-CNBC	Perceived Effectiveness Domestic Govt Support-CSTP	Perceived Effectiveness Domestic Govt Support-TRIPS
Perceived Effectiveness Domestic Govt Support-CNBC	Pearson Correlation	0.4958	0.6431	0.7462	0.3151	0.3972	0.7003	0.8873	1.0000	0.8936	0.5154
	Sig. (2-tailed)	0.0025	0.0000	0.0000	0.0652	0.0181	0.0000	0.0000	.	0.0000	0.0015
	N	35.0000	35.0000	35.0000	35.0000	35.0000	35.0000	35.0000	35.0000	35.0000	35.0000
Perceived Effectiveness Domestic Govt Support-CSTP	Pearson Correlation	0.6488	0.7008	0.7991	0.3586	0.5582	0.7898	0.8335	0.8936	1.0000	0.5664
	Sig. (2-tailed)	0.0000	0.0000	0.0000	0.0344	0.0005	0.0000	0.0000	0.0000	.	0.0004
	N	35.0000	35.0000	35.0000	35.0000	35.0000	35.0000	35.0000	35.0000	35.0000	35.0000
Perceived Effectiveness Domestic Govt Support-TRIPS	Pearson Correlation	0.4657	0.7017	0.5885	0.4627	0.8042	0.4604	0.6530	0.5154	0.5664	1.0000
	Sig. (2-tailed)	0.0048	0.0000	0.0002	0.0051	0.0000	0.0054	0.0000	0.0015	0.0004	.
	N	35.0000	35.0000	35.0000	35.0000	35.0000	35.0000	35.0000	35.0000	35.0000	35.0000
sqrtQIIIC1a	Pearson Correlation	0.7639	0.5705	0.6313	0.3251	0.5667	0.5408	0.2645	0.2496	0.4308	0.2822
	Sig. (2-tailed)	0.0000	0.0004	0.0001	0.0606	0.0005	0.0010	0.1306	0.1545	0.0110	0.1058
	N	34.0000	34.0000	34.0000	34.0000	34.0000	34.0000	34.0000	34.0000	34.0000	34.0000
sqrtQIIIC1b	Pearson Correlation	0.5533	0.7873	0.7282	0.4763	0.5801	0.4957	0.6657	0.5452	0.5366	0.5869
	Sig. (2-tailed)	0.0007	0.0000	0.0000	0.0044	0.0003	0.0029	0.0000	0.0009	0.0011	0.0003
	N	34.0000	34.0000	34.0000	34.0000	34.0000	34.0000	35.0000	34.0000	34.0000	34.0000
sqrtQIIIC1c	Pearson Correlation	0.6067	0.7518	0.7956	0.4219	0.5304	0.5929	0.7119	0.6459	0.6345	0.5227
	Sig. (2-tailed)	0.0001	0.0000	0.0000	0.0130	0.0013	0.0002	0.0000	0.0000	0.0001	0.0015
	N	34.0000	34.0000	34.0000	34.0000	34.0000	34.0000	34.0000	34.0000	34.0000	34.0000
sqrtQIIIC1d	Pearson Correlation	0.6772	0.7584	0.7142	0.4746	0.6505	0.5253	0.5112	0.4094	0.5227	0.5275
	Sig. (2-tailed)	0.0000	0.0000	0.0000	0.0046	0.0000	0.0014	0.0020	0.0162	0.0015	0.0013
	N	34.0000	34.0000	34.0000	34.0000	34.0000	34.0000	34.0000	34.0000	34.0000	34.0000
sqrtQIIIC1e	Pearson Correlation	0.6301	0.7619	0.7007	0.4727	0.7090	0.4501	0.5163	0.3886	0.5216	0.5756
	Sig. (2-tailed)	0.0001	0.0000	0.0000	0.0048	0.0000	0.0076	0.0018	0.0231	0.0016	0.0004
	N	34.0000	34.0000	34.0000	34.0000	34.0000	34.0000	34.0000	34.0000	34.0000	34.0000

Table A7, continued (Row 8, Col 9)

Correlation Matrix, International Variables (Parametric)		sqrtQIIIC1a	sqrtQIIIC1b	sqrtQIIIC1c	sqrtQIIIC1d	sqrtQIIIC1e
Perceived Effectiveness Domestic Govt Support-CNBC	Pearson Correlation	0.2496	0.5452	0.6459	0.4094	0.3886
	Sig. (2-tailed)	0.1545	0.0009	0.0000	0.0162	0.0231
	N	34.0000	34.0000	34.0000	34.0000	34.0000
Perceived Effectiveness Domestic Govt Support-CSTP	Pearson Correlation	0.4308	0.5366	0.6345	0.5227	0.5216
	Sig. (2-tailed)	0.0110	0.0011	0.0001	0.0015	0.0016
	N	34.0000	34.0000	34.0000	34.0000	34.0000
Perceived Effectiveness Domestic Govt Support-TRIPS	Pearson Correlation	0.2822	0.5869	0.5227	0.5275	0.5756
	Sig. (2-tailed)	0.1058	0.0003	0.0015	0.0013	0.0004
	N	34.0000	34.0000	34.0000	34.0000	34.0000
sqrtQIIIC1a	Pearson Correlation	1.0000	0.6496	0.6973	0.8380	0.7747
	Sig. (2-tailed)	.	0.0000	0.0000	0.0000	0.0000
	N	34.0000	34.0000	34.0000	34.0000	34.0000
sqrtQIIIC1b	Pearson Correlation	0.6496	1.0000	0.9330	0.9192	0.9080
	Sig. (2-tailed)	0.0000	.	0.0000	0.0000	0.0000
	N	34.0000	35.0000	34.0000	34.0000	34.0000
sqrtQIIIC1c	Pearson Correlation	0.6973	0.9330	1.0000	0.8768	0.8417
	Sig. (2-tailed)	0.0000	0.0000	.	0.0000	0.0000
	N	34.0000	34.0000	34.0000	34.0000	34.0000
sqrtQIIIC1d	Pearson Correlation	0.8380	0.9192	0.8768	1.0000	0.9629
	Sig. (2-tailed)	0.0000	0.0000	0.0000	.	0.0000
	N	34.0000	34.0000	34.0000	34.0000	34.0000
sqrtQIIIC1e	Pearson Correlation	0.7747	0.9080	0.8417	0.9629	1.0000
	Sig. (2-tailed)	0.0000	0.0000	0.0000	0.0000	.
	N	34.0000	34.0000	34.0000	34.0000	34.0000

ABOUT THE AUTHOR

Jonathan Liljeblad studies the connections between local and global phenomenon using interdisciplinary methods in law, politics, and sociology. His interests focus on the intersection of the internet, human rights, and international politics and law. He received his B.S. from the California Institute of Technology and his Ph.D. in political science, as well as his J.D., from the University of Southern California. He has taught at the University of California, Los Angeles and is currently a post-doctoral fellow at the School of Law of the University of New England in New South Wales, Australia.

qp

Visit us at *www.quidprobooks.com*.